Productive Objects

AN APPLIED SOFTWARE

PROJECT MANAGEMENT

FRAMEWORK

Productive Objects

AN APPLIED SOFTWARE

PROJECT MANAGEMENT

FRAMEWORK

Robert J. Muller

MORGAN KAUFMANN PUBLISHERS, INC.
SAN FRANCISCO, CALIFORNIA

SENIOR EDITOR   Diane D. Cerra
PRODUCTION MANAGER   Yonie Overton
PRODUCTION EDITOR   Cheri Palmer
EDITORIAL ASSISTANT   Antonia Richmond
COVER DESIGN   Ross Carron Design
TEXT DESIGN   Detta Penna, Penna Design & Production
COMPOSITION   Proctor-Willenbacher
TECHNICAL ILLUSTRATION   Technologies 'N' Typography
COPYEDITOR   Gary Morris
PROOFREADER   Jennifer McClain
PRINTER   Edwards Brothers, Inc.

Product or brand names used in this book may be trade names or trademarks. Where we believe that there may be proprietary claims to such trade names or trademarks, the name has been used with an initial capital or it has been capitalized in the style used by the name claimant. Regardless of the capitalization used, all such names have been used in an editorial manner, without any intent to convey endorsement of or other affiliation with the name claimant. Neither the author nor the publisher intends to express any judgment as to the validity or legal status of any such proprietary claims.

MORGAN KAUFMANN PUBLISHERS, INC.
Editorial and Sales Office
340 Pine Street, Sixth Floor
San Francisco, CA 94104-3205
USA
TELEPHONE   415 / 392-2665
FACSIMILE   415 / 982-2665
E-MAIL   mkp@mkp.com
WEB SITE   http://www.mkp.com
ORDER TOLL FREE   800 / 745-7323

© 1998 by Morgan Kaufmann Publishers, Inc.
All rights reserved
Printed in the United States of America
02 01 00 99 98   5 4 3 2 1

No part of this publication may be reproduced, stored in a retrieval system, or transmitted in any form or by any means—electronic, mechanical, photocopying, recording, or otherwise—without the prior written permission of the publisher.

LIBRARY OF CONGRESS CATALOGING-IN-PUBLICATION DATA
Muller, Robert J.
    Productive objects : an applied software project management framework / Robert J. Muller.
       p. cm.
    Includes bibliographical references and index.
    ISBN 1-55860-437-5
    1. Object-oriented programming (Computer science)   2. Applied software--Development--Management.   I. Title.
QA76.64.M847   1998
005.1'17'0684--dc21
                                                  98-15396
                                                        CIP

To M'Linn and Theo,

who organize my projects for me

Contents

List of Figures   xv

PART ONE

Systems and Projects

Chapter 1:   A General Systems Approach   4

Systems, Projects, and Value   5

Object Systems   7

The System and Kaizen   14

The Improvement Plan   28

The System Model   36

Readings   39   /   Questions to Think About   40

Chapter 2:   Reusable System   42

The Reusable System   42

The Reuse Repository   53

The Versioned System   57

Readings   60   /   Questions to Think About   61

Chapter 3:   The Project and Its Environment   63

The Project   63

The Project Deliverables and System Earned Value   67

The Project Stakeholder   74

The Project Repository   78

Readings   79   /   Questions to Think About   81

PART TWO

Process

Chapter 4: Process and Process Modeling — 84
The Task 84
The Process and Task Models 90
The Milestone 101
Readings 103 / Questions to Think About 103

Chapter 5: The Work-Flow Model — 105
Transaction Work-Flow Model 108
Ad Hoc Work-Flow Model 110
Administrative Work-Flow Model 112
Readings 114 / Questions to Think About 114

PART THREE

Plan and Scope

Chapter 6: The Project Document — 118
The Document 118
The Formal Project Document 122
The Document Template 124
Questions to Think About 127

Chapter 7: The Project Plan — 128
The Plan 128
The Project Plan 133
Readings 137 / Questions to Think About 138

Chapter 8: Statement of Work — 139
The Statement of Work 139
The Work Breakdown Structure 144
Readings 152 / Questions to Think About 153

Chapter 9: Quality Management — 154
The Quality Management Plan 154
The Quality Assurance Process Model and Process 156
The Test Plan 157
The Quality Environment 162
Readings 169 / Questions to Think About 170

PART FOUR
Schedule

Chapter 10: Project Scheduling — 174

The Project Schedule 174
The Time Chart 181
The Dependency Chart 183
Readings 187 / Questions to Think About 187

Chapter 11: The Schedule Task and Dependency — 189

The Schedule Task 189
Duration 192
The Dependency 194
Readings 197 / Questions to Think About 197

PART FIVE
Risk

Chapter 12: Risk — 200

The Risk 200
OO Development Risks 210
Readings 224 / Questions to Think About 225

Chapter 13: Risk Quantification — 226

What Are the Risks? 227
Risk Tolerance Quantification 236
Readings 242 / Questions to Think About 243

Chapter 14: Risk Management — 244

The Risk Management Plan 244
The Risk Management Method 247
Readings 252 / Questions to Think About 253

PART SIX
Software Development

Chapter 15: Software — 256

The Object 256
The Storage Organization 257
The Cluster 259
The Software System 264
The Product Document 267
Readings 270 / Questions to Think About 272

Chapter 16: Developing Object-Oriented Software — 273

The Development Process Model 273
Hacking 279
The Waterfall 281
The Spiral 284
The Fountain 286
Recursive-Parallel 288
Genetic 290
Readings 296 / Questions to Think About 297

Chapter 17: Development Documentation — 298

The Development Document 298
The Requirements Document 301
The Functional Specification 310
The Design Document 314
Readings 318 / Questions to Think About 320

Chapter 18: Development Environment — 322

The Development Environment 322
The Product Repository 325
Questions to Think About 329

PART SEVEN

Tools

Chapter 19: Work Calendar — 334

The Work Calendar 334
The Shift 338
Questions to Think About 340

Chapter 20: Repository — 341

The Repository 341
Schema 344
Questions to Think About 347

Chapter 21: Development Tool — 348

The Development Tool 348
Design Patterns 355
Readings 357 / Questions to Think About 359

Contents   xi

Chapter 22:   Information System and Modeling Tool   360
The Information System   360
The Project Management System   363
The Product Management System   371
System Modeling Tool   373
Readings   376   /   Questions to Think About   377

PART EIGHT

Change

Chapter 23:   Change Management Plan   380
The Change Management Plan   380
The Configuration Management Plan   383
Readings   385   /   Questions to Think About   385

Chapter 24:   Change Management   387
The Change Management Process   387
The Change Management Process Model   391
The Change Request   393
The Change Management System   395
The Change Report   396
Readings   398   /   Questions to Think About   399

Chapter 25:   Configuration Management   400
The Configuration Management Process   400
The Configuration Management Process Model   403
The Configuration Management System   408
Readings   416   /   Questions to Think About   418

Chapter 26:   Baseline   419
The Baseline   419
The Document Baseline   423
The Cluster Baseline   424
The Product Baseline   426
The Performance Evaluation Baseline   436
The Contract Baseline   439
Readings   442   /   Questions to Think About   442

PART NINE

Procurement

Chapter 27: Procurement — 446
  The Procurement Process 446
  The Procurement Process Model 451
  The Request for Proposal 452
  The Proposal 454
  The Assessment Criterion 456
  The Contract 457
  The Procurement Management Plan 464
  Readings 467 / Questions to Think About 468

Chapter 28: Contract Administration — 469
  The Contract Administration Process 469
  The Contract Administration Process Model 472
  The Contract Administration System 474
  The Contract Report 475
  Readings 477 / Questions to Think About 477

PART TEN

Organization

Chapter 29: Organization — 480
  The Organization 480
  The Functional Organization 491
  The Projectized Organization 496
  The Matrix Organization 501
  The Organization Chart 505
  Readings 506 / Questions to Think About 508

Chapter 30: Work Group and the Team — 509
  The Work Group 509
  The Team 519
  Readings 522 / Questions to Think About 524

Chapter 31: Management Culture — 525
  The Cultural Patterns 527
  Successful Pattern Matching 532
  Readings 536 / Questions to Think About 537

Contents   xiii

Chapter 32:	Policy	**538**

    The Policy   538
    The Design Standard   542
    The Coding Standard   545
    Readings   549   /   Questions to Think About   549

Chapter 33:	Organizational Environment	**550**

    The Organizational Environment   550
    The External Standard   554
    The Organizational Repository   555
    Readings   556   /   Questions to Think About   558

PART ELEVEN

Resources

Chapter 34:	Resource	**562**

    The Resource   562
    The Contractor   573
    The Skill   575
    The Skills Matrix   580
    The Role   582
    The Training Course   584
    Readings   588   /   Questions to Think About   590

Chapter 35:	Resource Assignment	**591**

    The Assignment   591
    The Staffing Plan   594
    The Responsibility Matrix   596
    The Effort Estimate   599
    Readings   602   /   Questions to Think About   603

PART TWELVE

Cost

Chapter 36:	The Chart of Accounts	**606**

    Readings   610   /   Questions to Think About   611

Chapter 37:	The Budget	**612**

    The Cost Estimate   612
    The Cost Estimation Tool   616

The Cost Budget   617
The Spending Budget   619
Readings   621   /   Questions to Think About   623

Chapter 38:   Cost Management ... 624
The Cost Management Plan   624
The Cost Management System   628
Readings   629   /   Questions to Think About   630

PART THIRTEEN

Communication

Chapter 39:   Communication Process ... 634
The Communication Process   634
The Communication Process Model   640
The Communications Management Plan   641
Readings   642   /   Questions to Think About   643

Chapter 40:   The Personal Interaction ... 644
Readings   646   /   Questions to Think About   647

Chapter 41:   Meeting ... 648
The Meeting   648
The Joint Review   651
The Communication Meeting   657
Readings   659   /   Questions to Think About   660

Chapter 42:   Progress Report ... 661
The Progress Report   661
The Timesheet   663
Readings   666   /   Questions to Think About   666

Chapter 43:   Communication Tool ... 667
The Communication Tool   667
The Online Repository   670
Readings   673   /   Questions to Think About   673

Bibliography   674

Index   683

List of Figures

FIGURE	CAPTION
1-1	Example of OOSD class diagram 8
1-2	Example of OOSD class diagram with object model 10
1-3	Example of system diagram for Brooks's law 12
1-4	Example of summary diagram for system model notation 13
3-1	Measurement of earned value 71
4-1	System model for project planning 99
4-2	System model for work breakdown structure generation 100
8-1	WBS generation and customization 148
9-1	The quality system 159
9-2	Quality approach relationships 161
9-3	x-R control chart 165
9-4	pn control chart 166
9-5	p control chart 167
10-1	Resource usage and availability histogram 178
10-2	Gantt chart 182
10-3	Activity-on-node dependency chart 185
12-1	Dependency chart with critical path 213
13-1	Risk assessment probability tree 230
13-2	Event tree example 233
13-3	Control decision tree example 235
13-4	A preference curve 238
13-5	Risk acceptance curve 239
15-1	The cluster pyramid 261
16-1	Hacking development process model 280
16-2	Waterfall development process model 282
16-3	The spiral development process model 285
16-4	The fountain development process model 287

FIGURE	CAPTION
16-5	The recursive-parallel development process model 289
16-6	The genetic development process model 294
17-1	QFD stakeholder-deliverable matrix 307
17-2	QFD House of Quality 309
25-1	The CM change process model 405
25-2	The release management process model 407
29-1	The functional organization 493
29-2	The projectized organization 498
29-3	The matrix organization 503
31-1	Cultural frontiers 533
34-1	Skills matrix for OO client/server group 580
35-1	High-level responsibility matrix for DTS project 598
37-1	The cost budget baseline graph 618
37-2	The spending budget baseline graph 619
38-1	Earned-cost graph 627

PREFACE

Object-Oriented Software Development

Turning and turning in the widening gyre

The falcon cannot hear the falconer;

Things fall apart; the center cannot hold...

> W. B. Yeats, "The Second Coming"

Bounteous plans and new deals

Wrapped with golden chains

Still I wonder

Who'll stop the rain?

> John Fogerty, "Who'll Stop the Rain"

There's something different about object-oriented (OO) software projects. Some take a hard line and say that people were reusing code in the 50s, that inheritance has been around since the '60s, and that there's nothing new under the sun. The fact remains, there is something *different* about OO software projects.

In casting about for the best way to organize my thoughts on OO project management (OOPM), it occurred to me that the problems with organizing a system for managing projects are very similar to the problems with organizing a software system. Since the object is to understand OO projects, why not construct a model of project management using OO techniques? In this book, therefore, I build a system of project management designed as an OO system. The form of the book thus reflects the form of the projects you will manage. This form gives you the same advantages as OO technology in software: extensibility and reusability. You can easily extend the model by adding more classes or by redefining the nature of a class. You can add your own classes, reusing the model classes already present. This book is thus a framework for project management that you can extend and mold to your own requirements, as with any OO system.

The book combines the perspectives of project management and systems theory to provide a unique look at managing *productive* OO projects. Systems thinking integrates a goal-directed, feedback-driven approach to management with the perspective of systems layered within systems. Project management adds key ideas that software management often neglects, such as risk analysis and management, a process-driven approach, and a metric-based system of determining how well you are doing through system feedback. In practice, what this gives you is the ability to improve the value that your projects produce and to improve your productivity in producing that value.

The book provides all the tools you need to manage any software project. It focuses on the application of those tools to managing OO software projects. This focus provides the strength of the book: an integrated, cohesive system of project management that aligns directly with the technology it manages.

The book provides examples of how the different objects work in practice. Mostly, I refer to many informal case studies from my career in object-oriented technology as examples, usually of what not to do. I will also have some examples from a made-up project to illustrate how to do something, such as construct a work breakdown structure. I intend these examples to help you to reify the abstractions in the class descriptions.

If you're like me, you've probably already read enough overviews of OO technology to make your eyes cross. The bibliography contains several good ones [Booch 1994; Cox; Jacobson; Meyer; Rumbaugh]. This book assumes a basic knowledge of OO concepts.

There are specific architectural differences in an OO system that contribute to the advantages of using it:

- Encapsulation of objects into classes and methods
- Structuring of objects into clusters and systems of clusters
- High degree of abstraction and interfaces
- Inheritance, single and multiple

These differences tend to reward revisiting objects at different points in development. This leads to a more *iterative* and *incremental* structure than in other methods. Commitment based on protoyping and risk management becomes much more useful than before. Finally, *reuse* of components is much easier.

The different styles of software and project management lead to several advantages:

- *Continuity* through real-world modeling, which means that design, analysis, and requirements have a much tighter relationship, leading to a continuity from the environmental market requirements to the working system and to an improved ability to accommodate change in the environment

- *Reusability* and *adaptability*, which directly impact productivity and time to market through reduced development time and software size, as well as the development process and planning activities

- *Simplicity* of design through reduction of objects and code to small units corresponding to well-understood requirements

- *Robustness* and *flexibility* in the face of environmental and internal change, through separation of interface and implementation, which in turn leads to component-oriented development
- *Maintainability* through encapsulated implementations that you can change without changing objects that use the changed object; this requires more analysis and design to perfect interfaces and suggests a prototyping approach
- *Quality* can be much better if you adapt your quality programs to take the entire life cycle into account and if you focus your quality efforts on reusable components rather than on system testing
- *Competitiveness*, when through a technology such as OO that has momentum, requires that you manage the use of the technology through such management techniques as continuous improvement and team organization

On the other hand, OO technology is still new and evolving quickly. The market chasm still looms. There is a shortage of people who have used the technology. OO projects thus need closer evaluation and stronger communication. The project manager must manage stakeholder expectations, including those of his or her management. It also means a great deal of training, at least for initial or early use of the technology.

The OO way of thinking about software differs from other ways such as structured or functional methods. This can be an advantage, since it is the paradigm switch that leads to the benefits above. It can also be a disadvantage if you have a great deal of legacy code and legacy coders, even legacy management. The legacy code makes opportunities for reuse if you can figure out how to make it compatible but a great deal of rework if you cannot. Training becomes more than just education—it becomes socialization into a different culture, a very different issue. A management that is less than supportive of new, faddish (to them) technologies such as OO may require a long period of trials and successful pilot projects. You may essentially have to deal with a legacy project management system as well as legacy technology in introducing OO technology into your development process. A good book on introducing new technology into an organization will help you with this process [Bouldin; Goldberg; Pressman].

This book assumes you have assessed whether to use OO technology or something else and have decided in favor of the former. Perhaps you want to enable higher productivity through stronger reusability of objects, or you want to improve maintainability through the advantages of encapsulated interfaces in components. Perhaps you want to use technology that your competitors are using and beat them at their own game. Perhaps you want to improve quality through higher-productivity OO quality assurance techniques. However you make your decision, this book assumes you've already made it, then helps you to organize for success.

- *Note:* While it is now clear to me that different techniques from the ones currently in use are needed to manage OO projects, I have also come to believe that the opposite is *not* true. That is, if you take the approach described in this book to managing *any* software project, OO or not, you will discover many synergies and advantages over your current methods. OO project management may be necessary for OO projects, but it is clearly useful for other projects as well. The author would be interested to hear from anyone who successfully applies any part of this book to other kinds of projects.

Comparing to Other Models

There are two major standards for the software development process and one major model of the project management process in the current management world: the Capability Maturity Model, the ISO-9000-3 model, and the Project Management Body of Knowledge. This section compares these models to the one I present in this book. You can use the tables in this section to orient yourself if you are familiar with the comparison model.

All of these models are *process models*. That is, the process provides the basic structure in the model. The organization of each model starts with a process and then breaks down the process into pieces. As in software design, this represents a paradigmatic difference with the OO approach. Instead of processes, this book sees objects and classes of objects. A process is one such class of objects. Comparing the models thus requires inverting the process model into the object model, never an easy thing to do. The following comparisons demonstrate the incommensurability of paradigms, though I've tried my best to match them up.

The Capability Maturity Model

The Software Engineering Institute of Carnegie Mellon University (SEI) developed the Capability Maturity Model (CMM), a comprehensive model of the software development process. The CMM outlines a set of processes and maturity levels of those processes. It is a normative model, a set of prescriptions that, if you follow them, will lead you on a clear, upward path to enlightenment: the Optimizing maturity level.

Maturity

The emphasis of the CMM is on *maturity:*

> Software process maturity is the extent to which a specific process is explicitly defined, managed, measured, controlled, and effective. Maturity implies a potential for growth in capability and indicates both the richness of an organization's software process and the consistency with which it is applied in projects throughout the organization. The

software process is well understood throughout a mature organization, usually through documentation and training, and the process is continually being monitored and improved by its users. The capability of a mature software process is known. Software process maturity implies that the productivity and quality resulting from an organization's software process can be improved over time through consistent gains in the discipline achieved by using its software process. [SEI 1993a, p. 4]

The maturity levels of the CMM reflect an interpretation of the way people work, not a fact. I feel, with Gerald Weinberg [Weinberg 1992, pp. 20–23], that the "maturity" in software development comes from applying the right model at the right time for the right reasons. No one model, including the one this book presents, is always "true" in any sense of the word.

The CMM defines the following maturity levels:

1. *Initial*
   The software process is characterized as ad hoc, and occasionally even chaotic. Few processes are defined, and success depends on individual effort.

2. *Repeatable*
   Basic project management processes are established to track cost, schedule, and functionality. The necessary process discipline is in place to repeat earlier successes on projects with similar applications.

3. *Defined*
   The software process for both management and engineering activities is documented, standardized, and integrated into a standard software process for the organization. All projects use an approved, tailored version of the organization's standard software process for developing and maintaining software.

4. *Managed*
   Detailed measures of the software process and product quality are collected. Both the software process and products are quantitatively understood and controlled.

5. *Optimizing*
   Continuous process improvement is enabled by quantitative feedback from the process and from piloting innovative ideas and technologies. [SEI 1993a, pp. 8–9]

The focus of the CMM on getting to a mature, optimizing state exaggerates the consistency of the everyday reality of most software shops. Some of the recommendations are useful most of the time; others are useful some of the time. The OO project management model in this book stresses optimization through applied judgment.

OO project managers must understand the nature of their systems, environment, and work cultures to make the best choices in a given situation. For example, many organizations can produce software with high value to stakeholders without collecting any measurements at all, or indeed without any formally stated process model. As software requirements grow in complexity and as customers become more demanding, the environment demands a different approach. A given project organization may or may not be able to move to a different maturity level through consistent gains in discipline; it is the project manager's job to judge whether the level of discipline is correct for the project. Focusing on maturity levels tends to obscure this responsibility. It can also be very expensive, perhaps unnecessarily so. Capers Jones regards artificial maturity levels as a major type of *risk* to software projects [Jones 1994, pp. 71–77]. As a project manager, you must pick and choose the things you work with. The OO model in this book provides a strong, flexible framework for organizing a project.

The smooth, evolutionary path that the CMM presents does not conform to the capability profile of a given organization at a given time. An organization may have pieces of any maturity level in place. For example, a project might be optimizing its budget while being ad hoc in its approach to scheduling. While the CMM notes this, it sees the profile ("assessment") as showing the *deficiencies* of the organization with respect to maturity, regardless of how much such "deficiencies" make sense in the given situation. It may make sense for project managers to become less CMM-mature as the environment and systems demand such change, while the CMM insists on a consistent, upward gain in discipline. This brings into question the reliance of the SEI on the concept of the maturity level as an *ordinal* scale; it is at best an unordered, *nominal* scale.

Comparing the specific maturity levels to the OO project management framework in this book doesn't work because the framework makes no assumptions about the overall state of optimization. Chapter 1 details the nature of system optimization. It shows how *value,* expressed in terms of vision, mission, and operational objectives, drives each system. It fully integrates the notion of risk into the system model (Part 5). The CMM discusses risk identification and management only tangentially, focusing on the software process assessment or capability evaluation as a means of identifying risks. That is, the CMM sees risk primarily in not being mature rather than looking at it as an essential feature of every system in a project.

The six patterns of management culture in Chapter 31 represent some aspects of the maturity levels, but there is no implied ordering of the cultures (Table 1). These cultural patterns are distinct combinations of management behavior and system relationships, particularly with respect to the way managers use feedback in the system [Weinberg 1992]. While they are systems and part of the model, they do not in any sense organize the model the way the maturity levels organize the CMM.

The model in this book presents the attributes and behaviors for each object in the system in a way designed to be of use to steering, anticipating, and congruent cultures. Variable and routine cultures may get some benefit from this book

Table 1 CMM Maturity Levels versus Management Culture Patterns

Maturity Level	Pattern	Pattern Description
Initial	Oblivious	No faint hint of concept of process
	Variable	No process, super-programmers
	Routine	Magical process; problems lead to panic and abandonment of process; linear thinking
Repeatable, Defined	Steering	Results-driven process based on managerial understanding and effective response to problems; nonlinear thinking
Managed	Anticipating	Experience-driven process; effective measurement
Optimizing	Congruent	Congruent process where everyone improves everything all the time

through exposure to effective project management. They probably will not be able to put these ideas to effective use without changing the culture, however. Similarly, the CMM stresses movement from Initial maturity to higher levels, and the techniques in the CMM apply mostly to those higher levels.

- *Note:* Given that CMM assessments usually show that about 90% of the organizations assessed are in the Initial stage, this focus is probably self-limiting for both the CMM and this book. We live in the hope of a better life, I guess. The encapsulation and cohesion in the present approach, however, should allow variable and routine organizations to make use of at least some parts of the model, while the CMM is probably not that flexible. It regards skipping maturity levels on the way up as "counterproductive." [SEI 1993a, p. 25]

Process Areas

The CMM maturity levels break down into process areas, clusters "of related activities that, when performed collectively, achieve a set of goals considered important for enhancing process capability" [SEI 1993a, p. 30]. These process areas in turn break down into key practices that achieve specific goals. Tables 2 through 5 relate the CMM process areas and their goals [SEI 1993a, pp. 59–64] to the classes in this book. The tables do not go to the level of detail of the key practices because that would take up too much room in what is already a wearisome preface. I have made an attempt, however, to be comprehensive in including all the classes that are relevant to each process area goal as represented in the key practices [SEI 1993b].

Virtually all the goals have *tasks, schedule tasks,* and entries in the *responsibility matrix,* so I make no reference to these. For example, allocating the system requirements to software requires that the manager establish a task (and a schedule task) and assign responsibility for accomplishing it to some individual or work group. Each of these is a class in the OO project management system that is therefore relevant to the requirements management process area of the CMM.

Policy class (32.1)

The "commitment to perform" common feature for each process usually defines a written *policy* (the Policy class) for the process. Since all processes have such a policy, I don't mention it in the tables explicitly.

The "abilities" common feature for each process area usually involves *resource assignments* (including people, hardware, and financial resources), *skills*, and *training* of resources in those skills, and for the sake of brevity the tables do not mention these either.

The "verification" common feature tends to mandate reviews for each process area at the senior management level, project management level, and quality assurance level. The abstract *Joint Review* class represents all these reviews.

Table 2   CMM Process Level 2 Goals versus OO Project Management Classes

Process Area	Goal	Object Class
Requirements management	System requirements allocated to software are controlled to establish a baseline for software engineering and management use.	Policy, Requirements Document, Technical Review, Baseline
	Software plans, products, and activities are kept consistent with the system requirements allocated to software.	Requirements Document, Project Plan, Deliverable, System Validation Test Suite*, Change Management Plan, Change Request, Management Review
Software project planning	Software estimates are documented for use in planning and tracking the software project.	Deliverable, Baseline, Milestone, Effort Estimate, Cost Estimate
	Software project activities and commitments are planned and documented.	Deliverable, Project Plan, Statement of Work, Work Breakdown Structure, Project Schedule, Risk, Risk Management Method, Organizational Environment, Development Process, Milestone, Policy
	Affected groups and individuals agree to their commitments related to the software project.	Stakeholder, Joint Review
Software project tracking and oversight	Actual results and performances are tracked against the software plans.	Project Plan, Development Process, Versioned System, Progress Report, Deliverable, Milestone, Improvement Plan
	Corrective actions are taken and managed to closure when actual results and performance deviate significantly from the software plans.	Project Plan, Development Process, Versioned System, Risk Management Method, Change Report
	Changes to software commitments are agreed to by the affected groups and individuals.	Stakeholder, Joint Review, Communication Meeting

Table 2 CMM Process Level 2 Goals versus OO Project Management Classes *(continued)*

Process Area	Goal	Object Class
Software subcontract management	The prime contractor selects qualified software subcontractors.	Procurement Process, Request for Proposal, Proposal, Assessment Criterion
	The prime contractor and the software subcontractor agree to their commitments to each other.	Joint Review, Contract, Change Management Plan, Quality Management Plan
	The prime contractor and the software subcontractor maintain ongoing communications.	Procurement Management Plan, Contract Administration Process, Communication Meeting
	The prime contractor tracks the software subcontractor's actual results and performance against its commitments.	Primary Process, Contract Administration System, Contract Report, Change Request, Milestone, Quality Management System, Acceptance Test Suite*, Configuration Management System, Improvement Plan
Software quality assurance	Software quality assurance activities are planned.	Quality Management Plan, Test Plan*
	Adherence of software products and activities to the applicable standards, procedures, and requirements is verified objectively.	Development Process, Technical Review, Test Plan*, Test Suite*, Improvement Plan
	Affected groups and individuals are informed of software quality assurance activities and results.	Test Report*, Quality Management System
	Noncompliance issues that cannot be resolved within the software project are addressed by senior management.	Risk Management Plan, Risk Management Method, Organization, Organizational Environment
Software configuration management	Software configuration management activities are planned.	Change Management Plan
	Selected software work products are identified, controlled, and available.	Deliverable, Versioned System, Baseline, Configuration Management Process, Change Management System, Product Repository, Reuse Repository
	Changes to identified software work products are controlled.	Change Request, Change Management System, Quality Management System*
	Affected groups and individuals are informed of the status and content of software baselines.	Change Report, Progress Report

*See Chapter 9.

Table 3 CMM Process Level 3 Goals versus OO Project Management Classes

Process Area	Goal	Object Class
Organization process focus	Software process development and improvement activities are coordinated across the organization.	Stakeholder, Organizational Environment, Organization, Procurement Process, Communication Meeting, Improvement Plan
	The strengths and weaknesses of the software processes used are identified relative to a process standard.	Process Model, Development Process Model, Improvement Plan, Policy, Organizational Repository, Information System
	Organization-level process development and improvement activities are planned.	System, Improvement Plan, Project Plan
Organization process definition	A standard software process for the organization is developed and maintained.	Development Process Model, Policy, Improvement Plan, System
	Information related to the use of the organization's standard software process by the software projects is collected, reviewed, and made available.	Repository, Information System, Improvement Plan
Training program	Training activities are planned.	Staffing Plan, Organizational Repository
	Training for developing the skills and knowledge needed to perform software management and technical roles is provided.	Role, Skill, Training Course, Procurement Process, Improvement Plan
	Individuals in the software engineering group and software-related groups receive the training necessary to perform their roles.	Resource, Training Course, Skill, Organizational Repository
Integrated software management	The project's defined software process is a tailored version of the organization's standard software process.	Development Process Model, Development Process
	The project is planned and managed according to the project's defined software process.	Work Breakdown Structure, Project Repository, Project Management System, Risk Management Plan, Reusable System, Procurement Management Plan, Project Schedule, Dependency, Progress Report, Improvement Plan
Software product engineering	The software engineering tasks are defined, integrated, and consistently performed to produce the software.	Development Process Model, Development Environment, Development Tool, Supporting Process, Improvement Plan

Table 3 CMM Process Level 3 Goals versus OO Project Management Classes (continued)

Process Area	Goal	Object Class
	Software work products are kept consistent with each other.	Deliverable, Integration Test Suite*, System Test Suite*, System Validation Test Suite*, Quality Assurance Process*, Quality Approach*, Test Report*, Improvement Plan, Quality Management System*
Intergroup coordination	The customer's requirements are agreed to by all affected groups.	Joint Review
	The commitments between the engineering groups are agreed to by the affected groups.	Development Process, Joint Review
	The engineering groups identify, track, and resolve intergroup issues.	Communications Management Plan, Work Breakdown Structure, Communication Meeting, Online Repository, Dependency
Peer reviews	Peer review activities are planned.	Work Breakdown Structure, Risk Management Plan
	Defects in the software work products are identified and removed.	Technical Review, Quality Management System*

*See Chapter 9.

Table 4 CMM Process Level 4 Goals versus OO Project Management Classes

Process Area	Goal	Object Class
Quantitative process management	The quantitative process management activities are planned.	System, Operational Objective, Process Model, Project Plan
	The process performance of the project's defined software process is controlled quantitatively.	Operational Objective, Progress Report, Project, Improvement Plan
	The process capability of the organization's standard software process is known in quantitative terms.	Project Repository, Organizational Repository, Baseline

Table 4 CMM Process Level 4 Goals versus OO Project Management Classes (continued)

Process Area	Goal	Object Class
Software quality management	The project's software quality management activities are planned.	Quality Management Plan, Test Plan*
	Measurable goals for software product quality and their priorities are defined.	System, Operational Objective, Risk Management Plan
	Actual progress toward achieving the quality goals for the software products is quantified and managed.	Quality Repository, Quality Management System*, Quality Assurance Process*, Test Suite*, Test Report*, Contract Administration Process, Contract Administration System, Contract Report

*See Chapter 9.

Table 5 CMM Process Level 5 Goals versus OO Project Management Classes

Process Area	Goal	Object Class
Defect prevention	Defect prevention activities are planned.	Organizational Environment, Risk Management Plan, Improvement Plan, Communication Meeting
	Common causes of defects are sought out and identified.	Risk, Test Report*, Technical Review, Improvement Plan, Quality Repository, Quality Management System
	Common causes of defects are prioritized and systematically eliminated.	Improvement Plan, Improvement Review, Risk Management Plan, Process Model, System, Operational Objective, Online Repository
Technology change management	Incorporation of technology changes are planned.	Development Environment, Organizational Environment, Improvement Plan, Procurement Management Plan
	New technologies are evaluated to determine their effect on quality and productivity.	Tool, Process, Organizational Repository, Project Repository, Quality Repository, Improvement Review
	Appropriate new technologies are transferred into normal practice across the organization.	Tool, Process Model, Procurement Process, Online Repository

Table 5 *CMM Process Level 5 Goals versus OO Project Management Classes (continued)*

Process Area	Goal	Object Class
Process change management	Continuous process improvement is planned.	System, Operational Objective, Improvement Plan
	Participation in the organization's software process improvement activities is organization-wide.	Project Organization, Improvement Review
	The organization's standard software process and the project's defined software processes are improved continuously.	Process, System, Project Plan, Repository, Improvement Review

*See Chapter 9.

The ISO-9000-3 Model

Rising above the CMM for a breath of air, this section considers a much less detailed standard, ISO-9000-3. This standard is a guideline for applying the ISO-9001 standard for quality assurance to the development, supply, and maintenance of software. The result is a guide to software development, one much less comprehensive and detailed than the CMM. Table 6 lists the headings of the standard and suggests the correspondence to the object classes in this book.

- *Note:* The main criticism of ISO-9000, aside from it being a waste of time, is that it addresses only process quality rather than product quality. The idea seems to be that if you get the process for producing value right, you will produce the right value. This seems to me to be a stretch. This book recommends looking at the value and risk in all project systems, process and product.

Table 6 *ISO-9000-3 Section Headings versus OO Project Management Classes*

Section No.	Heading	Object Classes
4.1	Management Responsibility	Policy, Organization (Responsibility Matrix), Improvement Review, Contract Administration Plan, Procurement Process, Joint Review
4.2	Quality System	Supporting Process, Policy, Development Process Model, Quality Management Plan
4.3	Internal Quality System Audits	Improvement Plan
4.4	Corrective Action	Test Plan*, Test Report*, Test Suite*, Risk Management Plan, Development Process
5.1	Life Cycle Activities	Development Process Model

Table 6 ISO-9000-3 Section Headings versus OO Project Management Classes *(continued)*

Section No.	Heading	Object Classes
5.2	Contract Review	Contract, Contract Administration Process
5.3	Purchaser's Requirements Specification	Requirements Document, Request for Proposal, Statement of Work, Contract Administration Process, Communications Management Plan
5.4.1	Development Planning	Development Plan (Operational Objective, Staffing Plan, Work Breakdown Structure, Project Schedule), Development Process, Joint Review
5.4.2	Development Plan	Development Process Model, Development Plan, Work Breakdown Structure, Project Schedule, Quality Management Plan, Change Management Plan, Cost Management Plan, Risk Management Plan, Procurement Management Plan, Staffing Plan, Communication Management Plan, Development Tool
5.4.3	Progress Control	Improvement Plan, Progress Report, Joint Review
5.4.4	Input to Development Phases	Development Process Model, Versioned System, Requirements Document, Functional Specification
5.4.5	Output from Development Phases	Development Process Model, Versioned System, Test Plan*, Test Suite*, Technical Review
5.4.6	Verification of Each Phase	Joint Review, Development Process, Risk Management Plan, Test Report*
5.5	Quality Planning	Quality Management Plan, Test Plan*, Change Management Plan
5.6.1	Design and Implementation	Development Process Model, Contract
5.6.2	Design	Design Standard Document, Development Tool
5.6.3	Implementation	Coding Standard Document, Development Tool
5.6.4	Reviews	Policy, Technical Review, Development Process Model
5.7.1	Testing and Validation	Risk Management Plan
5.7.2	Test Planning	Test Plan*, Test Case*, Technical Review, Test Environment*, Quality Tool, Quality Approach*, Resource, Skill
5.7.3	Testing	Test Data*, Quality Repository, Test Report*, Improvement Plan
5.7.4	Validation	System Validation Test Suite*
5.7.5	Field Testing	Field Test Suite*
5.8	Acceptance	System Acceptance Test Suite*, Joint Review, Contract Administration Process, Contract, Test Plan*

Table 6 ISO-9000-3 Section Headings versus OO Project Management Classes *(continued)*

Section No.	Heading	Object Classes
5.9	Replication, Delivery, and Installation	Contract, Development Process, Progress Report (partial coverage only)
5.10	Maintenance	Contract, Project, Versioned System, Product Repository, Quality Management System* (project-related coverage only)
6.1	Configuration Management	Configuration Management System, Versioned System, Change Request, Product Repository, Change Management Plan, Change Management Process Model and Process, Progress Report
6.2	Document Control	Project Document, Change Management Process Model, Change Management Plan, Policy, Development Plan
6.3	Quality Records	Repository, Improvement Plan, Test Report*
6.4	Measurement	Operational Objective
6.5	Rules, Practices, and Conventions	Project Process Model, Joint Review
6.6	Tools and Techniques	Tool
6.7	Purchasing	Procurement Process Model, Request for Proposal, Proposal, Contract, Procurement Management Plan, Contract Administration Process, System Validation Test*, System Acceptance Test*
6.8	Included Software	Procurement Management Plan, Contract
6.9	Training	Resource, Skill, Organizational Repository

*See Chapter 9.

The Project Management Body of Knowledge

The Project Management Body of Knowledge (PMBOK) [PMI 1996a] is a reference to the generally accepted knowledge and practices of modern project management. Everything in this guide applies to managing OO software projects, though the practices are general to every kind of project. The breadth of the current book takes its inspiration from this guide but changes the organization from a process organization to an object-oriented organization. Table 7 relates the project management context and process sections of the guide to object classes.

Table 8 relates the specific PMBOK knowledge areas to the corresponding classes.

Table 7 PMBOK Project Management Context versus OO Project Management Classes

Section No.	Header	Object Classes
2.1	Project Phases and the Project Life Cycle	Project, Project Process Model, Development Process Model
2.2	Project Stakeholders	Stakeholder, Organizational Environment
2.3	Organizational Influences	Organizational Environment, Organization, Management Culture, Functional Organization, Projectized Organization, Matrix Organization, Organization Chart
2.4	Key General Management Skills	Skill
2.5	Socioeconomic Influences	External Standard, Organizational Environment
3.1	Project Processes	Process, Process Model, Project Process Model
3.2	Process Groups	Process, Process Model, Project Process Model
3.3	Process Interactions	Process, Process Model, Project Process Model
3.4	Customizing Process Interactions	Process, Process Model, Project Process Model, Work Breakdown Structure

Table 8 PMBOK Project Management Knowledge Areas versus OOPM Classes

Section No.	Header	Object Classes
4	Project Integration Management	
4.1	Project Plan Development	Project Process, Stakeholder, Project Management System, Project Plan
4.2	Project Plan Execution	Project Plan, Policy, System, Skill, Project Plan, Joint Review, Communication Meeting, Progress Report, Versioned System, Change Request
4.3	Overall Change Control	Project Plan, Progress Report, Change Request, Change Management Plan, Change Management Process Model, Change Management System, Improvement Plan, Project Management System
5	Project Scope Management	
5.1	Initiation	Requirements Document, Organizational Environment, Policy, Project, Skill
5.2	Scope Planning	Statement of Work, Risk Management Plan, Change Management Plan

Preface   xxxiii

Table 8 PMBOK Project Management Knowledge Areas versus OOPM Classes *(continued)*

Section No.	Header	Object Classes
5.3	Scope Definition	Statement of Work, Project Plan, Stakeholder, Work Breakdown Structure
5.4	Scope Verification	Statement of Work, Joint Review, Milestone
5.5	Scope Change Control	Work Breakdown Structure, Progress Report, Change Request, Change Management System, Change Management Plan, Project Plan, System
6	Project Time Management	
6.1	Activity Definition	Work Breakdown Structure, Statement of Work, Stakeholder
6.2	Activity Sequencing	Work Breakdown Structure, Dependency, Project Plan, Project Management System, Dependency Chart
6.3	Activity Duration Estimating	Work Breakdown Structure, Resource, Skill, Assignment, Effort Estimate, Duration
6.4	Schedule Development	Dependency Chart, Duration, Resource, Assignment, Work Calendar, Project Management System, Time Chart, Schedule Task, Milestone, Project Schedule, Staffing Plan
6.5	Schedule Control	Project Schedule, Progress Report, Change Management Plan, Change Request, Change Management System, Duration, Effort Estimate, Versioned System, System
7	Project Cost Management	
7.1	Resource Planning	Work Breakdown Structure, Organizational Environment, Statement of Work, Organization, Policy, Resource, Staffing Plan
7.2	Cost Estimating	Work Breakdown Structure, Staffing Plan, Cost Estimate, Cost Estimation Tool, Cost Management Plan
7.3	Cost Budgeting	Cost Estimate, Work Breakdown Structure, Project Schedule, Cost Estimation Tool, Cost Budget
7.4	Cost Control	Cost Budget, Progress Report, Change Management Plan, Change Request, Change Management System, Cost Management System, Versioned System, Cost Estimate, System, Deliverable
8	Project Quality Management	
8.1	Quality Planning	Quality Approach*, Statement of Work, Policy, Organizational Environment, Quality Environment, Quality Management System*, Quality Management Plan, Operational Objective
8.2	Quality Assurance	Quality Management Plan, Quality Repository, Operational Objective, Quality Management System*, Improvement Plan

Table 8 PMBOK Project Management Knowledge Areas versus OOPM Classes (continued)

Section No.	Header	Object Classes
8.3	Quality Control	Versioned System, Quality Management Plan, Operational Objective, Test Suite*, Quality Management System*, Test Report*, Task, Improvement Plan, Process
9	Project Human Resource Management	
9.1	Organizational Planning	Organization, Skill, Task, Assignment, Organizational Environment, Stakeholder, Staffing Plan, Organization Chart
9.2	Staff Acquisition	Staffing Plan, Resource, Organization Chart, Assignment
9.3	Team Development	Resource, Project Plan, Staffing Plan, Progress Report, Work Group, Skill, System, Training Course, Organizational Environment
10	Project Communications Management	
10.1	Communications Planning	Organization, Stakeholder, Organizational Environment, Assignment, Work Group, Communication Tool, Communication Management Plan
10.2	Information Distribution	Progress Report, Versioned System, Communication Management Plan, Project Plan, Skill, Communication Tool, Project Repository, Information System
10.3	Performance Reporting	Project Plan, Versioned System, Progress Report, Project Repository, Communication Meeting, Deliverable, Change Request
10.4	Administrative Closure	Deliverable, Project Repository, System, Improvement Plan, Project, Process Milestone, Project Management System
11	Project Risk Management	
11.1	Risk Identification	Statement of Work, Project Plan, Stakeholder, Risk, System
11.2	Risk Quantification	System, Risk, Cost Estimate, Duration, Project Schedule, Risk Management Plan
11.3	Risk Response Development	Risk Management Plan, Risk Management Method, Contingency Plan, Reserve, Insurance Policy Provision, Contractual Provision, Contract
11.4	Risk Response Control	Risk Management Plan, Process, Versioned System, System
12	Project Procurement Management	
12.1	Procurement Planning	Statement of Work, Organizational Environment, Procurement Process Model, Procurement Management Plan, Contract
12.2	Solicitation Planning	Statement of Work, Procurement Management Plan, Request for Proposal, Proposal Assessment Criteria

Table 8 PMBOK Project Management Knowledge Areas versus OOPM Classes *(continued)*

Section No.	Header	Object Classes
12.3	Solicitation	Request for Proposal, Organizational Environment, Proposal
12.4	Source Selection	Proposal, Assessment Criterion, Policy, Contract
12.5	Contract Administration	Contract, Deliverable, Change Request, Change Management System, Contract Report, Organizational Environment, Contract Administration Process, Contract Administration System, Procurement Management Plan
12.6	Contract Close-Out	Contract Administration System, Contract Report, Improvement Plan, Contract Administration Process, Milestone

*See Chapter 9.

How to Use the Book

Generally, if you can read this sentence, you can use the book. Unlike software, books tend toward a standard technological solution to most problems, refreshingly, and everybody knows about that solution. There are some conventions that need explaining, however.

References to Other Works and the Bibliography

I have tried to minimize the impact of references to other works by simply embedding a name into the text in square brackets where necessary, such as this: [Weinberg]. This reference refers to a particular book by Weinberg that appears in the bibliography. Where there is ambiguity (two books, for example), I add the year: [Weinberg 1994]. Further ambiguity (two works in a year, for example) adds a distinguishing letter: [Weinberg 1994a]. If I am referring to a specific part of the work, I put the page numbers in the reference: [Weinberg, pp. 26–30]. Any comments I have about the book or its contents appear in the readings at the end of each chapter. There are no footnotes, a technology I reject.

There may be entries in the bibliography that do not appear as references.

Internal References

Bold marginal text appears when I refer to another part of the book. This marginal text will refer to either a chapter and section or a class, with the class name and number. Class diagrams also include the class name and numbers for cross-referential purposes.

Chapters have numbers, and system classes have numbers. No other sections in the book have numbers. This facilitates cross-references to classes by class number. The class number is the chapter number plus one or more incremental numbers depending on the position in the object hierarchy.

Figure numbers contain the chapter number and an incremental figure number. Figures should appear in the book somewhere around their first appearance in the text (Figure 2-1…).

Readings

[Humphrey]   Watts S. Humphrey. *Managing the Software Process.* Reading, MA: Addison-Wesley, 1989.

This book is the most complete version of the CMM, although the SEI has published a significant revision [SEI 1993a; SEI 1993b] that renders parts of it out of date. To fully understand the philosophy and detailed structure of the CMM, you need to read this book and the revised model in the SEI technical report.

[Kehoe]   Raymond Kehoe and Alka Jarvis. *ISO 9000-3: A Tool for Software Product and Process Improvement.* New York: Springer-Verlag, 1996.

While the ISO-9000-3 standard itself is the original source, this book adds glosses and suggestions that make it much more valuable. As with any book, take each suggestion as it is offered, with a grain of salt.

[PMI 1996a]   Project Management Institute Standards Committee. *A Guide to the Project Management Body of Knowledge.* Upper Darby, PA: Project Management Institute (+1-610-734-3330), 1996.

This recently revised version of the Project Management Body of Knowledge is a guide to the generally accepted knowledge and practices of project management. It is intended to be the reference for the PMI certification examination as well as a common lexicon for project management professionals. While short on details and references, this brief book gives a comprehensive, well-organized, and very useful overview of the field of project management. Any serious project manager should have a copy of this book and should be familiar with all the topics in it.

[SEI 1993a]   Mark C. Paulk, Bill Curtis, Mary Beth Chrissis, and Charles V. Weber. *Capability Maturity Model for Software, Version 1.1.* CMU/SEI-93-TR-24. Pittsburgh: Software Engineering Institute, Carnegie Mellon University (http://www.sei.cmu.edu), February 1993.

[SEI 1993b]   Mark C. Paulk, Charles V. Weber, Suzanne M. Garcia, Marybeth Chrissis, and Marilyn Bush. *Key Practices of the Capability Maturity Model, Version 1.1.* CMU/SEI-93-TR-25. Pittsburgh: Software Engineering Institute, Carnegie Mellon University (http://www.sei.cmu.edu), February 1993.

These technical reports are the latest version of the CMM. Anyone working with the CMM should have a copy of them as their basic reference. The CMM report gives you an overview of the model, focusing on maturity levels and process areas. The Key Practices report goes into detail on the process areas and their key practices. The detail is so great that you may benefit from cross-referencing to the indicated process areas in Tables 2 through 5 to get ideas for how to go about implementing some of the less detailed objects in this book. Be choosy, however, about adopting all of the CMM recommendations wholesale.

[Weinberg 1992] Gerald M. Weinberg. *Quality Software Management: Volume 1, Systems Thinking.* New York: Dorset House, 1992.

Weinberg's first volume of his magnum opus on software management is a clarion call for rationality in such management. I refer in this chapter to his analysis of patterns of software management culture and his criticisms of the capability maturity approach to process improvement. This book should be required reading for all software project managers.

Web Enhancement

To enhance this book's value as a practical reference to OO project management, the *Productive Objects* Web page on the Morgan Kaufmann Web site at *http://www.mkp.com/prodobj* offers some materials that can help you navigate around the project management classes.

First, you'll find two lists of all the classes. The first list is in alphabetic order by class, with the class number listed next to it. The second list is in numeric order by class number so you can look up the class by its number. The number includes the book chapter (class 23.1, for example, is the first class mentioned in Chapter 23).

Second, you'll find a diagram that merges the summary class diagrams you'll find in the part introductions. This diagram shows you the entire class hierarchy of the book arranged as nested classes. This Adobe Acrobat file lets you zero in on a particular cluster of classes that addresses your current interests.

Third, you'll find a complete list, again in Adobe Acrobat format, of all the visions, missions, and operational objectives in numeric order. This document gives you electronic access to the key reference elements of the classes, especially the metrics and objectives.

Creative use of these supplementary materials can greatly enhance your experience using the ideas in *Productive Objects*. Please don't hesitate to use them, and please send any suggestions for additional materials you think might be useful to Morgan Kaufmann or to the author at *muller@acm.org*.

Related Titles from Morgan Kaufmann

Understanding UML: The Developer's Guide with a Web-Based Application in Java

Paul Harmon and Mark Watson
1997; 300 pages; paperback; ISBN 1-55860-465-0

The Unified Modeling Language (UML) is a third-generation method for specifying, visualizing, and documenting an object-oriented system under development. It unifies three leading object-oriented methods and others to serve as the basis for a common, stable, and expressive object-oriented development method. This practical introduction to UML provides software developers and designers with an overview of this powerful new design method. It teaches Java programmers how to employ an object-oriented methodology to create Java applications—from analysis to design to final code.

Contextual Design: Defining Customer-Centered Systems

Hugh Beyer and Karen Holtzblatt
1997; 350 pages; paperback; ISBN 1-55860-411-1

This book introduces a customer-centered approach to business by showing how data gathered from people while they work can drive the definition of a product or process while supporting the needs of teams and their organizations. This is a practical, hands-on guide for anyone trying to design systems that reflect the way customers want to do their work. The authors developed Contextual Design, the method discussed here, through their work with teams struggling to design products and internal systems. In this book, you'll find the underlying principles of the method and how to apply them to different problems, constraints, and organizational situations.

PART ONE

Systems and Projects

"First thing to be done is to get rid of this bear, he's gummin' up the whole project."

"Dash it all, he IS the project!"

The wisdom of Walt Disney applied to project management
(The Many Adventures of Winnie-the-Pooh)

This part of the book introduces the basic terminology and ideas you need to understand to make sense of the rest of the book. It looks at systems and how you build them and improve them. It looks at how to make systems reusable. Finally, it describes the project and its components.

Deciding what the project is may be the most important aspect of creating OO software. Deciding how and when to reuse your systems is certainly next in line. This part introduces the two main classes of this book: system and reusable system. It develops the key elements of *kaizen,* or *continuous improvement,* through the improvement plan and its subclasses, all of which are project documents. The improvement plan depends on the one class in the book that is not a system by itself, the operational objective. This may not be a system, but systems all have operational objectives. Improvement plans also depend on system models, which represent the systems to improve.

The reusable system is at the heart of the OO approach to project management. Many classes in this book are subclasses of reusable system, and this is the source of much of the power of the approach. The versioned system is a kind of reusable system that lets you manage changes to systems over time. Many kinds of project management systems are versioned as well as being reusable in other ways. The reuse repository, a kind of storage organization, is key to the effectiveness of reusable systems.

Finally, Part 1 introduces the project and its stakeholders and deliverables. The project is a kind of task, meaning that projects represent some type of work. The stakeholders define what the work is to produce, the deliverables of the project. Deliverables are a kind of versioned object, meaning that you can deliver several versions of the object over its lifetime.

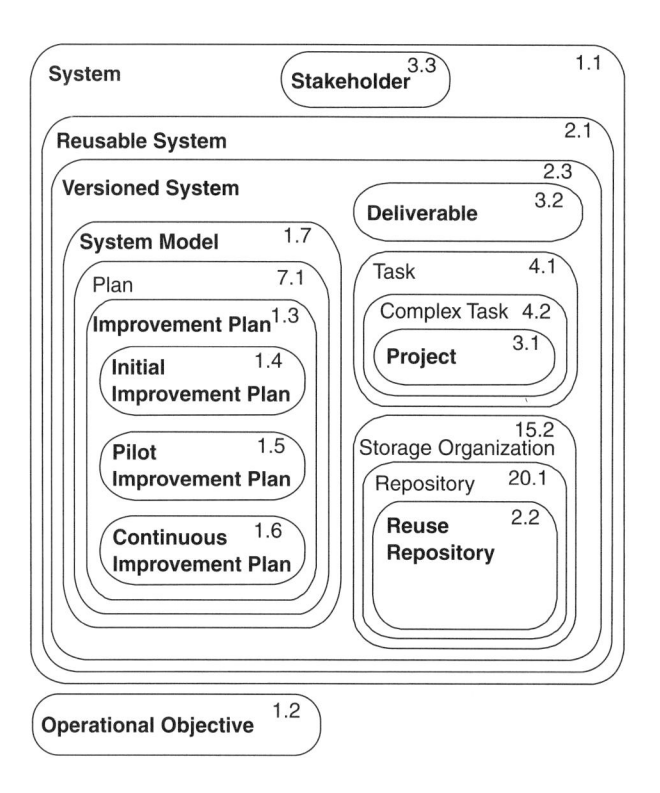

```
┌─────────────────────────────────────────────────┐
│ System          Stakeholder 3.3            1.1  │
│  ┌────────────────────────────────────────────┐ │
│  │ Reusable System                       2.1  │ │
│  │ ┌────────────────────────┐  ┌───────────┐  │ │
│  │ │ Versioned System  2.3  │  │Deliverable│  │ │
│  │ │ ┌──────────────────┐   │  │    3.2    │  │ │
│  │ │ │ System Model 1.7 │   │  └───────────┘  │ │
│  │ │ │ ┌──────────────┐ │   │  ┌───────────┐  │ │
│  │ │ │ │ Plan    7.1  │ │   │  │ Task  4.1 │  │ │
│  │ │ │ │Improvement1.3│ │   │  │Complex    │  │ │
│  │ │ │ │ Plan         │ │   │  │Task   4.2 │  │ │
│  │ │ │ │ ┌──────────┐ │ │   │  │ Project3.1│  │ │
│  │ │ │ │ │Initial 1.4│ │   │  └───────────┘  │ │
│  │ │ │ │ │Improvement│ │ │   │                 │ │
│  │ │ │ │ │Plan       │ │ │   │  ┌───────────┐  │ │
│  │ │ │ │ └──────────┘ │ │   │  │Storage    │  │ │
│  │ │ │ │ ┌──────────┐ │ │   │  │Org. 15.2  │  │ │
│  │ │ │ │ │Pilot  1.5│ │ │   │  │Repository │  │ │
│  │ │ │ │ │Improvement│ │   │  │       20.1│  │ │
│  │ │ │ │ │Plan       │ │ │   │  │Reuse  2.2 │  │ │
│  │ │ │ │ └──────────┘ │ │   │  │Repository │  │ │
│  │ │ │ │ ┌──────────┐ │ │   │  └───────────┘  │ │
│  │ │ │ │ │Continuous│ │ │   │                 │ │
│  │ │ │ │ │Improv.1.6│ │ │   │                 │ │
│  │ │ │ │ │Plan       │ │   │                 │ │
│  │ │ │ │ └──────────┘ │ │   │                 │ │
│  │ │ │ └──────────────┘ │   │                 │ │
│  │ │ └──────────────────┘   │                 │ │
│  │ └────────────────────────┘                 │ │
│  └────────────────────────────────────────────┘ │
│        Operational Objective  1.2               │
└─────────────────────────────────────────────────┘
```

■ *Note:* The illustration of the class hierarchy contains all the classes this part defines. Other parts of the book define and discuss classes not in boldface.

CHAPTER

1

A General Systems Approach

Managing an OO software project is not an easy task. Many busy project managers rise through the technical ranks to their positions without understanding either the special nature of software project management or the special needs of OO projects. This book systematically develops all the different aspects of managing such projects. It is for both the new or untrained project manager and the experienced project manager who needs to understand a bit more about OO projects.

To systematically develop a subject, there is nothing like organizing the discussion around the system. The following sections go into more detail on how systems are valuable to project managers. The chapters that follow go into even more detail on how to see every aspect of your project as a kind of system interacting with other systems and environments. Even reusability, that holy grail of the OO world, is a system characteristic. This systemic perspective will give you a strong, holistic understanding of the pieces of project management and how to put them together into a successful, valuable OO project.

■ *Note:* Most approaches to software development organize around processes, such as the Business Process Reengineering (BPR) approach, the CMM, ISO-9000, and ISO/IEX-12205. Why use the system instead of the process as the central concept? Systems are more general, as processes are systems, but not all systems are processes. Systems fit better with an OO model; the OO paradigm is all about things and relationships between things versus their behavior. Finally, systems provide some very useful concepts, such as purposiveness and feedback.

Systems, Projects, and Value

What does it mean to see a project as a system? Why does taking the system approach to project management make sense? What are the constructive principles behind the systems in this book? How can you measure the goals of a system? *Value,* both external and internal, plays a key role in understanding the project system and its management and is the fundamental focus of this book. The value of the project drives the project and the people who participate in it.

Value, and its synonym *quality,* are what projects are all about. If there is no value to a project, no one will undertake it. You define the success of a project by the value it delivers to its stakeholders, just as you define the failure of a project as the value the project fails to deliver.

Despite the clarity of this relationship between value and project success, it is still difficult to define the idea of value. Emotions, politics, culture, and other human qualities often obscure the concept. The actual meaning of value depends on your project vision and mission. Value can be as simple as the return on investment (ROI) on system deliverables, but usually that's too simple. A more sophisticated approach to economic or functional value such as *warranted equity value* or *earned value* can yield better results. If you have interests going beyond the economic world, such as social conditions or the environment, you need to include value along those dimensions as well.

Deliverable (3.2)

With software systems, value is a matter of the satisfaction of the needs of the people who use it. If user requirements and values drive OO software development, it produces a system you design to satisfy those needs. The system is thus a better, more valuable software product for the project stakeholders.

Value is not absolute, but relative to the observer [Weinberg 1975, pp. 51–85]. Even projects desperately inefficient at everything can deliver value to some observer, and often do. Because of this relation between projects in a global system, you should not *maximize* value in a given project but only *optimize* value for a project in a given environment for a given set of stakeholders or observers. What you're doing now may work but be suboptimal, and it may not work if the environment changes. Value is important because it drives the project, and measuring the value you deliver is important because it allows you to set an achievable goal. The absolute value involved, however, is less important than the optimization of the system that produces it.

Suppose there were two large software projects, both working in the general area of database software. Each project is producing software with similar functions, say the ability to represent complex objects and the ability to handle distributed transaction processing. The Theseus project has a strong organization that follows Total Quality principles and has a software maturity assessment of 3 according to the Software Engineering Institute (this is fiction, of course). The Minotaur project is three MIT students in a very dark room programming in Gnu C++ on Macintoshes.

While Theseus produces a feature-laden offering that certainly will satisfy the project's stakeholders, it is not out of the question for Minotaur to succeed in its project as well. Theseus will charge a high price for its software; Minotaur might well distribute its product as freeware across the Internet. Which will prove more popular? It probably depends on the real demand for the features. If Minotaur does enough to be useful, stakeholders will use it.

Some people will buy Theseus software and others will buy or simply download Minotaur software in a reasonably free market. The total amount of functionality (that is, software *value*) in the system will be higher than it would be if one project or the other did not exist. In fact, the way things work in the current environment, it is just as likely that Theseus would make a deal with Minotaur to integrate and resell their software at the system price level. This merger might even increase the total system value further.

Two years down the road, the MIT students will have graduated and gone on to well-paying jobs at Microsoft, Sybase, or Oracle. The Theseus project team will have completed two more projects, yielding yet more value to their stakeholders.

What does this economic fable really mean to project management? One moral, which might seem fabulous but is not, is that value is relative to the system, not to the specific project, and that you cannot therefore maximize value without reference to the environment of the project as a system. Even a badly run project can succeed in delivering value in a system where the project has some comparative advantage, and that is usually true. Evaluating your project as the value it delivers says very little about ultimate success and growth, nor about the overall capabilities of your organization. So what do you use to guide your project from within? You need to find a way to focus on understanding your comparative advantage and improving your advantage in other dimensions. This requires benchmarking your project against other projects, in turn requiring much formal organization, management, and data collection.

It also requires methods that focus on *improvement* rather than on absolute value. Absolute value is almost never useful in evaluating a software project. It fails in particular with OO software projects that produce code reusable in other projects or that reuse such code. Emphasizing improvement lets you focus on doing things better, with benchmarking making sure that you're doing it better than everyone else.

This book takes a normative approach to such methods for improvement, recommending what a project should look like, how to structure improvement efforts, and how you should measure value. It does this only within parameters that can vary a great deal. Without necessarily dragging in all the baggage associated with the Total Quality movement, the Japanese term *kaizen,* or *continuous improvement,* does seem to sum up the approach well. But no two organizations have the same way of constructing and valuing their development systems, and any method that rigidly prescribes a structure dooms itself. There are an infinite number of ways to organize a project to produce value. You will find that the proposals in this book can adapt to many different organizational cultures and structures.

In addition, this book takes an OO approach to structuring the systems of project management. As the following section discusses in more detail, this approach greatly facilitates applying project-management principles to OO development projects. The framework is flexible enough to accommodate the changes you need to make to adapt the techniques to your particular situation.

In this OO systems approach to project management, then, the focus is on the way a project achieves value through an adaptable and flexible set of object systems.

Object Systems

Taking an OO approach to talking about project management immediately immerses you in a way of thinking about managing OO software projects. That aligns you completely with the methods you are using to build your software, removing many of the usual barriers to successful optimization that you face as a project manager. The concepts of OO design provide the modeling notation for the book.

Each major section in this book describes a class of object. The section describes the class structure in both the *class model* (system of classes comprising the inheritance or type network) and the *object model* (a system of ownership and messaging relationships between objects).

An *object* is an individually identifiable thing with internal state and external behavior. The dynamic system comprises two or more objects interacting to produce the value of the system.

A *class* is a set of objects with the same properties. Each class has a set of *attributes* (simple objects) and *tasks* (pieces of work the object performs as part of its duties, its *contract* with the objects that use it).

The class model represents the type relationships between classes. That is, a class may be a kind of another class (a *subclass* of a *superclass*). For example, a project is a kind of system; it is also a kind of task that produces value. If a class has one parent class, the relationship is single inheritance; if it has two or more parent classes, the relationship is multiple inheritance. Inheritance means that the subclass inherits the properties (attributes and tasks) of the superclass.

- ■ *Note:* In this book, multiple inheritance is quite rare, with only one instance (the Matrix Organization class). The avoidance of multiple inheritance is good design, because it reduces the coupling of the class to other classes and reduces the complexity of meaning that the class inherits. See your local OO text for a full description of multiple inheritance.

Matrix Organization (29.4)

Design Standard (32.2)

An interesting if quirky aspect of OO modeling is that one spends very little time talking about objects; virtually all serious work gets done with classes. Since objects represent actual things, and classes represent the models for those things, designers spend a lot more time with classes. They want to model the system rather than see an actual system in motion. That is particularly true in this book, which deals largely in classes. You can use the book to examine parts of the project system in detail. You can see the overall workings of the project system through the interacting objects that the class descriptions call for. There are some system models that show the dynamics of object interaction. If you want to see actual objects performing their behaviors, though, plan and execute a project and map the results back to this book.

The following sections outline the notation the illustrations in this book use to supplement the text. In practice, there is no distinction between the class and object models; both appear in the same diagrams unless there is some reason to emphasize one or the other. For example, the introduction to each part of the book includes a class model to show the overall inheritance hierarchy of classes the part defines.

The Class Model Notation

The class diagrams in this book present the classes of objects in a modified OOSD notation [Wasserman], which Figure 1-1 illustrates for the class named "C." A box represents a class definition, with the name of the class in boldface in the top section of the box. The class reference number appears in the upper-right-hand corner of the box.

The rounded rectangles represent the superclasses of the class they surround [Harel], in this case classes A and B. The subclass inherits all the attributes and tasks of the superclasses, which do not appear in the diagram. You can cross-reference in this book to all the classes to find their attributes and tasks using the class reference numbers that appear in the upper-right-hand corner of the superclass rectangle.

Figure 1-1
Example of OOSD class diagram

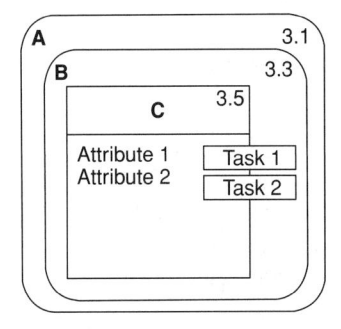

A class *attribute* is a property of a class that represents some basic data element that constitutes part of the object state, such as a number or text string. These are relatively rare in the project model, as most things are objects in their own right, not simple data elements. The second section of the class box lists these attributes by name (Attribute 1 and Attribute 2 in Figure 1-1). Please refer to the surrounding text for detailed discussion of the attributes.

A class *task* corresponds to a method or operation in standard OO design terminology. A task represents a unit of behavior of the objects that the class represents. In the project model, tasks represent the dynamic connections between the operating objects. When you see a project in operation, it consists of a series of tasks running, perhaps in parallel. The class task models this behavior, connecting the classes in a dynamic model. The notation represents tasks by small rectangles overlapping the class box in the lower section (Tasks 1 and 2 in Figure 1-1). The box contains the name of the task. Again, see the accompanying text for a detailed discussion of the task's behavior.

- *Note:* How much is enough? While the OO metaphor works in a book up to a point, one must walk a fine line and not descend into Lilliputian lunacy. OO design, for example, continues on from the method to define method arguments that then allow for method overloading, permitting several methods with the same name but different arguments in the same class. This would almost certainly confuse the issue in the project model, so I don't do it. Keep it simple, that's what they tried to teach me....

The Object Model Notation

The object model represents the relationships between objects, as opposed to the relationships between classes. There are two aspects to this: the related classes and the kind of relationship.

All the diagrams in this book represent the object model in simple, one-level diagrams. That is, you start with the class you are defining, show the objects that class owns or accesses, and leave it at that. On occasion, there may be a kind of shorthand that defines several classes together rather than pedantically doing separate diagrams; this conserves space and time, as all good objects must. Figure 1-2 illustrates the class definition of Figure 1-1 extended with its object model.

The boxes with boldface names connecting to class C represent *class references*. The class definition (class C) refers to objects of three other classes (D, E, and F). The references include a class number for cross-referencing within the book; all the classes are here somewhere.

The lines between the classes represent the object relationships. There are many, many ways of classifying object relationships. You can distinguish between objects the class definition owns versus those it merely accesses. You can distinguish one-way and two-way relationships (which object knows about the other).

Figure 1-2
Example of OOSD class diagram with object model

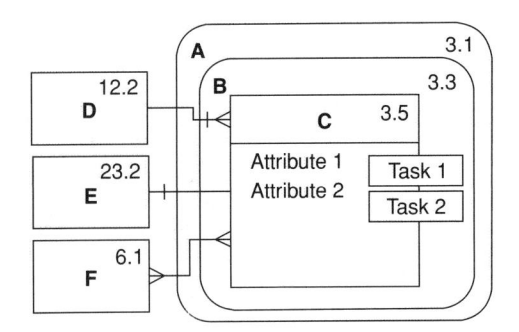

You can enumerate the objects, specifying how many there are on each end. You can specify whether the relationship is optional. You can even introduce concurrency concerns. I refer you to my previous note on simplicity.

The diagrams in this book use a relatively common entity-relationship (ER) notation that shows the enumeration and optionality of relationships. A crow's-foot at the end of a line indicates there may be several of the objects of that class relating to the original object. A crosshatch across the line means there must be at least one object. Table 1-1 lists the various possible relationships.

These relationships are familiar to database designers. For this book, they help you to see the structure between the classes without too much design detail.

For example, take the relationship between the schedule task and the people who work on it. The interesting thing about this is that it is many-to-many, required. You must have at least one person working on a task, and you can have multiple people working on it. The relationship object itself, the *assignment*, is central to the project. Its attributes include the kind of assignment, the estimated effort to complete the assignment, and so on. The assignment is the related object instead of the actual person assigned. That is, instead of linking the schedule task directly to the labor resource, the model links the schedule task to an assignment

Table 1-1 Relationship Types

Relationship	Description
One-to-one, optional	A single object perhaps relating to a single object
One-to-one, required	A single object definitely relating to another object (class C to class E in Figure 1-2)
One-to-many, optional	A single object relating to zero or more other objects
One-to-many, required	A single object relating to one or more other objects (class D to class B in Figure 1-2)
Many-to-many, optional	Several objects relating to zero or more other objects (class F to class C in Figure 1-2)
Many-to-many, required	Several objects relating to one or more other objects

and the assignment to the resource. The first relationship is one-to-many, required. The second is many-to-one, optional. A schedule task has at least one assignment, and a resource may have multiple assignments.

Using this basic notation, you can express most of the interesting elements of the system of project management.

The System Model Notation

The dynamic activity in the system represents a sequence of tasks the system's objects perform. Occasionally, the dynamic effects of the system in operation are important to understanding project management. While there is no overall system model in this book, it illustrates the important dynamic system relationships with a simple system modeling notation [Weinberg 1992; Abdel-Hamid]. The point of these diagrams is to show how dynamic operation through feedback affects interacting objects to produce surprising, nonlinear effects. Figure 1-3 is a system diagram that models Brooks's law (adding more people to a late project makes it later) [Brooks, pp. 21–26].

Slipping milestones cause a slower accumulation of earned value, which in turn causes the project to have a larger schedule variance. This causes the project to revise the project plan by revising the staffing plan, hiring additional resources, and increasing the number of assignments to work packages. To do this, however, the project plan also increases the number of levels of effort (that is, management or overhead tasks) and the number of personal interactions, meetings, and training courses for the pool of resources. These in turn reduce the availability of resources. Figure 1-3 does not show the mechanism by which reduced availability increases the duration of schedule tasks, which is quite complex. The increased effort spent on work packages, due to the lower availability of resources, actually increases the duration rather than reducing it. All this feeds back into the milestones, increasing the milestone date, which starts the whole circus over again.

■ *Note:* While it would be fascinating to develop a complete system model based on the class and object models in this book, it is well beyond the present scope. The system diagrams are illustrations that make a point about the impact of systems thinking on project management. They provide a dynamic model to add life to the more static class and object diagrams.

The ovals represent objects interacting in a system of objects. Overlapping ovals, such as Person or Personal Interaction in Figure 1-3, represent a pool of a particular kind of object. It is usually safe to assume that the real world is more complex than the diagram lets on, so please don't take the model too seriously. The lines between ovals represent feedback, relationships that change the object state in one of several ways. These relationships are messages that one system sends to another.

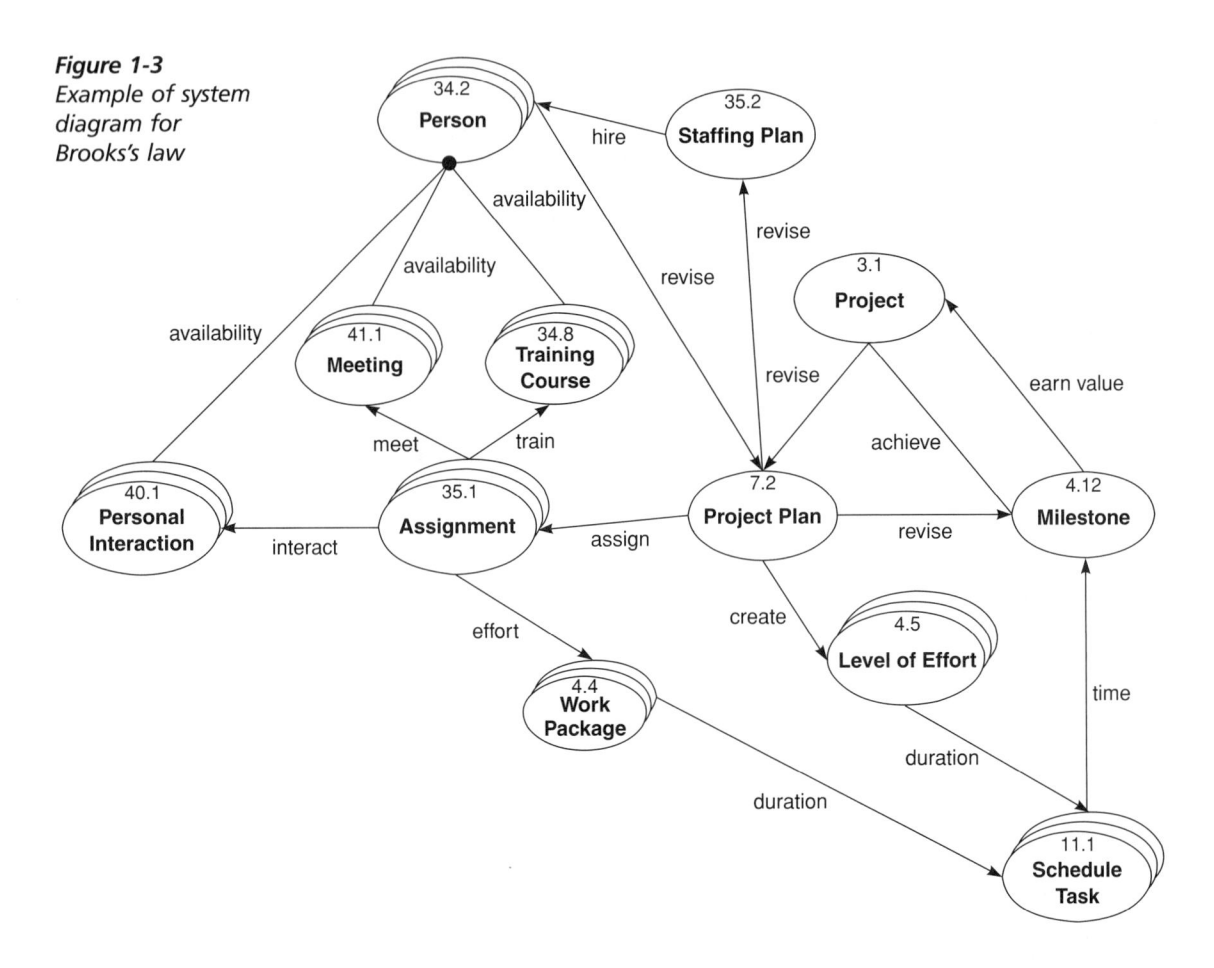

Figure 1-3
Example of system diagram for Brooks's law

First, feedback can increase or decrease the number of objects. In Figure 1-3, for example, the project-earned value feeds back into the labor pool by increasing the number of people in the pool ("adding more people to a project"). These new people increase the number of assignments to tasks, which in turn increases the number of communications in the project. These feedback relationships are usually "create", "generate", "close", "finish", or other such terms.

Second, feedback can increase or decrease some state within existing objects. In Figure 1-3, for example, the assignments increase the actual effort spent on schedule tasks, and for critical-schedule tasks, the finish dates for the tasks. That is, if you increase the number of resources assigned to a critical task, you increase the total amount of work. This is due to the effort that all resources must spend on communication and that experienced resources must spend on training. Since a critical task has no available slack, this increased effort extends the duration of the task by pushing out the finish date, taking into account availability of resources over the scheduled work time of the task. The label names the state variables that the feedback affects.

Third, feedback can initiate some behavior in a system. For example, in Figure 1-3, achieving a milestone earns value, increasing the earned value for the project system. Revising the staffing plan in turn causes the hiring of additional resources. The label on the feedback arrow is usually an active verb, such as "plan", "start", "execute", and so on.

An arrow on the feedback means *positive feedback*, increasing the state variable or number of objects or initiating a process. A solid circle means *negative feedback*, decreasing the state variable or the number of objects. The increased labor resources, increased assignments, increased communications, and increased total effort on critical-schedule tasks are examples of positive feedback in Figure 1-3. The decreased availability of people due to increased communications and the decreased project-earned value due to later critical-schedule tasks are examples of negative feedback.

■ *Note:* For the cognoscenti, this notation translates the usual state-variable notation into an object notation. That is, system diagrams usually show the variables changing as objects, not as relationships; and the diagrams usually do not show the objects to which they belong. I have transformed this to show the objects, putting the feedback in the context of the system of objects as relations between objects rather than seeing the system as a collection of variables. In software design, these diagrams are object diagrams as opposed to class diagrams; they show the dynamic flow of messages through the system instead of the system's static structure.

The Summary Notation

Purely as a matter of convenience, the summary notation summarizes a topic in a single graphic that lets you refer to discussions in other topics. Rather than the usual list of summary items, this summary notation organizes the contents of the topic as a fishbone diagram, as in Figure 1-4. This figure shows a summary for the previous section on "The System Model Notation."

"System Model Notation" section, p. 11

Figure 1-4
Example of summary diagram for system model notation

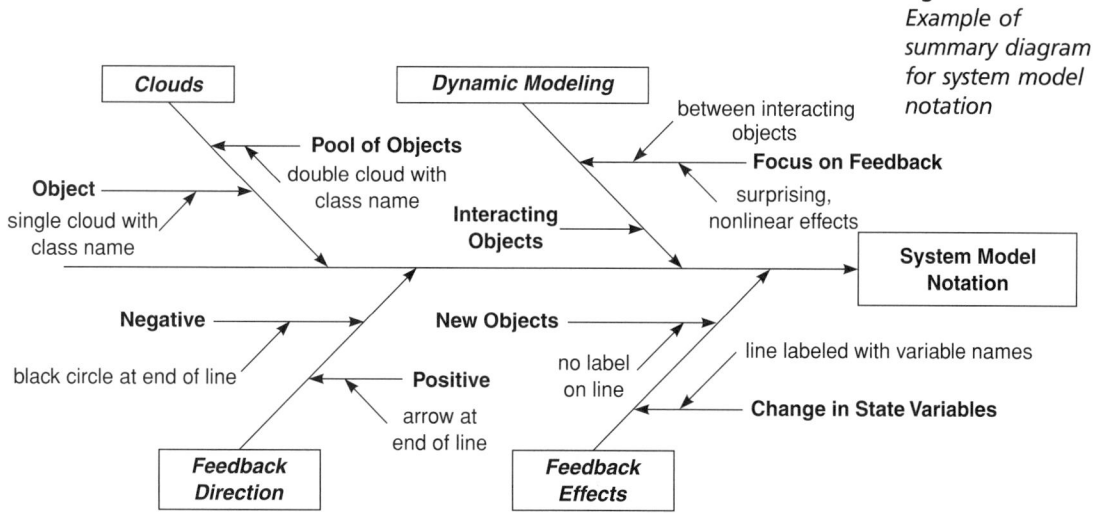

This is a version of the cause-and-effect diagram you use as a quality tool to identify the causes for problems in a system [Ishikawa].

The box to the right of the fishbone is the main point of the summary, the "head." This will usually contain the name of a class, but in some cases such as Figure 1-4 may contain the name of a major topic of some kind. The topic "Type" lists the superclass and subclasses of the class if the head is a class. The main bones of the fish skeleton are the main topics under the class or major topic: dynamic modeling, clouds, feedback direction, and feedback effects for Figure 1-4. Each main topic may have two or three subtopics, such as Object and Pool of Objects for the Clouds topic. Each of these may have two or three summary points coming off it, such as "black circle at end of line" or "single oval with class name." This is the lowest level of summary topic.

If any topic or point refers to some other section of the book, there will be a chapter or class reference number next to the box or line.

The System and Kaizen

If you reorient your thinking with system and OO ideas, you start seeing every object as a system to optimize. The smallest part of the project is a system dancing with the other parts of the project. The rest of the book builds on these system objects: all the different parts of the project system, each working as a smaller whole within the larger whole.

A *system*, in general systems theory, is a set of interrelated objects [Bertalanffy, pp. 55–56; Mesarovic, pp. 1–2 and 12–16]. The previous section defined the relations between objects, primarily inheritance and the different relationships between objects. Once you get relations into the act, the object becomes a system of constitutive objects. You need to see both the related objects *and* their relations with each other to see the workings of the system. This approach leads to the *emergent properties* of the system, properties that emerge from the objects as they interrelate. Without the relationships, these properties would not exist. The OO approach extends this notion of a constitutive system by hiding the internal objects and their relationships to present only the system as a whole to the observer. It does this by exporting only the emergent properties of the object.

An *open system* is one that has inputs and outputs; compare this to a closed system, which is entirely self-contained. All systems of interest here are open systems. Dealing with open systems introduces two fundamental systems theory concepts: equifinality and feedback.

An open system can reach a particular final steady state (a goal, for example) in a number of different ways. You can start with different initial states, and you can move through different paths to reach the same final goal. This is the principle of *equifinality*. In application, this principle means that you cannot determine the final state of the system by just examining its initial state. Both its inputs (interaction with the environment) and its relations (interaction between its internal objects) may contribute to the final state [Bertalanffy, pp. 132–133; Weinberg 1975, pp. 209–216].

You may find, for example, that no matter what you do, the system seems to always produce the same final, suboptimal state instead of achieving the goals you set. This may require changes to the environmental inputs, or to the internal structure of the system. In plain terms, you need to test your assumptions about the root causes of system behavior.

Similarly, an open system need not obey the second law of thermodynamics: increasing randomness or entropy. An open system can get energy or organization from its environment, leading to increasing organization within the system instead of to increasing randomness. In particular, this leads to the idea of feedback of information into the system. A *feedback,* or *goal-seeking,* system senses the results of its actions in the environment as additional inputs to the system, producing a self-regulating system [Bertalanffy, pp. 40–44; Mesarovic, pp. 3–4 and 6].

Finally, systems do not comprise only solitary objects, they can also contain other systems. That is, while a system is a set of interrelated objects, an object can be a system. A system that contains other systems is a *complex system* [Mesarovic, pp. 4–7].

Putting all these lessons from general systems theory together yields a system that you can characterize as a *complex, purposive, open system.* This kind of goal-seeking, self-regulating system is precisely the kind you want to have in project management. It leads to the notions of continuous improvement (*kaizen*) and optimized value for all the objects of interest. By getting at the root causes of problems, by making goals explicit, and by measuring and acting on the data in a feedback process, you can creatively optimize your project objects.

The *system* (Class 1.1) thus serves as a root class in the class model, since most of the other objects are a kind of system that you will improve and optimize over time. Each purposive system contains a vision, a mission, a set of operational objectives, an improvement plan, and a set of risks that constitute the ability of the system to respond to inputs with appropriately optimal outputs. Vision, mission, and operational objectives have their own sections below; consult Chapter 12 for a complete discussion of the risk.

Since most objects of a given type share the same vision, mission, and objectives, these are usually at the class level. Subclasses inherit the vision, mission, and objectives of their parents, perhaps replacing them with more specific versions or adding objectives specific to the subclass.

Vision: A system that produces value for its environment
Mission: To guide the system in producing optimal value at optimal productivity

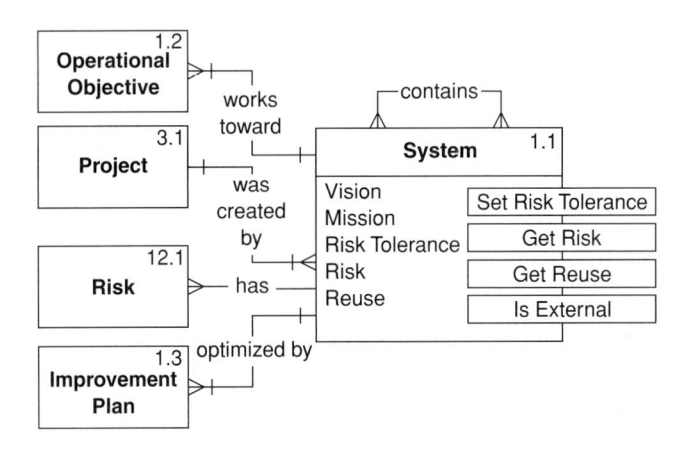

```
        1.2
  Operational
   Objective                    ─contains─
                    works
                    toward
      3.1                           System         1.1
     Project
                    was      Vision
                   created   Mission       Set Risk Tolerance
                     by      Risk Tolerance
      12.1                   Risk             Get Risk
      Risk          has      Reuse            Get Reuse
                                              Is External
              1.3  optimized by
       Improvement
          Plan
```

You can make these aspects of the system specific to a particular object. For example, you can construct a vision and mission for a project that is much more specific than the generic ones for all projects. Specific visions, missions, and objectives usually apply to the larger systems in the project. The further down the object tree you get, the less useful this seems. For example, you would not ordinarily have a specific vision for a particular assignment to a particular schedule task. It would not add much to the generic vision (work expended efficiently by a labor resource on a specific task to achieve the goals of the task). You might set a specific objective such as a deadline or a monetary goal for a small object, but you should carefully justify this before doing it.

Usually, you would subclass the object to make the vision, mission, and objectives more specific. For example, instead of creating specific objectives for your process model instance (the object you create that defines your development process), you would create a subclass of the process model that defines a specific mission. For example, you could define a corporate prototyping process model class. Its objectives would then apply to all instances of your process model, such as revisions or adaptations to special circumstances. This is a much more flexible approach to optimization than getting too specific.

Every goal-directed system in this book has an improvement plan. This plan is the internal memory that lets you optimize the system through the cycles of its existence.

Improvement Plan (1.3)

Risks are usually specific to the object, as they derive from the specific combination of objectives and internal systems within the object. Each system contains two attributes related to risk: the risk tolerance and the overall risk for the system. *Risk tolerance* is the probability that defines the boundary between tolerable and intolerable risk for the users of the system. That is, for every system, there are other systems that use or own the system. Those external systems depend in some way on the systems they use to achieve their internal missions. The risk tolerance

The System and Kaizen

Vision — **Definition**: meaningful statement of difference object makes
Requirements: single sentence, specific and clear
Declaration of Independence

System 1.1
- inputs and outputs
- emergent properties — **Set of Interrelated Objects**
- **Improvement Plan** 1.3 — inherited, overridden, or added vision, mission, and objectives — **Root Class**
- **Open System** — feedback, equifinality
- overall 12.1 **Risk** tolerance
- **Constitution**

System 1.1 — **Definition**: meaningful statement of how you intend to achieve vision through fundamental goal
Requirements: single sentence, specific and clear
Encapsulate

Mission

Operational Objective 1.2
- **Goal**
- **Approach**
- **Metric**
- **Target**

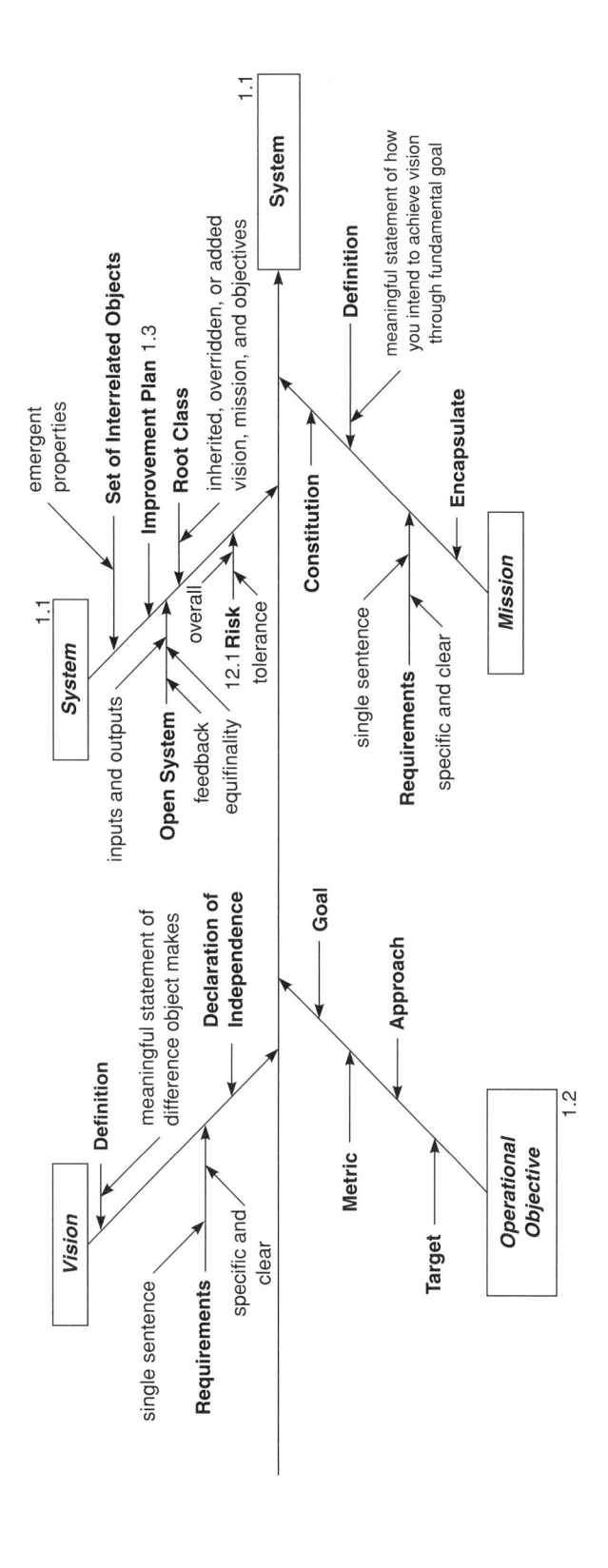

Risk (12.1)

Risk Management Method (14.2)

is the boundary set by the external systems that defines how much chance of failure they can tolerate in the system. The risk tolerance is the minimum tolerance of any using system.

The overall risk of the system is the probability that the system will fail to achieve its mission. This risk is the joint probability of the failure of the objectives and internal systems within the system (Chapter 12).

The Vision

The *vision* of a system states the difference that the system makes within its environment. The vision thus tells you what the system hopes to achieve in the best of all possible worlds.

A classic example of a strong vision is the Declaration of Independence of the United States of America. The first two paragraphs are very direct:

> When in the Course of human Events, it becomes necessary for one People to dissolve the Political Bands which have connected them with another, and to assume, among the Powers of the Earth, the separate and equal Station to which the Laws of Nature and of Nature's God entitle them, a decent Respect to the Opinions of Mankind requires that they should declare the causes which impel them to the Separation.
>
> We hold these Truths to be self-evident, that all Men are created equal, that they are endowed by their Creator with certain unalienable Rights, that among these are Life, Liberty, and the pursuit of Happiness—That to secure these Rights, Governments are instituted among Men, deriving their just Powers from the Consent of the Governed, that whenever any Form of Government becomes destructive of these Ends, it is the Right of the People to alter or to abolish it, and to institute new Government, laying its Foundation on such Principles, and organizing its Powers in such Form, as to them shall seem most likely to effect their Safety and Happiness. Prudence, indeed, will dictate that Governments long established should not be changed for light and transient Causes; and accordingly all Experience hath shewn, that Mankind are more disposed to suffer, while Evils are sufferable, than to right themselves by abolishing the Forms to which they are accustomed. But when a long Train of Abuses and Usurpations, pursuing invariably the same Object, evinces a Design to reduce them under absolute Despotism, it is their Right, it is their Duty, to throw off such Government, and to provide new Guards for their future Security.

The first paragraph above states clearly what the Congress hoped to achieve: the immediate and complete dissolution of the political relationship with Britain. The second paragraph expands on this basic vision with an enhanced view of the place of government in the world of men (I use the latter noun advisedly in this case). The phrase "Life, Liberty, and the pursuit of Happiness" has become the motto of the United States to such an extent that every individual citizen would probably recognize the phrase and attribute it correctly to this document. Yet it has no force in U.S. law. The document itself constitutes the severing of the political bonds between Britain and the U.S. It thus serves both as a legal act and as a clear, visionary statement of what the U.S. will become.

Every system object has a vision, a clearly defined statement of what will be different about the world because of the existence of the object. The vision statement should be a single sentence that states clearly how you see the world with this object in it. If your vision statement seems excessively vague or task-oriented, rethink it or eliminate the object as unnecessary. Without a clear vision for an object, there really is no point in expending effort on it.

For example, a project vision might be "delivery of a socially and economically valuable, unique product or service." A communication meeting might have the vision of "an informed set of stakeholders."

The Mission

The *mission* of a system states how you intend to achieve the vision through a fundamental goal or target. The mission statement corresponding to the Declaration of Independence is the United States Constitution:

> We the people of the United States, in Order to form a more perfect Union, establish Justice, insure domestic Tranquility, provide for the common defence, promote the general Welfare, and secure the Blessings of Liberty to ourselves and our Posterity, do ordain and establish this Constitution for the United States of America.

Without quoting the rest of the Constitution at length, this document clearly states the framework within which the U.S. government will operate. The preamble above is a classic one-sentence mission statement that states clearly what the U.S. is all about. The Constitution serves as the primary basis of the legal system of the United States. The Supreme Court is its interpreter, the Congress and people are its maintainers, and the President is its enforcer.

The mission statement for a project management object should be a single sentence that clearly describes the fundamental goal of the object.

Sometimes you will find mission statements that aggregate the goals from internal objects up to the highest level. In this OO approach, you should put the mission goal where it belongs rather than aggregating up the object tree. That is, you should not have a mission statement for an object that states both the goal of the object and the goals of the objects it contains. You should encapsulate missions just as much as you encapsulate the objects within the class. For example, the preamble to the Constitution above clearly states the mission of the Constitution as a whole. It does not delve into the executive branch or the right to bear arms, leaving that to the more detailed sections that apply to those objects.

As another example, your project mission should not include goals related to the processes or process models you will use in the project. The process model, for example, might have this mission: "To create a standard set of well-defined processes that all projects in the company will use to optimize process productivity and output value." The project might have this mission: "To create a unique product or service in a cost-effective way by using a standard set of well-defined processes that optimize process productivity and output value." Instead, the following statement is more direct: "To create a unique product or service that successfully provides value to the project stakeholders." This statement deals only with the actual project system goals, not with the goals of the systems that make up that object. For example, it might well be that there are other ways to optimize value than using standard process models. This is certainly true for very small projects that have very little technical complexity and few requirements. These projects can successfully provide value to stakeholders without using a process model at all, much less by optimizing process productivity and value.

The Operational Objective

The *operational objective* (Class 1.2) is a specific *goal* with the *approach* to achieving that goal, a *metric* for measuring its success, and a *target* using the metric that identifies the precise criterion for success of the objective. You can redefine or expand operational objectives as you move down the class model tree.

Making a system *congruent* with the vision and mission of its parents and its related objects results in a smoothly running, effective project. This follows from the nature of a purposive, open system. If the system's interacting objects strive toward conflicting goals, the system will only achieve its goals with difficulty.

A system may have more than one objective. Many systems have complex missions that break down into simpler objectives. Some systems may even have conflicting objectives. For a system with multiple objectives, you need to optimize the system by finding the right mix. This means prioritizing the objectives, or a trade-off decision, giving up some of one objective to achieve a greater part of another.

■ *Note:* The mathematically inclined should consider applying decision theory to systems with multiple, conflicting objectives [Keeney].

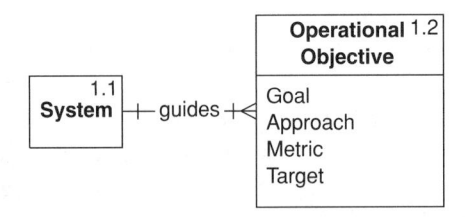

Unfortunately, the constitutional example tends to break down at this point. One could compare the system of laws, executive orders, and government regulations to the notion of operational objective, but the exercise would be unsatisfactory. Perhaps the lack of clear goals and measures is one of the things missing from this part of the United States government.

Goal

The *goal* is a brief, textual statement of a *measurable* purpose of some kind that contributes to the system mission. The goal expresses a *value*: to increase or decrease some quality, to optimize some value, and so on. You can also have *enabling goals* that create the potential for something else.

The goal should contribute in a reasonably obvious way to the overall mission of the system. In a single-objective system, the goal may be very similar to the mission. In a multiple-objective system, each goal should address a part of the overall mission, with the set of goals covering the entire mission.

A project plan, for example, might have this mission: "To specify in advance the method that a project will use to accomplish its mission." One goal of this class might relate to the quality of the specification: "To create a plan that specifies how to produce all the required parts of the project's output." Another goal might relate to the "in advance" part of the mission: "To create a plan that specifies the required tasks before the project resources undertake those tasks without delaying the delivery of the project's products and services." You could also have a productivity goal: "To produce a plan for the project using 10% less effort than the benchmark effort for this kind of project."

- ■ *Note:* The goal does not specify the precise target or targets for the objective; see the following section on "Target."

"Target" section, p. 26

Approach

The *approach* is the particular technique or method you use to achieve the goal. This is also a brief, textual statement that describes specifically how you will go about doing what you need to do. For example, Table 1-2 shows the three goals from the preceding "Goal" section and the corresponding approaches one might take.

"Goal" section, p. 21

You can have more than one approach to achieving a goal. Having multiple approaches makes it more difficult to interpret the results of your actions, however. You should use multidimensional modeling techniques (see the following section) to evaluate the independent and combined effects of multiple approaches to the goal.

Table 1-2   Example Goals and Approaches

Goal	Approach
To create a plan that specifies how to produce all the required parts of the project's output	Construct a statement of work, work breakdown structure, and specified subsidiary plans from a list of the deliverables and processes that the project uses to deliver them.
To create a plan that specifies the required tasks before the project resources undertake those tasks without delaying the delivery of the project's products and services	Conduct the planning process in a rolling-wave or transactional approach that specifies tasks and assignments incrementally based on the process model for the project.
To produce a plan for the project using 10% less effort than the benchmark effort for this kind of project	Use automated process templates to automate the plan creation process.

Metric

A *metric* is a method of measuring some empirical aspect of the real world. In this case, the metric for the objective measures the achievement of the goal. The data you collect by applying the metric to an object lets you represent the empirical status of the object with respect to the goal. In other words, the metric lets you *measure* how well the object is getting on.

Designing a valid metric for a particular goal is sometimes quite hard to do. If you intend to do much of this, you should become familiar with the basic mathematics of measurement theory [Coombs, pp. 7–30; Narens; Roberts]. In constructing a metric, you need to worry about three things:

- You must have goals that you can measure.
- You must have a metric that uses the right kind of *scale* for the type of goal you are measuring.
- You must have a metric that lets you make *meaningful* statements about the state of the object.

Some goals are not measurable, no matter how clever the metric. If your goals are vague, or if you can't specify the structure or theory for the goal, you will not be able to measure the results. If you can't get good empirical data with the metric, and if you can't relate that data directly to the objective, you do not have a valid metric. One of the biggest problems in total quality management is specifying clear objectives that you can measure. If you can construct such a metric, you can state your goal in a measurable way [Scholtes, pp. 5–38]. If you can neither construct a metric nor state a measurable goal, you should rethink your objective.

A common method for developing metrics is the *goal-question-metric paradigm* [Basili; Fenton; Goldberg; Henderson-Sellers 1996]. This way of developing metrics begins with a basic goal statement, such as "Identify a risk with optimal effort." You then frame one or more questions, the answers to which relate to achieving the goal. For example, the risk goal might have the questions "What kind of risk?" and "How much effort?" These questions then lead directly to one or more metrics, such as the type of risk (task-related, schedule-task-related, project-related, and so on) or effort-hours per risk identification. This approach lets you have multiple questions for each objective and multiple metrics for each question. Most assessment metrics, and most that appear in this book, are single metrics for the objective.

The addition of the approach provides an intermediate step between the objective and the questions. Instead of asking questions about the objective directly, your metric-directed questions should ask about the impact of the approach on the objective. For example, the approach to risk identification might take two directions, defining risks in advance for different types of objects and associating known process risks with process tasks before defining the plan from them. These approaches lead to specific questions about the effort saved by advance definition and process definition and to basic metrics that answer those questions. This focuses your metrics on the actions you plan to take to achieve the objective. If you change your approach, you should reevaluate your metrics for the objective.

A scale is a mapping from an empirical system to a numerical system. The *representation problem* is the determination that the mapping is a homomorphism, that the relationships between empirical elements is the same as the relationships between numerical elements [Roberts, pp. 54–55]. The *uniqueness problem* is how unique the homomorphism is. That is, what kinds of transformations can you apply to the data without destroying the representation? Measurement theory specifies a standard set of scale types it identifies by the kind of transformation. Table 1-3 shows the standard scales and their characteristics.

For example, your goal might be a simple true-or-false goal, such as "to deliver the object on time." You would use a nominal metric (1 or 0 for true or false). If your goal relates to an ordering, such as "to deliver the object under budget," use an ordinal metric (1, 2, and 3 for Under, On, or Over Budget). A goal with no zero value, such as "to deliver the object by the deadline," should use an interval metric such as the date the object was delivered. A quantifiable goal, such as "to deliver the object within 10% of the estimated effort," needs a ratio metric (actual effort in work-hours divided by the estimated effort in work-hours). Finally, an absolute goal of some kind, such as "to deliver thirteen objects to the stakeholders," requires an absolute metric (number of objects delivered).

- *Note:* The nominal and ordinal scales technically should be numerical. If you substitute number codes for the symbols, the numerical relation is again the

Table 1-3 Types of Measurement Scales from Measurement Theory

Scale	Characteristics	Example
Nominal	Any one-to-one transformation is possible; there is no ordering of numbers and no ability to add, subtract, or relate any two numbers other than a basic equality comparison; uses numbers as labels or names	Boolean values (True/False), categorizations (Good, Bad, Don't Care), alternative codes such as WBS numbers or object identifiers
Ordinal	Any order-preserving transformation is possible; only order is important, not the relative distance between numbers or the value of the numbers in themselves	Rankings (Good, Better, Best), grades, mineral hardness
Interval	Linear transformations of the type $\phi(x) = ax + b$ for $a > 0$; an ordered scale with an arbitrary origin b and a unit of measurement a, allowing you to compare intervals between scale values	Temperature (Celsius or Fahrenheit), time
Ratio	Linear transformation of the type $\phi(x) = ax$ for $a > 0$; scale values are unique with respect to an arbitrary unit of measurement a, allowing you to compare the numbers themselves; the scale fixes the origin (zero), however	Length, mass, absolute temperature, and similar physical quantities; time intervals; effort; most kinds of value where there is a concept of no (zero) value
Absolute	No transformations possible	Count of objects

rational numbers. If you use these scales with symbols, the mathematics may be somewhat tricky. One out is to regard the symbols as "interpretations" of the numbers; for the sake of those that use the data, define the interpretations and order carefully in your coding book or metrics documents.

You can also develop multidimensional models for metrics. Use statistical techniques such as distance metrics, principal components analysis, factor analysis, multidimensional scaling, or cluster analysis [Fenton]. These tools let you combine multiple scales into a single, multidimensional metric space that lets you better represent your goal [Osgood]. They do require much sophisticated statistical analysis and a solid understanding of rather complex goal and metric structures.

A metric measures some attribute of the system. In an OO model, that means the metric measures attributes of the object that owns the objective. It can also measure external attributes of internal systems of that object. An *internal attribute* is one of the several basic data elements of the class. An *external attribute* is a method on a class that returns an attribute value [Fenton, p. 43]. For example, the risk tolerance is an internal attribute of the class System, while the overall risk is an external attribute. You often calculate external attributes with models of two or more internal attributes, such as the productivity of a resource or the reliability of a system. Productivity, for example, is the average number of function points the resource produces per work-hour. It can vary over different time periods. You calculate it by aggregating the efforts for work assignments that are internal to the resource.

It doesn't do any good to try to measure achievement of a goal that has no meaningful characteristics. For example, controversy continues about the measurement of intelligence and in particular its application to determining the intellectual success of individuals. It is quite arguable that none of the words in the previous sentence are in themselves *meaningful,* much less measurable. Does IQ measure "intelligence," and if so, how? Effectively measurable goals should stick to relatively commonplace things in the real world, such as effort, time, and money. As the preceding section on "Systems, Projects, and Value" indicated, even the concept of "value" or "quality" has problems with measurability. You must carefully specify what you mean by these terms ("ROI," "Stakeholder Approval," "Zero-Defect," or whatever). It also doesn't do any good to try to apply metrics that use a certain kind of scale to goals that require a different scale. For example, if you had a goal "to deliver the object within 10% of the estimated effort," and you measure this with a metric that rates effort for an object as "Too Little, Just Right, Too Much," it is going to be hard to make the objective meaningful.

"Systems, Projects, and Value" section, p. 5

Table 1-4 sets out several characteristics that you can use to evaluate your metric [Henderson-Sellers 1996, pp. 33–38; Osgood, p. 11]. The more of these criteria your metric satisfies, the better is the metric.

Table 1-5 expands the goals and approaches from previous sections with some suggested metrics.

Once you've defined the goal, approach, and metric, you need to set the target.

Criterion	Definition
Objectivity	Does the metric yield reproducible data? Can different data collectors measure the same object with the same results?
Reliability	Does the metric yield the same results under the same conditions, within acceptable margins of error?
Validity	Can you validate the data that the metric yields with other, similar data that measures a similar kind of goal? Is there another metric that you can use to provide assurance that you are getting valid data?
Sensitivity	Does the metric yield data capable of distinguishing differences at the level of your goal?
Comparability	Can you apply the metric to all objects having the same or a similar goal?
Utility	Can you collect meaningful data at a reasonable rate and with reasonable effort?

Table 1-4
Evaluation Criteria for Metrics

Table 1-5 *Example Goals and Approaches*

Goal	Approach	Metric
To create a plan that specifies how to produce all the required parts of the project's output	Construct a statement of work, work breakdown structure, and specified subsidiary plans from a list of the deliverables and processes that the project uses to deliver them.	Coverage of required outputs by tasks (number of required outputs divided by number of required outputs associated with tasks)
To create a plan that specifies the required tasks before the project resources undertake those tasks without delaying the delivery of the project's products and services	Conduct the planning process in a rolling-wave or transactional approach that specifies tasks and assignments incrementally based on the process model for the project.	Date of task start subtracted from date of plan baseline that includes the task
To produce a plan for the project using 10% less effort than the benchmark effort for this kind of project	Use automated process templates to automate the plan creation process.	Effort in work-hours for all plan baselines divided by effort in work-hours for benchmark plan

Target

The target is a precise model of the criterion for success of the objective. The target specifies this criterion using the metric for the objective (see the preceding section) in a model. The model may take a number of forms, the most common of which are a single value equation or a tolerance range predicate.

A single-valued target is most appropriate for nominal and ordinal metrics, while a range is more appropriate for interval, ratio, and absolute metrics. For example, the single value may be Yes or No, or it may be High, Medium, or Low. This single value might be an appropriate aggregate metric, such as the median; for example, the median severity = Medium.

The tolerance range is a set of values that expresses boundaries of the space that satisfies the goal. Most ranges have two boundaries, the high and the low. The tolerance boundaries specify the highest tolerable value (5 defects per effort-hour, for example) but also the lowest tolerable rate (1 defect per effort-hour). This latter boundary is in place to detect development effort that is too efficient, presumably because it is also too expensive. The objective might be to achieve a low defect rate at a reasonable cost. The target is a predicate consisting of a conjunction of two inequalities:

$$\text{Metric} \geq \text{Low Boundary} \wedge \text{Metric} \leq \text{High Boundary}$$

You can also have a single-boundary tolerance if your interest is in just the high or low boundary. For example, the defect rate for a testing task might have only the low boundary to ensure that the testing is effective at finding defects. You don't want a high boundary, since the objective is to find as many defects as possible. Similarly, if you want to minimize effort for a task, you may only have a high boundary. This predicate is a simple inequality.

- *Note:* While it is tempting to frame targets as single-boundary tolerance ranges, it is much easier to get conflicting objectives if you have many such targets for system objectives. Often, if you consider the consequences of a very low or very high value, you can see ways to restate the objective to be more congruent with the system as a whole. Specifically, it is usually better to "optimize" than to "minimize" or "maximize" a value. If you use the latter two terms in a goal, think about the limits of what you're proposing.

A tolerance changes with time in a dynamic project system. The optimization cycle takes you through the stages of planning, executing, assessing, and feeding back the results into your system. This feedback process usually results in changes to targets.

You can introduce some statistical sophistication into your targets through the use of control charts to set ranges. Many of the metrics in this book refer to specific kinds of control charts, such as the x-R chart for standard ratio metrics or the p and pn charts for fractions and counts [Beauregard; Ishikawa; Ozeki]. The upper and lower control limits of the control chart correspond directly to the range targets.

- *Note:* Control charts are not really targeting mechanisms, they are statistical control tools. The ranges depend entirely on the statistical characteristics of the data you put into them. If your mission depends on meeting a specification of some kind, you need to set your targets to the specification, not to the control range. This may mean that you need to increase system capability to bring the control range into conformance with the target, rather than vice versa. Also, if you are going to use control charts, you should consult a textbook such as [Ozeki] for details on how to construct and use these charts.

Improvement Plan (1.3)

Your data may show that the system varies widely beyond your target. This can result from defining a target that is beyond the ability of the system to meet. For example, if your developer's training and skill level is medium to low, you may have trouble with a tight range of defects in code. Until you bring the staff up to the requisite level of skill, you should not establish tight targets. Through improvement plans, you can establish looser targets that your staff can meet, then gradually tighten the targets as your performance improves. You can also radically reengineer the system. Your decision will depend on how critical the results are to your mission. If the system is not likely to meet the target, and you persist with the target without any other change, you have set up the system to fail. Most people who have set personal Management By Objectives (MBO) targets should fully understand this comment.

Risk (12.1)

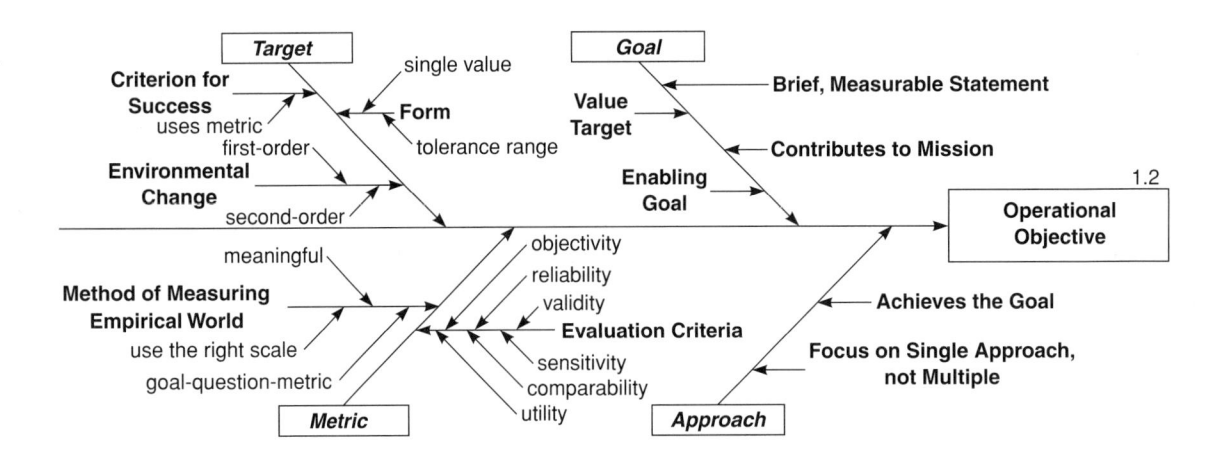

```
                    Target                      Goal
     Criterion for ─┘   single value    │     ─┘      ── Brief, Measurable Statement
       Success  ╲         ╲          Value  ╲
          uses metric╲    ── Form    Target  ╲
             first-order╲    tolerance range  ╲          ── Contributes to Mission
     Environmental      ╲         ╲         Enabling                               1.2
        Change           ╲         ╲          Goal  ╲                      ┌──────────────┐
             second-order╲          ╲                 ╲                    │  Operational │
                          ╲  objectivity               ╲                   │   Objective  │
           meaningful╲     ╲  reliability                ── Achieves the Goal
     Method of Measuring    ╲ validity
      Empirical World        ── Evaluation Criteria       ── Focus on Single Approach,
          use the right scale╱  sensitivity                    not Multiple
          goal-question-metric╱ comparability
                ┌────────┐    utility         ┌──────────┐
                │ Metric │                    │ Approach │
                └────────┘                    └──────────┘
```

Because this is a human endeavor in a changing world, things don't stay the same. As the environment changes, your systems must adapt to the changes or become irrelevant. This usually means changing the objectives of the system. Wholesale change can result in completely new objectives with radically different metrics and targets (*second-order,* or structural, change). Minor change can result in changed control ranges (*first-order* change). As part of system optimization, you must consider second-order as well as first-order change.

The Improvement Plan

Given a defined set of operational objectives, what do you do? The essence of a goal-seeking system is *feedback,* the use of information from the environment to control the direction of the system. The operational objectives let you collect the feedback; the *improvement plan* is a reusable project document that lets you plan and implement changes to the system to use that feedback. The improvement plan "closes the loop." To create an improvement plan, you must have data for the operational objective metrics and a clear idea about what you want to achieve and what you have to work with. Part of that clear idea comes from building the system model and part from aligning the system with its environment in the initial improvement plan.

An improvement plan is part of the project plan. You can also do improvement plans as separate projects, in which case the plan is a kind of project plan; but that is outside the context of OO project management.

Vision: A continuously improving, congruent project system that achieves its mission

Mission: To optimize the operation of a project system to better achieve its mission and to be congruent with its environment

The Improvement Plan 29

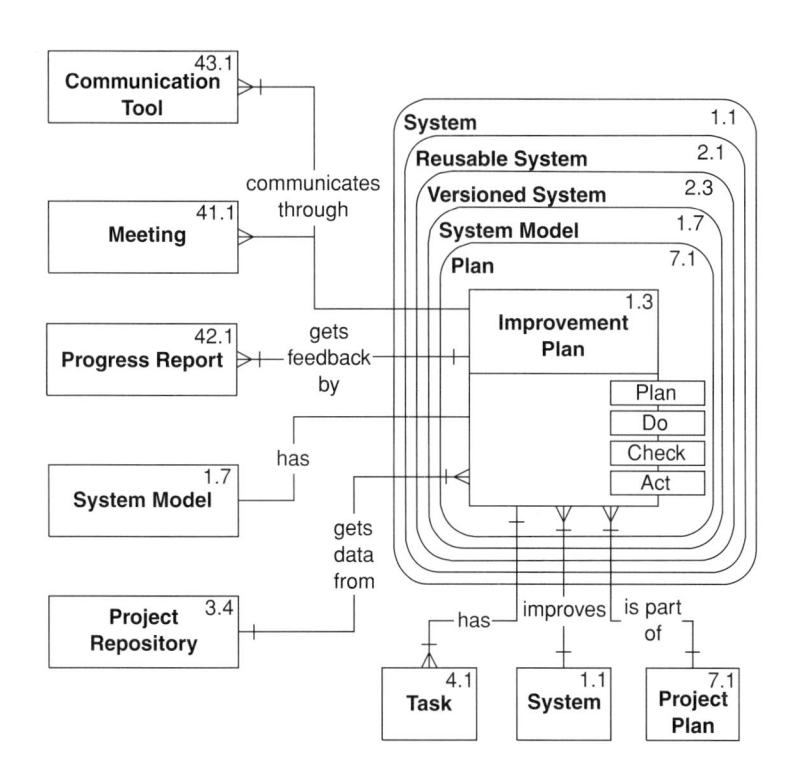

Table 1-6 shows the stages for system improvement [Beauregard; Deming; Scholtes].

Table 1-6 Tasks for the Improvement Plan

Task	Description
Understand the System	Describe the system and identify its vision, mission, and operational objectives
Align the System	Create or modify the system vision, mission, and objectives to be congruent with the objectives of systems that must use this system
Eliminate Errors	Make any simple changes to the system that eliminate problems
Remove Slack	Find and reduce the inefficiencies in the system
Reduce Measurement Variation	Eliminate special causes of variations in the system metrics and validate the metrics with a pilot project
Reduce System Variation	Eliminate special causes of variations in the operation of the system and validate the changes with a pilot project
Plan for Continuous Improvement	Create a plan that lets you continuously improve the system

Improving the system thus involves several different kinds of plans, all of which are subclasses of the abstract improvement plan. The *initial improvement plan* goes through the first four stages, standardizing the system. The *pilot improvement plan* tests changes to reduce variation, either in the metrics for the system or the operation of the system. The *continuous improvement plan* reduces variation in the system from common, random causes.

■ *Note:* This breakdown of types of improvement plan is my perception of how things work in practice. The particular structure of subclasses and the breakdown of the steps for system improvement you choose may reflect your own preferences and needs. This particular breakdown has made sense for me in the projects and organizations I have worked in.

All plans involve a simple management cycle: plan, do, check, act (PDCA). This is the standard Shewhart or Deming cycle from total quality management [Deming; Scholtes]. *Planning* is the process of building the improvement plan, including specifying the tasks, schedule, and resource assignments (a mini-project). *Doing* is the process you start by executing the plan. *Checking* is the set of tasks that monitors the progress and effectiveness of the improvement effort, including gathering system metric data and checking for weirdness (unexpected variation) in system operation. *Acting* is the set of tasks that evaluate the data and propose changes to the system. You document the success of the improvement, then fire off another planning effort by creating a next-stage improvement plan, hopefully reusing much of the current one.

Throughout the PDCA cycle, you must stress communication. Your improvement plan should contain tasks that reflect meetings, progress reports, and use of communications tools. There are three primary reasons for communication:

- *Coordination:* Making sure that all parts of the system are working together in the optimization process
- *Results:* Making sure the environmental systems understand how the system is working to improve itself and its congruence with them; in particular, communicating the results of improvement through success stories or cautionary tales
- *Leverage:* Building commitment and trust within both the system and the system's environment

Rather than giving examples here, the rest of the book shows how improvement plans might affect different systems.

■ *Note:* You can improve any system, but one class of systems is less amenable to it: the single-instance system. For example, a process is a single instance of a process model. That is, you can run through a process exactly once. Each run is a new process. Unless there is some kind of cycle within the process, there isn't much point in improving it: you improve the process model, not the process system it generates. Another approach to optimizing lets the improvement plan apply to the class of objects, not to each object. For example, you could improve all schedules as a group rather than improving a particular schedule. Position the improvement plan where it makes the most sense given the essential nature of the objects you want to improve.

The Initial Improvement Plan

The *initial improvement plan* gets the system to the point where you can improve it. If you don't understand how the system works, you can't do anything with it. You build an initial improvement plan, unsurprisingly, the first time you begin optimizing the system. But you also build an initial improvement plan whenever the system or its direct environment significantly changes. Change means what you used to do no longer applies, and you must rethink the system's vision, mission, and operational objectives and rebuild the system model.

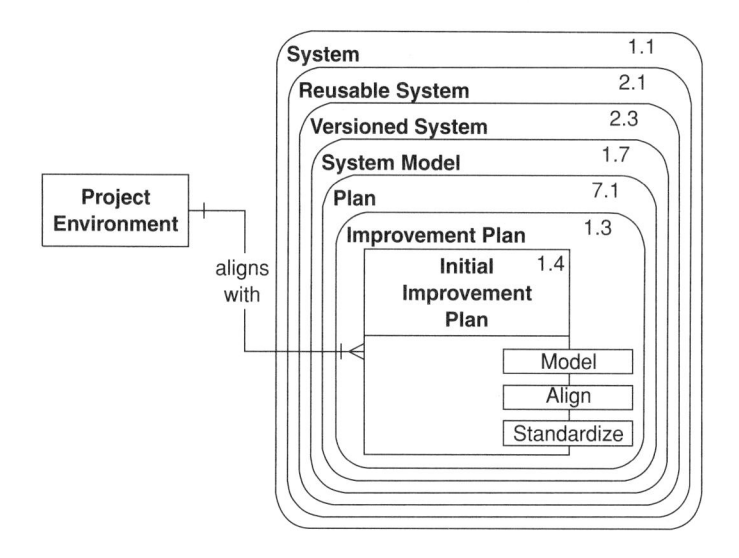

Vision: A well-understood, standardized system aligned with its environment

Mission: To understand and align the system with its environment

---

Objective 1.1: To optimize the congruence of the system with its environment

---

Approach 1.1: Adjust the vision, mission, and operational objectives of the system to increase the ability of the system to work with the systems in its environment (congruence).

Metric 1.1: Count of potential conflicts in the operational objectives of the systems that refer to the current system with the operational objectives of the current system

Target 1.1: Zero conflicts (in a perfect world, of course)

System Model (1.7)

The process of understanding the system is the process of *modeling* the components of the system and their interrelationships. You first need to identify the vision, mission, and operational objectives for the system. If there aren't any, you need to create them. That's the building block for aligning the system with other systems. You can't decide whether your system fits with others unless you understand its purpose and can measure progress toward that purpose.

Given that purpose, you look at the ways other systems use the system. You then align your vision, mission, and objectives with that environment. This is a balancing act, not an absolute. You must make trade-offs between the objectives.

After aligning the system, you standardize it by removing obvious errors and inefficiencies. Often this happens through producing the model. It forces you to organize the system. Standardization means developing a set of policies, usually some kind of standard. You should remove any system components that don't contribute to achieving the mission. When you've cleaned up the system to this point, you're ready to go on to reducing variation.

Policy (32.1)

The Pilot Improvement Plan

Although you have a standardized, efficient system, you still can't continually improve the system. You need to remove special causes of variation through a *pilot improvement plan*. A *special cause* makes the system vary its operation, or the data on its operation, in nonrandom ways. This can happen through a poor metric or a poorly performed task in the system. Special causes generally mean firefights. The cause of the fire is usually relatively obvious once you standardize the system. Knowing the cause lets you easily identify special causes with Pareto charts or control charts [Arthur; Beauregard; Ozeki; Scholtes], which are standard total quality tools.

Vision: An efficient, error-free system ready for continuous improvement under statistical control

Mission: To bring the system under statistical control

Objective 1.2: To bring the system under statistical control

The Improvement Plan

Approach 1.2.1: Reduce variation in the system measurement process by eliminating errors and inefficiencies in gathering data through the use of standard quality analysis tools.

Metric 1.2.1: Measurement variation for each metric in the system's operational objectives

Target 1.2.1: A control range identified by standard variance formulas that indicates the measurement process is under statistical control [Beauregard; Ishikawa; Ozeki]

Approach 1.2.2: Reduce variation in system operation by eliminating errors and inefficiencies through the use of standard quality analysis tools.

Metric 1.2.2: Mean and range for each metric in the system's operational objectives

Target 1.2.2: The upper and lower control limits in an x-R control chart

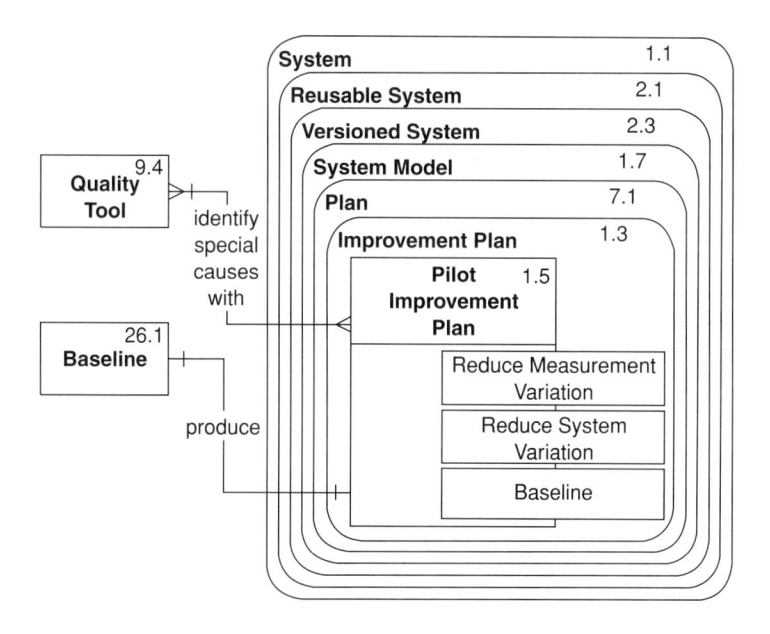

Variation in measurement comes from two different sources: invalid metrics and measurement error. The above section, "Metric," shows you how to construct metrics that adequately measure your objectives. Measurement error comes from several different sources (Table 1-7), all of which have to do with the mechanics of gathering data as your system operates.

Table 1-7 Sources of Measurement Error

Source	Description
Accuracy	How does the observed value *differ* from the true value? What is the bias of the measurement?
Repeatability	How do the observed values *vary* for the same true value? How do values vary for the *same* data collector collecting data on the same system with the same equipment?
Reproducibility	How *consistent* is the variation of observed values from the true value? How do values vary for *different* data collectors?
Stability	How *stable* is the variation? How does *time* affect measurement?
Linearity	How accurate is measurement over a *range* of values? Does a different scale kick in for different ranges? Do you need to calibrate measurement?

Eliminating special causes means testing your methods and changes through pilot studies. You continue with pilots until your data provides a useful baseline for continuous improvement. You may need to train people in measurement, for example. You may need to set up automated groupware that collects data without requiring fallible human interpretation.

Brainstorm cause and effect using cause-and-effect diagrams, then try things in pilot projects to eliminate the kinds of spikes and surges that come from special problems. For example, if one cluster in a system generates defects out of line with its weight in the system, consider rewriting or testing the module more thoroughly. If a particular policy seems to be being honored at best in the breach, find out why and fix it. In any case, build a pilot improvement plan for the project. The output of the acting phase of the plan is a baseline of the system metrics and targets that you can use to eliminate common causes of variation.

Baseline (26.1)

Continuous Improvement Plan

Once you have a baseline, you can create a *plan* for *continuous improvement*. This is a plan that continuously loops from acting to planning without needing a new plan. At this point, having eliminated errors, inefficiencies, and special causes of variation in the system, you need to adjust the system continuously to optimize its structure and operation for achieving its mission. You are reducing the effects of random causes of variation on the system. You then continuously plan, do, check, and act—forever or until the end of the project, whichever comes first. Or you can look at the environment and decide to begin an entirely new optimization sequence by restructuring the system completely, if the changed circumstances warrant it or if you have plateaued on improvement and want to shake things up to get to the next level.

The Improvement Plan

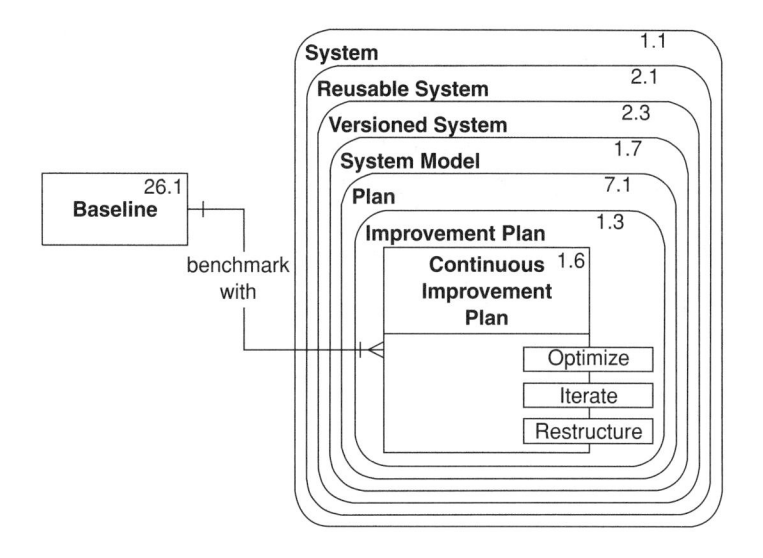

Vision: A system under statistical control continuously improving its ability to contribute value through achieving its mission

Mission: To continuously improve the system

Objective 1.3: To continuously improve the system

Approach 1.3.1: Reduce the effects of common causes of variation in the system by optimizing the capability of the system to achieve its mission and operational targets through the use of capability-enhancing tools and methods.

Metric 1.3.1: System capability index for a metric:

$$C_m = \min(C_{mu}, C_{ml})$$

where m is the operational objective metric, C_m is the capability index for that metric, C_{mu} is the capability index for the upper limit of a range target for the metric, and C_{ml} is the capability index for the lower limit of a range target for the metric.

$$C_{mu} = (\upsilon_m - \mu_m) \div 3\sigma_m$$

$$C_{ml} = (\mu_m - l_m) \div 3\sigma_m$$

where υ_m is the upper target for the metric m, l_m is the lower target for the metric m, μ_m is the mean of the measured data for m, and σ_m is the standard deviation (use the estimated mean and standard deviation). If the target is a single value instead of a range, use the appropriate minimum or maximum capability for a minimum or maximum target value.

Target 1.3.1: $C_m > 1.33$ [Beauregard, p. 129]; increase this as you continuously optimize your system

---

Approach 1.3.2: Improve the system capability for achieving its mission through drastic structural change requiring a new improvement cycle.

Metric 1.3.2: Improvement ratio: ratio of capability index from current improvement cycle to baseline from previous cycle

Target 1.3.2: Improvement ratio $\geq$ 1.2 (a 20% improvement in capability for a cycle); if you can't achieve this target, you should consider restructuring the system because you're topping out on capability with the current system

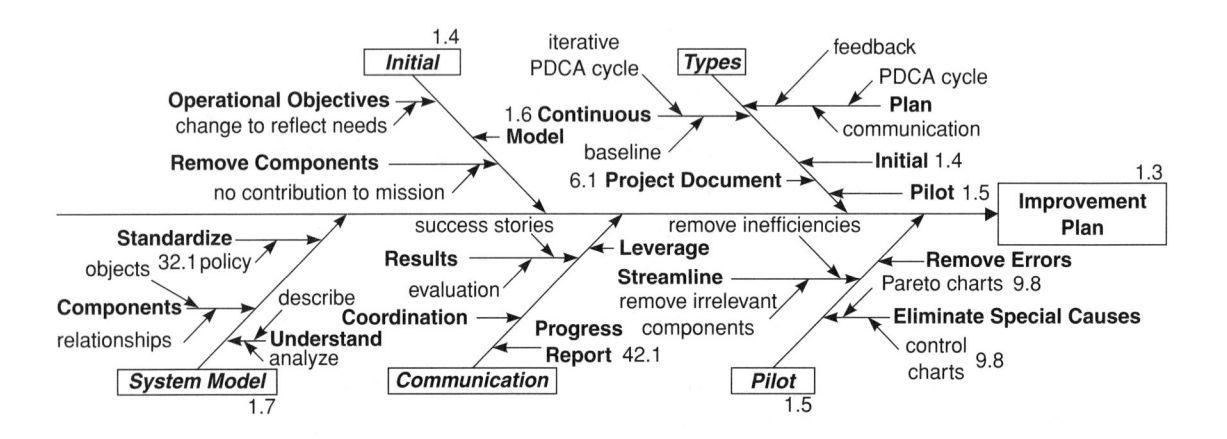

[Fishbone diagram showing the Improvement Plan 1.3 with branches for Initial 1.4, Types, Continuous Model 1.6, Pilot 1.5, System Model 1.7, Communication, and Pilot 1.5, with sub-elements including Operational Objectives, Remove Components, Standardize objects, Components relationships, iterative PDCA cycle, baseline, 6.1 Project Document, success stories, Results evaluation, Coordination, Understand/analyze, describe, Leverage, Streamline remove irrelevant, Progress Report 42.1, remove inefficiencies, feedback PDCA cycle, Plan communication, Initial 1.4, Pilot 1.5, Remove Errors Pareto charts 9.8, Eliminate Special Causes control charts 9.8]

The System Model

A *system model* represents a system and is itself a reusable, versioned system. All system models model a system as a relation between system components [Mesarovic], listing the components and their relationships. There are as many ways to do this as there are types of system, and potentially an infinite number.

Vision: A valuable, productive system you productively generate from a continuously improving model

Mission: To represent a kind of system that produces value that you want to reuse many times

---

Objective 1.4: To represent the objects and relationships in the value-producing system to allow generation of the system with optimal productivity

Approach 1.4: Model the target system with the objects and relationships that represent the generic qualities of the system that contribute to the system mission through achieving their own missions. Structure the model in a format that permits the generation of an instance of the model with as much detail as is optimally possible given your generic knowledge of the system. Improve the model continuously as your system knowledge improves.

Metric 1.4: System Representation Accuracy: the ratio of the median number of objects and relationships in the model version to the median number of objects and relationships in the systems you generate from the model version; this fraction could be greater than one if your model is more detailed than your actual system, but this is definitely an anomalous situation that you should avoid

Target 1.4: The upper and lower control limits in a p control chart for Metric 1.4

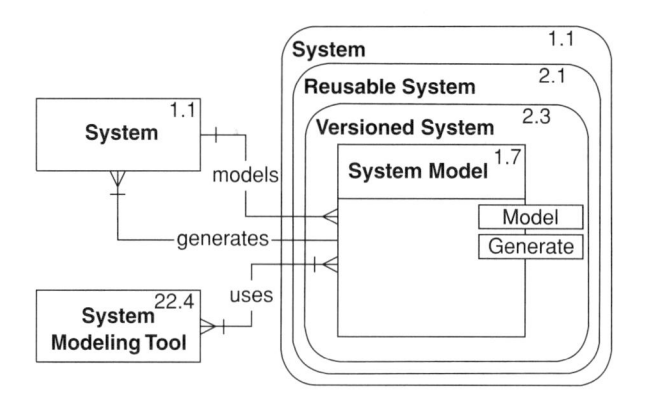

The key tasks for a system model are modeling the system and generating an instance of the system it represents. For example, understanding a process means building a process model that shows the tasks of the process and the flow of objects through those tasks. From this model, you can generate many processes that use the system model as the process structure. Understanding a document means building a document outline showing the different components of the document and how they relate. You can then generate documents from the template. Because the model is a versioned system, you can change it, tracking the different versions in the change management system.

System generation is reusing the model. Metric 1.4 is actually a reuse ratio: the percentage of the system you are generating from generic knowledge in the system model. To optimize productivity, you want to generate as much of the system as possible by spending a reasonable amount of time and money modeling. That is, by gathering a reasonable amount of generic knowledge, you can leverage the knowledge to generate new systems over and over again instead of starting from scratch. As well, when you generate systems from a standard model, you can leverage the standardization to improve the system using an improvement plan. The improvement plan for the model thus improves all the systems you generate from the system. Eliminating special and common causes of variation from the model eliminates them from the generated systems. As your generic knowledge increases due to improvement, your productivity in generation increases.

No knowledge is perfect, and no system model completely models the system it represents. When you generate the system, you thus need to add objects and relationships to adapt the generated system to the specific context in which you are using it. You need to customize or adapt the model to the situation [DeMarco 1982]. You thus need to trade off the cost of creating these objects and relationships to the cost of creating the knowledge needed to generate them over and over. For example, in creating a software development process, you might start with the generic processes of ISO-12207. Your initial processes will require much customization, since the model does not specify many of the relationships between the tasks, or indeed the content of the tasks themselves. The greater your experience in your project environment, the more you begin to understand about the generic qualities of your software development process. As your experience grows, your model acquires greater detail, and your processes get easier to generate. At some point, though, you need to stop modeling details, because the details change from project to project. The complexity you introduce into the model to handle these differences outweighs the productivity and quality improvements in process generation.

Process Model (4.7)
Task Model (4.9)
Project Process Model (4.8)
Design Pattern (21.2)
Document Template (6.3)

The most important system models in this book are the process model, the task model, the project process model, the document template, and the design pattern. Each uses a different system modeling tool to model the system objects and relationships, and each generates new systems from the model in different ways (processes, documents, designs, test cases, and technical systems). The test model hierarchy identifies several different models that contribute to test generation for different kinds of systems under test.

You have now seen the basic building blocks for project management of OO software. The purposive, open system with feedback introduces a dynamic, productive, value-based view of project management. The missions, visions, and operational objectives of these systems let you optimize the value they produce. Improvement plans guide you through to continuous improvement of the system. The next chapter introduces the *reusable* system, a kind of system with the mission of optimizing productivity as well as value.

Readings

[Abdel-Hamid]   Tarek Abdel-Hamid and Stuart E. Madnick. *Software Project Dynamics: An Integrated Approach*. Englewood Cliffs, NJ: Prentice Hall, 1991.

Abdel-Hamid and Madnick apply the Systems Dynamics simulation-modeling approach to understanding how software projects work. Although there is much to disagree with in the specifics of their modeling assumptions, the book is a landmark in applying simulation techniques to understanding complete project systems. Some of their conclusions about things like Brooks's law and the usefulness of deadlines and underestimation are fascinating.

[Bertalanffy]   Ludwig von Bertalanffy. *General System Theory: Foundations, Development, Applications. Revised Edition*. New York: George Braziller, 1971.

This is the most approachable work on general systems thinking, though it can be difficult in parts and is more of a collection of articles than a systematic exegesis of the topic.

[Cleland 1983]   David I. Cleland and William R. King. *Systems Analysis and Project Management, Third Edition*. New York: McGraw-Hill, 1983.

Cleland is the best general project management text that takes advantage of the systems approach. His technique of systems analysis, while a bit unsophisticated, helps put project management in the right framework.

[DeMarco 1982]   Tom DeMarco. *Controlling Software Projects: Management, Measurement, and Estimation*. New York: Yourdon Press, 1982.

Tom DeMarco has no equal as a writer or advocate of common sense in software projects. I took much of the inspiration for the system model class and its vision from this book, which devotes its Chapter 6 to a better explanation of system modeling than I could ever write. The book is also a major contributor to software development metrics, giving us both the Bang metric (an alternative to the function point) and the Chump metric (a binary measure whose value is True if the code is written in assembly language).

[Fenton]   Norman E. Fenton and Shari Lawrence Pfleeger. *Software Metrics: A Rigorous Approach, Second Edition*. Boston: International Thomson, 1997.

This is the best introduction to software metrics. It covers virtually everything of interest and does so with a rigor that should inspire all but the most resolutely anti-mathematical among us. While it is formal, it is very approachable; Fenton and Pfleeger never let the math interfere with the clarity of the points they make.

[Henderson-Sellers 1996] Brian Henderson-Sellers. *Object-Oriented Metrics: Measures of Complexity.* Englewood Cliffs, NJ: Prentice Hall PTR, 1996.

This is the best book available on OO software metrics. It relies a good deal on Fenton but extends his work to OO software. It is limited in detail on metrics other than complexity metrics, however.

[Mesarovic] Mihajlo D. Mesarovic and Yasuhiko Takahara. *Abstract Systems Theory.* Lecture Notes in Control and Information Sciences 116. New York: Springer-Verlag, 1989.

This is the best mathematical work available on general system theory. If you want to fully understand the theory, this is the place to follow up a close reading of Bertalanffy. It is, however, only for the mathematically sophisticated.

[Roberts] Fred S. Roberts. *Measurement Theory with Applications to Decisionmaking, Utility, and the Social Sciences.* Encyclopedia of Mathematics and Its Applications, Volume 7. Reading, MA: Addison-Wesley, 1979.

This is a wonderful book on measurement theory. Fenton relies on Roberts for his mathematics. The explanations of the different aspects of measurement are clear and exact. The later parts of the book apply the thinking to the social sciences in very interesting ways, and the book is well worth reading for its application to software metrics.

[Weinberg 1992] Gerald M. Weinberg. *Quality Software Management: Volume 1, Systems Thinking.* New York: Dorset House, 1992.

Weinberg's books are always a good read, and this one is a classic. It focuses on different aspects of applying systems thinking to software management, showing you how to rethink your approach. His introduction of cultural patterns as an alternative to Crosby's quality maturity model or the SEI's Capability Maturity Model provides a good deal of the rationale behind the approach to project management in this book.

Questions to Think About

1. List some different ways to measure the value of a project and the value of deliverables. Now list the advantages and disadvantages of each method. Does any particular method make more sense for OO software than for any other kind of software? Why?

2. Think of some relationships between classes and objects other than the simple ER relationships this book uses. How could you use these relationships to improve your management of OO projects?

3. Does your company/organization/team have a vision statement? a mission statement? If not, why not? What effect does the lack of such statements have on your understanding of the purpose of the project system? Can you effectively manage the project without a project purpose? Why?

4. Does your organization have a measured process? Do you have access to historical data from previous projects? If not, how could you introduce a sufficient level of record keeping to make such data available in the future?

5. Improvement plans come from a large literature on process improvement. What is the difference between improving a process and improving a goal-directed system? How does process improvement take the objectives of the process into account?

6. Models are objects that represent modeled systems through some kind of mapping. Can you name some models you use in everyday work life in addition to the ones that "The System Model" section lists, such as test models, process models, and templates?

CHAPTER

2

Reusable System

The Reusable System

Most discussions of reuse confine themselves to code reuse [Henderson-Sellers 1996]. Some expand the discussion to reusing other artifacts of the technical systems [Booch 1996; Jones 1994; Karlsson] such as design documents, test cases, or even project plans.

A rhetorical question: What does it mean to reuse a system? Since a productivity objective for a system often takes the approach of optimizing the reuse of component systems, it is very important to the system class. *Reusing* a system means using a system as a component to another system that is not a part of the task that originally created the reused system.

The HP 12C I've had sitting on my desk for years lets you enter a sequence of operations into its memory. This programmability lets the calculator do much more than its built-in functions suggest. For example, you can program the computer to do complex financial management rate-of-return calculations. But—you can have only one program in memory at a time. If you have two programs, you must reenter the first program when you want to reuse it. My personal computer spreadsheet program, on the other hand, lets me enter the program once. Then I can run it as often as I need it without reentering it, because it stores it in a special format on disk. When I reenter the program into my HP 12C, I am not reusing the program system, since I am recreating it. Since I type it in from a template of some kind (say, a sequence published in a financial calculations book), I am reusing the template but not the program. When I run the spreadsheet formula, I am reusing the stored system, as I created it separately.

In terms of programming productivity, the spreadsheet wins hands down over the calculator as a tool. Yet the calculator still sits on my desk, used every day.

It helps productivity in other ways than reuse, but I don't use it a lot for things that require programming.

Copying a system for later changes is not strictly reuse of the system, as it creates a new system within the "reusing" task instead of using the copied system. In practical terms, this means that if the original system changes, the copy does not. To maintain the "reused" system, you must put in place an extensive configuration management system to propagate changes from system to copy. You get an initial burst of increased productivity by copying the system; as time goes on, you lose some of that productivity increase through increased maintenance.

Similarly, versioning a system with changes is not strictly reuse of the system. Again, the new version is a new system. If you change the previous version, you have to propagate the change into the later versions, just as with a copy. Versioning makes the change management process easier, but it is not reuse.

Versioned System (2.3)
Change Management Process (24.1)

If you reuse a class through inheritance, most OO programming systems let you override the behavior of the superclass in the subclasses that inherit it. You thus reuse only part of the system.

For measurement purposes, you can also distinguish external from internal reuse: reusing a system within the project that created it versus outside that project. The system tracks the creating project and task as related systems.

There are several different proposals for measuring the amount of reuse in a system [Goldberg; Henderson-Sellers 1996], mostly as a predictive factor for estimating productivity and cost or for estimating the return on investment in reusable systems. There are at least four things wrong with this approach. First, measuring reuse in a system requires measuring size, and size is notoriously hard to measure. Optimally, you would measure the value added by the reused system; this is even harder to measure. Second, since you only know the amount of reuse *after* the system is complete, you can't use it to predict with any accuracy. Third, if you partially reuse a system by copying it, modifying it, versioning it, or inheriting from it with overriding behaviors, measurement gets a little tougher. Fourth, if you attempted to predict the reused portion in advance from other measures, you would need a more sophisticated model of reusability than is presently available [Karlsson], and you would be using an estimate to predict an estimate—shaky ground.

There are also some proposals to measure one or the other or both of external and internal reuse differently [Henderson-Sellers 1996, pp. 129–130; Jones 1991, p. 51]. For example, you could count only external reuse as reuse, or you could ignore externally reused components entirely as irrelevant to the current project. The idea is that one or the other style of counting yields a better estimate of system size to estimate cost. Unfortunately, no one has yet proposed and demonstrated a reliable model showing that this kind of reuse counting provides effective prediction of anything, particularly in OO systems.

So, while measuring actual reuse may be of some interest to management as a kind of propaganda tool, its value as a predictive tool is not high. You should almost certainly focus on *reuse potential* rather than on reuse in itself, and on measuring and optimizing *productivity*, not reuse. You can use measures of reuse effectively in a limited context that does not require extensive cross-system aggregation or predictive application. For example, the system metrics for the reusable system use actual system reuse counts as a statistical control variable. This use does not require aggregation of the reuse counts across systems.

Getting higher productivity requires optimizing reuse rather than maximizing it. This is as true in software as it is in physical processes. For example, reusing diapers is not necessarily the best way to achieve the goal of reducing the impact of a baby on the environment. Washing diapers wastes water and adds to water pollution, while using disposable diapers adds to ever-larger landfills, not to mention the environmental impact of producing paper diapers. Reusing a requirements document that doesn't satisfy a vital stakeholder, or reusing a test suite that has holes in it due to changes in the code, is not going to improve productivity in the long run.

Reusing a system requires the ability to use it outside the task that creates it. *Any* system that results from creative activity is a *potentially* reusable system, including tools, policies, project documents, repositories, organizational structures, resource skills, work groups, budgets, and the myriad plans (risk management, communications, and so on). You can generally reuse software clusters, classes, data, documentation, and frameworks. You can reuse design documents, design patterns, regression test suites, and requirements documents.

Some systems are inherently not reusable, such as meetings, reports, resources (as opposed to their skills), or processes (as opposed to process models). A project, for example, is not reusable; the project model that creates it is. Reuse is more prevalent than most managers might think. In any case, determining whether you are reusing a system requires knowing that the current task did not create the system.

Vision: A system that you can reuse to create value in many projects or tasks

Mission: To create a system with an optimal potential for reuse in multiple projects or tasks

Objective 2.1: To create trust in the system's ability to deliver value

Approach 2.1: Certify the system's ability to deliver value to optimize the potential for reuse given the intended domain, risk, and liability.

Metric 2.1: Reuse potential:

$$\text{Potential} = w_i P_i + w_d P_d + w_o P_o$$

The Reusable System

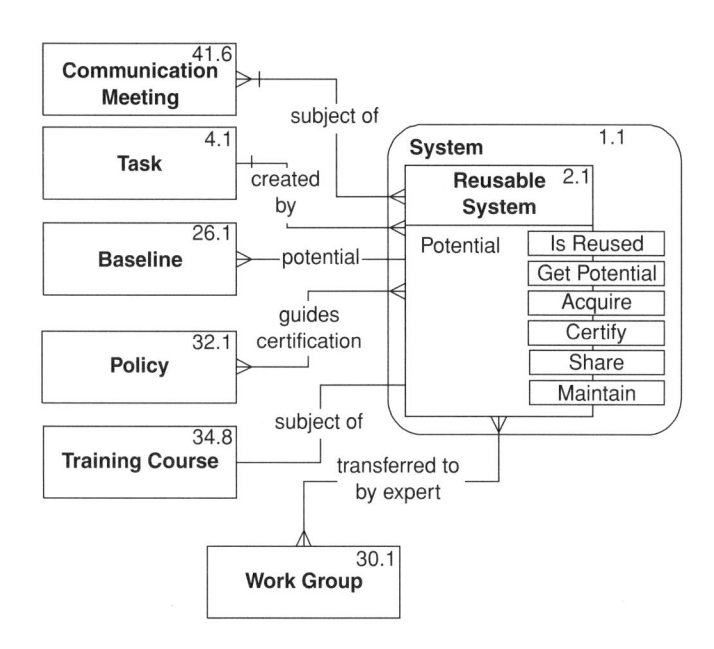

```
[41.6 Communication Meeting] ──subject of──┐
[4.1 Task] ──created by──────────────────┐ │
                                          ├─┤ System  1.1
[26.1 Baseline] ──potential──┐            │ │ Reusable System  2.1
                              ├─Potential─┤ │  • Is Reused
[32.1 Policy] ──guides        │            │ │  • Get Potential
               certification──┘            │ │  • Acquire
                                           │ │  • Certify
[34.8 Training Course] ──subject of────────┘ │  • Share
                                              │  • Maintain
                       transferred to
                       by expert
                              │
                      [30.1 Work Group]
```

where $w_i P_i$ is the weighted probability of inherent reuse, $w_d P_d$ is the weighted probability of domain reuse, and $w_o P_o$ is the weighted probability of organizational reuse (see text); the probabilities are Bayesian prior probabilities that you revise given actual reuse of the system; weights by default are all $1/3$, so the probabilities contribute equally, but you can vary the weights to emphasize one type of probability over another if that makes sense for the system, as long as the weights sum to one

Target 2.1: A reuse potential of 10% more than the current baseline for reuse potential in systems of the specific class; if there is no such baseline, then a reuse potential of 0.5 to start off with

---

Objective 2.2: To optimize the reuse of the system

Approach 2.2: Bring the reuse process under statistical control by measuring and acting on the actual reuse of the system. Measure both the actual reuse and the fraction of successful reuses versus total attempts at reuse, and use them to improve the reusability potential of the system and the knowledge of the system's availability and certification.

Metric 2.2.1: The number of reuses for the system

Target 2.2.1: No value outside the standard control limits in a pn control chart for Metric 2.2.1

Metric 2.2.2: The fraction of successful reuses versus total attempts at reuse of the system

Target 2.2.2: No value outside the standard control limit in a p control chart for Metric 2.2.2; this is a varying upper control level

---

Reuse Potential

Object-oriented projects focus on reusable technical systems as a major advantage of the approach. Whether or not this is true in practice, the focus is there; one job of an OO project manager is to facilitate and optimize reuse in the project. Measuring project reuse, however, should take all the different varieties of reuse into account that are of interest to achieving the mission of the project. For example, if a stakeholder such as a corporate executive is interested in increasing the profitability of the project through improving productivity, the project manager should look at the potential for reuse among *all* the reusable systems, not just the technical systems.

The potential for reuse is the probability that you will reuse the system. This depends on three reusability factors [Goldberg; Karlsson]:

- *Inherent reusability:* The probability of reuse due to *internal* properties such as the completeness of the system interface with respect to scenarios of use or the lack of coupling of the system to other systems (degree of encapsulation)

- *Domain reusability:* The probability of reusing the system because its functionality will support meeting the *requirements* of future systems; another way to say this is the probability that you will have similar requirements (domains) in the future

- *Organizational reusability:* The probability of reuse due to *organizational* factors such as repository facilities, communication, and reuse policies

The relative impact of each probability on reuse potential depends on the kind of system. If, for example, the system is heavily domain-dependent, such as a requirements document, you should weight the domain reusability probability higher. If the system depends less on a particular domain and more on its inherent interface, such as a low-level framework cluster of a linked list and its iterator classes, you should weight inherent reusability higher. The weight for organizational reusability depends on the overall impact of organizational factors on reuse; if you want to focus efforts on organizational aspects, weight this factor more heavily.

Certain characteristics of OO projects make more general kinds of reuse easier. The emphasis on encapsulation, for example, stresses the internal properties that lead to inherent reusability. The availability of inheritance makes it more likely that you will meet at least some future requirements even though you need to override certain features and add others. The focus of OO design on modeling domains leads to a high level of domain reusability. The cohesion you introduce with OO design is easier to communicate and document, leading to higher organizational reusability.

The common belief is that the most reusable kind of system is the system that provides the most value. Some believe that you should concentrate on really big components that make reuse worthwhile. I have little evidence for this. In my experience, systems get reused when they fit the need but don't impose their assumptions on you. I worked in one large software company that based several application system products on a massive application framework. It even tried to make this framework a separate product and sell it to outside developers. The framework imposed so many assumptions on developers and was so buggy that no one in the company wanted to use it. It actually *delayed* delivery of applications instead of improving productivity. While the framework delivered tremendous value through its extensive hierarchy of classes, it did so in a way that rendered the thing valueless in practice. Needless to say, the framework product never made it to market.

In developing reusable systems, you need to consider the potential reusers and their requirements. As with any kind of development project, you can never identify all the requirements or stakeholders. Someone will always come up with something new. What you can do is apply general design principles and patterns that make your system extensible and adaptable. Parameterize the system. Let users set options. Make classes easy to reuse through inheritance. Don't make too many assumptions about what people want to do. If you give reusers a chance, they will want to reuse your system.

Acquiring Reusable Systems

System *acquisition* is the process of creating the system. There are several different ways to get a reusable system. You can harvest systems after you use them the first time. You can do this at the end of the project, or you can put systems into the reuse repository as potential candidates for reuse and later develop them into fully reusable systems [Henderson-Sellers 1996]. You can buy off-the-shelf systems. You can build the system in-house, or you can outsource the job by contracting someone else to build the system.

In any case, you must determine who pays the bill for the system and when they will pay it. There are several different models for this as well. You can pay for system creation in the original project and use the resulting system elsewhere for free. You can amortize the cost by chargebacks to projects that reuse the system. You can fund system creation separately as a cost center. Part of the cost is the certification and sharing overhead that comes from the next two steps in the reusable system life cycle.

The decision to make a system reusable is often a part of the project process, usually involving extra process steps for generalization, certification, sharing, and maintenance.

- *Note:* Although the decision to make a system reusable is a project decision, the criteria for evaluating the decision must take a longer view. Since the current project does not realize the benefits of external reuse, you must estimate benefits from reuse in other projects to decide whether the extra effort to make the system reusable is worth it. The reusability decision thus should almost certainly be made in a joint effort with people from the project and organizational environment outside the project.

Certifying and Sharing the System

Certifying the system as reusable requires a certification policy that standardizes what you must do and analysis of several factors that establish *trust* in the system. Trust is essential for reuse; if you don't trust a system, you won't use it.

First, you must establish the *risk* level of the system. This answers the question: What is the probability that the system will do what it is supposed to do? Essentially, this means certifying that the system can achieve its mission within a certain level of risk (the risk tolerance of the reusing systems). To do this, you need to use the appropriate risk control approaches such as reviews and tests to reduce the system risk to the certified level. (See Part 5 on "Risk" for details of risk and risk management.) For example, for a cluster software object, you would certify the object's risk by a combination of code reviews and object and integration test suites that covered their test models to the required extent. For a process model, you would certify risk through a combination of process success metrics and reviews of the process model. For a compiler tool, you would certify risk through a defect rate metric. The reuser determines their risk tolerance, which in turn determines whether they can reuse the system at its indicated risk.

Second, you must provide a clear statement of the *goals* and *functioning* of the system. Generally, this requires the publication of the vision, mission, and operational objectives of the system. Those attributes of the system should be useful for potential reusers in determining whether to trust the system in a particular situation. Aside from the mission, reusers also want to know precisely what the system does, and to what domain or domains it does it. The operational objectives show reusers how the system approaches its mission and how it measures success, but there may be additional components of the system that provide useful information. For example, a software cluster, system, or tool usually has documentation that describes its use and functioning. This can be user documentation for a system, use cases and design documents for a system or cluster, or even a requirements document. For extensible and adaptable systems, you should include adequate documentation for adapters. You must certify that these collateral materials are complete and correct for reusable systems, usually through review. Sometimes the system contains accompanying reusable systems, such as regression test suites and their attendant baseline test results, that you can use to validate the system in its new setting.

A recent incident may illustrate the value of detailed functional certification. On June 4, 1996, the Ariane 5 rocket launched by the European Space Agency crashed about 40 seconds after liftoff. The cause: a software error in a reused component from an earlier system. A strong case can be made that the real cause was the lack of certification of this software, resulting in the inappropriate use of a 16-bit integer for a 64-bit floating-point number [Jézéquel]. There was no precise specification for the component that said it worked only in a 16-bit domain!

Third, you must provide a clear statement of responsibility for the system. That is, by publishing the system as reusable, you are offering a kind of "contract" to the reuser. Part of any contract are the promises you make regarding quality, quantity, performance, or legal title to a system. This warranty may range from the typical "as-is" warranty (no express or implied warranties including implied warranties of merchantability or fitness for a particular purpose) to a complete, express warranty of some promise. The warranty means that you accept responsibility for the problems of the system. The level of warranty often determines the level of trust the system user places in the system. For example, if you provide a reusable framework "as is," you take no responsibility for its problems. This almost guarantees that no one will reuse the framework. You can make some express warranties by guaranteeing some level of maintenance or by providing the reuser with enough detail that they can do the maintenance themselves if they so desire (the infamous source code in escrow, for example). Table 2-1 lists some standard areas for warranties of responsibility.

Certification must state for the reuser exactly what responsibility the source of the system assumes and what actions that source will take in what time frame if

Table 2-1 System Warranties for System Reuse Certification

Warranty	Description
Performance	The system will function at a certain level of risk (see the discussion on certification of risk), and it will do what it claims to do in the domains you've specified for it.
Title and Infringement	The creator of the system has the right to let reusers use it, usually with respect to intellectual property rights or exclusive use agreements (you need to reassure users they are not infringing your copyrights, for example, by using your test plans).
Disablement	There is no feature of the system that will disable functioning of the system.
Compatibility	The system will function in a particular environment stated in the description of the system.

there is a problem (see the following discussion of maintenance). You are informing the reuser of your accountability and thus establishing the third plank of trust in your system. You need to tell the user, for example, who the domain experts are that can answer questions about how the system fits into its intended domains. You need to supply experts and maintainers to keep the system operational.

Certifying a reusable system establishes trust, but only for those in the know. That is, if a potential reuser does not know about the existence of the system, it really doesn't matter how well you have certified it. The sharing step communicates the availability of the system to its potential reusers. The focus of the sharing step is the reuse repository, the storage facility in which you keep the systems. Usually this will be some kind of database with a set of associated browser and search tools. You need to classify and index the reusable systems to support these tools. See the section on "Reuse Repository" for a detailed look at these tools.

Reuse Repository (2.2)

But the repository is a passive communication tool at best. If you want to emphasize reuse as an approach to improving productivity, you need to sell your systems actively. You can do this with communication meetings, in which people familiar with what's available work with potential reusers to identify reusable systems of interest.

You can use training classes to train people in the systems they may want to use. Typically, project managers and architects get the most benefit from training.

You can also use organizational structures to transfer knowledge. For example, you can train resources in what's available for reuse, then assign those resources as reuse experts to work groups on projects. This cross-pollinates the work groups with resources that know what is available in the reuse repository.

The maintenance step is the final task you perform for the reusable system. Maintenance supports the warranties of your system certification with live bodies. Whether it is software, plans, process models, or resource skills, you must provide the appropriate maintenance services to fulfill your responsibilities. Usually this involves revising the reusable system in some way. But you can't stop there; you must propagate the changes to the reusers of the system. You must maintain a list of the systems that reuse your system to be able to inform those systems of changes. The model for the reusable system uses the system class relationship to

System (1.1)

other systems to represent this list.

Reusability Problems

As with all human systems, reusable systems are not always as effective as they might be. After slaving over a hot computer all day to generalize a framework so that everyone in the world will reuse it, it sometimes appears to the developer that his or her effort goes unrewarded and unappreciated. No one uses the work!

There are three basic problems that limit reuse in an OO project: lack of reusable systems, incompatible systems, and architectural mismatch.

Clearly, you can't reuse systems that don't exist. From the perspective of the prospective reuser, a system doesn't exist (1) if they can't find it or (2) if it really doesn't exist. The following section on the reuse repository discusses solutions to the problem of finding reusable systems. However, to find a system, it has to be in the repository. If you are just starting out with your reuse program, or if you are overly selective about what you put in your repository, you won't have many reusable systems. That's one of the reasons why you don't see a lot of reuse in the initial stages of developing OO applications: there's nothing to reuse until you've completed several systems.

Incompatibility is the inability of a system to work with its environment. This can be a technical problem, such as a bad interface to the operating or user interface system. It can also be an inherent problem in the system that renders it incapable of reuse in specific contexts. For example, if the mission of a project plan emphasizes delivering on schedule regardless of content or quality, and a project wants to reuse the plan but focuses on high-quality deliverables, the plan is probably incompatible with the project. If an object cluster uses an interface to the ORACLE relational database management system, but the reusing systems use an ODBC interface, the cluster is likely to be incompatible. Incompatibility is not an absolute; you can often provide extensions, workarounds, or exclusions that let you reuse the system. It's mostly a matter of degree.

For example, I worked with a great statistical analysis system in graduate school. The designers structured the system as a set of many small programs built around some basic data types and a relational database. This system let you reuse different pieces to put together a statisticial analysis that exactly suited your needs. Unfortunately, the designers wrote the system in PL/1 on an operating system that ceased to exist, and porting it proved difficult and uneconomic. The result: very few researchers use the system anymore. They use statistical packages on PCs and minicomputers with standard operating systems.

Architectural mismatch is a particular kind of inherent incompatibility: the conflicting, usually implicit assumptions that the reusable system makes [Garlan]. Implicit assumptions such as internal reliance on broad architectural relationships between parts of a framework or on the structure of external systems such as event loops can easily render a system unusable, if not completely incompatible. For example, reliance on large infrastructure libraries, only part of which the reusing system uses, can make frameworks too large, too complex, or too sluggish. Excessively detailed project plans can result in the need for excessive modification to fit new situations. Excessive numbers of policies in standards often force programmers, designers, and project managers to do things that they would not otherwise do, reducing productivity .

The main solution to architectural mismatch is to make the assumptions explicit as part of the certification process. The statement of system capabilities should include all potential assumptions that might affect reusers. Clearly, the

2.1 Reusable System

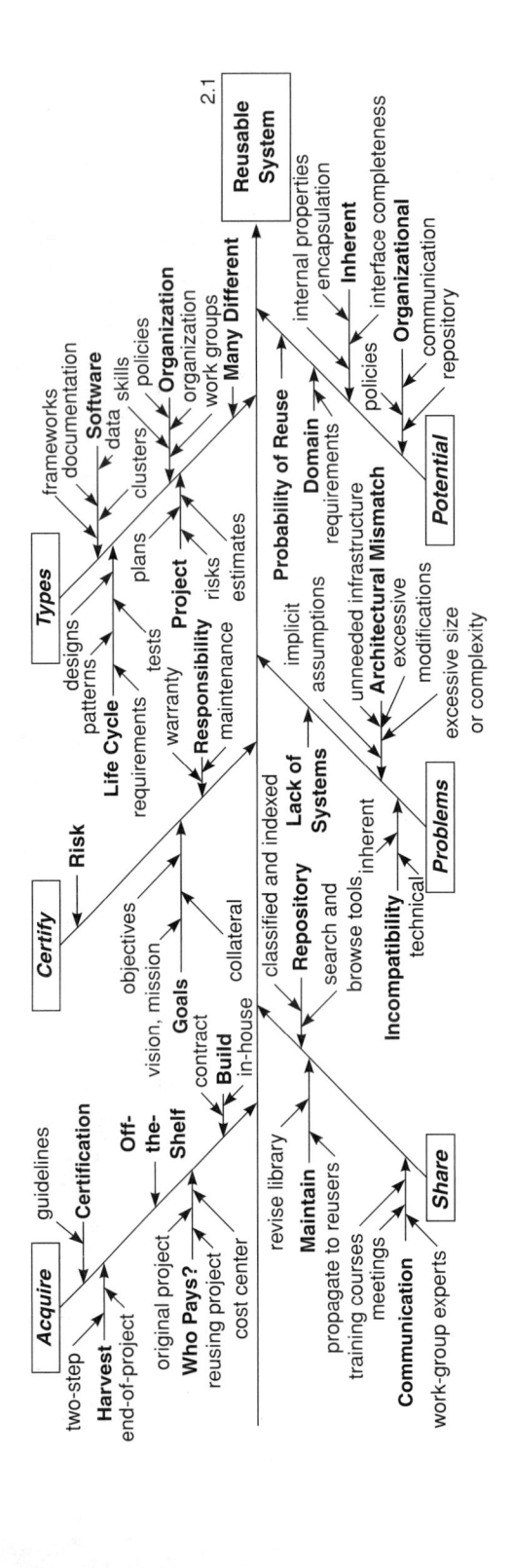

Acquire
- guidelines — **Certification**
- two-step — **Harvest**
- end-of-project
- original project
- **Who Pays?**
- reusing project
- cost center
- **Off-the-Shelf**
- vision, mission — **Goals** — objectives
- contract — **Build** — in-house — collateral

Certify
- **Risk**
- **Life Cycle**: requirements, designs, patterns, tests, warranty, maintenance — **Responsibility**
- **Types**: frameworks, documentation, plans, clusters, data, skills, policies — **Software**
- **Project**: risks, estimates — **Organization** — organization, work groups — **Many Different**

Problems
- revise library — **Maintain**
- classified and indexed — **Repository** — search and browse tools
- inherent — **Incompatibility** — technical
- **Lack of Systems**
- implicit assumptions, unneeded infrastructure, excessive modifications, excessive size or complexity — **Architectural Mismatch**

Potential
- **Probability of Reuse**
- requirements — **Domain**
- internal properties, encapsulation, interface completeness — **Inherent**
- policies, communication, repository — **Organizational**

Share
- propagate to reusers
- training courses, meetings — **Communication** — work-group experts

→ **Reusable System**

fewer assumptions you need to make, the more inherently reusable are your systems. This is one reason why large frameworks tend to aggravate reusers—too many assumptions about how things have to work together. You can also develop workarounds such as bridges, wrappers, or policy exceptions to eliminate specific problems. Designing a system to allow for different approaches—*negotiated interfaces*—is a good way to improve inherent reusability. Finally, focusing on reuse and developing a good, intuitive understanding of how things work together will let you design better systems. In other words, get *experienced* with reuse and you will build systems that have more reuse potential.

The Reuse Repository

The *reuse repository* is a kind of repository that contains reusable systems (*assets*). It also has their collateral *documentation*. The reuse repository permits the reuse of the systems in different tasks by storing and managing them. This repository is distinct from the product and project repositories because of its cross-product and cross-project nature and its storage of systems specifically for reusability.

Repository (20.1)

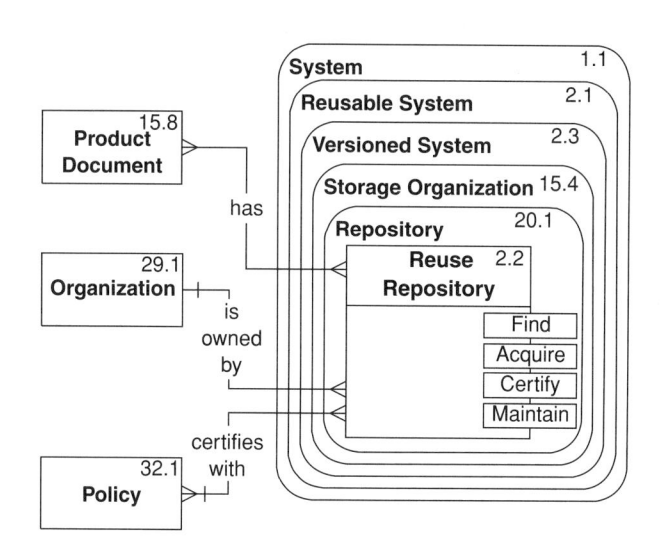

Vision: A set of well-ordered, reusable systems that any reuser can easily find and reuse

Mission: To enable the use of reusable systems

Objective 2.3: To enable the storage of reusable systems

Approach 2.3: Store the reusable systems in an appropriate storage organization that makes the systems available on demand in an appropriate format. Bring the system under statistical control by managing the fraction of reuses that requires some kind of conversion.

Metric 2.3: The fraction of reuses that involve a format conversion

Target 2.3: No value outside the standard control limit in a p control chart for Metric 2.3; this is a varying upper control limit for each group in the control chart

---

Objective 2.4: To organize the reusable systems for easy searching and browsing

---

Approach 2.4: Use the native repository facilities or off-the-shelf tools to provide standard search and browse facilities for the repository systems. Classify the systems using whatever classification method makes sense for your organization. Optimize the classification and the tools by bringing the search and browse process under statistical control and optimizing on the search success fraction and search time.

Metric 2.4.1: The fraction of searches that are successful at finding a reusable system that partially or fully meets the needs of the reuser

Target 2.4.1: No value outside the standard control limit of a p control chart for Metric 2.4.1; this is a varying upper control limit for each group in the control chart

---

Metric 2.4.2: The search time for reusable systems for searches that resulted in successful reuse of a system

Target 2.4.2: No value outside the standard control limits of an x-R control chart for Metric 2.4.2; these are the standard upper and lower control limits for the mean and range

---

The assets can have many different formats; for example:

- Text files
- Structured binary files
- Image files
- Relational or OO databases
- Paper

Any level of organization can own the reuse repository. For example, the reuse repository could be a corporate-wide database that several divisions or projects share. It could be a divisional or business-unit system that focuses on systems related to the product domain. It could even be a project library that stores systems that the project will reuse internally. You can also structure it at multiple levels, with each level taking responsibility for the systems of greatest interest to it. For example, the corporate database could contain general business rules, development policies, and software frameworks. The project level could contain domain-related clusters and project document templates. With a single repository, you don't need to go looking through many different places. Also, maintenance responsibilities are clear.

The primary services of the reuse repository system let you acquire, find, certify, and maintain the assets in the repository.

There are several models for acquiring the assets in a reuse repository [Goldberg; Henderson-Sellers 1996, pp. 22–23; Karlsson]:

- Generalize systems from a project for reuse in other projects as a *separate project,* charging generalization costs to designated stakeholders

- Generalize systems *within a project,* charging the stakeholders of the current project for generalization costs

- Generalize systems in a two-step process, first putting systems into a *potential* reuse repository and then generalizing them as needed in *new projects,* charging the generalization cost to the stakeholders of the generalizing project

- Produce reusable systems *independently* of projects in a *cost center,* charging projects for reuse through transfer fees or other mechanisms to recover costs over time; an "emerging technology group" approach [McTaggart]

- Buy reusable systems off-the-shelf or on a contract basis from vendors, charging projects by passing through licensing fees or amortized contract fees

Finding assets requires the repository to provide tools to search and browse the repository schema. Because the assets provide content-based services to the reusers, you generally want to provide search facilities that are more advanced than simple text searches. Generally this requires some kind of classification scheme [Goldberg; Karlsson]. Table 2-2 lists some possible schemes.

Whatever kind of classification scheme you use, you should make sure that it adequately links different reusable systems that relate to one another. For example, say you have a framework, its requirement document, and its regression test suite in your reuse repository. A search that turns up the framework should also turn up the document and test suite. Alternatively, you can use hypertext methods to cross-link systems in the repository schema. This lets you navigate from one system to another with a browser.

Searching generally employs online search tools and browsers, such as World Wide Web pages using standard search engines and languages. You can, of course, develop your own tools or acquire commercial tools for searching and

Table 2-2 *Reuse Repository Classification Schemes*

Scheme	Description
Category	You classify each asset in several different categories, dimensions, or domains using specific terms within each category. This lets you search by specifying terms in the different categories. Many World Wide Web search facilities now employ this kind of scheme. You should certainly use super- and subclass relationships as a domain in this kind of scheme.
Catalog	You classify each asset with a single catalog classification identifier that best describes the asset (libraries use this for book identifiers, for example). This scheme is appropriate mainly for searches for individual assets, but isn't very helpful for multiple-class searches. Searches generally work like searching a thesaurus; you go to the class that you think is likely to get a hit, then move around looking for things. This works well in library stacks, but isn't so wonderful for computer searches.
Keyword	You classify each asset with a set of keywords. Searches then become the art of guessing what words the classifier used to describe the reusable system. This is the standard for online searches in most libraries and online services, which use titles and names as keywords.

browsing. Newer search tools often incorporate "fuzzy" searching techniques that return not just matches but things that resemble your search criteria or are near it in some semantic sense [Karlsson].

While online tools are powerful, they are still not capable of finding what you want to find. Often, they are hard to use, buggy, and too simple. The result: there's still room for the help desk. A well-informed, well-trained person with good library skills is indispensable as part of your reuse organization. A good librarian is a jewel in the organizational crown. Also, any system must have adequate online help ranging from online documentation to bulletin boards or chat groups. These virtual hallways let people from all over the organization help each other to find reusable assets through personal interaction.

Part of finding reusable objects is effective marketing. The reuse organization must go out and present the system to its potential users through seminars and other kinds of communication meetings.

The organization that owns the reuse repository is generally responsible for certifying assets in the repository. It may contract the work out to the organization that creates the asset, but this is delegation of the responsibility. The repository stores the resulting project document that contains the certification materials. The reuse organization is also responsible for maintaining the set of reuse certification policies that creators use to certify their systems.

The systems in the reuse repository are not static; they change with time. The maintenance task drives the maintenance of the individual systems in the repository. That is, once you place an asset in the repository, you must go through the owner of the repository to change a system. Projects that reuse assets can change

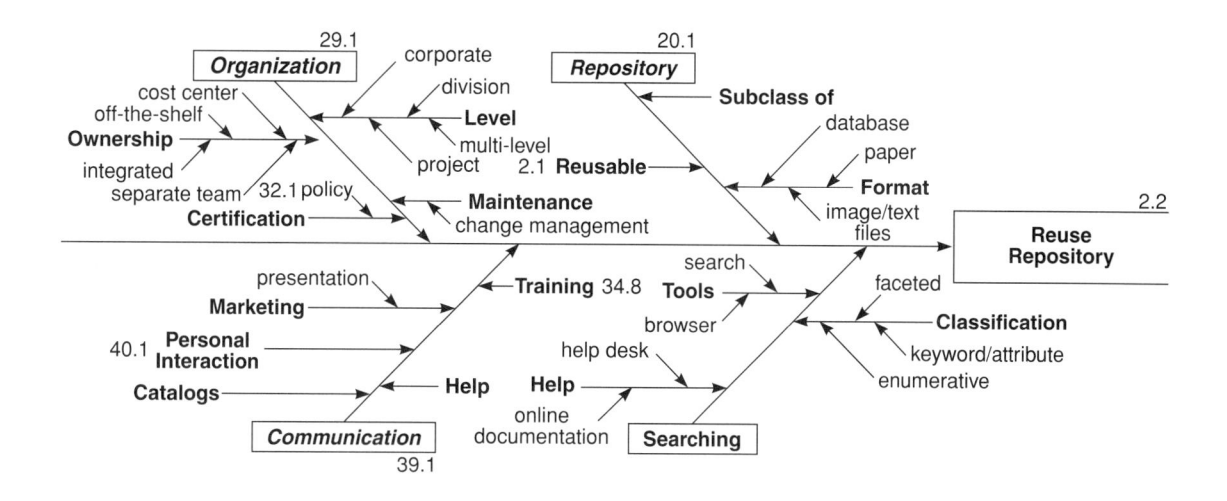

```
                        29.1              20.1
                   Organization          Repository
                             corporate
         cost center         / division        Subclass of
  off-the-shelf  \          /  Level                    database
  Ownership      \         /   multi-level             / paper
         integrated \     /    project  2.1 Reusable  / Format
         separate team / 32.1 policy \  Maintenance  / image/text
                      Certification    change management  files
                                                                    search         faceted
              presentation              Training  34.8  Tools                         Classification
         Marketing                                browser                            keyword/attribute
  40.1  Personal                                  help desk                          enumerative
        Interaction
        Catalogs                    Help       Help
                                              online
                              Communication   documentation   Searching
                                   39.1
```

                                                                                              2.2
                                                                                        Reuse
                                                                                        Repository

them, for example, and then place the revised assets back in the repository. This doesn't just happen, however; you need a change management process conducted by the reuse organization. This process will exist separately from the project change management process if the organization is outside the project.

Most organizations currently have some kind of reuse repository, even if it is only a floppy disk on a developer's desk (SneakerNet). The more formal the repository, the more likely you are to use it.

The Versioned System

Objects are not static. Even if a system is fully reusable as is, you must still maintain it. Many systems with less reuse potential change often through their lifetime. Rather than treating each change to a system as a new system, you need an intermediate way of referring to the dynamic changes.

A *versioned system* is a reusable system with a name and a version number. The name identifies the set of versions, while the name and version number together identify the particular object. When the content of the object changes as the result of a process task, the task increments the object's version number. The change management system should track these version numbers as part of its basic operation. The change management system and the subclass of versioned system coordinate on the storage of the different system versions.

Reusable System (2.1)

Change Management System (24.4)

Vision: A carefully orchestrated, reusable, and progressively more valuable system

Mission: To enable systems to optimally change their structure through reuse of their previous versions

Objective 2.5: To permit reuse of a system to incorporate changes that satisfy stakeholder needs

Approach 2.5: Represent the change as the difference between the previous and current systems. Associate a version number with each version, with the current version number being one greater than the previous version number.

Metric 2.5: Ratio of actual number of versions to expected number of versions, with the expected value being the median number of versions during similar control periods for this specific kind of system

Target 2.5: One (1)

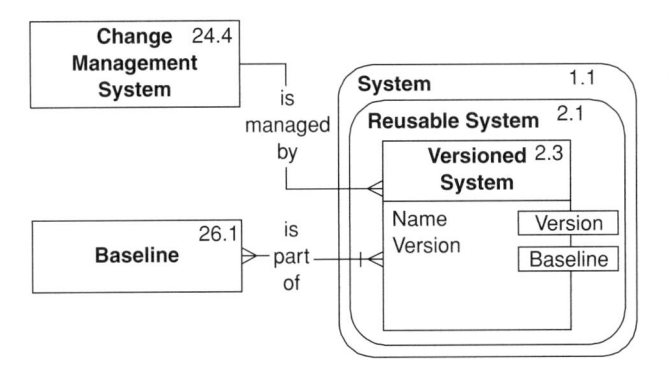

```
┌─────────────────┐
│ Change    24.4  │
│ Management      │
│ System          │──┐         ┌─────────────────────────────┐
└─────────────────┘  │is       │ System              1.1     │
                     managed   │ ┌─────────────────────────┐ │
                     by        │ │ Reusable System   2.1   │ │
                     │         │ │ ┌─────────────────────┐ │ │
                     │         │ │ │ Versioned    2.3    │ │ │
                     │         │ │ │ System              │ │ │
                     └─────────┼─┼◁┤                     │ │ │
                               │ │ │ Name    ┌─────────┐ │ │ │
┌─────────────────┐            │ │ │ Version │ Version │ │ │ │
│          26.1   │  is        │ │ │         ├─────────┤ │ │ │
│ Baseline        │▷─part──────┼─┼◁┤         │Baseline │ │ │ │
└─────────────────┘  of        │ │ │         └─────────┘ │ │ │
                               │ │ └─────────────────────┘ │ │
                               │ └─────────────────────────┘ │
                               └─────────────────────────────┘
```

The versioned system focuses on the reuse potential in systems that can change over time. That is, if a system accommodates change through versioning, you can reuse the system over and over with minor changes during each reuse. If you consider each new version as a completely separate system with no relationship to previous versions, you cannot roll forward changes from previous versions that change. Also, there is no way to relate the different versions to discover how change is affecting the system or to control that change. Versioned systems, of course, may also have other kinds of reuse potential beyond versioning, such as reuse in other domains or contexts.

Versioned systems are a general case of *configuration units,* systems under configuration control. For example, the military process model DOD-STD-2167A calls it the computer software configuration item (CSCI). The versioned system generalizes this by versioning items other than software, such as supporting documentation, system models, project standards, and so on. You need to decide whether the extra control is worth the overhead of maintaining versions in a configuration management system.

Many systems are complex, containing other systems. The containing system often treats a set of versions of its components as a distinct unit. The *baseline* is a set of versions with an emergent meaning relating to control and earned value: the baseline plan, baseline cost estimates, the alpha release, and so on. A version can belong to one or more baselines.

Baseline (26.1)

There are many complex versioning schemes to handle version branching and other requirements. With versioning, simplicity is a virtue. You must take object-level change into account in managing your project. You must control that change through change management. Versioning helps. Making versioning excessively complicated usually comes from trying to satisfy conflicting stakeholder expectations. The more complex your versioning scheme, the lower the inherent reuse potential.

I once worked in a financial software shop that catered to several major customers with a single product. Because each customer wanted a different set of features, the development manager branched the product. This resulted in several parallel-product deliverable baselines. It was nearly impossible to track which version of which deliverable applied to which customer. It took the efforts of three people full-time just to keep the configuration management system functional. When it came time to integrate the different streams, we couldn't do it, resulting in much rework.

You can extend the configuration process to handle project documents, procurement issues, calendars, and all the other systems that are part of project management. Introducing excessive complexity through branching will make this difficult. Keep it simple with a single, straight line of versioning and reasonably infrequent baselines.

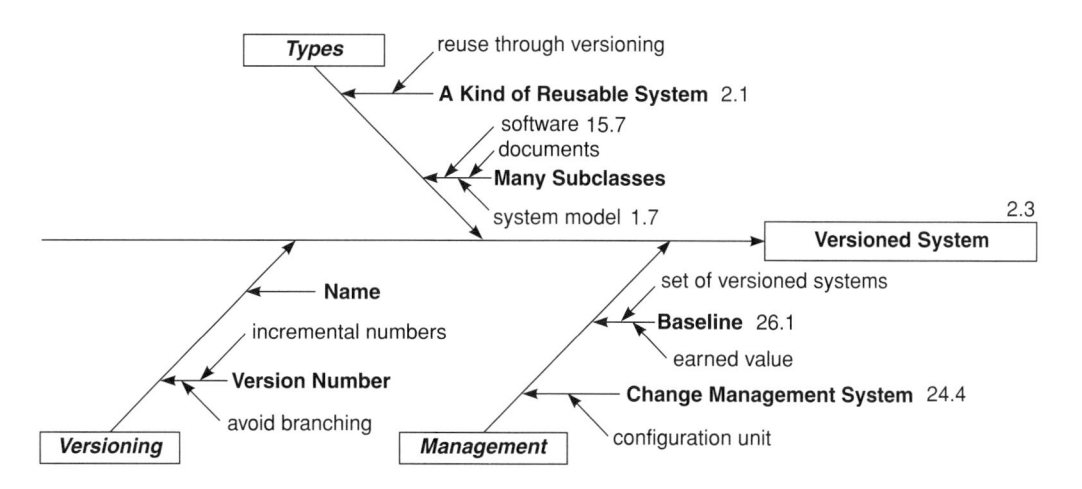

Readings

[Basili 1996]   Victor R. Basili, Lionel C. Briand, and Walcélio L. Melo. How reuse influences productivity in object-oriented systems. *Communications of the ACM* 39:10 (October 1996): 104–116.

This very recent article is the first step toward actually measuring the impact of reuse on productivity and quality. While it has serious methodological flaws (limited "student" data set, use of SLOC as measure of size and reuse, and a relatively vague set of reuse metrics), the article sets the context for the impact of software reuse very well. A notable conclusion: reuse explains 66% of productivity in a strongly increasing linear relationship.

[Biggerstaff]   Ted J. Biggerstaff and Alan J. Perliss. *Software Reusability*. Two volumes. New York: ACM Press, 1989.

This is the leading collection of articles on reusable software. Very academic. A must-have for anyone actually doing research, but of less interest to practitioners. There are several such collections of papers, and many more papers in the academic journals, testifying to the theoretical power of the concept of reuse, if not to its impact on practice.

[Garlan]   David Garlan, Robert Allen, and John Ockerbloom. Architectural mismatch: Why reuse is so hard. *IEEE Software* (November 1995): 17–26.

An excellent, well-written article that defines the concept of architectural mismatch and demonstrates how it affects the reusability of software. Must reading for anyone interested in reusability.

[Goldberg]   Adele Goldberg and Kenneth S. Rubin. *Succeeding with Objects: Decision Frameworks for Project Management*. Reading, MA: Addison-Wesley, 1995.

Goldberg and Rubin have two large chapters on reuse. Their approach to reuse certification and reuse potential is the source for those topics in the current chapter. Their chapter on the organization of reuse provides a good supplement to the project-related discussions of this chapter. Their discussion of classification schemes is particularly useful, though limited.

[Henderson-Sellers 1996] Brian Henderson-Sellers. *Object-Oriented Metrics: Measures of Complexity*. Englewood Cliffs, NJ: Prentice Hall PTR, 1996.

Henderson-Sellers has some good material both on ROI measures of reuse and on reuse metrics, though these are of limited value in practice.

[Karlsson]   Even-André Karlsson, editor. *Software Reuse: A Holistic Approach*. New York: Wiley, 1995.

Currently THE book on reuse, with more detail and case studies than you could ever ask for. The book is a bit dry and repetitious and certainly too long, but anyone starting a reuse program (and most of those who already have one) should read this book cover to cover. My one complaint is that the authors focus on how to do things in microdetail rather than on some major principles that will guide you. The result is that the authors often diffuse their point by failing to relate it to the rest of the book. I disagree with some of the approaches to metrics, and especially with the "reusability capability model," but the issues the book raises are comprehensive in scope and worth studying.

[Poulin] Jeffrey S. Poulin. *Measuring Software Reuse: Principles, Practices, and Economic Models*. Reading, MA: Addison-Wesley, 1997.

This is a good summary of the reuse literature as long as you ignore the principles that Poulin advocates for measuring reuse. His first rule is that reuse is external to an organization. This definition ignores the value of code one part of a project generates for reuse in another part, a major source of productivity. Poulin calls this just "good programming practice," not reuse. Defining reuse based on organizational boundaries is perhaps even more limiting, given the gray boundaries of software organizations. Finally, Poulin focuses primarily on measuring reuse itself, not on measuring reusability or the benefits of reuse. There is some material on return on investment, but it is not very detailed and seems to ignore common issues with return-on-investment analysis, such as the time value of money or, indeed, the nature of value itself.

[Tracz] Will Tracz. Tutorial: *Software Reuse—Emerging Technology*. Washington, DC: Computer Society Press, 1988.

This is also an interesting collection of academic papers on reusable software, though again of limited interest to practitioners.

Questions to Think About

1. Why is there so much focus on reusing code and so little on reusing other kinds of systems in software projects? Does code reuse contribute dramatically more to overall productivity than other kinds of reusable systems? How would you tell in your organization?

2. How would you measure partial reuse through inheritance? Why would you?

3. What kind of organization do you think would be better at reusing systems? Why?

4. Given the notion of architectural mismatch, is there any way to guarantee that your system is reusable (reuse potential of 100%)? What would need to be true for this to happen?

5. What kind of chargeback system does your organization have to transfer costs between business units? What are the implications of this for reuse and the reuse repository? Does the scheme provide incentives or disincentives for reuse?

6. Would a "reuse dictator" of some kind associated with the project help or hinder efforts to reuse systems in your organization? The reuse dictator reviews all systems with the power to force reuse of reusable systems.

7. Does your organization have a reuse repository? How does it charge for reuse? Is this structure a positive or negative motivation to reuse assets?

8. Does your organization branch versions of systems? Does it measure the impact of this branching on overall project productivity? If not, why not?

CHAPTER 3

The Project and Its Environment

The Project

A *project* is "a temporary endeavor undertaken to create a unique product or service" [PMI 1996a]. The "undertaken endeavor" part of this definition reflects a set of processes that organizes work into a system of tasks. The project is itself a complex task within the overall system of work done in your organizational environment. The objective of this complex task is to create a *unique* product or service, something that you have not done before and that you won't do again: a set of project deliverables. When you deliver these deliverables, the project is over: a project always has a definite ending point.

Projects don't just happen, or at least if you want them to deliver the right systems they don't. You need to plan them. The project plan is a project document that lays out the scope of work, the schedule for doing it, and all the different plans you need to have to make the project work. To build a project plan, you need to identify all the people and organizations that have a stake in the project: the project stakeholders. You also need to organize the people who will work on the project into a project organization. Together with the standard project process, all of this planning lets you create and run a project system, and that system in turn works within an organizational environment. The project management system stores and tracks project data in the project repository, letting you control the project as you execute it.

■ *Note:* Here is an example of a system that is *not* reusable, by definition. Since the project is a temporary endeavor to create a unique product, you can't reuse the entire project. You can, of course, reuse some of the systems that make it up, such as the project plan and certainly the deliverables, and your project process model is a system model that is certainly reusable.

Diagram

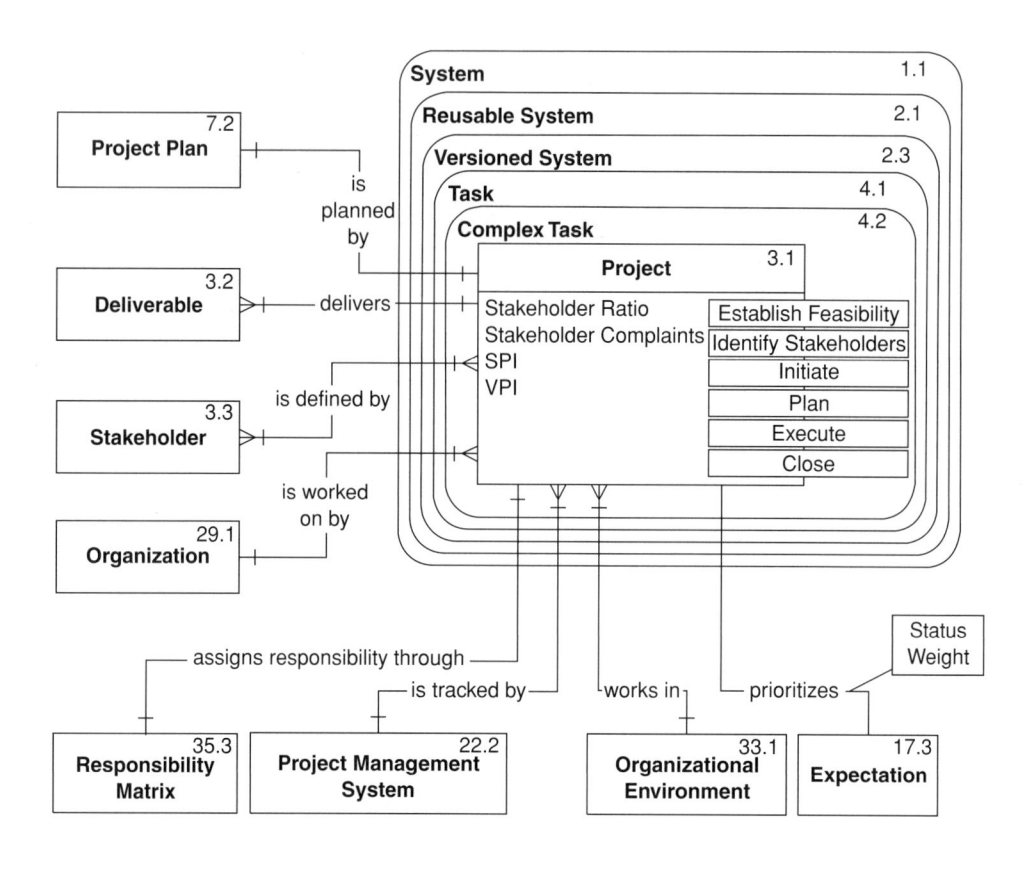

- **7.2 Project Plan** — is planned by —
- **3.2 Deliverable** — delivers —
- **3.3 Stakeholder** — is defined by —
- **29.1 Organization** — is worked on by —

Nested systems (outer to inner):
- System 1.1
- Reusable System 2.1
- Versioned System 2.3
- Task 4.1
- Complex Task 4.2
- **Project 3.1**
  - Stakeholder Ratio
  - Stakeholder Complaints
  - SPI
  - VPI
  - Establish Feasibility
  - Identify Stakeholders
  - Initiate
  - Plan
  - Execute
  - Close

Relationships from Project:
- assigns responsibility through → **35.3 Responsibility Matrix**
- is tracked by → **22.2 Project Management System**
- works in → **33.1 Organizational Environment**
- prioritizes → **17.3 Expectation** (Status, Weight)

Vision: A project that delivers optimal value to its stakeholders as a set of unique products and services

Mission: To create and deliver a set of deliverable objects that provide optimal value to the stakeholders of the project

---

Objective 3.1: To structure the set of deliverable objects to deliver an optimal amount of value to the stakeholders of the project given the environmental constraints of the project

---

Approach 3.1: Identify all the stakeholders of the project, and gather all their expectations. Structure these expectations into project objectives and requirements for deliverables, optimizing any conflicting expectations and constraints. Establish the feasibility of the plan. Identify clearly any stakeholders you decide to exclude from consideration.

Metric 3.1.1: Stakeholder Ratio: ratio of unidentified and misidentified stakeholders to identified stakeholders at the end of the project

Target 3.1.1: Zero to 5% (it takes experience to identify all stakeholders; as your experience grows, reduce the range toward zero)

Metric 3.1.2: Stakeholder Complaints: number of stakeholder complaints about missing or invalid requirements at the end of the project

Target 3.1.2: Zero to ten complaints (optimization means you will always have some dissatisfaction among stakeholders, so zero complaints is an ideal that will be hard to meet unless you have a poor stakeholder identification ratio)

Objective 3.2: To deliver the required deliverable objects to the stakeholders at the lowest possible cost

---

Approach 3.2: Plan the project to deliver the deliverables as the stakeholders require, given the optimization of Approach 3.1. Specify the scope of the project, the project schedule, and all the tasks that comprise the work of the project in this plan, including risk management tasks, communication tasks, quality assurance tasks, and so on. Execute the plan, revising it as necessary, to deliver the deliverable objects.

Metric 3.2.1: Schedule performance index (SPI): the ratio of total earned value to total planned value for the deliverables at the end of the project; this measures the efficiency with which you delivered what you planned to deliver at a given date (see the section on "The Project Deliverables and System Earned Value" for a complete definition of "earned value")

Target 3.2.1: Schedule performance index >= 1

Metric 3.2.2: Value performance index (VPI): the ratio of total earned value to total actual value for the deliverables at the end of the project; this measures how many "extras" you delivered (see the section on "The Project Deliverables and System Earned Value" for a complete definition of "earned value")

Target 3.2.2: Value performance index >= 1

Metric 3.2.3: Schedule variance (see the section on "The Project Deliverables and System Earned Value" for a complete definition of "earned value" and "schedule variance")

Target 3.2.3: At any given date during the project, 0 <= schedule variance <= 1% of value at completion

"The Project Deliverables" section, p. 67

While you can look at a project as a process, this book looks at it as a task with a set of processes taking place inside it. A process is a series of operations in the production of a product, while a task is a piece of work. Thinking of the project as a piece of work permits the unification of multiple projects in a network of tasks. It lets you place several different processes and life cycles within the project. Identifying a project identifies the products that the task produces. The *emergent* properties of the product as a system—the deliverables—thus contribute to making the task a project rather than just a task within a project.

The project plan provides the structure for the processes and tasks within the project. It shows the timing and dependencies of tasks as well as the budget and other control constraints on the project.

Process (4.6)
Process Model (4.7)

- *Note:* Most project management software does not structure work in processes but rather as a set of tasks. Software packages also usually have very complicated and arbitrary ways to embed projects within other projects or to work with multiple projects. Working with projects as tasks dramatically simplifies such structures, reducing the complexity to the more standard problems of distributed data management.

In the course of the life of the project, you have several tasks: establishing its feasibility; identifying its stakeholders; and initiating, planning, executing, and closing down the project.

Establishing feasibility creates the project. Before that, there was an idea and a guess that it might be possible. To reify the project, you must first *identify the stakeholders* and their expectations (see the following section on "The Project Stakeholder"). Then you set up the vision, mission, and operational objectives in interaction with the stakeholders. Once you've identified the objectives, you analyze them to a basic level to figure out if you should even attempt the project. The usual way to do this is to outline the plan to a basic level, including the budget and schedule. This first version of the project plan is the *business plan* or *project proposal*. It generally focuses on the probability of success of the deliverables satisfying the stakeholders. For example, the business plan for a commerical software product discusses the market for the system and projects how well the software will sell. The business plan for an internal application shows how the system meets the internal need that generated the project.

"Project Stakeholder"
section, p. 74

To *initiate* the project, the stakeholders review the business plan and decide whether they think the project is worth doing. The subset of stakeholders that hold the purse strings sign off on the project in the appropriate way. For example, this could be the signing of the contract between you and a stakeholder company buying a system. It could be the authorization of the senior vice president or chief executive of your company. While you can start a project informally, I've found that kicking off the project with formal approval from the stakeholders gives the project that extra seal of approval to make it more likely to succeed.

Once you initiate the project, the project manager *plans*, producing the complete project plan, including the work breakdown structure of tasks and a cost estimate for the deliverable. Usually, but not always, your stakeholders will insist that you finish the plan before you can execute the project. The plan can change throughout the execution of the project through the change management process.

When the plan is sufficient for the resources to begin work on planned tasks, you can *execute* the project, starting the planned processes. As the processes proceed and the deliverables accumulate, you are responsible for controlling the project by gathering information about deliverables and processes and feeding that information back into the processes.

When the project produces the desired product, or reaches a point at which someone with authority decides it is unlikely to do so under any circumstances, the project manager *closes down* the project. Closing the project is a series of tasks that verifies the deliverables are complete and satisfactory, formalizes the administrative aspects of project completion, and resolves any outstanding contractual issues.

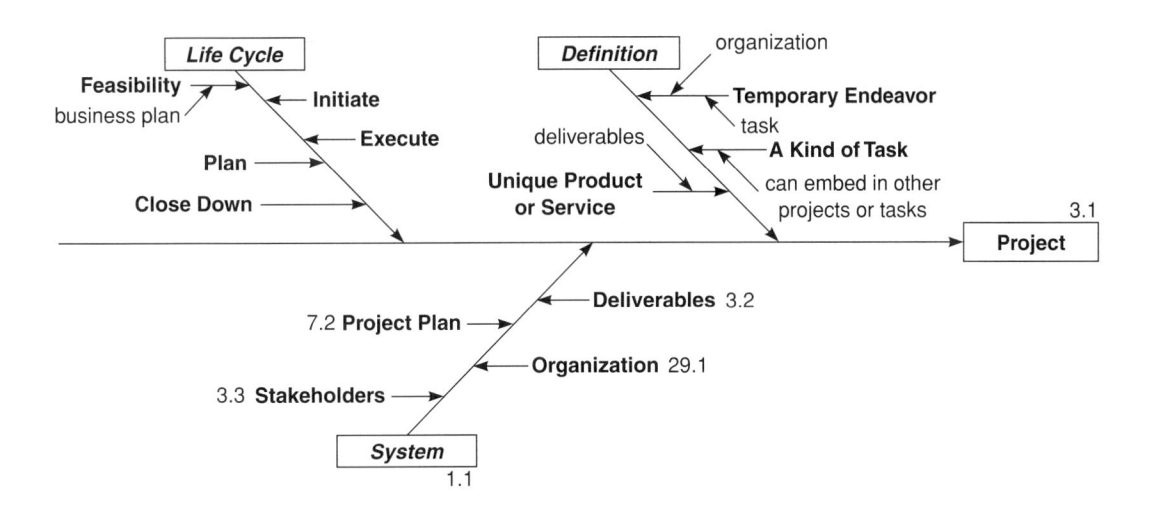

The Project Deliverables and System Earned Value

The unique product or service that a project produces is the set of *project deliverables*. The deliverable is not an off-the-shelf object; the project *creates* the deliverable through work, it does not just *manufacture and deliver* it. This added *value* is the rationale for doing the project.

Vision: A system that delivers its intended value to a stakeholder of the project

Mission: To provide value to stakeholders at a feasible cost to the project

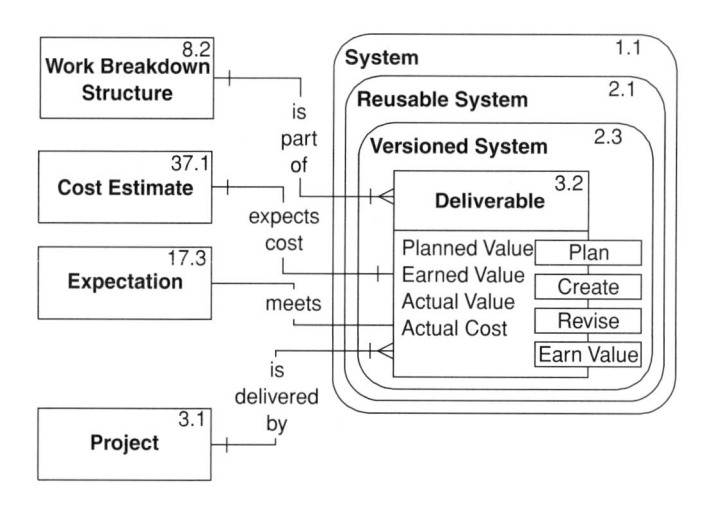

Objective 3.3: To plan, create, and revise the deliverable system to optimize the value it delivers to project stakeholders

Approach 3.3.1: Create a plan as part of the project plan to deliver the deliverable, making the deliverable a top-level component of the Work Breakdown Structure and estimating the value you intend to create and the cost you intend to incur in creating it.

Metric 3.3.1: Value: A system-specific scale representing the valuation of the system for the stakeholders, such as function points, price, or some other value metric; a generic one is warranted equity value:

$$WEV = \Sigma_{t=1}^{\infty}(ECF_t / (1 + CC)^t)$$

where *WEV* means "warranted equity value," *ECF* is "equity cash flow," and *CC* is the system cost of capital. Equity cash flow at time *t* is the earnings of the system during the period from time *t* – 1 to time *t* minus invested equity (the money the system puts into the continuing system during the period). The cost of capital is the risk-adjusted rate of return the system expects to get from its investment [McTaggart, pp. 299–312]. This measure of value gives you the net present return to the investors in terms of cash flow, a reasonable approach to evaluating a business system.

Target 3.3.1: A system with the value that the optimized stakeholder expectations require; delivering less value means that you abandoned intended features

Approach 3.3.2: Execute this plan to create and revise the deliverable system, measuring the progress through earned value analysis. Use this feedback to control optimization of deliverable value for the stakeholders.

Metric 3.3.2: Planned, Earned, and Actual Value: the planned value, planned value delivered, and actual value delivered at a given time, respectively (see text for details)

Target 3.3.2: A system that contributes an optimal value to the total value of the project; the target is thus set dynamically at any given time by the metrics of the project (schedule variance, SPI, VPI)

Approach 3.3.3: Measure the cost of producing the deliverable against the estimated cost to control the actual costs to deliver the system so that they do not exceed the budgeted costs.

Metric 3.3.3: Planned, Earned, and Actual Cost: the cost estimate, estimated cost delivered, and actual cost at any given time, respectively (see text for details)

Target 3.3.3: A system that you deliver on budget; the target is thus the current baseline budget estimate for the deliverable

---

A deliverable is a reusable system. You can have many tasks in your development process that deliver systems, but these are not necessarily *deliverable* systems. Deliverable systems are those that have innate *value* to the customer, that function by themselves as a system for a stakeholder. Usually, a deliverable is a working application with its documentation. You can also deliver application programming interfaces or other components that stand alone. To put all this another way, deliverable objects are systems you want to treat as systems in their own right rather than as components of other systems. The properties of the object that make it deliverable are thus *emergent system properties,* properties that come from the object as a system rather than from the individual parts that make up the system.

As an example, think about a client/server system that comprises four programs (a designer, a runtime client, a server module, and a maintenance utility) and a documentation set (user's guide and reference). No one part is useful without the others. Delivering the user's guide, for example, does not contribute any value without delivering the accompanying software, and vice versa. On the other hand, you could treat the runtime system as a separate product included with the development system for testing purposes. The runtime system has value on its own, but if you did not deliver the runtime system with the designer, the designer would be useless.

Deliverables thus have *value*. That is, you must have some way to express the contribution that the object makes to the overall value of the project. Value is an emergent property. You can express the value of a delivered software system and its supporting deliverables such as documentation, for example, in *function points,* a metric that represents the size of the software system. Any kind of deliverable system has a standard means of valuation, ranging from function points to potential sales to warranted equity value [McTaggart]. *Planning* the deliverable by putting it

Work Breakdown Structure (8.2)
Software System (15.7)

in the Work Breakdown Structure is the point at which you should establish the first estimate of value. You also break down the deliverable into its components, as far as you might know them. As you execute the plan, you "earn" the value by delivering the systems.

You allocate the function points to the deliverable objects, giving each object its functional contribution to the value of the overall system. You use this value in combination with planning and control to measure the *earned value* of a project: the amount of planned value you have actually delivered at a given point in the project.

The deliverable delivers value, but at a cost. Each deliverable system has a cost estimate and an actual cost. You make the cost estimate using the appropriate estimation tools and models. This estimate, and its rolling-wave allocation to the smaller packages that make up the deliverable, constitutes the project budget and spending budget. The actual cost accrues through the cost accounts as the project progresses [Kerzner].

Cost Estimate (37.1)
Cost Estimation Tool (37.2)
Cost Budget (37.3)
Chart of Accounts (36.1)

Deliverables have names and version numbers, as they are a kind of versioned system. *Creating* and *revising* the deliverable are primary tasks in the project, where the work of delivering value actually gets done. As with all versioned systems, you can baseline the deliverable at any time. When you revise the object, you get a new version of the object and a potential for earning value and cost.

Versioned System (2.3)

Figure 3-1 shows the measurement of earned value of a software system in terms of delivered function points. The horizontal axis shows time, and the vertical axis shows value in function points. You start the project with an initial value baseline, and you modify this baseline with new versions every so often as time progresses. At any given point in time, your work has delivered some amount of the value. You can also use a similar diagram to show the earned cost, substituting the costs for value measures.

The *planned value* at a specific date is the baseline value you planned to have complete by that date. This is the value of the baseline deliverable. For example, you might have planned to finish three systems by June 4, 1996, each of which was worth 65 function points, yielding a planned value for June 4 of 195 function points.

The *earned value* at a specific date is the amount of planned value you actually completed, or earned, at that date. *Earning value* requires a process of determining the completed value through some kind of decision process. (See the discussion below on ways you might approach this.) Continuing the example, if on June 4 you had completed only two of the three systems, your earned value is 130 function points.

The *actual value* at a specific date is the amount of value you have actually delivered, including systems that you did not plan to deliver according to the latest baseline. This represents total work done in some sense, and you can use it to compare with earned and planned value to determine your efficiency at delivering planned value. For this example, say you had also delivered a fourth system with an additional 45 function points that was not a part of the specification. Your actual value is 130 + 45, or 175 function points.

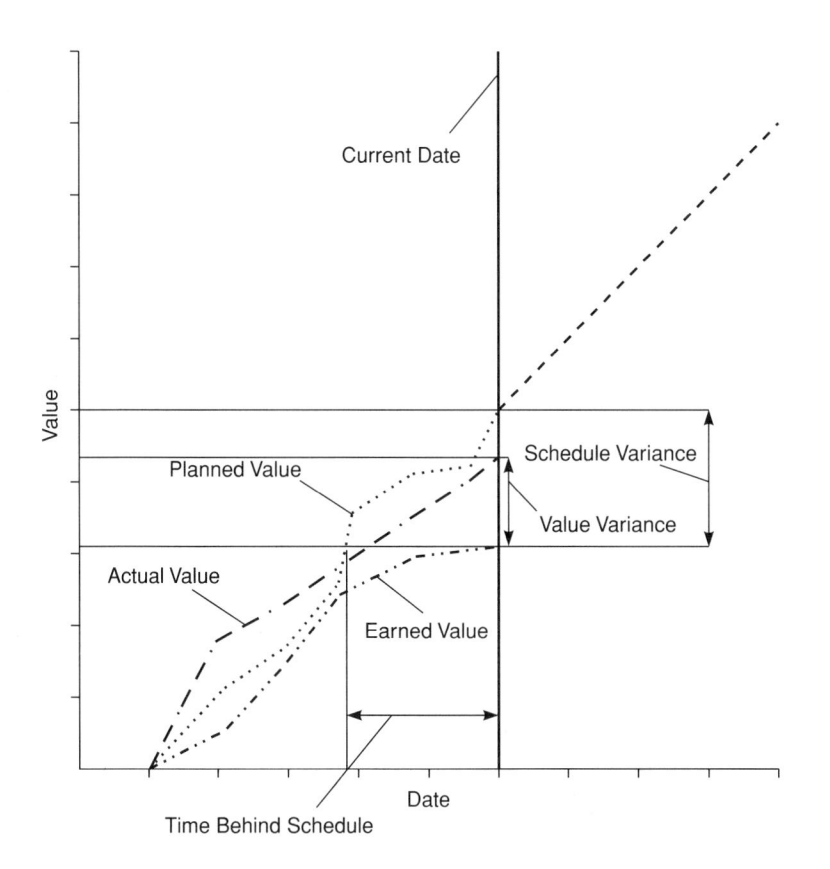

The Project Deliverables and System Earned Value 71

Figure 3-1
Measurement of earned value

The *estimated value at completion,* which is the sum of the current actual value plus the value your current baseline says you intend to deliver at the end of the project, tells you what total value will look like at the end of the project if you operate at perfect efficiency for the rest of the project. You can use this to rebaseline your schedule and as ammunition for controlling the wayward additions to unrequired value that are distending your current schedule. It shows you the impact of the value inefficiencies on the end of the project. In the continuing example, you might have five more systems to deliver with 100 function points each. The estimated value at completion is then the actual value (175 function points) plus the planned value for the not-yet-complete systems (500 function points), 675 function points.

The *schedule variance* is the difference between planned and earned value; in the example, this would be 195 – 130 = 65 function points. You can also compute the schedule delay by drawing a line down from the intersection of the earned value amount and the planned value line, although this is valid only within one baseline time period. Schedule variance is a measure of your efficiency at *delivering* required value. You can use schedule variance, as in Metric 3.2.3, to control your project as it moves forward. The suggested target range of Metric 3.2.3 uses the estimated value at completion to set the upper target bound, suggesting that your project should not have a schedule variance greater than 5% of that value. For example, given the estimated value of completion of 675 function points, you would not want the schedule variance to exceed 34 function points (0.05 × 675) at any point during the project. As time goes on and you establish your improvement program, you can reduce this target range toward zero (the perfect project).

The *value variance* is the difference between actual and earned value; in the example, this would be 175 − 130 = 45 function points. You delivered 45 function points more than what was required, presumably expending resources that could have produced required value. Value variance is a measure of your efficiency at *producing* required value.

You can also calculate the performance indexes (Metrics 3.2.1 and 3.2.2). These indexes provide ratios that measure delivery and production efficiency at a given date. Using these indexes, you can determine at any point how your project is doing with respect to its baseline plan of the moment.

- ■ *Note:* Using the relative target for schedule variance means that an increasingly inefficient production trend (that is, delivering value that wasn't planned) will increase your target schedule variance. You should combine control methods based on the value performance index (Metric 3.2.2) with the schedule variance to ensure that you are not getting out of control.

In Figure 3-1, the top line is planned value and the bottom line is earned value. These lines represent these values at different dates in the project, giving you a value history of the project. In this case, planned value zigs and zags with the changes to the baselined value. At the current date, the heavy black rule, earned value is much less than planned value, indicating something of a problem in delivery for the project. The schedule variance is the difference between the two.

- ■ *Note:* Classical earned-value calculations base these lines on planned estimated *cost* (the Budgeted Cost for Work Scheduled, or BCWS) and estimated cost for work performed (Budgeted Cost for Work Performed, or BCWP) [Fleming; Kerzner]. These definitions assume that cost estimates represent value, which seems unlikely given the poor quality of current cost estimation methods for software. As well, the use of cost ignores the different kinds of valuation available for different kinds of deliverables. These metrics derive from government programs concerned about cost and schedule overruns, not with delivering value. The assumption is that quality is constant and that projects always deliver what they promise, which is simply not true. Some large, contract-driven projects work this way, but many software projects do not. Many small-to-moderate OO software projects don't even have cost budgets. These assumptions are unlikely to be useful for OO software development, although you can certainly use them if cost control is a primary objective of your project. The approach in this book focuses on the actual delivered value (function points) and on the planning that goes into it, as well as on cost control.

The Project Deliverables and System Earned Value

The contribution of earned value to controlling projects is to focus on the value you planned to deliver and on how well you are doing at delivering it. That is the mission of the project system.

When do you earn the value for a deliverable? You can estimate earned value conservatively by accruing value only when you deliver, or you can more aggressively amortize the value over interim systems such as clusters having passed integration tests or even to each task that produces an output. The problem with these latter approaches is that not all task outputs make it into the systems of which they are ostensibly a part, so you might have to revise your figures later in the project as components wither up and die for lack of use. On the other hand, just measuring when you finish a system doesn't give you much lead time to judge your position in the project, especially if systems aren't complete until late in the project.

The key problem with a finer-grained distribution of value is that value relates to deliverables as a whole, not to the individual components of the deliverables. That is, value measures the size of the deliverable system as a whole, an emergent property of the system. If the software deliverable has 15 clusters that make it up for a total of 100 function points, and you have delivered 5 of those clusters, you have accrued 33 function points, right? No—you get 100 function points only when you deliver the system, because until then the system doesn't function. So, if you want to have a finer-grained control process, you must allocate the value in some kind of amortization process that makes sense given what you're trying to control.

The first thing you need to do is to specify the deliverables, so you at least have the value broken down as much as possible into its physical packages. This is the job of the Work Breakdown Structure. You break down the deliverables into work packages to the extent you can. You then use your allocation scheme to distribute the value for the deliverable to the different packages. You can, for example, use a fixed allocation scheme that gives an equal number of function points to each software cluster. You can estimate the cost, effort, complexity, or size of the cluster and use that as a weight, though this is fraught with measurement and prediction problems [Henderson-Sellers 1996]. You can generate random numbers, too, which is probably just as effective a method. Don't be too serious about these numbers, because they aren't real. Only the deliverable system itself is real.

Work Breakdown Structure (8.2)

- *Note:* Because planning and design is iterative, the structure of the deliverables changes as you move through the project. This can and will change your distribution of value and hence may affect your cumulative earned-value curve.

Another approach you can take to distribution is to design the internal systems as reusable deliverable systems in their own right. This lets you calculate value for each system in a meaningful way. The problem with this approach is that it requires you to treat the packages as systems, with full system tests and all the overhead of actually delivering a working system that others can use. This is a problem,

Reuse Repository (2.2)

but it is also a benefit as you move forward because you then have a solid, reusable set of reusable systems in your reuse repository.

Regardless of your method for determining value, you determine the *success* of the project mission only at the *end* of the project. Because the mission of the project is to *deliver* value, success means having delivered.

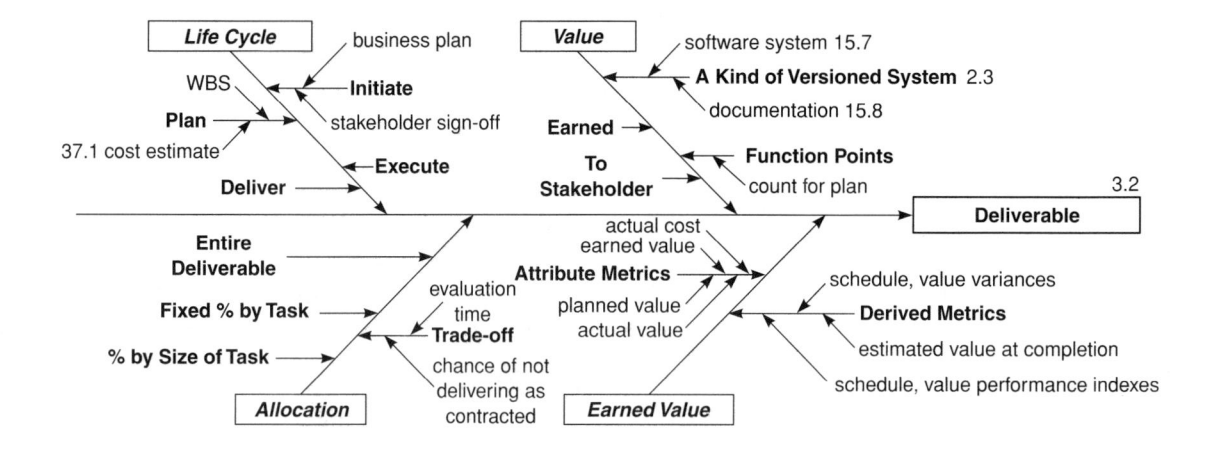

```
         Life Cycle        business plan      Value        software system 15.7
       WBS                ← Initiate                       A Kind of Versioned System  2.3
     Plan                   stakeholder sign-off Earned →  documentation 15.8
  37.1 cost estimate      ← Execute             To        Function Points
     Deliver                                    Stakeholder  count for plan              3.2
  ──────────────────────────────────────────────────────────────────────  Deliverable
     Entire                                actual cost
     Deliverable                          earned value
                          evaluation  Attribute Metrics      schedule, value variances
   Fixed % by Task    →      time      planned value         Derived Metrics
                          ← Trade-off  actual value          estimated value at completion
   % by Size of Task    →    chance of not                   schedule, value performance indexes
         Allocation          delivering as      Earned Value
                             contracted
```

The Project Stakeholder

Cui bono? Who cares? The *stakeholders* of a project define the objectives of the project by what they expect it to deliver. A stakeholder has interests that the project negatively or positively affects [PMI 1996a]. A customer, for example, wants the features of the product. A chief financial officer may impose a limit on the resources you can use. The more congruent the stakeholder's expectations are with the project objectives, the more successful the project will be at achieving those objectives. Two factors are certain to lead to failure:

- Stakeholders who do not participate in setting project objectives
- Stakeholders who set conflicting objectives that the project manager does not effectively manage

It is particularly important in OO projects to identify reusing stakeholders both inside and outside the project system.

Vision: A system that delights in the value that the project provides it
Mission: To get needed value from the project

Objective 3.4: To convey needs and expectations of the project to the project manager

---

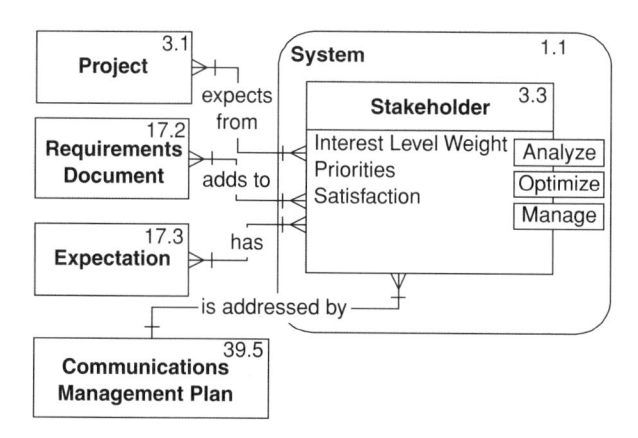

```
                3.1        ┌System              1.1 ┐
        ┌─────────┐        │
        │ Project │▷┐      │  ┌────────────┐
        └─────────┘ │      │  │ Stakeholder│  3.3
                  expects  │  ├────────────┤
               17.2 from   │  │Interest Level Weight│┌────────┐
        ┌─────────────┐    │  │Priorities           ││ Analyze│
        │Requirements │▷┐  │◁─┤Satisfaction         │├────────┤
        │ Document    │ │  │  │                     ││Optimize│
        └─────────────┘adds to│                     │├────────┤
                      │   │  └─────────────────────┘│ Manage │
               17.3   │has │                         └────────┘
        ┌───────────┐ │   │
        │Expectation│▷┘   │
        └───────────┘     │
              │           │
              └─is addressed by─┘
              │      39.5
        ┌─────────────┐
        │Communications│
        │Management Plan│
        └─────────────┘
```

Approach 3.4: The project manager identifies the different stakeholders for the project and rates their level of interest in the project. Each stakeholder then has the responsibility to communicate its prioritized expectations to the project manager. The project manager then optimizes the expectations of all the stakeholders and communicates the plans of the project to address expectations back to the interested stakeholders ("manages" expectations). The project manager clearly identifies expectations that are not technically or economically feasible and those that conflict with other expectations.

Metric 3.4.1: Interest Level Weight: an ordinal scale that identifies the degree to which the stakeholder is interested in the project deliverables as a whole: High, Medium, Low

Metric 3.4.2: Expectations Priority: an ordinal scale that identifies the degree to which the stakeholder values an expectation; values Essential, High, Medium, Low

Metric 3.4.3: Normalized Expectations Ratio: the ratio of the number of accepted stakeholder expectations to total feasible stakeholder expectations normalized by interest level weight; this measures the degree to which the project intends to satisfy stakeholder's expectations, or at least the ones that are possible to satisfy

Target 3.4: 1 for essential and high expectations; 0.75 for medium expectations; 0.5 for low expectations

---

Approach 3.5: On delivery of the project, the stakeholder evaluates the value of the deliverables against their expectations and communicates this evaluation to the project manager. The project manager feeds this back into the process evaluation for the project process.

Metric 3.5: Satisfaction: an ordinal scale that identifies the degree to which the stakeholder's expectations were met by the delivered systems: High, Medium, Low

Target 3.5: High satisfaction

Any given stakeholder is a role, not an individual. One person can be several stakeholders (customer, sponsor, and financier, for example). There is no room here to discuss all the varieties of stakeholder, but a partial list would include:

- Project manager
- Customer
- Performing organization
- Sponsor
- Reuser
- Other project managers for related projects
- Reusers of project systems
- Project work groups
- Senior management
- Unions and staff associations
- User groups
- Government departments
- Vendors

Not all have the same level of interest in a project. Usually, the central stakeholders are the customers of the project, the project manager, the sponsor, and the senior management. The project work groups and reusers follow closely behind [Thomsett, pp. 50–54].

One special variety of the stakeholder is the *project sponsor*: the executive or other authority figure within the parent organization that provides political support for the project. This is a key role in the project. The sponsor plays an active role in the planning stage of the project, influencing objectives, staffing, organizing, and prioritizing. The sponsor provides guidance on political and cultural issues and on standards and policies from the larger organizational environment. Since a major risk in OO projects is the political risk of adopting a new, unproved technology, you should choose a project sponsor who understands and trusts OO technology. Finally, the sponsor often serves as the interface between the project and its other stakeholders, particularly paying ones.

Risk (12.1)

An interesting situation arises when you have multiple project sponsors with conflicting expectations. I was on one project that was the focus of no less than five executives of a large software vendor, only two of whom had any idea what the technology meant. In retrospect, I probably should have developed strong ties to those two rather than trying to satisfy all the expectations from all the executives. One problem was that those two executives had little real interest in the project; their focus was on demonstrating success in the technology and on testing the mettle of the other managers, not on the actual project deliverables. This stuff gets very complex.

Another type of stakeholder is the *reuser*. External reusers reuse deliverables in their own projects. Internal reusers reuse systems in the current project. Identifying these reusers is a key part of the planning for an OO software project. I had one project that was developing a major framework for GUI development. The company had decided to market the framework as a product, and set up a separate project to develop it. The project managers in that project promptly ignored most of our requests for changes, enhancements, and so on. They also decided not to pursue a major operating system port that we needed for our project due to lack of resources and technical problems. These decisions made the framework useless for us, so we developed our own version of it from our original code. The framework product never made it to market, and our own project took three years longer than estimated, in large part due to low productivity.

Stakeholders have *expectations* for a project. The project manager must gather these expectations and then manage them through communication with the stakeholders during the project. Managing expectations means anything from defining or redefining expectations to setting the stakeholder's estimate of the probability of getting the expectation met.

Expectation (17.3)

The stakeholder is responsible for communicating its expectations and priorities. The project manager is responsible for making sure this happens. Meeting with stakeholders in joint reviews, the project manager can gather expectations and priorities and get feedback on progress toward meeting expectations.

Joint Review (41.2)

The project manager must then optimize the expectations. It may be that expectations from different sources conflict. There may be trade-offs between objectives—some may want high quality while others want more features in a short time. The project manager looks at each expectation to determine its feasibility. Some expectations are simply technically impossible with current technology. Others, while possible, are beyond the capabilities of the project given its skills, technology, and available budget. The project manager first must eliminate unfeasible expectations, and then clearly communicate the decision back to the stakeholders. It's generally a good idea to explain the reasons for rejecting an expectation as unfeasible.

The second step in optimizing is to turn the expectations into a vision, a mission, and operational objectives for the project. This results in the first version of the requirements document, which lists the expectations and constraints on the project. A preliminary risk analysis identifies the level of risk for each objective.

Requirements Document (17.2)
Risk (12.1)

The project manager then needs to identify the risk tolerance that is part of every system. The risk tolerance of the stakeholders is vital, because it drives the tolerances of the rest of the systems in the project. If the customer is risk averse, for example, you will need to increase risk management to meet their expectations.

System (1.1)

The risk tolerance of the project sponsor is essential to determining the project risk tolerance.

Knowing the objectives, risks, and risk tolerance, the project manager then must optimize the objective targets. This optimization could result in rejecting or revising expectations. Again, any decisions that affect expectations need to be communicated to the stakeholders.

One project I worked on had a very strong executive as project sponsor. He decided that his focus needed to be on delivering software on time, and he clearly communicated that to us. After a year of learning what really mattered, we had developed considerable skills at delivering on time, as we developed our risk management strategies around the schedule rather than around quality or features. One of the requirements of the project was to introduce OO technology into the product. The result of our risk management approach was to do very little new technology such as OO, resulting in an increasingly out-of-date product that did not do well in the market. But we delivered it on schedule!

Change Management System (24.4)

Change Request (24.3)

As the project progresses, the set of stakeholders and the set of expectations for each may change. Their risk tolerance may change as well. Tracking the expectation changes in the change management system is just as important as tracking the change requests they motivate.

Communications Management Plan (39.5)

As the project delivers its deliverables, the project manager must tell the stakeholders how the deliveries answer their expectations. The communications plan must show how this loop closes.

The Project Repository

The *project repository* stores those systems you use primarily in project management planning, execution, and control.

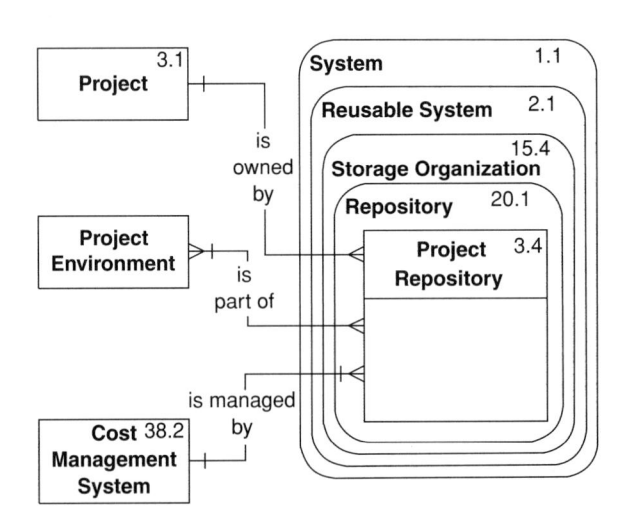

Vision: A set of secure, well-ordered project systems that any reuser can easily find

Mission: To enable the secure storage and easy retrieval of project systems in the project environment

It stores the persistent data from the project management system. It contains all the project documents, such as plans, development documents, project standards, timesheets, expense reports, and progress reports. It also stores contracts that relate to the project.

Project Document (6.1)
Contract (27.6)
Progress Report (42.1)

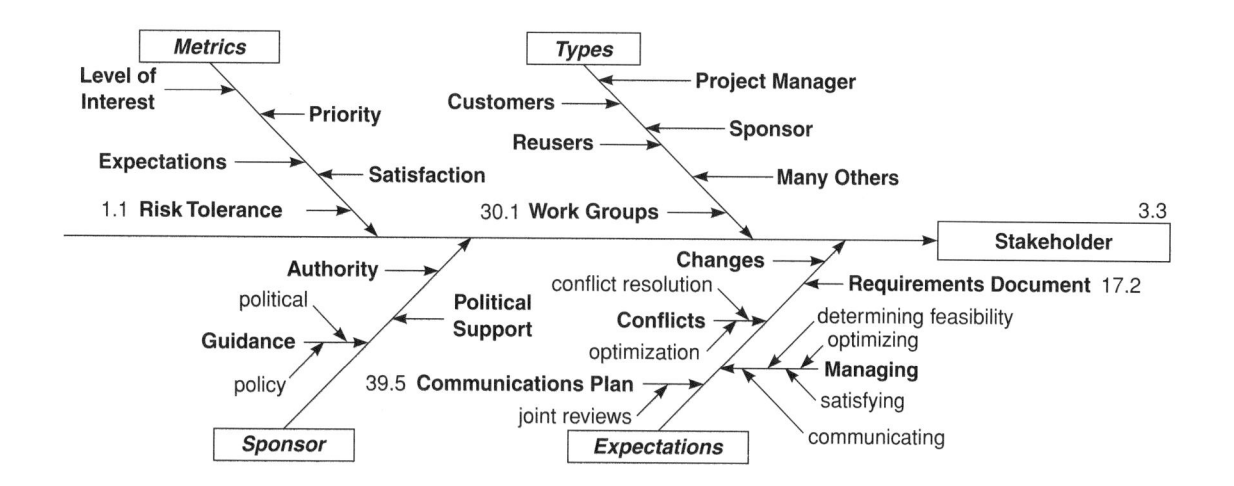

Readings

[Cleland 1983] David I. Cleland and William R. King. *Systems Analysis and Project Management, Third Edition.* New York: McGraw-Hill, 1983.

Cleland and King is a classic text on project management. It effectively uses systems analysis to organize a well-written and comprehensive book on general project management. All project managers should have this book.

[Dreger] J. Brian Dreger. *Function Point Analysis.* Englewood Cliffs, NJ: Prentice Hall, 1989.

This book is a tutorial introduction to counting function points. Dreger has some divergence from the standard IFPUG practices, which he clearly identifies, but this book is still useful in showing you how to count through its tutorial examples. Use it in combination with the *IFPUG Counting Practices Manual,* and follow their rules, not his.

[Fleming] Quentin W. Fleming. *Put Earned Value (C/SCSC) into Your Management Control System.* Humphreys and Associates (+1-714-955-2981), 1983.

This book is one of several that Quentin Fleming has done on earned value, and I find it the most useful. Fleming is the leading advocate of earned-value techniques for project performance measurement. While it is not easy to read, his book has everything you need to understand the C/SCSC system in its full bureaucratic glory. If you are a government contractor, you should be reading this book.

[IFPUG] International Function Point Users' Group. *IFPUG Counting Practices Manual, Release 4.0*. IFPUG (Blendonview Office Park, 5008-28 Pine Creek Drive, Westerville, OH 43081-4899, (+1-614-895-7130), January 1994.

This is the final arbiter of function point counting. While it does not take OO technology into account, you can use the techniques in this book at the system level without much trouble, as an OO system looks much like any other from the stakeholder's perspective. This manual is essential reading for anyone serious about using function points.

[Jones 1991] Capers Jones. *Applied Software Measurement: Assuring Productivity and Quality*. New York: McGraw-Hill, 1991.

Capers Jones is the leading advocate for function point counting. He has his own version of the counting practices, which this book overviews. While not as detailed as Dreger or the *IFPUG Counting Practices Manual*, this book is still useful for understanding the context of function point counting and some of the alternatives available. Look for the second edition rumored to be appearing in 1997.

[Kerzner] Harold Kerzner. *Project Management: A Systems Approach to Planning, Scheduling, and Controlling, Fifth Edition*. New York: Van Nostrand Reinhold, 1994.

This is the classic text on project management. It has an excellent section on earned value, as well as a very detailed explanation of projects, their components, and how they work.

[McTaggart] James M. McTaggart, Peter W. Kontes, and Michael C. Mankins. *The Value Imperative: Managing for Superior Shareholder Returns*. New York: Free Press, 1994.

This is an excellent general business book that takes a value-directed approach to business management. It focuses on shareholders as the sole stakeholder, which is a bit limiting, but the general principles of business-unit valuation and how to evaluate competitive and product position in the market is invaluable.

[PMI 1996a] Project Management Institute Standards Committee. *A Guide to the Project Management Body of Knowledge*. Project Management Institute (+1-610-734-3330), 1996.

The PMBOK is the bible for PMI certification as a Project Management Professional (PMP). It summarizes everything you need to know about project management in a few short pages, with excellent graphics and clear exposition. Every project manager should know this book by heart. It explains what a project is in gory detail and provides an excellent reference to the different components of the project.

Questions to Think About

1. If you consider a project as a process, where does planning fit in your process model? How would you integrate projects within other projects?

2. Think about the different kinds of systems your projects deliver. What kind of value do you think would best measure the contribution of that deliverable to stakeholder value? Is money the best measure? Functionality? Some other measure?

3. Think about how your organization deals with the costs of projects. Does the project budget deal with task-level cost accounts? How would you use the standard system of earned value using cost estimates within your budget process?

4. How does project sponsorship work in your company? Is it formal or informal? Do you have multiple sponsors with conflicting expectations? What happens if the CEO walks into your office and asks you to do something on the project?

5. How do you know when you have not identified major stakeholders and/or expectations?

6. What different kinds of communication structures can you use to communicate with stakeholders? Are these structures capable of two-way communication? Are there environmental constraints on such communication such as policies about talking with customers or geographical distance?

PART TWO

Process

> Improve constantly and forever the system of production and service, to improve quality and productivity, and thus constantly decrease costs.
>
> Dr. W. Edwards Deming, *Point 5 (Out of the Crisis)*

This part of the book introduces the fundamental systems that make everything work: the process systems and the process models on which they are based.

Processes, tasks, and work flows make up the project system. Modeling those objects gives you a way to engineer feedback into your process and hence to control it. The system model introduced in Part 1 provides the basis for the modeling in Part 2.

Your process models are the basis for your project plan and schedule. The structure of work, including work flow, is central to planning and scheduling the project. The process model lets you generate a project plan in a structured way. This in turn lets you control the planning process to reduce risk. The milestone, and especially the process milestone, gives you the feedback you need to control your schedule and delivery of value. The work-flow model lets you control the schedule planning process through its generation of dependencies in the project schedule.

Processes and process modeling are fundamental to effective project management. This part introduces a simple but effective way of integrating process models into your project management tool set.

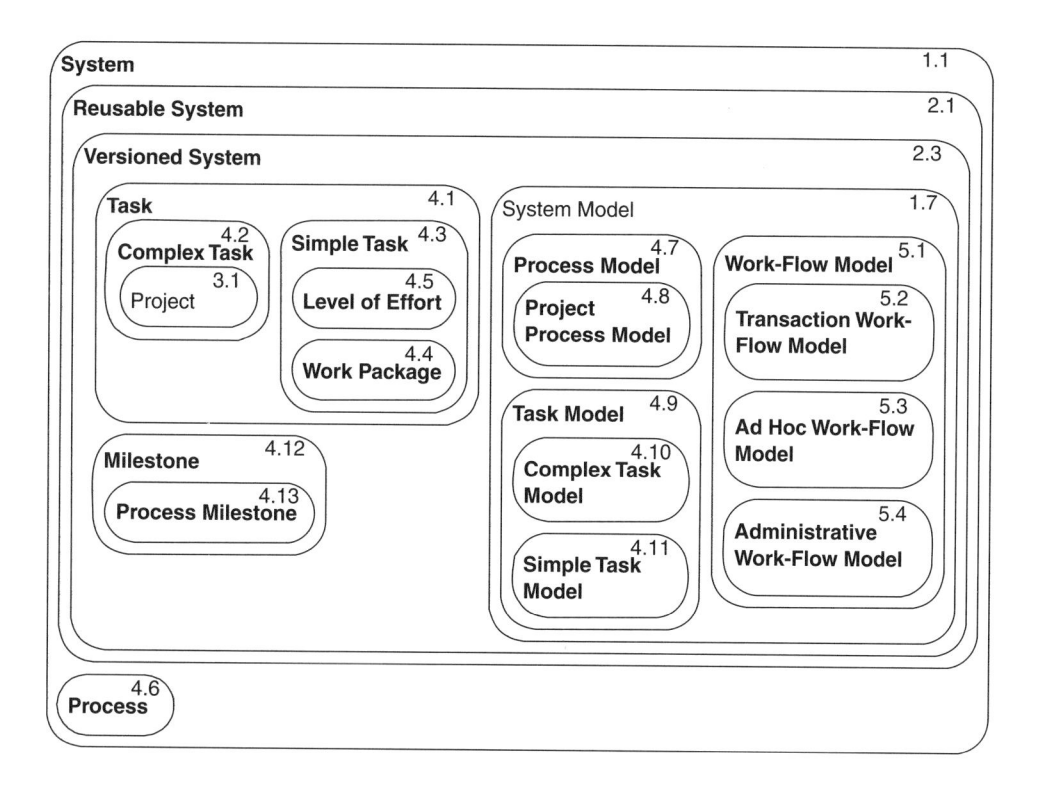

```
System                                                              1.1
  Reusable System                                                   2.1
    Versioned System                                                2.3
      Task                      4.1    System Model                 1.7
        Complex Task  4.2   Simple Task  4.3   Process Model  4.7   Work-Flow Model  5.1
          Project  3.1        Level of Effort  4.5   Project Process Model  4.8   Transaction Work-Flow Model  5.2
                              Work Package  4.4
                                               Task Model  4.9      Ad Hoc Work-Flow Model  5.3
      Milestone  4.12                            Complex Task Model  4.10
        Process Milestone  4.13                                     Administrative Work-Flow Model  5.4
                                                 Simple Task Model  4.11

    Process  4.6
```

- *Note:* The illustration of the class hierarchy contains all the classes this part defines. Other parts of the book define and discuss classes not in boldface.

CHAPTER

4 *Process and Process Modeling*

Business runs on process—or doesn't, without it. Project management depends essentially on process to structure the flow of project deliverables to the stakeholders [PMI 1996a]. This chapter and the next one discuss some of the general issues with process modeling, while the next part of the book applies the concepts to project planning. In OO project management, the process model serves as the structure for the project and its plan. The specific processes that apply to OO software development life cycles in Part 6 build on the process framework this chapter introduces.

Development Process (16.4)

The Task

The *task* is "a piece of work assigned by a superior or done as a part of one's duties" [AHD]. A task is a versioned system with an execution status that tells you about the state of the work. The task represents the work that your project plans to do. The process model generates tasks in the work breakdown structure to specify the scope and structure of work. The schedule then creates schedule tasks with start and end dates to plan and control the actual performance of the task in the project schedule.

Process Model (4.7)
Work Breakdown Structure (8.2)
Project Schedule (10.1)
Schedule Task (11.1)

The task status is usually a simple, nominal-scale scheme that represents the possible states of the task. An example: Not Started, In Progress, Finished, and Reviewed. These status values usually show up with the task name in progress reports.

Progress Report (42.1)

Vision: A manageable, productive unit of work in a process

Mission: To produce the results of work that contribute directly or indirectly to the value of the project of which they are a part

The Task

Objective 4.1: To produce work results with optimal productivity

---

Approach 4.1: Generate a task system from a process model with a vision, a mission, and a set of operational objectives that focus the system on the production of work results. The operational objectives should contribute to the operational objectives of the process to which the task belongs. Produce the work and add the task's contribution to the value and cost of the project.

Metric 4.1: Productivity: the amount of effort spent on producing a unit of value, with the value unit set by the deliverables to which the task contributes

Target 4.1: No value outside the standard control limits of an x-R control chart for Metric 4.1

Objective 4.2: To operate in a controlled, manageable manner

Approach 4.2: Track the status of the task for each reporting period using the internal status attribute.

Metric 4.2: Work status (Not Yet Started, In Progress, Finished)

Target 4.2: The status for the current date in the process baseline

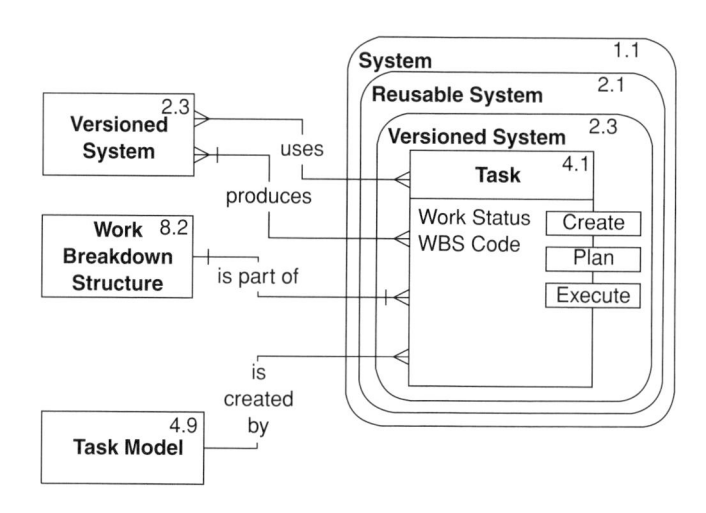

The task is a basic element of the work breakdown structure for the project. You create tasks in two ways. First, you generate tasks from a task model in a process model during the planning process; see the following section on "The Process and Task Models." Second, you generate tasks from specific planning, such as risk analysis, quality planning, and communications planning. These tasks may or may not derive from a task model.

"The Process and Task Models" section, p. 90

Planning a task sets the inputs and outputs of the task. Inputs and outputs are versioned systems. The task uses inputs to produce outputs.

- *Note:* A task as such does not necessarily produce deliverables, just versioned systems. Some of those versioned systems may be deliverable systems; others may be systems that support production of deliverable systems. Still others may be useless—you just don't know that yet! See the work package discussion that follows for tasks that produce deliverables.

You can reuse a task only through versioning. Each task that you create from a task model or plan has an initial take on what's involved in the task. As the project progresses through the OO life cycle of iterations, the plan changes to accommodate your increased understanding of what needs doing. Often this does not involve creating new tasks or deleting tasks but changing the current tasks. For example, you may realize at some point that the requirement that the task addresses actually requires something a little different than you originally thought. You then change the task description to accommodate it. That requires versioning the task. You thus reuse the task through versioning. You can continue versioning the task until you finish it.

The inherent reusability of a task thus derives mainly from the way you structure the work of the task. Executing the task means starting the work. Finishing the task stops work, and you can spend no further effort on the task. You should be careful to include all the work in the task that needs doing to call the task finished. For example, you can have a task that requires production of an output followed by a review followed by rework of the task. You should either include all this work in the task or separate these into separate tasks with clearly marked finishing points. Once you've completed the task, you can no longer version it and reuse it.

A *complex task* is one that contains a process. Its opposite is the *simple task*. The simple task can be either a work package or a level of effort.

The complex task represents a part of the project plan that is a separate process with a clearly demarcated start and finish. You create the complex task from a complex task model and its process model. The complex task does not represent any actual work in the project, just a higher level grouping of tasks. You use complex tasks to represent chunks of the project that you want to treat separately as processes but that still have inputs and outputs.

Project Process Model (4.8)

Project (3.1)

The complex task is a project if a project process model generates its process.

Planning and executing a complex task means planning and executing the underlying process that belongs to it. The hierarchical nature of the process-task relationship within the complex task leads to the hierarchical structure of the work breakdown structure for a project. For a project task, the project process has its own work breakdown structure. The WBS of the outer project does not include the tasks in the subproject, just a single task representing the whole project.

- *Note:* This structure has the implication that no task breakdown happens without a process surrounding it. That in turn leads to the assumption that the hierarchical breakdown of tasks is process driven. You can add tasks at each level to support the process-driven tasks, such as risk management tasks or communication tasks. These do not in turn break down into multiple tasks without having a process that structures those tasks. This structure contributes to more effective planning and execution of the tasks.

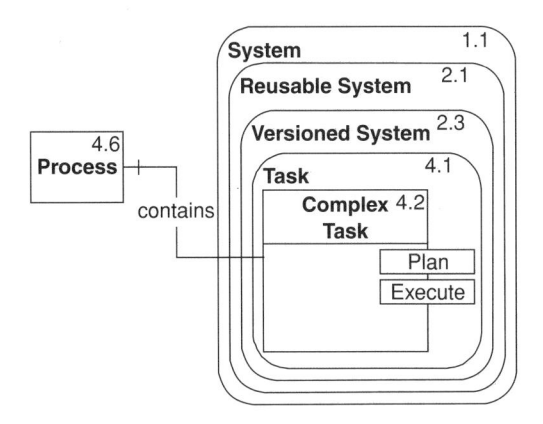

The *simple task* uses resources to produce its outputs, representing the work portion of the project plan. It accrues cost according to whatever method you are using to allocate costs for work done. Typically, a simple task is an amount of work that a person or a small team can do in a manageable control period, such as a week. A simple task can also be a distinct piece of short work such as a meeting or review. The effort for the task in combination with resource cost rates lets you calculate the cost of the task. Less typically, at least for a software project, the resources of the simple task contribute cost from sources other than effort: the *fixed cost* of the task. You can, for example, charge the task for using machine or other variable-cost, nonlabor resources, or you can allocate overhead to each task. The task of computing cost thus sums the costs contributed from each resource assignment and from any costs contributed by the task itself. You can also split cost into planned and actual costs—money you plan to spend and money you have actually spent. The planned amount comes from the cost estimate for the task in the budget, and the task relates to some account in the project chart of accounts that accumulates the cost.

Each simple task has a set of resources and a supervisor. The resources perform the work that the task represents in the project plan. The supervisor is responsible for executing the task: generating the outputs, coordination of resources, resolution of resource problems, and so on.

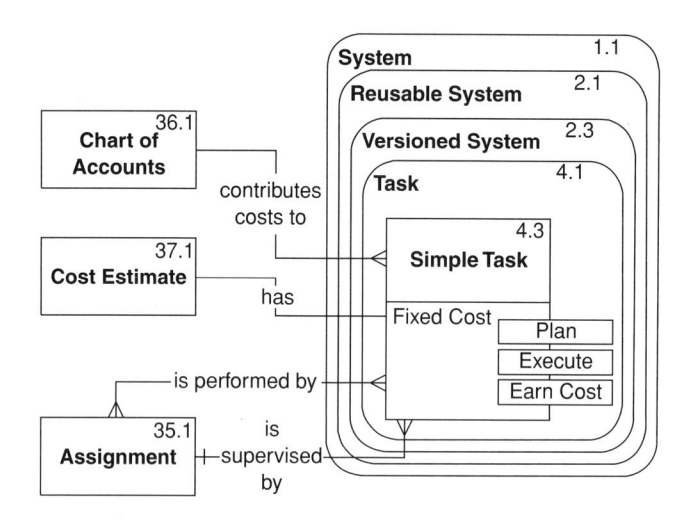

A *work package* is a simple task that consists of a single piece of work that contributes to a deliverable but does not break down into further tasks. The work package contributes to earned value through your scheme for accruing these amounts. For example, you can earn value when you finish the task. Alternatively, you can earn half the value when you have expended half the effort, then the other half when you finish the task.

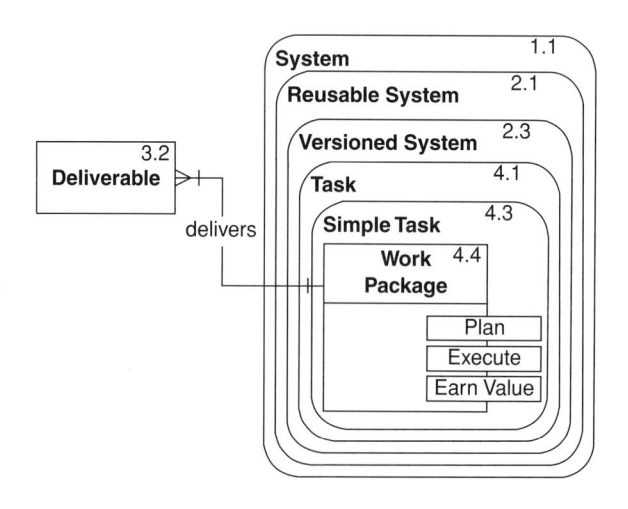

The Task 89

A *level-of-effort* task (government cost-accounting jargon, of course [Fleming]) is a simple task that represents work done in support of the primary work on deliverables. While a work package contributes directly to earned value and cost by work on deliverables, the level of effort contributes only indirectly to value. Levels of effort put resources to work on support products or nonproductive activities such as management. The level of effort does contribute directly to earned cost through being a simple task. Your allocation scheme for cost must take it into account through the relevant chart-of-accounts entries.

Chart of Accounts (36.1)

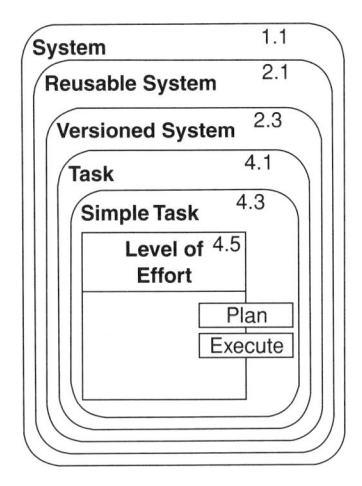

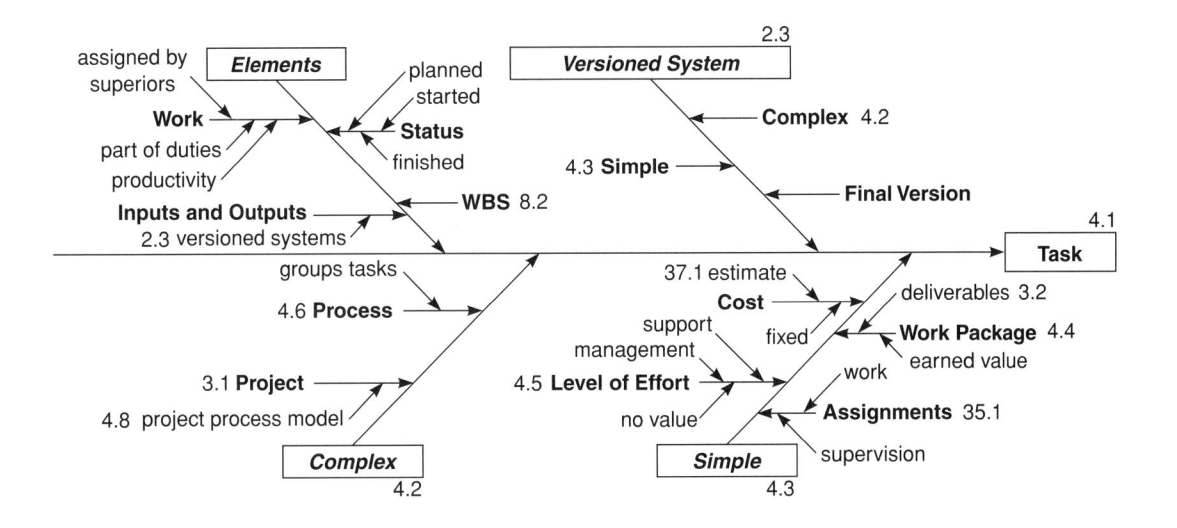

```
System                    1.1
  Reusable System         2.1
    Versioned System      2.3
      Task                4.1
        Simple Task       4.3
          Level of        4.5
          Effort
            ┌─────────┐
            │  Plan   │
            ├─────────┤
            │ Execute │
            └─────────┘
```

```
                                              2.3
assigned by   Elements      planned    Versioned System
superiors          \       started
    Work   ────→    ↘  ↙                ←──── Complex  4.2
part of duties    Status
productivity       finished     4.3 Simple
                            ←──────────────    ←──── Final Version
Inputs and Outputs ──── WBS 8.2                                    4.1
2.3 versioned systems                                             Task
                    groups tasks          37.1 estimate  ╱ deliverables 3.2
              4.6 Process            Cost              ←─── Work Package  4.4
                                  support    fixed            earned value
         3.1 Project ──→        management         ╲ work
4.8 project process model      4.5 Level of Effort  ←── Assignments  35.1
                                    no value      ╲ supervision
                  Complex                      Simple
                     4.2                         4.3
```

The Process and Task Models

The *process* is "a series of operations performed in the making or treatment of a product" [AHD]. A project-related process is a *sequence of tasks:* a partially ordered set of pieces of work. The process starts when the first task in the process starts, and it ends with the process milestone. The sequence of tasks is the work flow of the process.

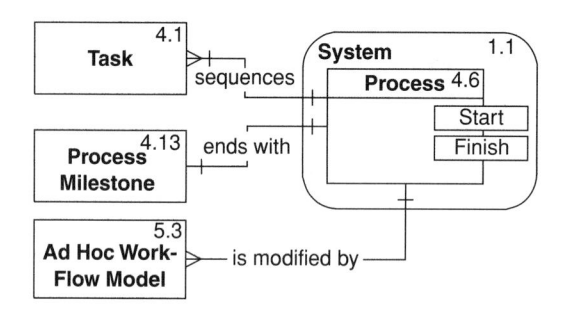

Vision: A productive work process that you execute and control to a successful completion

Mission: To manage the execution of a series of tasks to a successful completion

---

Objective 4.3: To complete a series of tasks successfully

Approach 4.3: Plan the tasks using the project plan, scheduling the tasks and assigning resources to do the work. Manage the process tasks, tracking and controlling progress on the tasks. Focus on earning the value or providing the supporting systems that the process produces through achieving the process milestone.

Metric 4.3: Whether or not the process achieves the process milestone. See the following section on "The Milestone" for details on defining milestone success.

Target 4.3: Success

A process is what happens when a project is under way. As a system, it is thus a one-time thing: the actual performance of work in the project. It's not a reusable system. Most of the things you want to do with processes as a project manager, however, seem to require a changeable, reusable system. What serves this purpose?

The Process Model

The *process model* is a system model that describes a process [Garg]. It's a structural template for generating a process. A process model is a sequence of task models and milestones, each of which ultimately corresponds to a task or milestone in the processes it generates. The sequence of task models is the work-flow model of the process. Processes and process models work together intimately in their project role, structuring the workings of the project through the project plan.

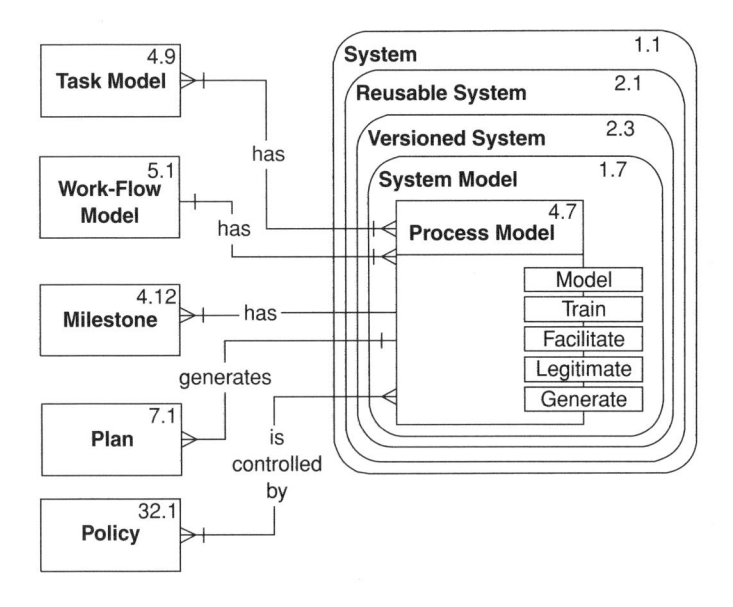

Vision: A valuable, reusable, productive process you productively plan from a continuously improving model

Mission: To represent a productive process that you want to reuse many times

---

Objective 4.4: To represent the process to allow planning with optimal productivity

---

Approach 4.4: Model the process with the tasks, milestones, and work flows that represent the generic work and structure of the process. Train anyone who participates in the process in how the process works, and facilitate the use of the process model at the appropriate organizational levels (team, project, functional, and so on). Legitimate the process model in the organization through communication, training, and participative, process modeling activities.

But you don't derive the process directly from the process model. That would be the equivalent of building a house while holding a copy of the *Contractor's Bible*. You *plan* first. The process model generates the process plan, which in turn executes the process. That is, for the process, system model generation is *planning*. Applied to project management, each process model contributes its mission to the overall project plan, which in turn drives the project.

Planning alone is not enough; you must also *do*. To apply the model, you must train all those who use the process in the process details. You can facilitate the use of the process with professional facilitators or consultants who understand how to make the components work. Mentoring the application of the process model in its initial stages is essential to its success.

The modeling of the process is a design task with the objective of creating a model with strong inherent reuse potential. To adequately model the systems the process controls, you must use participative design techniques with the process stakeholders, those who have some stake in the process. The best way to do this is the improvement plan for the model. Designing a process model that participants can understand and improve is the key to getting a reusable process model. Process stakeholders are often also the domain experts that can establish strong domain reusability. Designing the model with the participation of the experts is the best way to insure its ability to handle the situations for which you design it.

To succeed with an improvement plan, you must build a process model that reflects the reality of its participants. Process models that don't correspond to what people do or that participants can't improve are not trustworthy. You can't measure them, and you can't improve them. To achieve trust, you have to build it through legitimacy within the organization, facilitating organizational reuse. You build such trust by working with project and organizational stakeholders to create and enforce policies that apply the process model. Validating the process by recording and analyzing metric data in your improvement plan, and communicating the plan status, is a primary method of establishing trust. Planning and doing aren't enough—you must *check* and *act* as well.

The Project Process Model

The project is a complex task with an internal process. You generate that process from a special class of process model, the *project process model*. A project process document contains this model, which defines your standard project process. This process includes not only tasks for the standard software development process but for the planning process and any other project-related processes as well. The project process document thus documents all the project process models. Versioning any process also versions the project process document.

The Process and Task Models

[Diagram showing relationships between Project Document (6.1), Project Plan (7.2), Complex Task Model (4.10), and nested containers: System (1.1), Reusable System (2.1), Versioned System (2.3), System Model (1.7), Process Model (4.7), Project Process Model (4.8) with Generate. Labels: "is documented by", "generates", "has".]

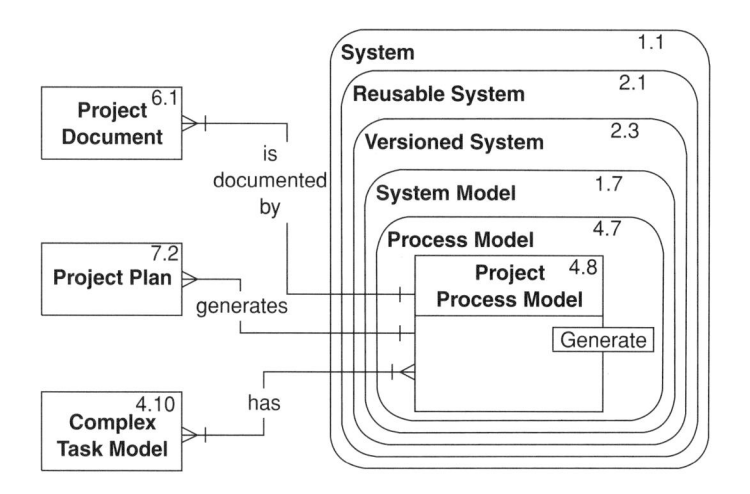

Vision: Valuable, productive projects you productively plan from a continuously improving, reusable model

Mission: To represent a productive project process that you want to reuse many times

---

Objective 4.5: To represent the project process to allow planning with optimal productivity

---

Approach 4.5: Model the project process with the complex tasks and work flows that represent the generic work and structure of the project. The project structure begins with the PMI project process structure and refines it with the appropriate OO software development process and any other customization that improves the productivity of the planning process.

- *Note:* The project process model is a very high-level model that should correspond very closely to the basic planning process of your project organization, and hence you should get a very close mapping between the project process model and the project plans you generate from it. These are "big picture" processes, not detailed practices. Your control chart ranges should come into control very quickly.

You use the project process model to generate the project plan by generating the individual plans corresponding to the project processes. Table 4-1 shows a possible structure for a project process, mapping the complex tasks of the project process to the corresponding project plan elements. Table 4-1 also points you to the part of this book that deals with the issues for each kind of task and plan element.

Table 4-1 Project Process Tasks and Project Plan Elements

Task	Plan	Part	Description
Quality Assurance and Control	Quality Management Plan	3	Test planning, test case development, quality reviews, testing, and test repository management tasks
Risk Control	Risk Management Plan	5	Risk identification, quantification, and control tasks
Software Development	Software Development Plan	6	Analysis, design, coding and testing, and documentation tasks for a deliverable, including both internal and product documentation
Change Management	Change Management Plan	8	System changes, configuration issues, change requests, change reporting, baselining tasks
Procurement	Procurement Management Plan	9	Proposal generation and assessment, contracting, and contract administration tasks
Staffing	Staffing Plan	10, 11	Hiring, training, resource allocation, organizational management, policy, and skill management tasks
Cost Management	Cost Management Plan	12	Budgeting, accounting, resource requirement planning, cost estimation, cost management system implementation tasks
Communication	Communications Management Plan	13	Personal interaction, meetings, progress reporting, and repository management tasks

You should organize the development tasks around the deliverables. The OO development processes in Part 6 develop software around a clustered architecture that builds the deliverables from components. Organizing the tasks around the deliverables sets the stage for such development. Each complex task thus represents the production of a single deliverable. You repeat the task for each deliverable. The work breakdown structure then has a complete set of tasks for delivering each deliverable system.

You may need to have several alternative development processes for deliverables of different kinds. The project process model should identify these different processes and the types of deliverables they produce as separate *development task models*.

The project process model describes every aspect of how your project organization does business. The brevity of this section should not mislead you: the rest of the book describes much of what goes into the project process model.

The Process and Task Models 95

```
              4.7                               1.1
       ┌──────────────┐                    ┌──────────┐
       │Process Model │  task models 4.9   │  System  │
       └──────────────┘                    └──────────┘
                      ← System Model 1.7       ↘ start
   7.1 Plan ──→         ↖ dependencies         ← Sequence of Tasks 4.1
                           ↖ train              ↖ finish
   generate in WBS ↗        Do                     ↗ defines success
                           ↖ legitimate         ← Process Milestone 4.13
       Check and Act ──→    ↗ facilitate                                   4.6
   ─────────────────────────────────────────── finishes process ──── ┌─────────┐
                                                                     │ Process │
                                                                     └─────────┘
                 9.1 Quality ──→  ← Risk 14.1        ↗ contains
                                  ← Change 23.1          ← Project Document 6.1
          16.2 Development ──→                  contains  ↖ documents all
                                  ← Staffing 35.2  ↗ subplans  project processes
         27.7 Procurement ──→                              ← Project Plan 7.2
                                  ← Cost 38.1
       39.5 Communication ──→
                          ┌──────────────┐          ┌─────────────────────┐
                          │ Project Plans│          │ Project Process Model│
                          └──────────────┘          └─────────────────────┘
                                7.2                            4.8
```

The Task Model

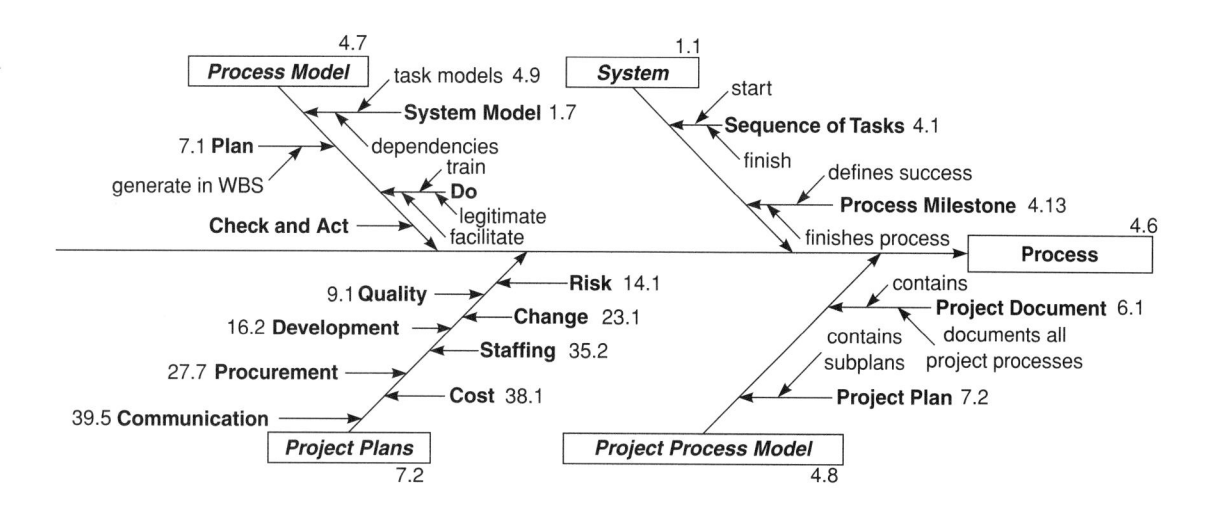

The *task model,* a system model for the task, represents the set of things you know about the task without actually applying it in a project. This generic knowledge includes several such items:

- *Resource roles:* generic placeholders for the resources you will assign to the task
- *Standard inputs and outputs:* generic placeholders for the things the task needs to perform its work and the things it will produce
- *Constraints:* generic limitations on the task, such as built-in costs or how long it has to take based on internal characteristics of the inputs and outputs
- *Risks:* generic risks that usually exceed the system's risk tolerance, such as the risk of inadequate class design or the failure of software integration or the risk of politics interfering with the task mission

Vision: A valuable, productive task you productively generate from a continuously improving model

Mission: To represent a task that you want to perform many times

---
Objective 4.6: To represent the task to allow process generation with optimal productivity
---

Approach 4.6: Model the process with the tasks and work flows that represent the generic work and structure of the process.

Metric 4.6: Process Representation Accuracy: the ratio of the median number of tasks and work flows in the processes you generate from the model version to the median number of tasks and work flows in the model version

Target 4.6: A ratio value between 1 and 1.5

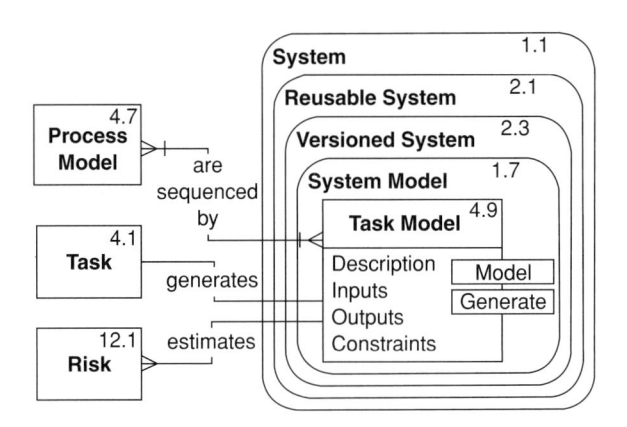

The risks are generic risks for the task and give an initial estimate of the risk probability. That is, the task model identifies risks for the type of task and estimates how likely those risks are to occur in the average project. You should flag those risks likely to exceed the system risk tolerance for the task. When you generate tasks from the task model, the tasks get an initial set of risks from these risk estimates.

A task model has more reuse potential when you model the generic characteristics of the task in immediately useful ways. Task models are most useful when you can generate virtually everything about a task from the model—resource assignments, inputs, outputs, constraints, and risks. The extent to which you have to modify the generated task reflects on the reusability of the task model that produces it. On the other hand, you can reuse a task model in more situations if you make its characteristics very general and domain independent.

An example is a task model I created for a documentation group. The first model was a very general model for creating any user document. It listed all the different kinds of inputs and outputs, such as requirements documents, developer interviews, previous documents, and so on. As time went on, the group decided there were at least four specific kinds of document-creation tasks, and we developed task models for each of these. The general model was useful, but it required too much work every time we had to adapt it to different kinds of documents. The less generic models led to a more complex process model but less work in applying the model. It also turned out to be easier to improve the more specific models because they related better to the kinds of documents we produced.

The task model classes mirror the task classes: the *complex task model*, the *simple task model,* the *work package model,* and the *level-of-effort model.* The task model contains all the elements you need to generate any task. The simple task model contains additional elements that let you generate both the simple tasks and their corresponding schedule tasks.

The complex task model contains a process model. When you build a task from the model, you also build a process and its tasks from the process model that the complex task model contains. The complex task model's reuse potential depends on the reuse potential of its process model.

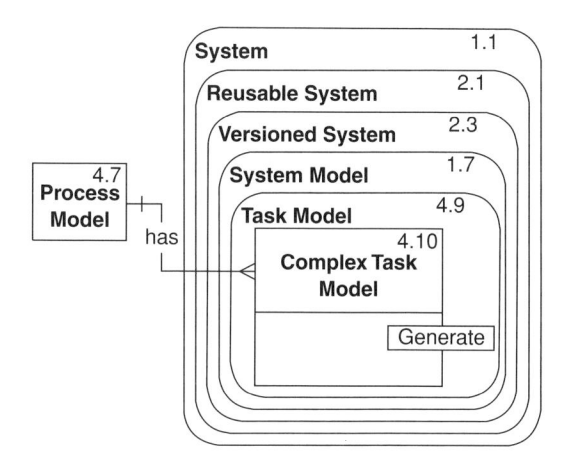

Simple task models can be either work package or level-of-effort models. The simple task model contains not only the basic elements of the task model, but also generic cost and value estimates. These estimates give you a ballpark estimate to use when you first generate your work breakdown structure.

Simple task models also contain duration estimates. Duration is the amount of work time the schedule task is likely to take given some assumptions about resources. Sometimes it is more efficient to estimate duration rather than effort, depending on how you do resource allocation and estimation. You can use these estimates to generate tasks with duration estimates even when you aren't using resource effort estimation to set up your schedules. This in turn lets you create schedule tasks in your project plan. The duration doesn't show up in the task but in the schedule task, as it relates to work calendars and other time-specific project elements.

Duration (11.2)
Schedule Task (11.1)

98   Chapter 4 / Process and Process Modeling

```
                              System                1.1
        4.9                    Reusable System       2.1
   Task Model
                               Versioned System     2.3
                               System Model        1.7
        3.2          has        Task Model          4.9
   Deliverable                                4.11
                                   Simple Task
                                      Model
       37.1                                    Model
    Cost                                      Generate
   Estimate    estimates
      11.2
    Duration
```

```
         Task Elements              Types
  Constraints →                       ← A Kind of System Model  1.7
  Inputs and         Resource Roles
  Outputs            probability estimate     ← Complex  4.10
                     Risks 12.1
  Reuse Potential                             ← Simple  4.11
  ─────────────────────────────────────────────────────────→  4.9
                                                          Task Model
                              37.1 Cost Estimate    work package model
        Process          Duration              Types
   4.7   Model    11.2   Estimate                   level-of-effort model
                                              Deliverables 3.1
                 11.1 for schedule task         value estimate
         Complex                     Simple
          4.10                        4.11
```

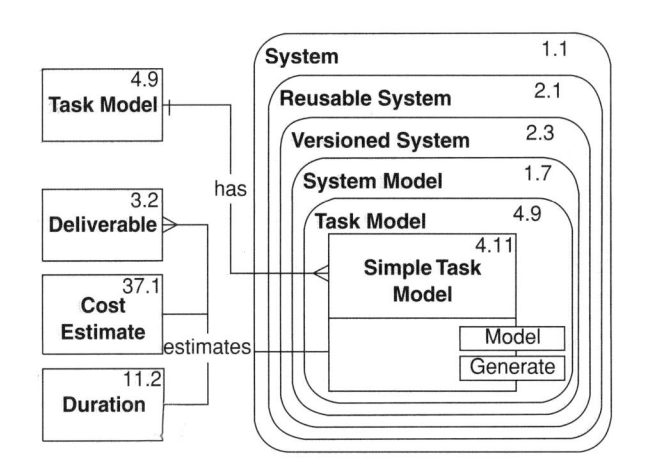

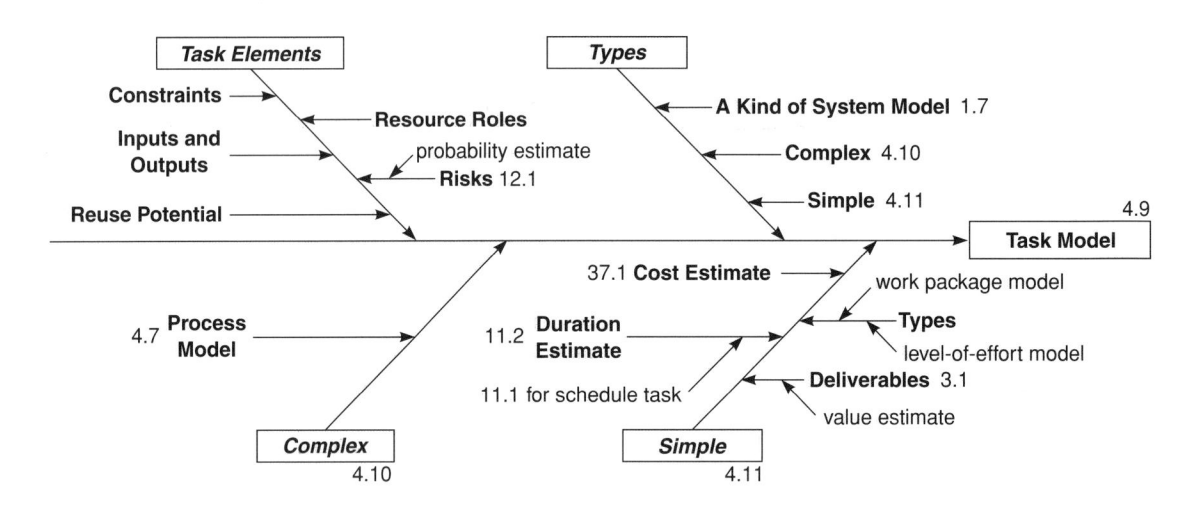

An Outline of Planning with Processes

To give you an overall picture of how the planning process works, here's a simplified description. Figure 4-1 illustrates the planning process as a system model.

Change Management System (24.4)

Document Template (6.3)

1. Retrieve the latest baseline for the project process document and its project process model from the organizational repository. Plan the project using the standards in this document.

2. Create the plan and its statement of work.

    2.1. Create the project plan document from its template.

    2.2. Collect the current set of requirements and create the statement of work in the project plan. Work out a preliminary list of deliverables

The Process and Task Models 99

for the project from these requirements. The deliverables are the actual software objects your project will deliver, such as the executables, dynamic libraries, help files, documentation, and installation templates.

Statement of Work (8.1)
Project Plan (7.2)
Deliverable (3.2)

3. Generate the work breakdown structure (Figure 4-2).

   3.1. Generate a task in the work breakdown structure from each nondevelopment, complex task model. These are complex tasks that represent the high-level processes for the project, not the processes that produce the deliverables.

   Work Breakdown Structure (8.2)

   3.2. Generate a development task in the work breakdown structure for each deliverable system the statement of work identifies. This development task is the software development process for the deliverable, and you generate it from the appropriate type of development task model.

   3.3. Generate a task in the work breakdown structure from each task model in the process for each complex task. This recursive process expands all the complex tasks and their processes into a hierarchical structure of tasks.

   3.4. Baseline the initial version of the work breakdown structure. This represents the standard structure for the project.

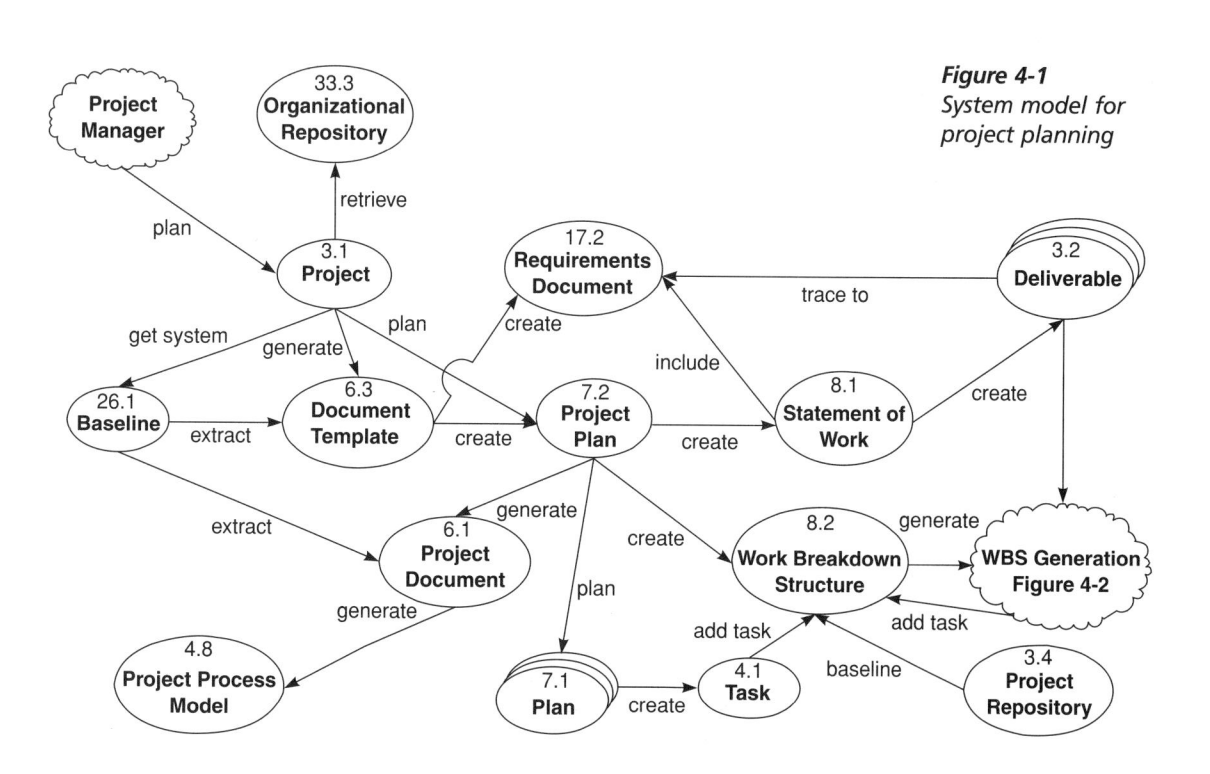

Figure 4-1
System model for project planning

Figure 4-2
System model for work breakdown structure generation

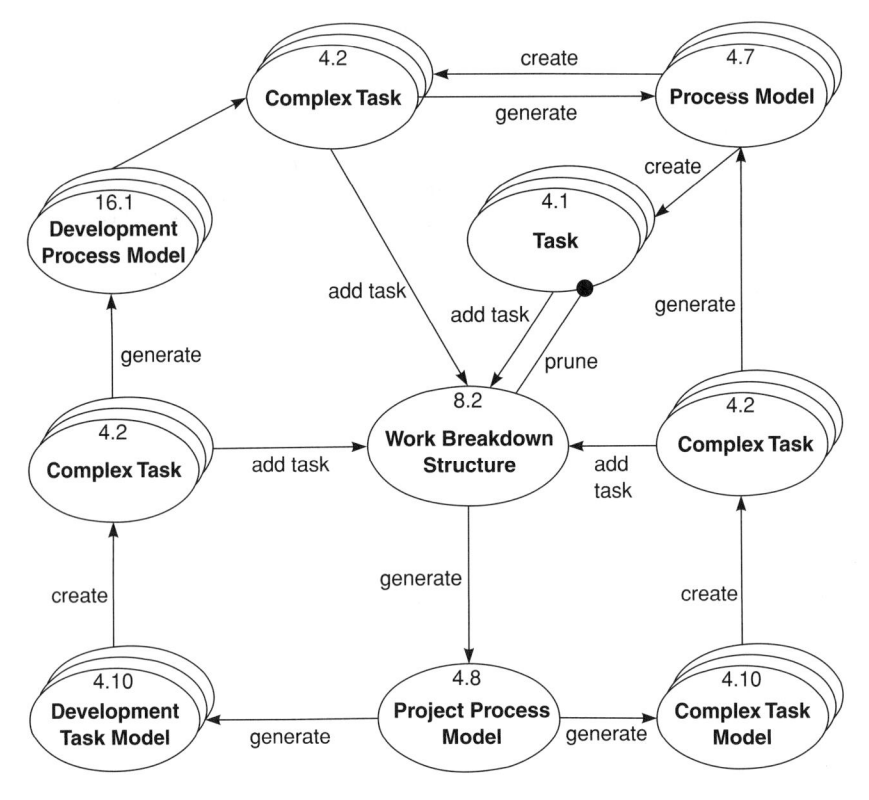

4. Customize the work breakdown structure.

   4.1. Examine each task in the work breakdown structure for relevance. If a task is not useful in the current project, remove it from the structure. As with any versioning work, you should add comments explaining why a standard task is not necessary.

   4.2. Plan out each of the subsidiary project processes. This planning process generates any additional tasks, such as risk management tasks, quality assurance tasks, or communications tasks, including repeating meetings and reviews.

5. Generate the project schedule from the work breakdown structure (tasks) and project process model (milestones).

6. Review and revise the project plan.

7. Execute the project plan. This includes revising the plan as required.

■ *Note:* Those who use project management software with integrated work breakdown structures should recognize the basic hierarchical structure of this planning process. The summary tasks in those programs correspond to complex tasks in the planning structure. The key difference is the emphasis on the combination of project process and deliverables as the drivers for the top level of the work breakdown structure. See Chapter 8 on "Statement of Work" for some examples of work breakdown structures.

As you might tell from this brief description, there is an intimate relationship between the process model and the project plan. While this relationship enables you to quickly build a comprehensive plan, it does not make you process bound. The process model applies a policy, and you can always have exceptions. The combination of process model and work breakdown structure lets you be very flexible about processes and work.

The Milestone

A *milestone* is a versioned system that represents an event at a time. A generic milestone is one that represents any arbitrary event. A milestone is *not* a task, nor does it appear in the work breakdown structure, since it does not involve work. It is purely a schedule-related object that you use to control some aspect of earning value or cost or some other aspect of the project objectives. The milestone is a time-related feedback mechanism for the project process.

There are two major purposes for the milestone, both of which relate to controlling the project. The first is to provide a benchmark for time, value, and/or cost that you can use to earn value. When you achieve the milestone, you earn value or cost. For example, if you are using an allocation scheme that allocates value to finished systems only, you get all the value when you achieve the system completion milestone. The second purpose is to focus attention on a process, and in particular on process completion. When you achieve the process milestone, the process is complete. You use this in scheduling to provide feedback on progress against the schedule. You use it in cost control to provide feedback on cost accrual. You use it in your improvement plans to drive the checking and acting portions of the PDCA cycle.

Project Schedule (10.1)
Improvement Plan (1.3)

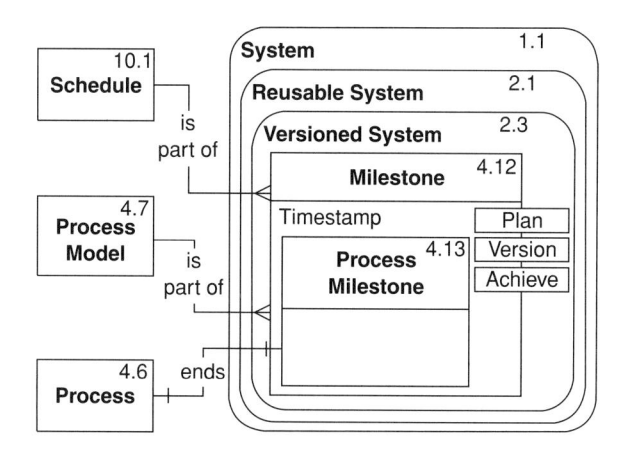

Vision: Clearly defined events that close the feedback loop for achieving success in the project

Mission: To control a project through timely feedback

Objective 4.7: To get feedback on the achievement of value and cost in a project

Approach 4.7: Add a milestone to the project schedule for each point at which you want to get feedback. Usually this will involve successful completion of a process or series of tasks, resulting in a deliverable, or at least a major, distinguishable part of a deliverable. In any case, collect the appropriate metric data and evaluate the success of the system on which you want feedback. Version the milestone as required to reset the timestamp. The last version of the milestone is the actual timestamp indicating when you achieved the milestone.

Metric 4.7: Feedback effectiveness: a nominal, subjective metric that evaluates the ability of the milestone to provide useful feedback; values High, Medium, Low, None

Target 4.7: High

You plan a milestone, setting its target date as a timestamp. You version the milestone whenever you change the event date. When you achieve the milestone, you create the final version of the milestone. After that point, you can no longer version the system.

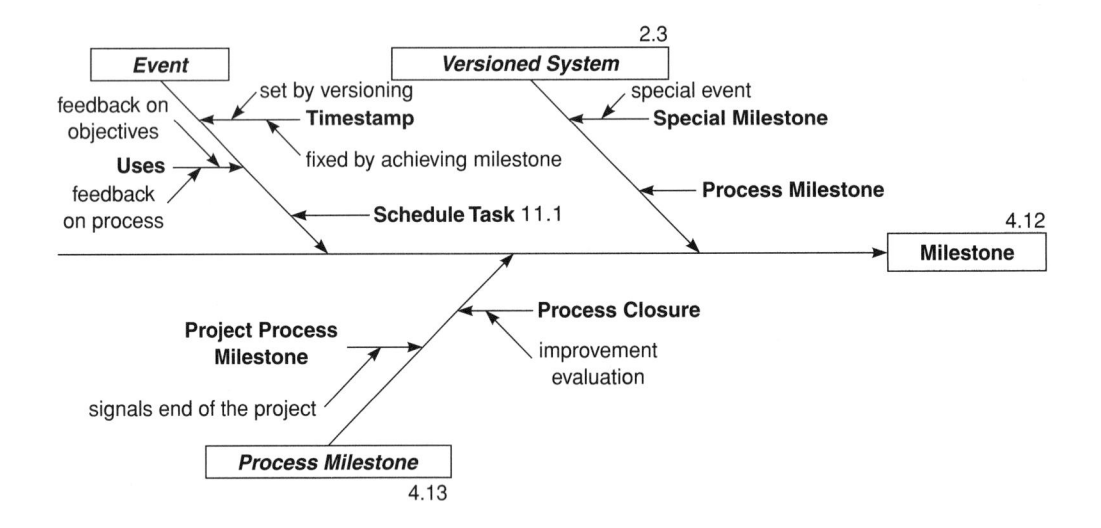

You have total power over the milestone. You can declare a milestone achieved whenever you like. This gives you a lot of flexibility in feedback. It also has its dangers: you can version the milestone beyond being effective as a feedback mechanism, rendering it useless.

A special kind of milestone, the *process milestone,* represents the closure of a process. It's usually when you finish the process milestone that the improvement plan for the process model kicks in to evaluate the process metrics. The most important process milestone is the project process milestone, which signals the completion of the project.

Readings

[Garg]   Pankaj K. Garg and Mehdi Jazayeri. *Process-Centered Software Engineering Environments.* Los Alamitos, CA: IEEE Computer Society Press, 1996.

This collection of readings is an excellent introduction to the current academic thinking about process models in the software engineering environment. While the practical aspects of applying models are less in evidence, the articles are useful in framing the issues in thinking about the impact of process modeling on projects.

Questions to Think About

1. Have you ever considered the separation of level-of-effort tasks from value-producing tasks in your project plans? What are the consequences of not distinguishing these two kinds of task?

2. While planning, can you usually specify all the inputs and outputs of tasks in your plan? If you specify a task with unknown inputs or outputs, what is the consequence to the people working on the task? to your ability to control the task? (Hint: If you don't know all the inputs and outputs, don't create the task; wait until you are more knowledgeable. Keep the value and budget in reserve at a higher level—the process or a higher-level task. Planning is not a one-time affair.)

3. Does your organization maintain a project process model document? a model document for each process that is part of the project process? If so, how do you currently use that document? Is it a bookend for other documents on your bookshelf? Does it change as your organizational processes change? Is it online?

4. Do you have a set of standard risks for the generic tasks in your process, or does your project risk analysis have to recreate these for each project? Could you save time by creating a reusable model of risks?

5. Think about the system you currently use to structure your work breakdown structure (if you have one). How does it differ from the system this book proposes? If possible, convert a plan from a previous project using the new method and look at the difference in the Gantt or PERT chart. How does the new system affect the organization of the plan compared to your current system?

6. How do you currently decide what milestones to have in your project? Do you always get feedback at the end of a process? at the end of the project?

CHAPTER

The Work-Flow Model 5

As you move into the more dynamic environment of parallel, recursive, and iterative OO development, it is no longer enough to have a simplistic structural view of your project. You must model and control its dynamics to be able to optimize it. The *work flow* of a process connects process tasks through the flow of input and output systems between tasks. The work flow also positions the milestone events in the flow of tasks and their outputs. The project schedule represents work flow through the dependencies in the project schedule. A *work-flow model* is a system model that models the generic structure of tasks and milestones in a process model. The planning process transforms this model into the dependencies in the project schedule.

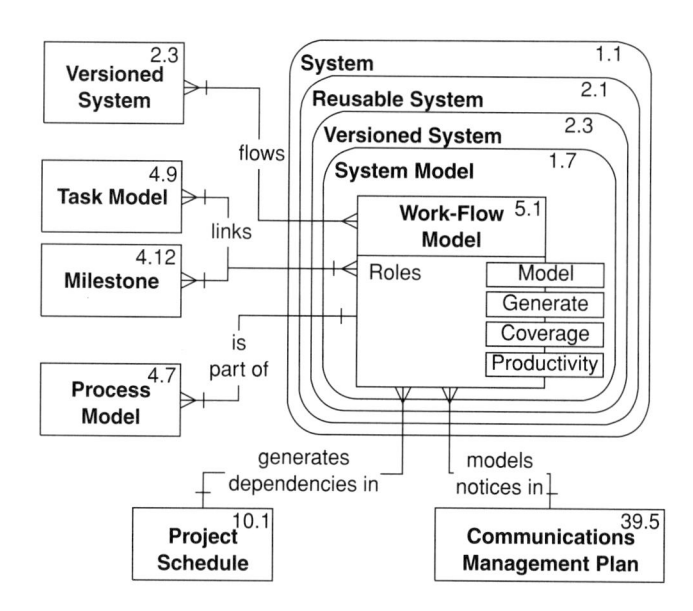

105

Vision: A process that delivers value in an optimally productive way

Mission: To sequence the flow of systems through the activities that produce them in an optimally productive way

---

Objective 5.1: To model the flow of versioned systems through a series of tasks that add value to the systems

---

Approach 5.1: Model the flow of versioned systems between tasks and milestones with a modeling tool. Show how each task adds value to the input systems to produce the output systems.

Metric 5.1: Model coverage: the ratio of paths through the work-flow network that represent the complete transformation of a system's value to the total paths through the network; complete transformation means that each task on the path adds value to the system until the completion of its life cycle (that is, until you completely consume or effectively use the system in producing other systems or until it emerges from the process as a deliverable system)

Target 5.1: Complete coverage: each path in the work-flow model represents a complete transformation

---

Objective 5.2: To model the flow of versioned systems to optimize the productivity of the tasks

---

Approach 5.2: Ensure that all the work flows in the process are necessary and sufficient for the tasks they connect. Model any constraints, such as lead or lag times or amounts of input systems that improve the ability of one or more tasks to transform the versioned system inputs to outputs. Balance the need for minimal inputs against the need for high availability of inputs in the production process.

Metric 5.2: Estimated total task productivity: the sum of the estimated values added to each output system over the estimated effort or duration of the task

Target 5.2: No value outside the standard control limits in an x-R control chart for Metric 5.2

- *Note:* The classes in this chapter represent the basic nature of the work-flow model, but not the detailed structure. Please consult the work-flow literature [Khoshafian] for discussion of details and references to the extensive academic literature on the structure of work flow. This chapter gives you an overview of the general nature of work flow but makes no attempt to model the very complex details.

The Work-Flow Model

The work-flow model shows how the input and output versioned systems flow from task to milestone to task in a process. Work-flow steps contain source and target resource roles as well as the explicit link between tasks or milestones. For example, if you link a class design document to a cluster coding process, you should specify who among the resources on the cluster team is to get the document, such as the "cluster team leader."

Work flows also permit *retraction* and *reassignment* of the flow to another task as a versioning process on a dependency. This usually happens when, for one reason or another, the first task failed to accomplish the required work. The retraction thus serves to let the work flow recover from problems. You model the retraction possibilities as prioritized, alternate flows in the work-flow model. When a task fails in its mission related to the input system, you can retract the system and reassign it in the schedule, creating another dependency in the project process.

Modeling a work-flow system requires a modeling tool with the right characteristics. There are several notations for showing work flow, including process models, functional or data-flow models, and flowcharts. Some are better than others in the OO world, since the focus is on the systems that flow between tasks. Flowcharts, for example, tend to focus on the processes, not the flowing systems. Data-flow models represent the systems as "data stores," which may be a bit mechanistic. Whichever representation method you choose, the work-flow model must link two tasks, including complex tasks with nested processes. It must specify what versioned systems flow from task to task. It also models important events within the work flow through milestones.

Generating the work flow for a process identifies the specific dependencies on task outputs in the project schedule. The cluster that one team builds, for example, may be the input to the building of another cluster or to the integration of several clusters into a system for system testing. The production and distribution of project documents for communication, review, and approval is another example.

When you generate the schedule dependencies from the model, you fill in the roles through assignment, and your communication plan shows how to notify resources when input systems become available. On a milestone event, the flow notifies a person or role of the event, perhaps transmitting the versioned objects from the flow or some other information about the flow. This notification approach becomes part of the communication plan.

As a reusable system, a work-flow model increases its reuse potential through all the different aspects of reusability. Reuse of the model occurs every time you use the model in a different process, as well as when you version the model to incorporate improvements. Inherent reusability improves through the level of completeness of specification of flows. That is, the better organized the work-flow model, the more valuable it becomes. A model that contains no excess steps and little waste has a lot of potential for reuse in different processes. Organizational factors may also

Communications Management Plan (39.5)

play a big role in reuse of the work-flow model. As teams grow used to a certain model of work flow, and as their managers become familiar with its communication needs and control points, the organization will use the model in different processes.

The work-flow model also improves its reusability through being relatively domain independent where possible. The more the model describes a generic process, the more likely you will be to reuse it in different process models. The work-flow model is somewhat domain dependent in that it depends on the types of versioned systems and tasks. Ultimately, the domain reusability depends on the domain reuse potential of the entire process model.

Transaction Work-Flow Model

The *transaction work-flow model* represents a logical unit of work consisting of a network of simple tasks that move versioned systems through a well-defined, atomic process. The organization usually defines this kind of process in a set of policies or standards in the organizational repository.

Vision: A well-defined atomic process that limits the risk of mission failure for its deliverable systems

Mission: To model the work flow of a process consisting of simple tasks to limit the risk of failing to deliver the process deliverables (not necessarily project deliverable systems, just versioned systems that are process outputs)

Objective 5.2: To model a transaction flow of simple tasks

Approach 5.2: Model a work flow as a network of simple tasks and versioned systems. Produce policies in the organizational repository that specify guidelines or standards for the work flow. Generate dependencies in the project schedule from the appropriate flows and add the appropriate constraints to the schedule and to the project plan.

Metric 5.2: System representation accuracy (see Metric 1.4)

Target 5.2: See Target 1.4

Objective 5.3: To limit the risk of mission failure of a process

---

Approach 5.3: Use improvement plans to focus work-flow modeling on limiting the risk of failing to reach the process milestone or failing to deliver the versioned systems that are the output of the process. Identify and quantify the generic risks for the process, and use the appropriate risk management methods to structure the process work flow as a network of simple task models that represent the risk management actions needed to reduce process system risk below risk tolerance.

Metric 5.3: Risk of the process model that includes the work-flow model
Target 5.3: Risk ≤ Risk Tolerance

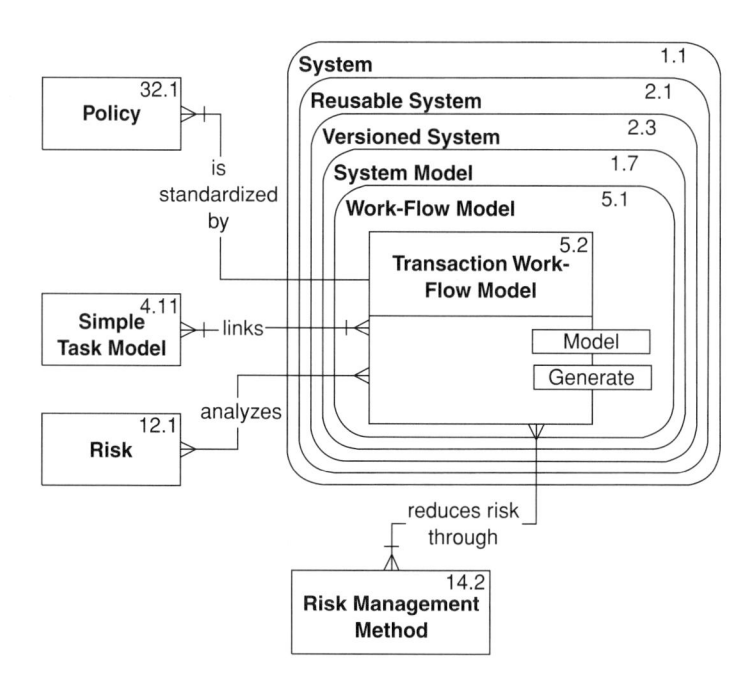

The transaction work-flow model typically manages some kind of risk. The set of policies that models the work flow represents a risk management method. For example, a common transaction work flow is the production of the plan. This is a series of tasks for producing a document in a standard format that then goes through a structured review and approval process. This process reduces the risk of the plan failing to meet stakeholder expectations. It also reduces the risk of plan failure due to insufficient communication of the plan elements.

Transaction work flows are part of any well-developed process model, not just OO ones. Certain risks associated with OO projects do require certain transaction work flows, however. For example, the cluster architecture requires an integration process that goes through a sequence of steps, including checking in code, building the cluster, executing integration test suites, and judging whether the cluster passed the test criteria. This is a standard transaction work flow that ends with acceptance or rejection of the integration attempt.

Along with the basic reuse potential of the work-flow model, the transaction model benefits from the completeness of the risk analysis and planning. The more the contribution of the model structure to limiting risk, the more valuable it becomes.

Ad Hoc Work-Flow Model

The *ad hoc work-flow model* represents a series of simple tasks you create on the fly. You may, on the spur of the moment, decide to get the reaction of a marketer to a proposed enhancement to a component. You might iterate a design and need to communicate the plan changes to those affected. You might want to gather project documents as inputs to a new design task that arises unexpectedly, and you might need to establish new plan dependencies based on the result of the task. All of these are nonstandard collections of tasks connected into a work flow by the ad hoc transmission of systems between the tasks. The process model that contains the work flow is an informal model at best, though it does exist. These ad hoc flows represent changes in the needs of the processes rather than standardized approaches to managing risk.

Needs change due to improved technical knowledge, insights into organization of tasks from improvement plans, singularities in the process, and changes in the environment. New needs may lead to new tasks or milestones that you must integrate into the process work flow. They may also suggest revisions to the standard work flow for this particular process.

Ad hoc work flows let you creatively manage the process as it unfolds. On the negative side, they move you away from standard processes, reducing your ability to bring the process under statistical control. Too many ad hoc work flows mean an out-of-control process. Too few mean an inflexible one. Ad hoc work flows tend to add risk to a project because of their locally optimal nature. You may not see the forest for the trees when making ad hoc decisions deep in the ongoing process. Where your risk tolerance is low, such as in a mission-critical process, you should avoid excessive ad hoc work flows to limit your risk.

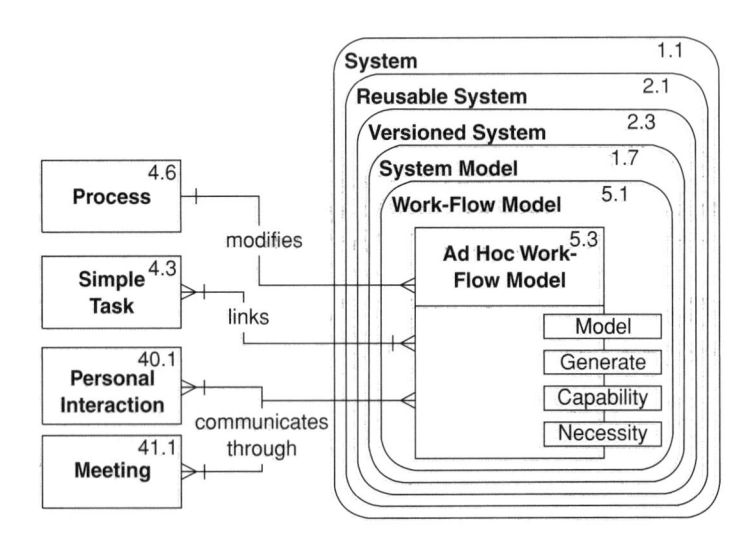

Vision: A process that adapts to changing software development needs in a timely manner

Mission: To adapt a process to a new need

Objective 5.4: To adapt a process to a new need for movement of systems from task to task

---

Approach 5.4: Create new links between tasks and milestones in an active process and its schedule. Minimize the changes to the schedule dependency structure by ensuring that each change moves a needed versioned system into a task that can use it.

Metric 5.4.1: Capability contribution: process system capability difference from adding the ad hoc work flow (how much capability does the ad hoc work flow add to the process?)

Target 5.4.1: A material capability difference relative to the process system capability target

---

Metric 5.4.2: Necessity: the project value added by the ad hoc work flow, as calculated from the value of the deliverable systems the ad hoc work flows enable

Target 5.4.2: A material value difference relative to the total value the process contributes to the project deliverables

---

OO projects tend to involve quite a few ad hoc work flows, particularly for prototyping and design sequences. The iterative nature of such design leads to changes in the needs of tasks further down the line, and hence to ad hoc work flows.

By definition, ad hoc work flows have a low reuse potential. Reuse for these systems is generally through versioning as your plan changes to reflect new ideas and realities. If you see the potential for an ad hoc work flow to make a difference in future projects, you should standardize it into a new transaction work-flow model.

Ad hoc work flows do not participate in the communications plan, they just happen. Ensuring the appropriate level of feedback to resources and managers is thus a critical part of managing the work flow. Creating personal interactions and meetings increases the overhead of the work flow but is necessary to ensuring the effectiveness of the flows.

Personal Interaction (40.1)
Meeting (41.1)

In a company with a strong process model, I found a particular process was having problems applying the standard task sequence to produce working code in a client/server application interface. On looking into the problem, I discovered that the standard process model did not take into account the error handling needs of the software we were using. Each class in this particular system required an additional coding process step that introduced generated error handling code into the classes. This step was not part of the standard model, since that model used software tools that didn't require this kind of error checking or code generation. I directed the engineers to include the error-code-generation step, and the process changed. This need came about because the architect of the system had never used client/server APIs in OO design and did not realize the process needed adjustment, thus leading to an ad hoc work-flow change. I suggested that the development team develop a new process model for client/server projects to incorporate the full needs of such projects into the policies of the organization, primarily to limit the risk of schedule failure in future projects.

In a small project to develop an OO Web interface, the engineers were constantly finding problems with the APIs they were using. Each problem created a new task (working around the problem) and new dependencies, often shifting the work flows on a daily basis. Due to both resource availability constraints and changing tasks, the team leaders had to retract deliverable systems and reassign them on the fly as new issues forced changes to the work flow.

Administrative Work-Flow Model

The *administrative work-flow model* represents the flow of administrative tasks, which are levels of effort. These are tasks you link by transmission of forms such as timesheets, vacation requests, or expense reports. OO projects are not unique in having administrative requirements. Administrative work flows generally belong to the organizational environment rather than to the project itself.

Vision: A smoothly functioning process

Mission: To provide the administrative infrastructure that underpins the work packages with moving versioned systems that are not deliverables between level-of-effort tasks

---

Objective 5.5: To model the flow of administrative systems through a process to ensure the smooth functioning of that process

---

Approach 5.5: Separately model the standard flows of administrative systems such as timesheets and expense reports. Communicate the standards to all resources that will produce such systems, and track the delivery of the systems to ensure that they are necessary and complete.

Metric 5.5.1: Necessity: the ratio of the necessary work flows to total work flows in the model, as judged by the process resources (how necessary are the administrative systems to the project mission?)

Administrative Work-Flow Model 113

Target 5.5.1: Optimize the ratio, trading off political and organizational control concerns with the effort required to produce the administrative systems

---

Metric 5.5.2: Compliance: the ratio of actual flows to required flows (how well do the resources comply with administrative requirements?)

Target 5.5.2: A ratio that stays within the control limits of a p control chart

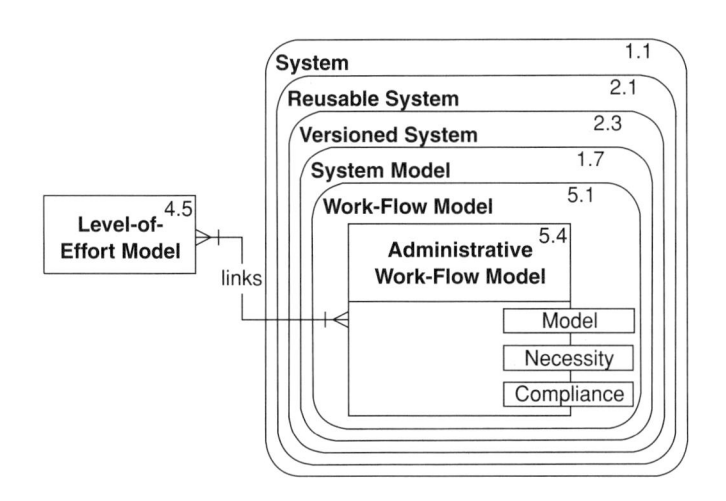

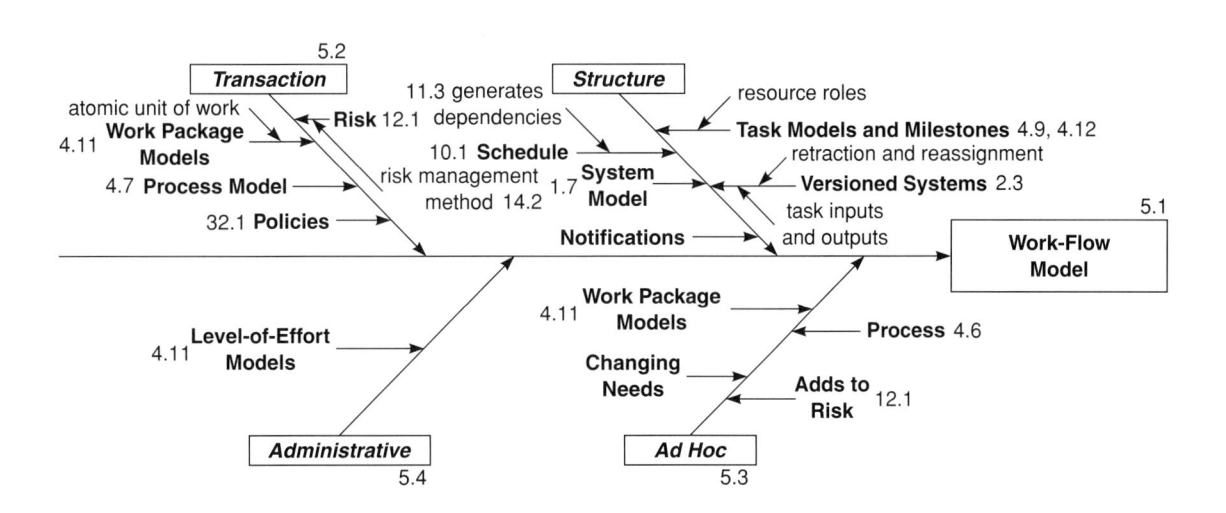

Readings

[Khoshafian]   Setrag Khoshafian and Marek Buckiewicz. *Introduction to Groupware, Workflow, and Workgroup Computing*. New York: Wiley, 1995.

This book is an excellent introduction to the new technologies of groupware, work flow, and work-group software systems. Much of the work-flow structure of this chapter comes from here. The only limitation of this clearly written and otherwise excellent book is the lack of a complete analysis of available tools and systems. The ones they do discuss are a bit out of date. You should supplement the book by researching current vendor offerings or attending seminars and conferences on the subject, as the commercial software world is moving rapidly to create new software in this area.

Questions to Think About

1. How do you construct your schedule dependencies in your project schedules now? How would using work-flow models change this?

2. Can a process contain several "transactions" in the sense of multiple units of work? Why or why not? What is the relationship between processes, transaction work flows, and system deliverables?

3. Why do ad hoc work flows add to the risk of the process? Do you think that OO projects are more likely to be at risk because of the ad hoc nature of the life-cycle work flows? How can you reduce the ad hoc nature of the work flows (hint: see Chapter 16)?

4. How can you encourage people to follow the administrative work-flow model? How does compliance with the model benefit people working on tasks?

5. How can you limit the necessity for administrative work flows?

PART THREE

Plan and Scope

> The plan is nothing, planning is everything.
>
> Dwight D. Eisenhower

This part of the book develops the systems that are central to the everyday work of the project manager. No, not people: *documents!* A vital way to improve your productivity as a project manager is to identify the specific project documents you need to create. By carefully justifying them, you reduce their impact on your overall time.

The key document for the project manager is the project plan. The plan, a kind of system model, is where you organize your thinking and the work of the project. The project plan contains all the planning for your schedule, budget, communications, risk, and all the other aspects of the project you must control.

The first part of the plan is the statement of work. The structure in this book has the statement of work consisting of two components: the requirements document and the work breakdown structure. In Part 2, the process model generates processes through the plan's work breakdown structure. In this part, you get the details of that and some examples that will help you structure your own plan.

The last chapter in this part summarizes a huge subject: quality management. This could be a part on its own, or a book. That book has already been written, and this chapter refers you there. It introduces a key part of the project plan, the quality management plan, and summarizes the test and quality planning that is a part of it. It also discusses the quality environment and the quality tools that you use in any OO project.

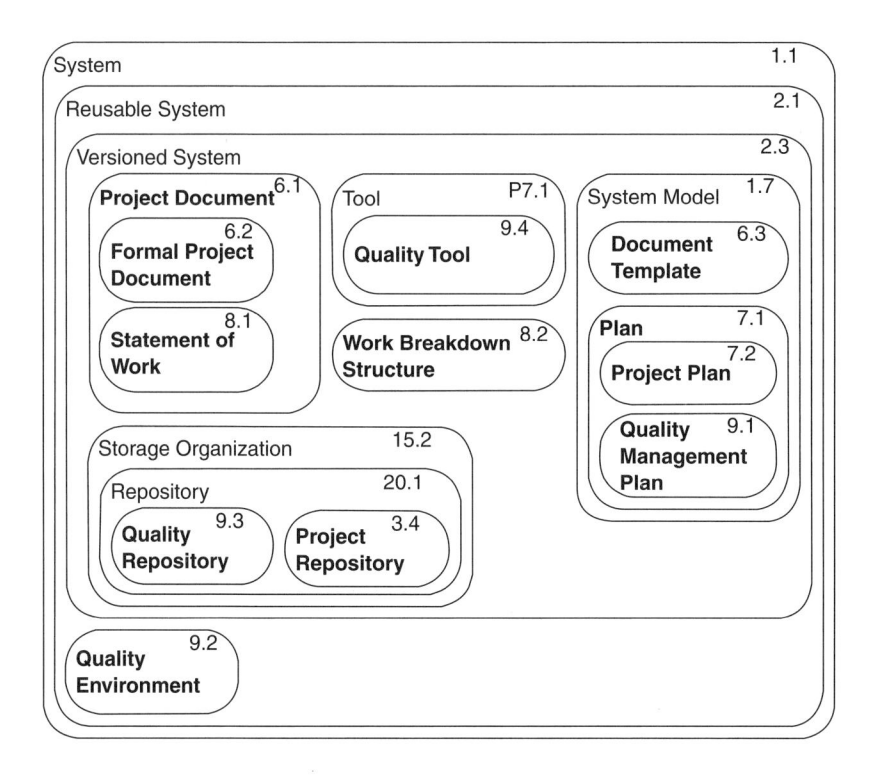

```
┌─────────────────────────────────────────────────────────────┐
│ System                                                 1.1  │
│ ┌───────────────────────────────────────────────────────┐   │
│ │ Reusable System                                  2.1  │   │
│ │ ┌─────────────────────────────────────────────────┐   │   │
│ │ │ Versioned System                           2.3  │   │   │
│ │ │  ╭────────────────╮ ╭────────────╮ ╭──────────╮ │   │   │
│ │ │  │Project Document│ │Tool    P7.1│ │System    │ │   │   │
│ │ │  │            6.1 │ │            │ │Model 1.7 │ │   │   │
│ │ │  │ ╭────────────╮ │ │ ╭────────╮ │ │ ╭──────╮ │ │   │   │
│ │ │  │ │Formal  6.2 │ │ │ │Quality │ │ │ │Doc   │ │ │   │   │
│ │ │  │ │Project     │ │ │ │Tool 9.4│ │ │ │Templ.│ │ │   │   │
│ │ │  │ │Document    │ │ │ ╰────────╯ │ │ │ 6.3  │ │ │   │   │
│ │ │  │ ╰────────────╯ │ ╰────────────╯ │ ╰──────╯ │ │   │   │
│ │ │  │ ╭────────────╮ ╭──────────────╮ │ ╭──────╮ │ │   │   │
│ │ │  │ │Statement of│ │Work Breakdown│ │ │Plan  │ │ │   │   │
│ │ │  │ │Work    8.1 │ │Structure 8.2 │ │ │  7.1 │ │ │   │   │
│ │ │  │ ╰────────────╯ ╰──────────────╯ │ ╰──────╯ │ │   │   │
│ │ │  ╰────────────────────────────────╯           │ │   │   │
│ │ │                                                │ │   │   │
│ │ └─────────────────────────────────────────────────┘   │   │
│ └───────────────────────────────────────────────────────┘   │
└─────────────────────────────────────────────────────────────┘
```

- *Note:* The illustration of the class hierarchy contains all the classes this part defines. Other parts of the book define and discuss classes not in boldface.

CHAPTER

6

The Project Document

Paperwork—you can't live with it and you can't live without it. This chapter tells you how to focus your paperwork, or more grandiosely, your *documentation,* on the things that matter. It also tells you how to be more productive at paperwork.

- *Note:* The project document in all its variations is just a system like all the others in your project. It has a vision, a mission, operational objectives, and risks. Those system elements should tell you whether you need the document at all. For small projects, for example, the effort of producing tons of documents is not worth their contribution to the value of the project. You need to carefully evaluate all the different documents in the context of your project to understand what your project needs. You do not create value by producing worthless documents but by creating great software.

The Document

Development Document (17.1)
Project Plan (7.2)

The *project document* is a versioned object that standardizes the structure of all documents relating to a project. The project plan and the set of development documents, for example, are project documents—requirements, functional specifications, design documents, test plans, and so on.

The project document unifies the structure of all documents on the project. This helps to reduce overlooked document elements, such as dates or version numbers. It enables creation of templates to reduce effort in document production. The project and reuse repositories should contain all project documents under change management.

Document Template (6.3)
Project Repository (3.4)
Reuse Repository (2.2)

Vision: An optimal amount of paperwork that communicates project information effectively and productively

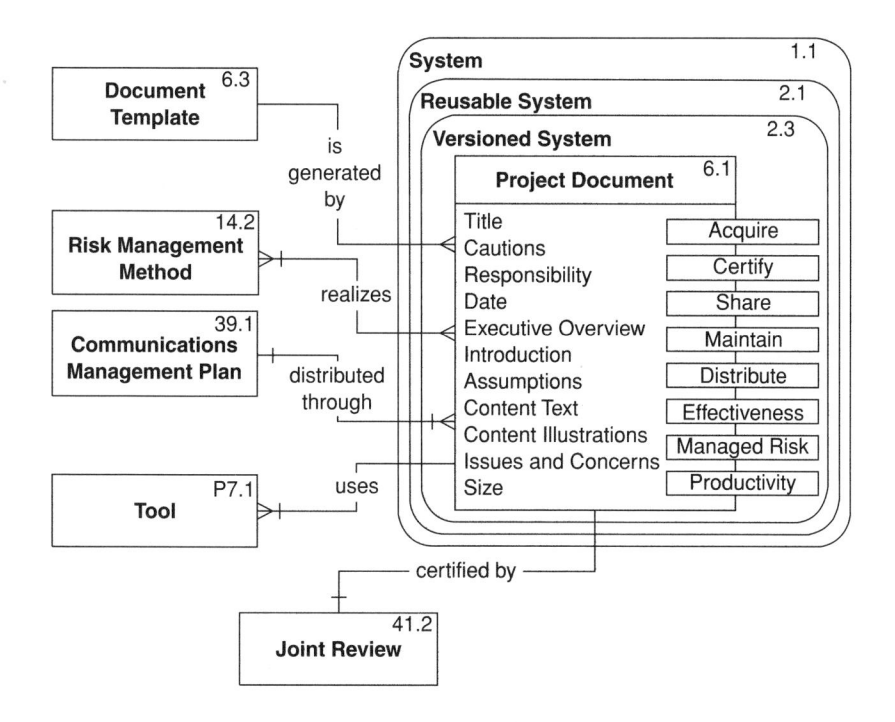

The Document

```
                                    System                    1.1
  ┌──────────────┐ 6.3                                          
  │  Document    │              Reusable System         2.1
  │  Template    │                                              
  └──────┬───────┘           Versioned System           2.3
         │                                                      
         │       is          ┌─────────────────────┐ 6.1
         │    generated      │  Project Document   │           
         │       by          │  Title              │  ┌──────────┐
  ┌──────┴───────┐ 14.2      │  Cautions           │◁─│ Acquire  │
  │    Risk      │           │  Responsibility     │  │ Certify  │
  │  Management  │▷┐         │  Date               │  │  Share   │
  │    Method    │ │         │  Executive Overview │◁─│ Maintain │
  └──────────────┘ │         │  Introduction       │  │ Distribute│
                   │ realizes│  Assumptions        │  │Effectiveness│
  ┌──────────────┐ 39.1      │  Content Text       │  │Managed Risk│
  │ Communications│          │  Content Illustrations│◁│          │
  │ Management   │┬──────────│  Issues and Concerns│  │Productivity│
  │    Plan      │ distributed│ Size               │  └──────────┘
  └──────────────┘  through  └─────────────────────┘           
                                                                
  ┌──────────────┐ P7.1        uses                             
  │    Tool      │▷────────────────                             
  └──────┬───────┘                                              
         │           ─── certified by ───                        
         │              ┌─────────┐ 41.2                        
         └──────────────│  Joint  │                             
                        │ Review  │                             
                        └─────────┘                             
```

Mission: To communicate essential project information effectively and productively

---

Objective 6.1: To communicate effectively

Approach 6.1: Identify the communications you intend to make through a document in terms of content, sources, and targets in the communication plan. Execute that plan as you execute the project plan and monitor the results. Improve the document as you learn more about what communicates and what doesn't.

Metric 6.1: Comprehension: a test of the communication targets for their relative understanding of the content of the document as a percentage of total understanding; note that effective communication depends on both the quality of the content and on how much of it there is given the time constraints of the communication targets

Target 6.1: Comprehension of the document within standard p control chart limits, with a minimum comprehension level of 80%

Objective 6.2: To communicate essential information

Approach 6.2: Identify the risks that the document manages. If these risks do not contribute to raising the system risk beyond its risk tolerance, eliminate the communication or the whole document if no communications remain in it. Note that a document can be redundant as a risk management measure, but only if the absence of the communication would raise the risk of communication failure beyond the system risk tolerance.

Metric 6.2: Managed Risk: What percentage of project or system risk does the document effectively manage?

Target 6.2: Managed risk within standard p control limits

Objective 6.3: To communicate productively

Approach 6.3: Use a document template to build initial versions of the document. Be terse. Use illustrations sparingly where they are most effective at conveying real information. Use productive writing and drawing tools.

Metric 6.3.1: Text size: number of words in the document

Metric 6.3.2: Illustration size: number of illustrations in the document

Metric 6.3.3: Text productivity: words/effort-hour

Metric 6.3.4: Illustration productivity: illustrations/effort-hour

Target 6.3: Productivity within standard pn control chart limits for both text and illustrations

---

The project document includes these sections:

- *Title:* the name of the document
- *Cautions:* the copyright notice, confidentiality policy, and so on
- *Responsibility:* the people responsible for the document's acquisition and maintenance
- *Date:* supplements the version number for time-sensitive materials
- *Executive overview:* summarizes the document for the terminally busy person
- *Introduction:* summarizes the document for the normally busy person
- *Assumptions:* the things the authors assumed in acquiring the document
- *Textual content:* the textual meat of the document
- *Illustrations:* graphics that convey content or illustrate the text
- *Issues and concerns:* statements about problems that are unresolved or risks that may cause the document or project mission to fail

You will usually put the version number of the document into the printed representation of the document for reference, though you should always be able to retrieve the version number of a given document through the repository.

The actual form of the document should meet its needs. An online document in a repository is highly accessible from anywhere in the world. You can easily put it under change control. A paper document is highly accessible when computers are not necessarily available or capable of effective display. A combination of both online and paper editions of a document gives you the best of both worlds. There are several possible formats for project documents:

- Paper
- ASCII text file
- Word processor or document publishing system file
- HTML page(s) for World Wide Web access
- Adobe Acrobat or other page display software formats for online access

■ *Note:* For a document to be fully reusable, it must have an online form. Email and Web access have become the standard methods for making project documents available. Without an online form, you can't send the document to stakeholders through email or set up access to the document on a Web site.

Reusability of the project document depends largely on its content, in terms of both inherent reusability and domain reusability. You can reuse a project document in two ways.

First, you can reuse the document in its entirety. For example, if the document is part of a software cluster—say a design document—you can just refer to it as needed. To do this, you can't have any requirements for different structures (a changed executive overview, for example, or a different title). You have to reuse the document as it is.

Second, you can reuse the document by modifying it, either through a revision or by copying elements into a new document. Revisions are better, since you make the changes under version control. Just as with copying software, if you make changes, you need to remember to change the copied bits as well—either that or deliberately ignore them.

Many project documents contain proprietary or confidential information. The repository for the documents should give you the security capabilities you need to protect your documents from sabotage or theft. Be sure you understand your access requirements and make use of the appropriate repository features.

Certain kinds of project documents, such as the project plan and its subplans, are inherently not reusable. Usually your tools focus on these kinds of documents, as that is where they can be most productively put to use—in generating standard documentation.

The tools you use to create documents often have a dramatic effect on your productivity. If your target is online documentation, for example, you should choose desktop publishing tools capable of generating online format files such as HTML or Acrobat. Not all do. Also, choose a drawing tool that helps instead of getting in your way. Finally, choose a change management system that is capable of handling documents. There are several well-engineered document management systems on the market, such as Documentum, FileNet, PC DOCS, or Open Text; or work-flow systems that manage documents, such as DEC's LinkWorks or IBM's FlowMark. You must combine these with effective configuration and change management tools to manage reusable documentation.

Change Management System (24.4)

The project document has the basic operations of any reusable system. You can acquire a document by checking it out of the reuse repository. You can also create a new document. You certify a document by reviewing it for accuracy and completeness through a joint review. You share a document through the reuse repository. You maintain it as part of the ongoing project and organizational processes.

When is enough for a document? When it no longer helps you to manage risks. The flow of documents as work products in the work flow of the project enables the communication of the content of the document. To communicate effectively, you integrate all project documents into the communications management plan, which should contain matrixes of documents and distribution lists. The distribution of project documents comprises a vital part of your project work flow.

Risk (12.1)

This communication translates into risk management if you think about its enabling properties with respect to the system mission. That is, what is the risk of mission failure if a particular communication fails? What won't happen if the resources on a task don't know something? What will happen to the project if task resources must recreate knowledge every time they need it rather than referring to a project document? The document's contribution to managing risk is thus an excellent surrogate for Occam's razor: a way to keep it simple. Measure the risk reduction from the presence of the document. If having the document does not contribute substantially to reducing system risk, you don't need it.

Communications Management Plan (39.5)

The Formal Project Document

Sometimes having the paper isn't enough; you have to have it *signed,* too.

The *formal project document* is a special kind of project document that adds approval to the basic document. If your process requires sign-offs, you need a formal project document to sign off. Usually, only major documents are formal with sign-offs, because otherwise you can bureaucratize your project. Routine cultures (pattern 2) can overdo this because of their focus on magic. These cultures often see signatures as a talisman that guarantees process success or the commitment of the signatories to the process. Of course, as with all talismans, this really depends on which side of their bed the Project Gods arose that day.

Management Culture (31.1)

The Formal Project Document

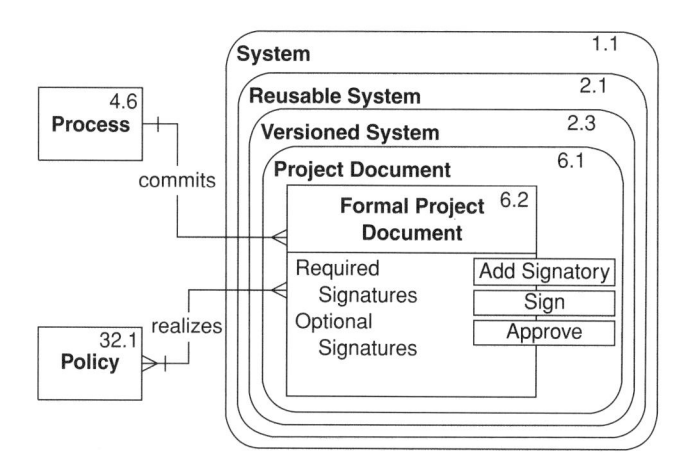

Vision: Strong commitment to the content mission of a project document

Mission: To formalize commitment to the content mission of the document

---

Objective 6.4: To obtain strong commitment from the organization

Approach 6.4: Add signatories to the document that represent all the authority on the project. After reviewing and revising the document, obtain the signatures required for approval by your approval policy. Communicate the achieving of the approval milestone to broadcast authoritative commitment to the project throughout the organization.

Metric 6.4: Commitment: How strong is the actual commitment of the signatories?

Target 6.4: Very strong

The organization will usually have a set of policies that specify the different approvals a document requires. One policy may determine which project documents are formal; another may indicate who has to sign each document. Some documents may have a set of both required signatures and optional ones. Each person signs the document. When the document has all the required signatures, it is approved.

Formal documents are almost always associated with a process, usually as an output. The process milestone occurs when the signatories approve the document. This approval milestone is the basis of the phased development processes such as the waterfall model or the spiral model. The end of the phase represents the stakeholders' commitment to proceed with the project.

Formal documents are by definition not reusable. You may be able to add a signature page to a document. But the very nature of the approval process is a one-time event.

There are plenty of cautionary tales about formal documents. One large company I worked for had a strong process policy that included formal approval of specifications and other major documents. On the one hand, this signified a strong commitment to the project by the executives that signed it. On the other hand, the project manager did not distribute the documents to the resources, so no one really knew who was committed to the project or why.

Another company I worked for had a middling-strict process, with one major approval point—the functional specification. All authority resided in the senior vice president in charge of the software organization, and his signature was all that was required for approval. Because he perceived something of a commitment problem with the organization, he had all the people in the organization sign the document. While this was laudatory, the controversy that ensued when various team members complained about their lack of belief in the specification and their unwillingness to put their name to it led to some interesting consequences. The vice president obtained all the signatures and the project went ahead, though it was shortly thereafter canceled by the vice president who replaced him. Commitment is, after all, relative.

The Document Template

The system model you use as the basis for generating your project document is the *document template*. This template can be as simple as a word processor document with the appropriate sections and format styles. You copy it and off you go. It can also be as complex as a repository-driven system for generating documents from CASE diagrams and annotations. The tool you use for document generation determines the structure of the model. You keep the template in the reuse repository.

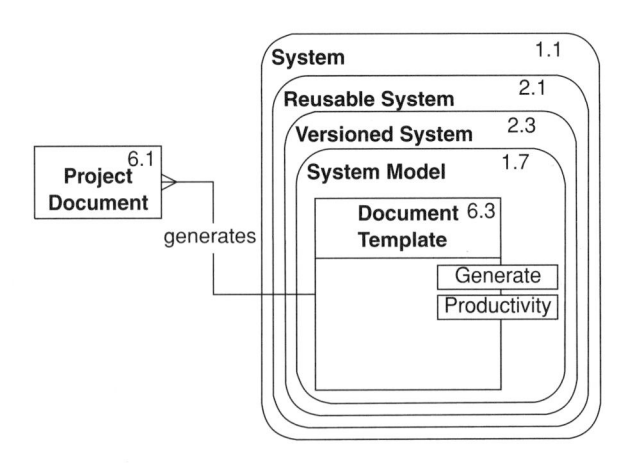

The Document Template

Vision: A project document created quickly and efficiently

Mission: To represent the pieces of a project document in a format that lets you quickly create the basic document

Objective 6.5: To create an initial version of a project document quickly and efficiently

Approach 6.5: Create a document in one or more word processor formats with all formatting and document components in place, as specified in organizational policies. You can parameterize the document through wizards and other techniques that make the template more effective. If you can, generate the complete text and illustrations; if not, at least generate the basic structure of the document.

Metric 6.5: Productivity: documents per effort-hour

Target 6.5: Productivity within standard pn control chart limits

There are two aspects to reusability of templates. First, as reusable systems, you can reuse the templates in different projects or in different stages of the project. The template becomes the operational aspect of the documentation policies of the organization. Maintaining the model means changing the template to suit changes in policy. Second, as system models, the template creates documents that, while they are not strictly reused, bring similar productivity improvements. You are reusing the creation process of the documents, if not the documents themselves.

Many CASE tools such as Software through Pictures or Teamwork can generate project documents from the diagrams and annotations in the CASE repository. For the most part, these are technical project documents. Most project management systems have similar capabilities for more general project documents such as work breakdown structures, organization charts, and budgets. They also have basic report writers that let you define your own documents. The more effective ones, such as Microsoft Project, Project Scheduler, and Time Line, provide an interface to database tools. You can then build information systems of any sort to produce and manage the documents using database report writers and application development tools.

Project Management System (22.2)

Information System (22.1)

The policies that are the basis for the template include standards for the structure of the target documents. You also generally have policies for the standard legal cautions on a document:

- The copyright notice
- Trademark and service mark notices
- Acknowledgment of licenses to use copyrighted material
- Notices to internal users about trade secrecy and limited distribution
- Notices to external users about licenses and trade secrecy
- General notices about dropping the document on things in bigger projects

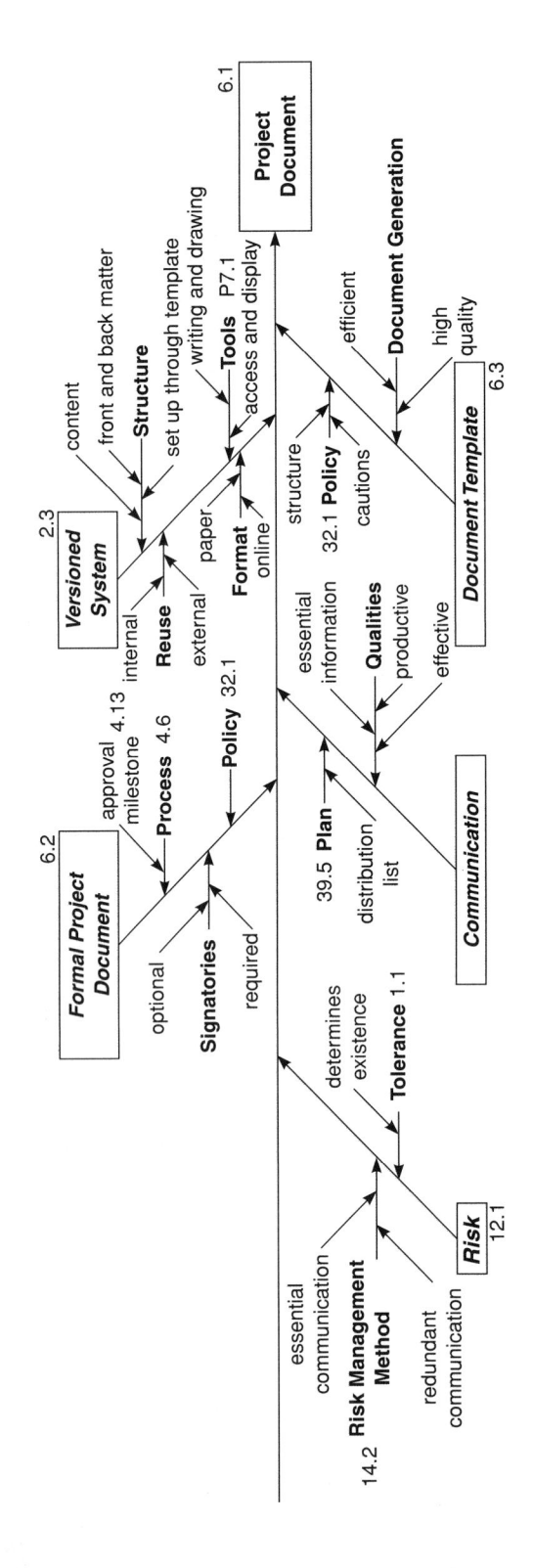

Chapter 6 / The Project Document

Project Document 6.1
— content
— front and back matter **Structure**
— set up through template
— writing and drawing **Tools** P7.1
— access and display
Document Generation — efficient
— high quality
Document Template 6.3
— structure
— **Policy** 32.1
— cautions
— paper
Format
— online
— external **Reuse**
— internal
Versioned System 2.3
— approval 4.13
— milestone **Process** 4.6
— **Policy** 32.1
Formal Project Document 6.2
— optional **Signatories**
— required
— essential information
— **Qualities** productive
— effective
Communication
— 39.5 **Plan**
— distribution list
— determines existence **Tolerance** 1.1
Risk 12.1
— essential communication
14.2 **Risk Management Method**
— redundant communication

Questions to Think About

1. Can you think of other methods for deciding whether a document is worthwhile? What metric and target let you decide this? Does the method suggest another objective for the project document as a class?

2. What is the real basis for commitment of resources to a project? How do you establish commitment and trust in your organization? Do signatures on documents contribute much to this?

3. Do you like to do paperwork? Anticipating your answer, why not? Is the paperwork you do really needed? If not, why do you do it? Would training in the skills involved in good documentation help? Would more effective document templates and tools help? What about training the recipients of the documents in the skills they need to use them?

CHAPTER

7 The Project Plan

The Plan

A *plan* is a "detailed scheme, program, or method worked out beforehand for the accomplishment of an object [AHD]." It is yet another system model, this time a model of the task structure of a specific process [DeMarco 1982]. You use a plan to guide the process to a successful conclusion.

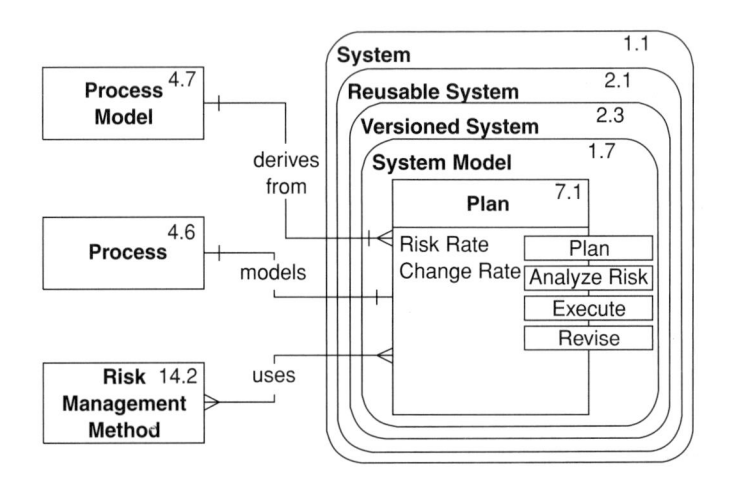

A plan is an intermediate system model that comes between the process model and the process it represents. While the process model represents the general structure of a process, the plan represents the specific model for a specific process. For example, the level of detail and the focus on accomplishment are two factors that distinguish a plan from a process model. While a process model is a once and future scheme to produce a product, it has none of the pragmatic and specific details (the actual resources, the current legal constraints, the specific delivery times) that you need to guide an operating process. The plan also contains all the exceptions, additions, and deletions from the standard process model. The process needs this level of adaptation before it executes—no process model is 100% of everything you need to do in a process. The plan is the highest level of risk management in a system, as it directly addresses the issue of mission success or failure through the tasks it contains.

Vision: A process brought to a successful conclusion, achieving its mission by delivering its products

Mission: To bring the process model for a system to bear on successfully achieving its mission

Objective 7.1: To translate a process model into a set of tasks likely to achieve the mission of the process

Approach 7.1: Set the risk tolerance of the process. Generate a plan from a process model, laying out the tasks and dependencies of the process in the required amount of detail. Analyze the risk of the plan and add tasks to manage that risk as required. Review the plan with the project stakeholders that the process will affect as a way to validate the risk-reducing qualities of the plan. Execute the plan and collect feedback to improve it.

Metric 7.1: Risk Rate: rate of change of process risk relative to planning effort

Target 7.1: A rate of change that brings the process risk below the risk tolerance of the process in a reasonable time frame (that is, before you execute the process and incur the risk) with a reasonable amount of effort

Objective 7.2: To provide a mechanism for accommodating change in a process

Approach 7.2: As you execute the plan, collect feedback both from the execution of the plan through milestones and from the process environment. Make required changes after evaluating their impact on the uncompleted tasks in the plan, again analyzing risk.

Metric 7.2: Change Rate: rate of change of the plan during execution of the plan

Target 7.2: A stable rate of plan change within control limits of an x-R control chart. The better your plan, the more stable it will be during the course of the project.

There are many plans in any given project, mostly corresponding to the different processes in the project:

Improvement Plan (1.3)

- *System improvement plans:* plans to improve a system

Development Plan (16.2)

- *Development plan:* a plan to produce software and documentation deliverables

Quality Management Plan (9.1)

- *Quality management plan:* a development plan to manage the quality of project systems and products

Change Management Plan (23.1)

- *Change management plan:* a plan to manage change in a project

Configuration Management Plan (23.2)

- *Configuration management plan:* a change management plan to manage change in the integration of deliverable systems such as hardware and software systems

Cost Management Plan (38.1)

- *Cost management plan:* a plan to manage system costs in a project

Staffing Plan (35.2)

- *Staffing plan:* a cost management plan to manage the resources of a project, including hiring and assignment of resources and the organizational structuring of resources into work groups

Communications Management Plan (39.5)

- *Communications management plan:* a plan to manage internal and external communication in a project

Risk Management Plan (14.1)

- *Risk management plan:* a plan to manage risks in a project

Procurement Management Plan (27.7)

- *Procurement management plan:* a plan to manage the acquisition of systems, tools, and materials for a project, including contract administration for outsourced deliverables, licensed tools, and hardware resources

■ *Note:* There is no such thing as a standard for a project plan. The Project Management Body of Knowledge [PMI 1996a] is as close to a standard as you can get, and the above set of subsidiary plans comes from there. Most software development planning is nowhere near as complete as this, and most plans take shape from the tools that produce them. The point of this book, however, is to take control of your project systems through system mission and objectives. You should determine the format and contents of your plans through these goals and not just accept the primitive capabilities of current planning tools such as Microsoft Project or ManagePro. Good as these tools are, they supply only part of your needs. You should think about planning from your perspective, not theirs.

Modeling, in this case, means planning: generating the plan model from the process model. A formal process model gives you a well-structured set of tasks in your plan. A less formal process model, or no process model at all, gives you less help in structuring your project. With little or no process modeling, you must model your process in an ad hoc manner.

On a project to deliver an OO version of a non-OO product, we were working with a set of process models that varied in formality. The model for one part of the project was thorough and up-to-date, and the resulting plan was comprehensive and workable. (My department, of course!) The model for another part of the project was less formal, and the plan reflected the vagueness of the model. A complication was that the less formal part of the planning was also the part of the project with the least experience and training with OO technology. As project manager, I had to compensate for the lack of planning through other risk management techniques, such as stepped-up communication and more thorough reviews. This resulted in a somewhat unbalanced management style for the project, with some groups feeling more "managed" than others.

Planning provides the main mechanism for evaluating risk in a process. Getting the level of detail right is the hardest thing to do in planning, and risk analysis can help you do that. Go to the level of detail you need to identify and manage the risks of the process. Stop planning when your process risk is below your risk tolerance for that process. If your process has little risk without the plan, don't plan at all. Check yourself, however, through reviews. You may not perceive all the risks involved, especially with complex technical or financial processes. Get stakeholders involved and ask them if there are any risks you have not identified that are mission-threatening. If there are, go back and change the plan to manage those risks.

Watch your rate of change of risk (Metric 7.1). If the impact of your planning on process risk is not effective, you should weigh two options. First, consider doing something other than planning to cut risk, such as reducing requirements or revising the process model. Second, consider canceling the process entirely: it may be that the risk is simply too high. All the planning in the world will not make an unfeasible process work. On the other hand, planning to a certain level can clarify the problems in your project.

For example, my first serious development plan was to port an interactive database application from a relatively modern operating system to an old, batch-oriented operating system running under a TP monitor. Given the dependence of the application on specific vendor tools, the project quickly became an exercise in identifying failure. The company's management wanted to move the system because the customers all used the older operating system. The development managers believed that the project was feasible but did not have enough experience to estimate the schedule or budget. Working out the development plan to a reasonable level of detail convinced both managements that the project would fail, both because of technology risks and because of the lengthy project's interference with producing upgrades to the current product by sucking up resources. Upper management canceled the project based on this development plan.

For OO projects, planning will identify technology areas that lack trained resources or well-thought-out requirements. Planning is particularly important for

Risk (12.1)

acquisition processes because of the high risk of failure due to ineffective tools (the Silver Bullet syndrome). It is also useful to handle some of the risks of estimation failure. Working out a plan in detail can often provide estimates where standard cost estimation techniques cannot due to lack of data or validated models.

Generating the process from the plan means, essentially, executing the plan. You assign responsibility for the project tasks and authorize the resources to continue with them. Plans are versioned objects that change as the plan executes. Beware of change before execution: thrashing the plan endlessly is the management equivalent of endless prototyping. You go on and on trying different things, and the world just grows older without the benefit of any results or products. This is like a noble heading for the guillotine, looking for the Scarlet Pimpernel at every crossing.

Executing the plan is what gives you the opportunity to collect feedback. Feedback, in turn, lets you change the plan effectively and meaningfully. However, you need to balance change against risk: Metric 7.2 versus Metric 7.1. If revising the plan does not significantly affect risk, don't bother, even to accommodate change in the process environment. The plan does not need to reflect reality, just risk.

Plan reuse depends on process model reuse. Even though plans connect single-time processes to process models, the plans can come largely from the reuse repository. If the process model on which you base a plan is stable and complete, you can often reuse a previous plan. Therefore, process design is the most important way to increase inherent and domain reuse potential in a plan.

The versioning of a plan lets you reuse previous versions of the specific plan. The degree to which this is useful depends on how robust the plan is in the face of feedback and change. By taking change into account in your original planning, and by thoroughly analyzing risk, you can improve the stability of your plan and hence its reuse potential within the current project. The less you have to alter the plan to accommodate failure and change, the less work you have to do and the better quality your process has.

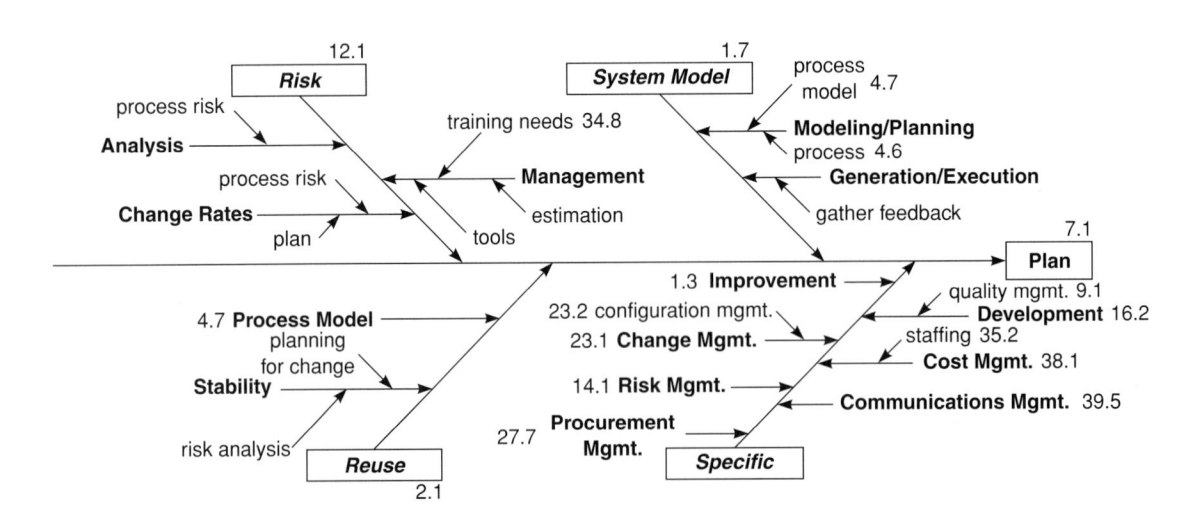

The Project Plan

The *project plan* contains all the planning effort of the project. It is an umbrella plan that contains all the other plans of the project, such as the communications management and risk management plans. The project plan contains the statement of work, which in turn contains the requirements document and the work breakdown structure. It contains the project schedule, which combines all the tasks in the work breakdown structure in schedule tasks on a project time line.

The project plan contains the project calendar, which determines the structure of work time for the duration of the project. It also contains the organization chart, which tells you the organizational structure of the project.

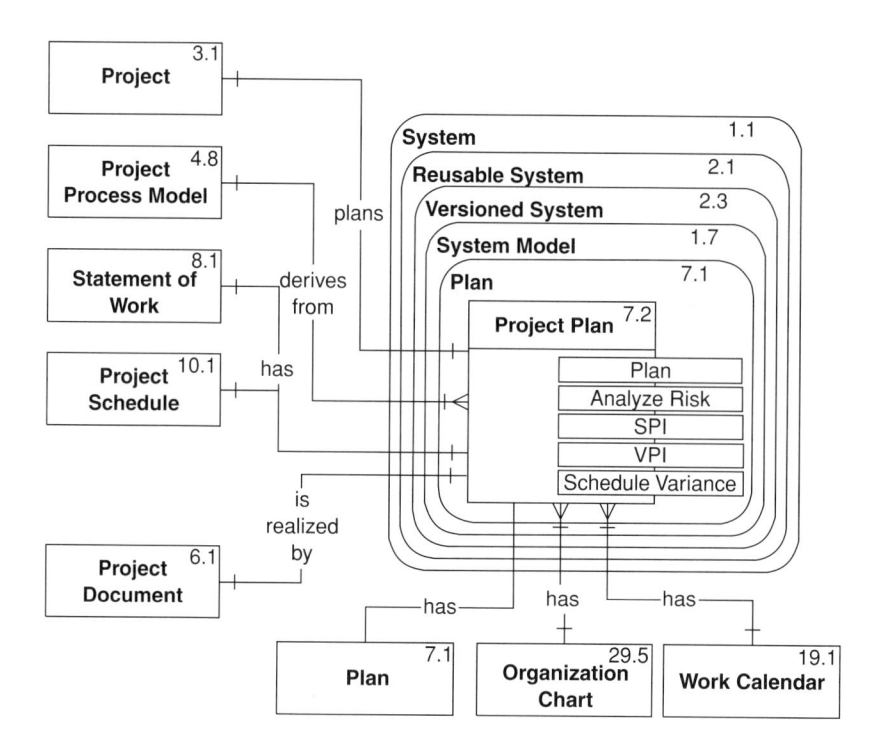

You represent all this abstraction in a single project document, also called the project plan. As with any project document, you standardize the content structure with a template. The document might, for example, have the following content structure:

- Statement of Work (Requirements and WBS)
- Schedule
- Development plan

- Quality management plan
- Change management plan
- Cost management plan
- Communications management plan
- Risk management plan
- Procurement management plan

■ *Note:* The project plan satisfies the requirements for a quality plan in the ISO-9000 standards (9000, 9001, 9004, and 9000-3).

Vision: A project that delivers value on time and under budget

Mission: To structure a project process that produces deliverable systems that create value for the project stakeholders

---

Objective 7.3: To create a project process likely to achieve the mission of the project

---

Approach 7.3: Plan the project. Create the statement of work from the requirements document and the component plans' contribution to the work breakdown structure. Set up the organizational structure most likely to achieve the project mission. Develop a work calendar for the period of the project. Develop the schedule for the project from the work breakdown structure, the organization chart, and the work calendar. Baseline the statement of work (including its cost estimates) and the schedule. Revise the plan as required during project execution, baselining again as needed.

Metric 7.3.1: Project Risk Change Rate: the rate of change of project risk relative to planning effort

Target 7.3.1: A rate of change of project risk that brings that risk below the risk tolerance of the project in a reasonable time frame with a reasonable amount of effort

---

Metric 7.3.2: Baseline change ratio: the current baseline time and cost over the original baseline time and cost values

Target 7.3.2: A value near 1 varying within standard p control chart limits

---

Metric 7.3.3: Baseline rate of change: the rate of change of the baseline change ratio with respect to time

Target 7.3.3: Rate of change decreasing with time (that is, the change ratio rate of change diminishes as the project executes)

The Project Plan 135

Objective 7.4: To create project deliverables on time and under budget

Approach 7.4: Execute the project plan, tracking the schedule and budget. Manage the statement of work to ensure that the project creates all required system deliverables according to schedule and budget, taking into account required change. Manage the organization and the work calendar to provide the most effective use of resources on the project.

Metric 7.4.1: Schedule performance index (SPI): the ratio of total earned value to total planned value for the deliverables at a specific time in the project (see Metric 3.2.1 in Chapter 3)

Target 7.4.1: Schedule performance index >= 1

Metric 7.4.2: Value performance index (VPI): the ratio of total earned value to total actual value for the deliverables at a specific time in the project (see Metric 3.2.2 in Chapter 3)

Target 7.4.2: Value performance index >= 1

Metric 7.4.3: Schedule variance at a specific time in the project (see Metric 3.2.3 in Chapter 3)

Target 7.4.3: At any given date during the project, 0 <= schedule variance <= 1% of value at completion

---

The project plan document is the central object the project manager deals with throughout the project. Despite that fact, it is really more interesting as a container object than in its own right.

The planning task starts at the project plan level and works its way down through the statement of work, the schedule, the organization chart, the work calendar, and the various subsidiary plans. The project initiates planning through its high-level plan task. It generates project metrics from the plan for specific milestones. If issues between subsidiary plans arise, the project manager and the project stakeholders resolve the conflict at the project level as part of the planning process. Conflicts can arise because the subsidiary plans, such as the quality plan, often come from organizations not subject to the authority of the project manager. This can cause all kinds of headaches and political conflicts on projects.   **Organization (29.1)**

For example, a project to develop a new PC application ran into some planning conflicts between the quality plan and the development plan. The development manager had an aggressive plan for delivering software components based on the stakeholders' need for an early release date for the software. The quality manager was in the process of building a strong quality organization and process model, however. She wanted to apply the new process to the project, particularly as the plan specified the OO components to be reusable in other projects. The result called into question the aggressive delivery dates from development, as it became clear that (1) the quality schedule was too optimistic, and (2) the real impact of quality assurance on the project would result in a high rework ratio. That is, if the quality assurance group applied its process to the current level of software quality, it would result in many more defects being found and fixed. This would in turn result in schedule delays, as no resource additions were possible.

The project manager, in this case, was also the development manager. The resolution of the issue at the project level was very political in nature. The development manager refused to allow the quality manager to implement her plan and took over quality assurance for the project. Eventually, this forced the other manager to leave the company. The product came out two years late and was not a shining example of quality software.

The project plan is the source for risk analysis in the project. The plan risk tolerance comes from the project risk tolerance. Risk analysis combines the standard risks from the process model and the specific risks for the current project into a comprehensive survey of the risks that the project faces. The risk management plan quantifies the risks and specifies risk control methods for the risks that exceed the risk tolerance.

First, the project manager identifies project-related risks, those that apply to the project as a whole. Project risks come from the project process model (standard risks) or from the project environment (specific risks). As planning works through the subsidiary plans, these plans in turn analyze risks in their process to produce a comprehensive survey of risk to the project from all sources. The risk analysis task identifies and quantifies these risks, and the risk planning identifies the control measures to take to bring total risk below the project risk tolerance.

Risk (12.1)

Risk Management Method (14.2)

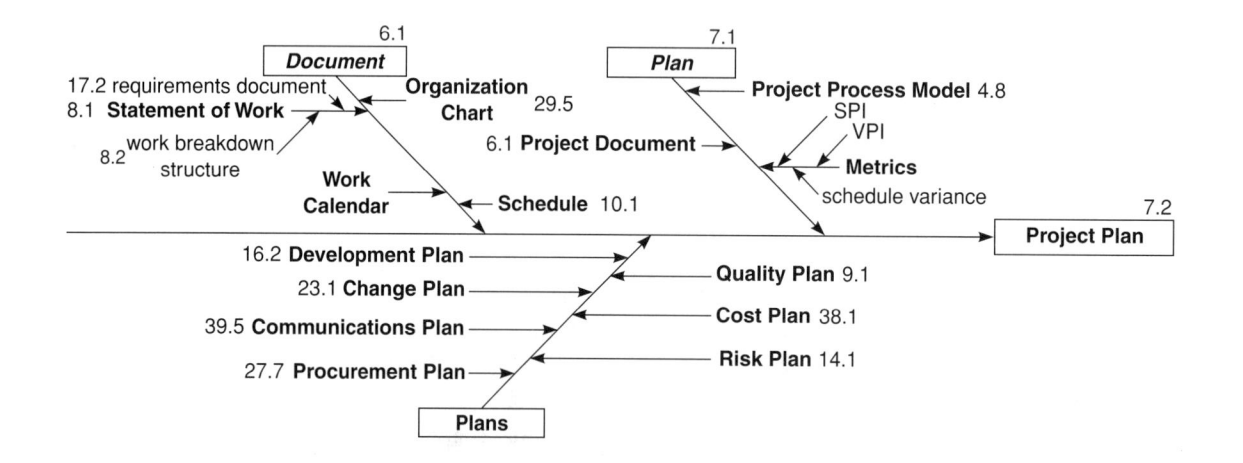

The various project plan metrics provide you with the feedback you need during execution of the plan. These metrics are the same as those for the project. Instead of waiting until the end of the project, however, you can get interim values through the plan. At the final project milestone, the plan metrics are identical to and the source for the project metrics. That is, you evaluate the project in the end by evaluating how well the actual project performed to its plan.

Project (3.1)

Readings

[DeMarco 1982] Tom DeMarco. *Controlling Software Projects: Management, Measurement, and Estimation.* New York: Yourdon Press, 1982.

DeMarco's book on metrics and project control contains an entire chapter on project plans as system models (Chapter 13). While he does not separate process model and plan explicitly, much of his discussion is relevant to this chapter. He suggests some specific ways to implement the system modeling that are useful, if extreme.

[Kerzner] Harold Kerzner. *Project Management: A Systems Approach to Planning, Scheduling, and Controlling, Fifth Edition.* New York: Van Nostrand Reinhold, 1994.

Chapter 11 of Kerzner's book addresses the different aspects of planning in a systematic and practical manner. Kerzner introduces all the different parts of a project plan and tells you what you need to know to make best use of them as a project manager. The material isn't well structured, but close study does pay off in a better understanding of the planning process.

[PMI 1996a] Project Management Institute Standards Committee. *A Guide to the Project Management Body of Knowledge.* Project Management Institute (+1-610-734-3330), 1996.

The Body of Knowledge gives an excellent summary of the different plans you must include in any project plan. While the detail isn't there, the scope is. Often getting the big picture helps more than getting bogged down in details, and that's usually true with planning.

[Thomsett] Rob Thomsett. *Third Wave Project Management: A Handbook for Managing the Complex Information Systems for the 1990s.* Englewood Cliffs, NJ: Prentice Hall PTR, 1989.

Thomsett's Chapter 3 devotes 22 pages to a very insightful discussion of the project planning process, including setting the development approach, risk analysis, building the work breakdown structure, and cost estimating. This is one of the clearest descriptions of the process I've read.

Questions to Think About

1. Have you ever done a project of any substantive size without a plan? (Remember the definition of a plan: a detailed scheme worked out beforehand.) How did the project succeed without a plan (or how did it fail because of the lack of a plan)?

2. How many of the different kinds of plans have you actually done in practice? Why haven't you done the kinds you haven't done?

3. If you have ever done a formal risk analysis, how did you integrate the results of that analysis into the project? Did you do it through the project plan? Why or why not?

4. What is the key element that risk analysis and planning share? (Hint: What makes risk risky?)

5. Propose some different structures for your standard project plan document and justify the choices you've made. What kinds of issues arise in considering this kind of standard plan? How does it change with application to specific situations?

CHAPTER

Statement of Work 8

The Statement of Work

The *statement of work* is a project document that describes the *scope* of the project: the set of products and services that constitute the deliverables of the project. This document is a part of the larger project plan.

Vision: A project that delivers a clearly defined solution to stakeholder needs

Mission: To define the boundaries of the project through specifying the products and services that are the deliverables of the project and the work needed to produce those deliverables

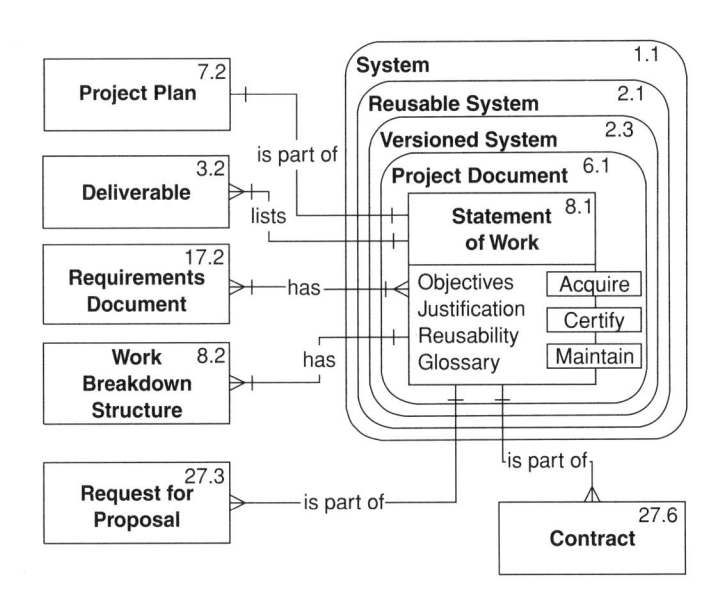

Objective 8.1: To specify the deliverables of the project that address stakeholder needs

Approach 8.1: Summarize the project objectives. Justify the scope of the project by relating it to stakeholder needs (market analysis, cost-benefit analysis, and so on). Produce a requirements document that states the stakeholder needs (the problem to solve). Produce a list of deliverables that, as a system, meets the requirements of the project.

Metric 8.1: Stakeholder Assessment: Do the stakeholders agree that the statement of work fairly describes the problems they want to address? Yes or no.

Target 8.1: Yes

Objective 8.2: To specify the work required to produce the set of deliverables

Approach 8.2: Break down the deliverables into tasks to produce them, and continue breaking down the structure until you reach a set of simple tasks (work packages and levels of effort) from which you can estimate the cost and the schedule of the project.

Metric 8.2: Traceability Ratio: the ratio of number of requirements satisfied by work to produce deliverables to total number of requirements

Target 8.2: 1

In line with its mission, the statement of work contains the requirements document and the work breakdown structure. Together, these elements provide enough detail for a reasonable person (do you know any?) to figure out whether the organization can do the project. "Do" implies doing successfully, not just working away at it for years until somebody pulls the plug. This is a very real danger with OO and other iterative projects. People get into the flow and iterate endlessly, losing track of the fact that a project has to end at some point.

Usually, this problem comes under the shibboleth of "creeping requirements" [Jones 1994]. I've been in many OO projects where, at each stage in the growth of the project, managers again try to assert through some variation on the statement of work that "this is it," drawing the line in the sand. I used to believe in the Alamo myself, but I've come regrettably to the conclusion that things change. You can either accept change or get out of the way. On the other hand, you need to have some way of understanding how change affects the project. Accepting change is what the statement of work does. It is the central place where you accumulate changes and communicate them to those that need to know. It is the place where you record changes and get acceptance from stakeholders of their consequences to work (and the project schedule and budget).

- *Note:* The statement of work is definitely *not* the place to make decisions about delivery. Obviously, at some point you need to deliver a product. Scope changes can go on forever. But the statement of work just *describes* the scope. It represents the net effect of the decisions you make with stakeholders about the value of the project. It is not a protective shield against the vagaries of fate. Focusing on the statement of work as a way of limiting your project is self-defeating. Instead, focus on the value of the project to stakeholders, and then develop the scope to deliver that value.

The reusability that the statement of work picks up from being a versioned system lets you move the statement of work forward as change occurs. While you act on change, you don't need to redefine the project completely every time something changes.

For example, I worked on a project that merged with another project that was a year late, three years into the project. By merging the projects, management (the primary stakeholders) wanted to refocus development on a clear target, encourage reuse, and integrate the division into a single, focused unit. The statement of work for the original project was a combination of a reference manual requirements document and a work breakdown structure in the project management system the organization used. The reference manual expanded to include the new features from the new project. The new teams integrated their work breakdown structures into that of the original project. The result was a complete statement of work available in about a week after the decision to merge the projects. The project ultimately failed because management did this three more times over two more years. Great statement of work, lousy control.

The statement of work has some other sections besides the two main ones. The statement of work is where you write down the objectives of the project. It's also the place where you summarize the justification, or business case, for the project. Both of these sections should be just a page, no more. If you think you need more, create a separate document and refer to it. Then put it on your internal Web system and track hits and learn something.

Optionally, you can develop a general structure for reuse on the project in the statement of work. It is, after all, the scope of work that is the subject of the document. Suggesting reuse of major systems or components from the reuse repository reflects some key assumptions about how you will go about the project. Developing for reuse is also an issue that reflects additional development time for generalization of the components you produce.

A glossary of terms you have invented to describe the wonderful ideas of the product team is always useful. If nothing else, you can advertise your team's ability to invent truly awful acronyms. Unfortunately, most OO projects tend to avoid acronyms these days; the names of things tend to reflect "real-world" structures and to use real-world words. The words, of course, do not necessarily mean what everyone else thinks they mean, so you still need a glossary.

■ *Note:* Be careful to define the term "object" in your glossary. A little controversy livens up a project with any class.

Acquiring the reusable statement of work means getting it from the reuse repository, building it from components you find there, or building it from scratch. This acquisition process drives the development of the requirements document for the project as well as of the work breakdown structure. This in turn drives the scheduling and cost estimation processes for the project.

Certifying the document has two parts. First, you must conduct one or more joint reviews of the document with the stakeholders to validate the content of the document. Metric 8.1 is a binary metric that indicates that the stakeholders have signed off on the requirements. Second, you must certify the internal consistency of the requirements by analysis of the work breakdown structure and its feasibility. Can you fulfill the requirements? Is there any contradiction between requirements? What are the risks associated with the development choices you've made? Metric 8.2 is a ratio metric that describes the relationship between the tasks in the work breakdown structure and the requirements.

Most books on software practice describe a technique called the *traceability matrix*. This method, usually a quality assurance method, traces the relationship of artifacts at one stage of development back to artifacts at another stage. The classic system traceability matrix connects deliverables at the end of the project to requirements at the beginning of the project.

You typically build a traceability matrix as a spreadsheet with one row for each deliverable-requirement combination. You can then search for particular requirements or look at all the requirements for one deliverable. For example, Table 8-1 shows part of the traceability matrix for an example defect tracking system. This example shows the deliverable name and its WBS code, and then lists the requirement scenario or use case it satisfies and the particular step within the use case. The complete matrix should have at least one row for each step in the set of use cases and at least one row for each deliverable.

The traceability ratio in Metric 8.2 provides a measure of this traceability in the planning of the project. That is, after building the statement of work, the proposed work in the work breakdown structure should map to the requirements through the deliverables. The section below on the work breakdown structure provides some suggestions about ways to ensure that this happens

Certification, aside from addressing the needs of the current project, also addresses the concerns of reusing projects. By certifying the statement of work, you

The Statement of Work   143

WBS	Deliverable	Requirement Scenario	Step Number
DTS-3	DTS.EXE	Logon	1
DTS-3	DTS.EXE	Logon	2
DTS-3	DTS.EXE	Menu	1
DTS-4	PERSON.DLL	Enter New Person	1
DTS-4	PERSON.DLL	Enter New Person	2
DTS-4	PERSON.DLL	Enter New Person	3
DTS-4	PERSON.DLL	Enter New Person	4
DTS-5	PRODUCT.DLL	Version Product	1
DTS-5	PRODUCT.DLL	Version Product	2
DTS-5	PRODUCT.DLL	Link Failure to Product	1

Table 8-1
Part of the DTS Traceabilty Matrix

are showing potential reusers that the work breakdown structure and requirements document are internally and externally valid, at least for the specified domain. Reusing the statement of work in a similar domain then becomes more feasible.

Versioning the statement of work—maintaining it—is more than useful, it is necessary. A key difference between the iterative nature of OO systems and the static nature of other development methods is in their ability to handle change. The statement of work is a focal point for change. Both the requirements and the way you will go about satisfying them through the work tasks change as you iterate through clusters and systems of deliverables. The change management plan identifies the process and mechanisms through which you manage change to the statement of work. The change management process can involve change requests, a change control team, and other controls.

Change Managment Plan (23.1)

Change Management Process (24.1)

The statement of work has three potential roles in any project. The above discussion focuses on the role of the document in defining the general scope of project work. In the context of projects that involve multiple contractors, the statement of work becomes part of the procurement process. The procuring organization creates requests for proposals that incorporate a statement of work for the contractor to bid on. As well, the contract you eventually sign contains a statement of work (or at least it should) that specifies the deliverables and work for the contractor to perform. Typically, these statements of work are for portions of the overall project. In these situations, it might make sense to have a structured statement of work, with contracted portions clearly identified within the overall project document. In any case, you must make sure all these statements of work reconcile. You wouldn't want a contractor working on something you didn't need, would you?

Request for Proposal (27.3)

Contract (27.6)

The Work Breakdown Structure

The *work breakdown structure* (WBS) is "a deliverable-oriented grouping of project elements which organizes and defines the total scope of the project" [PMI 1996a]. It is the part of the statement of work that shows how the project tasks relate to the processes and deliverables of the project.

There are dozens of ways of constructing work breakdown structures. Usually the structure of the WBS reflects the underlying purpose of the scope definition effort. For example, breaking down life-cycle phases into finely grained tasks is a standard way to construct a software development WBS [Kerzner; PMI 1996a]. A task-driven WBS reflects the desire of management to manage by phase approval. This approach packages the work into behemoth approval steps according to a waterfall process model. Such packaging usually leads to strange-looking schedule charts and much fudging as people try to do what they need to do even though a phase is finished or not yet begun. The management accounting people also like task-oriented WBSs, which they see as cost-accounting structures (charts of accounts). They can aggregate accounting information right up the tree, making the jobs of budgeting and auditing much easier.

Chart of Accounts (36.1)

Unfortunately, most of these structures make it much more difficult to build effective plans. They also make it harder to arrange work in plans and to figure out the status of the work and report on it. A Navy study suggested another approach:

> …traditional work breakdown structures simply broke down an existing work process into more detailed tasks. These were aggregated vertically, often reflecting the craft-based production organization. The task and the object being worked were usually rigidly locked together as a WBS element. Accountability for the pieces of the process was possible only as long as the rigid structure was not violated. Such a language described processes but had little flexibility for accommodating the inevitable changes that occur in the course of a project. The team concluded that the individual components of a ship (motors, pumps, etc.) needed to be identified separately from the work tasks applied to them. Once this was done these component units (CUs) provided a convenient and consistent structure upon which all work could be planned, packaged, and executed, whatever the stage of production. [Luby, page 39]

Vision: *A statement of work that clearly identifies the tasks needed to achieve stakeholder requirements*

Mission: *To break the project down into manageable tasks that achieve stakeholder requirements*

Objective 8.3: To create a set of tasks that is detailed enough to allow the project to achieve stakeholder requirements

---

Approach 8.3: Given a list of deliverable systems that achieves stakeholder requirements, create a WBS node for each such system, and then break that node apart by applying the process models for processes required to produce the deliverable. Generate tasks from the process models to a level that reflects your current knowledge of the deliverable structure (rolling-wave planning). By the time you execute them, the tasks should reflect a predictable and controllable level of detail.

Metric 8.3: Level of Detail: a partially subjective, ordinal metric with values Too Much, Correct, Not Enough, None; None means you only know the deliverable, Not Enough means you have a set of tasks but not at a deep enough level to be able to estimate or control the tasks, Correct means you have a set of tasks that you can estimate and control, and Too Much means that you have too many tasks at too fine a level to control effectively (usually because you get bogged down in bookkeeping activities)

Target 8.3: Correct

Objective 8.4: To create a set of tasks that contribute a known amount of value to the project

---

Approach 8.4: Assign an appropriate value measure to each deliverable node (function points, monetary value, warranted equity value, or whatever kind of value is useful). Allocate the value across the tasks you generate from your process model, breaking it down to a level appropriate for control feedback (usually process milestones) and baselining it. Develop a weighting system that lets you compute a reasonable earned value at appropriate control milestones.

Metric 8.4: Baseline value ratio: the ratio of baselined value in the WBS to the total desired value of the project (an external project number determined by the business case)

Target 8.4: Within tolerance limits around 1; over time, within control limits of a p control chart of the ratio (changes should produce changes in value, but within control limits)

Objective 8.5: To create a set of tasks that you can use to create an effective schedule and budget with an appropriate level of risk

---

Approach 8.5: For each simple task (work package or level of effort), create a schedule task in the project schedule. Assign resources to the tasks. Estimate the effort for each simple task given the assigned resources. Create the project schedule by estimating schedule task start and end dates and durations. Create the project budget by estimating the cost of each task (or the appropriate higher level of the WBS for a larger project).

Metric 8.5.1: Schedule Risk: the total risk of mission failure of the project schedule

Metric 8.5.2: Budget Risk: the total risk of mission failure of the project budget

Target 8.5: A level of risk that (together with other sources of risk) is below the risk tolerance of the WBS, which the statement of work sets (ultimately, this comes from the risk tolerance of the project and project plan); this metric represents the level of confidence you have in the ability of the tasks in the WBS to produce the deliverables on time and under budget

---

The WBS is a versioned system that you baseline and change as the project progresses. For example, as you move from architectural to detailed design, you may change the basic structure of the system. This is the basis for *rolling-wave planning*. With this iterative planning style, you plan to a level that matches your current understanding of the project, keeping any processes you have not yet worked out at a high level. This of course results in higher risk for those parts of the project. To manage this risk, you put in place various risk management methods, such as reserves ("fudge factors"). As you iterate, you expand these parts of the WBS. You estimate costs and schedules. You eliminate risk through planning and knowledge acquisition. You then transfer the reserves or other risk controls into their appropriate form.

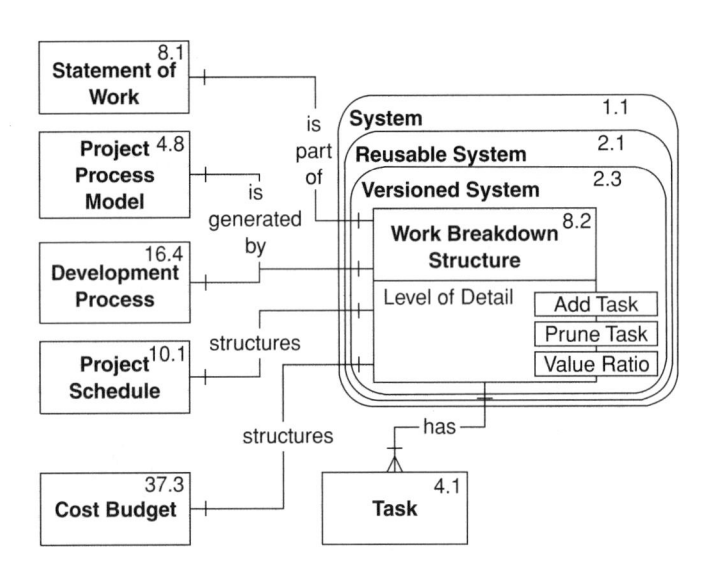

For example, I did a project to develop an OO parsing system for a database language. I was not sure what kind of query optimization I would need to handle the kinds of queries likely in an OO DBMS. My WBS contained a component called the *query optimizer*, but it had no detail, just a basic time estimate (a schedule reserve). As I developed the class hierarchy for the expression parsing and query representation attributes, I began to understand in some detail what kinds of structural and cost-based optimizations might be possible. I also spent some time doing a literature search and research into query optimization for relational, OO, and hybrid database managers. The combination of schedule reserve and increased knowledge let me work out a better plan for delivering the query optimizer. As it turned out, the task was too great for the deadline of the project. A full optimizer based on graph-theoretic analysis would be too much work. So, we revised the functional specification to include only minimal structural query optimization for the first release of the product (another method of risk control). I then revised the work breakdown structure to remove the optimization component and to include some tasks in the expression parser for representing basic query structure.

Iteration gives project managers headaches, particularly using project management software to represent WBSs and schedules. Most software now handles repetitive tasks such as weekly status meetings, but only if you can specify a scheduling period. Task iteration is much more difficult to handle, however, as it is not periodic in nature. The risk-based nature of rolling-wave WBS development lets you handle iteration directly. Each iteration on some result adds tasks to the WBS baseline, versioning the system. You can provide for a certain number of iterations or perhaps for cost or schedule reserves that you can allocate to any needed iterations. In any case, the focus on risk management gives you an immediate method for planning, feedback, and control of iterative, OO projects.

You can potentially reuse the WBS in multiple projects, but because the tasks are very domain dependent, this is difficult at best. You can break the project down to a relatively high level, and then keep that baseline as a reusable WBS in your reuse repository. When you plan a new project, you can start with this partially expanded WBS and specialize it to the specific deliverables. This strategy limits the domain dependencies in the reusable WBS by keeping the processes at a relatively high and innocuous level. Reuse also depends on the stability of the project processes across projects. If you change the process that generates the WBS, you will not be able to reuse a WBS generated with a prior version of the project process.

The section "An Outline of Planning with Processes" laid out the full planning scenario, which included the following steps within the WBS:

"An Outline of Planning with Processes" section, Chapter 4, p. 98

1. Generate the work breakdown structure (Figure 8-1).
    1.1. Generate a task in the work breakdown structure from each nondevelopment complex task model. These are complex tasks that represent the high-level processes for the project, not the processes that produce the deliverables.
    1.2. Generate a development task in the work breakdown structure for each deliverable system the statement of work identifies. This development task is the software development process for the deliverable, and you generate it from the appropriate type of development task model.

1.3. Generate a task in the work breakdown structure from each task model in the process for each complex task. This recursive process expands all the complex tasks and their processes into a hierarchical structure of tasks.

1.4. Baseline the initial version of the work breakdown structure. This represents the standard structure for the project.

2. Customize the work breakdown structure.

2.1. Examine each task in the work breakdown structure for relevance. If a task is not useful in the current project, remove it from the structure. As with any versioning work, you should add comments explaining why a standard task is not necessary.

2.2. Plan out each of the subsidiary project processes. This planning process generates any additional tasks, such as risk management tasks, quality assurance tasks, or communications tasks, including repeating meetings and reviews.

Figure 8-1
WBS generation and customization

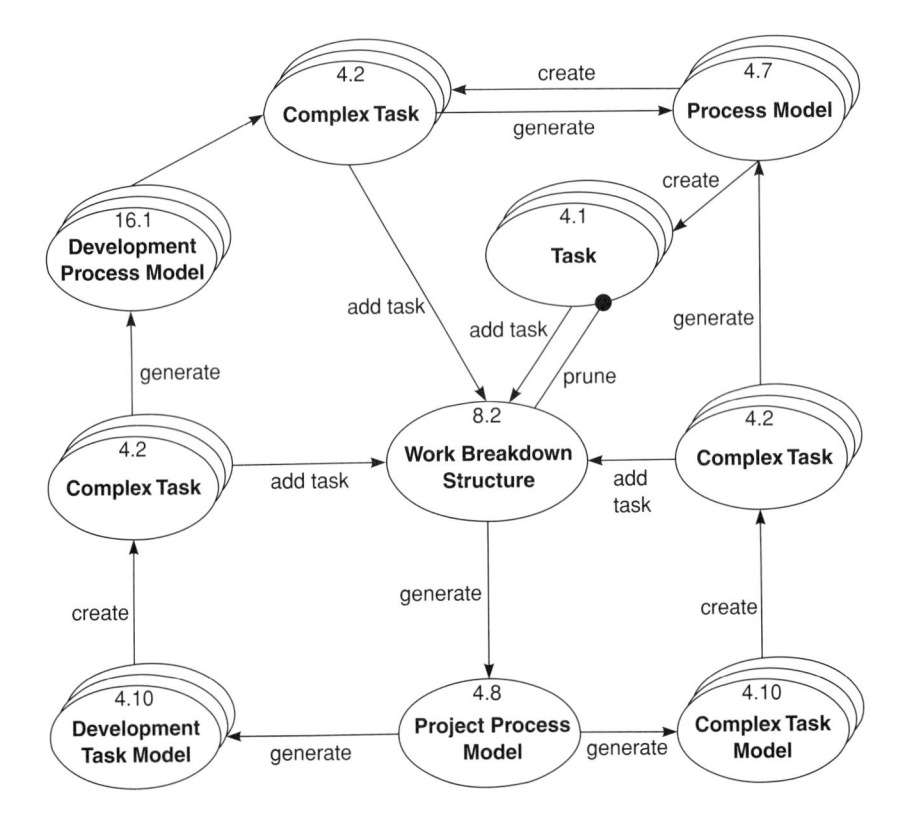

The top level of the WBS consists of the project deliverables and any project process tasks outside the deliverable production systems. The second level of the WBS consists of the complex processes through which the project delivers its deliverables. Each subsequent level of the WBS breaks down the complex tasks ultimately into simple tasks that produce the deliverables and the intermediate products that lead to them.

Each task in the WBS should have a unique identifying code, the *WBS code*. A standard format for this is <Project Abbreviation>-<Level 1 Number>.<Level 2 Number>....

As an example of an OO WBS, consider a project to develop a product that provides fault and failure tracking for software products (the Defect Tracking System, or DTS). This relatively small-scale system consists of an executable, a set of dynamic link libraries (DLLs), and a user manual. The project process uses a simple version of the recursive-parallel life cycle.

The top level of the initial WBS might look like this:

```
DTS-1 Analyze Feasibility
DTS-2 Plan
DTS-3 Develop DTS.EXE
DTS-4 Develop PERSON.DLL
DTS-5 Develop PRODUCT.DLL
DTS-6 Develop PROBLEM.DLL
DTS-7 Develop DTSTOOLS.DLL
DTS-8 Create User's Guide
```

The first two tasks, DTS-1 and DTS-2, are project-level tasks outside the deliverable structure. The rest of the tasks are the complete set of deliverables, including the user manual. Planning then applies the development process to DTS-3 through DTS-7 and the document creation process to DTS-8. The next level of DTS-4 might look like this:

```
DTS-4.1 Analyze Person Subsystem
DTS-4.2 Design Person Subsystem
DTS-4.3 Develop Employee Cluster
DTS-4.4 Develop Customer Cluster
```

The high-level architecture for the Person subsystem breaks the classes into Employee and Customer class hierarchies under the Person class. That much we know right now. Say, for example, the architect had an idea what the Customer cluster required but was uncertain about the scope of the Employee cluster. The DTS-4.3 breakdown might look like this:

```
DTS-4.3.1 Develop Employee Cluster
DTS-4.3.1.1 Analyze Employee Cluster
DTS-4.3.1.2 Design Employee Cluster
```

```
DTS-4.3.1.3 Code Employee Cluster
DTS-4.3.2 Redevelop Employee Cluster
DTS-4.3.1.1 Reanalyze Employee Cluster
DTS-4.3.1.2 Redesign Employee Cluster
DTS-4.3.1.3 Recode Employee Cluster
```

Together with the development team for this cluster, the project manager could allocate a reasonable amount of effort to these tasks. The DTS-4.3.2 task is an iteration that would apply knowledge gained from the DTS-4.3.1 task. It might also represent a development split that handles some dependency on another cluster. The first part could be everything that didn't depend on the other cluster, and the second part the rest. This structure increases parallelism and reduces the time to market (and the risk).

You might have noticed that there are no testing or documentation tasks in the WBS at this point. That's because, at least for this project, such tasks are risk management or quality assurance planning tasks. These come as part of the customization structure.

For example, QA planning might decide that recoding the employee cluster (DTS-4.3.1.3) would require a full-scale integration test. The cluster would then be ready for integration with higher-level clusters and subsystems. Perhaps there needs to be at least one iteration on integration testing. As well, risk management planning might determine that the employee design is risky. It should have a formal design document and review. Finally, the reuse planning process might add both an analysis document and a formal certification step. The revised portion of the DTS WBS might look like this:

```
DTS-4.3.1 Develop Employee Cluster
DTS-4.3.1.1 Analyze Employee Cluster
DTS-4.3.1.1.1 Document Analysis
DTS-4.3.1.1.2 Review Analysis Document
DTS-4.3.1.1.3 Revise and Review Analysis Document
DTS-4.3.1.2 Design Employee Cluster
DTS-4.3.1.1.1 Document Design
DTS-4.3.1.1.2 Review Design Document
DTS-4.3.1.1.3 Revise and Review Design Document
DTS-4.3.1.3 Code Employee Cluster
DTS-4.3.2 Redevelop Employee Cluster
DTS-4.3.1.1 Reanalyze Employee Cluster
DTS-4.3.1.2 Redesign Employee Cluster
DTS-4.3.1.3 Recode Employee Cluster
DTS-4.3.1.4 Integration Test Employee Cluster
DTS-4.3.1.5 Revise Employee Cluster
DTS-4.3.1.6 Integration Test Employee Cluster
DTS-4.3.1.7 Certify Reusable Employee Cluster
```

The Work Breakdown Structure

This example WBS is actually quite high-level compared to a real one. For example, the reviews (DTS-4.3.1.1.2, for example) are really complex processes in their own right. You first need to produce and distribute the review materials. Then you need to schedule the review and acquire its resources (meeting room, LCD projector, and so on). Next you conduct the review. Then you distribute the approved minutes of the review. The level of detail depends entirely on your needs in controlling the project.

- *Note:* For very large projects, it is usually not useful to have even this level of detail in your WBS. Instead, you develop only the very high-level processes for each subsystem. Represent the lower-level tasks as aggregations. You control the project through tracking statistics on aggregate task completion and value creation rather than individual tasks. As with any large system, you create lower-level structures to handle the lower-level details (subprojects, for example).

You can also prune standard tasks from the WBS. Consider the User's Guide, for example. Say the standard process contained a step for creating online text from your desktop publishing system. Perhaps your marketing department has decided for various value-related reasons (to be charitable) not to include online material with the product. You could prune this standard task from the WBS even though policy requires it. This exception might or might not require some kind of stakeholder approval.

Once you generate it, the WBS becomes the most important element of your project plan. Virtually everything else in the plan depends on this list of tasks: the project schedule, the budget, and the iterative planning that you will do as you execute the project. Starting from a firm, well-developed base is essential to good planning.

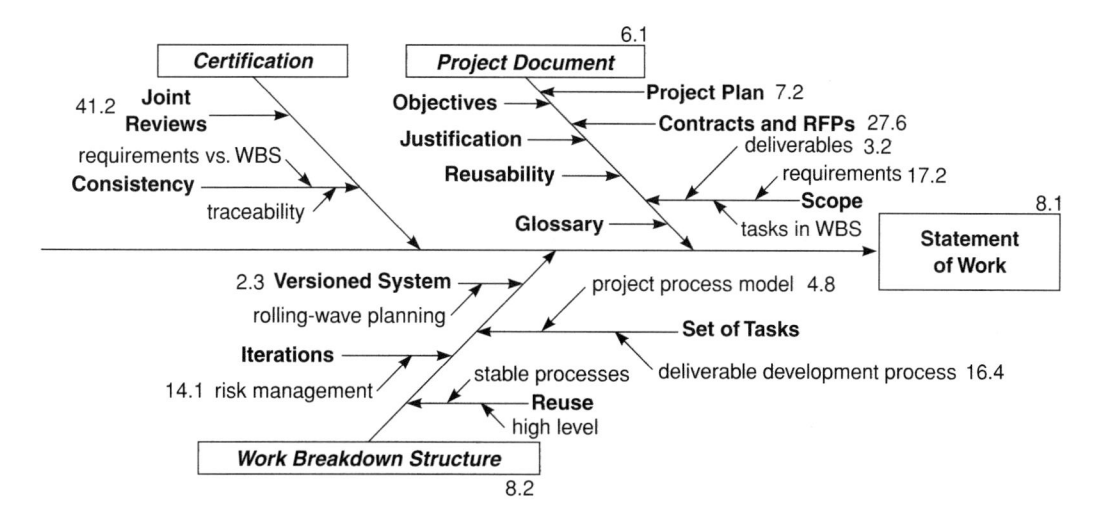

Readings

[Katz] Barry Katz and Naftali Lerman. Building a three-dimensional work breakdown structure. *Data Base* (Summer 1985): 14–17.

An old but fascinating article describing a three-dimensional structure for the software WBS. The three dimensions are project phase, software architecture component, and output. Each WBS item is thus a combination of process element, software element, and deliverable. It also provides a value-based metric for measuring progress. Much of my thinking about the WBS system started with this seminal article.

[Kerzner] Harold Kerzner. *Project Management: A Systems Approach to Planning, Scheduling, and Controlling, Fifth Edition.* New York: Van Nostrand Reinhold, 1994.

Section 11.7 of Kerzner's book deals specifically with the statement of work. He quotes extensively from the NASA guidelines for the SOW and demonstrates how complex the process can be if you try. Section 11.10 deals with the WBS, although in a rather confusing manner. Kerzner considers the WBS as primarily a structure for cost accounting, though he notes you also use it as the basis for almost every aspect of planning and control.

[Luby] Robert E. Luby, Douglas Peel, and William Swahl. Component-based work breakdown structure (CBWBS). *Project Management Journal* (December 1995): 38–43.

This article is an interesting case study of a WBS scheme organized around deliverable systems. The article develops a WBS grammar able to describe the characteristics of any industrial process, providing a strong theoretical basis for a WBS-based project management system.

[PMI 1996a] Project Management Institute Standards Committee. *A Guide to the Project Management Body of Knowledge.* Project Management Institute (+1-610-734-3330), 1996.

The Body of Knowledge sees the statement of work, specifically, as the procurement specification. It defines a separate scope statement for the main definition of project requirements. Both sections are very relevant to the material presented here, however.

[Wilson] David N. Wilson and Mark J. Sifer. Structured planning—project views. In [Reifer], pages 187–193. Originally published in *Software Engineering Journal* 3:4 (July 1988): 134–140.

A short paper that outlines a model of project management, including a strong model of the work breakdown structure. The model applies "structured design" techniques to modeling the project system, much as this book applies "object design" methods. For the WBS, this translates into a top-down partitioning scheme based on life-cycle phases. Reading this article in conjunction with the present book shows the same paradigmatic differences that you find between developing functional software and developing OO software. The WBS that results from structured planning follows closely the structure of the life cycle you choose. The WBS that results from object planning follows closely the structure of the system(s) you deliver. The rest of the paper contains a work-flow model that integrates with the WBS to provide complete project-planning capabilities.

Questions to Think About

1. How have projects with which you've been involved related requirements and tasks? Was the relationship implicit or explicit? Can you think of negative and positive consequences of the choice?

2. How else might a project communicate the work to do to stakeholders and contractors?

3. Name three different ways of organizing the tasks in a project. What are the advantages and disadvantages of each method? How does each method relate tasks to processes and process models? schedule? budget?

4. What is the impact of project size on the WBS structure? Is it a linear or nonlinear relationship between project size and WBS complexity? Why?

5. Suggest some other kinds of WBS coding schemes that you might find useful. Justify them by impact on other elements of the project.

6. Do you think some kind of automated iteration support in your project management system would be helpful? Why or why not? What would be the impact on risk management? control of the project tasks? planning productivity?

CHAPTER

9 *Quality Management*

Quality in OO software development is particularly rewarding. The structure of OO projects lends itself well to effective quality management. OO quality management is so interesting, it's worth a whole book in itself. This chapter summarizes that book [Siegel] and connects the quality management subsystem to the project management subsystem.

■ *Note:* Siegel's book uses the same systems approach that this book uses, and this book fits with Siegel's book like a hand in a glove. If you're interested in quality, you should have Siegel's book as well as this one.

OO quality management is very different from the quality management you find in earlier technologies. The focus is much more on object and integration testing and less on system testing. Instead of waiting until the end of the project, you take advantage of the iterative, incremental development of clusters and of reuse to build tested, safe platforms for development. When you get the whole system to test, everything's already been thoroughly certified; all you need to do is test the system as a whole in a real-world context to judge whether it satisfies its requirements, performs well, and works in the required configurations.

The Quality Management Plan

The *quality management plan* is a component plan of the project plan. It contains the set of test plans for the software system. It applies the quality process model to the deliverables to produce plans for assuring the quality of those deliverables through a quality process. That process is a risk management method that addresses the technical risk of the deliverable. The quality management plan also

The Quality Management Plan

includes the preventive measures and improvement plans you will undertake to prevent the risky events from occurring. Tests and reviews find problems; other risk management methods and improvement plans prevent them.

Risk Management Method (14.2)

Improvement Plan (1.3)

Each test plan includes a quality approach and a test model for its target, the *system under test*. Depending on the level of detail in your test plans, you can either include them directly in the project plan or refer to them from that plan.

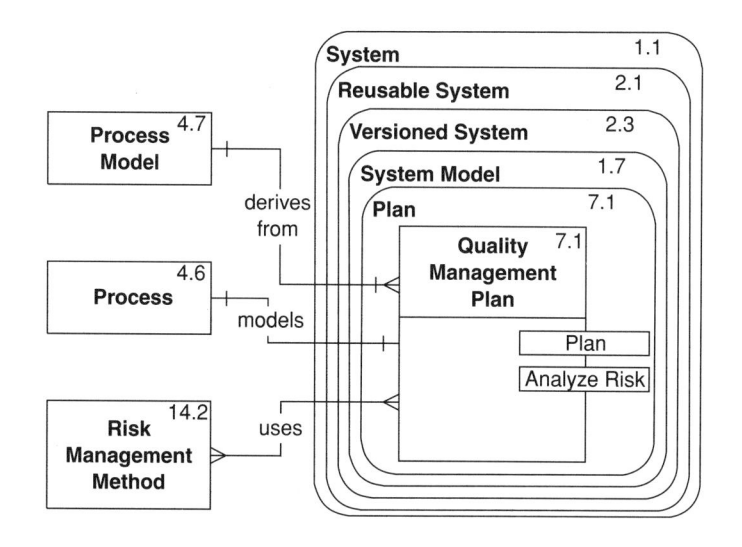

Vision: A contract with stakeholders to provide assured value through the project's ability to achieve its mission successfully

Mission: To reduce technical risk below the project tolerance for such risk

---

Objective 9.1: To specify risk management methods and the tasks that implement them to reduce technical risks for a deliverable

---

Objective 9.2: To provide a mechanism for accommodating change in a quality process

---

- *Note:* The metric and target for Objectives 9.1 and 9.2 are the same as for the Plan class Objectives 7.1 and 7.2. Only the specific type of processes measured changes.

Usually, the set of test plans mirrors the system architecture. As you iterate through your project, you expand your WBS with additional clusters and systems.

You also add test plans to the quality management plan. You then generate new tasks in the WBS from the quality assurance process models that apply through the test plan. A lower or higher risk tolerance may permit you to limit testing. Double-check your risk evaluation with a review, as this should happen very seldom.

On a relatively complex OO project with many facets, the project manager decided that due to a relatively high level of risk tolerance and a low impact for failure, we would not need to test certain elements of the system. He got away with it. I'm still not sure whether this indicated that the components in question were irrelevant or just very well programmed.

Conversely, I managed several projects with a QA manager who was highly risk averse. She wanted to test everything, no matter what. Her QA process model required absolute delivery of all materials by alpha release. That meant, for example, that the online documentation needed to be on the alpha release directory in testable form, as she insisted on testing it as part of alpha acceptance testing. The result was dislocation in the other processes. To deliver online documentation, the technical writers needed complete documents two weeks before delivery. That meant that they needed to have their documents complete two weeks *before* the software. Stakeholders, and particularly the corporate executives, could never understand why I claimed that, for us, online documentation made the process slower. I could produce better, faster printed documentation than online, given this process model, because we didn't have to print by alpha release. This situation shows the need to evaluate risk tolerance on a collective level, not in isolated processes. Systems interact, and a simple thing in your process may lead to complex things in other processes.

The Quality Assurance Process Model and Process

The ISO-12207 standard [ISO 1995] identifies several quality-related processes as "supporting" processes: quality assurance, verification, validation, joint review, auditing, and problem resolution. These quality-related processes are all part of a larger life cycle of quality management that starts with market research and ends with product disposal. The ISO-9000 standards also provide a comprehensive approach to quality systems and life cycles.

External Standard (33.2)

The *quality assurance process* assures stakeholders that the deliverables and processes of the project conform to requirements and standards. Quality assurance consists of *product assurance, process assurance,* and *system assurance,* all in line with ISO-9000 requirements. The *verification process* determines whether the outputs of a task satisfy the requirements imposed by previous activities (verifying code against design, design against requirements, and so on). The *validation process* determines whether a system meets its expectations ("requirements for intended use"). Both of these processes produce a *quality evaluation document* that analyzes process results and measurements of quality criteria for success. The *joint review process* is a meeting to review a document or software object. The *audit process* lets internal or external auditors assess the processes and their deliverables for compliance with plans and requirements. Audits identify successes and failures in a systematic review of any or all project processes. This audit process provides feedback to planning that enables you to improve processes for the next project or process iteration. Auditing is a central feature of the improvement plan. It also ensures compliance with your quality policies, which in turn assures you that your policy decisions are having their intended effects.

Joint Review (41.2)
Improvement Plan (1.3)

- *Note:* Problem resolution is outside the scope of project management. It is a part of ongoing operations.

The quality assurance process for a particular deliverable executes the quality plan you derive from the quality process model. Tasks you add to the WBS as a consequence monitor the results of other processes to determine whether they comply with quality standards. The quality plan is also the source for most improvement plans. For an OO project, the quality assurance process mirrors the development process.

The Test Plan

The *test plan* for a system contains the quality approach for that system and the quality models and test cases you base on that quality approach. Your first step is to identify the systems that you want to test through the risk management plan. You need to test—that is, evaluate the quality of the system—if the risk of failure exceeds the system's risk tolerance, and you have some kind of evaluative test as a potential risk management method.

Risk Management Plan (14.1)
Risk (12.1)
Risk Management Method (14.2)

You develop test plans as part of the quality management plan. As you develop the test plan, you insert the testing tasks into the WBS through plan process generation. As the project progresses, the test plans become increasingly complete through iteration and incremental extension. You may discover new risks that require additional tests for systems that did not have them before. You add these risks to the risk management plan. You then create additional test plans in the quality management plan and through that add tasks to the WBS.

Quality Management Plan (9.1)
Task Model (4.9)
Work Breakdown Structure (8.2)

When you reach the baseline delivery milestone for the system, your test models should be complete enough to serve as the basis for the review, test scripts, or whatever specific technique the plan calls for to evaluate the system. The WBS tasks then undertake the evaluation and produce the test results, evaluating the deliverable system through its quality criteria.

The Quality Approach

The *quality approach* is the particular scheme you intend to use to model a software system for quality evaluation. Most people will assume that "testing" means running the executable code for a software system or cluster. That's a very limited definition. The quality approach includes any method or tool for evaluating the quality of a system—any system. There are many systems, such as design documents or requirements documents, that you cannot test with software, so you use review methods to evaluate them.

Joint Review (41.2)

Testing executable code has its own specific test methods. Often when programmers approach testing, they test the code, and the quality criteria are things like *code coverage:* the number of statements exercised over the total number of executable statements in a module. This approach to code testing has only one limitation—it doesn't work.

Testing a program is somewhere between a science and an art form, probably leaning more toward the latter. The state of the art is, however, much beyond simple code coverage. *Branch coverage,* for example, requires a simple understanding of the control flow of a block of code. The usual coverage criterion is to test each path through the control network at least once. The more complex the code, the more testing it requires. The difference between testing the code and testing the logic is the introduction of an intermediate system model: the test model. This model represents the things of interest to the tester, not the programmer: the branches, for example, rather than the simple statements. The test model models the actual code (or other structure, such as inheritance hierarchy or object relationships). Figure 9-1 shows the relationships between some of the different quality system objects.

OO systems introduce various relationships into the testing cauldron, including inheritance, containment, clusters and subsystems, and object interaction. The standard quality methods work for OO systems, but you can usually do better by taking the OO structures into account. You should concentrate your efforts on requirements and design reviews and object and integration testing for several reasons. First, because of the iterative and recursive nature of OO development, testing each component requires such reviews and testing, not system testing. A cluster is not a software system, and system test methods don't apply. Second, each level of the system builds on the components you've already developed. The risk reduction you get from testing objects and the integration of components also reduces risk in the rest of the development process. Third, reuse—whether external or internal—requires certification, not system testing. If you concentrate on system tests, you are almost certainly not certifying reusable components at the right level.

The Test Plan 159

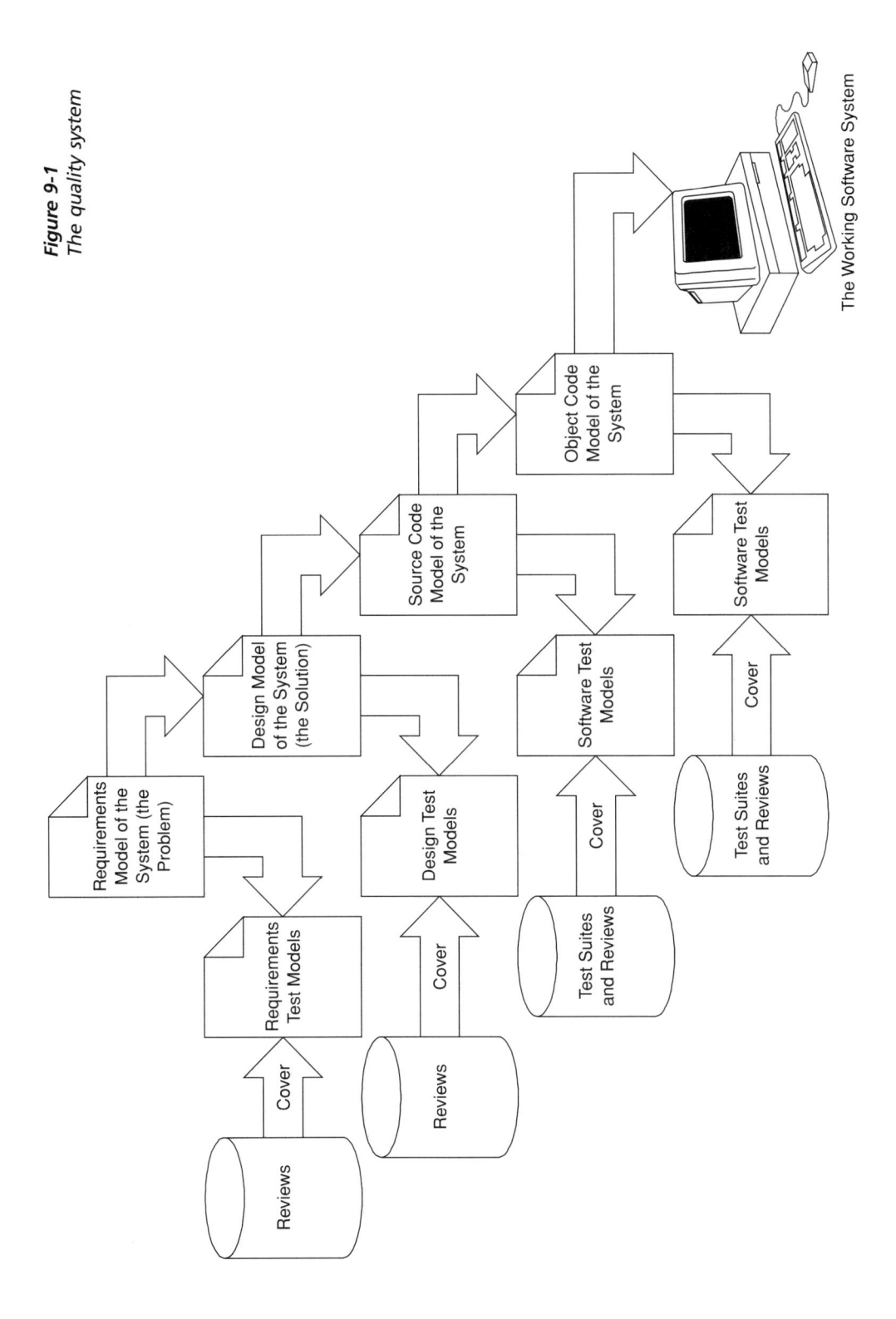

Figure 9-1
The quality system

From another perspective, reuse also introduces decision points into your quality planning. When you reuse components, such as external ActiveX controls or Java applets, in your system, you need to look at their reuse certification to decide whether to test them as systems. If the certification is satisfactory, there is no need to test. If there is no certification, test thoroughly. On the supplier side, if you are supplying a reusable system, your certification process should contain the appropriate quality measures that reusers will want to see.

There are usually several kinds of test model that you can apply to a system. The quality approach specifies the models you intend to use in this instance. The approach also specifies the *quality criteria,* the metrics and targets you use to judge whether a quality suite has successfully verified the system (branch coverage, for example). The quality approach may refer to a policy for the project containing test modeling standards.

The Test Model, Test Case, and Test Suite

The *test model* is a representation of a system using a modeling technology suitable for producing review documents, test cases, and test scripts. The *review document* is a project document that presents information about the system structured for quality review. The *test case* is a particular configuration of the model, such as a single path through a control-flow or state-transition graph. The *test script* is a software object that applies the test case to the software object as part of a *test suite,* a collection of test scripts. All of these objects exist in the quality repository. Figure 9-2 shows the relationships among the four objects for a software object, for example.

Table 9-1 lists the several classes of test suite or review document.

Table 9-1 The Test Suite Classes [Siegel]

Test Suite	Description
Object	A kind of test suite that tests test cases from some kind of single-class test model
Conditional	A kind of object test suite that tests test cases from test models of specific conditions in a class
Hierarchical-Incremental	A kind of object test suite that tests test cases from test models of some part of a class in the context of a class hierarchy
Integration	A kind of test suite that tests test cases from test models of a cluster of multiple interacting classes
Functional	A kind of integration test suite that tests functional integration (vertical integration) of a cluster; usually a review document
Abstraction	A kind of integration test suite that tests abstraction integration (horizontal integration) of a cluster; usually a review document
System	A kind of test suite that tests cases from test models of a system rather than a cluster

Table 9-1 The Test Suite Classes [Siegel] (continued)

Test Suite	Description
Validation	A kind of system test suite that tests whether a system fulfills its requirements
Acceptance	A kind of system validation test suite that is a contractual requirement for accepting delivery of procured software
Verification	A kind of system test that tests whether a system implementation performs to an acceptable level of risk
Capability	A kind of verification test that tests specific capabilities of a product
Performance	A kind of capability test suite that tests the performance capabilities of a product
Configuration	A kind of capability test suite that tests the ability of the system to perform on target hardware and software configurations
Installation	A kind of configuration test suite that tests the ability to install the system on target hardware and software configurations
Field	A kind of configuration test suite that tests the ability of the software to function under target conditions in the field
Regression	A collection of previously run test scripts and test reports, usually a kind of integration or system test suite

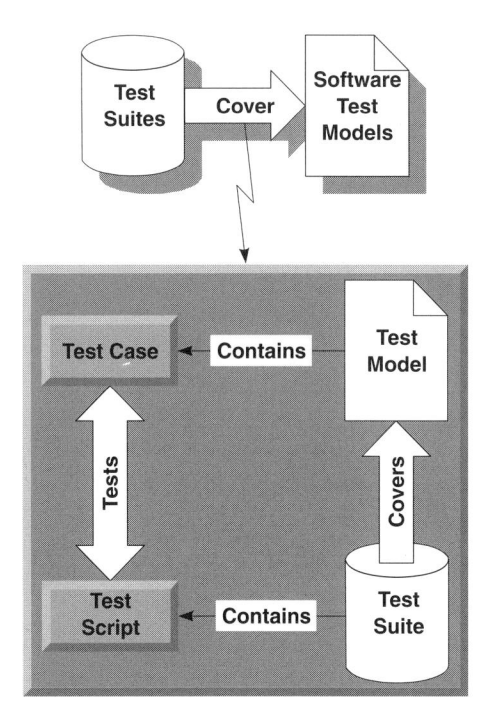

Figure 9-2
Quality approach relationships

The Quality Environment

The *quality environment* contains the policies, repository, and tools that the quality processes use. The quality environment is a reusable system. It is part of the general project environment that multiple projects share, so each project has access to the reusable components from the environment.

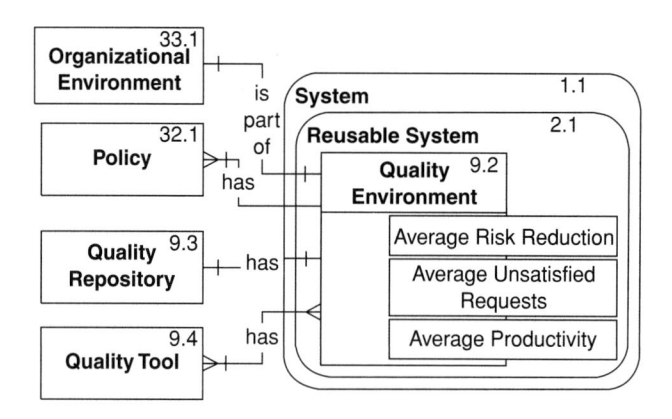

Vision: *A set of valuable, low-risk project deliverables that satisfy stakeholder expectations*

Mission: *To provide the infrastructure that allows quality processes to achieve their missions*

Objective 9.3: To ensure that all projects achieve a certain level of risk

---

Approach 9.3: Create a set of quality policies that standardize the application of quality processes to projects.

Metric 9.3: Average Risk Reduction: the cross-project average difference in risk between systems to which you apply the policies and the equivalent systems with the policies not enforced

Target 9.3: A significantly negative average difference between the control limits of an x-R control chart

---

Objective 9.4: To ensure that cross-project quality data is available for systems either for reuse or for improvement plans

---

Approach 9.4: Create a quality repository for test data, test results, and quality statistics.

The Quality Environment 163

Metric 9.4: Average number of unsatisfied requests for quality-related data

Target 9.4: A low count within control limits of a pn control chart

---

Objective 9.5: To ensure that each project has effective and efficient tools for implementing standard quality processes

---

Approach 9.5: Acquire and maintain a set of quality tools, including test frameworks, test tools, and quality management tools for use in all projects.

Metric 9.5: Average productivity of quality processes

Target 9.5: A value within control limits of an x-R control chart

---

Quality Repository

The quality repository contains the test suites, test data, and test results for a project. Each project may keep a separate repository, or several projects may store their information together. The repository may be a single database accessible with a standard set of tools, or it may be different databases and file directories. As all these systems are versioned systems, the change management system tracks the changes to them.

The quality repository is usually also the place you keep information about failures and faults in the software systems, the ubiquitous bug database. This works together with the product repository to let you track and control problems in your products.

Product Respository (18.2)

Product Management System (22.3)

Quality Tools

There are many different kinds of quality tools. Here I focus on three particular kinds: the statistical process control tool set, the testing framework, and test modeling and scripting tools.

Statistical Process Control Tools

The *statistical process control tools* are charts and analysis systems that you use in improvement plans to identify and resolve quality problems. The main set of these tools in their current format has been around for decades [Arthur; Beauregard; Ishikawa; Ozeki]. Table 9-2 lists the several tools and describes them.

The control chart is the tool most of interest in this book, as several classes use it to define the targets for their objectives. Table 9-3 lists the different kinds of control charts.

Table 9-2 The Statistical Process Control Tools

Tool	Description
Checksheet	A simple form that lets you collect counts and other data about processes, either manually or automatically
Pareto Chart	A bar chart, where the bars represent interesting categories such as clusters or classes and the numeric dimension represents the control variable, such as effort, cost, number of defects, and so on; the bars are sorted on the control variable, so the category that contributes most to it is obvious, as are the diminishing returns to the other categories
Ishikawa Diagram	A fishbone chart; the summary diagrams in this book are Ishikawa diagrams; mostly used to analyze the causes of a problem, but also the organization of a process or other system
Line Graph	A two-dimensional graph that relates two variables with a line connecting the data points, usually time and some other control variable such as cost, effort, number of defects, and so on; used to show trends and other relationships between the variables
Scatter Diagram	A two-dimensional graph that relates to variables as a set of points in the joint space; used to distinguish relationships between the variables
Pie Chart	A circle divided to show the contribution of several parts to a whole, with the slices of the pie being categories and the size of each slice being that category's contribution to the control total, whatever it might be
Histogram	Bar chart that shows the distribution of control data, relating two variables; the Pareto chart is a special case of the bar chart, ordered by the control data
Control Chart	A chart of aggregate values divided into groups that shows how the average and variance of the groups vary; control limits come from statistical formulas that depend on the particular type of control variable
Flowchart	A standard method for visualizing processes

Table 9-3 Control Charts

Chart	Application
x-R	Mean or median and range; charts measured dimensions on a ratio or interval scale
x	Values; charts individual data elements instead of groups for hard-to-measure or costly data
pn	Counts; charts the number of control items in fixed-size samples
p	Percents or ratios; charts the fraction of items to some total control set in samples of varying size
c	Counts; charts the number of control items in a specific unit over a specific period of time
u	Count per unit area; charts number of control items in a varying-size unit over a specific period of time

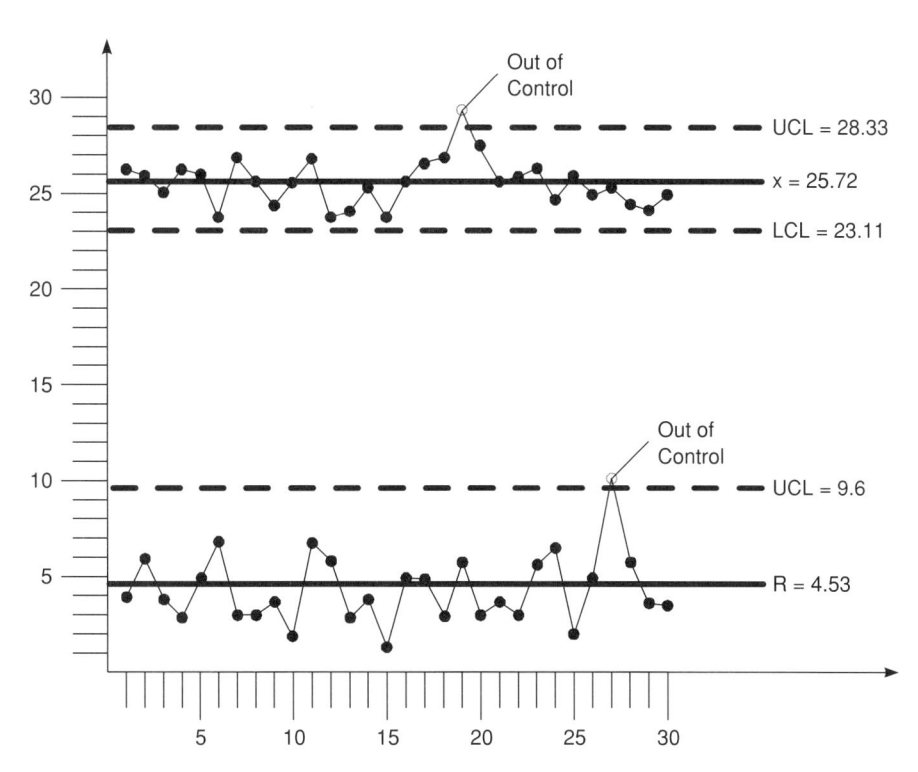

Figure 9-3
x-R control chart

Figure 9-3 is an x-R control chart that graphs the mean and range of a control item such as effort or productivity. The top line shows the mean, while the bottom line shows the range. Each data point is the mean or range of a group of measurements. That is, you take a sample of, say, five measures of effort, and take the mean and range of that group. Keeping the groups in a fixed size and making sure they are as random as possible is a good idea. The solid line is the mean of the means or the mean of the ranges. The broken lines are the upper and lower control limits, computed as some number of standard deviations from the mean of the mean or range. Using these limits, you can identify processes that are not in control by finding means and ranges that extend beyond the control limits [Beauregard; Ishikawa; Ozeki].

Figure 9-4 is a pn control chart. You use pn control charts to chart data on the absolute scale, the scale of counts. Number of defects, for example, is a classic application of pn control charts. These charts require a fixed sample size for the control groups. Each data point in Figure 9-4 represents the count of things in the control group. The center line is the mean of these counts over the set of groups. The control limits represent some number of standard deviations from the mean. Usually, there is no lower limit, as it would be negative.

Figure 9-4
pn control chart

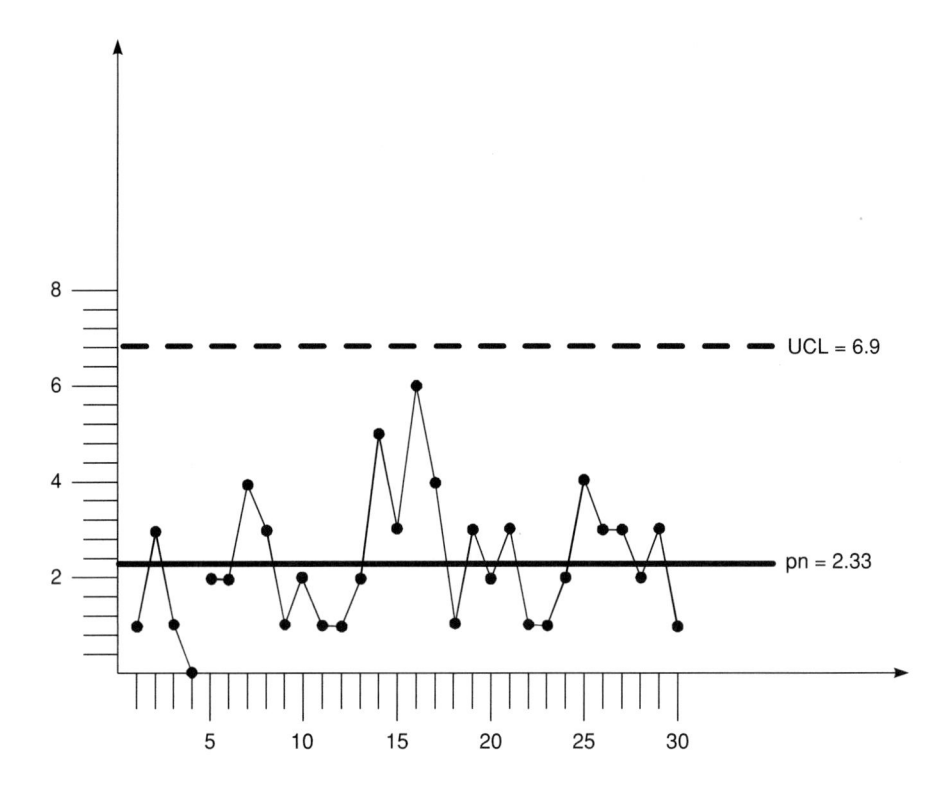

[Chart showing pn control chart with UCL = 6.9 and pn = 2.33]

Figure 9-5 is a p control chart. This lets you chart ratios, rates, and similar data you derive from counts using varying sample sizes. You group the data and calculate the ratio or rate for the group. For example, in a group of three clusters, you might have 20 defects for a defect rate of 6.67. That would be the data item for that group of clusters. The closer you come to a fixed size, the better. In Figure 9-5, the data is the rate for each group, and the center line is the mean of the ratios. A major difference in this control chart is that each group has its own control limit, which you calculate as some number of standard deviations within the group data. Again, the lower control limit may be negative and thus irrelevant.

Testing Frameworks

A *test framework* is an automated testing tool that lets a software or quality assurance developer test a software system. As most OO programs are compiled, this usually translates into some kind of program framework that adds code to the software.

The architecture of test frameworks depends on the features of the OO language you are using. One common architecture is the parallel-class architecture, which declares a test class for each system class. There are two criticisms of this approach. First, it doesn't address higher-level systems such as clusters, subsystems,

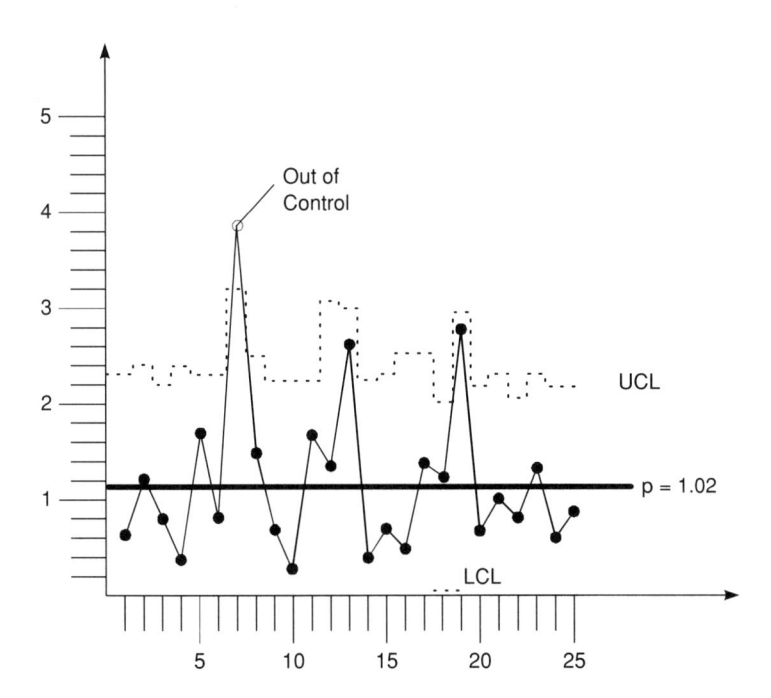

Figure 9-5
p control chart

and systems, providing no help in integration testing. Second, it produces a tremendous amount of code, which in turn adds a tremendous amount of work to the project. Depending on your system, this may or may not be productive. A key metric for a test framework is testing productivity: the number of failures per effort-hour of testing.

An alternative architecture is the invasive approach, in which you add test code to the classes (and other systems) themselves. Often, this takes the form of assertions, conditional statements in the code that fail if there is a problem. You can encapsulate test code through a separate, reusable test-driver system. Alternatively, you can use reusable test data in your quality repository to drive the testing process. Again, the architecture and language of your system often determines the most productive approach.

Test Modeling and Scripting Tools

A visual programming environment is fine for developing code, but not so great for developing test models, test cases, test scripts, and test suites. Given a test framework integrated into your programming environment, you can at least automate running your test scripts. That doesn't help you create them, however.

There is a whole range of test modeling tools that help you understand what you need to test in a system.

At the highest level, you can use CASE tools such as Rational Rose or Software through Pictures to represent high- and low-level designs, which you test through design reviews. There are even requirements modeling tools coming on the market that expand the inspection approach to the requirements analysis process. Most serious CASE environments have repositories and consistency checking tools that let you verify the consistency of a design, and most interface to desktop publishing systems to permit easy generation of documentation for review.

At the implementation level, there are several tools on the market, such as the T tool from Aionix, that analyze code to produce test models and even test cases, measuring coverage as they go. These tools are not cheap, but if they fit your specific coding model, they can save developers much time in object and integration testing.

For user interfaces, there are several graphical user interface (GUI) testing tools on the market. These tools permit you to record test scripts in your quality repository, and then play them back in regression tests. They permit you to develop highly reusable test scripts for GUI-based systems.

For system testing, many of the same companies that produce GUI testing tools also produce tools to analyze and test performance, particularly for client/server OO systems. The various combinations of CORBA, DCOM, network technology, and "distributed objects everywhere" will increasingly make these testing tools a necessity [Lewis].

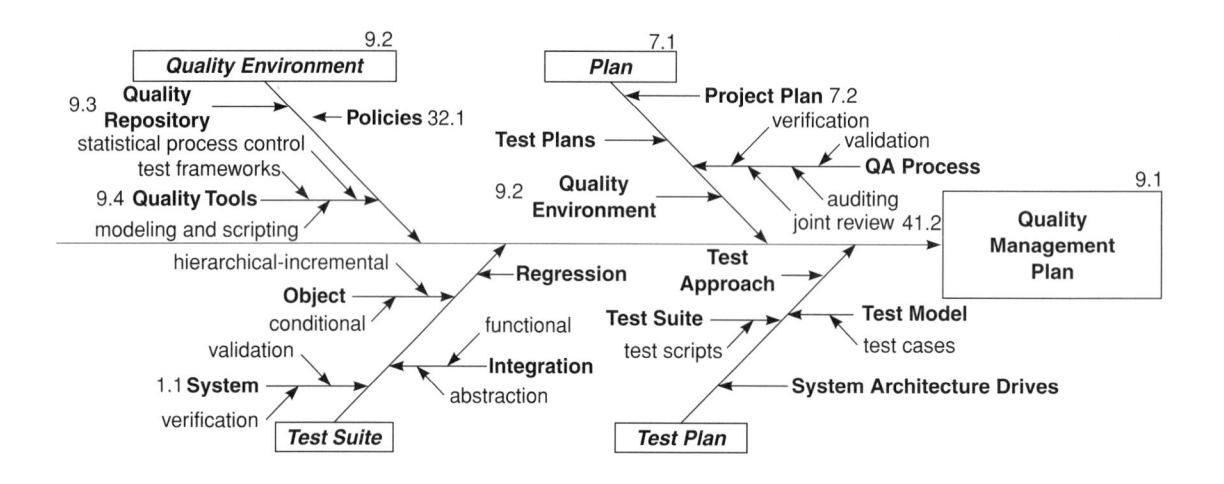

Readings

[Arthur] Lowell Jay Arthur. *Improving Software Quality: An Insider's Guide to TQM.* New York: Wiley, 1993.

This is the best all-around book on the application of Total Quality Management (TQM) methods to the software industry. While the present book goes much more into detail on the applications of process improvement, Arthur's book has a lot of detail on the tools and techniques themselves.

[Beauregard] Michael R. Beauregard, Raymond J. Mikulak, and Barbara A. Olson. *A Practical Guide to Statistical Quality Improvement: Opening Up the Statistical Toolbox.* New York: Van Nostrand Reinhold, 1992.

This is a rather advanced textbook for students and researchers in the area of statistical process control. It contains all the tools and all the statistical theory on which they are based. The references in this book are particularly useful for understanding the mathematical and practical underpinnings of statistical process control.

[Ishikawa] Kaoru Ishikawa. *Guide to Quality Control.* Asian Productivity Organization, 1976 (available through UNIPUB, 800-521-8110).

A guide to statistical process control tools written for shop supervisors, this book has the benefits and flaws of extreme simplicity. It explains how to use the tools, but it does not give you the statistical detail to develop a real understanding of them. Nevertheless, this is a very useful book to have for reference or training.

[ISO 1991] International Standards Organization. *ISO 9000-3, Guideline for Application of ISO 9001 to the Development, Supply, and Maintenance of Software.* ISO, 1991.

[ISO 1995] International Standards Organization. *ISO/IEC 12207, Information Technology—Software Life Cycle Processes.* ISO, 1995.

These two ISO standards are the most important standards for quality processes in software. Both tend to focus on process quality rather than on product quality, but the general organization and techniques in the standards are broadly applicable to both types of quality assurance.

[Ozeki] Kazuo Ozeki and Tetsuichi Asaka, editors. *Handbook of Quality Tools: The Japanese Approach.* Cambridge, MA: Productivity Press, (+1-617-497-5146), 1990.

This is an intermediate-level textbook for managers who need to understand the details and context of the statistical process control tools. It provides step-by-step instructions for a truly impressive array of tools. It also explains the basic statistics behind those tools and gives you the management and organizational context behind their use. This is a very useful book if you are using these tools on a daily or weekly basis.

[Siegel] Shel Siegel with contributions by Robert J. Muller. *Object-Oriented Software Testing: A Hierarchical Approach.* New York: Wiley, 1996.

This book originated the approach the current book takes of developing management processes using OO methods. The material in the current chapter derives from the work done in this book, filtered through my own systems and total quality thinking. The current book also has a more elaborate model for reuse of quality systems than the Siegel book. Any project manager who wants to understand the full scope of quality management for OO systems should own this book. It goes into detail on the different testing models and test criteria, focusing on adapting everything to OO systems. It also contains references to the most important books and articles relevant to managing and implementing OO software quality.

Questions to Think About

1. Under what circumstances would you eliminate quality assurance processes for a deliverable?

2. How closely should the quality assurance team work with the development team? Should they be completely separate teams, one and the same, or something in between?

3. How do you set your testing criteria right now? Are such criteria at all related to your risk assessment for a deliverable? Why or why not?

4. Why do you think that statement coverage is not sufficient to test a class?

5. How do you think you can take advantage of inheritance in testing? What are the implications of inheritance for testing a specific subclass? Do you need to retest all of the methods of the class and its parents?

6. What are the implications of code reuse for testing? (Hint: Think about both sides of the question, the impact on producing new code for reuse and the impact of reusing certified code.)

7. What is the relationship of certification of reusable components to quality assurance? (Hint: It's not just testing.)

PART FOUR

Schedule

Remember, that time is money.

Benjamin Franklin, *Advice to Young Tradesman,* 1748

The schedule is at the center of project management because time is money. The amount of money spent on scheduling in projects probably exceeds the total value of those projects. While not gainsaying the importance of the schedule, as a set of classes, it does not occupy much space. Keeping your schedule simple is one of the ways you can increase your productivity and ability to respond to change.

The schedule, a kind of plan, organizes your work along the dimension of time and links tasks and milestones with work-flow dependencies. You build the schedule from WBS tasks and baseline it. This provides the key baselines for computing earned value in your project. You display the schedule in any of a variety of time and dependency charts, both to communicate it to others and to organize your thinking.

The schedule task encapsulates the simple tasks of the project, those involving real work. The separation of work-related task from date-related task makes various relationships easier to understand.

Duration is a complex object, encompassing a time interval and various kinds of relative calendar calculations.

The dependency is a versioned system that represents work flow in the project. The dependency links between tasks and milestones let you build the schedule network that is at the center of technical project management.

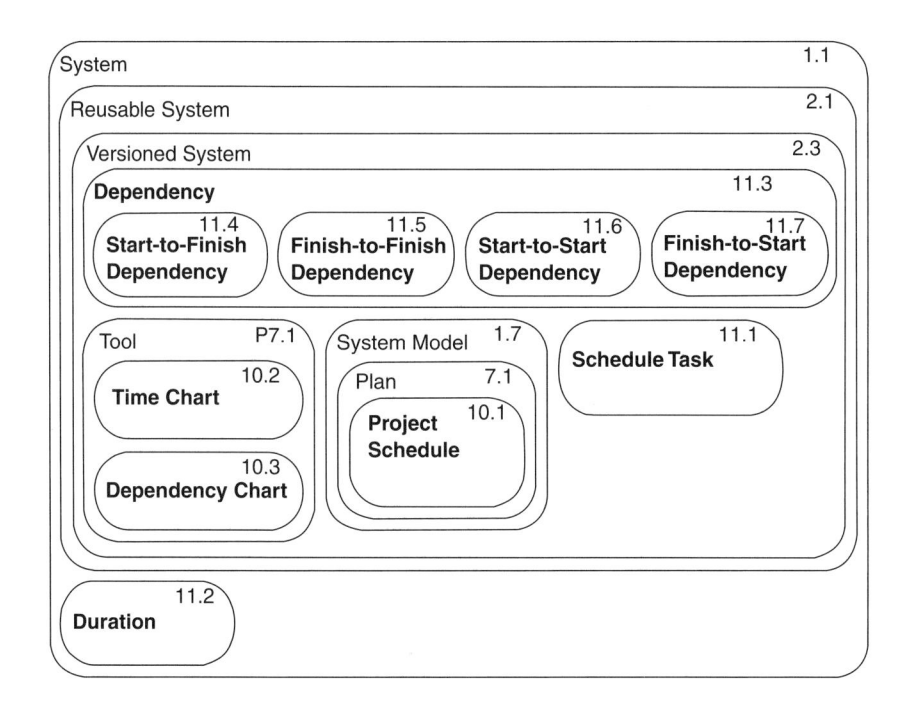

```
┌─ System ─────────────────────────────────────────────── 1.1 ──┐
│ ┌─ Reusable System ──────────────────────────────── 2.1 ──┐  │
│ │ ┌─ Versioned System ─────────────────────────── 2.3 ──┐ │  │
│ │ │ ┌─ Dependency ───────────────────────── 11.3 ─────┐ │ │  │
│ │ │ │   11.4          11.5          11.6        11.7 │ │ │  │
│ │ │ │ Start-to-Finish Finish-to-Finish Start-to-Start Finish-to-Start │
│ │ │ │ Dependency    Dependency    Dependency  Dependency │
│ │ │ └───────────────────────────────────────────────┘ │ │  │
│ │ │ ┌─ Tool ──── P7.1 ─┐ ┌─ System Model ── 1.7 ─┐      │ │  │
│ │ │ │         10.2     │ │ ┌─ Plan ──── 7.1 ─┐    │  11.1│ │  │
│ │ │ │ Time Chart       │ │ │        10.1    │    │ Schedule Task │
│ │ │ │         10.3     │ │ │ Project        │    │      │ │  │
│ │ │ │ Dependency Chart │ │ │ Schedule       │    │      │ │  │
│ │ │ └──────────────────┘ └─────────────────────────┘      │ │  │
│ │ └───────────────────────────────────────────────────┘ │  │
│ │                                                        │  │
│ │ ┌─ 11.2 ───────┐                                       │  │
│ │ │ Duration     │                                       │  │
│ │ └──────────────┘                                       │  │
│ └────────────────────────────────────────────────────────┘  │
└───────────────────────────────────────────────────────────────┘
```

■ *Note:* The illustration of the class hierarchy contains all the classes this part defines. Other parts of the book define and discuss classes not in boldface.

CHAPTER

10 *Project Scheduling*

The Project Schedule

The *project schedule* is a plan of the temporal aspects of the project. It is a system model comprising schedule tasks, milestones, and dependencies between them. The *tasks* in the schedule are date-oriented versions of the process task. The *milestones* in the schedule come from your processes. The *dependencies* represent input-output relationships between tasks. The schedule represents its contents with a *time chart* to display the project time line and a *dependency chart* to display the dependency constraints on tasks. The *work calendar* declares the time available to work on the project. It specifies holidays, work shifts, and other resource-related information.

Vision: A project that delivers its products and services on time

Mission: To schedule the work of the project to ensure its efficient delivery on time

Objective 10.1: To enable the on-time delivery of products and services

Approach 10.1: Model the temporal dimension of the product by transforming tasks into time-oriented schedule tasks and linking them through dependencies. Add milestones to the schedule to model the specific control events for which you want time-oriented feedback, such as process milestones and desirable or mandatory end dates.

Metric 10.1: Project Finish Date: the date of the final completion of the project

Target 10.1: A project finish date within the range of dates acceptable to the stakeholders

The Project Schedule

Objective 10.2: To reduce the risk of failing to deliver according to schedule

Approach 10.2: Given the schedule developed by Approach 10.1, arrange the tasks within the constraints to optimize the risk of schedule failure. Level resource assignments to distribute work in a reasonable manner, improving productivity. Arrange tasks within the dependency and resource constraints to optimize the *float*—the time you can delay a task without delaying the project end date (that is, the delivery of the products and services). Float is also known as *slack*. Build time and dependency charts to both validate relationships and communicate relationships more effectively.

Metric 10.2: Risk Rate: see Metric and Target 7.1

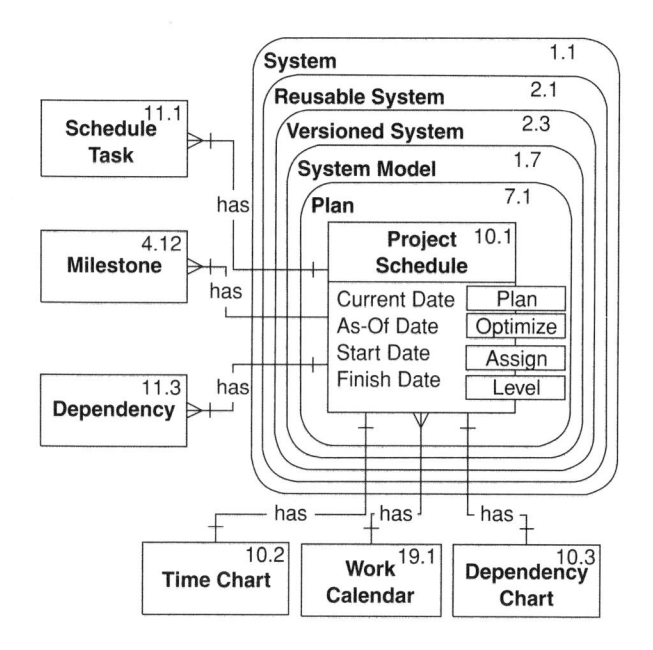

The *current date* of the schedule is the actual moment. The current date is the separating point between work done and work to do. What is past is done and what is future is to do. The current date is the real status of the schedule. The *as-of date* lets you see the project status "as of" that date, regardless of the current date and the actual status. The as-of date lets you get project-level information at dates other than the current one, such as earned-value information.

Planning the schedule generates the model from the WBS and process models, and then optimizes the schedule and levels resources. It follows that you can start real planning only after you have a basic statement of work in place as well as having a development process model. WBS generation lets you create the tasks in the WBS from a process model. At the same time, you create schedule tasks for the tasks in the WBS and the milestones from the process model. These milestones include the process milestone and any intermediate milestones for the process. You create the dependencies in the schedule from the work-flow model in the process model. You then create any technical dependencies from relationships between inputs and outputs specific to this project.

Work Breakdown Structure (8.2)

There are two milestones that directly constrain scheduling, the start date and finish date of the project process. The schedule fixes the *start date* once you start a project. It is the point at which you began the first actual task in the project. The schedule either fixes the *finish date* or not, depending on its nature. For example, if you must deliver your software package by a certain date for marketing or legal reasons, your project schedule fixes the finish date. You thus constrain your schedule by both dates.

The finish date in Metric 10.1 is perhaps the most controversial of these milestones. It measures the success of the project in meeting the stakeholders' temporal needs. "On time" in the context of project management means at a time *acceptable* to the stakeholders. Time is money. Unfortunately, you may find that OO software project stakeholders may not agree with each other's perceived temporal needs. Certain stakeholder factions may require the building of a small temporal device that enables the project developers to be in three places at once. This is, of course, how Scotty managed to keep the Enterprise going, but it's unlikely to be useful in the 20th (or 21st) century. A key part of managing stakeholders' expectations is the balancing of those expectations relating to the delivery date.

Stakeholder (3.3)

■ *Note:* Classic software project management assumes that the delivery date and project finish date are the same. Many projects, and especially OO projects, may be able to deliver systems at several points in the project, depending on the context. The project boundaries need not constrain your delivery schedule. For example, you might be able to deliver one piece (the most important) of a full system to the users, followed by documentation, followed by other, less important pieces. You can use staged delivery to ease some of the stakeholder pressures to deliver on time.

Once you have an initial plan, you can then assign resources to the schedule tasks. During the generation of the WBS, you should have already produced effort estimates for the tasks. For each schedule task in the project, you now assign one or more resources from your organization, usually consulting the resources and their managers. This introduces the resource constraints on your schedule, since resources work within the confines of space and time (although you wouldn't think so to look at many project plans).

Schedule Task (11.1)
Assignment (35.1)

■ *Note:* While it is possible to develop effort estimates and to assign resources without consultation, you are unlikely to have an effective schedule as the result. Bottom-up scheduling is usually better than top-down scheduling [Whitten].

Optimizing the plan is the process of arranging the tasks to optimize the overall risk in the schedule, taking into account its dependency and resource constraints. There are myriad ways to rearrange schedule tasks without changing the basic work in them:

- *Delaying* tasks by moving their start dates ahead in time, usually up to the point when there is no more float for the task
- *Advancing* tasks by moving their start dates back in time, usually not before the current date (unless you have one of those temporal devices I mentioned, or at least a forgiving auditor)
- *Splitting* tasks by rearranging the work involved to occur in pieces rather than all at once through a task calendar
- *Extending* tasks by increasing the duration of the task while reducing the effort per day through a task calendar

You can also change the basic tasks in several ways:

- *Modifying* tasks by changing the inputs, outputs, or technology associated with the task
- *Assigning* additional resource effort to a task
- *Deleting* tasks by removing them from the schedule and WBS and reconnecting any dependencies lost as a result
- *Combining* tasks by taking advantage of any redundancies that have made it through your deep and clever reuse analysis

Schedule Task (11.1)
Work Calendar (19.1)

You could, for example, reduce the risk of failing to deliver a critical component by advancing another task. Doing that task earlier might free up some resources that you could then assign to the critical task. Or you could extend a task, freeing up part of its resources' effort to spend on another task during the same period.

In OO projects, iteration provides many opportunities for schedule optimization. For example, you can plan on three iterations on a component. After the first and second iterations, you can evaluate the success criteria for the component and decide whether the rest of the iterations are necessary. If not, you can eliminate them. You should base such a decision on object and integration test criteria, however, not on the need for schedule optimization. That is, don't start chopping iteration due to schedule pressure. OO projects need iteration to be successful. If you must, cut features before cutting iteration and testing.

Depending on how your tools and methods for resource assignment work, you must also make sure that resources are working at reasonable levels during the plan. Resource *leveling* is the process of ensuring that the schedule reflects adequate resource usage. The effort of any given resource or pool of resources is not available in infinite amounts at any time during the project. People have vacations, take holidays, and work on other things. People come into the project and leave the project at different times. The amount of work available from a resource or resource pool

Resource (34.1)

during a specific time is the availability of the resource. You derive this availability from the work calendar for each resource.

Figure 10-1 shows a histogram chart that graphs the availability of a resource over time along with the planned resource usage. When a bar extends past the availability line, it means you have scheduled the resource to spend more effort than they have available. The line across the chart is availability, and the bars show resource usage. Most project management systems provide an availability tool for leveling.

There are two sides to availability—too much and too little. If you are overusing a resource, your schedule calls for a resource to exert more effort than is available during the scheduled task. Lack of available effort may be due to too much work being required from that task, or to the unavailability of the resource due to other work or time off.

But you can also be underusing a resource. You don't want a resource to be sitting around if you can avoid it. You motivate people by giving them rewarding work, not by long periods of inactivity. Look for gaps in resource usage. You can also use gaps in work schedules for training.

You use the same set of techniques for manipulating the schedule tasks and dependencies to reduce or increase the required work until it fits the availability closely. Using splitting and extending, you can have resources working on multiple tasks without exceeding their availability. You also have the option of reassigning

Figure 10-1
Resource usage and availability histogram

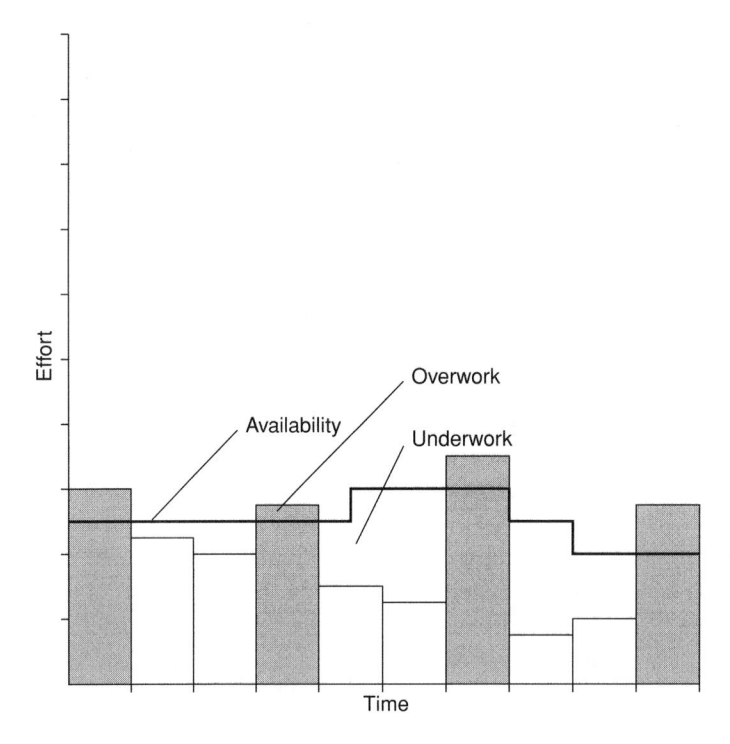

resources or of moving resources around to balance the load among different ones. This works as long as all the resources you assign to a task have the skills appropriate for accomplishing the task. Especially in OO projects, skills do not distribute equally among all the resources in a project.

Skill (34.5)

You can manage availability to some extent by manipulating the work calendar, either for the project or for the resource. Overtime is the ability of the resource to expend more effort than is available. By assigning overtime, you allow the explicit overuse of the resource. Overtime can come from time off, from vacations, or from holidays. There are, ultimately, only so many hours in the day and so many days per year. Too much overtime, and your people burn out. Use it sparingly. Stress and overwork are becoming a social problem in our chronically time-challenged society.

You can also use effort reserves as a risk management method for schedule tasks. That is, you can reserve a certain amount of a resource's availability for work you have not yet planned. This ensures that you have resources available when you change your WBS or increase your effort estimates. There are several ways to represent such a reserve. You can lower the availability of the resource, and then raise it when you need it. You can increase the duration of the task beyond that resulting from the scheduled effort. You can add an effort buffer to the effort estimate for the task.

You can also optimize the schedule by modifying the dependencies between tasks or the resource assignments on tasks.

Dependency (11.3)
Assignment (35.1)

Developing the project schedule is an ongoing process that takes full advantage of the rolling-wave approach to planning. As your understanding of the work needs of the project grows, you can develop better schedules. You should focus your scheduling on a period during which your planning can effectively reduce risk, usually four to six weeks. This short-term focus in scheduling lets you produce effective working schedules for project resources while preserving your options for the longer term.

Reusing the project schedule is largely a versioning issue, since the time-specific characteristics of the schedule are project specific. You may be able to reuse project schedules to some extent with project management tool templates. For example, if you have a standard process for a deliverable, you can often generate the initial schedule for that deliverable using a previously developed template schedule based on the standard process.

Revising the project schedule has several interesting aspects. A typical revision updates the current date to a new date and changes the schedule characteristics of the various schedule tasks and milestones according to project status. These project status revisions update the schedule to reflect the current reality of the project. You can also revise the schedule by optimizing it to reflect new resources or new understanding of schedule relationships. Finally, when the WBS changes to reflect a changing requirement or lower-level planning, you change the schedule to reflect the task changes.

Baselining the schedule baselines all the schedule tasks in the schedule. This baseline lets you calculate earned value as your project moves forward.

I was a functional manager and in charge of the project planning for my piece of a project. I was managing a small team of five people who had little or no project experience and relatively little experience with the technology we decided to use. By the middle of this nine-month project, I had abandoned project management entirely and was focusing on delivering my products. I did so, with no time at all to spare.

What had happened to make a fully committed project manager abandon everything he knew to be needed? My team simply ignored the schedule. Because they had no exposure to working to a plan, they did not organize their work according to the assigned tasks. I would ask for task status on a weekly basis, only to find that everyone had been doing other things half of the time. Things were getting done, but they weren't necessarily the things I'd planned on being done. There was so much parallelism possible in the underlying structure of the tasks that people could pretty much work on anything they wanted and still make forward progress, at least in their own minds. By the middle of the project, I was spending all my time revising the plan every week or running around getting people to focus. Since I had clearly defined the deliverables, I decided that it would be easier to just deliver them and try to do better next time. After a year of ongoing team building, discipline, and training, the team finally began to acquire a disciplined approach to project work. Shortly thereafter, we were all laid off. We learned, but the company didn't.

In a different project, I briefly assisted another project manager in developing a project schedule. The project manager was also the chief architect for a Web-related OO project involving a complex, distributed OO architecture including CORBA, Java, and a relational database. He didn't have time to develop the schedule, unsurprisingly. What was surprising, at least to me, was the unwillingness of anyone involved with the project to specify what they were going to deliver. The project manager had me put "use case" development into the plan, and then ignored these tasks and dived directly into design and development. There was broad disagreement not only over the architecture but over what the distributed deliverables would be. None of the Web developers knew anything about the CORBA architecture and what it entailed. At this point the project sponsor stepped in and insisted on delivery of a "prototype" system (no distributed objects) within two weeks. Everyone got to work and delivered it. I learned two lessons from this project. The first was that some projects don't need plans. The second was that some projects, no matter how complex or involved, won't have plans that people follow. These projects are not likely to achieve their mission. They will deliver, but not what you expect them to deliver.

The Time Chart

The *time chart* shows you how time affects the project, and vice versa. This chart is an essential part of the project schedule because a time chart is much more effective than any other method of communicating the schedule.

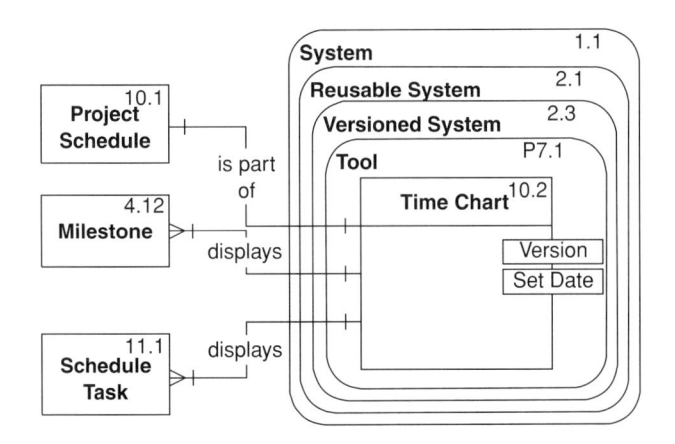

Vision: A clearly communicated work schedule for a project

Mission: To communicate the temporal aspect of a project schedule efficiently and effectively

---

Objective 10.3: To display the temporal aspects of the project schedule efficiently and effectively

---

Approach 10.3: Graph the schedule tasks and milestones of the project schedule along a time line, showing the start date and finish date for each task and the milestone date for each milestone. Highlight the current date through a rule graphic or other method.

Metric 10.3: Effectiveness: an ordinal, subjective measure of effective communication; users of the chart answer the question, "Please rate the effectiveness of this chart in giving you the schedule information you need to do your job." Values: Highly Effective, Moderately Effective, Somewhat Effective, Not Very Effective, Useless

Target 10.3: Highly Effective

There are a number of graphical methods for showing schedule tasks.

The Gantt chart is a very old method for displaying schedules (turn of the twentieth century, coming out of the Taylor method of manufacturing management). Figure 10-2 shows a Gantt chart. Each bar represents a task. The vertical rule shows the current date. Most modern project management versions of this chart associate the chart with a spreadsheet of task information, with the bars lining up with the task row in the spreadsheet. The graphic thus displays both tabular and graphical information, concentrating as much information as possible into a powerful diagram. Figure 10-2 shows how you can also include dependency information in the chart, with the small arrows between tasks representing dependencies.

You can use graphics very effectively in Gantt charts to display all kinds of schedule information. The bars in Figure 10-2 show you the critical path in a different color, for example. You can add shadow bars to show actual work done on the task, labels with names, WBS codes, or any other task-related information, graphics for float, and myriad other adornments.

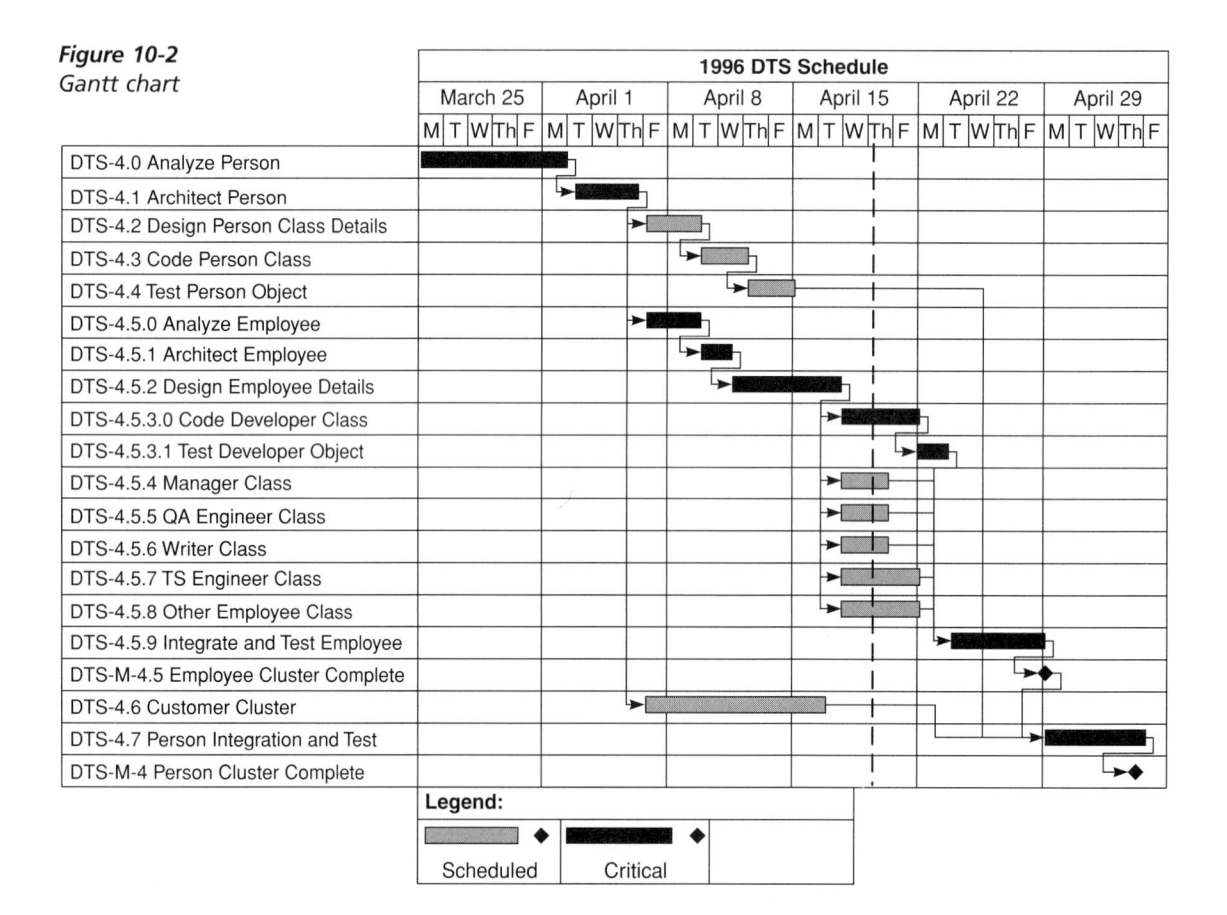

Figure 10-2
Gantt chart

■ *Note:* Most of the popular project management packages, including Microsoft Project, Time Line for Windows, Project Planner, and Project Scheduler, let you build your WBS in the task spreadsheet of the system, and then combine that with the Gantt chart. This combination lets you summarize the tasks into parents. It can, however, interfere with effective communication of the basic schedule information. Trying to do too much in these charts seems to be the current blind spot in this software industry corner.

You can also use a PERT chart (see the following section on "The Dependency Chart") to represent temporal information by aligning the task boxes along a time line. This variety of time chart is a bit bulky and less effective than the Gantt chart.

A third variety of time line uses the standard calendar layout to display tasks. You thus see a wall calendar for a month or week at a time with the task bars laid out across the day boxes. This works up to a point, but there are spatial limitations to its effectiveness. Its advantage is that you see time in a familiar layout.

You can, of course, reuse the chart tool in any project, as it is part of your organizational repository. You will find that you can generally reuse the specific chart setup through a template or some kind of attribute database (resource file, initialization file, and so on). You should be able to regenerate the chart automatically without making any changes in it aside from setting the current date.

The Dependency Chart

The *dependency chart* is a project management tool that represents the dependency network of the project schedule graphically. Schedule dependencies derive from process work-flow models and from the internal technical relationships between schedule tasks. The dependency chart is a necessary component of the project schedule system because it presents the dependency information much more efficiently than a simple list of dependencies.

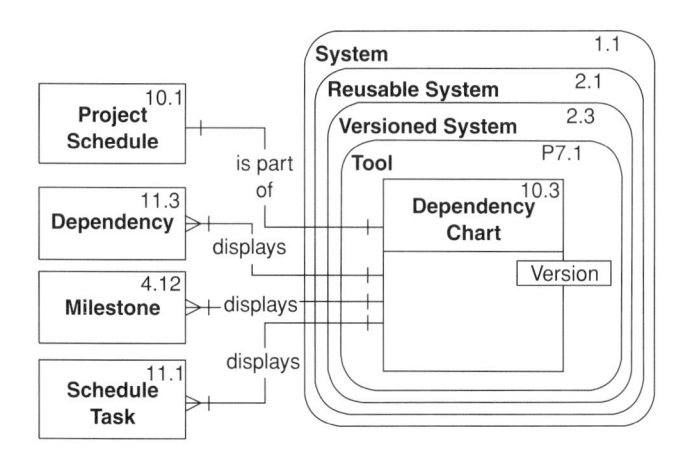

Vision: A project work flow that achieves its mission

Mission: To understand and to communicate the dependencies of a project schedule effectively and efficiently

---

Objective 10.4: To display the work-flow dependencies of the project schedule efficiently and effectively

---

Approach 10.4: Graph the dependencies of the project schedule, showing the schedule tasks and milestones they connect.

Metric 10.4: Effectiveness: an ordinal, subjective measure of effective communication; users of the chart answer the question, "Please rate the effectiveness of this chart in giving you the schedule information you need to do your job." Values: Highly Effective, Moderately Effective, Somewhat Effective, Not Very Effective, Useless

Target 10.4: Highly Effective

There are two primary tools for showing schedule dependencies, the *activity-on-node chart* and the *activity-on-arrow chart*. The underlying logic of these tools is the same: to represent the network of schedule tasks and dependencies, and specifically, to identify the critical paths through the network.

A *critical path* of a dependency network is a series of tasks and/or milestones "which determines the earliest completion of the project" [PMI 1996a, p. 162]. This definition has at least two different pragmatic definitions. One is that a critical path is a path through the network such that, if you delay the finish of a task or milestone on the path, you delay the finish date of the project. Another is that a critical path is a path through the network such that all activities on the path have a zero float. Mathematically, these are the same. A network may have several critical paths, depending on its exact structure.

The critical path gets its name from its function: to show you those tasks and milestones in the schedule that are critical to finishing the project on time. The dependency chart helps you to see the critical path by displaying it, usually in a different pattern or color. The overall schedule risk then depends solely on the critical tasks.

Unfortunately, reliance on critical path analysis has caused more problems than it has solved in software project management, and particularly in OO projects. Because of their highly parallel and iterative nature, OO projects tend to have many tasks operating in parallel. The result is that the critical path is quite sensitive to minor schedule changes. If you delay one task, you may find that the dependency chart displays an entirely different set of critical paths. You therefore must take the critical path with a grain of salt.

Most software project managers know the activity-on-node chart through their project management software. Microsoft Project, Time Line, and all the other

The Dependency Chart

major packages use this kind of chart, which shows schedule tasks and milestones as nodes in a network. The arrows between the nodes are the dependencies between the tasks and milestones. Figure 10-3 illustrates a simple activity-on-node chart.

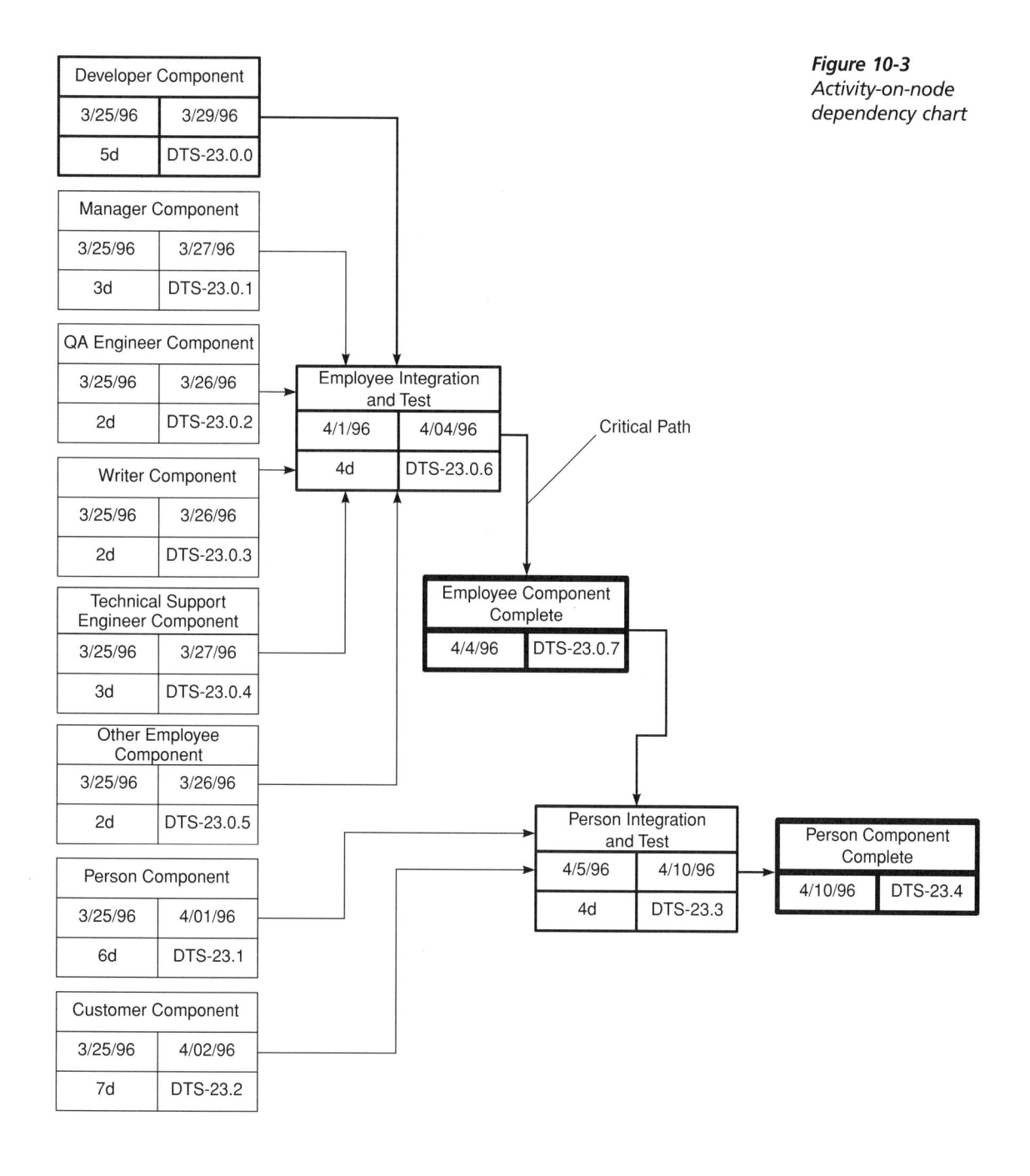

Figure 10-3
Activity-on-node dependency chart

Developer Component	
3/25/96	3/29/96
5d	DTS-23.0.0

Manager Component	
3/25/96	3/27/96
3d	DTS-23.0.1

QA Engineer Component	
3/25/96	3/26/96
2d	DTS-23.0.2

Writer Component	
3/25/96	3/26/96
2d	DTS-23.0.3

Technical Support Engineer Component	
3/25/96	3/27/96
3d	DTS-23.0.4

Other Employee Component	
3/25/96	3/26/96
2d	DTS-23.0.5

Person Component	
3/25/96	4/01/96
6d	DTS-23.1

Customer Component	
3/25/96	4/02/96
7d	DTS-23.2

Employee Integration and Test	
4/1/96	4/04/96
4d	DTS-23.0.6

Employee Component Complete	
4/4/96	DTS-23.0.7

Person Integration and Test	
4/5/96	4/10/96
4d	DTS-23.3

Person Component Complete	
4/10/96	DTS-23.4

Critical Path

■ *Note:* Activity-on-node charts often are called PERT charts, after a particular government method of project management that used such charts. PERT (Program Evaluation and Review Technique) involves a lot more than just charts, though [Kerzner; Moder].

The activity-on-arrow chart represents dependencies as nodes and the schedule tasks as arrows. The arrows thus intuitively represent an interval of work that begins at one dependency and ends at another. Critical path analysis uses this graph structure to calculate float, identifying activities that are critical (without float) and the amount of float you have for an activity.

■ *Note:* Virtually no one uses activity-on-arrow charts in software project management, so I do not discuss these charts further. If you are building your own project management information system, however, you may want to look at the literature on the Critical Path Method (CPM), which uses these charts extensively [Moder]. Also, activity-on-arrow charts are not good at representing milestones, since events have no duration. The arrows thus become one-dimensional for no good reason. This might, of course, explain the tendency of some projects to approach milestones like black holes.

I saw an interesting approach to dependency networking on a client/server project. The functional manager for the client/server group developed a dependency network that ordered the tasks by resource. That is, he took the tasks and linked them by dependencies because the resource assigned to the task could do only one thing at a time. Thus, the dependencies represented not the inherent work flow of the project but the structure of the organization doing the project.

Another OO subproject I worked on had almost complete parallelism. No one task really depended on any other task. I developed a network diagram that had a start milestone, a group of tasks connected to it, and the same tasks connected to a finish milestone. The critical path in this subproject was shifting on a daily basis. Parallelism is good, but hard to manage, particularly with fewer resources.

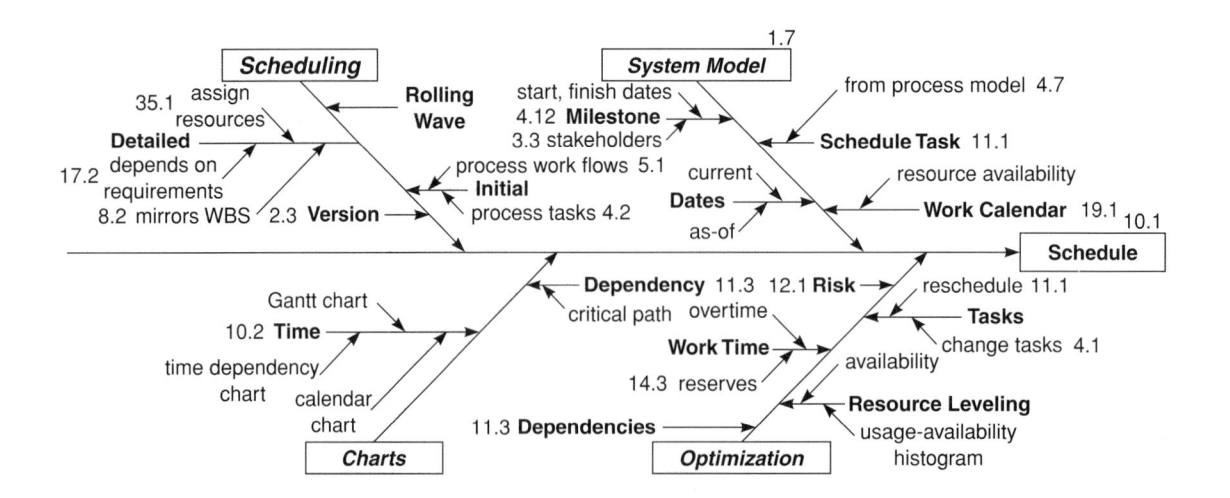

Readings

[Kerzner] Harold Kerzner. *Project Management: A Systems Approach to Planning, Scheduling, and Controlling, Fifth Edition.* New York: Van Nostrand Reinhold, 1994.

Kerzner is relatively weak on the practical aspects of scheduling, but he has a strong discussion of the use of slack or float time (Section 12.2).

[Moder] Joseph J. Moder, Cecil R. Phillips, and Edward W. Davis. *Project Management with CPM, PERT, and Precedence Diagramming, Third Edition.* New York: Van Nostrand Reinhold, 1983.

If you want the gory details of precedence diagramming, this is the book. Chapter 7 on "Resource Constraints in Project Scheduling" is of particular interest, though the technical approaches are somewhat out of date.

[O'Brien] James J. O'Brien. *Scheduling Handbook.* New York: McGraw-Hill, 1969.

This is the book on scheduling for the technically minded. Although very out of date, much of the material is as relevant today as it was in 1969. Go to this book if you really want to understand the mathematics of scheduling and resource allocation.

[Whitten] Neal Whitten. *Managing Software Development Projects: Formula for Success, Second Edition.* New York: Wiley, 1995.

Whitten's excellent and pragmatic book has a great chapter on scheduling, with many practical lessons about what to do and what not to do. While I don't agree with all of his suggestions, most are right on target.

Questions to Think About

1. When you think about project management, do you think primarily about the schedule? Look at your favorite project management tool and estimate the amount of attention the tool pays to schedule versus other parts of the product. Now look at the number of pages in this book devoted to schedule and scheduling. Where's the beef? (Hint: People, risk, change, communication, organization, procurement, and process. Software has a long way to go.)

2. Can you effectively schedule a project without assigning resources to schedule tasks? (Hint: Look at "Duration" in the following chapter.)

3. With so many different ways to affect the schedule through schedule tasks, how do you choose which method to use for a given situation? (Hint: Artificial intelligence is NOT the answer.)

4. Do you consider time or precedence more important in determining the best schedule? Why?

5. Consider the idea of calendar time charts. Do you think they would be effective in communicating your typical project schedules? Why or why not?

6. Review the different project management software you've used and seen. Why do you think that software tends to use precedence diagramming and activity-on-node charts almost exclusively?

7. What is the impact of the calendar on effective scheduling? (Hint: When was the last time you scheduled a delivery for Friday afternoon instead of Monday morning? When was the last time you scheduled a delivery for December 27th?)

CHAPTER

The Schedule Task and Dependency 11

The Schedule Task

The *schedule task* is a date-oriented container for a simple task. It wraps the process-generated WBS simple task with start and finish dates, schedule dependencies, and milestones. Changing the schedule thus does not version the underlying tasks, just the schedule tasks. This permits you to maintain several schedule baselines separate from the work breakdown structure baselines. Each task contains a reference to an element of the WBS, which in turn may refer to a process task.

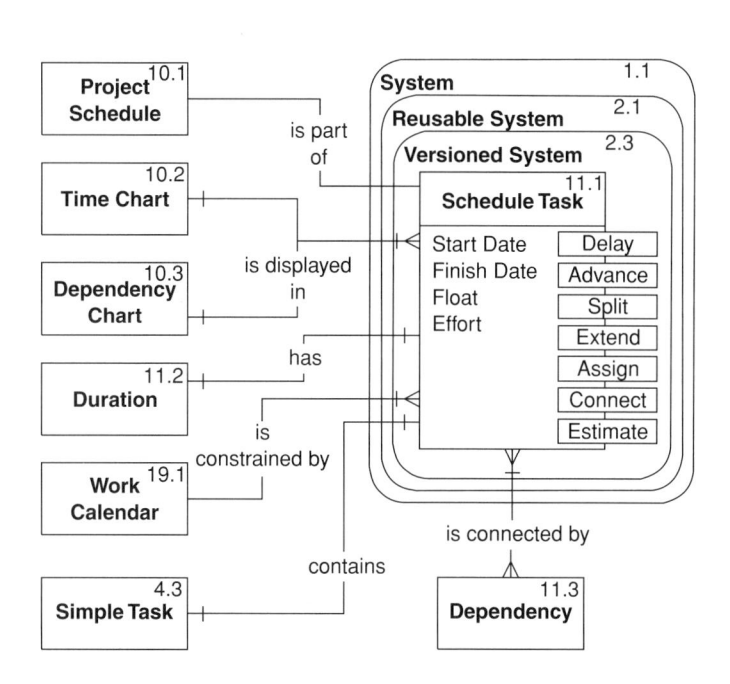

Vision: *An easily maintained schedule that accurately represents the temporal aspects of the project*

Mission: *To represent the temporal aspect of a task for use in the project schedule*

Objective 11.1: To enable the task to be a part of the project schedule

---

Approach 11.1: Encapsulate the start and finish date and accompanying duration interval in the schedule task that the task generates. Develop duration estimates based on the task and its resource assignments, work calendar, and cost estimates. Use an optional task calendar to constrain the dates and duration in special ways, overriding any resource or project work calendars.

Metric 11.1: Enabled: Does the simple task participate effectively in the schedule? Yes or no

Target 11.1: Yes

Objective 11.2: To enable efficient maintenance, baselining, and change control of the project schedule

---

Approach 11.2: Encapsulate the start and finish date and accompanying duration interval in the schedule task, and change these volatile elements there, not in the underlying simple task. Version and baseline the schedule task as required by the schedule without doing anything to the underlying task.

Metric 11.2: Productivity: effort-hours per version of the schedule task, measuring the amount of work spent to make a single change to the schedule by versioning the schedule task

Target 11.2: A value within control limits of an x-R control chart

---

The *start* and *finish dates* provide the key information for the project schedule. There are various schemes for identifying the earliest and latest possible start and finish dates for a task, each of which constitutes a milestone in the project schedule. Usually, a project schedule treats these milestones as invisible parts of the task node rather than as separate schedule elements.

The task *float* is the amount of calendar time that you could delay the task without delaying the project finish milestone. The *critical path,* for example, is the path through the dependency network of schedule tasks with zero float. Another word for float is *slack,* as in slack time. Understanding the float of a task is critical to being able to evaluate the schedule risk of the task. Many of the schedule task actions depend on the float of the task.

The effort of the task is the effort you spent creating the current version of the task. This includes all the time spent in estimating duration and placing the task in an appropriate place in the schedule by delaying it, advancing it, and so on.

The task duration is the duration of this version of the task. The task connects to other tasks or to milestones through its set of dependencies. These connections can be in either direction, to a task or from a task. The task calendar is an optional work calendar you can use to impose special time constraints on the task. It overrides the calendars of the resources assigned to work on the task or the project work calendar.

The schedule task appears graphically within the time and dependency charts.

The schedule task enables you to both estimate the duration of the task and to arrange the task's position in the project schedule.

To estimate duration, you must take into account the following things:

- The task cost estimate
- The effort and availability of the resources assigned to the task
- The task calendar constraints
- The dependencies, including any start or finish constraints or leads or lags

You can also estimate the duration directly. Theoretically, you would do this only for tasks that have some time-related component unrelated to the actual work to do. However, in larger projects, you may find it impossible to make resource assignments on every task. You could also use simple duration estimates as a preliminary scheduling technique to get a basic schedule without having to assign resources or make extensive cost estimates.

■ *Note:* Do not use tasks to represent time leads and lags. Instead, use the lag attribute of the dependency. For example, if you schedule a review, and you want to specify that it start no less than a week after distribution of the review materials, you connect the task to the distribution task with a lag dependency of one week. The schedule task itself has the duration only of the meeting, not of the lag and the meeting time.

Delaying the task is moving the start date of the task to a later time. This is the most common way to handle resource overloading problems. You usually have the choice of delaying one of several conflicting tasks. Your decision about which to delay should depend on your assessment of the risk of the schedule task. Will the task being late affect the end of the project? Is the schedule sensitive to small changes in this schedule task? Usually, you delay tasks with the most float available, as this is a direct measure of schedule risk.

Advancing the task is moving the start date of the task to an earlier time. You can move the task backwards in time up to the current moment or to a point where another task constrains it through a dependency. You would usually do this if a work gap had appeared in the resource usage available for the task due to another schedule change.

Splitting the task is micromanaging the effort spent on the task into well-defined pieces. You usually do this when an overloaded resource overworks during only part of the task's duration. For example, if a quality developer works on two components at the same time, and one component is twice as long as the other, and the longer one has some float, you can split the effort so the developer can work on the first task, then the second, then the first again. The effect of this is to lengthen the duration of the split task, hopefully in a way that will not affect the rest of the schedule. You can also split a task if the resources need a break. For example, a review of a particularly complex component might take 12 hours. Instead of having a single, 12-hour meeting, you break up the review into six two-hour meetings. You could of course break the task into six tasks, but really it's just a single task split into six effort groups.

Extending the task means reducing the effort on the task, lengthening the duration. You usually do this when you cannot split the task, either for logical or temporal reasons. At some point, you reach a limit on the amount of effort that is practically useful. For example, say you extend a coding task to the point where a developer is spending less than an hour or two a day on it. You may find that the effort is less productive because the resource doesn't have the chance to get into the task. This effect is very similar to what happens in poorly engineered multi-tasking operating systems that try to do too many things at once.

Assigning resources to the task means that you either create additional resource assignments in the underlying simple task or remove some existing ones. This can affect the duration of the task. For example, if the current resource assignment is to a resource overloaded with work or away from the job for an extended period, you can reassign the task to a different resource with more availability.

Duration

The *duration* of the schedule task is the time interval the task takes. This is not a simple number, as the number is relative to several different work calendars. Also, you can consider it a random variable with an average value rather than as a single-valued variable. The actual time interval is a value expressed in specific time unit precision such as hours or days.

Vision: A schedule that clearly expresses the calendar time it will take to deliver the project products and services

Mission: To express calendar time in a clear and direct manner

Objective 11.3: To express calendar time in a clear and direct manner

Approach 11.3: Compute or estimate the duration of a task or a lag in calendar or work time. Express the time in a time interval unit of hours or days, which are more amenable to date arithmetic than longer units.

Metric 11.3: Number of problems: count of the number of problems you have in calculating start and finish dates from durations and vice versa, including problems deriving from increased risk incurred by interval calculation precision

Target 11.3: Approaching zero, or at least within control limits of a pn control chart near zero; time is always difficult, even at the best of times

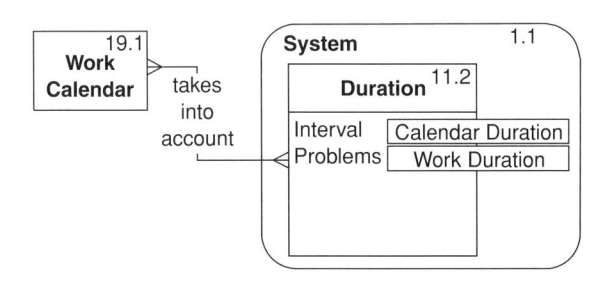

The *calendar duration* is the absolute calendar time between the actual start and finish dates of the schedule task. The *relative work duration,* or *project duration* [Moder], is the amount of actual work time the schedule task occupies. This calculation depends on the start time in combination with the various work calendars (task, resource, and project) that separate calendar time into work time and time off.

For example, say that you schedule a task for designing a component to start on Thursday, December 21, and end on January 4. The calendar duration is 15 days. The relative working duration is anything from an hour to 15 days, depending on how the calendars structure the working time. For example, you might have three holidays during that period (Christmas, the day following Christmas, and New Year's Day), you've got weekends in there, and almost certainly some vacations.

As it is obviously very complex to calculate, what would interest you in working duration? When your boss asks you how long it will take to code a class, you will usually answer him or her with hours or days of effort. What your boss hears is the day you'll finish, assuming you'll work time-and-a-half on the task. If you're smart, you'll ask, "Starting when, and how important is this?" You've just estimated a relative work duration.

If you estimate your schedule entirely with durations rather than by using resource cost estimates, you are estimating the working duration of the task. The calendar duration changes depending on where you position the task in the schedule. If you think about the implications of calendars and work structure on this number, you can see why estimating this way often leads to more schedule risk. Because of the impact of calendars and varying work schedules, using work duration makes it much more difficult to predict the true calendar duration. You can predict the finish date only when you know the start date. That means you have less flexibility in scheduling to eliminate risk. If it's the best you can do because you can't assign resources directly, then you have to take the variability into account.

■ *Note:* There is also the special subclass of duration, vendor duration. Vendor duration is the absolute calendar time plus a very large random-variable time interval. Vendor duration is the inverse of stoplight duration, the time between the change of a stoplight and the idiot behind you honking. Boston stoplight duration is also the definition of negative infinity.

Approach 11.3 calls for expressing duration in hours or days. You will often see durations in months or weeks. This is a bad idea. Consider the calendar. How many weeks are there in a year? a month? How many days are there in a month? The only answer to these questions is, "It depends." It depends on the year, or the month, or the century. Hours and days don't have this problem. Therefore, you should express calendar duration in hours or days of calendar time. If this leads to a scale problem with very large numbers, use metrics: hundreds of hours or tens of days. (Decadays? sounds like a bad sitcom.) I suppose milliseconds are a possibility…for Internet projects.

■ *Note:* The SQL 1992 standard [ANSI] has an excellent definition of the time interval data type. It requires you to specify the precision in various mutually incompatible units of time. Anyone seriously considering working with software to handle time should examine and understand this standard.

Time Interval (19.2)

The Dependency

The *dependency* is a versioned system that represents a directed link between two schedule tasks or milestones. The standard interpretation is that the finish date of the first task must come before the start date of the second. There are other interpretations (the start date of the first task must come before the start date of the second, for example). A dependency may have a *lead* or *lag time* that constrains the schedule even further.

Vision: A schedule that clearly reflects the true flow of work in a project
Mission: To represent the work flow of a project

Objective 11.4: To represent the work flow of a project

Approach 11.4: Build a network of tasks and milestones connected by directed arrows. These arrows represent the flow of inputs and outputs between tasks and milestones.

The Dependency

Metric 11.4: Spurious: Does this dependency represent something other than the actual flow of work?

Target 11.4: No

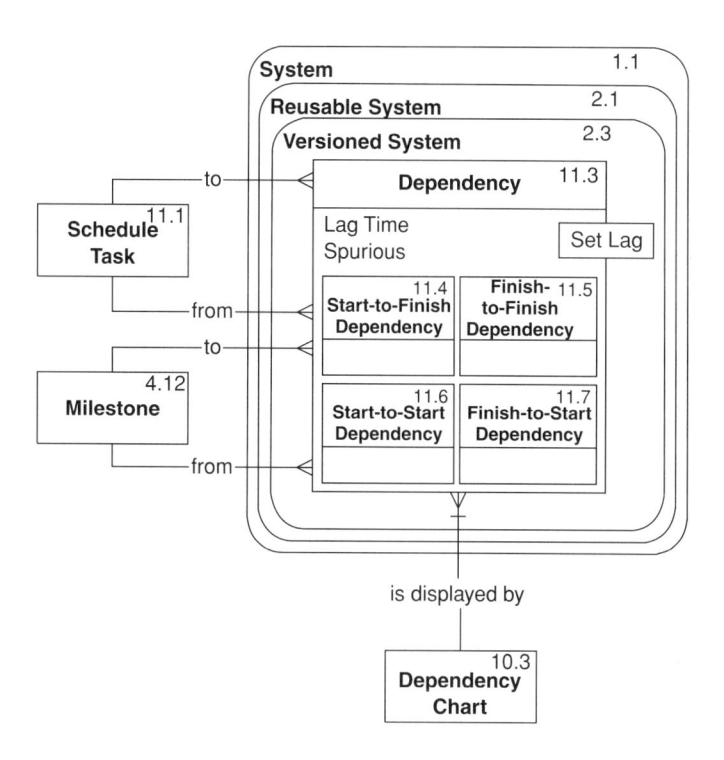

A link between tasks or milestones in a work-flow model generates the equivalent dependency in the schedule. As well as these standard process dependencies, you add dependencies for ad hoc work flows. These work flows come about due to timing, risk management, or other issues that arise during the project.

There are four types of dependency, as Table 11-1 describes. These are subclasses of the parent dependency class. The subclasses constrain particular dates within the tasks or milestones dependent on one another.

Table 11-1
Dependency Types

Type	Description
Start to finish	The second task finishes when the first task starts
Finish to finish	Both tasks finish at the same time
Start to start	Both tasks start at the same time
Finish to start	The second task starts when the first task finishes

The *lag time* of a dependency is the duration of the dependency itself. For example, if your design task depends on the task of ordering CASE tools, and the shipping time is one week after order placement, the lag on the dependency is one week. The lag is a duration, a time interval that may depend on a calendar of some kind. For example, the lag may be five "working" days. A negative lag time, or *lead* time, is a time that the two tasks overlap in some way.

The dependency represents the work flow of versioned systems through the executing process. Part of the operation of the dependency is its conditional nature. If the target task fails in some way, often you can retract a versioned system from the task and reassign it to another task in the process. The retraction alternatives appear as part of the work-flow model. You can also represent this sort of process as an ad hoc work-flow model. Retraction means that you need not version the dependency unless the actual work flow of the project changes.

■ *Note:* Most project management software does not support any kind of retraction mechanism other than the usual one: revise the schedule by hand when the failure occurs. As work-flow techniques become more prevalent in software, this situation should change to let you model contingency in a less time-consuming way. Contingent approaches should also contribute to a better understanding and management of risk in projects.

Other than changing the lag time or connecting the tasks and milestones differently, there are few ways to reuse dependencies. Insofar as you can reuse the entire project schedule, you can reuse the dependencies in it. Because the dependencies are often specific to a particular combination of tasks in a project, their reuse potential is low.

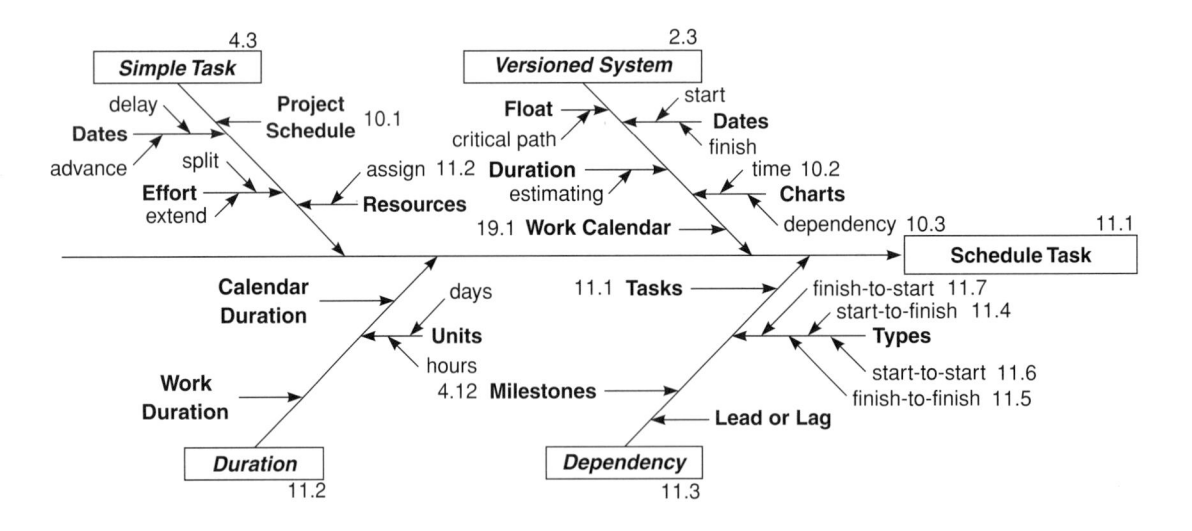

Readings

[Moder]   Joseph J. Moder, Cecil R. Phillips, and Edward W. Davis. *Project Management with CPM, PERT, and Precedence Diagramming, Third Edition.* New York: Van Nostrand Reinhold, 1983.

Moder's Chapter 3 discusses "Time Estimates and Level of Detail," focusing on duration estimation. Interestingly, he leaves it to a later chapter (7) to integrate resource constraints as an "advanced" topic, which seems typical in the duration-fixated project management world.

Questions to Think About

1. What kind of tasks become schedule tasks? (Hint: Not all tasks represent actual work or scheduled work.)

2. Do schedule tasks need to connect to at least one other schedule task or milestone through dependencies? (Hint: There is more than one answer. Consider the project start and finish milestones, for example, and what is dependent on them.)

3. Many books express work in terms of man-months. Are man-months in fact mythical [Brooks]? Think about men, and think about months, and think about alternative units for awhile. Now, think about why industry decided to express things this way. I have not been able to find the original source of this English expression, but it's very interesting to consider its implications.

4. Can you think of other uses for the basic duration concept? How does duration differ from the underlying time interval concept?

5. Think about your last few projects. What kind of dependencies did you have in that project? What was the most common type? If it wasn't finish-to-start, why not? Did you have lags or leads, and if so, why? What kinds of behavior in OO projects lead to leads and lags?

PART FIVE

Risk

If you can make one heap of all your winnings
   And risk it on one turn of pitch-and-toss,
And lose, and start again at your beginnings
   And never breathe a word about your loss.
…

If you can fill the unforgiving minute
   With sixty seconds' worth of distance run,
Yours is the Earth and everything that's in it,
   And—which is more—you'll be a Man, my son!

Rudyard Kipling, "If—"

When not walking with kings or Kipling, the project manager has the duty to take a more responsible view of life than one turn of pitch-and-toss. As project management has matured as a discipline, and as other fields have developed the techniques and methods, the project manager has acquired the ability to deal with risk to the heap of winnings in a very direct, foresighted way.

This part introduces the basics of risk analysis, quantification, and management. There is a very large literature now on risk in general and software development risk in particular. While this literature gives you a strong background in many of the elements of risk, I've found it unnecessarily complicated for everyday project management. In this part, I present some simplifying assumptions about quantifying and managing risk. The system approach to risk is the risk of failing to achieve the system mission. This approach means that you can greatly restrict what you need to calculate to analyze and manage risk in your projects.

The risk class itself is a relatively complex class internally but quite simple from the project manager's perspective. As well, it is a reusable system that you can develop once and reuse in many projects.

There are several classes of risk that apply specifically to OO development, and Chapter 12 goes into some detail on these, giving examples from my own projects.

Chapter 13 details my approach to risk quantification, which uses Bayesian likelihood and joint probability estimation to quantify that most basic risk: failing to achieve the system mission. It also shows you how the project manager assigns a risk tolerance to the project and to all the systems within the project.

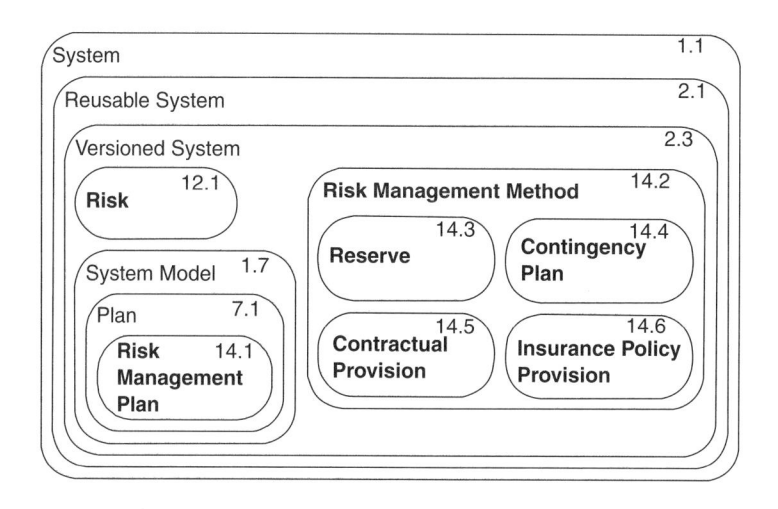

```
┌─System─────────────────────────────────────1.1─┐
│ ┌─Reusable System──────────────────────────2.1─┐ │
│ │ ┌─Versioned System───────────────────────2.3─┐ │ │
│ │ │  ┌─────────12.1─┐  ┌─Risk Management Method──14.2─┐ │ │ │
│ │ │  │ Risk         │  │    ┌──────14.3─┐ ┌─────14.4─┐ │ │ │ │
│ │ │  └──────────────┘  │    │ Reserve   │ │Contingency│ │ │ │ │
│ │ │  ┌─System Model─1.7─┐  │    └───────────┘ │ Plan     │ │ │ │ │
│ │ │  │ ┌─Plan────7.1─┐ │  │    ┌──────14.5─┐ ┌─────14.6─┐ │ │ │ │
│ │ │  │ │ ┌Risk──14.1┐│ │  │    │Contractual│ │Insurance Policy│ │ │ │
│ │ │  │ │ │Management││ │  │    │ Provision │ │ Provision │ │ │ │ │
│ │ │  │ │ │ Plan     ││ │  │    └───────────┘ └──────────┘ │ │ │ │
│ │ │  │ │ └──────────┘│ │  └──────────────────────────────┘ │ │ │
│ │ │  │ └─────────────┘ │                                   │ │ │
│ │ │  └─────────────────┘                                   │ │ │
│ │ └────────────────────────────────────────────────────────┘ │ │
│ └────────────────────────────────────────────────────────────┘ │
└────────────────────────────────────────────────────────────────┘
```

The last chapter in this part develops the several varieties of risk management. These, too, are reusable systems. You can develop standard methods for dealing with risk, ranging from reserves of time, people, and money to contracts and insurance policies. Contingency planning lets you build work-flow retraction and other contingent techniques into your project risk management plan.

You can't avoid risk. You *can* manage it. And you may still own the Earth and everything in it.

- *Note:* The illustration of the class hierarchy contains all the classes this part defines. Other parts of the book define and discuss classes not in boldface.

CHAPTER

12 *Risk*

The Risk

A *project-related risk* is the potential for a situation that befalls a system in a project. To be a risk, this situation must cause undesirable and negative consequences of some kind to the system. To be a project-related risk, the system must be a part of a project.

There is a tremendous variety of risks in the world and a like number of ways to manage them. Not all are project-related. Project managers deal primarily with acquisition, supply, and development risks. Projects do not involve operations and maintenance processes. Although these are perfectly good risks, they are not *project* risks: they do not have a negative impact on the project. Similarly, there are risks in things that happen outside the project that affect things within the project, such as process modeling or reuse repository management. These risks are also outside the scope of project management.

The word "potential" specifies that *uncertainty* is a fundamental aspect of risk. If you are certain something will happen, it's not a risk, whatever its impact.

With purposive systems, risks relate directly to the mission of the system. To restate the definition of project risk in system terms, risk is the joint probability of the failure of the mission of the system. This definition leads to three assumptions about risk and systems.

First, if a system has no purpose, it has no risk. Without a purpose, the system does not contribute any value to the project, and therefore it cannot fail to deliver value. I assume away this kind of system, since all the systems in this book are purposive and have missions. In a project situation, any object that does not contribute value should not exist.

The Risk

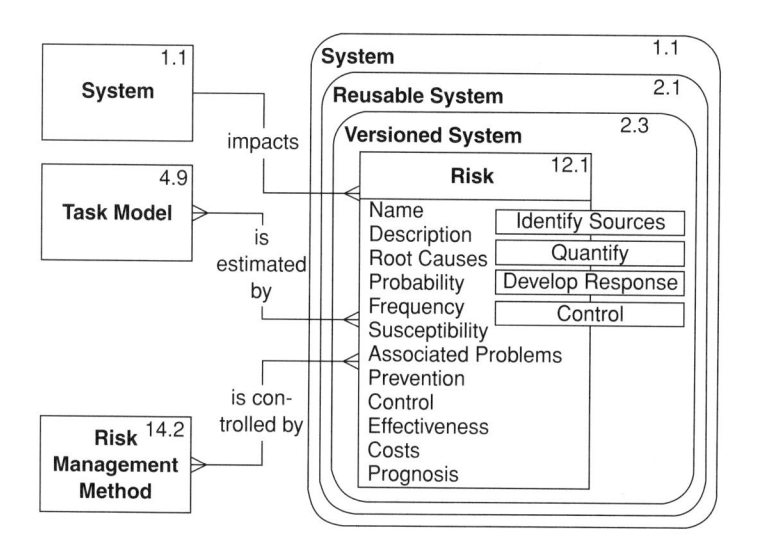

[Diagram: System (1.1) impacts Risk; Task Model (4.9) is estimated by Risk; Risk Management Method (14.2) is controlled by Risk. Risk (12.1) is contained within Versioned System (2.3), Reusable System (2.1), System (1.1). Risk attributes: Name, Description, Root Causes, Probability, Frequency, Susceptibility, Associated Problems, Prevention, Control, Effectiveness, Costs, Prognosis. Operations: Identify Sources, Quantify, Develop Response, Control.]

Second, if a system's objectives are not measurable or do not have targets for their metrics, then the objective does not contribute to risk. This assumption is necessary for the quantification of the risk, but it is not particularly restrictive. You should be able to measure any objective. Even a purely subjective, nominally scaled metric that answers the question behind the objective is a valid measure, though it must meet the basic criteria for measurement. Targets may be absolute, but usually targets are control ranges that specify an acceptable set of values, not a single value. The target reflects the range of acceptable values for the objective, defining the impact of the objective on the system mission.

Third, the target value must identify a risk that exceeds the tolerance of the system for risk. That is, you need only concern yourself with risks that worry you. In the stock market, brokers define this as "sleeping at night." I quantify the term "worry" with the idea of a system *risk tolerance:* the probability of mission failure beyond which the consequences become too serious to ignore.

Vision: A project manager able to easily identify, quantify, communicate, and control a project risk

Mission: To identify, quantify, communicate, and control a specific project risk

Objective 12.1: To identify a risk with minimal effort

Approach 12.1: Standardize common risks in a generic risk analysis in the project environment. Associate generic risks with elements of the process model, where appropriate.

System (1.1)

Metric 12.1: Effort to identify the risk in effort-hours

Target 12.1: A control range for effort-hours per risk that represents a minimal effort

---

Objective 12.2: To quantify the potential for system mission failure due to the situation that is the root cause of the risk

---

Approach 12.2: Estimate the probability of failure using Bayesian prior estimation techniques. Combine probabilities for multiple risk events that comprise the risk situation using appropriate joint probability laws to calculate the unconditional probability of failure.

Metric 12.2: The posterior probability of the hypothesis that the risk situation will result in mission failure given data about the situation and the failure, not necessarily from this project

Target 12.2: A posterior probability greater than the risk tolerance of the system at risk

---

Objective 12.3: To communicate the risk to those affected by possible failure of the system

---

Approach 12.3: Identify the project stakeholders that the system's failure would affect. Communicate the risks to those stakeholders along with the quantification and risk control methods you intend to apply. Ensure that stakeholders are comfortable with the level of risk and with your strategy for dealing with that risk.

Metric 12.3: Stakeholder awareness: a subjective metric that evaluates how aware the stakeholders are of the risks in the project that might affect them; this could be a random survey listing specific risks and control methods, for example

Target 12.3: A value showing good awareness, such as 90% of all risks understood and accepted; you can use the appropriate control chart for continuous sampling throughout the project to make sure the communication process is stable and consistent

---

Objective 12.4: To control the risk to bring it under the risk tolerance for the system

---

Approach 12.4: Use the externally set risk tolerance to compare with the independent risks. For those risks that exceed the risk tolerance, develop control strategies in the risk management plan and execute the control tasks as part of the project work.

The Risk 203

Metric 12.4: The frequency of the risk (how many times the risk occurs) as a dependent variable in a model of the risk management methods you use to control the risk

Target 12.4: A risk frequency under the risk tolerance of the system and an appropriate level of statistical significance for the multidimensional control factors you used to control the risk (that is, you need to know that the control methods are working, and you determine that by statistical methods in the multidimensional model)

Because risk is a versioned object, you can change the various characteristics of a risk as you learn more about its true colors and impact on your projects. Most risks are inherently reusable, with only a few being domain dependent. One of the best ways to reuse risk objects is to embed them in task models. As you develop and apply your process models as part of your organizational repository, you learn about the risks to the various tasks in the processes. Embedding this knowledge in the process model through associating specific risks with specific task models lets you reuse your risk analysis in multiple projects. It also ensures the increasing relevance of the process models for your projects, improving the reusability of the models as well.   Task Model (4.9)

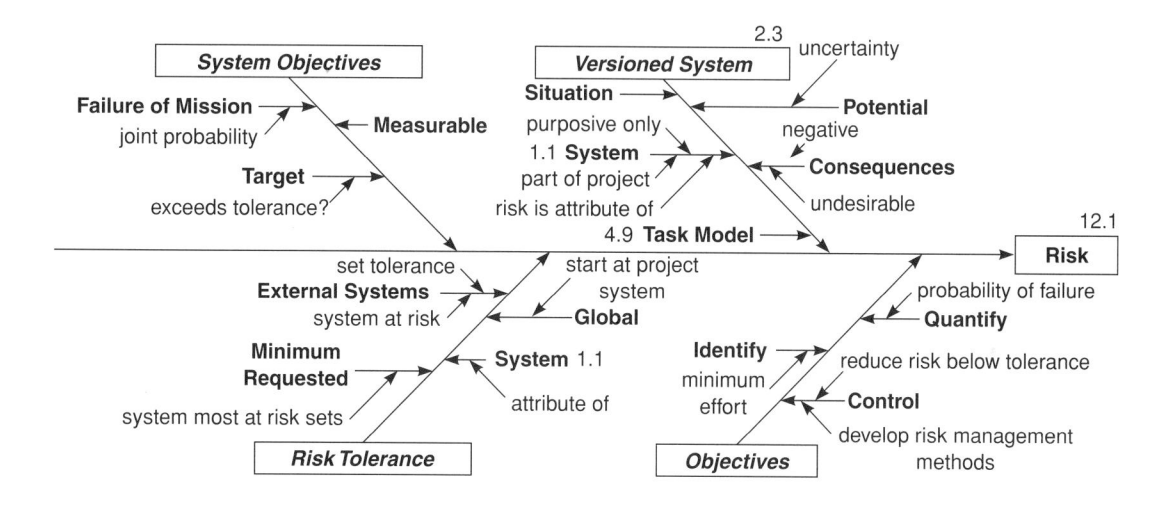

Risk and Systems

Risk does not exist by itself; a *system* is at risk. In OO terms, the system *owns* the risk. A system may own several risks that derive from independent situations. For example, a task depends on three things to achieve its mission: time, work, and quality. A situation may involve any one of these factors or any combination of factors.

You could constrain time, for example, by setting an inappropriate finish date for a process milestone. This by itself doesn't involve work or quality, though the measures you take to mitigate the risk may. The time risk is thus a separate, statistically independent risk. Another risk might be lack of OO skills, which leads to quality problems or low productivity or both; this risk involves work and quality jointly but does not necessarily involve time. The overall system risk, an external system attribute, is the joint probability of failure of all the independent risks.

Risk Quantification

A key element of the situation is the target for the metric. The target specifies a criterion by which you can evaluate the success or failure of the objective. If a data value falls within the control range, you have succeeded in your objective; if not, you have failed. That ties the target directly to risk. The joint probability of failure takes the objective into account through the quantification of the unconditional or conditional probability of failure of the specific objective. Each objective probability in turn may depend on the probability of failure of one or more metrics.

The risk thus takes both the objectives of the owning system and the situation that potentially causes failure in those objectives into account.

Every purposive system in the project can own risks. Not every system has risks that you must worry about, since they may fall below the system's risk tolerance. The project system, however, is not a random collection of objects but a highly structured hierarchy of objects, each of which uses other systems. This has some direct implications for risk quantification. When you compute the overall risk for a system, that risk is an external attribute of the system. The objects that own that system combine the risk of failure of their own objectives with the risks of system failure of the systems that contribute to its mission. Thus, the risk rises up the object hierarchy to the project. Project risk is thus the joint probability of the objectives of the project in combination with the systems that are part of the project system.

See Chapter 13 for a complete discussion of risk quantification, including the metric for judging whether you have successfully identified a risk. Chapter 13 also discusses the various ways to compute risk probabilities, including summing up the hierarchy. Finally, it gives you some tools to estimate prior probabilities for different classes of objects.

Chapter 13, Risk Quantification, section "Kinds of Risks," p. 227

The Risk Paradigm and OO Development

Thinking about risk is a paradigm. Risk permeates the crust of the world of project management to such an extent that you will find it difficult to see if you're not looking for it.

Consider, for a moment, the processes for software development in the ISO-12207 standard [ISO 1995]. Nowhere in that standard does the term "risk" even appear. Now think about the various quality assurance processes: verification,

The Risk 205

validation, joint review, and audit. What is the purpose behind these processes? To assure that "the products and processes are in conformance with their specified requirements and adhere to their established plans." Why? If you are thinking about risk rather than about processes, you should begin to realize that the sole reason for the existence of the supporting quality assurance process is the *risk of failure of the primary process*. Similarly, the system documentation process exists as a method for managing the maintenance risks for the software.

Development Process (16.4)

Both ISO-12207 and ISO-9000-3 [ISO 1991] thus implicitly devote a large portion of their processes to managing risk. The standards do not, however, contain the word "risk." Again, all this points to a different way of thinking. The project management world has turned to explicit risk management as a fundamental way of thinking about projects [PMI 1996a], and I adopt this paradigm here.

Part of modern risk management is the use of decision theory. Over the past 30 years, operations researchers have developed this mathematical tool to help with making management and policy decisions based on probabilities and expected values [Bernstein]. You use probability distributions, decision trees, and simulation tools to analyze risk [Charette; Holloway; Karolak; PMI 1996a]. If you're not thinking about risk, you're missing a large part of the toolset for managing projects.

Chapter 13, Risk Quantification

Combining the risk paradigm with the system paradigm creates a method for risk that suits OO development well. As the iterative planning moves forward, the project manager can easily use the risk methods to assess the current state of project system risk, as the spiral life cycle requires.

As a practical matter, risk assessment happens in several different places. When you develop process models, part of the model consists of the generic risks the process faces. These risks are reusable risks. Every time you generate a plan from the process model, the generic risks come along for the ride. The risk analysis for these risks happens in two phases. The group that develops the process model

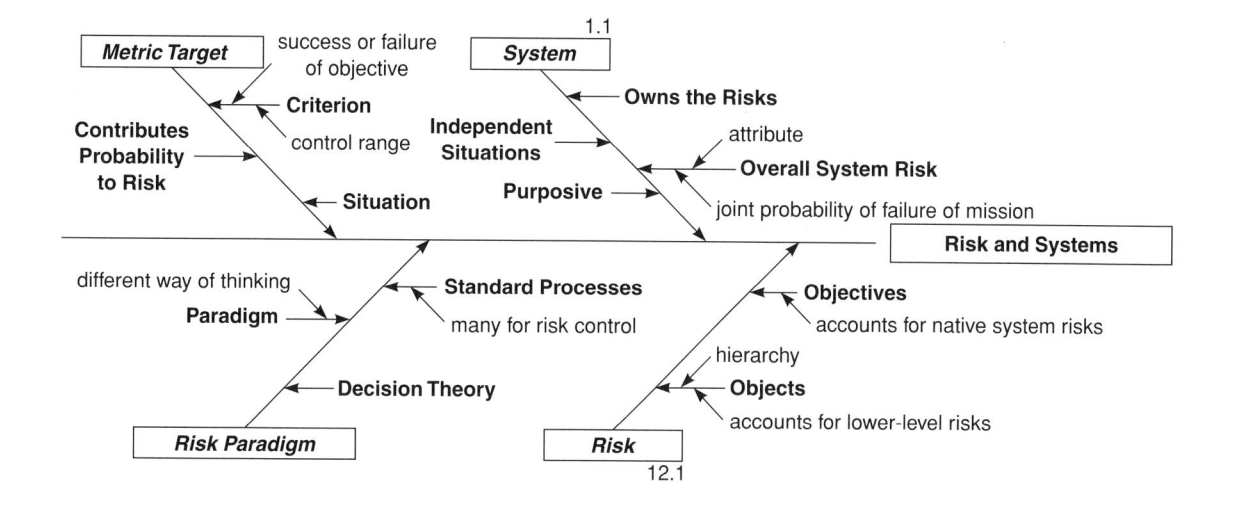

Process Model (4.7)

works out the list of risks and estimates the typical probability of failure. When you plan, you start with this and adjust the probability to the specific situation, and then compare it to the risk tolerance of the system at risk.

The rest of risk assessment occurs during planning. You can either do it all yourself as project manager, or you can divide the work along with the subsidiary plans, making each manager responsible for identifying and assessing the risks in their part of the plan. Ultimately, the risk management plan needs to integrate the risks and their management methods, which is the job of the project manager. If you're lucky and are working on a large project, you may be able to create a special risk manager job to which you can delegate these planning tasks.

Risk Attributes

The attributes of the risk represent all the information you know about the risk. The structure follows the approach of Capers Jones that he bases on the medical desk reference model [Jones 1994]. You can use the information in these attributes to figure out your management options and how much they will cost. Table 12-1 lists the risk attributes and their meanings.

Table 12-1 Attributes of the Risk Class

Attribute	Description
Name	The name of the risk
Description	A brief textual description of the risk
Root Causes	The situations or combinations of events that lead to the negative consequences of the risk
Probability	The probability that the risk will cause the mission of the system to fail
Frequency	How often the risk occurs in generic situations; you can use this to estimate the prior probability
Susceptibility	The kinds of objects that are most susceptible to the risk
Associated Problems	Other risks that tend to occur simultaneously with this one
Prevention	Ways to forestall the events that place the system at risk
Control	Ways to minimize mission failure due to the events that place the system at risk
Effectiveness	How well the control methods work in practice, and what methods are better than others
Costs	How much the control methods cost to apply
Prognosis	How well your project should do if you apply the effective control methods

You start identifying risks with the objectives and internal systems of a particular kind of object (the system at risk). Think about how the failure of these systems might affect the mission. For example, a task mission usually is to produce the outputs by a baselined time with a baselined cost at an acceptable quality. This mission breaks down into several objectives:

- To produce the outputs
- To meet the baselined cost budget
- To meet the quality criteria for the outputs

Each of these objectives has an approach, metric, and target. The targets reflect the priorities of the project. For example, if the project manager must meet strong quality criteria but can be flexible on cost, the control range for the quality targets will be tight but the control range for the cost targets will be loose.

The next step in identifying risks is to look at the objects the system contains. Again looking at a task, a task contains the resource assignments, the input versioned objects, and the output versioned objects. Looking at each internal object of the task, you identify the risks from their objectives and objects and quantify them recursively. The overall risk for each object contributes in some way to the risk of the task system.

Using the metrics and targets and the risks from the internal objects, you can identify the risks fairly easily. The technology may not be capable of producing the outputs. Perhaps the tools aren't good enough, or the skill levels of the engineers may not permit them to understand the task. This latter issue can cause problems with all the objectives. Perhaps there aren't enough engineers to complete the task on budget, or the funding for hardware is lacking. Perhaps the vendor that supplied the framework the task uses as an input was weak on testing, and defects in it could affect output quality. And so on.

Every risk has some kind of *root cause,* a situation in the project system or its environment that causes the event to happen. This situation will consist of objects in particular configurations, either within the project system or in its environment, that put the system at risk. As you think about the system at risk, you analyze it to determine what root causes could produce failure. This leads to a set of specific, independent risks for the system. If the root causes for several risks overlap, you have not identified independent risks, and you should combine them according to root causes.

A *generic risk* is one you associate with a process task model. This risk lets you characterize a task's risks as part of the process model from which you derive the task. You can thus generate multiple task risks from a single risk in the task model. That is, when you create the WBS elements from the process model, you create risks corresponding to the generic risks in the model. You can then customize those risks for the specific task as you customize the objectives and internal objects of the task. You then analyze the task further to see if there are any risks specific to the task situation that were not present in the process task model.

Another way to classify risk is to distinguish errors of *commission* from errors of *omission*. For every kind of risk, you actually have two risks: the risk of doing something that leads to failure, and the risk of not doing something that leads to failure [Weinberg 1982, p. 4]. While inaction may seem preferable to action, as action is likely to be more visible, you should take a balanced approach to the choice. Don't blindly assume that you must do something, but don't also blindly assume that you can't do something. Try both alternatives in your risk analysis and response development to see which produces a better overall result for your total project risk. Would it be better to risk alienating a major customer by leaving out a feature or to risk schedule delays by putting the feature in? Would it be better to risk technical failure by using a new compiler or to risk cost overruns by using the old one that is much less efficient, requiring more engineering to take up the slack in performance?

Chapter 13, Risk Quantification

The final step in identifying risks is to quantify them.

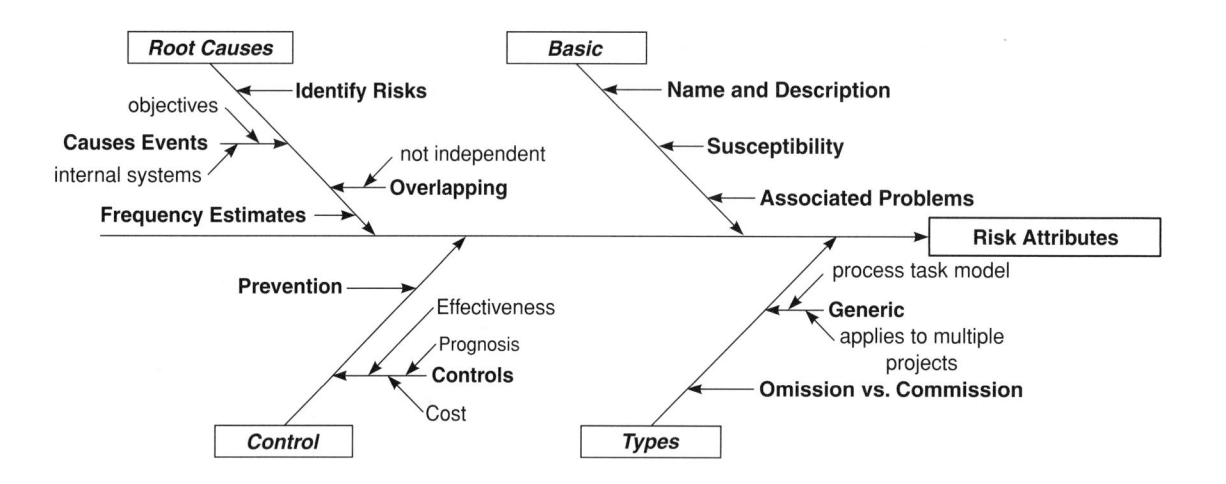

Risk Control

Risk Management Plan (14.1)

After quantifying the risks in the project, you can create or revise the risk management plan by developing responses to the risk.

Developing risk responses identifies the risk management methods that you can use for this risk. Any particular method may apply to many risks, particularly those with similar root causes. The objective is to reduce the risk below the system's risk tolerance. For any particular risk, you need to choose among three control approaches (Table 12-2).

The avoidance and mitigation approaches are not mutually exclusive. You can reduce the probability of occurrence to some extent, and then put in place mitigation measures to handle any event that does occur. You should take this combined approach when prevention or control measures alone are not enough to reduce the risk below your tolerance. The combination may be able to reduce it.

The Risk

Risk Response	Description
Avoid	*Prevent* the risk from occurring by taking forestalling measures (see the Prevention attribute for a list of known measures); this reduces the probability of occurrence to a small value
Mitigate	*Reduce the impact* of the risk occurrence by taking controlling measures (see the Control attribute for a list of known measures); this reduces the impact of the occurrence to a small value
Ignore	Accept the consequences of the risk occurrence, presumably because the risk falls below your risk tolerance

Table 12-2
General Risk Control Approaches

Ignoring the risk is appropriate when it falls within your tolerance level. You do not eliminate the risk; you specify that you are ignoring it. This communicates your strategy and understanding of the risk to the stakeholders through the management plan. Without the risk in the plan, stakeholders may misunderstand; they may think you don't understand the risks. Ignoring a risk means that you associate no risk management methods with the risk.

Given these approaches, as the task progresses, you are now able to control the risk by taking action through the risk management methods. Usually this will involve executing tasks that the risk management plan adds to the WBS during planning.

The several attributes that describe the characteristics of control are effectiveness, costs, and prognosis. The *effectiveness* of a set of controls describes how well the controls work in practice. The *prognosis* describes the positive effects on the project of applying the control methods. The *cost* details how much money you can expect to spend to apply the methods. These attributes describe the joint characteristics of a set of controls, not just a single control, which is why they are attributes of the risk rather than the risk management method. These methods work together, with joint effects, so you have to consider the results and costs as joint, not singular.

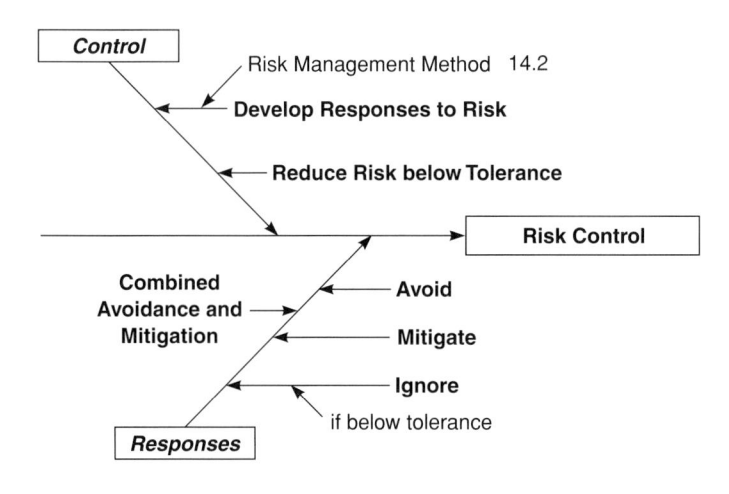

OO Development Risks

OO software development exposes you to much the same risks as would any kind of software development. This section details two kinds of OO-relevant risks. First, OO projects are at specific risk in certain areas due to the nature of OO technology and projects. The use of OO technology is the root cause of the potential for the negative event. Second, OO technology or project management techniques might reduce the potential for some risks by changing the causal factors behind the risk. Consult the several excellent books on software risk management [Charette; Jones 1994; Karolak; Roetzheim] for a broader analysis of software development risk.

- *Note:* The subsections discuss particular causal situations that lead to risks in project systems. Ultimately, you could build a class hierarchy of these causal situations as subclasses of the Risk class. I do not attempt this, as a general causal theory of risk is beyond the scope of the present book. You could also build a shadow hierarchy of risks based on the system class hierarchy, with each class of risk belonging to a class of system at risk. The structure below reflects such a structure but I make no attempt to distinguish these as separate classes. There is not enough behavioral or structural difference between them to justify it here.

The Project Risk

A *project risk* is one that affects the entire project system. It is a risk that prevents the project from achieving its mission. While other risks in this chapter are project-related, these risks affect the project as a whole rather than its parts. The usual situation that leads to a project risk is when some object missing from the project causes mission failure. For example, if you fail to identify a stakeholder, the project can fail to meet that stakeholder's expectations. This isn't a stakeholder failure, because no existing stakeholder has failed. It's a project failure, because you failed to include a stakeholder in the project. Other project risks derive from external forces in the environment that affect the project as a whole, such as a changing market or legal environment.

Project (3.1)

Low Stability

Stakeholder expectations may change so much during the project that the work already done in the project becomes valueless. This is usually due to excessively long project terms or possibly to rapid change in the target market. This project risk is *less* likely to occur in OO projects. First, OO technology can (not will) reduce the time to market. Second, the iterative nature of OO technology and its development life cycle can track requirements changes better than less flexible technologies and processes. Technical tasks are thus less likely to encounter unwelcome changes requiring rework.

Stakeholder (3.3)

You can run into situations in which your project gets into trouble with the budget as it adapts to an increasing number of new requirements and expanded scope. Budgets aren't as flexible as customers, in most cases; OO projects must balance new requirements with budgetary limitations. This takes a global project perspective on the budget, as it requires reallocation of resources and replanning at a high level.

An example of stability risk was a project I participated in for a year and a half. The project had existed for a year prior to my joining it, and it went on for another year after I left. During this time, the company discovered that its target market did not exist, so it redefined the nature of the product several times, searching for a viable product. The OO framework for the project grew and grew, eventually becoming a separate product in its own right that was in turn canceled.

Several subsystems came and went as expectations changed. For example, the second major revision of the system called for a portable database interface that could function on three target operating systems. By the fourth major revision, the company was targeting only one operating system. The system architect decided that buying a database manager that ran only on that system was preferable to finishing the database interface project, which was canned, costing the project about four work-years of wasted effort. The product eventually came to market and was reasonably successful. The company was sold and has returned to profitability.

Poor Tools, Methods, and Tool Acquisition

You may waste much of the money you spend on tools. You can spend $100,000 on CASE tools that prove inadequate and wind up on a shelf, for example. This kind of waste is endemic in software companies [Jones 1994].

You may find that the tools available are not completely up to the job. For example, although the cluster is the fundamental object in the OO life cycle, most configuration management, CASE, and quality assurance tools do not support the concept. These tools generally manage files, not objects. Even OO repository technology is notoriously difficult to apply effectively to OO life cycles and objects. This means that you must face the risks of either adapting your processes to fit your tools or building tools at great cost to support your processes. This latter possibility means the tools you bought go on the shelf.

Tools (P7.1)

The generally poor state of tools and the hyperbole you find among tool vendors leads to the risk of acquiring tools that do not meet your technical needs or that are incompatible with other tools. This acquisition task risk is higher for OO systems because of the lack of standards and the lack of adequate acquisition techniques that take OO requirements into account. On the other hand, the documented return on investment for reusability and OO languages is good to excellent [Jones 1994, pp. 496–498]. That means that the risk of making a poor technology investment in OO tools and methods is probably lower than for investments in other paradigms of software development.

I have experienced shelfware in every company I've worked for. Most companies do not have a serious acquisition process, particularly when buying tools to support new technology. Most companies using OO technology do not focus much on cost, and so are willing to waste a certain amount of money on shelfware if there is a chance of finding a tool that will help them get to market faster. However, one company had a more formal acquisition process that prevented the investment of hundreds of thousands of dollars in compilation technology that proved to be very buggy during the acquisition evaluation process.

Milestone Risk and the Silver Bullet

Milestones are almost always events signaling either the end of a process or of a series of tasks within a process. Within the network of schedule tasks leading to the milestone, the dependencies determine the *critical path*. This is the path through the process from the first task to the milestone that contains all the tasks that can delay the achievement of the milestone. That is, if any task on the critical path lasts longer than its planned finish date, the schedule will delay the milestone date beyond its planned value. The *milestone risk* is the potential for a schedule delay that causes the mission of the milestone to fail.

Dependency Chart (10.3)
Milestone (4.12)

Figure 12-1 shows a sample critical path through a component development process. If the Developer component lasts longer than five days, this failure delays the remaining tasks on the critical path. Thus, the integration and testing of the Employee component gets a five-day delay, which in turn leads to a five-day delay in the Person Component milestone.

The Silver Bullet

The successful selling of OO technology can lead to the risk of too much schedule pressure on milestones. When your boss or your customers hear you are going to use OO technology, their first reaction will be to praise you. The second will be to say how much sooner they want your project to finish. Capers Jones calls this the "Silver Bullet Syndrome" [Jones 1994, pp. 526–533; Brooks, pp. 189–190]. Particularly with your initial projects, which will exhibit less reuse, this can lead almost immediately to schedule pressure. Such pressure results in milestones that you are unlikely to meet.

The flip side of schedule pressure is the risk of optimism. Because *you* selected OO technology to solve your problems, you may expect it to solve all your problems *now*. That's unlikely; it's another Silver Bullet. In particular, if you put too much faith in the claims of technology vendors, you may find the lycanthrope at your throat when the Silver Bullet doesn't work. This will be particularly true on the first few projects until you get a high rate of reuse. This kind of risk is frequently present in Routine cultures, which often believe in magic rather than in measurement.

Management Culture (31.1)

OO Development Risks

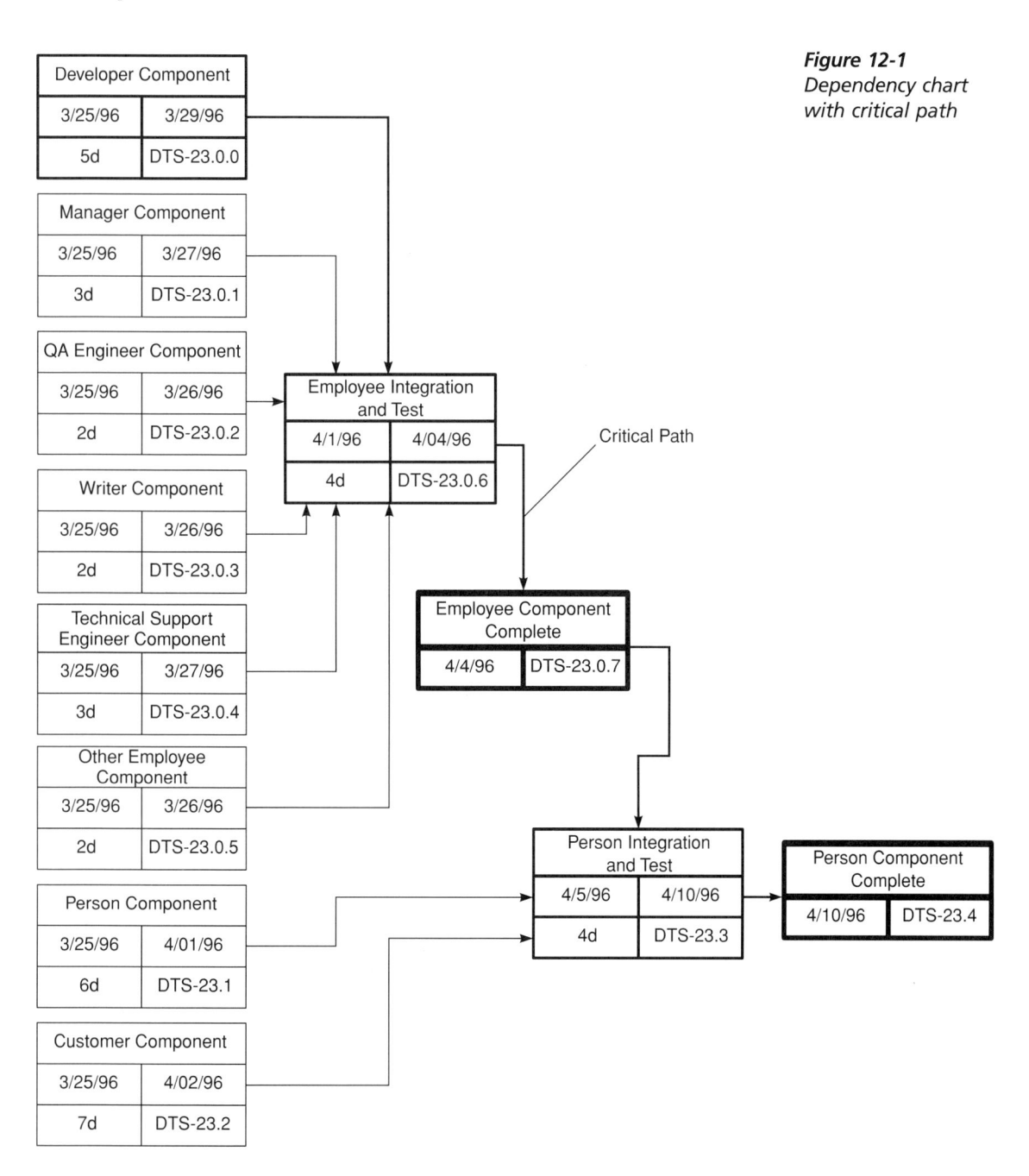

Figure 12-1
Dependency chart with critical path

Developer Component		
3/25/96	3/29/96	
5d	DTS-23.0.0	

Manager Component		
3/25/96	3/27/96	
3d	DTS-23.0.1	

QA Engineer Component		
3/25/96	3/26/96	
2d	DTS-23.0.2	

Writer Component		
3/25/96	3/26/96	
2d	DTS-23.0.3	

Technical Support Engineer Component		
3/25/96	3/27/96	
3d	DTS-23.0.4	

Other Employee Component		
3/25/96	3/26/96	
2d	DTS-23.0.5	

Person Component		
3/25/96	4/01/96	
6d	DTS-23.1	

Customer Component		
3/25/96	4/02/96	
7d	DTS-23.2	

Employee Integration and Test	
4/1/96	4/04/96
4d	DTS-23.0.6

Critical Path

Employee Component Complete	
4/4/96	DTS-23.0.7

Person Integration and Test	
4/5/96	4/10/96
4d	DTS-23.3

Person Component Complete	
4/10/96	DTS-23.4

I met with a subtle version of the Silver Bullet. I was working on a large, OO application, adding relational database technology. The nontechnical manager understood neither OO technology nor relational databases. The integration of the two technologies proved as difficult as it usually does, but the project manager had counted on a smooth, easy transition (I found out later). Someone had made Silver-Bullet technological promises. The project manager canceled the project after it failed to meet its first milestone. He decided that all parties were incompetent.

Stakeholder Friction

Milestone risks lead to friction between project management and stakeholders, especially senior management. If your schedule falls behind, the first thing that happens is an increase in dissatisfaction in senior executives and customers. This can in turn lead to poor morale, increased turnover, and yet lower productivity because of the lack of stakeholder support for the project. These effects feed back into milestones again as they cause further schedule delays.

Poor Technical Skills

The main impact of poor technical skills is on tasks, but there is an impact on milestones as well. When you build a milestone that reflects an assumption that all effort is at the same skill level, you seriously risk delays in completing technical tasks. With skills in OO technology at a premium, your resource pool will almost always have a maldistribution of OO skills. That means that your resource assignments are at risk, which in turn leads to the risk of task failure, which in turn leads to milestone failure through the delay of schedule tasks. This cascade of risks ties together the task and milestone risks.

Skill (34.5)

Poor Project Management Skills

The current state of knowledge of standard project management in the software industry is relatively weak [Jones 1994]. The kinds of skills represented by the classes in this book are even less common. Knowledge of OO project management is thus at risk. This in turn leads to the risk of developing milestones that do not reflect the needs of OO technology because the project manager bases them on an insufficient understanding of those needs. Such plans will invariably diverge from reality.

One of the worst problems I have seen in real-world projects is the inability of the participants to focus on tasks. The plan and schedule lay out the tasks clearly, with inputs and outputs, and the project manager communicates these clearly to team members in communications meetings. And yet, when you examine the work done, the teams spend most of their time doing other things only vaguely related to the tasks: rebuilding their computers, fielding technical questions from Japan, writing nifty new classes that aren't relevant to the task, and so on. These kinds of activities are characteristic of a Variable culture. I used to believe that this was merely people doing what they want to do instead of working, but I have come to believe that

OO Development Risks

people in Variable and Routine cultures are genuinely unaware of the need for focus. They simply don't have the skills needed to understand the purpose underlying a task assignment and to focus on that purpose. Part of this is commitment, part is bad communication, part is low productivity, but a big part is not being able to say no. The inability to say no, to explain why, and to make it stick leads to massive risks for milestones, and it comes directly from poor project management skills on the part of both the project manager and the team members.

Poor Project Management Tools

Project management tools have not caught up with technological tools in managing the OO project. Given the state of the latter tools, this is not a generous evaluation. Unfortunately, most project management tools provide little in the way of flexible process management. Most tools do not yet recognize the impact of processes on planning. This makes schedule maintenance very difficult, if not impossible. Many tools also do not provide the flexible reporting necessary to effective communication.

Project Management System (22.2)

For example, try generating a simple report that automatically informs each person working on multiple projects what tasks they should work on during a particular week, with the tasks ordered by start date. Combine this problem with the iterative and recursive nature of planning and scheduling in an OO project, and you magnify the risk of tool failure by a large factor. The risk here is not so much the risk of developing a poor schedule as the inability to control your project to meet milestones. This leads directly to milestone risk, as your project spirals, unwatched, out of control.

Poor Estimation

You can estimate schedule tasks and milestones in a number of different ways. You can

Cost Estimate (37.1)

- develop the milestones from a system size estimate using a cost-estimation model and a baseline process-scheduling model.
- work out a full WBS and assign resources to tasks, and then use tools to derive the durations for the schedule tasks.
- estimate durations of tasks in the WBS by consensus estimates from the people that will do the work.
- guess.

However you estimate your schedule, with OO technology, you are going to be working with less data than you otherwise would. As well, there are few predictive models from which you can develop schedules [Goldberg; Henderson-Sellers 1996]. This leads directly to milestone risk, as your estimates may vary widely in accuracy.

Until I recently started using function points as a system size metric, I based my estimates either on lines of code or number of classes. I used the COCOMO predictive cost-estimation model and used the results to check the consensus estimates I got from the developers. The two usually differed by an order of magnitude. Sometimes COCOMO was closer, and sometimes the developer was closer. The estimates always required serious risk management.

There's Hope

On the positive side, you may find that you can increasingly reuse other things besides code if you use OO methods. OO methods tend to reduce the impedance mismatch between the phases of development. Analysis models often represent the same classes you wind up coding and testing. The result is that when you build reusable components, the requirements, functional specification, design documentation, and test plans tend to represent the same structure. That means that you can reuse them in new projects just as you reuse the code. This reduces the risk of milestone slips by increasing productivity.

One key result of a milestone slip, particularly the product shipment milestone, is that your product has an excessive time to market. This leads in turn to revenue shortfalls and canceled projects. As your use of OO technology matures, you will find that the risk of excessive time to market falls. With increased productivity due to better quality and higher reuse, you will be able to shorten your project schedules, reducing the risk of cancellation due to milestone failure. If you benchmark the competition and use your optimizing techniques to push productivity far above the benchmark, you should have very little risk of excessive time to market. OO technology alone is not a Silver Bullet, but the combination of OO technology and effective project management may be.

Finally, the iterative and recursive nature of OO projects leads to an iterative planning style. You baseline, but you rebaseline in systematic ways as well. This means that, at any given moment, your milestones are in error. It also means that as the plan progresses, you have a chance to correct these errors based on new information. In more rigid processes, this chance does not exist, and OO projects gain a reduction in milestone risks as a result.

The Schedule Task Risk

Schedule Task (11.1)

The schedule task is the wrapper around a task that contains the temporal aspects of the task, such as duration, start and finish dates, and the dependencies between tasks. Risks to schedule tasks come from the failure of the schedule task mission, to accurately and reliably represent the timing of the work of a task. Schedule task risks can lead to milestone risks if the schedule tasks are on the critical path, but the focus for these risks is the failure of the schedule task, not the milestone.

Lack of Well-Defined Process

You may not be able to develop an effective schedule due to the lack of a well-defined process model. Most companies have an SEI level of 2 or less, meaning that they do not have a well-defined, effective process. Without such a process, you will find it difficult to develop a well-organized WBS. Without such a WBS, you will find it difficult in turn to develop a sensible schedule. You develop schedule tasks that artificially constrain tasks with meaningless dependencies to get them to behave.

Project Process Model (4.8)

This is a more serious problem for OO systems because, while some companies have a well-defined process, the chances of it being a well-defined *OO* process are not good.

Poor Duration Estimation

You can base schedule task duration estimates on effort and availability of resources, or you can estimate the duration based on the size of the outputs. Duration estimation is difficult because there are few validated OO duration predication models. Also, because OO technology is new, your company is unlikely to have collected any applicable historical data, no matter how mature it is or how much data it has collected. You may be using excessively simplistic metrics such as lines of code. This leads to the risk of schedule task failure as the duration estimate becomes highly unreliable.

Cost Estimate (37.1)

I've relied on resource effort estimates and a tool-based resource leveling to set durations. This works well for small projects. It does not scale well to large projects. Large projects normally require using duration estimation, usually with Monte Carlo analysis to get the best estimate. As OO projects get bigger and bigger, it will be necessary to develop stronger predictive models for duration estimation from system size and complexity [Henderson-Sellers 1996].

Procurement Risk

Certain schedule tasks relate to procurement of systems. In an OO project, you are likely to want to go outside the project itself for reusable components. You may also want to subcontract a component to an outside contractor, as this becomes easier with the component architecture of an OO system.

Procurement Process (27.1)

Aside from the obvious risks of procurement failure, you must deal with the extra risk of schedule failure due to late delivery or poor quality on a part of the project outside your direct control. You estimate the probability of failure in the same way you would for your own tasks. If you have statistics on previous projects that the contractor has worked on, you can use those to get better estimates of the risk. Usually, you use contract provisions, contingency plans, and reserves to manage these risks.

Contractual Provision (14.5)

Reserve (14.3)

Contingency Plan (14.4)

The Task Risk

The simple task (a work package or level-of-effort) is the central object in the project system. It is where the real work gets done in the project. Tasks focus on quality and production of outputs but are also at risk from resource assignments (see the following section, "The Resource Assignment Risk"). Tasks do not involve schedule-related risks; these are part of the schedule task and milestone risks (see the preceding sections).

Simple Task (4.3)

Poor Quality

OO technology is new, and there are few validated predictive product metrics for such technology. The result is to increase your risk of a lower rate of defect removal, which in turn leads to a higher risk of an unacceptable project deliverable. The tasks that remove defects and the tasks that produce acceptable project deliverables are at risk.

Most OO projects I've worked on have relied on a combination of instinctive developer unit testing and a system test. For systems with significant amounts of internal reuse, this has invariably caused excessive defects and rework in the reused code. Using OO testing techniques at the object/class level, I was able to deliver a large, reusable cluster with very few defects for the system test to find.

High Complexity

OO systems tend to have lower complexity than other kinds of systems [Henderson-Sellers 1996] because of the OO design features of encapsulation, abstraction, and inheritance. This lower complexity leads to a less risky error rate for tasks that produce clusters compared to modules, their logical equivalent in other styles of design. Thus technical tasks that produce clusters will tend to be less risky in OO systems.

Poor Use of Prototyping

Your project process may not permit the level of prototyping you need. If you fail to prototype in situations where requirements are not clear or where you cannot resolve design issues through analysis, you increase technical risks for those tasks. If you fail to construct a process that can accommodate such prototyping, you cannot even identify the risks for those tasks. In either case, the technical tasks with unclear requirements or outstanding design issues are at risk.

On the other hand, some development organizations go overboard on prototyping [Goldberg]. You can go around and around on a prototype, yet never quite converge to a deliverable product. The risk of endless prototyping is reasonably high in organizations that encourage prototyping. Since the mission of a prototyping task requires convergence, the task is at risk.

Inadequate Skills and Training

The newness of OO technology means that skills related to it are rarer than standard technology skills. This means that you may risk technical failure due to lack of knowledge within the team assigned to the task. You should assess the knowledge and experience of your team in OO technology. You can use this assessment to see whether a technical task is at risk due to lack of skills.

Skill (34.5)

You also run the risk of slow technology transfer due to the paradigmatic nature of OO technology and the cognitive dissonance that this change engenders. This can in turn reduce productivity and increase cost on specific tasks. It can also increase the time to market for the project as a whole.

If your team possesses few OO skills, there is a high risk of *technical malpractice:* performing the at-risk tasks using obsolete and ineffectual techniques [Jones 1994]. This goes beyond simple lack of knowledge. It represents the unwillingness of team members to abandon their favorite practices, especially if they remain untrained, unsocialized, and subject to intense schedule pressure. This can not only make for bad technology, it can cost you thousands of dollars in rework and retraining. It also leads to poor morale and lowered productivity in all technical tasks.

Lack of Standards

These tool-related risks relate to an even harder-to-handle risk: the lack of OO standards. There is not one standard for an OO language currently on the books of the major international standards organizations. This leads to the risk of failing to use the ultimately correct standard for developing your system. Generally, standards run about three to five years behind the state of the art [Jones 1994]. In the case of OO technologies, it seems to be more like seven to eight years. For example, the basic text on the C++ language came out in 1986 [Stroustrup]; the revised version that serves as the basis for the ANSI standard came out in 1990 [Ellis]. Subtract a year for transforming the state of the art into a book, and compare to the current year (1997), in which there is no C++ standard. The C++ draft standard does not include any standard for even a basic framework for developing applications. The other major OO languages and databases are in worse shape.

Low Reuse

You may not be able to reuse code for technical reasons. There are many such roadblocks to reuse. You cannot develop reuse on a project-by-project basis [Goldberg]; you must do it for all projects in the project environment. Thus, any one project has only limited control over reuse and reusability of software. But the biggest reuse issue is architectural. First, it is very hard to design reusable components to match unknown requirements. Second, it is hard to produce components that are 100% compatible with other components [Garlan]. Even when you have a reuse program, you face the risk that it will not measure up to your needs. Tasks that could benefit from reuse risk not being able to do so.

Reusable System (2.1)

Another form of reuse risk is that of not being able to reuse data [Jones 1994]. Your system may depend on data that already exists, such as corporate records, data sets, or historical project data. You may need to use this data without converting it. Unfortunately, OO architecture is largely incompatible with current databases. There are reports of successful integration with relational databases [Goldberg], but in the context of the wider universe, you almost certainly run the risk of data problems. Using an OO database is not really an answer, since most existing data is definitely incompatible with OO databases. Tasks that must be compatible with existing data are thus at risk.

Poor Tools, Methods, and Tool Acquisition

There is also a risk of inadequate methods to support OO development. There is certainly no accepted, standard method for developing OO technology. There is some data available on a case-by-case basis for some methods but little in the way of empirical validation of the methods as a whole. When you choose a method, you are taking a technical risk that the method will produce the results you intend in the technical tasks to which you apply the method. This risk extends to testing methods, which are still weak for OO technology. You cannot simply reuse the old, tried-and-true structured unit and integration testing methods for OO classes, objects, and clusters [Siegel]. This is a second-order risk: the risk of risk management techniques failing to achieve their technical objectives.

Development Tool (21.1)

The Resource Assignment Risk

A resource assignment is the relationship between a resource (labor, physical, or any other kind) and a task. A key part of the resource assignment is the estimate of the cost of the assignment. For people, this means effort times burdened cost of labor for the resource. For physical resources, this means the depreciated cost of the item allocated to this task. Risks to resource assignments come mainly from the potential for cost overruns, which lead to the mission failure of the budget.

Assignment (35.1)

■ *Note:* Fixed and overhead costs can also generate risks, though at the project level, not the individual assignment level. Overhead may come from fixed or variable costs that accrue along with the variable costs; risk analysis of the variable costs should take variable overhead into account. The budget and baseline costs for resource assignments should therefore reflect all variable cost and overhead, not just the pure resource costs. This book ignores the fixed cost, as it usually is not a significant source of cost risk in OO software projects.

Poor Cost Estimation

Cost estimation is difficult because there are few validated OO metrics and cost-estimation models. Also, because OO technology is new, your company is unlikely to have collected any applicable historical data, no matter how mature it is nor how much data it has collected. You may be using excessively simplistic metrics such as number of classes or number of use cases, or worse, lines of code. If so, you are that much more likely to inaccurately estimate your cost.

Cost Estimate (37.1)

Poor Project Management Skills

As with milestones, you can run into cost-estimation and control difficulties because of lack of OO project management skills. There are several implications of the OO development process for estimating the effort for different assignments.

Because you should aim for an optimal level of reuse, you must cost the system to promote such reuse. You need to allocate more effort to new components to ensure they are reusable designs. You must allocate less effort to components that should reuse previously developed components. To make sure all this works, you need to track the tasks with an understanding of the reuse objectives. If the project manager isn't focused on reuse, the cost estimates will not reflect these objectives.

Because of the different structure of OO systems, project managers must work with costs and earned value on an iterative basis. A project manager without understanding of this iterative process fixes costs and baselines early in the project. He or she is not flexible enough to revise those costs and baselines as new structures emerge. This will result in the earned value not adequately reflecting the true value of the software developed. There is no way to predict whether it represents more value or less value, either. This is a project cost risk.

Without an understanding of the structure of OO systems, the project manager is likely to adopt organizational structures that do not align well with these systems. You will find teams that overlap in responsibility for a cluster, divided responsibilities for classes and clusters, and functional assignments that come and go with functional rather than object needs. The lack of alignment between the organization and its responsibilities leads directly to an increase in the cost of producing the deliverables. It also becomes much more difficult to track and control work on the deliverables because of the mixed responsibility. You should analyze assignments to see where this organizational alignment risk is greatest.

Poor Tools, Methods, and Tool Acquisition

By selecting OO technology, you have entered the world of high-tech marketing claims. This is reality versus hype: not all the tools you buy will lead to the increase in productivity the vendor has led you to expect. Thus, you may run a risk of cost overruns if you expect too much from your tools, or indeed from OO technology itself. This is a version of the Silver Bullet again, but this time affecting resource assignments.

High Maintenance Costs

A big advantage of OO development is that it reduces the risk of high maintenance costs. For a maintenance project, a key risk factor is whether you are maintaining an OO system or a system developed with standard or hybrid technology. Well-designed OO software lets you reuse code to enhance the software. It also lets you easily identify the faults in the components that result in failures in the field and reduces the amount of effort you need to spend to fix those faults. Thus, in a maintenance project, you can eliminate many cost risks from consideration on resource assignments.

Here's a story to counterbalance optimism. Although I was not at the company when this happened, I encountered what I think was a silver bullet lodged in the heart of a software product. A company founder had rewritten in C++ large parts of the code he had originally written in C. Unfortunately, the architecture of the product reflected its developer's lack of knowledge of OO design techniques. According to later developers working on maintaining and enhancing the system, the code was a mass of spaghetti with objects strewn about like meatballs. The maintenance efforts quickly dominated the technical work at the company, destroying any hope of getting new products to market in a reasonable time frame.

Excessive Politics

Larger companies that harbor both OO projects and other technologies are at risk for corporate politics interfering with the project. Because OO projects represent a different way of thinking and doing things, you will often find yourself in politically heated situations. This can lead to cost overruns because your team will perform less efficiently. You will get less cooperation from other projects or departments than you need to perform at peak efficiency. You should give this risk to assignments involving meetings with people outside the project. You should also give it to assignments that depend on external deliverables, objects that come from teams outside the project.

Poor Change Management

The real impact of not understanding the OO development process is in rework costs. If you are not controlling changes to the appropriate objects, such as clusters, you will find that it costs more to rework the objects when you have faults. You may be able to restore a module to a certain revision. If that module is part of a cluster, and your change management doesn't track clusters, you will have extra work to make sure the entire cluster is at the right state. You will have to redo integration tests that you might not with adequate configuration management.

Change Management Plan (23.1)

OO Development Risks 223

OO Development Risks

Project Risk
- Low Stability
- Poor Tools, Methods, and Tool Acquisition

Schedule Task Risk
- Lack of Well-Defined Process
- Poor Duration Estimation

Milestone Risk
- The Silver Bullet
- Poor Technical Skills
- Poor Estimation
- Higher Reuse

Task Risk
- Poor Quality
- Poor Use of Prototyping
- Lack of Standards
- Poor Tools, Methods, and Tool Acquisition

- Stakeholder Friction
- Poor Project Management Skills
- Poor Project Management Tools
- High Maintenance Costs
- Inadequate Skills and Training
- Low Reuse

Resource Assignment Risk
- Poor Cost Estimation
- Poor Project Management Skills
- Poor Tools, Methods, and Tool Acquisition
- Excessive Politics
- Poor Change Management

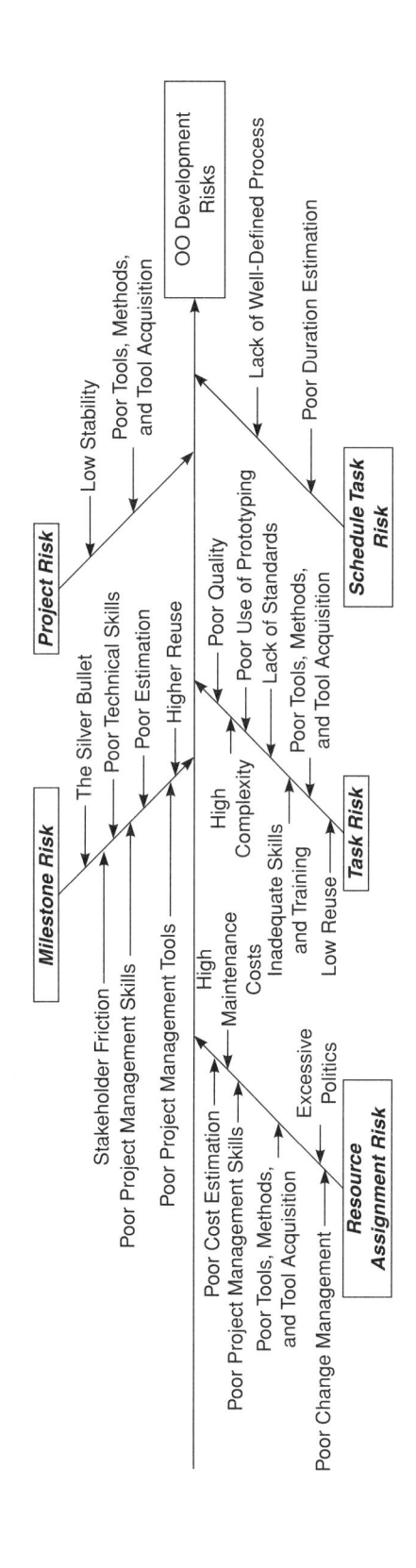

Because OO systems handle requirements changes easily, it is all the more important to track these changes. In other kinds of projects, changes happen infrequently, so tracking the changes is not necessarily critical. As you scale up to larger projects, change management becomes critical to ensure communication of changes and to track delivery. With the kind of iteration possible in OO projects, this scaling happens to much smaller projects. Change management becomes essential to meeting your budget without much rework or sudden discoveries of additional effort that needs doing.

The lack of effective change management can potentially affect all the assignments in the project. The later assignments should have a higher risk factor due to the larger number of objects that should be under control.

Readings

[Carbonell]   Nelson Carbonell. Managing the net risk of your development project. *Object Magazine* 6:12 (February 1997): 58–60.

This very interesting article addresses the risk evaluation problem from a slightly different perspective. Carbonell proposes the concept of net risk, the combined risk from all project components. Net risk management minimizes this overall risk. While I agree with his reasoning, I think an OO model of risk, with its encapsulation and hierarchical risk evaluation, provides a much easier and more suitable approach for managing risk in OO projects. His discussion of risk myths is very enlightening.

[Charette]   Robert N. Charette. *Software Engineering Risk Analysis and Management.* New York: Intertext Publications, McGraw-Hill, 1989.

This book is the best overall introduction to software risk management. Although the book is somewhat disorganized, it has everything you need to understand the basics of risk management. Appendix B has a useful table of the different risks associated with software engineering, with an impact magnitude scale describing the potential impact of several technical, cost, and schedule failures.

[Jones 1994]   Capers Jones. *Assessment and Control of Software Risks.* New York: Yourdon Press, 1994.

Capers Jones has developed an impressive list of risks. The organization of this book follows the Public Health Service medical model, and I've used his categories to organize the attributes of the risk class. Unfortunately, many of these "risks" are really the situations or problems that lead to risks, not the risks that you would consider for the milestones and tasks themselves. The book lists these problems in alphabetical order, which is both an advantage and a disadvantage (look up "Inadequate" and you find 15 things, for example). The biggest problem with the book is the total lack of an index, making it impossible to find references to specific risk management techniques. The book would also benefit from a chapter on the causal relationships between risks. There are two terrific initial chapters on "The Most Common Software Risks" and "The Most Serious Software Risks" that should be required reading for all software project managers.

[Karolak]   Dale Walter Karolak. *Software Engineering Risk Management.* Los Alamitos, CA: IEEE Computer Society Press, 1996.

Karolak provides a good, simple introduction to risk analysis and management and a comprehensive, though oversimplified, system of risk identification and quantification. The method provides a factor-driven approach that identifies general risks and quantifies them for the project as a whole rather than for specific situations within the project.

[Kerzner]   Harold Kerzner. *Project Management: A Systems Approach to Planning, Scheduling, and Controlling, Fifth Edition.* New York: Van Nostrand Reinhold, 1994.

Kerzner's Chapter 17, "Risk Management," is a good summary of the way project managers use risk management and includes many of the specific techniques found in the other books in this bibliography. If you're a project manager, you probably ought to have this book anyway, and this chapter is a good place to start at understanding risk and risk management.

[Roetzheim]   William H. Roetzheim. *Structured Computer Project Management.* Englewood Cliffs, NJ: Prentice Hall, 1988.

This is a general book on project management with a good section on risk analysis. The last chapter contains a couple of excellent sections giving advice on specific kinds of failure.

[Rowe]   William D. Rowe. *The Anatomy of Risk.* New York: Wiley, 1977.

This is the main reference book on risk and risk management. Although it is oriented more toward physical risk (the risk referent Rowe cites most is the risk of being hit by a meteor), Rowe defines the major pieces of the risk puzzle with a wealth of examples and detail that no other book offers.

Questions to Think About

1. Consider a project from your past work that failed in some way. Can you identify the primary risks that the project manager should have foreseen and managed? How would you identify these risks during planning, and how would you manage them?

2. Identify additional technical, cost, and schedule risks that you have seen in your projects. How easy was it to come up with the risks? How complete do you think the Jones and Charette (Department of Defense) lists of risks are? Why?

3. Think about the ultimate causes of the different OO risks. Do the risks stem from a tremendous number of different causes, or are there relatively few? Can you think of any way to manage risks by attacking the causes rather than the symptoms? Does this require organizational change outside the context of a specific project? How would you go about this?

CHAPTER

13 Risk Quantification

Why put numbers on risk? Isn't this just too much effort for too little reward?

First, joint probabilities often yield unintuitive results. The human mind tends to focus on one thing at a time, isolating the effects of one risk to a system. Systems, however, are collections of objects, all of which are at risk themselves. The interactions between the different systems necessary to achieving the objectives of the system yield an emergent system risk apart from the risk of the parts that make up the system [Dörner]. We have trouble figuring out how many black balls come out of an urn, much less how much value is going to come out of a project. Quantifying all these risks gives you an overall risk for the system that reflects the risks of both the parts and the whole.

Second, putting numbers on risk allows you to make a quantitative judgment about the impact of all of your potential failures on your project. By comparing your risk estimate with your risk tolerance, you can more easily decide whether you need to take some kind of risk-averting action.

The *risk quantification* is the part of the risk management plan that evaluates the impact of the risk in each system and the likelihood of its occurrence as a quantitative value. On one hand you quantify the risk tolerance of the system; on the other, the risk of failure. You then can specify risk management methods to reduce the risk below the tolerance.

- *Note:* The methods that this chapter uses for risk quantification are much simpler than the usual methods, though you can use more complex methods if you want to get more sophisticated. If you don't feel comfortable with the math in this chapter, you have two choices: ignore risk quantification and lose the benefits, or acquire the simple math skills this chapter uses through going to the references. I strongly recommend the second approach, because the benefits of risk quantification are great enough to justify some brain pain in learning the math. In any case, reading this chapter will acquaint you with the basic issues and techniques you can use to quantify risk.

Risk Management Plan (14.1)

What Are the Risks?

If you use most of the risk management literature as a guide, figuring out the risk in a system can seem very complicated. One problem is that there is an infinity of risk. There are so many things that can go wrong, it's virtually impossible to take them all into account. The simplifying assumption here is that you're really only interested in one risk—the risk of the system failing to achieve its mission.

- *Note:* Of course, if you don't know what the mission of the system is, or you cannot measure it through operational objectives, you can't simplify risk analysis. This is one of the primary reasons for developing your mission and objectives for each system at risk.

You can see the risk of the project as a decision tree of risky alternatives. Each project component has a risk of failure, and each component of that component has a risk. The binary alternatives (failure or success) lead to binary expected payoffs (value) in the project, with different payoffs coming from different potential failures in project components. This tree is so complex that you must simplify it to be able to do anything with risk quantification. You do this by analyzing risk system by system and encapsulating the internal risk of systems with a single risk number for the system.

- *Note:* Most approaches to software development risk take the standard approach from Rowe (or a simpler version of it). This approach develops a risk metric comprising the probability of failure and the impact or consequence of failure [Charette; Karolak; Rowe] for each risk separately. Because of the mission-risk approach in this book, impact is uniform—the system fails to achieve its mission. This is a simple, binary, mutually exclusive event, which simplifies calculations dramatically. You only need to structure the tree of conditional probabilities within each system to calculate the distribution of risk within the system. Each system has a single risk probability that then becomes the basis for higher-level system risk.

When you begin analyzing risk as part of risk management planning, you start with the project system and work your way down the tree systematically. The planning process identifies the standard risks that come from the various process models that generate the WBS. Given these risks, you look at each system and identify additional risks that might affect the system.

Kinds of Risk

In each system, there are two kinds of risk: risk to objectives and risk to components. If an objective fails, the mission fails. If a component fails to achieve its mission, the failure has some effect on the ability of the system that uses the component to achieve its mission. It may be that there are joint effects as well. Perhaps a combination of failures is more potent, making the system much more certain to fail.

Perhaps there are redundancies that allow one component to fail without consequence to the system mission. These are the emergent risks of the system, effects that exist at the system level rather than in the parts of the system.

Objective Assessment

Objective risk is the risk that the system will not achieve the target for the objective. To evaluate this risk, you look at the objective and determine any risk events that might prevent the system from reaching the target. A common risk event is simply setting the target too high, so you should always evaluate this risk for each objective. List out the risks, and then evaluate each one for its contribution to the total risk for the objective.

For example, any reusable system has the Objective (2.1) to create trust in the system's ability to deliver value. You measure this objective with reuse potential, the weighted probability of inherent, domain, and organizational reuse. The target is a reuse potential of 10% more than the current baseline for such potential for the class. Say you were going to create a requirements document that you intend to be reusable in future projects. Your benchmark for requirements reuse suggests a baseline potential probability of 0.3, a 30% chance of reuse. To evaluate the risk of this objective, you look at the system and decide what the chances are of it meeting the target. In this case, you ask what the chances are of the requirements document having a reuse potential of 40% or more. Looking at the inherent, domain, and organizational factors, you decide the chances of a 40% reuse potential are quite good. You assess a prior probability of 95% for this system objective's being successful and a 5% chance that it will fail.

As another example, consider the complex task of developing the object model cluster for a project management system. This was a real-world task I managed as part of a larger OO effort. The first objective of this task is to create a software cluster that models the various application objects you need in a project management system, such as the Task, the Resource, the Project, and the Resource Assignment. Table 13-1 lists several OO-related risks for this objective along with an estimate for the probability of the event occurring.

Let's take the assessments one by one.

The quality record on this project was not good. No one could tell me the frequency of failure or of defects, since no one tracked such things during development, but from talking with people, I realized that knocking code out was more important than testing. There were no design reviews and no code reviews. Each programmer was responsible for his or her own object testing. There were no quality criteria for checking code into the source control system, however, so there was no verification of object testing. The people working on this task were nice but inexperienced developers. This leads to a strong chance of poor quality. Fortunately, most faults in the code we were working on could be easily caught and corrected, so the impact on the objective was only moderate (35%).

Risk Event	Event Probability
Poor quality	75%
Poor use of prototyping	80%
Inadequate skills and training	90%

Table 13-1
Risk Assessment for a Complex Task's First Objective

The company did not use prototyping. The typical pattern of development started with a functional specification containing a picture of some UI feature. The developer would design this using the features of the GUI framework we were using, code it up, and check it into the system. For the particular task we were to undertake, the specification was difficult to use. We needed to pull together the object needs of the different objects, reusing some of the previously developed classes for these objects as templates. This surely would have benefited from a prototype and several iterations to get the model right. The lack of prototyping also meant that we had no feedback from stakeholders about missing requirements until very late in the project. Because of the iteration of the design, however, the system itself acted as a kind of prototype in-the-large for the object model. I therefore assess this risk at 80%, since we do get some prototyping in most cases.

The developers in my group were all relatively inexperienced. One had never worked with object models before; the other was right out of school. I thus assessed the risk of lack of training at 90%.

Figure 13-1 shows the probability tree for this collection of risks. This graphical representation of the problem shows the possible combinations of the risks. You need to assess a probability for each branch in the tree with the objective of getting the probability of the joint event for each possible combination of risk events. To get this joint probability, you multiply the probability of the first event by the second, and so on through each branch. The top branch in Figure 13-1, for example, shows the probability of all three risks occurring. The first probability is 75%, the second is 80%, and the third is 90% (from Table 13-1).

■ *Note:* The example assumes the risk events are independent, meaning that knowing the probability of one does not affect the estimate for the probability of another one. This results in the probabilities being the same for Prototyping in the two branches in which it appears (good quality and poor quality). If the events are not independent, you must estimate each of these branches separately.

To get the joint probability, you multiply these in decimal form: $0.75 \times 0.8 \times 0.9 = 0.54$, 54%. The final piece of the puzzle, the last branch, is the probability of the objective failing given the previous three risk outcomes. You need to estimate this conditional probability for each branch of the tree. Table 13-2 shows the conditional probabilities of objective failure for Figure 13-1's final probability branches.

Chapter 13 / Risk Quantification

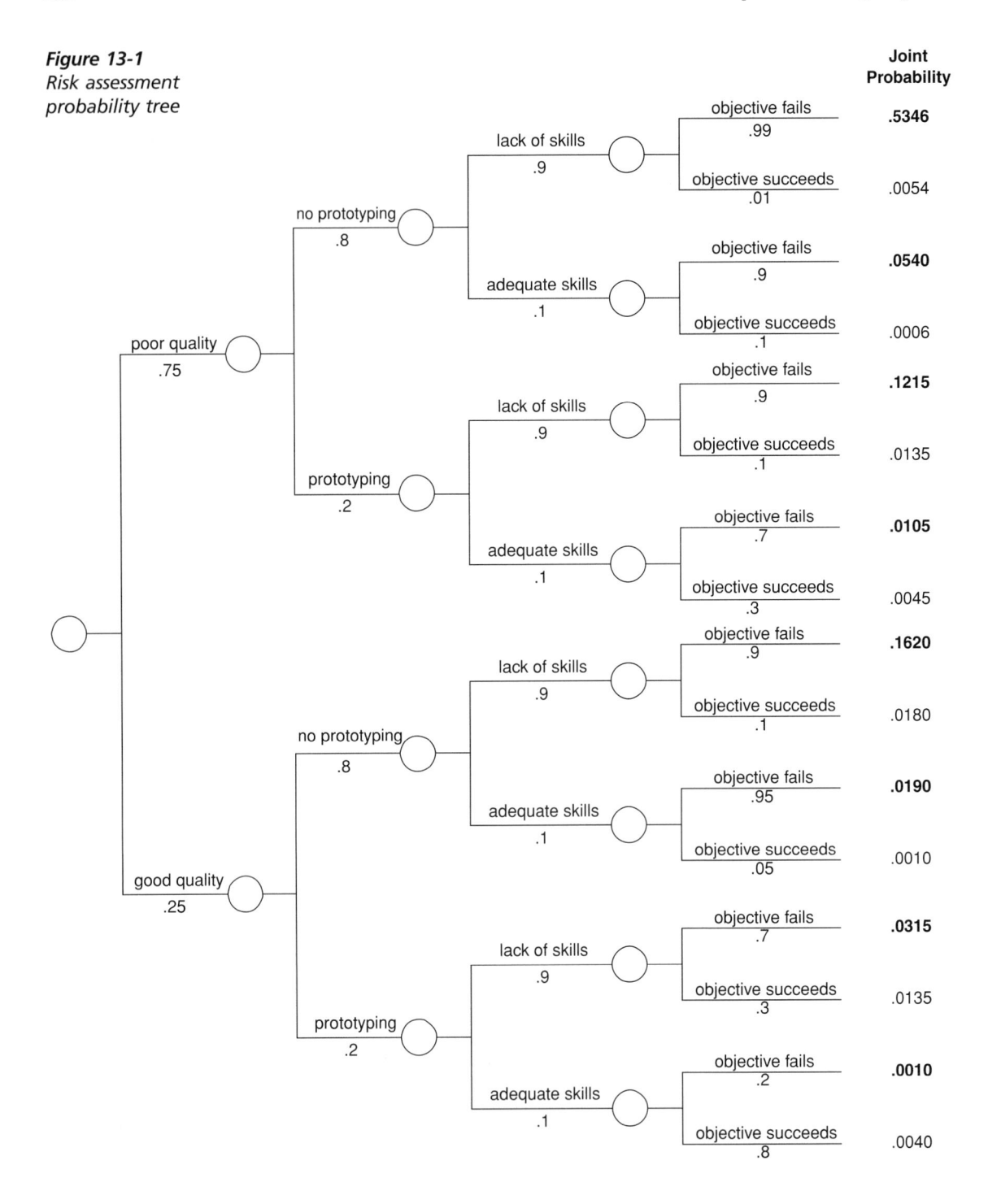

Figure 13-1
Risk assessment probability tree

	Joint Probability
poor quality .75 → no prototyping .8 → lack of skills .9 → objective fails .99	**.5346**
→ objective succeeds .01	.0054
→ adequate skills .1 → objective fails .9	**.0540**
→ objective succeeds .1	.0006
→ prototyping .2 → lack of skills .9 → objective fails .9	**.1215**
→ objective succeeds .1	.0135
→ adequate skills .1 → objective fails .7	**.0105**
→ objective succeeds .3	.0045
good quality .25 → no prototyping .8 → lack of skills .9 → objective fails .9	**.1620**
→ objective succeeds .1	.0180
→ adequate skills .1 → objective fails .95	**.0190**
→ objective succeeds .05	.0010
→ prototyping .2 → lack of skills .9 → objective fails .7	**.0315**
→ objective succeeds .3	.0135
→ adequate skills .1 → objective fails .2	**.0010**
→ objective succeeds .8	.0040

What Are the Risks?

Risks Occurred	Conditional Probability
All	99%
Quality, Prototyping	90%
Quality, Skills	90%
Prototyping, Skills	90%
Quality	70%
Prototyping	95%
Skills	70%
None	20%

Table 13-2
Conditional Probabilities of Objective Failure for Complex Task Objective Risks

You get the conditional probabilities in this table by estimating the probability of not meeting the objective if the specific combination of risks occurs. For example, I've estimated the probability of objective failure at 99% if all three risks occur, but only 75% if just the quality risk occurs. If none of the risks occur, there is still a 20% chance of failure.

By multiplying the previous result by these numbers, you get the final joint probability of objective failure, the numbers to the right of the tree branches. The first branch is now 0.75 × 0.8 × 0.9 × 0.99 = 0.5346, 53.46%. By summing the failure probabilities (in boldface in the diagram), you get the total probability of failure: 53.46 + 5.4 + 12.15 + 1.05 + 16.2 + 1.9 + 3.15 + 0.1 = 93.41%.

This is not a pretty picture. There is a 94% chance of failing to achieve the objective! In retrospect, I was far too complacent about the issues in this project. I did manage to get an experienced quality developer attached to the group to work with my developers on quality, reducing the probability of poor quality greatly. I insisted on design reviews but was not able to persuade the other managers to build a prototype incrementally. I sent one developer to training in the software framework we were reusing and trained the other in object modeling to a certain extent. Nevertheless, the task faltered, due mainly to requirements issues and the lack of some infrastructure such as error handling in the resulting code due to inexperience.

Ultimately, however, the task failed due to something I hadn't foreseen. The GUI framework in which we were working made some assumptions about the internal structure of the operating system common dialogs. As it turned out, we needed to change the logic of those dialogs to handle persistence issues. When we integrated our code into the user interface, the system crashed. We were never able to resolve the issue and had to go back to rework the design using another framework for persistence.

The risk here was my inexperience at risk assessment. I should not have been as complacent about some of the technical risks. I should not have accepted the claims of the framework experts that there would be no problem with the dialogs. Prototyping would have turned this up, but I should have included the risk until I had firm evidence.

Component Assessment

After looking at the objectives for the system, you look at each of the components of the system to determine the risk of the system. In a way, this risk evaluation is simpler; from the perspective of the current system, you simply ask the component system for its risk. What this means in a practical sense, however, is that you switch to the component system and begin over, evaluating its objectives and components. You continue this process down the tree until you reach leaf systems; then you navigate back up the tree, reporting back system risks to using systems. When you get back to the project level, you know the risk for each component of the project and for all the project objectives. Now you can calculate the joint probability of project mission failure.

For example, say you have a project with a single deliverable, the software fault tracking system you're building with C++. After evaluating the risk to the project objectives, you start looking at the components. First, you evaluate stakeholder risk for each major stakeholder. Then you evaluate the risk for the deliverable software system. This leads to an evaluation of the risk for the development process (and its model) and of the component processes and systems that make up that development process. Each cluster has a risk, as does each of the processes associated with the cluster (quality, communication, and so on).

The Event Tree

The failure of a system to achieve its mission comes from the failure to achieve objectives or from the failure of a component of the system. Each system mission can either succeed or fail, so for each system there are two mutually exclusive possible outcomes. The risk of the system is the probability of the failure event, and the probability of success is one minus that probability. The risk in turn depends on the probabilities of failure of the objectives, which depends on the probabilities of failure of the system components in whatever combination. These mutually exclusive, conditional probabilities make up the event tree for the system. Calculating the risk requires you to estimate all the conditional probabilities, and then add them up to get the unconditional probability of system failure.

The event tree in Figure 13-2 shows an example cluster with two classes, one of which helps the other to succeed. This is a list class and its iterator. The list class can succeed in its mission without the iterator succeeding, because the list does not

Figure 13-2
Event tree example

Joint Probability

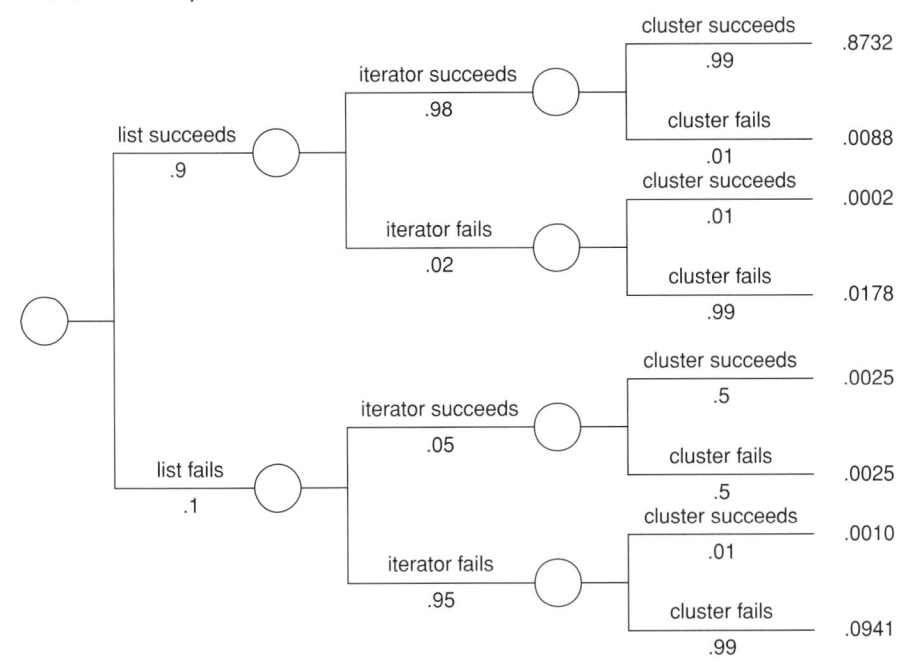

```
                                          cluster succeeds
                                                .99          .8732
                    iterator succeeds
                           .98
                                          cluster fails
      list succeeds                             .01          .0088
           .9
                                          cluster succeeds
                                                .01          .0002
                    iterator fails
                          .02
                                          cluster fails
                                                .99          .0178

                                          cluster succeeds
                                                .5           .0025
                    iterator succeeds
                           .05
                                          cluster fails
      list fails                                .5           .0025
           .1
                                          cluster succeeds
                                                .01          .0010
                    iterator fails
                          .95
                                          cluster fails
                                                .99          .0941
```

access the iterator. But the iterator needs a successful list class to deliver on its mission of iterating over list elements. The list cluster in turn requires both classes to succeed, as its mission depends on both having a list and being able to iterate through it.

■ *Note:* In this simple case, there is a single objective. Failing to achieve the objective results in failure to achieve the mission of the cluster. Clearly, the more complex your objectives, the more complex your risk becomes. Keeping objectives simple is thus a good thing.

The risk of the list failing is 10%, perhaps due to bad design or a coding fault risk due to unfamiliarity with the C++ language or to the inability of tools to build the feature. You might have a general defect rate of 10%, for example, that you use as the prior probability of failure. The risk of the iterator succeeding given a successful list is 98%, leaving a 2% risk. Given an unsuccessful list, the iterator risk becomes 95%.

Given a successful list and iterator, the cluster has a 99% chance of succeeding. The 1% risk reflects some kind of integration fault risk that comes from putting the two classes together into the cluster system (an emergent risk). The other paths reflect a similar logic. One notable probability here: if the list fails and the iterator succeeds, it probably means that the list has some kind of internal problem, but you can still iterate through it successfully. This means a higher probability of the cluster fulfilling its mission, and hence the 50-50 split.

The probabilities to the right of the tree are the joint probabilities of each path through the tree. These are simply the multiplication of the probabilities along the path. The sum of these eight probabilities is 1. To calculate the unconditional risk of the system, you sum up all the paths in which the cluster fails: 0.0088 + 0.0178 + 0.0025 + 0.0941 = 0.1232. The cluster has a 12.3% risk of failure.

Controlling Risk

Given this risk, you now need to compare the risk to the system risk tolerance (see the following main section). If the risk is greater than the tolerance, you need to put in place risk control measures that lower the risk. This creates a decision tree that shows the various risk management methods as decisions with appropriate changes in the probabilities of success and failure of the components. As with any OO system, you can simplify calculations by encapsulation.

"Risk Tolerance Quantification" section, p. 236

For example, in the list cluster, the greatest contributor to the risk is the path where both list and iterator fail. It may be possible to reduce this risk dramatically by reducing the unconditional risk of list failure. You could add an object test suite for the list to the system to see what effect it might have. This changes the probabilities of the list failing without changing anything else. Figure 13-3 shows the resulting decision tree.

Each of the two parts of the tree now sum to 1, but the distribution of risk is very different. Because you've changed the initial probabilities of list success and failure, the path risks change, and the unconditional system risk becomes 4%. By adding the object test suite, you've reduced the risk by 8%.

There are four important things to note here. First, you take control measures only if the system risk is greater than the risk tolerance. For example, if your tolerance for the list cluster was 20% because it isn't that important a part of the system, then you would not bother to add the object test suite. Second, by focusing on the greatest contributors to risk using the standard Pareto approach, you can quickly identify those risk management methods that will have the biggest impact on system risk. This lets you ignore components that contribute little to system risk. Third, by encapsulating risk management, you simplify your calculations and magnify the impact of your decisions on system risk.

> ■ *Note:* It is essential to understand the basic nature of probability here. By using tolerance, you are combining your preference for risk with the subjective estimation of actual risk. That does not mean that you are eliminating risk; it means *you are taking just the risk you want to take.* Any risk is still risk. Even though you successfully execute your object test suite, there is still a 1% chance of failure. One out of 100 times, the list will fail. You took your risk and failed. There is no guarantee of success, only a guarantee that you have your risk under control.

Figure 13-3
Control decision tree example

Joint Probability

Path	Joint Probability
no object test suite → list succeeds (.9) → iterator succeeds (.98) → cluster succeeds (.99)	.8732
no object test suite → list succeeds (.9) → iterator succeeds (.98) → cluster fails (.01)	.0088
no object test suite → list succeeds (.9) → iterator fails (.02) → cluster succeeds (.01)	.0002
no object test suite → list succeeds (.9) → iterator fails (.02) → cluster fails (.99)	.0178
no object test suite → list fails (.1) → iterator succeeds (.05) → cluster succeeds (.5)	.0025
no object test suite → list fails (.1) → iterator succeeds (.05) → cluster fails (.5)	.0025
no object test suite → list fails (.1) → iterator fails (.95) → cluster succeeds (.01)	.0010
no object test suite → list fails (.1) → iterator fails (.95) → cluster fails (.99)	.0941
object test suite → list succeeds (**.99**) → iterator succeeds (.98) → cluster succeeds (.99)	.9605
object test suite → list succeeds (**.99**) → iterator succeeds (.98) → cluster fails (.01)	.0097
object test suite → list succeeds (**.99**) → iterator fails (.02) → cluster succeeds (.01)	.0002
object test suite → list succeeds (**.99**) → iterator fails (.02) → cluster fails (.99)	.0196
object test suite → list fails (**.01**) → iterator succeeds (.05) → cluster succeeds (.5)	.0003
object test suite → list fails (**.01**) → iterator succeeds (.05) → cluster fails (.5)	.0003
object test suite → list fails (**.01**) → iterator fails (.95) → cluster succeeds (.01)	.0001
object test suite → list fails (**.01**) → iterator fails (.95) → cluster fails (.99)	.0094

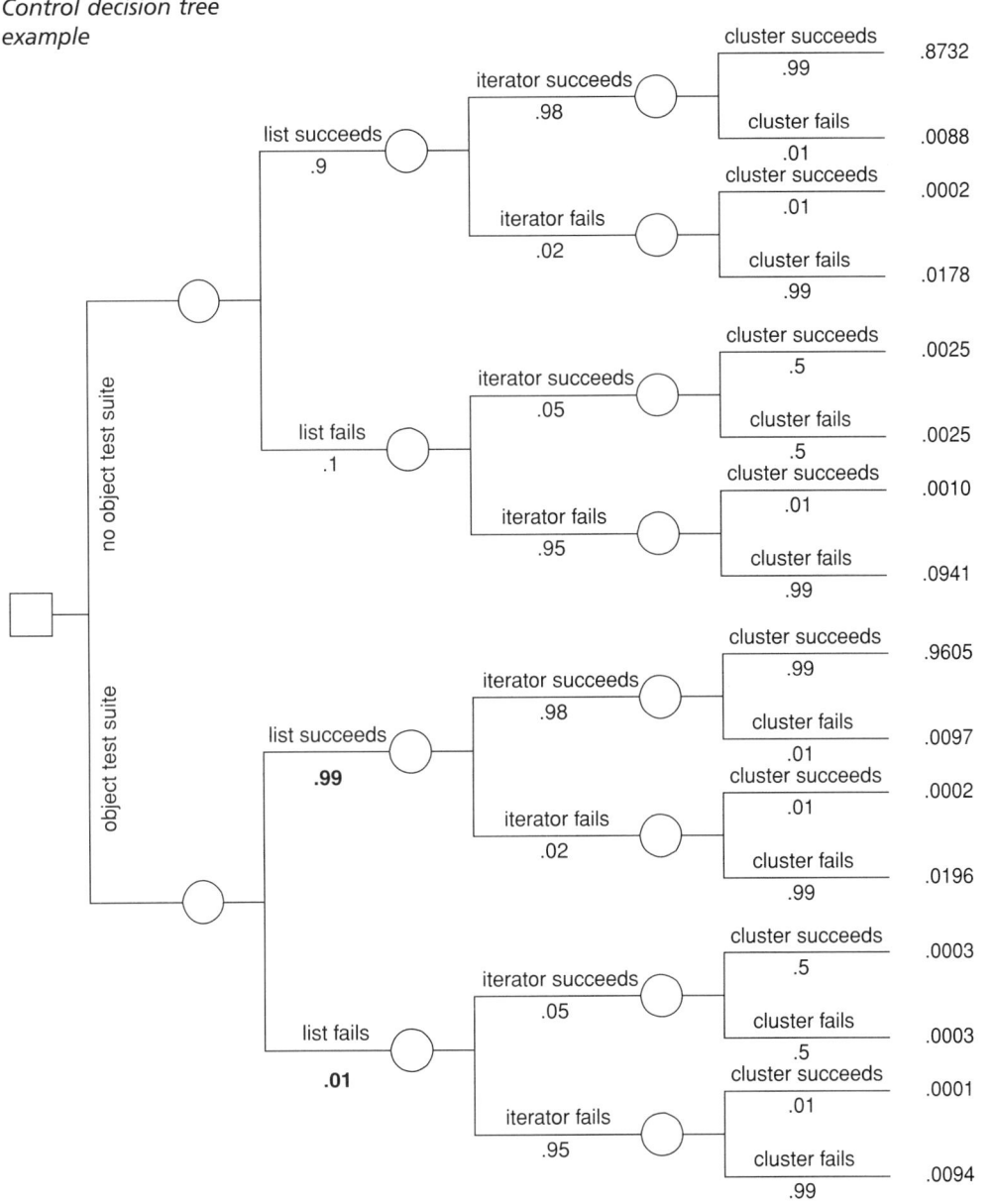

Fourth, most of the probabilities you estimate are subjective in nature. They represent your best guess about the true probabilities. There are various ways to improve your estimates. You can, for example, run simulations using PERT, Monte Carlo, or other methods based on probability distributions and random number generation to compute probabilities. You can also use Bayesian statistical analysis to combine prior probability estimates with data-based likelihoods to obtain posterior probability distributions [Helm; Holloway; Phillips]. As your data accumulates for various kinds of systems in your organizational repositories, you can start with better and better estimates of risk.

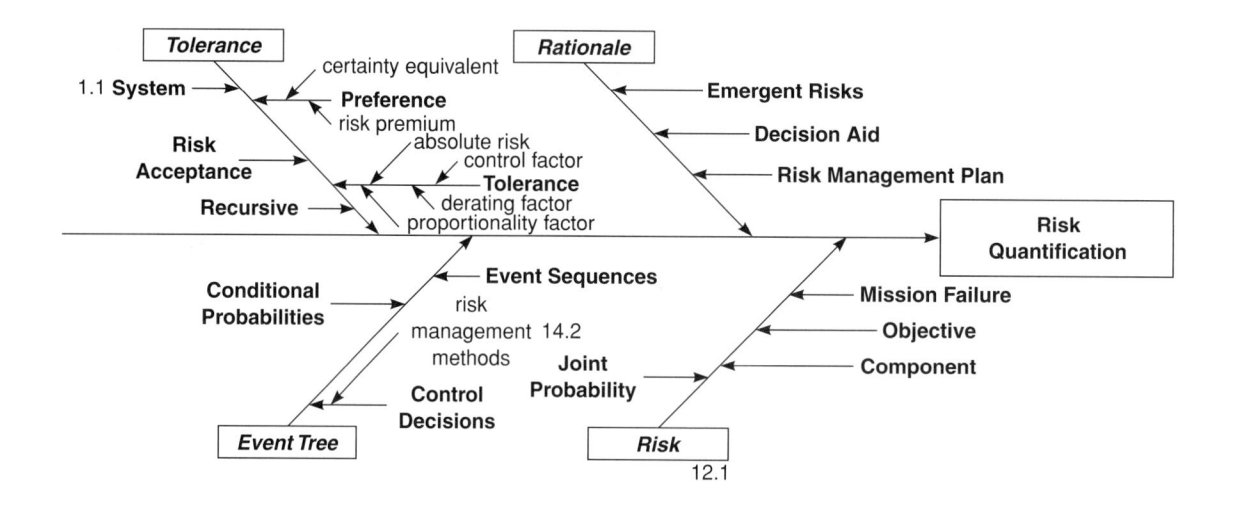

Risk Tolerance Quantification

The risk tolerance of a system is the probability of failure that it will accept. If the risk is below this level, the system can sleep at night, so to speak.

Preference, Certainty, and You

Decision theorists generally divide people into risk averse, risk neutral, or risk seeking based on their preference curves for an event. A preference curve shows the relationship between certainty equivalents and preference. A *certainty equivalent* for an uncertain event is the certain value, in whatever units, that you are just willing to accept in place of the roll of the dice represented by the event. For example, say you are building an OO system that you must be able to move between two different graphical user interfaces. Your architecture comes down to a choice between not being portable or acquiring and integrating a third-party class library for $1,000. Your research on the class library shows that there is some probability of the class library failing under some extreme conditions. Your marketing department tells you that having the portability is worth $50,000 in revenue. Your development manager tells you that the cost of using the library would be about $20,000.

The certainty equivalent for this situation is a value that is equivalent to the uncertain event, reusing the portability library. On the one hand, if you successfully use the library, you make $30,000. On the other hand, if you fail, you lose $20,000, the development cost of the system. Your certainty equivalent is the amount of money that you would take in place of having to make this decision. How much of a bird in the hand would it take to make you not care whether the library would fail? If no amount of money would, you're probably not suited to being a software project manager—you're too risk averse. The certainty equivalent in this case is probably somewhere between a moderate loss and a moderate gain, say between losing $5,000 and gaining $10,000.

Another way to think about the certainty equivalent is insurance. Say an insurance agent walked into your office and offered you this deal. If you develop using the class library and end up making less than $10,000 on it, the insurance company will pay the difference. If you make more, they take the excess. If you think this is a reasonable deal, $10,000 is your certainty equivalent, since you are now certain of getting $10,000. Moving this value up and down until you are just at the point of turning the deal down is the exact certainty equivalent of the decision.

The *risk premium* is the difference between the expected payoff of an event and the certainty equivalent of that event. In the above example, if the expected payoff is $50,000 and your certainty equivalent is $10,000, the risk premium is $40,000. That's what you'll pay to the insurance company for letting you sleep at night. If you are *risk averse,* you have a positive risk premium.

Preference is a ratio scale that measures the preference of the decision maker for alternatives. Another way of saying this is that the preference scale measures the probability of winning a certainty equivalent for a reference gamble. The preference curve is a relationship that translates certainty equivalents into preferences. Figure 13-4 is a preference curve for the portability decision. The straight line represents the risk-neutral preference curve, where the certainty equivalent is the expected payoff. The risk premium is the difference between this expected payoff and the certainty equivalent for a particular preference. Note that the premium grows to a certain point, and then declines as the expected payoff grows. People tend to have relatively higher certainty equivalents for relatively higher payoffs, not surprisingly.

For instance, if the preference for the $50,000 is 1 and the preference for the $20,000 loss is 0, and there is a 50-50 chance of failing (risk probability), then the expected preference is .5 ((0.5 * 1) + (0.5 * 0)). If your certainty equivalent is $5,000, your risk premium is the distance between the expected value ((0.5 * $50,000) + (0.5 * –20,000) = $15,000) and the certainty equivalent ($10,000). The preference curve shows the smoothed risk premiums for the entire range of preferences and certainty equivalents.

Figure 13-4
A preference curve

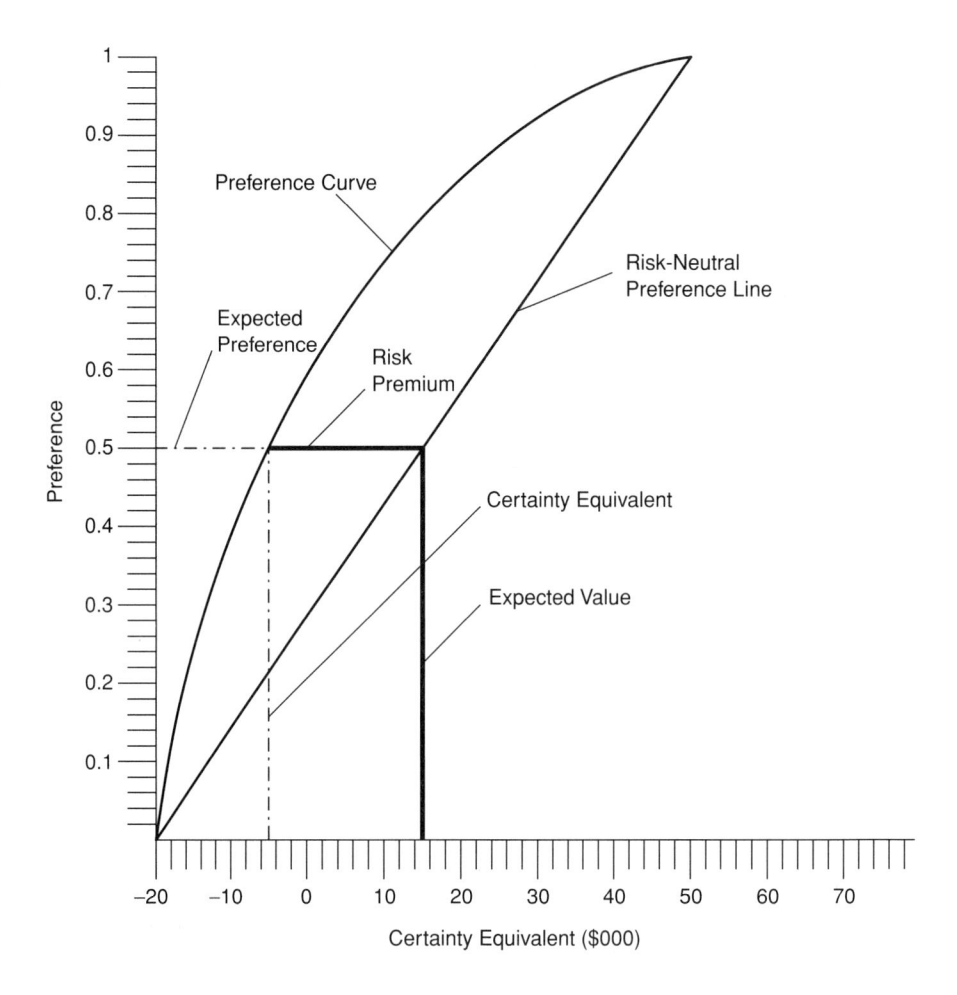

Tolerating Risk

The *risk tolerance* of a system is the probability of failure of the mission of the system that you are willing to accept. By "you," I don't necessarily mean you personally, but rather your system and the systems that use your system. Your own preferences might have you sleeping at night when your system doesn't. You should always use system preferences, not personal ones, in making system decisions. The risk tolerance varies from system to system within the project depending on the impact of that system on the systems that use it.

System (1.1)

In the case of the portability example, the system is the high-level cluster that reuses the library. The mission of that system is to provide some value in function points to the system. Failing to achieve that due to library defects on different platforms, for example, means mission failure. This, in turn, means that the system will fail to provide certain functions on certain platforms. For example, clicking on a certain button to initiate some GUI feature might crash the system on the Mac but might work fine under Windows. How much risk could you tolerate here?

A system consists of component objects, and various other systems use the system as a component object. The risk tolerance of the system at risk must take into account the effect of its mission failure on all the objects that use it. It is the job of those objects to tell the system what their tolerance for failure is. The system then uses the least tolerant object to set its own tolerance.

To set a risk tolerance, you must have some kind of reference risk to which to compare your risk preference. Inverting the standard preference curve from the last section, you get the risk acceptance profile. This graph shows the relationship between the tolerance level for the risk event and the qualitative consequence of the event (Figure 13-5) [Rowe, pp. 168–169].

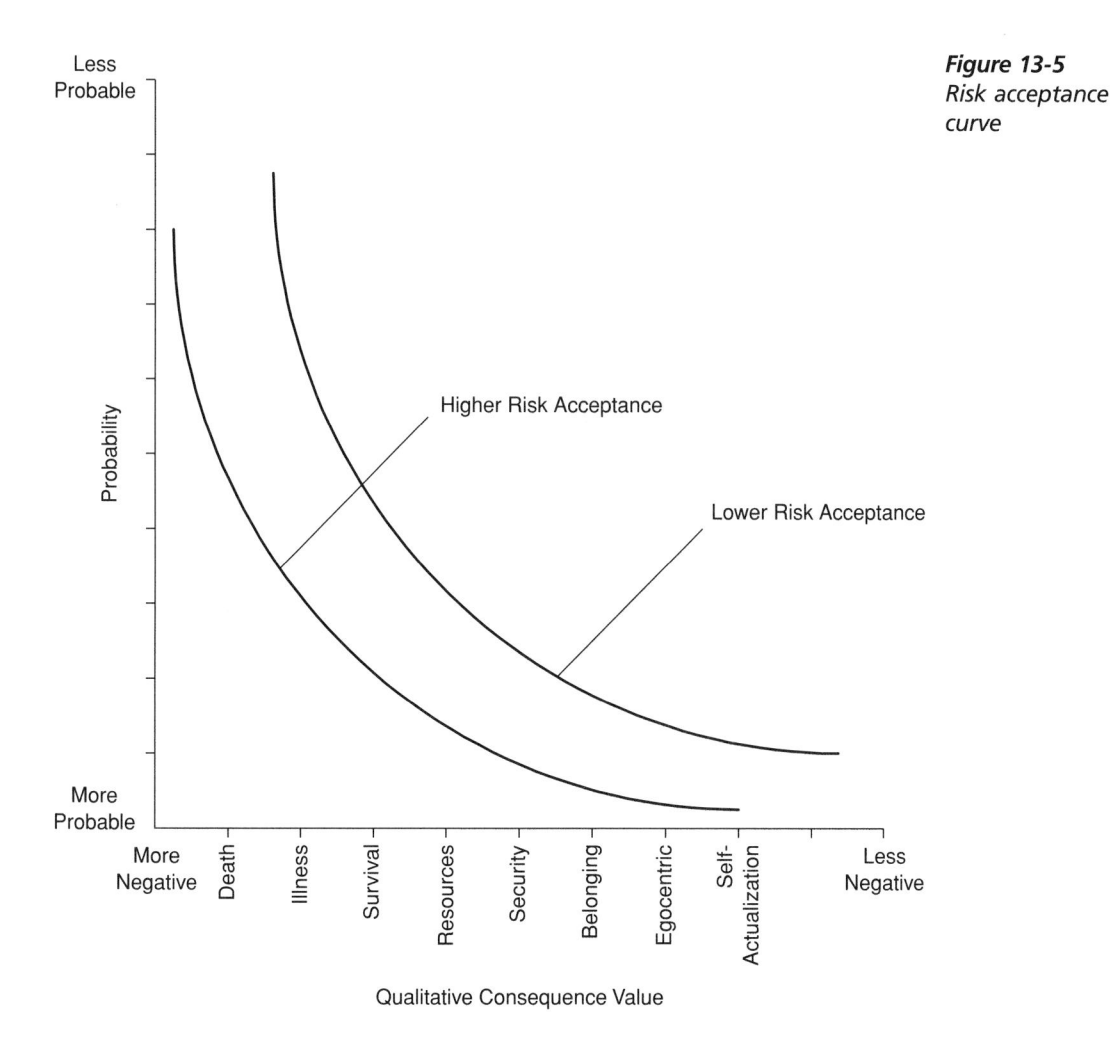

Figure 13-5
Risk acceptance curve

The consequences of risk fall into various Maslowian categories, depending on the nature of the system at risk and its position in other systems. A software component that you use in a mission-critical system such as a controller for a potentially deadly X-ray machine or a spacecraft can cause death, so your risk tolerance will be quite low. A communication plan for a minor, 10-week development project for an internal software bug-tracking application might affect your relationship to others in your organization in a noncritical way. This might lead to a moderate-to-high risk tolerance. A training course might affect your self-actualization, leading to a relatively high tolerance for risk.

Another way to understand the system risk tolerance is as the threshold of risk beyond which you have sufficient concern to take risk avoidance or mitigation measures.

Rowe has developed a general equation for risk tolerance [Rowe, p. 375]:

```
Risk Tolerance = AR × PF × DF × C
```

where AR is an absolute risk reference, such as the risk of being laid off (say, 10%) or hit by a meteor (10^{-14}%), whichever seems most appropriate; PF is a proportionality factor that represents the additional amount of risk your organization will accept for a very beneficial indirect benefit; DF is a derating factor for the proportionality factor that adjusts for indirect cost-benefit balances (favorable = 1, indecisive = 0 .01, unacceptable = 0.0001); and C is the overall desirability of control based on the approach, degree, implementation, and effectiveness of available risk management methods.

For example, the absolute risk reference for our ongoing example system might be the mean risk of GUI failure through operating system flaws, say 1×10^{-3}. Since the system is new but there is software reuse of a certified class library sold as a commercial, warranted product, the proportionality factor is probably reasonably high, near 1 (a doubling of risk is acceptable to get the benefit). The fact of certification and sale as a commercial product shows the favorability of the indirect cost-benefit balance, giving a derating factor of 1 as well. The available risk management methods include OO design, tools for inspection and verification such as a test bed and reference regression tests, and OO risk management through quality assurance, training and certification, and design and code reviews. This leads to a control factor close to 1 as well.

The overall risk tolerance is thus $1 \times 10^{-3} \times 1 \times 1 \times 1$, or 1×10^{-3}. You can accept a risk of system failure of 0.001, or 0.1%.

The proportionality factor could decrease, for example, if the decision involved an uncertified class library of dubious value. You might have a proportionality factor of 0.1 reflecting the dubious value and a derating factor of 0.2 reflecting the lack of certification (and thus the unacceptability of the cost-benefit balance resulting from possible defects). You might have a situation where you had no available means of systemic control of risk, leading to a control factor of 0.1. This situation would result in a risk tolerance of $1 \times 10^{-3} \times 0.1 \times 0.2 \times 0.1 = 2 \times 10^{-6}$. This is a much lower tolerance for risk, reflecting your unwillingness to take system risks to get dubious benefits. You would need to demonstrate that the class library had this level of risk of failure to accept the decision to use it.

The tolerance setting is part of the recursive, global risk analysis. Starting with the stakeholders, you determine the tolerance for the project system. Your risk reference should come from the general stakeholder environment, preferably from some kind of measurable acceptable risk of failure, such as a competitive benchmark available through an industry association or market research reports. Having determined the risk reference, you now set the tolerance for your project system. You then determine the risk tolerances for the different system components (plan, deliverables, process, organization, information system, and organizational environment). You assign the tolerance, and those systems take over and transmit the tolerance down the hierarchy as required to meet that tolerance.

For example, say you are developing an OO system for managing manufacturing plant designs. You benchmark the industry to determine the acceptable risk of failure to stakeholders, which might be as high as 10 or 20% (software fails with abandon in the current market). In other words, customers, executives, and employees are willing to live with 10–20% risk of system failure in the deliverables. You then build your risk tolerance for the project from the various factors in combination with this reference. For example, you might have a proportionality factor of 0.9 because of the terrific productivity benefits of your product to its stakeholders and a derating factor of 0.1 due to the marginally favorable cost-benefit analysis for the particular industry you're aiming at (steel, say, or toy making). As well, you know your organization has an SEI rating of 1 and little knowledge of OO methods, so you know controlling risk will be a problem, leading to a control factor of 0.1. Your project risk tolerance would be $0.2 \times 0.9 \times 0.1 \times 0.1 = 1.8 \times 10^{-3}$.

You then turn around and set the risk tolerances for the different parts of your project according to their contribution to system risk. For example, your organization contributes much risk due to lack of knowledge of OO methods. The organizational risk tolerance should be equal to or less than your project tolerance. On the other hand, as the overall project management requirements for the project are small, the impact of the project management system is not that great, so you can tolerate more risk there. Generally, however, the stakeholder risk adjusted for benefits and control should determine the tolerance of system components.

As you progress, you may set the risk tolerance for a system multiple times, since multiple systems may use that system. Each such system sets its risk tolerance as the minimum risk tolerance requested by any system. That is, if the requested tolerance is less than the current tolerance, reset the tolerance to the new value; otherwise, ignore it. That ensures that the system risk tolerance reflects the impact of the using system that would suffer the most from the system's mission failure.

Risk Management Plan (14.1)

Once you have set all the system tolerances, you can develop and compare the internal risks and overall risk to the tolerance. This lets you decide whether to ignore the risk or to put in place risk management methods. This is part of developing your risk management plan.

Readings

[Dörner]   Dietrich Dörner. *The Logic of Failure: Why Things Go Wrong and What We Can Do to Make Them Right.* New York: Metropolitan Books, 1996 (originally published in German in 1989).

Dörner's fascinating psychological study of the impact of systems on policy failure should be required reading for every project manager. Seeing how and why seemingly thoughtful, intelligent people get blindsided by systems is a sobering exercise. This book advocates a balanced approach to planning, standardization, data gathering, and action oriented toward finding our way through the system thicket. Risk analysis in particular is a way to prevent ballistic behavior, where feedback leads to increasingly extreme and bizarre actions.

[Helm]   Leslie Helm. Improbable inspiration: The future of software may lie in the obscure theories of an 18th century cleric named Thomas Bayes. *Los Angeles Times,* October 28, 1996. Available on the World Wide Web at http://hugin.dk/lat-bn.html.

This article has an extensive and well-written discussion of one application of Bayesian statistics, the Bayesian network. Researchers at Microsoft have developed some interesting tools using Bayesian methods that will help software learn how to do a better job for people. The same methods are the basis for much of modern decision theory [Holloway].

[Holloway]   Charles A. Holloway. *Decision Making Under Uncertainty: Models and Choices.* Englewood Cliffs, NJ: Prentice Hall, 1979.

This book is an introductory textbook on decision theory. It is the book you should go to for an understanding of the basic probability mathematics behind this chapter, both for the probability calculations and the approach to preferences. Holloway takes the theory developed by Raiffa and others and makes it very comprehensible, with many examples from the real industrial world. There are still many urns filled with balls, but there are integrated-circuit components, oil wells, and stock investments as well.

[Phillips]   Lawrence D. Phillips. *Bayesian Statistics for Social Scientists.* New York: Crowell, 1973.

This text is an excellent introduction to Bayesian statistics. It has very clear explanations and examples of how to develop priors, likelihoods, and conditional probability distributions. Reading this in conjunction with another text on decision theory such as [Holloway] will give you an excellent mathematical basis for risk analysis.

[Rowe]   William D. Rowe. *The Anatomy of Risk.* New York: Wiley, 1977.

Rowe is extremely detailed on developing risk referents (tolerances), particularly for health- and welfare-related risks such as airplane accidents or pollution. Rowe developed the risk-referent analysis based on Maslow's hierarchy of needs that I use here. You should go to Rowe for much detail and fully worked out examples of the risk tolerance equation.

Questions to Think About

1. Are you risk averse, risk neutral, or risk seeking? What kinds of behaviors do you think each of these personality types exhibits in software development?

2. If you do not use the idea of risk tolerance, how else could you decide how much risk to take?

3. Is it possible to take risks without realizing it?

4. Would you be willing to adjust your risk tolerance for a system if you found you could not reduce the system risk to your initial tolerance? What are the implications of your answer to your risk acceptance curve?

5. What is the most direct risk management method of all? (Hint: If you don't have a system, you don't have any risk.)

6. Are you comfortable with the fact of using subjective probability estimates for risk analysis? What are the alternatives?

CHAPTER 14

Risk Management

The Risk Management Plan

Given the list of quantified risks, the *risk management plan* develops approaches to managing those risks, either by lowering the probability of the risk or by mitigating the risk's impact, or both. Virtually every supporting process in the software project process relates to some kind of risk response. The risk management plan identifies the processes and tasks that address specific risks by applying the risk management process. Risk is a choice, not a fate [Bernstein].

The risk management plan contains a set of risks and a set of risk management methods. Each method has its own relationships to various other kinds of systems. The plan is a part of the project plan.

Vision: *A project brought to a successful conclusion despite the slings and arrows of outrageous fortune*

Mission: *To identify and control all risks that affect the successful delivery of the project's products and services*

Objective 14.1: To identify all risks that affect the success of the project system

---

Approach 14.1: For each system in the project plan, analyze the risks to the system mission. Identify those likely to affect the project. Start with standard risks from the project process models and add any risks that are specific to this project. Quantify the risks and determine whether the risk exceeds the system tolerance for risk.

Metric 14.1.1: Relative risk ratio: the ratio of identified risks to a benchmark of project risk in comparable projects; this metric tells you whether your risk analysis is in line with the usual amount of risk for this kind of project

The Risk Management Plan 245

Target 14.1.1: A relative risk rate near 1 within limits on a pn control chart over the life of the plan

---

Metric 14.1.2: Red flag rate: the number of unanticipated events per month having a material effect on a major system in the project; this metric gives you immediate feedback on your plan's effectiveness in identifying the real risks of the project

Target 14.1.2: A red flag rate within control limits of a p control chart, with a value approaching 0

Objective 14.2: To control all risks that affect the success of the project system

---

Approach 14.2: For those risks that exceed their system's risk tolerance, estimate the causes, outcomes, exposure, and consequences of the risk [Rowe]. Using decision trees or other aids to comparison of alternatives, develop risk management methods that reduce the risk in the system below the risk tolerance. Build the risk management methods into the WBS and project process. Monitor the results of these tasks for effectiveness. Modify the plan as required to accommodate changes in risk or in understanding of risk.

Metric 14.2: Risk control ratio: the ratio of identified risk events that did not occur to the total number of identified risk events

Target 14.2: A risk control ratio below the risk tolerance of the project

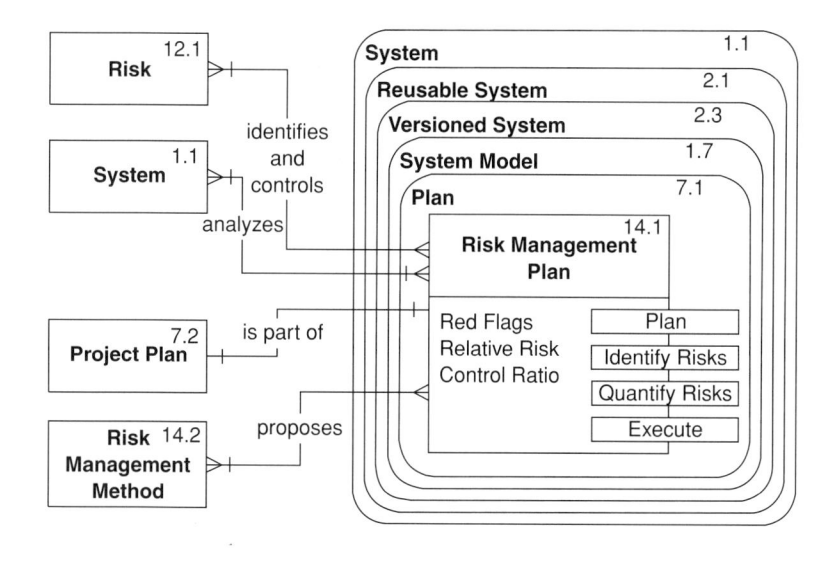

Risk management planning identifies project risks and quantifies them. An *identified risk* is one that you estimate will exceed the risk tolerance of the system at risk. The job of the risk management plan is to identify risks and control them, bringing the total project risk under the project risk tolerance.

Quantification is the intermediate step that lets you decide what risk management methods are most useful in controlling the risk. You first determine the probability of the risk. You then compare that probability to the risk tolerance. You can ignore risks that fall within the tolerance of the system. For those that do not, you must identify risk management methods that reduce the risk below the system tolerance. Usually, you focus on those parts of the system with high risk, and you use risk management methods optimally to balance their cost and benefits.

■ *Note:* You can accept excessive risk in some systems within a project if you can find a way to bring the risk of the entire project under your risk tolerance. Just don't become a fugitive from the law of averages.

There are several specific areas in which you should concentrate your risk management plan:

- Stakeholders
- Deliverables
- Statement of Work
- Schedule
- Budget
- Procurement Processes

Your risk management plan should clearly identify the major risks in these areas. What is the risk of missing an important stakeholder? of stakeholders changing their expectations? of deliverables not being feasible? of requirements changing? of schedule overrun? of budget overrun? How likely are you to fail at acquiring important pieces of your system or tools for building it?

Once you've identified and quantified the risks, you have a set of risk management methods to apply to the project. Executing the risk management plan places the tasks from the risk management methods into the WBS and tracks their success in dealing with risk. Generate the tasks in the WBS from each method, using either the standard process model task generation or the special task generation from specific risk management methods.

Revising the risk management plan comes from the feedback you get from the risk management methods. As the project unfolds, you will see some risks appear that you didn't anticipate. You will see risks disappear as their systems disappear. You will see risks change in probability or impact as their causes shift. All of these changes feed back into the risk management plan, resulting in more changes to the WBS.

- *Note:* The risk management plan is an active document, like any plan. You don't just plan and shelve. The metrics let you understand how effective your plan is, which lets you adjust it to changed conditions or understanding of risk.

Just as with any of the subsidiary parts of the project plan, you can reuse the risk management plan insofar as the plan addresses the domain of the new project. Your organizational repository should certainly collect the results of applying risk management methods to risky situations. This will give you data to use to build effective risk management plans in new situations that involve old risks.

My first experience with a risk management plan was on an OO project in a company that exhibited most of the risks described in Chapter 12. After developing my WBS for the project, I used the standard risk-analysis method of listing the risks for the task, and then quantifying them by estimating probability of occurrence and degree of impact. My risk management plan laid out the risks that were higher than a rather high tolerance for risk. I was very proud of that risk plan. My director called me in and said, "Bob, you seem to be very worried about things. Can we talk about it?" After some discussion, I realized that he thought about risk from the perspective of a platoon commander about to send his men (but not himself) out into the jungle. It wasn't so much a difference in risk tolerance as a fundamental lack of understanding of the idea of managing risk [Bernstein]. "Taking risks" was what this man's life was all about. I don't know whether this attitude contributed to the eventual delay of the project by two years, as I left the company soon after.

The Risk Management Method

A *risk management method* is a kind of versioned system that lets you control project risks. You can apply a single method to several systems to control the risks in those systems. You can control risk in a particular system with a combination of several risk management methods.

Vision: A system that achieves its mission by judicious management of the risks it faces

Mission: To control a risk or set of risks by lowering the probability of risk or the impact of risk on the system missions of systems controlled by this method

Objective 14.3: To lower the probability of mission failure in one or more systems

Approach 14.3: If there is a process model associated with the method, expand it into the WBS as a set of risk control tasks. Add any other tasks specific to this particular method. Estimate the effect the method will have on system risk relative to the system risk tolerance. Monitor the effectiveness of the tasks at actually controlling the risk.

Metric 14.3: Risk reduction ratio: the ratio of the risk after applying the method to the risk before applying the method

Target 14.3: A ratio materially less than 1; materiality implies a significant participation in the lowering of system risk in conjunction with other risk control methods

---

Objective 14.4: To mitigate the impact of a mission failure on systems that use the system at risk

---

Approach 14.4: Apply the method to the systems at risk. Monitor the effectiveness of mitigation when the risk event occurs. Reset the risk tolerance of the system and of the systems it uses as appropriate.

Metric 14.4: Risk mitigation: Does the method effectively mitigate the impact of a risk event on systems to which you apply it?

Target 14.4: Yes

Risk reduction lowers the probability of mission failure in a system at risk. *Risk mitigation* lowers the impact of an event on a system mission. Both methods are effective in controlling risk, though they take different approaches. The first addresses risk directly; the second addresses the risk tolerance of the system.

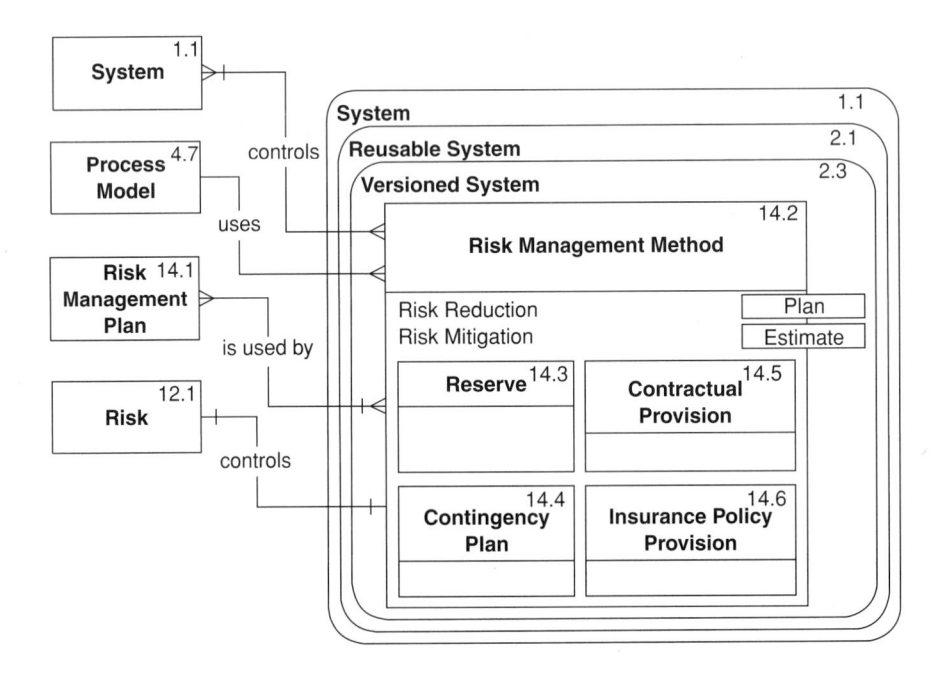

The Risk Management Method

Planning uses the risk management method to construct tasks or other systems in the project to reduce or mitigate risk. Because such methods can benefit many systems and control many risks at once, you apply them outside the context of individual system risk. Once you understand the risks in your systems, you can address them efficiently using a well-structured set of management methods. Such methods range from quality assurance to reserves to insurance policies.

Any risk management method may contain a process model that describes the risk management process. For example, the quality-assurance process model is part of the quality-assurance risk management method. If the method supports this kind of process model, you can apply the process model to your project plan in the usual way, generating the WBS tasks from the process model.

Process Model (4.7)

Some subclasses of the generic risk management method provide specific ways to control risk. Often, these take the form of specific tasks or other systems you must create in your project. For example, you might have a schedule risk coming from buying a class library from a third-party vendor. You can put a contract provision in place that imposes penalties for late delivery or poor quality. This can prove unacceptable to the contractor, however, as they will fear the risk that you will take money away from them for unjustified reasons. A better approach would be the combination of a firm, contractual milestone for delivery and a contingency plan or reserve that will let you recover from failure to meet the contract.

Estimating the impact of the method on the systems at risk means quantifying the risk with decision models. These models let you decide whether it's worth applying the control measure. Since many control methods work together, you have to estimate both the usefulness of the method in isolation and in conjunction with other methods. The risk management plan drives this global estimation process.

Your reuse repository should contain most risk management methods as reusable systems. By carefully developing your risk control process models, you can build in inherent reusability across a range of projects. Many risk management methods are domain independent, requiring little in the way of adaptation when reusing them in different areas. Many methods are even organizationally reusable, depending on how general they are.

The Reserve

A *reserve* is a cost or effort estimate separate from the primary cost and effort estimates for assignments.

Cost Estimate (37.1)
Assignment (35.1)

The actual method by which you put a reserve in place can vary depending on the nature of the system at risk. If you are dealing with simple tasks, you can add the reserve to the estimated duration, effort, or cost of the task or to the resource assignments on the task. If you are dealing with complex tasks, you can add the reserve to the process duration or cost. Dealing with items at a higher level of aggregation may require creating specific systems that represent the reserve. For example, you may have an account in the chart of accounts that represents the cost reserve from which you can draw money. You may have a labor pool from which you can draw reserved resources on demand.

A *budgetary reserve* is an amount of money you formally set aside to handle contingent events. There are two kinds of budgetary reserve: the management reserve and the undistributed budget. The *management reserve* is outside the baseline budget, so you don't use it when computing project-earned value [Fleming] using cost valuation. The *undistributed budget* is money you include in the budget with every intention of using but without allocating to a specific cost account or task. You use undistributed budget reserves, for example, when your rolling-wave planning has not yet specified the full work breakdown for a deliverable or process. You may have a valid cost estimate based on some kind of statistical model, but you have not actually allocated the budget. The management reserve, on the other hand, is for dealing with operational risk. This money becomes available when you need it to pay for the implementation of contingency plans or other responses to events.

A *schedule reserve* is an amount of time, or duration, that you associate with some schedule element. You can do this at the project level by extending the project finish milestone to a point later than your scheduling algorithm indicates. The effect of a project schedule reserve is to increase the total float time in the project, distributing the increased flexibility evenly throughout the tasks still to be done. You can also add a schedule reserve to a particular task or milestone in the schedule. The effect is to add float to that part of the schedule.

With one OO project I worked on, the management stakeholders were very sensitive to meeting schedules for political reasons. They thought that making the date was more important than delivering quality software, for better or worse. The result was a much lower risk tolerance in schedule-related systems in the project. This in turn resulted in quite a few reserves being put into task estimates. Unfortunately, some stakeholders also wanted the software delivered as soon as possible—"sooner is better than later." This resulted in a much higher risk tolerance in schedule-related systems in the project. As scheduling seesawed back and forth between these competing expectations, risk management became a casualty of politics. It became very difficult to manage schedules at all, because no one was willing to either commit to a schedule for an intermediate task or tell the truth about what was really happening with a task. The only schedule dates that really mattered in this project were the delivery milestones, making the process basically unmanageable. We had no control over the iterations within the major milestones, which meant no assurance that we would meet those milestones. Development managers were not willing, in fact, to put iteration into the process model we were following, as this would force them to be explicit about planning and scheduling intermediate milestones.

This story points up the difference between a reserve and the common project management technique called the "fudge factor." A reserve is a risk management method. A fudge factor is a creative tool ("lie") about a cost or duration estimate.

You can justify, track, and control reserves; you cannot do that for fudge factors. Also, as any contractor will tell you, neither of these terms have anything to do with the project profit, which is separate and inviolate—at least to the contractor!

The Contingency Plan

A *contingency plan* is a risk management method that specifies what you will do *if* a specific risk event occurs. This can be anything from tapping a reserve to claiming insurance. The contingency plan adds tasks to the WBS on a contingent basis—if some event occurs, execute the task.

One application of the contingency plan is *retraction,* the ability to retract a work-flow task from a resource and give it to another resource. If one resource proves unable to complete a task, another can take over on a certain date or after the first resource spends a certain amount of money or time on the task.

Work-Flow Model (5.1)

The Contractual Provision

A *contractual provision* is a part of a contract that relates specifically to a risk event in the risk management plan. Usually, you need to have risk-related provisions in place in a contract when you initially sign it, as it becomes difficult to negotiate such clauses later when the risks become apparent. That means that your risk analysis needs to happen up front before signing the contract.

Contract provisions are very formal. They are, in fact, a way to distribute risk from supplier to buyer and vice versa. Consequently, the more provisions you place in your contracts to distribute risk, the more difficult and expensive the contract becomes to negotiate. People get lawyers involved to look over the language. People disagree over the exact distribution of risk. People get delusions of power and security that don't really exist.

Also, contractual provisions, while very useful in recovering from a risk event, can often involve protracted and very expensive legal action. Therefore, you should not rely primarily on a contractual provision to manage risk unless it is the only option for doing so.

A special case of the contractual provision is the *warranty clause* of a contract or license. This clause specifies the explicit guarantees a supplier makes about a product.

Contract (27.6)

The Insurance Policy Provision

An *insurance policy provision* is an element of an insurance policy that relates specifically to a risk event in the risk quantification. Many insurance policies include *standard provisions* for basic risk management in a project.

There are very few standard insurance policies specifically oriented toward object-oriented software development, or any other kind. If you choose to use insurance to manage risk, you will usually need special *riders* to your insurance policy. You must negotiate these individually with your insurer and you must pay additional premiums for them, if you can get them at all.

Flexibility is not a hallmark of the insurance industry. It is best to rely on insurance for either standard risks (fire, theft, and so on) or very special and expensive risks that you are willing to pay a premium to manage through riders.

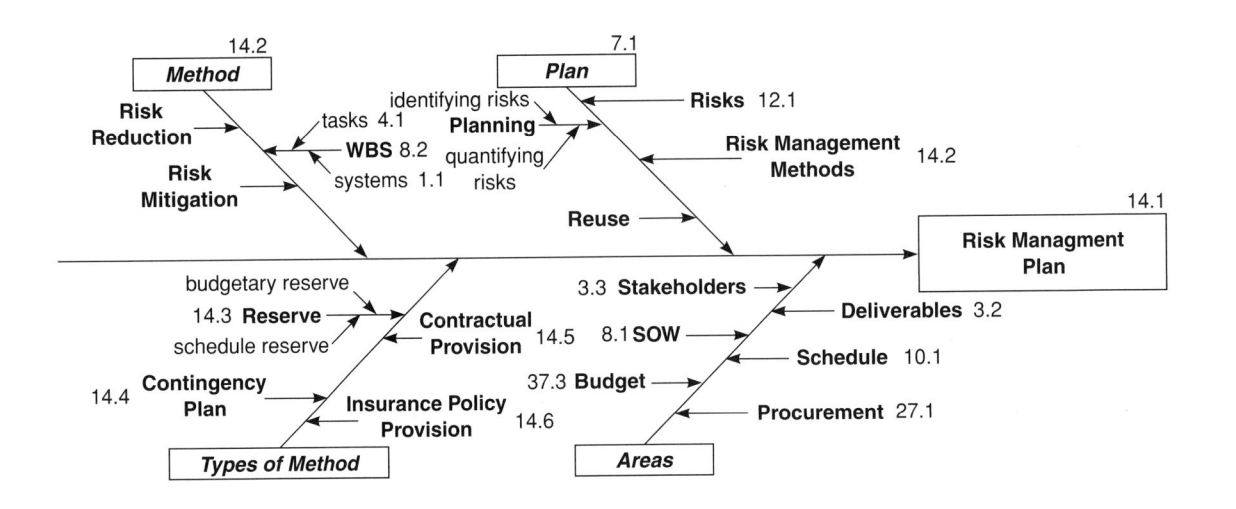

Readings

[Bernstein] Peter L. Bernstein. *Against the Gods: The Remarkable Story of Risk.* New York: Wiley, 1996.

This is a very readable history and essay on the philosophy of risk and risk management. Bernstein's thesis is that before the advent of the mathematics of probability, society believed in fate rather than risk: something that controlled you as opposed to something you could control. Risk management has dramatically transformed world society in myriad ways.

[Jones 1994] Capers Jones. *Assessment and Control of Software Risks.* New York: Yourdon Press, 1994.

If your project has risk, this book probably describes it in detail and gives you several different alternatives for control. Based on a medical textbook format, this book is a comprehensive guide to understanding and dealing with risk in the software world.

Questions to Think About

1. Can you think of a single risk management method that manages multiple risks at once? Is this fortuitous or is the method designed that way? Does it take advantage of some kind of domain similarity of the risks?

2. How many red flag events happen in your typical project? Do you track this figure? Why or why not?

3. How much of a typical WBS consists of risk management tasks as opposed to productive tasks?

4. If you are familiar with the ISO-9000 or CMM models of software process, compare their approaches to the risk management approach in this book. Why don't these methods mention risk? What parts of their methods are risk management methods? What difference does considering these methods as risk management make in their application? (Hint: You only need to manage certain risks, not all of them.)

5. Read a standard shrink-wrap license agreement. What kinds of risk does this agreement address? Are any of them on the buyer side? Why do you accept these one-sided risk distributions in most cases?

6. Have you ever seen an insurance policy provision that insures you against a late delivery or cost overrun? Have you tried to get an insurance rider for a special risk, such as the risk of injury or death due to your software?

PART SIX

Software Development

> The ideal project design, then, would avoid having all its parts in the same stage of programming at the same time. However, if one were to believe typical management texts, one would get precisely the opposite impression. What saves us, more often than not, is the lack of true boundaries between these stages, so that a little debugging is already going on during problem definition and a little problem definition is still going on during debugging. The same kind of "smearing" is done by the good programmer—whether consciously or unconsciously—so that when he runs into an obstacle in one area of activity he switches to another. Indeed, one mark of a poor programmer is that he can be found sitting around doing nothing whenever there is machine trouble and he cannot get his programs run. If he can't do the one thing scheduled for today, he is lost.
>
> Gerald Weinberg, *The Psychology of Computer Programming*

This part examines the high-level details of OO software development itself. *Software*, the purpose behind everything, consists of objects, clusters, classes, and a group of systems called storage organizations (files, databases, and repositories). Deliverables, systems with inherent value to the stakeholders, come in two varieties: software systems and product documents.

To produce software, you need a development process model and its consequent development plan. A large part of developing software is the creation of supporting documentation in development documents, including a requirements document, a functional specification, and one or more design documents. The requirements document is the location of the set of expectations, the things the stakeholders want from the project.

All of this critical mass of the project happens within the context of the development environment. This environment contains not only the tools and policies for developing the software but the software itself in the form of the product repository, a kind of reuse repository for deliverables.

The following chapters give you an overview of the nature of OO software development. After reading these chapters, you will understand the structure of OO software and the development processes that produce it. You will also see some of the ways that developers adapt older processes and documents to new uses for OO software development, getting closer to Weinberg's ideal programming project.

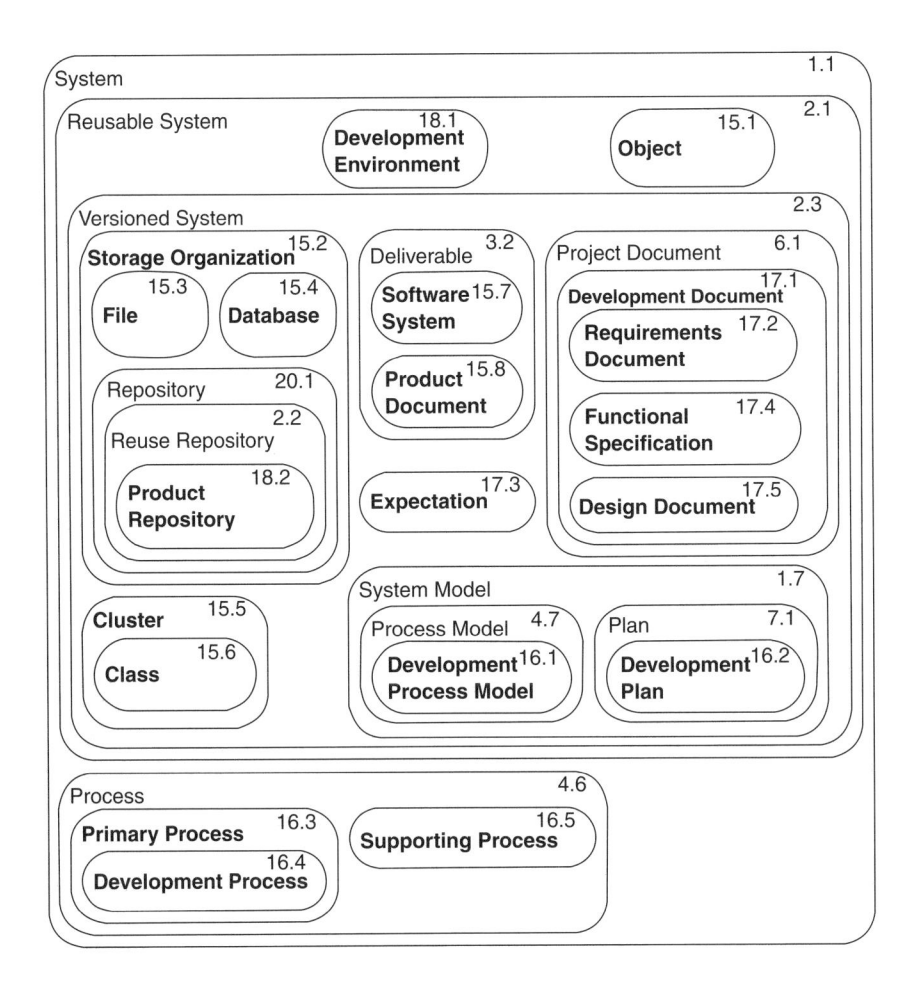

■ *Note:* The illustration of the class hierarchy contains all the classes this part defines. Other parts of the book define and discuss classes not in boldface.

CHAPTER

15 Software

There are several different kinds of software objects. Each is of interest to project managers as part of the products their projects produce. The structure of software defines object-oriented software systems.

- *Note:* The following sections clarify the architecture of a software system without taking a position in the word wars. I make no attempt, for example, to define "framework," a highly sacred word, but I do class it as a cluster. The management approach in this book uses these concepts, needing no others. You may want to add subclasses and management methods to fit your design needs. Also, as the properties of software other than reuse are irrelevant to this book, I don't go into detail on metrics, patterns, development methods, and the like.

The Object

The *object* is the basic unit in the running OO system. The system consists mainly of compiled objects interacting through messages. Objects are not themselves versioned objects; the classes that create the objects or the files that contain those classes are.

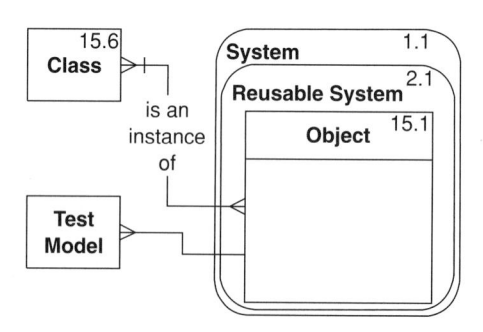

Vision: A well-designed, functional object that performs a needed function in an operational software system

Mission: To represent the working functionality of some part of the software system

>Objects are reusable systems. Reuse depends on architecture:
>
>- Using an object through a distributed object architecture such as CORBA by which you maintain and access object state through some kind of interprocess messaging mechanism
>
>- Using an object through a persistent object mechanism by which you maintain the state of the object between uses in different processes
>
>- Using an object by maintaining it in memory such as a heap or other special memory that persists beyond the specific instance on the stack

Other possibilities probably exist, though these are the main ones I know about. Most of this, while fascinating from the perspective of the software architect, is largely irrelevant to the project manager. The project manager manages the development of the classes, clusters, and storage organizations. Running the software system results in the objects, which are under the management of the stakeholders, not the project manager, and usually after the project is done at that.

The one exception is testing. Objects are the focus of certain kinds of object, integration, and system testing. Test design models the relationships between objects, and testing using working objects makes sure that these objects perform their functions properly, are compatible, and are well designed.

The Storage Organization

The *storage organization* is a versioned system that consists of one or more persistent objects of some kind. *Persistence* is the ability of an object to exist in time and/or space beyond the existence of the system that created it. From the perspective of time, the object continues to exist after the system that created it ceases to exist. From the perspective of space, the object exists at a location other than the one where you originally created it. There are two varieties of storage organization of interest here: files and databases.

Vision: A well-designed, functional system that represents persistent objects

Mission: To provide persistence for objects of any kind

> ■ *Note:* Other storage organizations are certainly possible. I focus on files and databases because they are the two varieties commonly found in OO systems. Each class has many subclasses: relational databases, ORACLE or SYBASE relational databases, UNIX files, DOS files, Windows 95 files, and so on.

```
┌─────────────────────────────┐
│ System              1.1     │
│ ┌─────────────────────────┐ │
│ │ Reusable System    2.1  │ │
│ │ ┌─────────────────────┐ │ │
│ │ │ Versioned System 2.3│ │ │
│ │ │ ┌─────────────────┐ │ │ │
│ │ │ │ Storage    15.2 │ │ │ │
│ │ │ │ Organization    │ │ │ │
│ │ │ │ ┌──────┐ ┌────┐ │ │ │ │
│ │ │ │ │File  │ │Read│ │ │ │ │
│ │ │ │ │ 15.3 │ ├────┤ │ │ │ │
│ │ │ │ │      │ │Writ│ │ │ │ │
│ │ │ │ └──────┘ └────┘ │ │ │ │
│ │ │ │  ┌──────┐       │ │ │ │
│ │ │ │  │ 15.4 │       │ │ │ │
│ │ │ │  │Datab.│       │ │ │ │
│ │ │ │  └──────┘       │ │ │ │
│ │ │ └─────────────────┘ │ │ │
│ │ └─────────────────────┘ │ │
│ └─────────────────────────┘ │
└─────────────────────────────┘
```

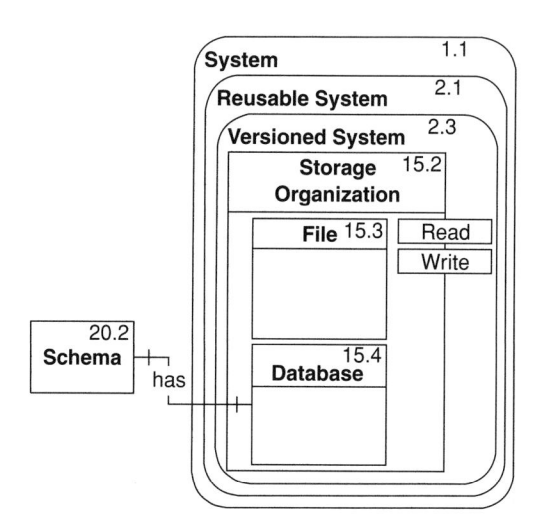

[20.2 Schema] —has— connects to Database

A *drive* is a physical or logical volume identifier for a root file hierarchy you access through the operating system. A *directory* is a group of files and additional directories. A *file* is a sequential sequence of stored data elements. A file has a drive and a directory, collectively known as a *path*, as well as a name.

A file-oriented version control system stores the initial version of the file and a series of version files. These files store the difference between the initial version and the current version (or the last version). There are many variations with associated advantages and disadvantages. You should be able to retrieve a specific version of the file from the repository, whatever its format.

- *Note:* Version control systems could store other kinds of storage organization such as databases. The problem is that complex documents, databases, and other such storage have internal structure that the simple, text-based version control systems cannot handle without adding a great deal of additional code. I know of no systems that have tried to add complex objects to their versioning capabilities.

A *database* is a storage format you access through a database access language of some kind, either through an API or a higher-level programming interface. Databases in turn have many types, the most prevalent of which are relational, hierarchical, network, and OO databases. There are also "flat-file" databases that are really just files with additional access mechanisms available.

The system organizes the storage of most system objects into logical *repositories*.

Repository (20.1)

- *Note:* The relationship between storage organization and reusability is one of enabling. To be reusable, a system must have a persistent object representation, by definition. The reuse repository storage organization fulfills that need for most reusable objects.

The Cluster

Although the runtime system comprises only objects you create from classes, many of the things that objects do apply to several classes and storage organizations. This group of objects is the *cluster,* a versioned system. For example, a single class encapsulates its data and operations. But it also inherits data and operations from its superclasses. It often interacts closely with other classes through messaging.

- *Note:* There are various things called "clusters" that you should not confuse with this unit of software architecture. One kind of cluster is a cluster of hardware processors, such as the VAX cluster. Another is part of a statistical technique for multidimensional classification, cluster analysis.

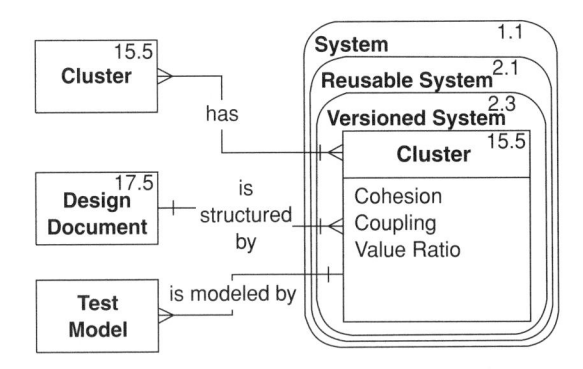

Vision: A well-designed, cleanly separated part of the deliverable software available for reuse

Mission: To design and build a cohesive set of objects that interact with other clusters in a well-structured, independent way

---

Objective 15.1: To design and build a cohesive set of objects

---

Approach 15.1: Choose a design method that works for you in designing cohesive clusters [Booch 1994; Booch 1996; Champeaux; Goldberg; Jacobson; Rumbaugh]. Apply the method religiously (I use the term advisedly). Focus on the semantics of the cluster. How does the cluster represent some cohesive aspect of the solution to the problems posed by requirements? Review your clusters (design and code reviews) to ensure successful application of the method. Generalize your solution as much as possible to promote internal reusability.

Metric 15.1: Cohesion: a subjective measure that describes how well the system "hangs together" in a semantic and pragmatic sense

Target 15.1: A value that ensures a strong inherent reuse potential, usually toward the high end of a cohesion metric

---

Objective 15.2: To design and build a decoupled set of objects

---

Approach 15.2: Choose a design method that works for you in designing clusters with as little coupling to other clusters as is reasonable, as in Approach 15.1. Focus on structure: how does the cluster interact with other systems? How can you reduce such interaction without sacrificing functionality, quality, or performance? Review and generalize your cluster as in Approach 15.1.

Metric 15.2: Coupling: a measure indicating the degree to which the cluster interacts with other clusters in the deliverable system

Target 15.2: A value that ensures a strong inherent reuse potential, usually toward the low end of a coupling metric

---

Objective 15.3: To add value to the deliverable software system

---

Approach 15.3: Trace the design elements of the cluster to requirements in the statement of work. Add only those objects needed to support required functions, to add cohesion, or to reduce coupling. Allocate function points to the cluster based on your approach for amortizing the value of the full deliverable system to its parts.

Metric 15.3: Value ratio: the percentage of the total value of the deliverable systems to which this cluster contributes; this represents the value in function points that this system adds to the deliverable systems

Target 15.3: A value ratio that reflects the true impact of the cluster on the deliverable software systems to which it contributes

---

■ *Note:* I make no attempt to define the cohesion and coupling metrics here. There are several attempts in the literature to define these, none entirely successful [Champeaux; Goldberg; Henderson-Sellers 1996]. You should study these references and the articles they cite to determine what measure will work best for your cluster design metrics.

A cluster can be one complete class hierarchy, with the classes relating to each other through inheritance. It can perform a core function or represent a logical or physical architectural component, with the classes interrelating through messaging relationships. Most clusters consist of classes relating to each other with a combination of inheritance and messaging relationships. There are subclasses of the cluster

The Cluster 261

that may be of interest in specific systems, such as the framework, the subsystem, the layer, or the interface.

There is always some *cohesion* that makes the collection of objects a cluster: there should be no object unrelated to the others in the component (see Objective 15-1).

Clusters build upon other clusters as you create your software systems. Figure 15-1 illustrates the pyramid of clusters in a deliverable system. Building the series of clusters may happen bottom up, top down, or inside out, without any order necessarily imposed by a process. If you want to build top down or inside out, you can stub the clusters on which the cluster you're building depends. If you allocate earned value to objects below the level of a working system, the cluster is the object at which you should stop. You should not recognize earned value for a cluster until the clusters on which it depends are complete. The configuration management process bases itself on collections of clusters, not of objects or classes [Booch 1996, pp. 44–45].

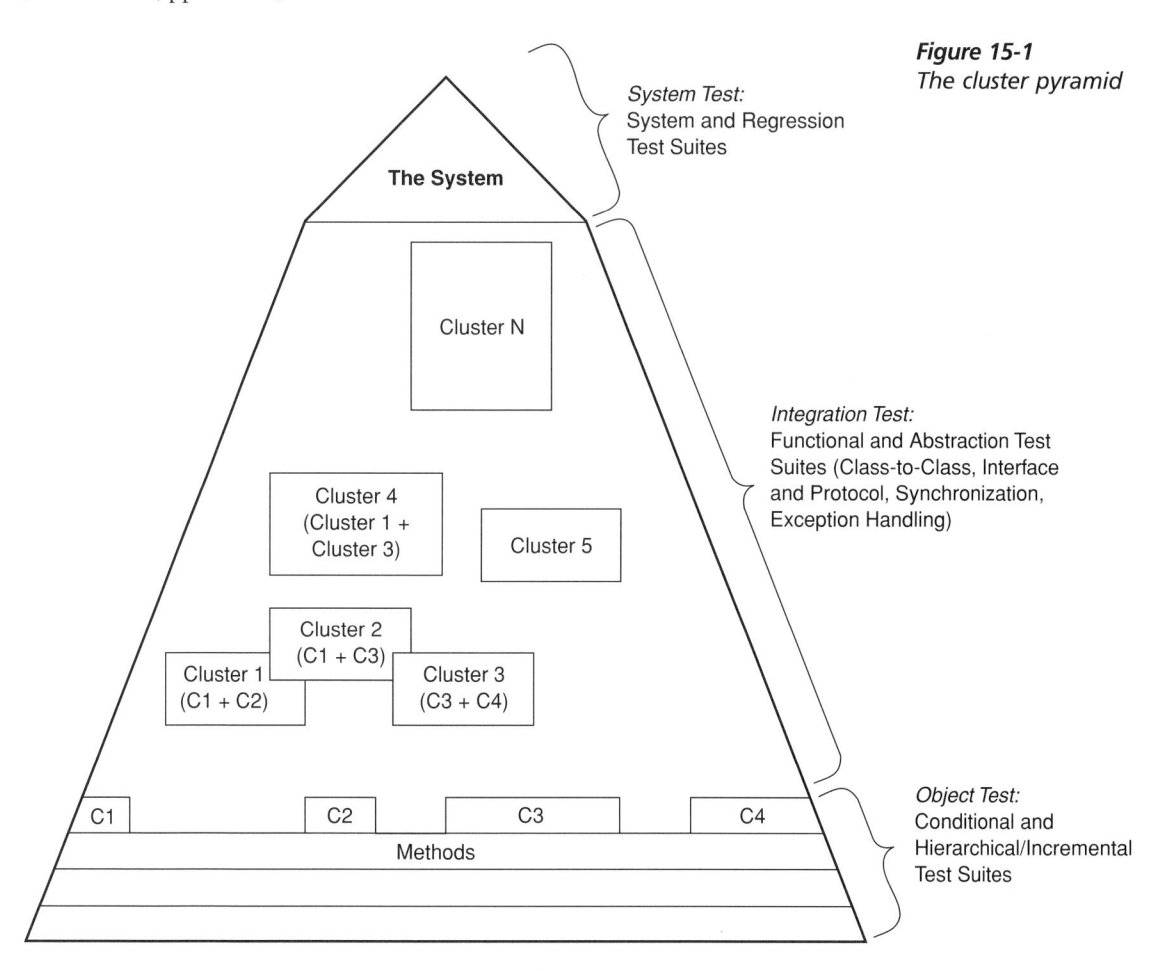

Figure 15-1
The cluster pyramid

Table 15-1
Reusability Properties of a Cluster

Reusability Property	Definition
Safety	The level of technical risk or risk exposure; the probability of technical failure multiplied by the cost impact of such a failure
Understandability	The degree to which a developer who wants to reuse the cluster feels confidence that he or she understands how to do so
Compatibility	The degree to which a cluster fits into the target system; depends on two underlying characteristics: architectural compatibility and coupling compatibility (the fit of the design and the fit of the code with the target system)
Validity	Whether the cluster correctly implements its requirements, as expressed in a functional specification such as a use case model, which must accompany the cluster

The cluster is the basic object of software reuse. The inherent reusability of the cluster comes from optimizing several cluster properties [Goldberg, p. 235]. Table 15-1 lists the most important of these properties. Certifying the cluster means validating and verifying these properties along with the domain and organizational reuse properties of the cluster.

Certification is relative to the situation in which you intend to reuse the cluster. For example, you can certify the cluster for use in specific domains, or you can certify it for use in situations that do not threaten human life. You need to be very clear on this certification model so that you do not falsely reassure potential reusers about the reusability of the cluster.

The safety property requires a thorough risk assessment. Once you've identified and quantified the risks of technical failure, you must set up and execute a risk management plan that produces a level of risk below the tolerance of the cluster. For reusable clusters, that level is going to be way below what your risk tolerance might ordinarily be for a given project. Remember, this cluster is going to have to convince a large number of other developers that it is safe. To do this, it must have a higher level of quality than an ordinary application cluster. The target system in which developers will use the cluster is unknown, and therefore you don't know the mission and risk tolerance of that system. That means that you must focus on reducing probability of failure to a very low level [Goldberg; Karlsson; Love; Siegel]. You should benchmark risk tolerance for the target domains and organizations to get some idea of the acceptable level of risk. You should also spend some time understanding the different kinds of missions to which the cluster might contribute.

Risk (12.1)

Risk Management Plan (14.1)

One way to reduce risk is to provide the source code and data for the cluster. Table 15-2 shows the categories of clusters using this technique for reducing risk [Goldberg; Love, p. 219].

Category	Definition
Black Box	The cluster comes without source code and data; you must reuse the cluster by linking your software to it and using only the external interface; this limits risk only to the extent that the original cluster limits risk, aside from the standard OO feature of letting you extend the cluster with additional subclasses and data
Glass Box	The cluster comes with source code and data but limits you to using only the unchanged external interface; this permits you to know what is going on under the covers but not to change it, reducing risk of making errors in understanding and letting you reuse code by inheritance without incurring high risk
White Box	The cluster comes with source code and data without limits; this limits risk by permitting you to change the code and data to fix problems or to add features to the cluster without having to extend the hierarchy or database

Table 15-2 Categories of Clusters

Although making full source available, or acquiring it, is a good way to reduce certain technical risks, you lose part of the advantage of reusing the cluster. You must maintain changes to the source, possibly in parallel with changes by the cluster vendor. In addition, you incur all the risks associated with new development and maintenance. Black Box reuse is the most effective kind of reuse, but it does require a high level of confidence in the cluster.

The Class

The *class* is a cluster that represents the intensional structure of a set of objects: the properties the objects share. Properties consist of attributes (data) and operations (behavior). Classes relate to one another through an inheritance hierarchy of superclasses and subclasses.

"Object Systems" section, Chapter 1, p. 7

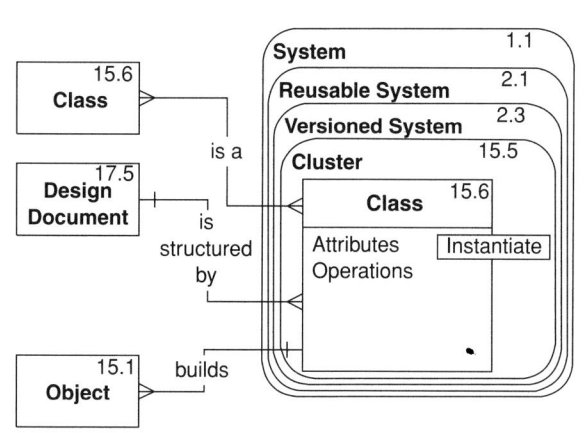

Vision: A well-designed system that represents the intensional structure of a set of objects

Mission: To represent the internal structure of a set of objects, including the type and object structure

Classes are the building blocks with which you make clusters and software systems. They are not themselves the basic architectural units, however, except insofar as they represent a cluster. Class design and building always take into account the other classes and data clustered with the class you are building, either through inheritance or messaging.

The Software System

A *software system* is a complete, working deliverable system made up of clusters that delivers viable value to its users. By *viable*, I mean that the system can perform its function by itself, without being combined with any other system at its own level. The difference between a cluster and a software system is qualitative rather than quantitative. While clusters are systems, they are not deliverable software systems in the sense of being viable in themselves. They are always *parts* of a working system. A user can actually use a deliverable software system, while he or she may or may not be able to use a cluster by itself.

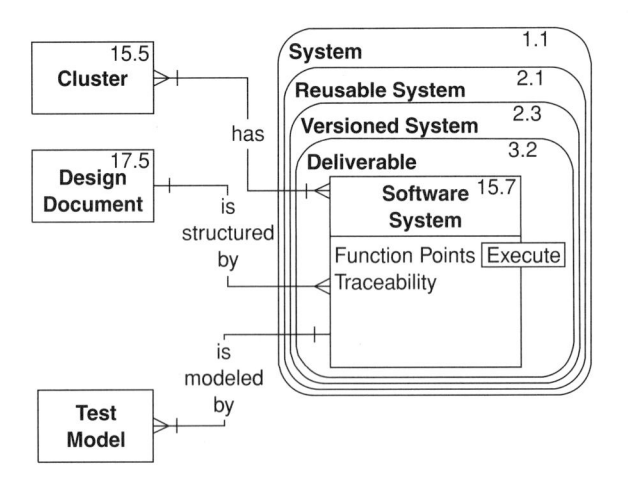

- *Note:* Viability is hard to define in practice. For example, any application theoretically can stand alone—except for the operating system, network software, and all the other software layers needed for it to run on your hardware. Can you separate the software from that hardware? Like most things, you know it when you see it. Something that comes in a pretty package, or that you download over the Net in a ZIP file, or that you install in one installation—that's a software system. You can also see programming libraries as software systems, since they tend to stand alone in this way as well. The key is value: does the system, by itself, deliver actual value to its consumers?

Vision: *A software system that delivers its intended value to a stakeholder of the project*

Mission: *To provide value to stakeholders*

Objective 15.4: To provide value to stakeholders

Approach 15.4: Deliver a working software system that does what its requirements say that it should do.

Metric 15.4.1: Function point: a subjective, ratio-level measure of functional value of a software system based on a system of external counting and weighting developed as a standard by the International Function Point Users Group (IFPUG)

Target 15.4.1: A function point number close to the planned number of function points

---

Metric 15.4.2: Traceability ratio: the number of function points in the software system that you can trace to function points in the requirements document from which that system derives over the total number of function points in that document

Target 15.4.2: A value within control limits of an x-R diagram, converging on 1

A key difference, for example, between a cluster and a system is where you apply system testing techniques. The elements of the software you test in a system test are emergent properties of the system, such as system performance and system behavior under different configuration environments. You can validate the system against user requirements only at the system level, since user requirements are at that level and do not take internal architecture into account.

Function points measure the size of a software system by counting specific things in the user interface and architecture of the system [Dreger; IFPUG; Jones 1991], as Table 15-3 lists.

After counting the basic function points for a data object or transaction, you multiply it by a complexity multiplier that you determine based on the complexity of the data object or transaction. You then adjust this value using the value adjustment factor, a multiplier you calculate by ranking the application according to 14 general system characteristics, as Table 15-4 lists.

Table 15-3 Function Point Counting Types

Type	Description
Internal Logical File	A logically related set of data or control information that the application you are counting maintains, such as a master file or database table to which the application writes data
External Interface File	A logically related set of data or control information that the application you are counting does not maintain, such as a file or database table that provides read-only lookup information for the application
External Input	A transaction that processes data or control information coming from outside the application you are counting, such as entry into input fields in a form or reading a record from a data file
External Output	A transaction that generates data or control information and sends it outside the application you are counting, such as generating a report, displaying an error message, or generating a backup file
External Inquiry	A transaction that is a combination of input and output using a simple key, not a range, with immediate response and no update (request and retrieval), such as a menu, a help screen, or an SQL SELECT query statement

Table 15-4 General System Characteristics for Function Point Value Adjustment Factor

Characteristic	Description
Data Communications	The way the system uses data communications protocols
Distributed Data Processing	The way the system shares data with other systems
Performance	The nature of performance requirements for the system
Heavily Used Configuration	The nature of configuration requirements for the system
Transaction Rate	The rate of transaction processing the system must support
Online Data Entry	The amount of interactive data entry in the system
End-User Efficiency	The presence of various aids to the user in the system
Online Update	The way the system updates internal files
Complex Processing	The degree of presence of complex things such as logic, math, security, exceptions, or multimedia
Reusability	The degree to which you design the system for reuse (that is, how much you have to generalize the system)
Installation Ease	The degree to which the installation and conversion of prior systems is easy or hard

Table 15-4 *General System Characteristics for Function Point Value Adjustment Factor (continued)*

Characteristic	Description
Operational Ease	The degree to which the operation of the system is easy or hard
Multiple Sites	The degree to which you designed the system for installation and operation at different customer sites, ranging from the custom application to vendor mass-market software for multiple operating systems with customer support requirements
Facilitate Change	The degree to which you designed the system so that the operator can change it (flexibility and extensibility of the system)

You then calculate the final function point count. There are variations of this for new systems, enhanced systems, and application systems that don't count conversion function points.

- *Note:* I have heard from several reviewers and clients that there is a general belief that function points are problematic with OO software. I have not been able to find anything in print that addresses this issue. On the surface, I can't see why this should be true. Function points measure the external appearance of the software, not the internal structure. The whole point is to measure size independent of the implementation method; that's why function points are better than lines of code measures. I suppose it could matter if you were measuring APIs, since those are structured differently, but function points don't measure APIs, they measure user interfaces and reports. There are several other criticisms of function points relating to the adjustment factors and their subjectivity and inappropriateness for different kinds of software applications, but this also has nothing to do with OO versus other kinds of software.

The Product Document

A *product document* is a kind of deliverable system. You can classify product documents into several kinds of system:

- User manuals
- Reference manuals
- Tutorials
- Online help
- Online documents and Web pages
- Release notes

A document usually consists of a set of topics. Each topic usually has a section to itself. The topic is the level at which the operational objectives operate. Document size is a two-part metric consisting of number of words and number of illustrations, and you measure productivity in words per effort-hour and illustrations per effort-hour.

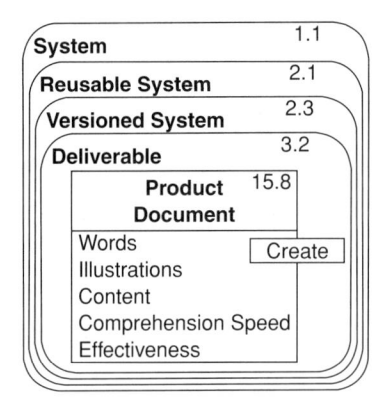

```
System                     1.1
  Reusable System          2.1
  Versioned System         2.3
    Deliverable            3.2
      Product              15.8
      Document
        Words          [ Create ]
        Illustrations
        Content
        Comprehension Speed
        Effectiveness
```

Vision: *A document that helps users of a software system to learn and use that system quickly and effectively*

Mission: *To provide information to users of a software system to help those users learn and use the system quickly and effectively*

Objective 15.5: To provide information to users

Approach 15.5: Create a document with a clearly defined mission and audience that contains all the information needed to achieve that mission.

Metric 15.5: Content: A subjective measure of the completeness of content; the actual metric depends on the subclass. For example, a reference manual must have one topic for each element of the system it documents. A user's guide must have one topic for each concept the user needs to know about to use the system. And so on.

Target 15.5: A content value within control limits on an x-R control chart of similar documents

---

Objective 15.6: To provide information that helps users to learn and use the system quickly

---

The Product Document 269

Approach 15.6: Focus the creation of the document on conveying the precise information required in clear and unambiguous language. Use practical examples and develop material in a logical sequence for the intended audience. Write well.

Metric 15.6: Comprehension speed: the average number of minutes required for a user to master the average topic

Target 15.6: A value within control limits on an x-R control chart of similar documents; the value should approach a benchmark of industry documentation comprehension speed, as the document is a competitive tool

---

Objective 15.7: To provide effective information

Approach 15.7: Take a similar approach to that of Approach 15.6, but focus on the target audience to make sure the presentation is at the correct level and that the information uses modern educational communication methods to reach the optimal set of people. Use examples for different types of learners, and supplement text with pictures, audio, and other multimedia techniques as appropriate.

Metric 15.7: Document effectiveness: a multiple-item survey that tests the user of a document for his or her ability to use the system after exposure to the document

Target 15.7: A value within control limits on an x-R control chart of groups of survey administrations; the value should approach any standard you can set by benchmarking industry documentation effectiveness, since this is a competitive tool

---

You should not confuse the *product* documentation with the *development* documentation. The former is the product of the primary development process. The latter is part of the supporting documentation process.

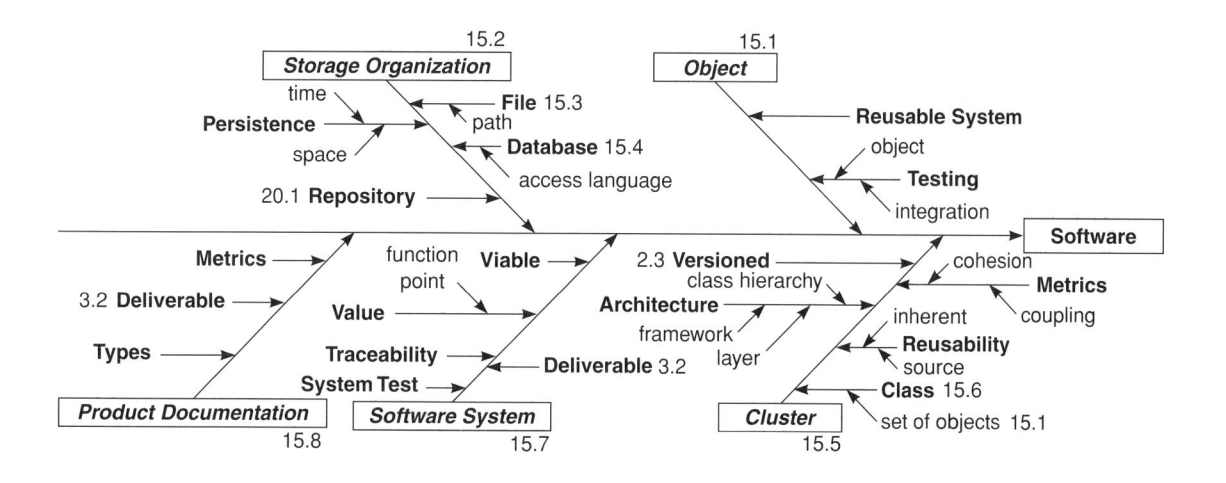

Readings

- *Note:* If you read all the readings below, you will understand the full range of object-oriented software technology, and especially its impact on reusability of software objects and systems. You will also be a year older. I'm not sure which is more important in the long run, but here it is.

[Biggerstaff]   Ted J. Biggerstaff and Alan J. Perliss. *Software Reusability.* Two volumes. New York: ACM Press, 1989.

This is the leading collection of articles on reusable software. Very academic. A must-have for anyone actually doing research, but of less interest to practitioners. There are several such collections of papers, and many more papers in the academic journals, testifying to the theoretical power of the concept of reuse, if not to its impact on practice.

[Booch 1994]   Grady Booch. *Object-Oriented Analysis and Design with Applications, Second Edition.* Redwood City, CA: Benjamin/Cummings, 1994.

Booch is one of the main textbooks on OO design. It is less useful for analysis, and unless you're a homeowner interested in building your own heating system, probably not much use for coding. Very good on design, though.

[Booch 1996]   Grady Booch. *Object Solutions: Managing the Object-Oriented Project.* Reading, MA: Addison-Wesley, 1996.

This is the material that Booch couldn't include in his design book. I'll cite it again in the development process chapter, where it applies most. From the software perspective, Booch goes into detail on some aspects of design that you should not miss. In particular, pages 44 and 45 discuss the issue of clusters, or as Booch terms them, "class categories."

[Champeaux]   Dennis de Champeaux. *Object-Oriented Development Processes and Metrics.* Englewood Cliffs, NJ: Prentice Hall, 1997 (published in 1996).

Champeaux has written an excellent book on the development processes for OO software, including the metrics and coding details that sophisticated developers should use in their work. Particularly for those interested in developing their own heating systems, this book will reward serious study. If you ignore the coding examples and read the 100 pages of text on process, you will learn virtually everything you need to know about process management for development processes. If you focus on the coding and design examples, you will see how C++ works as an OO language. Something for everyone. There are also some spirited critiques of the OO stars that you should not miss.

[Dreger]   J. Brian Dreger. *Function Point Analysis.* Englewood Cliffs, NJ: Prentice Hall, 1989.

Dreger is an excellent tutorial introduction to function point counting. Using this book in addition to the IFPUG manual [IFPUG] is an excellent way to learn. Dreger occasionally departs from the IFPUG standard, but explains why when he does. You decide.

Readings

[Garlan]	David Garlan, Robert Allen, and John Ockerbloom. Architectural mismatch: Why reuse is so hard. *IEEE Software* (November 1995): 17–26.

An excellent, well-written article that defines the concept of architectural mismatch and demonstrates how it affects the reusability of software. Must reading for anyone interested in reusability.

[Goldberg]	Adele Goldberg and Kenneth S. Rubin. *Succeeding with Objects: Decision Frameworks for Project Management.* Reading, MA: Addison-Wesley, 1995.

Goldberg and Rubin discuss most of the interesting aspects of OO software development. Reading this in addition to one of the design books provides an excellent introduction for technical managers. The chapters on software reuse are particularly good.

[IFPUG]	International Function Point Users' Group. *IFPUG Counting Practices Manual, Release 4.0.* IFPUG (Blendonview Office Park, 5008-28 Pine Creek Drive, Westerville, OH 43081-4899, (+1-614-895-7130), January 1994.

This is THE book on function point counting. It's available from IFPUG only and is overpriced, unfortunately, but is well worth the money if you are serious about function points. IFPUG also runs conferences, tutorials, and other programs relating to function points.

[Jacobson]	Ivar Jacobson, Magnus Christerson, Patrik Jonsson, and Gunnar Overgaard. *Object-Oriented Software Engineering: A Use Case Driven Approach.* Reading, MA: Addison-Wesley, 1992.

This is currently the best book on OO design available, in my humble opinion. Though it is based on all kinds of practical techniques instead of on theory, it somehow works. Practice tends to be that way.

[Jones 1991]	Capers Jones. *Applied Software Measurement: Assuring Productivity and Quality.* New York: McGraw-Hill, 1991.

This book provides an excellent rationale and history for function points. Read it if you need to justify use of function points to stakeholders and management. There is also an excellent function point example in the appendices.

[Karlsson]	Even-André Karlsson, editor. *Software Reuse: A Holistic Approach.* New York: Wiley, 1995.

Currently THE book on reuse, with more detail and case studies than you could ever ask for. The book is a bit dry and repetitious and certainly too long, but anyone starting a reuse program (and most of those who already have one) should read this book cover to cover. My one complaint is that the authors focus on how to do things in microdetail rather than on some major principles that will guide you. The result is often to diffuse the point the authors are trying to make due to lack of cohesion in relating the point to the rest of the book. I disagree with some of the approaches to metrics, and especially with the "reusability capability model," but the issues the book raises are comprehensive in scope and worth studying.

[Lewis]   Ted Lewis. *Deploying Distributed Business Software.* New York: SIGS Books, 1996.

Lewis has written an invaluable book on client/server computing, and in it he discusses most of the interesting architectural issues and products confronting the OO architect who is interested in two- and three-tier solutions, as well as the manager who wants to know the buzzwords that architect likes to use.

[Love]   Tom Love. *Object Lessons: Lessons Learned in Object-Oriented Development Projects.* New York: SIGS Books, 1993.

Love's book is a good background book for early experiences in OO technology. Love was one of the original architects of Objective C.

[Meyer]   Bertrand Meyer. *Object-Oriented Software Construction.* Englewood Cliffs, NJ: Prentice Hall, 1988.

This is one of the original texts of the OO revolution, and the basis for the Eiffel programming language. Its prescience is astonishing, though the details are getting old fast.

[Rumbaugh]   James Rumbaugh, Michael Blaha, William Premerlani, Frederick Eddy, and William Lorensen. *Object-Oriented Modeling and Design.* Englewood Cliffs, NJ: Prentice Hall, 1991.

Rumbaugh et al., with [Booch], is one of the primary references for OO architects. Booch, Jacobson, and Rumbaugh have combined their notations into a single one which they are in the process of publishing. Rumbaugh has an excellent discussion of modern state-transition diagramming as a representation of object behavior, as well as a useful focus on the data relationships between objects. His discussion of higher-level architectural issues leaves something to be desired [Champeaux], but overall this is an excellent text.

[Tracz]   Will Tracz. Tutorial: *Software Reuse—Emerging Technology.* Washington, DC: Computer Society Press, 1988.

This is also an interesting collection of academic papers on reusable software, though again of limited interest to practitioners.

Questions to Think About

1. Do you think about objects first when you are designing systems or classes? Why?

2. What kind of subclasses of cluster can you see in systems that you've worked on?

3. Is there one key thing you should do to make software reusable? If not, what is your best strategy for reusability?

4. Is product documentation part of a product or a separate deliverable? Why?

5. Should you read everything written about OO design to fully grok the field? Why or why not? (Hint: Does good software come from reading or doing?)

CHAPTER

Developing Object-Oriented Software 16

The Development Process Model

The OO *development process model* is the process model by which you develop OO software system deliverables. When you generate the WBS through the project process model, it is a development process model that generates the tasks for each software system the project will deliver. The following sections discuss the different kinds of software processes currently in use for developing object-oriented software. Each represents a particular modeling of the sequence and content of the tasks you undertake to develop the software system.

Work Breakdown Structure (8.2)

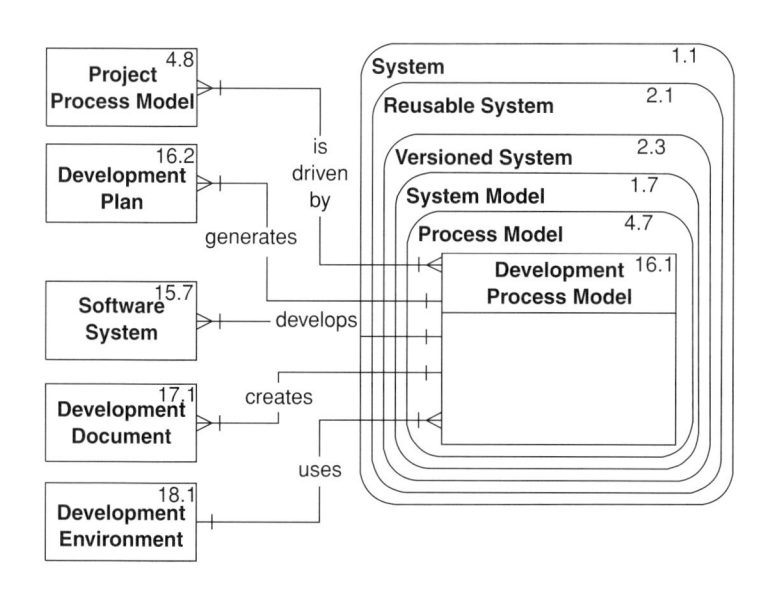

273

■ *Note:* You could do a whole book on OO development processes [Goldberg; Booch 1996]. There are many variations on them. Doubtless there are many other possible ways to organize software development. This chapter presents the outlines of the most popular processes in use in today's OO projects. Some processes are better than others at different times for developing OO software, primarily because of the cluster-based, iterative, incremental nature of that software. I make no attempt to develop these process models into full classes with all the attendant complexity; instead, I suggest the outlines of the process model in the class description.

Vision: A productive software development process that you execute and control to a successful completion

Mission: To manage the execution of a series of software development tasks to a successful completion

The development process model generates the development plan, a vital component of the project plan. The model and the tasks it generates use the development environment that contains analysis, design, coding, and reuse tools. It creates development documentation.

The development process interacts with the project process model and software system deliverables. As project planning goes on, you create a development process using the process model for each deliverable system in the project. As with all planning, you plan to the level of knowledge you have and baseline your plan as needed.

The Development Plan

The *development plan* is the part of the project plan that controls the production of the software deliverables. You generate the development plan from the development process model for each deliverable software system.

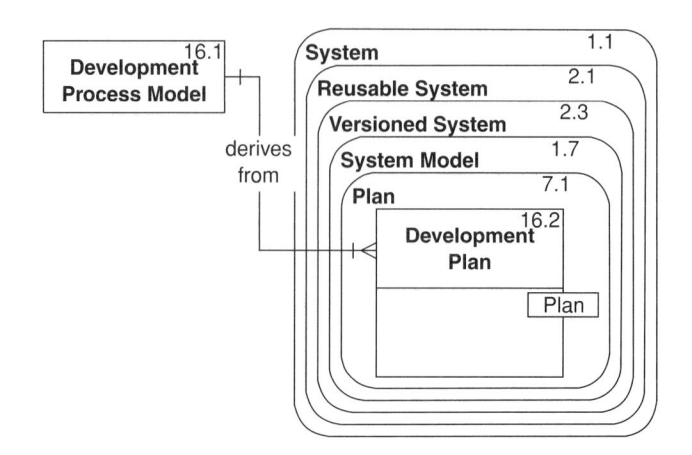

Vision: A development process brought to a successful conclusion, achieving its mission by delivering its software system

Mission: To bring the development process model for a system to bear on successfully achieving its mission

Process Model (4.7)

Process Policy and the Development Plan

The set of standards and guidelines relating to process models from the organizational environment determines what specific process models you use. These standards include both external standards such as ISO/IEC-12207 and internal standards for implementing process models (the ISO-9000-3 *Software Process Handbook*, for example [Kehoe]). These policies define the approach to use in planning and executing your project.

Policy (32.1)

- *Note:* Rather than burden this chapter with sections with process model details, I subsume them all within this class. Hence, these process models do not have separate class numbers or diagrams. The specific objects they use appear in the development process model diagram. When developing your own process model, you should develop subclasses with details appropriate to the specific processes you want to define as part of that model.

There are two major standards for the software development process: ISO/IEC-12207, *Information Technology—Software Life Cycle Processes,* and ISO-9000-3, *Guideline for Application of ISO 9001 to the Development, Supply, and Maintenance of Software*. These standards specify names and definitions for software processes and tasks, but they do not impose any process model. The process comprises three kinds of complex task: primary processes, supporting processes, and organizational processes. Not all the processes are relevant in the project context; some relate to ongoing operations. Software projects also include other project-related processes not mentioned in these standards.

The *organizational processes* form the bedrock of project management: management itself, infrastructure, improvement, and training.

- *Note:* The following sections do not discuss the organizational processes in detail, as they appear elsewhere in the book.

The various management plans and their corresponding planning and control tasks are *management* processes. There are other management processes, primarily relating to human resource management, that are part of the organizational environment rather than of the project. These are ongoing activities related to operations of the firm.

Plan (7.1)

The structure and use of process models reflects the dominant management pattern of the organization. Using Weinberg's patterns, for example, Oblivious or Variable organizations often have little in the way of a process model. Routine organizations have magical models (if you follow them, things will come out right,

Management Culture (31.1)

Organizational Environment (33.1)

Development Environment (18.1)

Quality Environment (9.2)

Tool (P7.1)

Improvement Plan (1.3)

but nobody knows why, and when they don't work, you panic). The structure of the process model thus reflects the cultural status of the organization. It is not a static, unchanging "right way to do things." In an open system, the culture should take advantage of its ability to learn from experience to create the culture it needs to succeed.

Infrastructure appears in the several environments (organizational, development, quality). Environments include the tools you need to do your job, whatever it might be.

Improvement enters this book through every system's improvement plans. Every process you generate has such a plan, as do all the tasks and other objects that those processes use. The process model itself has an improvement plan, letting you continuously improve your ability to plan and control projects.

Training appears in two places. First, the training task for process models trains people in using those models for planning and execution of project processes. Second, the training course class provides resources with the training they need to do their jobs.

The Primary Process

A *primary process* is a prime mover in the production of software. There are three kinds of primary process in OO software projects: acquisition, supply, and development. Acquisition and supply are the mirror images of each other, the procurement process seen from two different perspectives. The supply process is another name for the project task's process, which is the entire subject of this book.

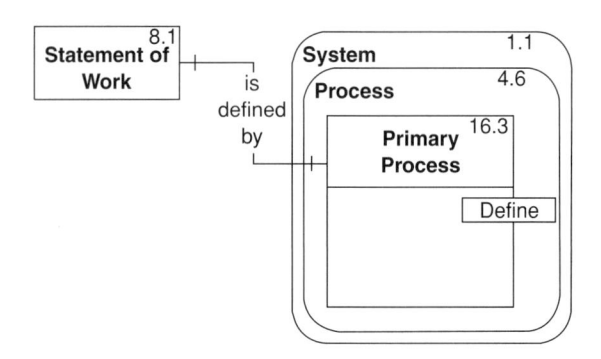

Procurement Process Model (27.2)

The Procurement Process

Acquisition is the process of acquiring software products and services. The procurement process executes the plan you derive from the procurement process model. This process includes contracting, bidding, getting bids, contract administration, and contract reporting.

OO software projects use acquisition to get reusable software or even reusable plans, designs, or requirements. You can also acquire parts of the software through subcontracting or "outsourcing" your development process through an acquisition process. There are, as always, risks associated with using off-the-shelf software or software built by others: some tools won't measure up, and you won't be able to reuse everything you acquire for reuse.

Reusable System (2.1)
Risk (12.1)

The Development Process

The *development* process is the central process for software project management. It sequences all the tasks required to produce a software deliverable and any other deliverables such as product documentation, training materials, or whatever.

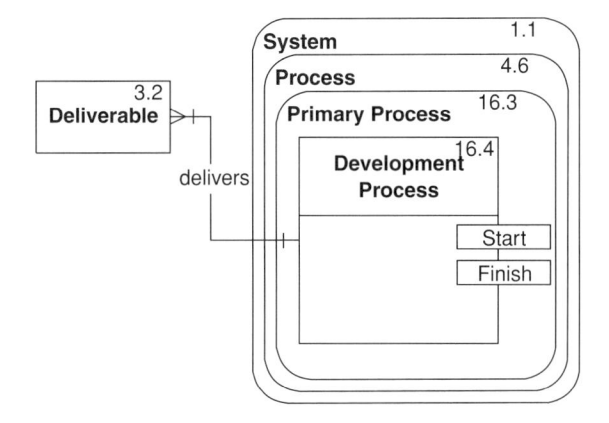

The ISO-12207 standard calls for the several tasks as part of the development process, specifying no particular order. Table 16-1 lists these complex task models.

Task	Description
Process implementation	Planning, process modeling, and process execution
System requirements analysis	Specification of the intended use of the system as a whole
System architectural design	Top-level architectural design of the system as a whole
Software requirements analysis	Specification of the intended use of the parts of the system (the clusters or "configuration items")
Software architectural design	Top-level architectural design of the parts of the system

Table 16-1
ISO-12207 Development Process Tasks

Table 16-1
ISO-12207 Development Process Tasks (continued)

Task	Description
Software detailed design	Design of lower-level clusters that you can code and test
Software coding and testing	Coding and testing of lower-level clusters
Software integration	Integration of one or more clusters into higher-level clusters
Software qualification testing	Integration testing of an integrated cluster
System integration	Integration of the software system deliverable
System qualification testing	System testing of the software system deliverable
Software installation	Installation of the deliverable as the contract specifies
Software acceptance support	Support of the acquiring organization's acceptance review of the installed deliverable software, including acceptance testing and training

You execute the development plan to start the development process, and you finish it up at the development process milestone at which you deliver the deliverables.

The Supporting Process

A *supporting process* provides some service or product for another process in a distinct, purposive way.

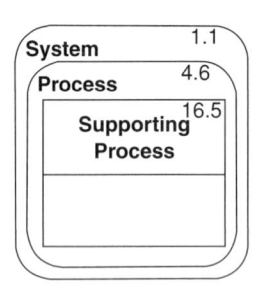

```
System                    1.1
  Process                 4.6
    Supporting           16.5
    Process
```

Table 16-2 lists the ISO supporting processes.

Process	Description
Documentation	Produces documents containing information needed by project resources and stakeholders
Configuration Management	Identifies, defines, and baselines software items; controls versioning and delivery of software items; and reports status of items and modification requests
Quality Assurance	Provides assurance that the software and processes conform to requirements and adhere to plans
Verification	Determines whether clusters or software systems fulfill the requirements or conditions imposed on them in previous activities
Validation	Determines whether the requirements or a software deliverable fulfills its intended use
Joint Review	Evaluates the status and products of a task
Audit	Determines compliance of software or processes with requirements, plans, and contracts
Problem Resolution	Analyzes and resolves problems discovered during any other process to ensure resolution of all problems

Table 16-2
ISO-12207 Supporting Processes

These resolve into three basic project processes: documentation, configuration management, and quality assurance. Adding to the ISO-9000 processes, there is a fourth supporting process: communication. The tasks in these processes are generally level-of-effort tasks, not work packages.

Development Document (17.1)
Change Management Process (24.1)
Quality Management Plan (9.1)
Communications Management Plan (39.1)

Hacking

A great deal of OO development gets done by *hacking*, just writing the code and revising it until it satisfies you or until you think you can deliver the result to the stakeholders with some assurance that they will accept it. Often, this is the approach that Oblivious or Variable organizations take. Routine cultures often profess a waterfall model but in practice follow a modified hacking strategy.

Management Culture (31.1)

Figure 16-1 illustrates the very simple hacking process model. The process iterates through a never-ending series of code and deliver cycles. More sophisticated hackers decide to deliver based on some kind of system validation test. Less sophisticated hackers decide to deliver whenever they wish.

Vision: A delivered system

Mission: To deliver the system ("just do it")

Figure 16-1
Hacking development process model

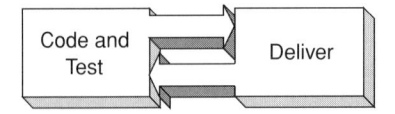

[Code and Test → Deliver]

Objective 16.1: To deliver the system

Approach 16.1: Code what you think the stakeholders want. Test it as required and deliver it to them.

Metric 16.1: Delivery: yes or no

Target 16.1: Yes

The hacking model is best for very simple systems or for situations with few and simple stakeholder needs. Stress *simple* here. For example, my personal accounting system is done pretty much with a hacking model. No one cares about it except my accountant and myself. On a slightly grander scale, I developed an internal system for a company reusing various classes from other internal tools. Others cared but were not concerned with delivery, reuse potential, or any other characteristics except having the tool available on occasion. Some were concerned with performance, which I addressed as I found time. Others just hacked up their own tools to replace the one I did.

One major disadvantage of the hacking model is that the hacker usually has free rein to decide what to reuse. Usually, this leads to one of two things happening in OO systems:

- The developer reuses very little
- The developer reuses his own tools and components, ignoring others

On the other hand, misapplying the hacking model can have severe effects on system viability. If you try to deliver complex software or software that must meet relatively high expectations from stakeholders, you will run into trouble using the hacking model.

One company I worked with organized its development around individual developers, with each one taking responsibility for one piece of the system. The system was a collection of independent clusters integrated through a uniform graphical user interface. Each developer was free to develop any way he or she wanted to as long as the cluster delivery milestone was met. There was no formal integration testing, only an alpha system test of the whole software system. This was a hacking model contained within a larger waterfall process.

The results from this process model were predictable only in their unpredictability. The functionality, value, quality, and delivery schedule depended entirely on the skill level and commitment of the developer. The environment of this project distanced the developers from all stakeholders except their manager, a senior executive. His priority was schedule, not value. The result was not much value and usually late milestones due to rework. Many clusters looked completely different from what the project manager originally intended.

There was one cluster that completely failed to integrate into the user interface. When asked about this failure, the developer in question responded that it wasn't his job to integrate it into the user interface. He believed this UI was wrongheaded and needed redoing (by him, as he believed the original developer was an idiot). This cluster did not make it into the final system, along with about half of the other clusters in this project. The whole project was the subject of some mirth among the technical management, which is itself an indicator of the hacking process model being applied.

Another company I worked for, a major software firm, organized much of its early development this way. To make it work, they hired only geniuses and super-programmers. They quickly weeded out those who could not cut it. Those who did cut it got every perk in the book. This style took the company from a very small start-up to a very successful midsize corporation, when things got so complicated they couldn't do it that way anymore.

Hacking is a very personal process, and while it can be successful given the right person, you shouldn't bet the farm on it for OO projects.

The Waterfall

The waterfall process model is a phased series of processes, each of which ends with an approval milestone that determines whether the process proceeds or stops. Boehm's statement of this life cycle, Figure 16-2, is the standard description [Boehm 1981, pp. 35–50].

Vision: A predictable software development process that you execute and control to a successful completion

Mission: To manage the execution of a sequence of software development tasks to a successful completion

---

Objective 16.2: To enable the successful prediction of the project schedule and budget

---

Approach 16.2: Organize the standard software development tasks in a linear sequence. Separate the tasks with formal milestones that represent "go-no go" decisions. Plan the project, permitting only limited iteration and maintaining the linear sequence whenever possible. Baseline the plan once and execute the plan to that baseline.

Figure 16-2
Waterfall development process model

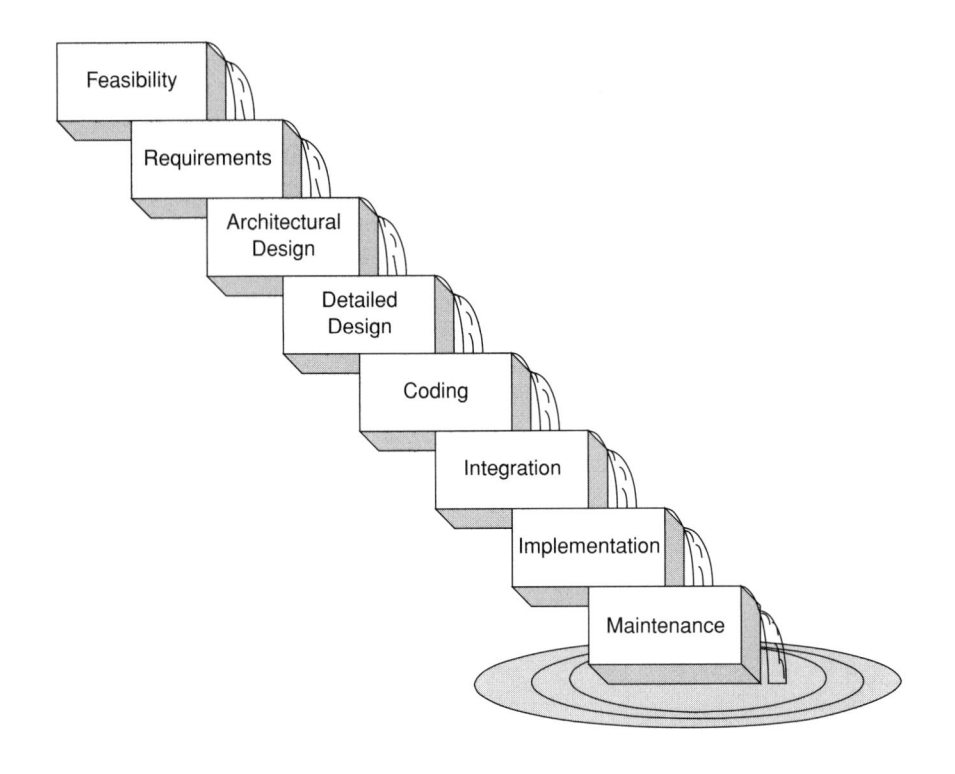

[Figure: Waterfall diagram showing cascading stages: Feasibility → Requirements → Architectural Design → Detailed Design → Coding → Integration → Implementation → Maintenance]

Metric 16.2: Cost performance index (CPI): planned cost divided by actual cost at the development process milestone, where the planned cost is the baseline cost from the initial plan for that milestone

Target 16.2: CPI ≥ 0

The mission of the waterfall is to limit the scope of change to a manageable and predictable level by maximizing the amount of salvageable work in case of problems [Royce, p. 2]. From the economic perspective, the waterfall model improves predictability by minimizing the cost of finding and fixing problems. The earlier you find and fix a problem, the less it costs [Boehm 1981, pp. 39–41], in terms of both time and money. Fixing problems early reduces their impact on the project schedule and budget.

Each process in the sequence of complex tasks results in a baseline of the product. Each has a verification and validation test that the process has delivered the right product built in the right way. The work-flow model is one way. If the test fails, you iterate through the process one more time. If the test succeeds, you pass through the process milestone, and you cannot execute that process again. For example, say you complete and validate the software requirements analysis, then go on with design. For various reasons, design fails. Using the waterfall model, you cannot return to software requirements analysis to fix design problems. You have to try to address them within the current phase.

While this strategy manages certain risks, it increases others. You may, for example, find a problem in testing that requires massive design or requirements changes. The risk is to the budget or schedule: you have to go back to redo the whole series of processes [Royce, pp. 2–3]. Royce suggests some additional risk management methods to address this risk:

- Add a preliminary program design step between requirements and analysis. This forces consideration of architectural issues in the analysis stage, making it much less likely to discover design problems after finishing analysis.

- Document the design. This improves communication, forces commitment, and provides evidence of completion. It represents the tangible output of the process—no document, no design. It provides concrete inputs to later stages.

- Do it twice. If you're doing a completely new system, do it again before you deliver it to stakeholders. That is, plan on two projects: one to prototype the whole system, and one to reengineer it for the real world. This is similar to one of Brooks's conclusions: plan to throw one away [Brooks].

- Concentrate on test planning to achieve full test coverage of the system.

- Get commitment from stakeholders through joint reviews after preliminary design (system review), full design (critical software review), and testing (acceptance review).

Since the essence of OO projects is incremental and iterative development, it is not obvious why anyone would want to apply the waterfall model to OO software projects. They really don't work that way. You can adapt the process to some extent by adding incrementalism: simply repeat the entire process for each increment of the product. This works for large-scale increments but not for the many smaller-scale increments typical of an OO project. As well, the iteration typical of good OO design and development is anathema to the predictability of the waterfall approach.

Many of the companies I've worked for have relied on the waterfall model. For better or worse, most have honored it more in the breach than in the observance. The common perspective of all of these companies is to eliminate the risk of making a mistake by being thorough. The common reality is that, first, people aren't thorough, and second, change happens. You can manage lack of thoroughness through torture and other modern management techniques; change is much harder to manage in the context of a rigid sequence of tasks.

On a project to implement a new and quite theory-ridden feature in an OO database management system, the project team went over and over the requirements to make sure to get them right. The project had a major stakeholder in a major computer vendor that had licensed the software, and they provided critical database theory input—several times in conflicting ways. In the end, the developer doing the work redid the requirements willy-nilly as he descended into the depths of the real system on which all this had to work. The feature was six months late by the end of the project. (The computer vendor subsequently restructured, losing all its software functions and all the theorists it had employed, so by the end of the project, no one cared about the requirements input from the year before.)

One thing you must watch for is the political waterfall. Instead of optimizing the risk of problems down the line, this waterfall preserves the ability of stakeholders to say no. I worked in a commercial software vendor environment with a senior executive and a quality assurance manager who wanted to gain control over the development process. They did this by imposing major milestones at key process points, effectively putting a waterfall model in place. They gave themselves complete authority to say yea or nay to the project moving forward. This was not a matter of being sure of being right, but of being sure of being in control.

This strategy might have worked had it not been for the ultimate mission of the project: to deliver the software on schedule. This objective turned the so-called gatekeeper milestones into opportunities for the executives to nod and say "just do it." They really had no option other than to completely cancel the project, which happened once or twice.

These examples point up the fundamental problem with the waterfall model: it handles risk, but at much too high a level in the project system.

The Spiral

The spiral process model is an iterative, risk-based series of complex tasks. Each complex task contains a risk assessment task, a prototyping task, an approval milestone that determines whether the process continues or stops, and a development task or process followed by a validation and verification test. Figure 16-3 illustrates the spiral process. The horizontal line is the "commitment partition," which divides the complex tasks with milestones. The vertical line is cumulative cost, showing the increasing cost of the system as development spirals outward [Boehm 1988].

Vision: *A low-risk software development process that you execute and control to a successful completion*

Mission: *To manage the risk of a software development process to a successful completion*

Objective 16.3: To manage the risk of a software development process

The Spiral

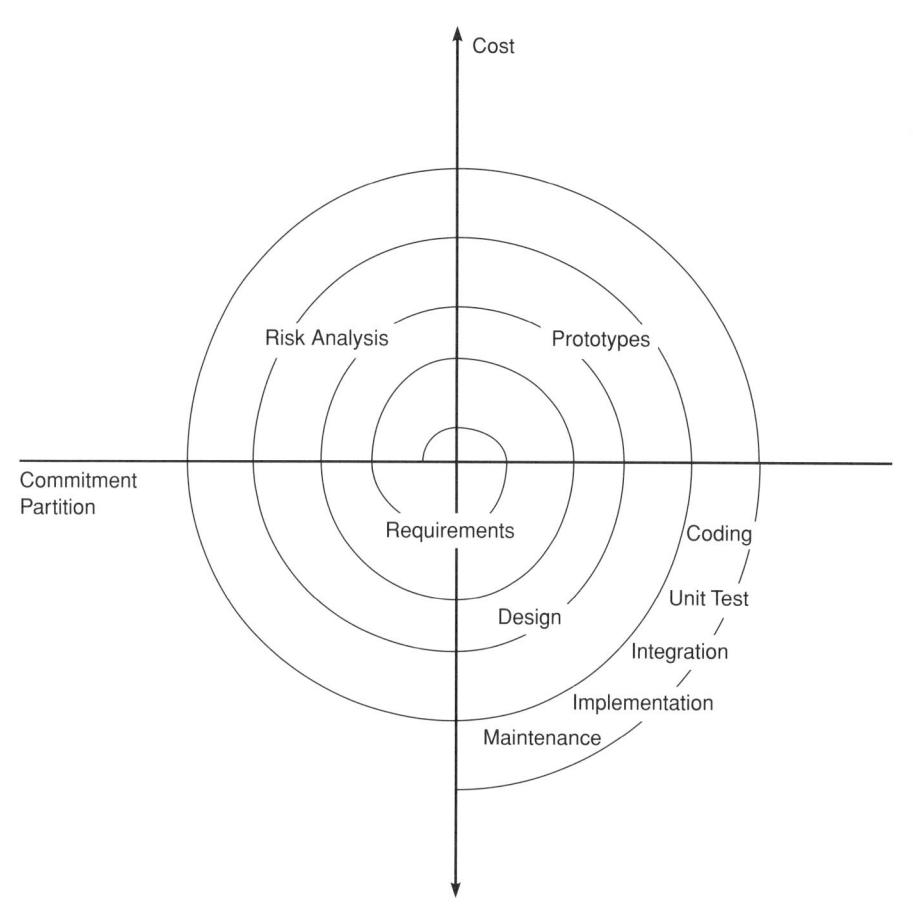

Figure 16-3
The spiral development process model

Approach 16.3: Organize the software development tasks in a series of iterations. In each iteration, focus on risk analysis and risk management through prototyping or other risk management method. Conduct the development tasks indicated by the risk analysis. At the end of the iteration, review the results with stakeholders to obtain commitment to proceeding with the next iteration. Plan the project as a series of iterations, basing the plan on a continuing risk analysis.

Metric 16.3: Risk: the system risk of the software development process generated by the process model

Target 16.3: A risk below the risk tolerance of the process model system

---

Each iteration of the process contains these complex tasks:
- Analyze the risks during the iteration.
- Apply risk management methods such as prototyping to resolve any risky issues.

- Execute the appropriate development process, such as analysis, design, or coding.
- Validate and verify the results of the development process.
- Plan the next iteration in detail.
- Commit project to next iteration with a review of the results of this one.

Boehm explicitly includes the potential for dividing the software into incremental partitions, adding a third dimension to Figure 16-3 [Boehm 1988, p. 64].

The primary advantage of the spiral model is its adaptability. You can change the process to do whatever your risk analysis and management indicates that you should do. While preserving the economic benefits of the waterfall, the spiral model thus puts much more flexibility into the process.

There are some other pluses of the spiral model [Boehm 1988, p. 69]:

- It encourages reuse by focusing attention on different ways to accomplish development.
- It allows change easily through its ability to reevaluate and replan.
- Because risk analysis requires understanding of goals and constraints, the model provides a way for you to integrate quality into the process.
- It finds problems early, reducing cost and risk.
- It lets you decide among alternatives using well-understood criteria.
- It lets you spend just as much time and money as you need to based on well-understood criteria.
- It is just as effective for maintenance as for original development.

The benefits of this approach seem so clear that I have fully integrated the approach into the entire project management approach, not just the development portion of the project. The risk management plan manages all the different risks of the project. The "rolling-wave" style of planning that this book advocates is very similar in many ways to the spiral process model applied in-the-large.

Risk Management Plan (14.1)

I suspect that only Steering, Anticipating, and Congruent cultures could use the spiral process. Each of these cultures drives its process through the kind of feedback that the spiral model encourages. Oblivious, Variable, and Routine cultures do not. Except, of course, for the famous "death spiral."

Management Culture (31.1)

The Fountain

The fountain model [Henderson-Sellers 1990, 1993] is a model specifically designed for OO projects. In particular, the fountain model focuses on reuse—doing it and making it possible. Figure 16-4 illustrates, somewhat fancifully, the fountain model. This model is quite new and is just finding its way into the literature [Goldberg] and into OO projects.

The Fountain

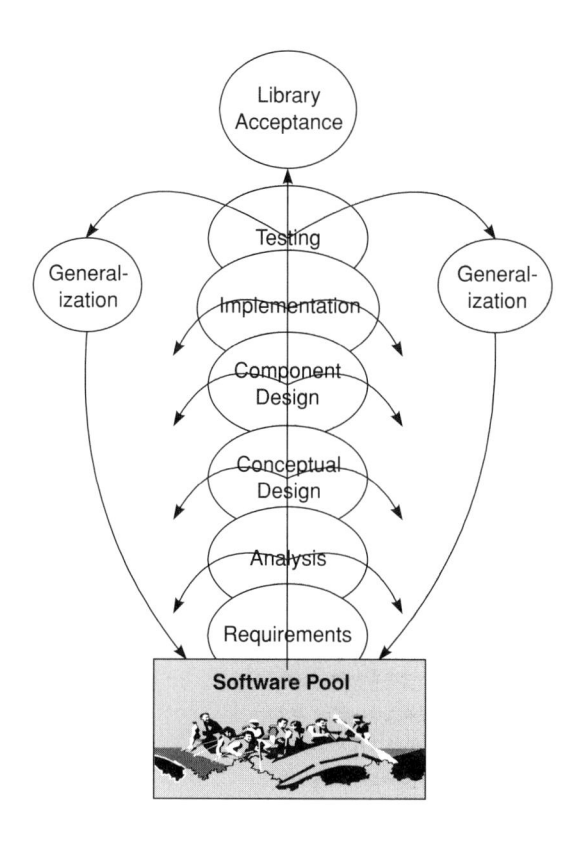

Figure 16-4
The fountain development process model

Vision: Reusable components used and useful in this and future products

Mission: To manage productively the creation of reusable components and systems

---

Objective 16.4: To manage productively the creation of reusable components and systems

---

Approach 16.4: Organize the software development tasks in a series of inter-linked, nested tasks. Start the process by reusing available components. Move up and down the fountain of tasks as required by the nature of the work. When you complete a deliverable, take an extra step to generalize and certify it before installing it in the reuse repository.

Metric 16.4: Reuse potential of deliverable systems

Target 16.4: Values within the limits of an x-R control chart; project average ≥ a benchmark of organizational reuse potential

Reuse Repository (2.2)
Software System (15.7)
Cluster (15.5)

The fountain emerges from a pool of existing software that the project reuses, the reuse repository. The fountain applies to the system as a whole. It also applies to the individual clusters. As each cluster moves through requirements, analysis, design, implementation, and testing, work can fall back into previous phases. Only when testing is complete and the project has generalized the system, however, does it place it into the reuse repository.

The goal is to develop the full reuse potential for the software clusters and systems you create. Thus, this process model is most suitable for those OO projects with a high proportion of reusable deliverables. If you intend to build your reuse repository with the deliverables of a project, you should organize their delivery through this process model. Usually, this means casting many more of your clusters as deliverable software systems instead of just clusters within a software system.

This model is much more flexible than the waterfall and spiral models for OO software. From any point, you can go to any other point, as long as you understand why you are doing it. This reflects the general approach to OO software of incrementing and iterating over your clusters as they develop. It is not supposed to be a matter of discovering flaws and going back to previous stages to fix them, but rather a process of carefully extending the clusters in a controlled and flexible manner to accommodate your increased knowledge. Thus, the time you spend in the different development processes is the same but distributed differently relative to time [Henderson-Sellers 1990, pp. 157–158].

The fountain model does have some disadvantages. Its focus is somewhat unbalanced from the project manager's perspective. Everything is reuse, and there is nothing in the model about risk, particularly the risks of failing to meet stakeholder expectations and of schedule failure. You have to balance the generalization of components for reusability with the need to deliver systems. That is, after all, the ultimate point of development. Striking a balance between the needs of the current project and those of future projects is the main challenge of the fountain model. Planning should use risk analysis to identify the parts of the process likely to iterate; it should also identify clusters with a high risk of low reuse potential. You can either adjust the process to increase their potential, or revise the process toward cluster delivery and away from reuse generalization.

Recursive-Parallel

The recursive-parallel life cycle reflects the architecture of the system you are developing [Berard]. The idea formalizes a well-known approach: "analyze a little, design a little, implement a little, test a little." Figure 16-5 illustrates this model.

Vision: A simple, easy-to-manage OO software development process

Mission: To generate a simple, easy-to-manage development process

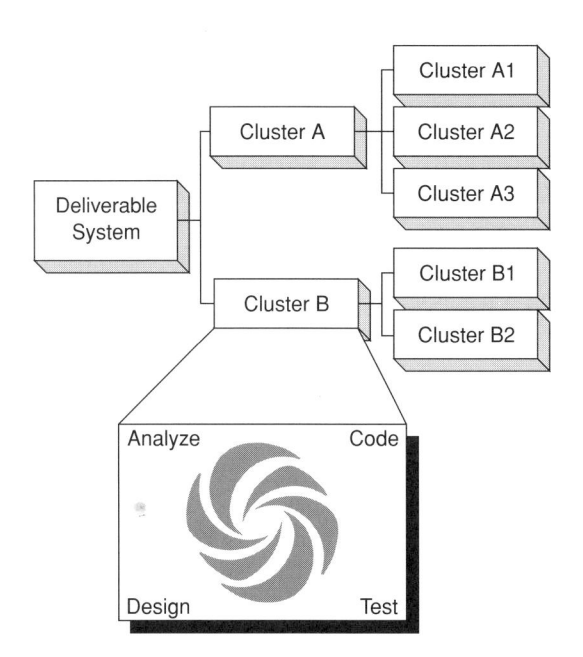

Figure 16-5
The recursive-parallel development process model

Objective 16.5: To generate a simple, easy-to-manage development process

Approach 16.5: Focus on the cluster architecture of the deliverable system. Break down the top-level clusters into finer-grained clusters and organize the development processes around those clusters. Recursively define clusters until you reach an appropriate level. Execute the plan to deliver clusters in parallel to optimize the schedule.

Metric 16.5: Management process effort: the amount of effort spent in level-of-effort management tasks relating to development in the project

Target 16.5: Values within the limits of an x-R control chart; project average ≥ a benchmark of management effort

The goal of this model is to build an easy-to-manage development process that reflects the architecture of the system. This model is a generally top-down approach. First, you decompose the problem into clusters. Then, you recurse on each cluster to decompose them further, as required. Then, you apply your process (analysis, design, code, and test) to each cluster in parallel. You continue this process until you deliver the clusters and the deliverable systems.

The top-down nature of this approach is not strict. You can, for example, compose or aggregate clusters if the architecture calls for it. You can generate new cluster requirements as you design through a discovery process. The general philosophy is to do what is necessary to get a good design, a design reflecting highly independent clusters and systems.

Also, the distribution of effort among the parts of the process for a cluster depend on the nature of the clusters. Some clusters require more analysis, others require more coding, and still others require more testing. Often the analysis and design tasks merge, as the OO approach tends to make them indistinguishable. If the cluster is small and "obvious," you may just code and test it. If there is a reusable component in the reuse repository that accomplishes the mission of the required cluster, you can skip the whole thing, or modify it as required.

The negative side of the recursive-parallel model is its informality. It provides no particular mechanism other than "good design" for creating reusable systems. It provides no context for risk analysis and management. It has little focus on reuse. Also, while it implicitly permits rework of the developing clusters, the focus on top-down development tends to lock in architectural decisions early in the project.

I've taught this and the other OO methods in language and management courses several times. Almost every time, the OO-knowledgeable participants saw their previous efforts as recursive-parallel rather than as hacking, waterfall, spiral, or fountain. This model is close to the "natural" development process for OO experts. On the other hand, most of the projects people mentioned were simple, or prototypes, or pilot projects to demonstrate OO technology. They definitely were not complex, large projects involving hundreds or thousands of clusters.

If your management culture is decentralized, you may be able to match this development process to your organizational culture by distributing authority and responsibility along process lines. If each cluster takes responsibility for itself and for integrating with the clusters that use it, the project should manage itself. Now about that bridge I wanted to sell you....

Genetic

Having reviewed the competition, each of the proposed life cycles for OO projects leaves something to be desired. The hacking cycle doesn't scale beyond a single person. The waterfall delivers, if you can wait. The spiral ignores reuse and is too formal. The fountain ignores risk. The recursive-parallel ignores risk and is too top down, as well as being a bit too informal.

The genetic development process is my first attempt at integrating some of these diverse strands into a unified approach to developing OO software.

Vision: A productive OO software development process that you execute and control to a successful completion

Mission: To provide a structure for planning and execution of an effective, productive OO software development process

Genetic

```
┌─System ──────────────────── 1.1 ──┐
│ ┌─Process ───────────────── 4.6 ──┐│
│ │ ┌─Primary Process ────── 16.3 ─┐││
│ │ │ ┌─Development Process ─ 16.4 ┐│││
│ │ │ │                        16.6││││
│ │ │ │    Genetic Development     ││││
│ │ │ │         Process            ││││
│ │ │ │                            ││││
│ │ │ │  Process Effectiveness     ││││
│ │ │ │  Failure Potential         ││││
│ │ │ │  Risk Rate                 ││││
│ │ │ │  Risk Reduction Rate       ││││
│ │ │ │  Process Productivity      ││││
│ │ │ │  System Reuse Potential    ││││
│ │ │ │  Alignment                 ││││
│ │ │ └────────────────────────────┘│││
│ │ └──────────────────────────────┘││
│ └────────────────────────────────┘│
└──────────────────────────────────┘
```

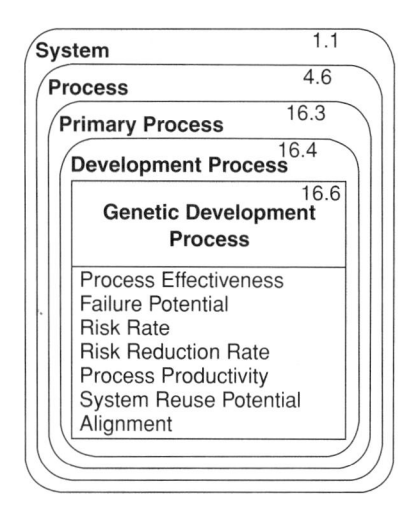

Objective 16.6: To ensure process effectiveness

Approach 16.6: Adapt to the organizational culture by modifying standard tasks, work flows, and milestones to the requirements of the culture, the customers, and the work domain.

Metric 16.6: Process effectiveness: a multiple-attribute metric that includes attributes for the issues of interest to the management culture, such as quality (fault rates, capability benchmarks), stability (schedule variance), or cost effectiveness (cost per delivered value unit)

Target 16.6: Individual metrics for the attributes that baseline current values of the attributes of the process, with each attribute being within control parameters of the appropriate type of control chart

Objective 16.7: To identify the potential for common failures in standard tasks, milestones, and dependencies

Approach 16.7: Identify and quantify common risks to tasks, work flows, and milestones you create in Approach 16.6. To identify a risk, analyze the objectives and components of the system to understand how it might fail. To assess the risk, estimate the probability of failure given historical data or a priori assessments of the general probability of failure as opposed to the specific probability of failure in a given project. These risks serve as reusable systems when you plan a project. The planning process assesses the risk taking the specific project and situation into account.

Metric 16.7.1: Failure potential: a prior probability estimate for the failure of the system mission for all the systems in the process model

Target 16.7.1: A potential within the risk tolerance for the development process model

---

Metric 16.7.2: Risk rate: the rate of growth of development process model risks with respect to time

Target 16.7.2: A low and stable value indicating diminishing risk discovery over time

---

Objective 16.8: To provide methods to avoid and mitigate potential failures that exceed your tolerance for risk

---

Approach 16.8: Identify your general tolerance for risk in the development process as a probability of mission failure that you are not willing to exceed. For any standard risks with probability of failure greater than your tolerance, identify a set of methods that either reduce the probability of failure directly or through mitigation of the impact of the failure on the mission.

Metric 16.8: Risk reduction rate: the rate of change of the ratio of risk after introducing risk management methods into the development process model to the prior risk (Metric 16.7.1) with respect to time

Target 16.8: A negative rate, indicating that the model is consistently diminishing risk over time in a material way, eventually stabilizing at a low rate of change

---

Objective 16.9: To be highly productive in the current project

---

Approach 16.9: Acquire and reuse systems wherever possible in the project, either through a capable reuse repository or through an acquisition process. Avoid new development if there is a system available that will do the required job.

Metric 16.9: Process productivity: the value from the current project delivered from processes that the model generates per effort-hour

Target 16.9: A high value within control limits of an x-R control chart of the process productivity over time

---

Objective 16.10: To be highly productive across all the projects you plan and execute using this process model

---

Approach 16.10: Assess the reuse potential of each system you create through a process task. Assess the reuse benefits and costs using cost-benefit, return-on-investment, or cost-avoidance methods [Poulin]. Generalize and certify those systems that will justify the effort spent and deposit them in a reuse repository for use in other tasks in the project and in other projects.

Metric 16.10: System reuse potential: the median reuse potential from all projects delivered from processes that the model generates, adjusted by posterior distributions of actual reuse of systems across all projects

Target 16.10: A high system reuse potential for the model

Objective 16.11: To align the development process with the structural requirements of OO systems

---

Approach 16.11: Structure your process work-flow standard to accommodate the iterative, incremental, recursive, and parallel nature of OO and RAD development. Create internal processes within the model that apply to encapsulated clusters within the software systems, and build the process model from these processes. Define a strategy for systematically developing the system (top-down recursion, bottom-up integration, inside-out nuclear growth). Place milestones at the end of each internal process and at decision points, points in the process where you decide whether to iterate, to finalize, or to abandon the cluster using risk analysis of the prototype software. Integrate clusters explicitly through integration processes flowing from milestones that you reach by satisfying exit criteria. Generalize and certify clusters for reuse in an explicit process that flows from the integration milestone.

Metric 16.11: Alignment: a subjective metric based on the satisfaction of the people working with the process with the process structure; if you must, weight your survey with experience or skill weights, or use a Delphi technique of interviewing experts rather than just random surveys

Target 16.11: A high alignment within control parameters of an x-R control chart of alignment ratings from users of the process

---

The objectives must address the following issues:

- A healthy mix of formality and informality appropriate to the management culture of the organization
- Integration of risk assessment and management into the planning process to ensure successful delivery

- A focus on reuse, both in terms of reusing systems in the project and developing systems for reuse in other projects, as the central approach to improving productivity and quality
- Integration of the iterative, incremental, recursive, parallel structure of OO and RAD development into the development process to align that process with the nature of the work

These objectives lead to the following OO life cycle, which I call the "genetic life cycle" because the resulting project looks like the growth of an organism from its genetic code. Figure 16-6 shows a slightly ornate first attempt at representing this development process.

The genetic process model starts at the center with the same feasibility analysis and initial requirements gathering that any software project requires. As the

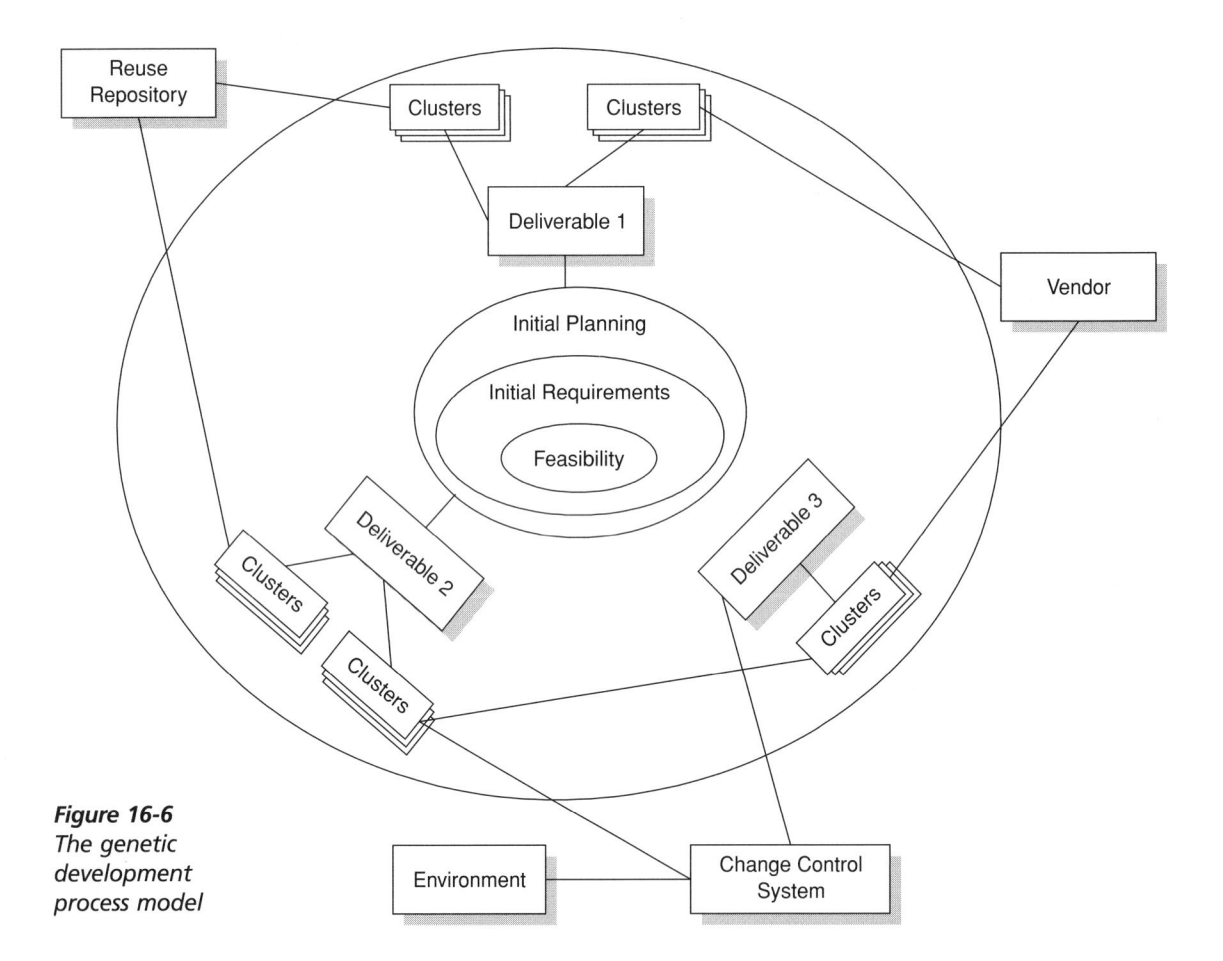

Figure 16-6
The genetic development process model

project builds, the software systems and product documents that comprise the deliverable system grow out from this center. Depending on your approach to developing the clusters, the system may develop center-out (a top-down method) or may grow by filling in the middle (bottom-up or inside-out). In any case, each cluster grows by increments and iterations as you build prototypes, evaluate risks, and integrate clusters.

At a certain level of integration, you generalize and certify a component and deposit it in the reuse repository for use in other tasks, both within the project and in other projects. Additional requirements and other changes come into the project system from its environment, controlled by the change management system of the project. As the project progresses, project management extends the project plan, plans new processes within the system, and baselines performance evaluation measures to generate planning feedback to management. The planning map to this structure is the work breakdown structure, which organizes all the work in the project into a network around the system deliverables.

This development process describes the ideal process behind many of the projects I have managed. One functional manager I worked with, at a facilitated session on building a department-wide development process model, suggested that a simple process was best. On my asking where the iteration was in this process, he said that we could assume it was there, because that's what the developers would do anyway. I held my peace at the time, but I've always felt strongly that a process model should look at least vaguely like the reality it models. For me, the genetic process comes closest to this ideal. It serves my purpose, and I hope to refine it over the next few years into a strong, realistic approach to developing OO software.

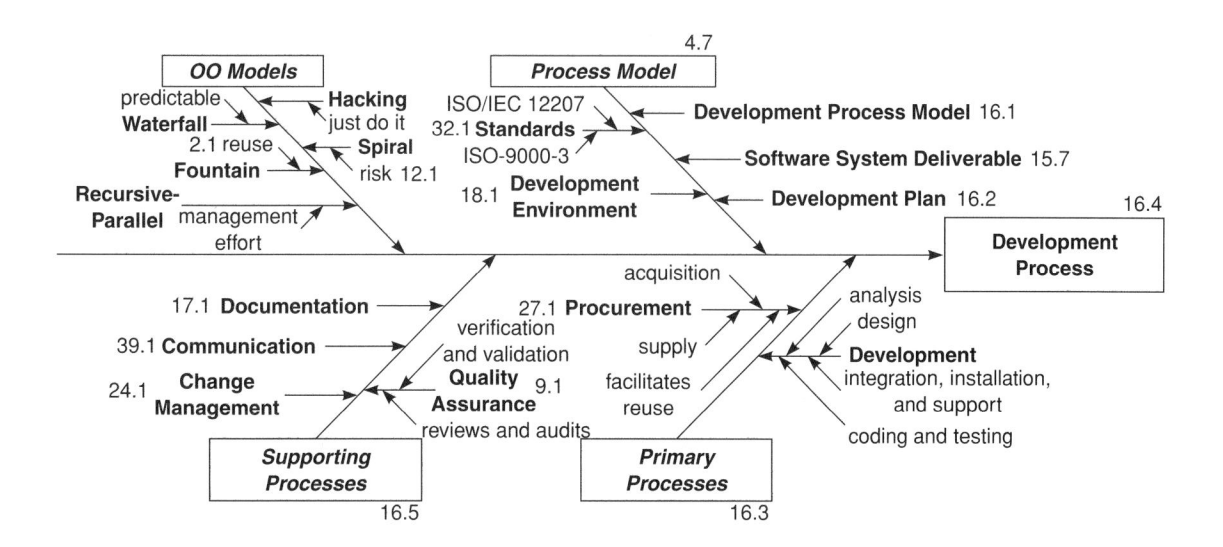

Readings

[Berard] Edward V. Berard. *Essays on Object-Oriented Software Engineering, Volume I.* Englewood Cliffs, NJ: Prentice Hall, 1993.

This book is a collection of essays that Berard released over the Internet over a period of years while researching OO methods. It is an individualistic, opinionated, and quirky introduction to OO technology, readable if a bit diffuse. Chapter 5 discusses the recursive-parallel life cycle.

[Boehm 1981] Barry W. Boehm. *Software Engineering Economics.* Englewood Cliffs, NJ: Prentice Hall, 1981.

The primary purpose for this book is the COCOMO method of cost estimation for software systems. To develop and justify that method, Boehm delves into most aspects of the economics of software production and development, including the details of the waterfall life cycle. There are few discussions of the life cycle that are better.

[Boehm 1988] Barry W. Boehm. A spiral model of software development and enhancement. *Computer* 21:5 (May 1988): 61–72.

This is the best of several similar articles that Boehm has published on the spiral model. It clearly defines the model, applies it to a case study, and sets out the advantages and disadvantages of the model. It also nicely summarizes the other life-cycle models from Boehm's perspective.

[Henderson-Sellers 1990] Brian Henderson-Sellers and Julian M. Edwards. The object-oriented systems life cycle. *Communications of the ACM* 33:9 (September 1990): 142–159.

This article lays out the basic needs of OO development. It goes through most of the development tasks in detail, showing how they break down for OO software. It discusses OO development methods and their requirements from process models. It then proposes the fountain model for both system and component development.

[Henderson-Sellers 1993] Brian Henderson-Sellers and Julian M. Edwards. The fountain model for object-oriented systems development. *Object Magazine* 3:2 (1993): 72–79.

This is a more accessible and less detailed presentation of the fountain model.

[ISO 1991] International Standards Organization. *ISO 9000-3, Guideline for Application of ISO 9001 to the Development, Supply, and Maintenance of Software.* ISO, 1991.

This is an addendum to the ISO-9000 standard that goes into detail on how to apply ISO-9001 to software development. It is the main international standard for software development processes.

[ISO 1995] International Standards Organization. *ISO/IEC 12207, Information Technology—Software Life Cycle Processes.* ISO, 1995.

This is a new standard designed to replace earlier process standards. It details the various software development processes without insisting on any particular method for applying them. The primary intent is to define terms and to establish a common vocabulary for standardizing development processes.

[Kehoe]	Raymond Kehoe and Alka Jarvis. *ISO 9000-3: A Tool for Software Product and Process Improvement.* New York: Springer-Verlag, 1996.

This book is a gloss on [ISO 1991] that explains in detail what is required to claim that you adhere to the ISO-9001 standard for software development. While I disagree with some aspects of their presentation, the book is invaluable in interpreting the standard as applied to the real world.

[Royce]	Winston W. Royce. Managing the development of large software systems: Concepts and techniques. In *1970 WESCON Technical Papers, Vol. 14*. August 25–28, 1970. Session A, paper A/1. WESCON, 1970.

This is the original article on the waterfall process model. Much of the justification for and detail of the model appears here and not elsewhere, so it is well worth reading. The technology is a bit out of date, but the management concerns are still with us.

Questions to Think About

1. Why are there so many different ways to organize the software development process?

2. Have you ever used a process that guaranteed on-time, under-budget delivery of software? What kinds of guarantees does a process model give you?

3. The process orientation of the ISO software development standards says very little about product quality, focusing instead on process quality. Do you think this focus is adequate for delivering valuable software? Why or why not?

4. Before reading the next chapter, do you think the processes of this one are document-centric? Why or why not? What roles do the various documents play in the different process models? (Hint: How do tasks communicate? How do people communicate? How do people communicate between tasks?)

5. What would the impact be in your current work environment of proposing to follow the spiral model as Boehm presented it?

6. Compare the spiral, fountain, recursive-parallel, and genetic approaches with respect to reuse. What are the advantages and disadvantages of each?

7. Which process model comes closest to the methods you've used in the past? Why did the methods you have used differ from the models here?

CHAPTER 17

Development Documentation

The Development Document

The *development document* is a project document that records the information a development process produces. This includes requirements definition, functional specification, or design. You use a document template to produce the initial version, as with any project document. The document represents everything of interest about the process [Royce, p. 5]. For example, when you think of a design, you really think of a design document. The "functional specification" is usually a document, not a process, to those who review it. It documents the systems that the process produces and any aspects of the process itself that are of interest.

Vision: A technical community well informed about a software system and making use of that information in building the system

Mission: To communicate information about a software system that its developers can use in their efforts

---
Objective 17.1: To communicate information developed as part of a development process

---

Approach 17.1: Identify the audience for the document. Create the document using a document template according to the plan you generate from the process model that produces the document. Create the content of the document using an appropriate mix of text and graphics. Review the document with a technical review. Evaluate the document in the review using the criteria for the particular kind of document. Revise the document as required. Repeat the review/revision tasks until the document is acceptable.

The Development Document 299

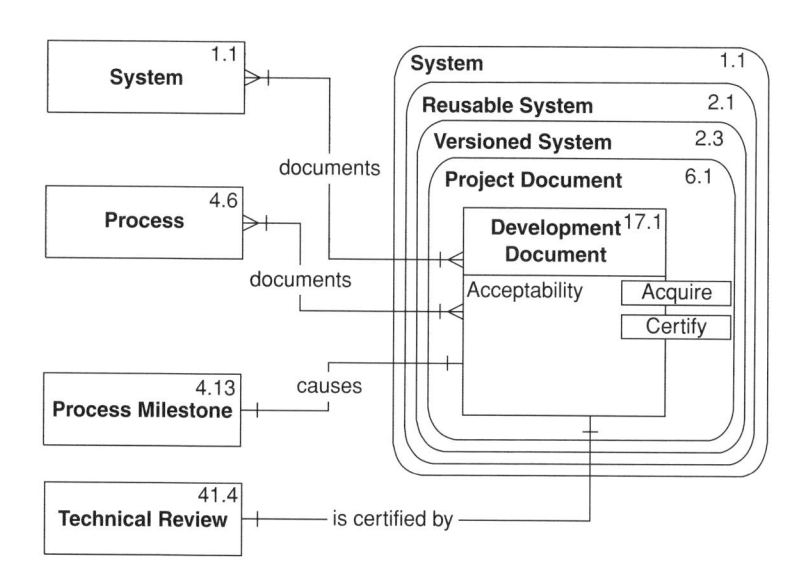

Metric 17.1: Acceptability of document: a nominal metric with values Acceptable, Acceptable with Revisions, Not Acceptable

Target 17.1: Acceptable

Objective 17.2: To provide information of use to developers in building a software system

---

Approach 17.2: Evaluate the subject matter of the document for feasibility, testability, consistency, and traceability. Provide a clearly detailed analysis of the quality of the subject matter for the next stage in the development process.

Metric 17.2.1: Feasibility: the probability that the development processes that depend on this document will accomplish their mission given the information in this document (a measure of system risk)

Target 17.2.1: A feasibility probability higher than 1 minus the risk tolerance for the target software system, with the value within control limits of an x-R control chart of feasibilities for similar software systems

---

Metric 17.2.2: Testability: a ratio metric that estimates the cost of lowering the risk of the target system to its risk tolerance (the cost of quality [Jones 1991, p. 286])

Target 17.2.2: A cost within the limits of an x-R control diagram of similar target system costs of quality

---

Metric 17.2.3: Internal Consistency: a count of internal contradictions between elements of the document

Target 17.2.3: Zero

Metric 17.2.4: External Consistency: a count of contradictions between elements of the document and external system elements, usually in a source document that supplies the basis for the internal elements

Target 17.2.4: Zero

Metric 17.2.5: Traceability: a ratio of the number of elements traceable to an input source of elements (tracing analysis objects to requirements or design features to analysis elements, for example) to the total number of elements

Target 17.2.5: A value within control limits of a pn control chart

---

■ *Note:* Every development has myriad internal content objects that derive from the particular method you are following. These include use cases, state-transition diagrams, flowcharts, classes, relationships, interactions, flows, and on and on. Since there are so many variations, and since this book is already too long, I do not deal with the document contents as objects. Each object in a document has its own technical metrics and targets. There are various aggregate metrics for collections of objects for testability and feasibility, for example, [Champeaux; Fenton; Henderson-Sellers 1996]. Usually, these metrics are for the technical manager or developer, not the project manager. You can often use them to understand risk and other project issues. An example is class complexity in analysis and design documents. Developers can use this metric to evaluate their designs for feasibility. Project managers can use it to evaluate the risk of the development process tasks and to adjust the schedule and budget accordingly.

There are three major uses for development documents: forcing the systematic review of the information you are creating, reviewing the information in technical reviews, and using them as input into another process.

Having now written many documents and several books, I firmly believe, with Brooks, that writing down your thoughts is essential [Brooks, p. 111]. The human mind likes shortcuts, and most shortcut decisions lead to failure [Dörner]. Writing down your thinking forces you to be clear, to fill in gaps, to resolve issues, and to make decisions. With a document, you have thought; without, you have nothing.

Technical reviews are the major method of confirming or testing concepts. Compared to code, concepts are hard to test. It is almost impossible to automate the testing of the designer's mind, for example. Documents provide a way to validate concepts directly. There are other ways, such as prototypes, storyboards, or even spoken interactions. Documents are more effective and more permanent. Having an acceptable technical document is the event that the process milestone represents, and you can't leave the process without it.

Technical Review (41.4)
Process Milestone (4.13)

If you are the only person working on a system, you need not document it. Think twice, though. Reread the paragraph above about writing down thoughts. If you are not the only person, then you need to communicate with others. For training alone, documents are vital. They also provide essential information—names, purposes, relationships—that other people need to know to do their jobs. Most documents provide handy checklists for evaluating systems, particularly for testing or reuse evaluation.

Development documents are an essential part of certification for reuse. The document provides information essential to reusing other systems—source code comments, class hierarchy design, messaging structure, or test results, for example. A development document is also a reusable system itself, and you acquire it and certify it as you would any reusable system. You certify a document with a technical review and any other tools that apply.

Reusable System (2.1)

A document may or may not be acceptable going into a review. It must be acceptable if you use it as input to any other task. It must also be acceptable to certify it as reusable.

■ *Note:* In documentation, as in all things, moderation is all.

The Requirements Document

The *requirements document* states the stakeholder requirements for the software system in terms that a stakeholder can understand and approve. This document explicitly contains all the stakeholder expectations as distinct elements, including the metrics by which the project manager and stakeholders can determine whether the software system has fulfilled each expectation. The requirements document is part of the statement of work. It is the basis for the work breakdown structure (WBS). The requirements document also contains the top-level architecture of the product: the deliverables and any of the top-level clusters in those deliverables that clarify some role in meeting stakeholder expectations.

Vision: A vision of the product that takes strategic stakeholder expectations into account and produces deliverables that satisfy and delight stakeholders

Mission: To communicate a clear, unambiguous statement of strategic stakeholder expectations and their relationship to the project deliverables, leading to a product that satisfies and delights stakeholders

---

Objective 17.3: To create an unambiguous statement of strategic requirements for the deliverables

---

Diagram

- Stakeholder [3.3] — lists →
- Expectation [17.3] — lists →
- Deliverable [3.2] — lists →
- Statement of Work [8.1] — is part of →

System [1.1]
  Reusable System [2.1]
    Versioned System [2.3]
      Project Document [6.1]
        Development Document [17.1]
          Requirements Document [17.2]
            - Ambiguity
            - System Usability
            - Satisfaction
            - Acquire
            - Certify
            - Strategic Value
            - Risk-Adjusted Value

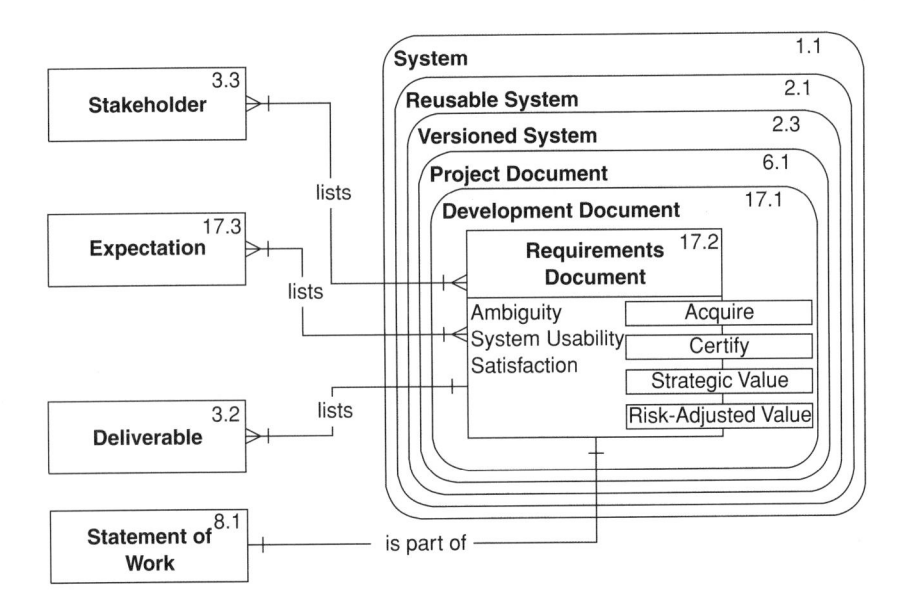

Approach 17.3: Create a list of stakeholders. For each stakeholder, create a list of unambiguous, strategic expectations: those expectations that (1) you are likely to be able to meet; (2) create strategic, substantial, and material value for the stakeholders; and (3) relate directly to your chosen business strategy (business and regulatory environment, market, competitiveness, product mix, pricing, growth rate, and so on). Communicate these lists to stakeholders through the requirements document and list their reactions, revising and integrating the feedback as required.

Metric 17.3.1: Strategic value ratio: the ratio of strategic function points (those satisfying the criteria in Approach 17.2) to total estimated function points for the system

Target 17.3.1: A number within control limits of an x-R control chart of similar product deliverables for your organization or industry

---

Metric 17.3.2: Ambiguity: the diversity of interpretation of the set of requirements, measured by polling a reasonably diverse set of stakeholders on the cost of the system that would satisfy the stated requirements in the requirements document; ambiguity is the relative range of values [Gause]

Target 17.3.2: A level of ambiguity within control limits of an x-R control chart of similar products for your organization or industry

---

Objective 17.4: To prioritize deliverables to deliver the optimal amount of value to stakeholders, taking into account risks of those deliverables

Approach 17.4: Develop a set of criteria for prioritizing deliverables, such as priority of expectation, deliverable cost, technical difficulty, or competitive pressures. Develop the set of deliverables with which you propose to satisfy stakeholder expectations. Analyze the relationship to prioritize the deliverables according to your criteria. Make the appropriate decisions about specific expectations and communicate those decisions to stakeholders through the requirements document.

Metric 17.4: Risk-adjusted value: the value of the project to stakeholders multiplied by the project risk

Target 17.4: A value acceptable compared to a risk-free return-on-investment analysis for the project

---

Objective 17.5: To satisfy and delight stakeholders

Approach 17.5: Plan your project using the insights, requirements, and deliverable priorities in the requirements document. Deliver the product in incremental releases and survey stakeholder response to each release with usability tests and satisfaction surveys, feeding this information back into a revised requirements document.

Metric 17.5.1: System usability: a multidimensional, subjective evaluation along several dimensions of stakeholder expectations relating to use of the product (performance, ease of use, and other such system characteristics)

Target 17.5.1: An increasing usability rating within control limits of an x-R control chart of similar products from your organization and industry

---

Metric 17.5.1: Stakeholder satisfaction: a multidimensional rating of the current product version based on stakeholder response to the approaches to delivering specified requirements (that is, rate the product on stated expectations, not on vague or subjective "satisfaction" measures)

Target 17.5.1: A satisfaction level within control limits of an x-R control chart of delivered versions and/or delivered products over several projects

---

While the requirements document and its contents are object-oriented because of this book's approach, there is nothing different between the requirements document for an OO system versus that for any other kind. Requirements, after all, have nothing to do with the way you build your system. However, as you will see below, the basic architecture does affect some ways of relating requirements to the system to build. This in turn feeds back into your understanding of which requirements you want to meet.

It is unusual to have architectural statements appearing in the requirements document. I have come to the conclusion after going through several tries at requirements that it is essential to build a list of deliverables as part of the requirements. Can you fully develop requirements without having done a database design? What about the work breakdown structure? How can you base it on deliverables if the requirements document doesn't list them? Of course, this makes the document iterative. As you move through architectural design, you will revise your list of deliverables, showing how they contribute to expectations. It is essential that, as you do so, you revise the requirements document that drives the work of the project.

Whitten adds a separate product document called the *product objectives*. Its purpose is to reduce the amount of rework and waste later in the project [Whitten, pp. 241–255]. The operational objectives of the deliverables you define in the requirements serve this purpose, though you can separate them as Whitten does. They clarify issues, forcing them to the surface early in the project. They provide a connection between the project and its stakeholder environment. They also provide a clear baseline for change control throughout the project.

Stakeholder Expectations

A stakeholder has a set of expectations for a project. These expectations form the basis for the requirements document. Each expectation is a requirement. A given stakeholder may have expectations for several projects, and he or she may expect the same thing from multiple projects. When the project delivers, the deliverables meet the expectations.

Vision: A project that delivers value to its stakeholders

Mission: To express the things that stakeholders value about a project

---

Objective 17.6: To express a stakeholder expectation

Approach 17.6: Get the stakeholder to state his or her expectation unambiguously.

Metric 17.6: Ambiguity: the diversity of interpretation of the expectation, measured as in Metric 17.2.2

Target 17.6: A level of ambiguity within control limits of an x-R control chart of similar expectations for your organization or industry

---

In format, an expectation is usually a simple text in the words of the stakeholder, not those of the project manager, development managers, or developers. When the stakeholder reviews an expectation, he or she should be able to read it, understand it, and approve it.

The Requirements Document

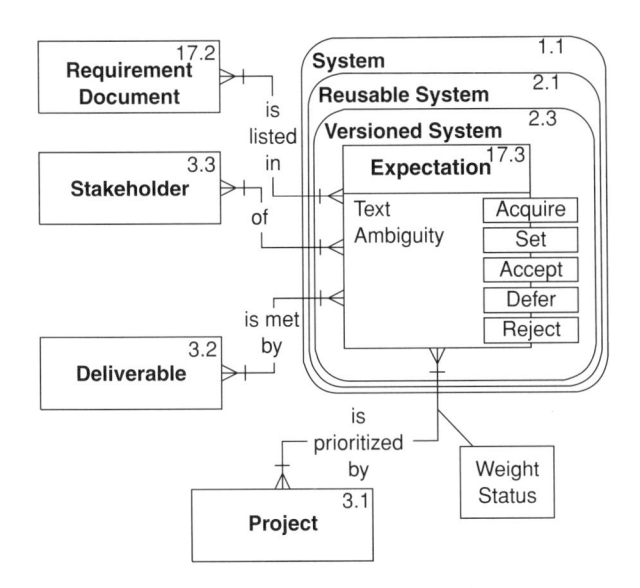

You can acquire expectations in all sorts of interesting ways [Gause]. There are two essentials: breadth and precision. Your excavation of expectations should try to reach all the potential stakeholders you can find. You should be careful to probe as deeply as you can for the true structure of those stakeholders' expectations. This is not a system that benefits from keeping it simple. The complexity makes it even more important to resolve the ambiguities inherent in human communication. Being precise in stating expectations is the essence of the art of gathering them. Helping others to be precise is a large part of that art.

There are many tricks and techniques to this kind of analysis, most related to removing ambiguity in the list of expectations. There are specific kinds of questions you should ask. There are specific people whom you should involve. There are many techniques for developing both expectations and ways to address them, such as brainstorming and mind mapping. You can develop this into a science through various kinds of ambiguity and stakeholder satisfaction measures.

Once you've stated an expectation, you need to decide what to do about it. The same expectation may apply to several projects. Each project may weight the expectation differently, and each project may set the stakeholder's expectations differently. For example, one project may defer the expectation, weighting it very low. The next project, to which you deferred the expectation, increases the weight and makes the expectation status active.

You have three choices about what to do with an expectation. You can

- accept the expectation, stating your intention to meet it with the deliverables of your project.
- defer the expectation to a later project.
- reject an expectation entirely.

It is usually a good idea to state the reasons for deferring or rejecting an expectation. This communication at least makes the attempt to satisfy the stakeholder by reducing his or her priority for the expectation. Saying nothing at all is likely to leave a stakeholder feeling rejected, which can cause communication and support problems later in the project.

Many commercial software companies have problems with this level of communication. A project I managed, for example, had a series of expectations from various stakeholders that the system would become easier to use through adoption of OO technology. As the architecture and proposed deliverables developed, it appeared that the OO approach of the product would make the product harder to use, mostly through poorly defined inheritance relationships. When I brought up the issue of expectations, the project sponsor responded, "Those expectations are from the wrong customers. Let's focus on the important customers." This kind of situation calls for "spin control" by product marketing. I seriously doubt that going out to the customers and telling them they aren't the right ones is going to be an effective way to set expectations. Personally, I'd rather meet the expectations than explain why I can't. If I can't, I'd like to have a better reason than unwillingness to deal with a customer.

Quality Function Deployment

One tool for developing a strong requirements document is quality function deployment (QFD). Also known as the "House of Quality," QFD is a set of tools from the total quality movement that relate stakeholder objectives to development features. Recasting this a bit into the OO framework of this book, we see stakeholder expectations related to deliverable systems and clusters. Let's take one piece of the puzzle at a time to make the overall QFD framework comprehensible. This example again uses the defect tracking system for tracking faults and failures in a software product.

To construct the basic QFD matrix, you need to relate stakeholders to architectural design features and deliverables that contain them (Figure 17-1) [Hauser].

First, identify the stakeholders. Next, list their expectations. These become the QFD *customer attributes,* the vertical categories of the matrix. In the defect tracking example, there are several stakeholders:

- External customers who buy the software product
- The project sponsor
- Development managers
- Developers

Each of these stakeholders has a set of expectations for the system. For example, external customers want to report failures and track fixes to their failures. The

Figure 17-1
QFD stakeholder-deliverable matrix

Legend	
Strongly Positive	++
Positive	+
No Effect	
Negative	-
Strongly Negative	--

		PROBLEM						PERSON	
		Enable Failure Tracking	Enable Fault Tracking	Enable Fix Tracking	Enable Causation Tracking	Improve Tracking Impact	Eliminate Duplicate Faults	Enable Fix Notification	Enable Assignments
Customer	Report Failures	+				++			
	Track Fixes			++				++	
Sponsor	Raise support productivity	++	+	+	+	++	+		
	Raise maintenance productivity		++	-	+	-	++		
Development Manager	Track failures	++			+	+			
	Track faults		++		+	+	++		
	Track fixes			++	+		+	+	
	Prioritize faults		+			+	++	++	
	Prioritize fixes			+		+		++	
	Assign failures	+							++
Developer	Track assignments	++	++						++
	Update fix information			++		-			

project sponsor wants to raise the productivity of the support and maintenance organizations. The managers need to track failures, faults, and fixes. They need to prioritize faults and fixes and to assign failures for investigation. The developers need to track assignments and update fix information. Figure 17-1 lists these expectations going down the left side of the matrix.

Next, you must identify the system deliverables. This is one of the first tasks that development architects must undertake in the project. Without knowing the deliverables, it is difficult to develop an effective WBS. It is also difficult to prioritize the stakeholder expectations. This top-level architecture is in many ways a simple feasibility analysis for the project. If you can't figure out the basic deliverable structure that will satisfy an expectation, you should remove the expectation from the project.

Under each deliverable (or cluster, if it is useful to go a level or two further down), you list the operational objectives of the system. For example, Figure 17-1 identifies the PROBLEM.DLL and PERSON.DLL deliverables. One objective is to enable tracking of problems (faults and failures) and the links between them. Another objective is to improve the impact of this tracking by separating faults from failures. This approach lets you prioritize faults based on failure rate rather than on a simple priority scheme. A third objective is to raise maintenance productivity by eliminating duplicate faults through the separation of failures from faults. A product can fail many times based on a single fault. And so on through the rest of the deliverables.

Now, you have a matrix. In the cells of the matrix, place symbols that show how the objective satisfies a stakeholder expectation. The legend in Figure 17-1 shows one possible set of symbols on a five-point ordinal scale from "strongly positive" to "strongly negative." Leaving a cell blank means no impact. For example, enabling fix tracking has no impact on customer reporting of failures, a strongly positive impact on customer fix tracking, and so on. As an example of a negative impact, enabling fix notification means adding complexity to the work done by maintenance developers, who must now link fixes to failures when they fix a fault. This objective thus has a negative, but not strongly negative, impact on raising developer productivity, so the project sponsor may have a problem with this objective.

■ *Note:* The manufacturing systems for which the total quality toolsmiths developed QFD tend to have many trade-offs, unlike a software system. The most common are things that impact performance, where high performance is a stakeholder expectation. The abstract nature of software tends to make it easier to meet expectations than in harder industries.

Besides showing you how objectives relate to expectations, the full House of Quality (Figure 17-2) tells you several things:

- How to measure objectives (referring to system metrics in the statement of work)
- How you and your competitors compare on these metrics
- How stakeholders perceive you and your competitors' ability to satisfy their expectations with your current product
- How deliverables relate to one another
- How to prioritize the deliverables taking expectations, technical difficulty, costs, competitive pressures, and other factors into account
- Targets for objectives

The perception ranking to the right of the matrix shows how each of several competitors ranks on the expectation. The measures section shows the metrics and how you and your competitors currently rate. The summaries below this section show the different factors for each objective and the targets for the metrics to which these factors lead you.

The Requirements Document

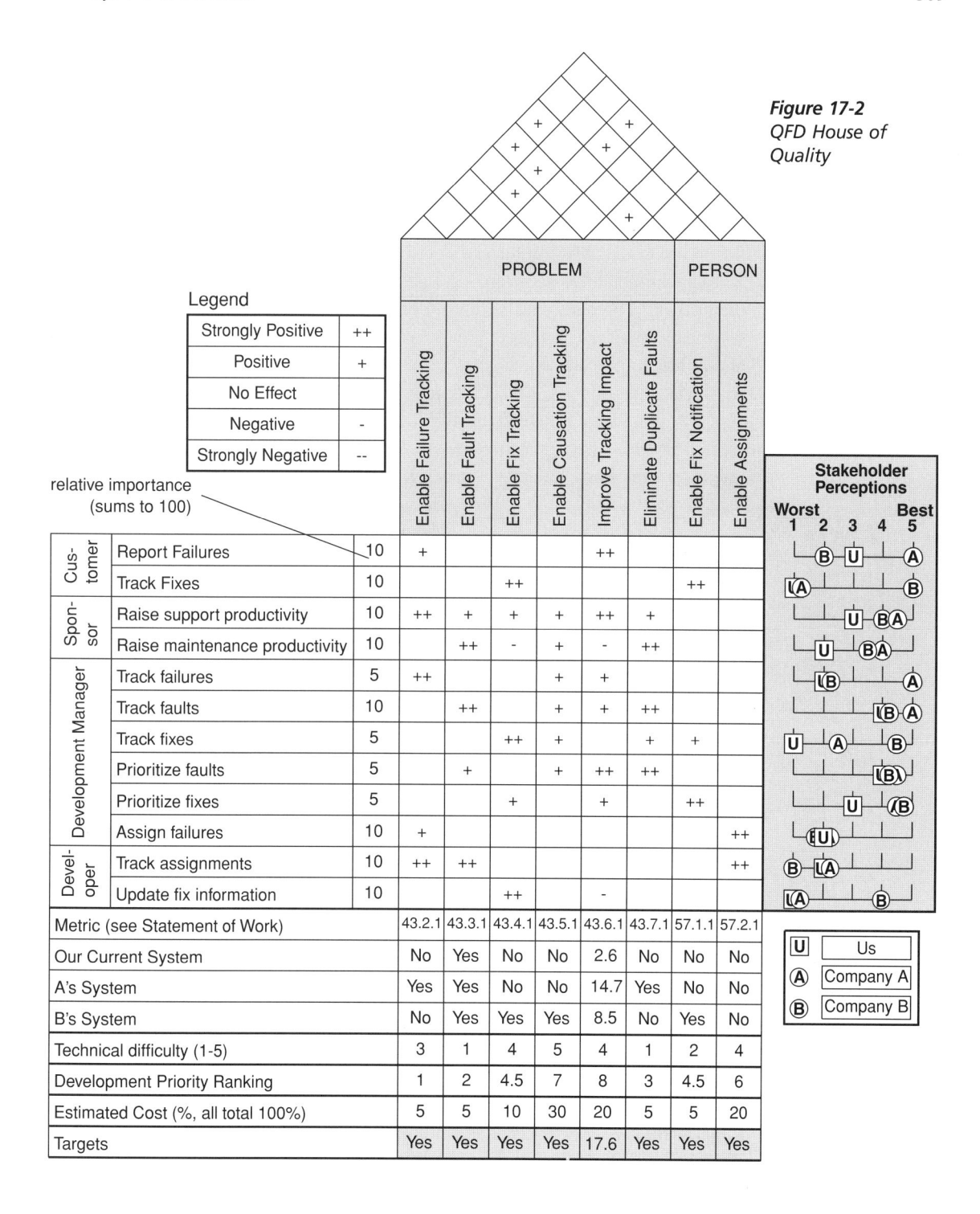

Figure 17-2
QFD House of Quality

Legend	
Strongly Positive	++
Positive	+
No Effect	
Negative	-
Strongly Negative	--

relative importance (sums to 100)

		Rel. Imp.	Enable Failure Tracking	Enable Fault Tracking	Enable Fix Tracking	Enable Causation Tracking	Improve Tracking Impact	Eliminate Duplicate Faults	Enable Fix Notification	Enable Assignments
Customer	Report Failures	10	+				++			
	Track Fixes	10			++				++	
Sponsor	Raise support productivity	10	++	+	+	+	++	+		
	Raise maintenance productivity	10		++	-	+	-	++		
Development Manager	Track failures	5	++			+	+			
	Track faults	10		++		+	+	++		
	Track fixes	5			++	+		+	+	
	Prioritize faults	5		+		+	++	++		
	Prioritize fixes	5			+		+		++	
	Assign failures	10	+							++
Developer	Track assignments	10	++	++						++
	Update fix information	10			++		-			
Metric (see Statement of Work)			43.2.1	43.3.1	43.4.1	43.5.1	43.6.1	43.7.1	57.1.1	57.2.1
Our Current System			No	Yes	No	No	2.6	No	No	No
A's System			Yes	Yes	No	No	14.7	Yes	No	No
B's System			No	Yes	Yes	Yes	8.5	No	Yes	No
Technical difficulty (1-5)			3	1	4	5	4	1	2	4
Development Priority Ranking			1	2	4.5	7	8	3	4.5	6
Estimated Cost (%, all total 100%)			5	5	10	30	20	5	5	20
Targets			Yes	Yes	Yes	Yes	17.6	Yes	Yes	Yes

Stakeholder Perceptions

Worst 1 2 3 4 5 Best

U	Us
A	Company A
B	Company B

The roof of the house relates the deliverables to one another. Certain deliverables may share clusters, for example, leading to a positive relationship. An example is the code that enables fault tracking and the code that enables causation (fault causes failure) tracking. Other deliverables could negatively affect each other, but this is rare. Conflicting architectures might lead to a negative relationship between objectives.

Having the QFD diagram in your document and statement of work gives you the ability to make well-informed decisions about what to include in your project. You can immediately see from the matrix which objectives are more important than others. The rating at the bottom of the matrix gives you some quantification of your priorities. The targets you set carry through to all the development tasks and guide developers to a successful result. The relationships let you identify the technical trade-offs you need to make. The competitive information jumps out at you, clarifying what you're doing right and what your competitors are doing right.

The QFD analysis also shows traceability of architectural design to requirements. It thus both validates the design and sets the stage for further validation tests down the road, such as the system validation test.

Finally, the objectives and their targets become the basis for further system development in the WBS and development plans. They can also help with identification of technical risk and risk management planning by clarifying risk tolerance and the impact of specific risk management methods.

■ *Note:* This all-too-brief introduction to the House of Quality may seem overwhelming. I urge interested readers to go to sources with more detail [Arthur, pp. 32–36; Bossert; Haag; Hauser]. Understanding the tool will pay great dividends in helping you to decide what your real objectives should be in an OO project.

The Functional Specification

The *functional specification* documents the results of the analysis process. It represents your best attempt to meet the expectations of the stakeholders as expressed in the requirements document. Requirements analysis takes the requirements document, analyzes it, and specifies the system and cluster requirements [ISO 1995].

Vision: Clearly defined requirements for building a software system

Mission: To define clearly and consistently the requirements for building a software system

---

Objective 17.7: To define software system requirements

The Functional Specification *311*

Approach 17.7: Use the analysis method of your choice to define a system that satisfies the expectations in the input requirements document. You should define the functions of the system as well as system requirements, database structure, and user interface. The document should support the list of deliverables in the requirements document. Review the document for feasibility of architectural design, testability of the specification, internal consistency, external consistency with requirements, and traceability to the requirements.

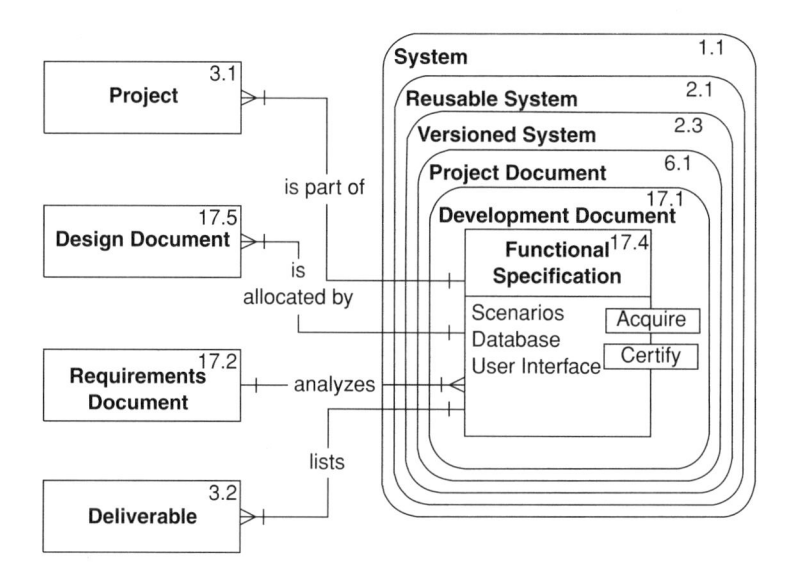

Not all the expectations that the requirements document expresses relate directly to the software. The functional specification isolates those that do. It formalizes them using some kind of functional representation. An emerging standard in OO software is the *use case* or *scenario* that specifies a sequence of actor-driven transactions through the software system. This works with class diagrams and interaction diagrams to show how objects interact in scenarios [Jacobson]. This approach better suits OO development than the process- or data-related styles of functional specification.

There are many different ways of thinking about analysis. One school believes analysis addresses the problem space while design addresses the solution space. Another school, prevalent in OO methods, says that design is extended analysis, more a matter of level of detail than of conceptual difference [Booch 1994; Jacobson; Rumbaugh]. Several OO methodologists claim this as a benefit of OO analysis and design—the lack of a transition barrier in moving from analysis to design. Protoyping moves the coding and testing process into this universe without boundaries as well.

In this book, I arbitrarily divide the two areas by the documents they produce. I don't take a strong position on the structure of the documents. The vision and mission of each document is clear: the functional specification defines software system requirements, while the design document defines the structure of the system and clusters. Many methods contradict each other in this respect, having different views of what constitutes analysis and what constitutes design. As long as you choose a method and stick with it, this should not be an issue. If it becomes an issue, use your operational objectives to resolve it.

It may be possible to start with multiple functional specifications, though in my experience this is very unusual. Project sponsors and other stakeholders like to see the system in one place.

In analyzing the requirements, you need to specify all the elements in Table 17-1.

In OO systems, you specify the functions of the system through class definitions, scenarios, and interaction diagrams. Class definitions provide the structure for the objects that scenarios use. Scenarios, or use cases, specify transactions that system agents initiate and interact with through the user interface. Interaction diagrams link class diagrams and scenarios, showing how the scenario uses objects [Jacobson].

In most client/server OO systems, you need to define the database early in the process. The functional specification is a good place to do that. The database definition often takes the form of class diagrams that bear a strong relationship to the ER diagrams of standard client/server design. Many client/server methods distinguish

Table 17-1 Kinds of System Requirements in the Functional Specification

Requirement	Description
Functions	The set of user and system functions that the system must perform
Database	The set of persistent data structures available to the program
User Interface	The structure and appearance of the user interface of the system
Ergonomics	The usability requirements for the system
Security	The requirements for limiting access to functions and the database
Safety	The requirements for safe operation and maintenance
User Documentation	The requirements for user documentation (user's guide, reference, online help, online documentation, tutorials, and so on)
Maintenance	The requirements for fixing problems with the system
Installation	The requirements for installing the system at user sites
Acceptance	The requirements for the user's accepting the system

between the logical design and the physical design. The former are class or ER diagrams and the latter are relational database (RDBMS) tables and constraints. I've used both as part of the functional specification. When the user can extend the database schema or access it with other tools, you must define the database structure as a system requirement. If you are using the database internally without direct user access, then you need not put the database design into the functional specification.

Since the requirements document has already listed the deliverables, you can start with that list and expand it as your requirements grow. The list of deliverables serves as the basis for your analysis of the user interface. In this part of the functional specification, you need to specify the grammar or appearance of the interface through which agents interact with the system. For example, most functional specifications contain prototype bitmaps that show field arrangements, controls, menus, and other graphical user interface elements. These graphics, or text descriptions of them for the technologically impaired, serve as part of the basis for function point counts along with the database structure.

The actual format of the functional specification varies with your method. It is usually a mixture of graphics and text. The sections represent the different kinds of requirements and the objects within those sections. A common alternative format is to write a prototype of the user documentation for the system, such as a reference manual and/or user's guide. While this has the benefit of conveying to the user the true nature of the system, it does not have the level of technical detail you need. On the other hand, combining this kind of preliminary user's documentation with additional specification documents has several benefits. As well as helping to specify the system, it provides a starting point for the user documentation process and a working manual for system testers.

Product Documentation (15.8)

When you review the functional specification, you need to establish values for the four measures of document success: feasibility, consistency, traceability, and testability. If the functional specification is feasible, you should be able to design and build each requirement in it with the methods, tools, and resources available to the project. If it is consistent, it is complete, correct, unambiguous, and at the right level of detail. If it is traceable, you should be able to trace each requirement to some expectation in the requirements document. If it is testable, you should be able to state criteria for a system test to validate a requirement (test whether the delivered system meets the requirement). You should evaluate the functional specification for risk of change and identify any risk management methods you can use to reduce the risk of failure due to changing requirements. This is always a problem in OO systems, with their emphasis on incremental and iterative development.

When you complete your review of the document and revise it to acceptability, you create a baseline that establishes the content of the system. This baseline is the first point at which you can define earned value, because it is the first point at which you have formal metrics for size, such as function points. It provides a baseline for the verification of the design. It also provides the set of system requirements against which you validate the system when you deliver it.

Reviewing the document should establish its certification as a reusable document. That means that it must clearly identify those elements that detract from its reuse potential. Inherent reuse potential in the functional specification usually has to do with the consistency issues. Domain reuse relates both to traceability and to the level of domain specificity in the document. If the requirements apply only to a very limited domain, the document is much less reusable. Finally, reuse depends on the capabilities of the organization for storing the document, retrieving it on demand, reuse policies, and the management culture.

I was appointed project manager of a commercial OO system with several prior versions going back ten years. Every project manager before me had left the company, either in anger or disgrace. The corporate culture was, to put it mildly, Variable. We had a bright, shiny new development process model and a forward-looking commitment to quality from upper management. My point in this encomium is the functional specification: this was an ongoing product with virtually nothing changing from release to release and a stable process model. And yet every project manager developed a completely new specification in a completely new way.

The project manager before me, for example, developed a multimedia database that made the functional specification available as a series of topics. By the middle of that project, these topics had become irrelevant because they did not represent what the developers were doing. It crashed all the time, too. I decided to abandon this approach because of its technical problems, instead developing a pseudo-user's manual with a high level of detail. I was not able to reuse any material from the previous specification, as none of it had been certified (or reviewed) and most of it was inaccurate or could not be moved into my publishing system. As it turned out, the exercise would have been irrelevant. The Variable culture was not capable of following the functional specification in any case, which is why project managers in this company had a half-life of months. The point: documentation such as a functional specification works only if those it is intended to serve use it. Documents depend on legitimacy and consensus for their success in most software companies and IS shops.

The Design Document

The *design document* documents a design process. It applies to either the system (*high-level* or *architectural design*) or to an individual cluster (*low-level* or *detailed design*). Design starts with the functional specification. It then proceeds iteratively using design tools from the development environment. The design uses any technical standards that apply to the process.

Vision: Clearly defined structures for building a software system

Mission: To define clearly and consistently the requirements for building a software system

The Design Document

Objective 17.8: To define software system architecture

Approach 17.8: Use the design method of your choice to define a system that satisfies the expectations in the input functional specification. Review the document for feasibility of implementation, testability of the design, internal consistency, external consistency with, and traceability to the functional specification.

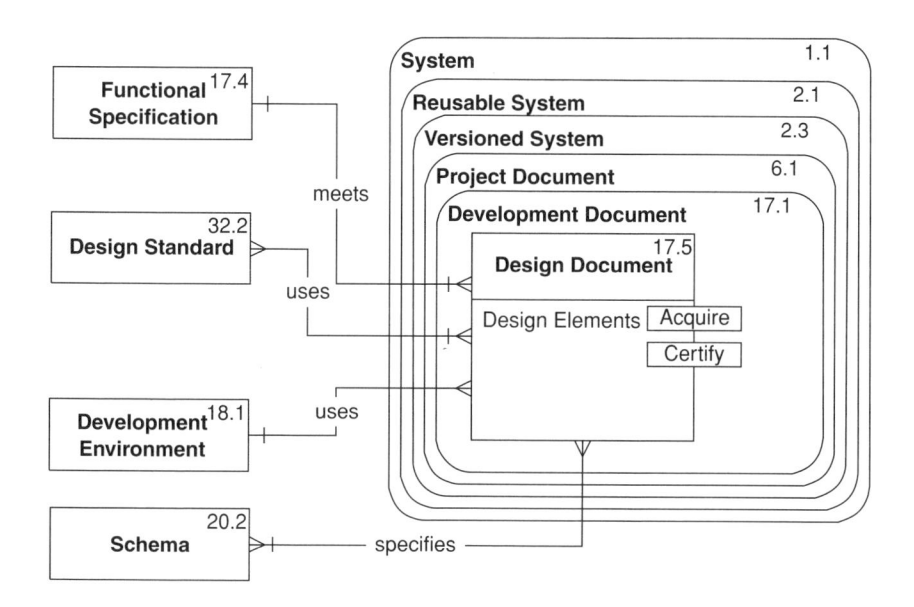

Architectural design identifies the top-level clusters of the system. This includes identifying components, allocating requirements, specifying system and major cluster interfaces, and designing database schemas. Detailed design for each cluster specifies it to a level that permits coding and testing of the cluster. This design includes class and cluster design, allocating requirements to classes and clusters, and specifying low-level cluster interfaces.

Design is inherently different for OO software development. The typical design has an object or class model and a basic object architecture showing system interaction through messaging. Class and cluster design uses detailed OO design techniques that fully specify the structure and behavior of the cluster. These use models ranging from state-transition models to class and object structure models. Whether you proceed top down, bottom up, or inside out, the design process is always incremental and iterative. As you learn more about the universe you're trying to model, you expand and extend clusters, move functions around to different classes, and add classes and clusters to add to your initial understanding.

Table 17-2 Kinds of Design Elements

Requirement	Description
Functions	Design elements that satisfy functional requirements from the functional specification; these are the meat of the design and include everything from classes to operations to clusters
Interfaces	Design elements, usually classes, that provide a programming interface to a cluster or system
Database	The full specification for the schema for the database, usually either in standard SQL or in the target database definition language, such as C++ or Smalltalk for OODBMSs
Test Models	System models that represent each system or cluster in terms of test-oriented structures
User Documentation	A preliminary cut at reference manuals, online help, user's guides, and other user documentation that assists users in learning how to use the software system deliverable; this is usually a part of architectural design, as the external elements are part of the architecture, not part of the low-level components of the system

You will often find multiple design documents for a project's functional specification, with each document relating to a specific software system deliverable or cluster. It is possible to have only one design document, but it is unusual.

In designing a system or cluster, you need to specify all the elements in Table 17-2.

A system design is complete when you can trace all requirements in the functional specification to design objects. An individual design document for a cluster or system contributes to the system design being complete but is complete itself when you have specified all the elements in Table 17-2.

One advantage of the OO approach to analysis and design is the relative ease with which you can allocate requirements to design objects. Most OO analysis methods specify a class hierarchy and relationships between these classes. You move this into design by extending the classes, adding new ones, and clustering the classes. Your design process can move down from the system level or up from the class level, or both. In any case, the transition from analysis to design is straightforward.

There is much confusion in the OO software community about when to do various elements such as database schema design, test models, the user interface, and user documentation. The answer is that you do them when you need them. You need a logical schema design as part of the functional specification, for example, if it is going to be a feature of the deliverable system. Similarly, you need a complete UI specification as part of the functional specification for two reasons: to enable function point counting and to specify the external interface on which design depends for guidance. Leaving UI design to the low-level design process, or worse, to the coding process, is not a good idea. Remember, however, that all of this is iterative and incremental. The point is not so much *when* to do it as *where* to do it. You do it at the logical time in the project when the information you need becomes available, whenever that might be. But the UI belongs in the functional specification, not in a design document.

The same logic applies to test models and user documentation. You should develop system test models and user documentation when you have a functional specification of the system, and you should iterate those models with the iterations of that specification.

- *Note:* There is a curious reluctance by both developers and technical writers to develop documentation early in the project. This is a fundamental mistake from the perspective of project management. I've worked on several projects as both a technical writer and a documentation manager. Most of these projects could have had complete documentation available for alpha release, but writers seemed reluctant to put what they knew down on paper because it might change. Of course it changes! That's why we use desktop publishing systems instead of quill pens. For example, writers are reluctant to take screen shots for fear of having to redo them. It takes me about four hours to supply the screen shots for a 200-page manual. This is not a large risk factor in delivering the document. The same logic applies to documentation and testing as to development: iterate and increment; don't expect everything to get done all at once at the end of the project. Learn to embrace change instead of resisting it.

When you review a design document, you need to review it to establish values for the four measures of document success: feasibility, consistency, traceability, and testability [Freedman]. If the design is feasible, you should be able to code and test each class and cluster in it with the development tools and resources available to the project. If the document is consistent, it is complete and correct with respect to functions, interfaces, and schemas. If the document is traceable, you should be able to trace each design element to some requirement in the functional specification. If the document is testable, you should be able to develop a test model for each design element. As well, you should evaluate the design for risk of change and identify any risk management methods you can use to reduce the risk of failure due to iterative changes.

The technical review certifies the design document for a reusable system. Most reusable systems and clusters require a design document as part of their certification, as reuse generally requires the communication of design elements such as interfaces and database schemas. The design document can be a reusable system in its own right irrespective of its implementation if it has strong internal cohesion, a reasonably broad domain reuse potential, and a strong probability of reuse within the organization. OO technical design metrics [Champeaux; Goldberg; Henderson-Sellers 1996], such as class or cluster complexity and cohesion, provide a good basis for evaluating inherent reuse potential.

OO database managers provide a unique opportunity for reusable design. Because the schema for the database component becomes part of the object model, it is difficult *not* to reuse it in later projects. An OO database schema thus becomes a key part of your reuse repository with very little effort on your part. I developed an OO schema for a CASE tool to support OO development methods. The schema became the fundamental architectural basis for the product, even when the underlying DBMS technology was replaced. This enabled later work to expand the original concept through expanding the original schema in a classic, inheritance-based reuse process.

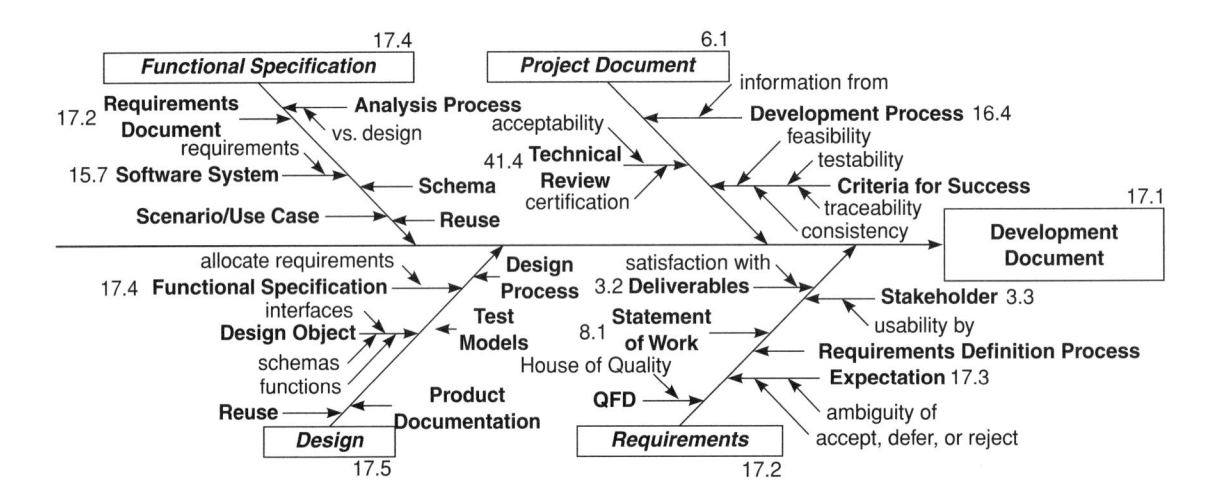

Readings

- *Note:* There are dozens of books on OO analysis and design. Any technical bookstore can provide you with more books than you can read in a lifetime. I have listed some of the books I've found useful in defining my own approach to analysis and design, but I make no claim that these are the best. One stops reading and starts analyzing and designing at some point in one's career unless one becomes a methodologist, which I'm not.

[Booch 1994]   Grady Booch. *Object-Oriented Analysis and Design with Applications, Second Edition.* Redwood City, CA: Benjamin/Cummings, 1994.

[Booch 1996]   Grady Booch. *Object Solutions: Managing the Object-Oriented Project.* Reading, MA: Addison-Wesley, 1996.

These two books provide an excellent introduction to architectural and low-level OO design. While I'm not a fan of the notation, it has become a standard in the OO software industry, and is part of the basis for the new UML design notation being proposed as a standard through the Object Management Group, along with Rumbaugh's and Jacobson's notations. The design method and explanation are clear and cogent.

Readings

[Bossert]   James L. Bossert. *Quality Function Deployment: A Practitioner's Approach*. ASQC Quality Press (Marcel Dekker, Inc., 270 Madison Ave., New York, NY 10016), 1991.

This book is an excellent, if elementary, introduction to the tools and methods of quality function deployment. While not as well done as the Hauser article [Hauser], it has a lot more detail on the various quality tools you will find useful in QFD.

[Champeaux] Dennis de Champeaux. *Object-Oriented Development Processes and Metrics*. Englewood Cliffs, NJ: Prentice Hall, 1997 (published in 1996).

This book focuses on the process and measurement of design but includes a full-scale design example based on the home-heating system that Booch uses in his books as well. The detail of the example is both an advantage and a disadvantage. While it detracts from the process and metrics, it provides those interested in learning about OO design with an excellent tutorial example.

[Freedman]   Daniel P. Freedman and Gerald M. Weinberg. *Handbook of Walkthroughs, Inspections, and Technical Reviews: Evaluating Programs, Projects, and Products, Third Edition*. New York: Dorset House, 1990.

This is the classic book on technical reviews. It also happens to be the best description of technical documentation that I've found. Freedman and Weinberg describe the evaluation criteria for most kinds of documents in great detail, which is of as much use to those creating them as to those reviewing them. For example, they reproduce several checklists for functional specifications and design documents from companies with which they've worked.

[Gause]   Donald C. Gause and Gerald M. Weinberg. *Exploring Requirements: Quality Before Design*. New York: Dorset House, 1989.

This is one of the best books on requirements gathering I've seen. While it does not explicitly address OO requirements analysis, it does provide a practical introduction to the techniques you need to reduce ambiguity in stakeholder expectations. The sections on brainstorming and mind mapping alone are worth the price of the book, as is the part on clarifying expectations.

[Haag]   Stephen Haag, M. K. Raja, and L. L. Schkade. Quality function deployment usage in software development. *Communications of the ACM* 39:1 (January 1996): 41–49.

This survey article describes the application of QFD to software and also surveys the state of adoption of QFD among major software manufacturers. Read in conjunction with [Hauser], you will get the idea behind QFD applied to software.

[Hauser]   John R. Hauser and Don Clausing. The house of quality. *Harvard Business Review* 66:3 (May-June 1988): 63–73.

This article clearly describes and illustrates the "House of Quality" method for developing requirements. Anyone interested in pursuing this approach should read this well-written article.

[Jacobson]   Ivar Jacobson, Magnus Christerson, Patrik Jonsson, and Gunnar Overgaard. *Object-Oriented Software Engineering: A Use Case Driven Approach.* Reading, MA: Addison-Wesley, 1992.

This is an essential book for those interested in analysis and design. The book suffers from a certain lack of detail, but its approach is practical enough to be of great importance in understanding the issues of analysis and design. In particular, this book introduces the "use case" or scenario and the interaction diagram, which are rapidly becoming fundamental parts of OO analysis. There are relatively few other places that explain use cases in this detail, in fact. Jacobson is a member of the triumvirate that has proposed the new UML design notation.

[Rumbaugh]   James Rumbaugh, Michael Blaha, William Premerlani, Frederick Eddy, and William Lorensen. *Object-Oriented Modeling and Design.* Englewood Cliffs, NJ: Prentice Hall, 1991.

This is another essential book. The major contributions of this one are its notation, which is better than Booch's or Jacobson's, and its chapter on state-transition diagramming for OO analysis. I use this book all the time. It is flawed; Champeaux, for example, critiques certain aspects of the approach to architectural design for multiprocessing systems. Rumbaugh has also written several articles expanding the approach, most in the *Journal of Object-Oriented Programming* over a period of years since he published this book. He is part of the triumvirate pressing for adoption of the new UML design notation.

[Wirfs-Brock] Rebecca Wirfs-Brock, Brian Wilkerson, and Lauren Wiener. *Designing Object-Oriented Software.* Englewood Cliffs, NJ: Prentice Hall, 1990.

This book is an excellent introduction to OO design. While the approach is somewhat informal, it is also very practical, and many of the techniques proposed by the book have become standards in the design community. The use of a contract model, the description of classes and subsystems through short descriptions (CRC cards), and the subsystem as a major architectural feature are all elements proposed by this book.

Questions to Think About

1. Which is more important about a development document, communication or content? That is, should you design the document primarily for communicating its information or containing every bit of information in a process?

2. Should there be one document per process? How would you decide this?

3. Why is traceability an important criterion for all development documents? (Hint: Reread the section "The Project Deliverables and System Earned Value" in Chapter 3.)

4. How do you see the difference between analysis and design? Is there a real need for two separate documents? What about requirements versus analysis?

5. If ambiguity is the central problem in requirements gathering, what is the central problem in functional specification and in design? Do the documents in this chapter address this problem?

6. Many CASE tools provide automatic documentation tools. How effective do you think these tools can be at producing the documents described in this chapter? What benefits do these tools provide in terms of risk management?

CHAPTER

18 *Development Environment*

The Development Environment

The *development environment* is a reusable system that provides the context for development processes. The environment contains the reuse and product repositories that store software products. It also contains the set of tools that developers use to develop software. The development environment links the quality environment and the organizational environment with development tools to provide the infrastructure for an OO software project.

Vision: *A supportive bed of reusable tools that enables the organization to develop valuable software with optimal productivity*

Mission: *To provide an integrated system of tools, repositories, and other infrastructure that enables the productive execution of the primary and supporting development processes*

Objective 18.1: To provide an integrated system of reusable tools, repositories, and infrastructure

---

Approach 18.1: Use procurement processes to acquire the tools you need to develop OO software, such as compilers, CASE tools, testing tools, software frameworks, database management tools, change management tools, and hardware. Build a reusable product repository, or set up the one you've already got to store the software deliverables. Link to the reuse, quality, and organizational repositories to access reusable systems, quality-related systems, and policies and other organizational systems. Certify, share, and maintain the tools and repositories.

The Development Environment

Metric 18.1: Environment Faults: the number of faults in project software deliverables with a cause relating to inadequacies of the development environment, such as compiler bugs, lack of test tools, ineffectual CASE tools, and so on

Target 18.1: A value within control limits of a p control chart of faults for this and similar development environments in your organization and industry

---

Objective 18.2: To enable productive execution of primary and supporting development processes

---

Approach 18.2: Evaluate tools with a focus on productivity. Use improvement plans to continuously improve productivity in your use of the development environment. Procure additional tools based on a return-on-investment analysis that emphasizes productivity and return to stakeholders. Extend these activities to the full range of primary and supporting development processes to ensure that all processes are as productive as they can be given their infrastructure.

Metric 18.2: Project productivity: effort-hours per unit of project-earned value

Target 18.2: An increasing value within control limits on an x-R control chart of project productivity for projects using this development environment; a value greater than a benchmark of the productivity of similar projects in your industry

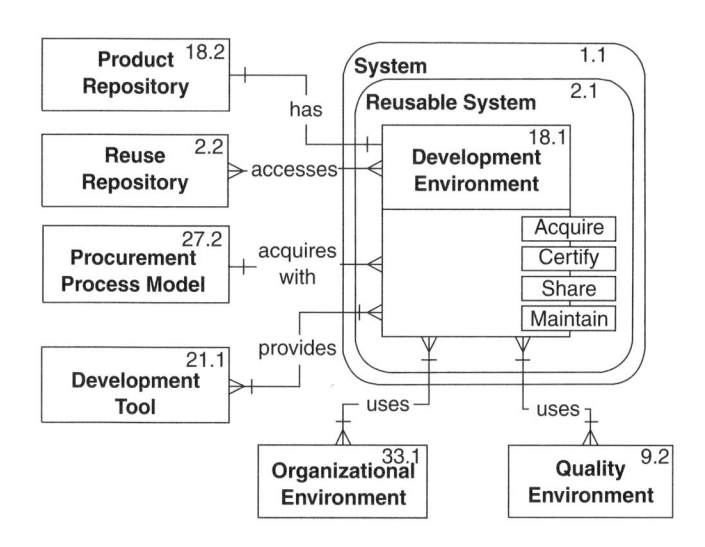

Infrastructure is the system of objects that lets you deliver value. A large part of the infrastructure is the development environment. Acquiring and using an effective set of tools is critical to OO development.

Risk (12.1)

Procurement Process Model (27.2)

OO projects have several risks associated with tools and repositories. You are at risk with OO tools because OO technology is new and the tools are newer. Until recently there were few effective compilers for OO languages. That's changed dramatically in the last couple of years. In the news as I write (April 1997) is the war between Microsoft and Sun on Java tools, right next to the war between Microsoft and everybody else on CORBA versus ActiveX and DCOM. A major complaint from OO developers using Java is the performance of the system on different operating systems. There are also incompatibilities of the various virtual machine implementations, particularly Microsoft's [Gaudin; Hayes]. Things change very quickly in this environment.

Acquiring your development environment is one of the primary tasks for functional and team managers. If you can, you should have a staff member in charge of the development environment. The acquisition process should be a standard procurement process.

Sharing the development environment requires both communication and training. You should set up a Web page or similar online system that keeps developers up-to-date on acquisitions and changes in the development environment. This is also a good way to link to other environments, such as the organizational environment for access to up-to-date policies or the quality environment for test tools and scripts. Taking your environment online helps to integrate it, providing a synergy between the different parts. Tool training courses may or may not be necessary, depending on the sophistication of your developers, but it's always a good idea to consider it as part of the cost of tool acquisition.

In particular, you need to make sure everyone understands the configuration management tools. These tools often provide the major way developers work together—they are a primitive form of groupware.

I worked in an OO development organization that used C++ with a state-of-the-art configuration management system. The organization had a policy of integrating the system every night after the developers went home (yeah, right—home, what's that?). Every other morning saw the gathering of the developers at the espresso machine while those at fault tried to figure out why integrating their small change to a class header had broken the system and crashed everyone in the shop. Part of the rite of passage in this organization was the ritual flaming of new developers silly enough to check something in without "testing" it. This was, of course, almost impossible for a newbie to do, since you had to know the rather complex ropes involved in making sure your system was completely up-to-date with respect to the version control database. Also, since there were no regression test scripts available, you had to engineer your own, which everyone did after the first couple of flaming sessions. It didn't help that virtually every class in the system included a single header file that defined all the constants in the system. When you added a new constant using the bit-flag scheme developed in the mists of history, all the code required recompilation, and it was very easy to break something. My conclusion from this project was that the development environment and its interaction with the development processes is critical to productivity. It's also a key archeological dig site for understanding the organizational culture of the development team.

Maintaining the development environment as a reusable system is a critical activity in your projects. When a tool breaks, work stops. When work stops, projects fail. That said, there are times when you don't want to maintain your environment. The most common reason not to keep your environment up-to-date is to prevent forward compatibility problems. Particularly with OO software tools, the next release always has more features but is likely to break something you've already done. Part of your maintenance process model should be the acceptance testing and phase-in of tools in the development environment. Instead of just installing and bringing the new tool version online, you should test it using a system test bed of some kind, and then cut over.

Some shops have unfortunate limitations on maintenance. I worked at a major software vendor that developed OO tools as well as the system I was developing. There was a corporate policy to use company products rather than competitors' products, on the theory that if we used our own products we'd make them insanely great. This didn't take into account that different divisions of the company still saw themselves as completely different companies. Even getting support on the OO compiler we had to use was difficult, because the separate support organization would only interact with us through email. When we ran into a major floating-point bug, we got the same answer as any other customer: upgrade to the next release. As with any other customer, that release had introduced incompatibilities with our current system that would bring our project to a halt for days, if not weeks. We eliminated a feature from our product and moved on.

- *Note:* Certain OO development tool vendors are notorious for both bug-ridden software and release incompatibilities. Your acquisition process should probe in this area quite deeply so that you understand the risks you are incurring by acquiring a particular tool. If you can, talk to reference sites that have upgraded their tool a couple of times at least.

Configuration Management System (25.3)

The Product Repository

The *product repository* is a reuse repository that stores the project deliverables and the intermediate deliverables you reuse to produce the project deliverables. The product repository contains all the deliverables (classes, objects, clusters, files, databases, software systems, and product documentation). It links to the quality repository for objects such as test plans, test data, test scripts, and test results. Finally, it contains supporting deliverables such as development documentation and anything else useful for constructing the product or delivering it to the stakeholders. Anything you distribute to stakeholders belongs in the product repository. The change management system and in particular its configuration management tools manage the product repository.

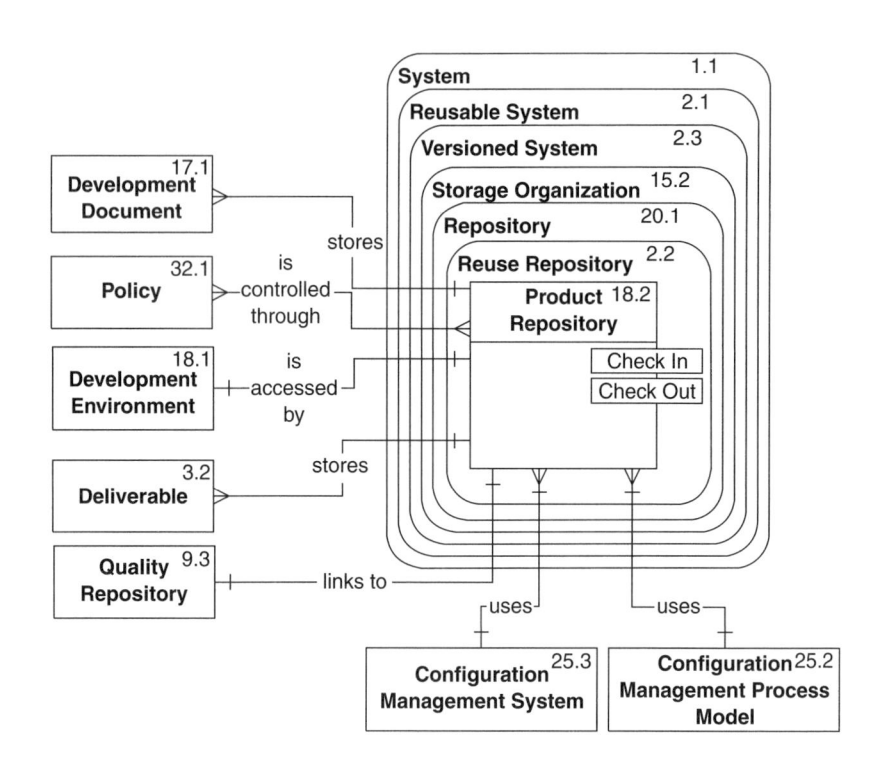

Vision: A set of well-ordered, reusable software systems and product documentation that is well protected from inadvertent harm

Mission: To enable the use of and to protect reusable software systems and product documentation

---

Objective 18.3: To enable the storage of reusable software systems and documentation

---

Approach 18.3: Store the reusable systems in an appropriate storage organization that makes the systems available on demand in an appropriate format. Put the systems under configuration management control.

Metric 18.3: Reuse Faults: the number of problems that require maintenance of the repository

Target 18.3: Values within control limits of a pn control chart of problems with this and similar repositories

---

Objective 18.4: To organize the reusable systems for easy searching and browsing

Approach 18.4: Use standard search and browse tools to make the software and documentation available to those who need it. Use the configuration management system to establish both read-only copies of systems and checked-out versions for modification. Use development tools to manipulate and browse the systems as required. If you use a file hierarchy as the product repository, set up a directory hierarchy that makes sense given your project organization.

Metric 18.4.1: The fraction of searches that are successful at finding a reusable system that partially or fully meets the needs of the reuser

Target 18.4.1: A value within control limits of a p control chart of searches of this repository

---

Metric 18.4.2: The search time for reusable systems for searches that resulted in successful reuse of a system

Target 18.4.2: A value within control limits of an x-R control chart of searches of this repository

---

Objective 18.5: To protect deliverable versions of software systems and documentation

---

Approach 18.5: Implement a configuration management process model for the repository. Ensure, through enforced policies and quality assurance, that the systems in the repository meet the quality criteria for deliverable systems.

Metric 18.5: Reuse Faults: the number of problems that require maintenance of the configuration management aspects of the repository

Target 18.5: Values within control limits of a pn control chart of problems with this and similar repositories

---

Some organizations are careful to distinguish between two product repositories: internal and external ones. An internal repository is one that only developers and project resources can access. An external repository is one that contains software that you will give to stakeholders. By separating the two repositories, organizations attempt to control the risk of distributing software that fails. This strategy has its pluses and minuses. On the plus side, the quality organization can control the software and test it thoroughly without the risk of developers changing it. On the minus side, the code freeze that the separate repository mandates diminishes project flexibility greatly, particularly when there are strong policy constraints on the external repository.

I worked in a Variable culture that had this kind of arrangement. The version control tools were primitive, and only one or two team leaders understood how to use them effectively. Developers had gotten into the habit of moving code around without any change control or documentation. Inevitably, there were many problems with building the deliverable systems. This led to a fire wall approach. The team leaders would check in all the code, compile it, clean up any problems, and then declare a code freeze. They would then let the quality assurance team copy the files to a separate file server (in a different country). The quality group would then integrate and build the system, test it, log failures, and loop back to the developers if the system failed their test criteria. This approach had the desired effect, but it meant that managers had almost no flexibility once code freeze was declared. This is a variation on the waterfall model. Up to code delivery, the process was OO, iterative, and incremental. After delivery, it was the strictest waterfall you could imagine. I agreed with this, as the organizational structure did not permit any better solution to the problem then.

- *Note:* One moral of this story is that an OO project is a system. The company could not take full advantage of its OO development process without having the rest of the system in place, such as organizational culture, policies, change management, and the other aspects of a fully functional OO project environment.

Reuse happens in at least three ways. First, the product repository holds the clusters that you produce as part of the current project and reuse internally in that project. At some point during the project, you decide whether to certify the clusters for external reuse and move them to an external reuse repository. Second, the product repository acts as the repository for the versioning system for the project deliverables, giving you a storage and access mechanism for incremental reuse. Third, the product repository acts as the archive for previous versions of the deliverables. You use these as input into new projects, either to maintain the deliverables or to expand or transform them into new deliverables.

The inherent reuse potential of the product repository depends in large part on the reuse potential of the systems it stores. The more your project reuses internal clusters or prior deliverables, the greater the reuse potential of the product repository. Domain reusability is high by the nature of the repository, as all systems reflect the same domain, the domain of the project. Organizational reuse depends on policies and organizational factors, not the least of which is the actual storage technology you use. The better access you have, and the more control you have, the more likely you are to be able to reuse systems from the product repository. See the story above about the code freeze for an example of policy limits to organizational reuse for the product repository.

The physical structure of the product repository can be quite complex. I worked for an OODBMS vendor that had set up their product repository as a set of directories on a UNIX file server. The first thing you noticed was that each port of the system had its own hierarchy, and that each of these hierarchies mirrored each other in structure. The second thing you noticed was the complex system of UNIX scripts for generating make files and other elements required to use and structure the hierarchies. This was by far the most complicated system I'd used. It allowed the program librarian to type "compile" and have the whole repository compiled on appropriate machines, which generally took hours and brought the network to its knees. This worked well until the company decided to do a DOS/Windows port, and the system couldn't handle the integration of the very different file structure and network access required.

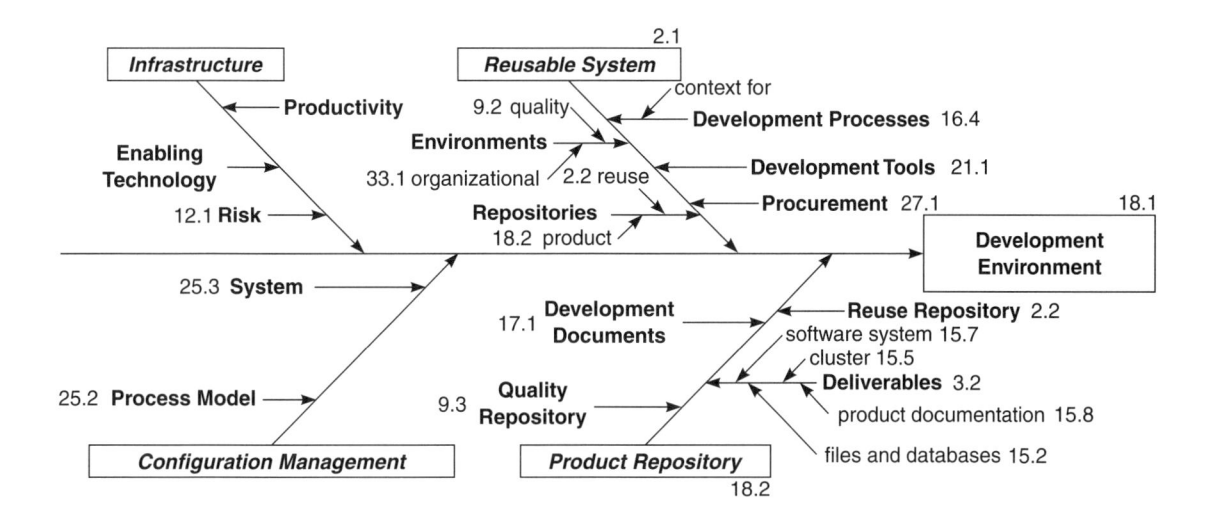

Questions to Think About

1. What risks besides tool-related risks can the development environment address?

2. Does your organization have a person whose job it is to run the development environment? How about the configuration management system? Why or why not?

3. List some systems other than those listed by the text that might appear in the product repository in your organization, such as make files.

4. How would you use a database storage organization as part of the product repository?

5. Is there a physical distinction between the quality repository and the product repository, or could you integrate them in the same storage structure? Explain the reasoning behind your answer.

PART SEVEN

Tools

> Give us the tools, and we will finish the job.
>
> Winston Churchill, February 9, 1941; to President Roosevelt

Configuration Management Tool (25.2)
Quality Tool (9.4)
Organizational Calendar (32.3)
Project Calendar (32.5)
Communication Tool (43.1)

Tools are essential in technological work. Tools are the infrastructure on which we build the technological feats that make our society what it is. This part of the book discusses various classes of tool, a versioned system, that the project system uses. The procurement process applies to tool acquisition as much as to component acquisition. The general tool class thus contains tasks to evaluate tools and to make a buy-build decision as part of the acquisition task.

■ *Note:* Some of the specific kinds of tools that you use in software projects appear in other parts of this book. This part focuses on project management and development tools.

Vision: People getting their jobs done

Mission: To provide leverage to effort in achieving project tasks

Objective P7.1: To add value to a task

Approach P7.1: Acquire the tool using an evaluative procurement process that estimates the value that the tool will add to your work. Train people to use the tool. Work the use of the tool into policies and plans. Improve the impact of the tool on value through improvement plans. Maintain the tool and dispose of it when it no longer can add value to your work.

Metric P7.1: Value Added: the amount of value you generate from tasks using the tool that you could not have generated without the tool

Target P7.1: A value within control limits on an x-R control chart of similar tools from your organization or industry; the value should reflect a positive internal rate of return on investment as well

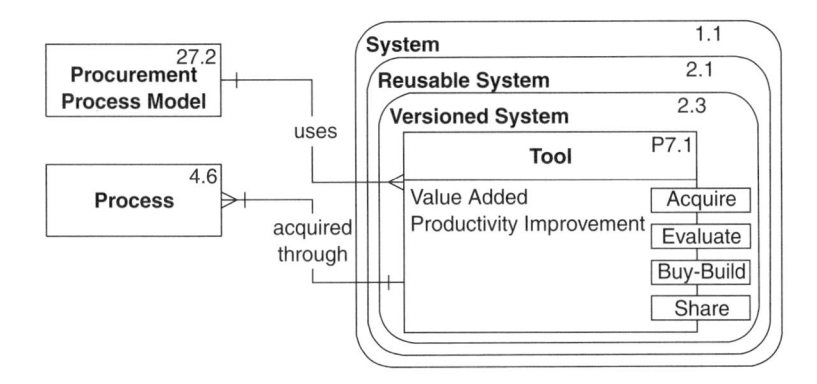

Objective P7.2: To improve productivity in achieving a task

Approach P7.2: Proceed as in Approach P7.1, except for focusing on productivity instead of value.

Metric P7.2: Productivity Improvement: the ratio of mean productivity (effort-hours per unit of value produced) while using the tool to productivity while not using the tool on similar tasks

Target P7.2: A value within control limits on a p control chart of similar tools from your organization or industry; the value should be materially greater than 1

Acquiring a tool means evaluating the needs, risks, and alternatives for the tool, and then making a buy-build decision about whether it is better to acquire the tool or develop it yourself. If you take the acquisition path, you use a procurement process model to structure the acquisition process.

As with any investment analysis, you must make the decision to acquire the tool based not just on the characteristics of the tool itself but also on the characteristics of alternatives to the tool. You may have a compiler, for example, that improves productivity by 10%. There may be another compiler that improves it by 100%, or there may be a different way to think about the problem that improves productivity by 1000%.

Sharing a tool means making it available through the appropriate environment (development, organizational, or quality). In its role as a reusable system, sharing the tool means communicating with others about tool use and availability, training, and policies about tool use. It also means using the tool as an input to a task in a project.

As with any system, a tool has an improvement plan. Evaluating and using the tool produces this plan, and you should work with your vendor or toolsmith to improve the tools you use over time. Part of your project process improvement plan should be to improve the tools available to the project.

There are broad classes of tools you will use as part of your general infrastructure:

- Writing and publishing tools
- Illustration, graphics, and drawing tools
- Online communication tools (browsers, email, and so on)
- Time management tools
- Financial analysis tools
- Presentation tools
- Operating systems
- Network operating systems
- Basic computer hardware in all its glorious variation

Work calendars and shifts are central to most project management tools. With these, you can easily describe the availability and cost of resources to projects. This improves your schedule and budget accuracy. Calendars and shifts depend on time interval systems to measure the passage of time.

Repositories and their schemas are everywhere. Other parts of the book develop specific kinds of repositories (quality, product, organizational, and reuse). This one develops the general class. It also introduces a system model, the schema, that models the intensional structure and content of the database.

Development tools are the focus of much of a manager's budget excepting resource expenses. Design and coding tools are the biggest part of the development environment. Design patterns let you design and reuse standard problem solutions.

Information systems are the backbone of your project. Without information, you have no feedback. These tools help you to manage information in your repositories. The project management system is the key software for project managers to use in managing their projects. The product information system is the critical connection between the project and the larger organization that markets and supports products.

Several system modeling tools are important to project management. Process modeling, planning, document templates, and schemas are all examples of system models that benefit from automated tools for modeling. Some project management systems are beginning to expand their modeling activities beyond planning to process modeling, raising the importance of good modeling tools.

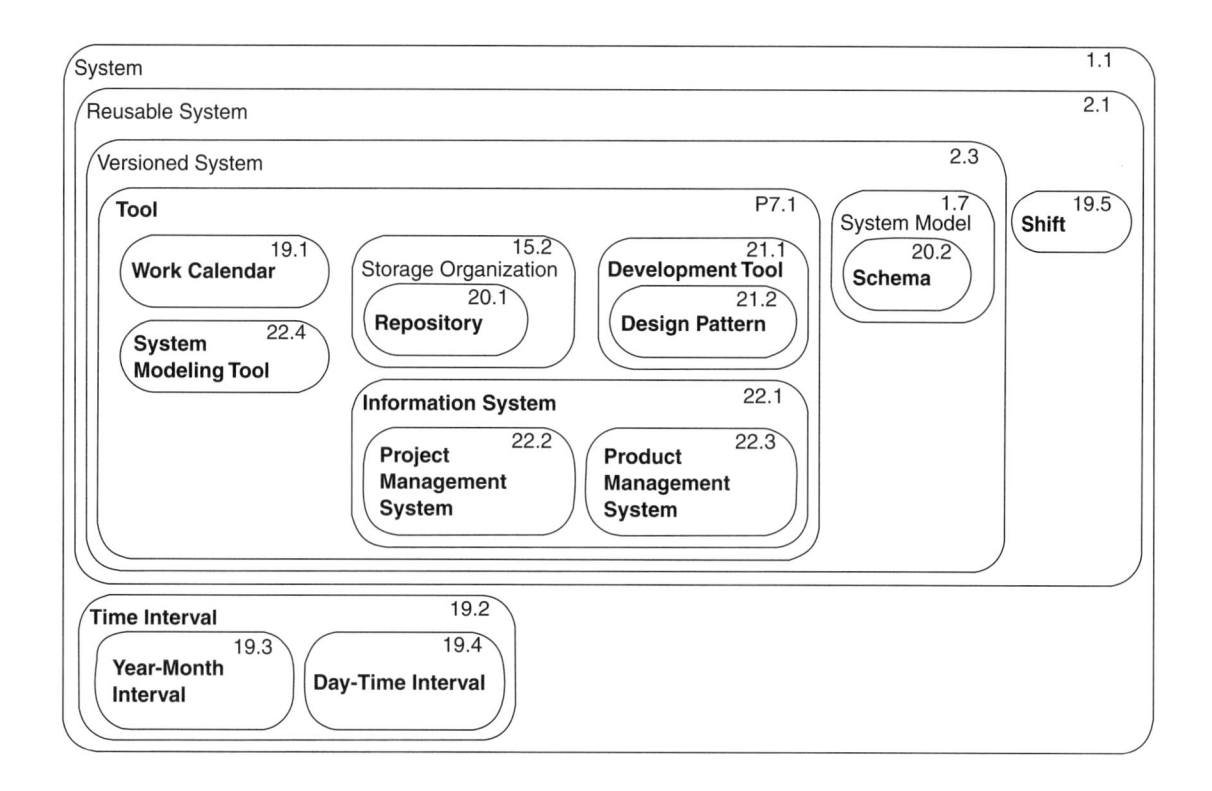

```
┌─ System ─────────────────────────────────────────────────── 1.1 ─┐
│ ┌─ Reusable System ──────────────────────────────────────── 2.1 ─┐│
│ │ ┌─ Versioned System ──────────────────────────────── 2.3 ───┐ ││
│ │ │ ┌─ Tool ──────────────────────── P7.1 ┐  ┌─ 1.7 ─┐ ┌19.5┐ │ ││
│ │ │ │                                     │  │System │ │Shift│ │ ││
│ │ │ │  (Work Calendar 19.1)               │  │ Model │ └─────┘ │ ││
│ │ │ │                                     │  │ (Schema 20.2)│  │ ││
│ │ │ │  (System Modeling Tool 22.4)        │  └──────────────┘  │ ││
│ │ │ └─────────────────────────────────────┘                    │ ││
│ │ │  (Storage Organization 15.2)   (Development Tool 21.1)     │ ││
│ │ │    (Repository 20.1)             (Design Pattern 21.2)     │ ││
│ │ │  ┌─ Information System ──────────────────── 22.1 ┐         │ ││
│ │ │  │ (Project Management   (Product Management     │         │ ││
│ │ │  │  System 22.2)          System 22.3)           │         │ ││
│ │ │  └────────────────────────────────────────────────┘         │ ││
│ │ └────────────────────────────────────────────────────────────┘ ││
│ │ ┌─ Time Interval ──────────────────── 19.2 ┐                   ││
│ │ │ (Year-Month Interval 19.3)  (Day-Time Interval 19.4)│         ││
│ │ └──────────────────────────────────────────┘                   ││
│ └────────────────────────────────────────────────────────────────┘│
└──────────────────────────────────────────────────────────────────┘
```

- *Note:* The illustration of the class hierarchy contains all the classes this part defines. Other parts of the book define and discuss classes not in boldface.

CHAPTER

19 Work Calendar

The Work Calendar

The *work calendar* is a tool that describes the time line for a project with work, availability, or cost time intervals.

Work time is time that the object to which the work calendar relates (tasks, projects, resources) is active in working on some task. *Availability* is an interval of time during which some system is available for work. *Cost* is a monetary amount that stays the same for some interval of time. You use cost intervals to describe things like cost rates, currency exchange rates, and other money rates.

Each work calendar can inherit from another work calendar, giving you the ability to have multiple calendars at different organizational and task levels. Each work calendar may belong to a system, allowing that system to inform its subsystems what calendar to use. Usually, the calendar belongs to a resource or schedule task, including a project schedule task, but any system can have a calendar. An organization, for example, has a calendar that serves as the basic time policy for the organization (standard shifts, holidays, and so on). The primary effect of work calendars is on work duration, the amount of work time a schedule task takes.

Duration (11.2)

Vision: A schedule productively organized around the resources of the project

Mission: To leverage the ability of the project manager to effectively organize the project resources

Objective 19.1: To improve the productivity of the project

The Work Calendar

Approach 19.1: Organize the resource work on the project using the various work calendar intervals (standard time, overtime, holiday time, special time, availability, and variable cost). Load resources with work to the desired level to optimize the schedule through effective scheduling of tasks and to optimize productivity through reducing overwork and burnout [Abdel-Hamid].

Metric 19.1: Project Productivity: work-hours per unit of delivered value

Target 19.1: A value within control limits of an x-R control chart of project productivity from your organization and industry

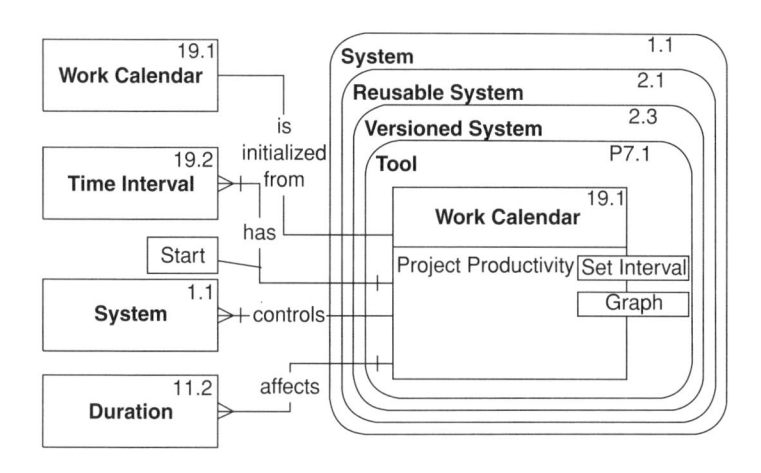

A calendar may take its initial time intervals from another calendar, and then add its own intervals to override those of the parent. Using this relationship, a system can feel the effects of more than one calendar through its default values coming from parent calendars.

The calendar sequences the time intervals, tying each to a specific starting date and time. The intervals are continuous from the beginning to the end of the project.

■ *Note:* Most project management systems provide all kinds of different calendars, giving you a fine degree of control over the structure of work time. Many project managers do not use these tools effectively, I've found. This is partially due to managers often not realizing the impact on the project schedule of effective resource organization. If you don't manage resource scheduling, you don't worry about calendars. If you understand the patterns of time for your resources, you are much more capable of scheduling those resources. If your computer-based scheduling tools effectively represent this time-related information, you're even better off.

The increased parallelism and incrementalism in an OO project makes tracking work intervals even more important than in the usual project. Parallelism in a project results in many more conflicts between schedule tasks. Unless you have tools to optimize the distribution of resources among these parallel tasks, you will have a hard time organizing your resources properly. Calendars are part of this tool set. Without them, you will find your resources alternately not having enough to do or being radically overworked and burning out.

A special case of interest is the very small project. Ordinarily, you would not think that using project management software and work calendars would be useful with one or two people. If you structure the project with many parallel tasks, however, you will quickly overload the small group of available resources. A work calendar lets you level the load by delaying or otherwise reorganizing tasks. Without it, you waste time while you switch from task to task without any idea how it's going to affect your schedule in the long run.

Time Interval

Work calendars get their time line from the standard calendar of days, weeks, months, and years. Instead of accounting for time in simple time intervals, however, a work calendar has several different kinds of complex time interval describing a specific work, availability, or cost pattern. A *time interval* is a period from one instant to another instant of real time.

```
┌─────────────────────────────────────────────┐
│              System                    1.1  │
│  ┌───────────────────────────────────19.2─┐ │
│  │           Time Interval                │ │
│  │ Precision                              │ │
│  │  ┌──────────────19.3┬──────────────19.4┐│ │
│  │  │  Year-Month      │  Day-Time        ││ │
│  │  │   Interval       │   Interval       ││ │
│  │  ├──────────────────┼──────────────────┤│ │
│  │  │ Year             │ Days    Hours    ││ │
│  │  │ Month            │ Minutes Seconds  ││ │
│  │  └──────────────────┴──────────────────┘│ │
│  └────────────────────────────────────────┘ │
└─────────────────────────────────────────────┘
```

***Vision**: Clearly defined relationships between time and project resources*
***Mission**: To model an interval of time*

There are two different kinds of time interval that are mutually incompatible. A year-month interval measures time in units of years and months. A day-time interval measures time in units of days and time (hours, minutes, and seconds).

You should use one or the other, but not both, in your projects. First, the different number of days in a month makes for many arithmetic headaches. Second, if some intervals are in months and others are in days, you have many problems converting between the two when you need to combine them or use them in different contexts. I strongly recommend you make all time intervals day-time intervals, using only days and hours as time units.

■ *Note:* There are many possible kinds of time interval. Since much of the logic of these subclasses is application dependent, I'll leave the full definition to you in your project. The class hierarchy is quite complicated, with many variations on the basic temporal elements of the interval. Table 19-1 shows some of the possible types of time interval.

Table 19-1
Types of Time Interval

Interval	Description
Standard Work Shift	A work time interval in a work calendar that occurs in repeating periods representing work done at the standard cost for the resources
Overtime Work Shift	A work time interval in a work calendar that occurs in repeating periods representing work done at the overtime cost for the resources
Holidays	An off-time interval in a work calendar that occurs at specified, reasonably regular dates generally treated as overhead cost for all resources; if a resource works during a holiday, you accrue overtime or some other special cost for the resource
Special	An off-time interval in a work calendar associated with a specific resource that occurs at variable dates, generally treated as overhead cost for the resources and never as work time
Fixed Cost	Cost that varies only by time
Availability	The work time for a resource that varies by both time and the number of units of the resource; the interval contains both number of units and the amount of available work time
Variable Cost	Cost that varies by both time and the number of units of the resource; the interval contains both number of units and the cost
Lead and Lag	A time interval you associate with a dependency between two schedule tasks to specify a time gap between start and finish dates on the tasks
Duration	A time interval you associate with a schedule task that specifies the calendar and work time that the task will take in the current schedule

The Shift

A *shift* is a periodic set of intervals of work time. That is, the shift specifies time intervals (usually in minutes or hours) during which a system is available for work on a regular, repeating basis. The "day shift," for example, might be from 8–12 and 1–5 Monday through Friday. The shift permits you to describe standard work time and off-time throughout a project with a very simple model, letting you quickly specify the availability and cost characteristics of resources. You can then make exceptions to the shift in calendars you attach to specific objects.

There are many different possible shifts, as many as there are innovative ways to specify the repeating patterns of intervals. Some fix on the day of the week; others vary based on time-on and time-off relationships with no particular day requirements. The structure can be quite complex, including recursive references to shifts: a shift as a varying combination of several other shifts. For example, you can have a shift that varies every three months, with each three-month period having a set of three different shifts. Every three months, these shifts change to other configurations.

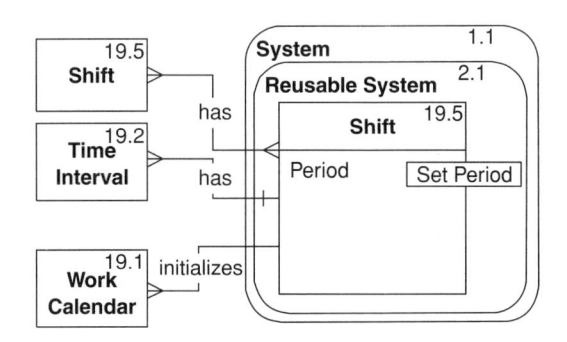

Vision: An easily defined work calendar

Mission: To model work time and off-time in a systematic way that you can use to provide the default time intervals for a work calendar

Objective 19.2: To model work time systematically

Approach 19.2: Create a shift using a period and shift structure that accurately represents the default time arrangements of your systems. Trade off simplicity of the shift structure with accuracy. Use the shift in the appropriate work calendars and make exceptions as required in those calendars.

Metric 19.2: Exceptions Ratio: number of exceptional time intervals to the shift over the total number of time intervals in the work calendar

Target 19.2: A value within control limits on a p control chart of time intervals in the work calendar

---

The shift defines a standard, periodic time at which a system is available. It lets you define a whole work calendar without specifying any particular time interval. You use it, for example, to assign people to tasks, thus determining the possible start- and finish-date milestones given the amount of effort you assign to the task, without touching the work calendar.

The shift can also define the boundary of regular work and overtime. You can use shifts to describe various kinds of resource rate differentials, not just overtime as such.

- *Note:* Shifts are relatively unusual in software projects, which are famous for the "dedication" of their denizens. Larger companies often have stricter shifts, as do many organizations outside the United States. Nevertheless, you may find it difficult to build a realistic model that describes your periodic time setup, even holidays. If your projects involve multiple countries, good luck. If you find yourself constantly asking how to account for time spent at strange hours, ignore shifts and deal with simple calendar intervals instead. Since most project management systems depend on shift structures in their calendars, this can be quite difficult.

Shift reusability comes mostly from the accuracy of your modeling effort. If your shift accurately represents a time interval structure that your organization uses, the shift will have high inherent, domain, and organizational reuse potential.

My most interesting shift situation came about when I managed a group of technical writers that was half in the United States and half in the United Kingdom, eight hours apart. The U.K. crowd stuck pretty closely to a standard U.K. shift, while the U.S. crowd was more flexible. It turned out that the software we used to schedule had no ability to understand time zones. It also had some interesting assumptions about the timing of multiple resource assignments. When I assigned one U.K. writer and one U.S. writer to a single task and then automatically leveled resources, the task moved out to positive infinity. The reason: the shifts did not overlap, and the scheduler assumed that the resources had to work together, literally, at the same time. This led to a complete inability to schedule the task, as one resource would never be available. I had to choose between maintaining the time difference and using the resource leveling or producing a much more complicated schedule by breaking apart the tasks. I chose the latter and pretended the U.K. writers were on California time, reducing my planning accuracy.

340   *Chapter 19 / Work Calendar*

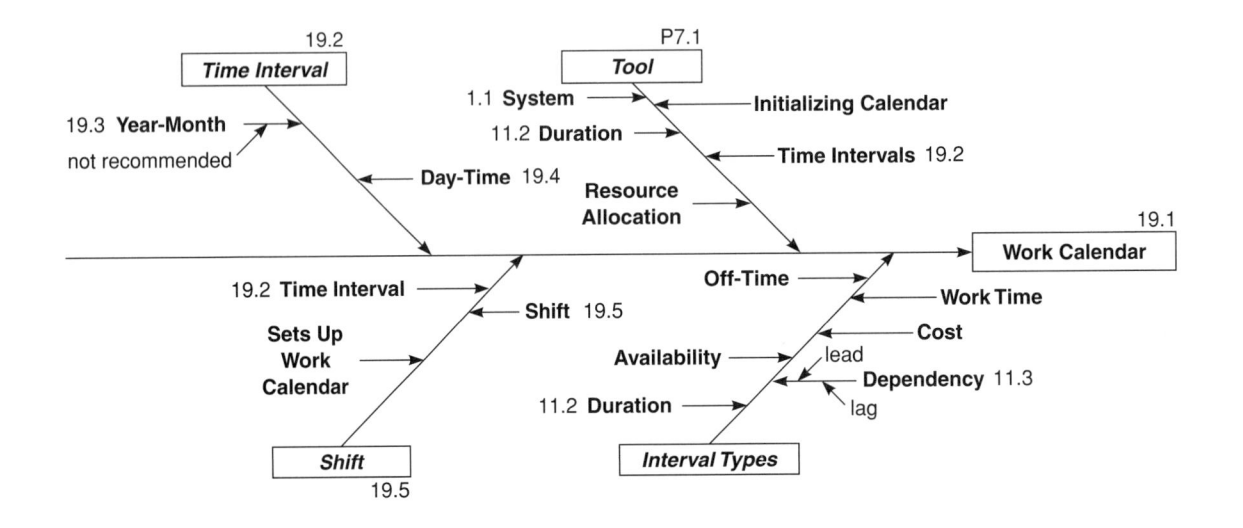

Questions to Think About

1. Do you pay your programmers overtime? If so, do you use your time-tracking forms to generate productivity and other data based on effort spent? Do the timesheets have a way to relate effort spent to a specific work package or level of effort?

2. Does your project management package support calendars? On what kinds of objects? Do you have standard calendars that everyone in your organization uses?

3. For very large projects, it is common to use resource pools instead of individual resources to allocate resources to schedule tasks. How can you handle the situation where several resources in a pool have different work calendars? What is the effect on the schedule?

4. Can you think of any additional types of time interval that a work calendar might contain?

5. Describe your current organizational shifts using the scheme presented here. How complicated is the period? Can you improve your planning ability by considering a simpler kind of shift? a more complex shift? getting rid of shifts altogether?

CHAPTER

Repository 20

The Repository

A *repository* is a storage organization that stores systems in a way organized for finding and using or reusing them. The schema of the repository models the stored systems and their relationships. Repositories serve the storage needs of the people and systems that operate in the project, going beyond the simple storage mechanisms to provide a comprehensive ability to find what you're looking for.

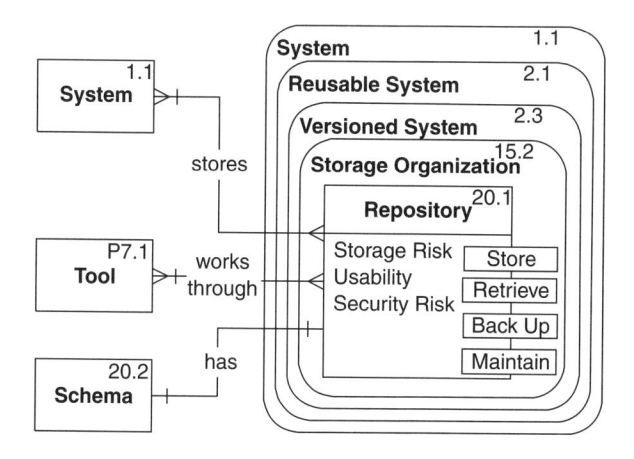

Vision: A set of secure, well-ordered systems that any reuser can easily find

Mission: To enable the secure storage and easy retrieval of systems in an environment

341

Objective 20.1: To enable system storage

Approach 20.1: Acquire a set of storage tools that are capable of storing a set of systems. Acquire or build any tools necessary for the storage process and share them with the organizations that will store the systems. Back up and maintain the systems to optimize risk.

Metric 20.1: Storage risk: the probability of failing to store a needed system

Target 20.1: A storage risk under the risk tolerance of the repository, which should be very small due to the important contributions of system storage to project risk

Objective 20.2: To make system retrieval easy

Approach 20.2: Acquire a set of retrieval tools for the repository technology. Share the tools with organizations that need to retrieve systems from the repository through communication and training.

Metric 20.2: Usability: a subjective, ordinal measure based on the question, "How easily can you find systems in the repository?" Values: Very Easily, Somewhat Easily, With Some Difficulty, With Great Difficulty, Not At All.

Target 20.2: Very Easily

Objective 20.3: To make the stored systems secure

Approach 20.3: Acquire a set of tools that imposes a security mechanism on the storage organization (encryption, authentication, access control, privilege control, and physical protection, for example). Share whatever parts of this system users of the repository must be aware of and keep the rest secret. Loose lips sink ships! Often, improvement means making people aware of the consequences of security breaches rather than changing the security mechanism.

Metric 20.3: Security Risk: the risk of the repository being compromised through a security breach, determined by risk analysis and study of benchmarks of similar security schemes for their frequency of security breaches with compromising effects

Target 20.3: A value below the risk tolerance of the repository for security breaches

Putting systems in, getting systems out, and protecting sensitive systems all interfere with one another. For example, many indexing schemes make system access faster but slow down adding systems. Security often gets in the way of easy access.

The storage for a repository can be anything: files, databases, or anything in between. A repository has a set of tools that implement the repository. You can, for example, build a repository with a relational database. The schema would consist of the data dictionary containing the tables and columns and any integrity constraints. The storage and retrieval mechanisms would consist of SQL and the interfaces necessary to using it. Alternatively, you could build it with an OO database using the native schema and object retrieval and storage, such as object faults and unpinning. A lower-tech alternative might be to store the objects as files on a network. You could then have a file that serves as a table-of-contents schema. You could store and retrieve files using the application tools that generate the files (a word processor or drawing tool, for example). This scheme would only work for smaller projects.

One good alternative for a repository is groupware. Lotus Notes, the product that defines a major part of the groupware software category [Khoshafian], provides a proprietary repository format suited to storing complex documents and other systems. It has an extensive programming interface. Many third-party tools use it to implement all kinds of different functions of interest to project managers. It has some very useful data replication features that let you take systems offline and later come back and reconcile changes in the shared repository. It has specific tools for managing group work through forums, topics databases, and email. Other tools in this category include Collabra Share and Microsoft Exchange, which may not have the full repository capabilities that Lotus Notes offers, depending on your needs [Lewis].

- *Note:* Lotus is now a part of IBM, which is continuing to develop the technology as part of its OO software focus.

The retrieval mechanism integrates the schema, the access methods, and tools for finding systems. There are many schemes for getting systems out of repositories. The more intelligent systems give you ways to search freely within the repository. Some of the new Web-based search engines show great promise in this regard. The World Wide Web provides an excellent example of a repository. Because of its infinite scope, the Web is difficult to search. Its usefulness, on the other hand, makes up for this difficulty. Becoming adept at searching the Web can yield great benefits. Similarly, becoming adept at searching your project repositories can yield great benefits to the project manager. A key difference between the Web and a project repository is that the Web doesn't have a schema.

Schema (20.2)

There are several logical repositories for projects:

- The *project* repository stores project-related systems.
- The *quality* repository stores quality-related systems.
- The *reuse* repository stores reusable systems.
- The *product* repository stores deliverable systems.
- The *organizational* repository stores policies and other organization-related systems.

Reuse Repository (2.2)
Project Repository (3.4)
Product Repository (18.2)
Quality Repository (9.3)
Organizational Repository (33.3)

These repositories can overlap; they need not be physically distinct repositories. I separate them here because each has its own objectives and mission. Some systems with multiple purposes may exist in multiple repositories. For example, the quality repository stores test results and test scripts. Since they are also part of a reusable system certification, they also appear in the reuse repository.

The reuse potential of the repository is almost by definition quite high. Persistence is a central attribute of any storage organization. One key to reuse of a repository is the ease of finding systems. If you can't find what you're looking for, you won't use the systems in the repository. While this is critical for the reusable systems in the reuse repository, it is just as critical for objects in the other repositories. If you can't find the part of the project plan you're looking for, you won't use it. If you can't locate test scripts, you won't run them. The second key is simply whether the system you're looking for is there. Many projects carefully maintain repositories but don't put critical systems in them, for one reason or another. This makes the repository less useful and hence less reusable.

- *Note:* Backup of repositories is critical. Not having a system in the repository is bad enough. Not having one there that should be there but which you lost through misadventure, disaster, or calculated mischief is worse, because it is preventable. The risk of data loss is great in most storage organizations. Manage this risk. Back up your repository. Think of this as baselining and versioning the system. A monthly backup becomes a baseline; incremental backups are versions. Back up at times that represent the logical versioning of the system.

Schema

The *schema* is the system model of a repository. The schema provides the users and maintainers of the repository with a metamodel of the repository's structure. It also enables repository tools to access the repository in interesting ways using information about the structure of the repository.

Vision: *A carefully organized repository accessible through smart tools*

Mission: *To represent the intensional structure of the repository to enable smart tools and people to use the repository effectively*

Objective 20.4: To enable tools and people to use the repository effectively

---

Approach 20.4: Build a system model of the repository, representing the various kinds of systems and their relationships. Share the schema with the tools and people that use the system. Maintain the schema automatically where possible and manually where not.

Schema 345

Metric 20.4: Effectiveness: Does the schema provide all the intensional information that tools and people need to access the repository? Values: Yes or No

Target 20.4: Yes

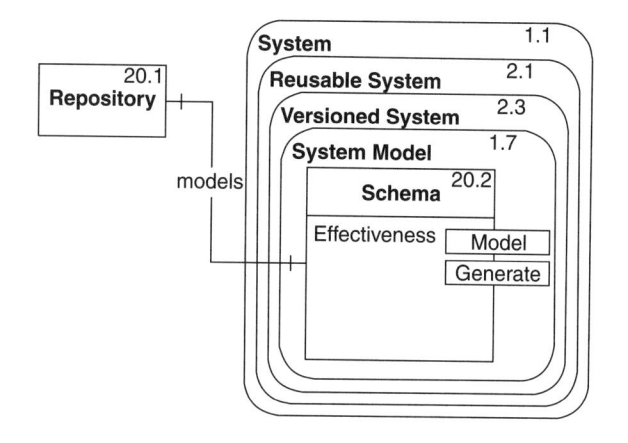

Schemas are a vital part of any repository. You can't effectively retrieve information if you don't know its structure. Free text databases, for example, are useful up to a point; that point being the effectiveness of the free text search tools. Building a second-order index or table of contents, however, increases the usefulness of the text repository substantially, as well as providing a faster access method. Schemas are usually themselves systems stored in the repository.

- *Note:* The terms "schema" and "metamodel" are equivalent. You find the latter term in academic or statistical databases or in computer science classrooms. Some scientists might quibble: a metamodel, they will say, contains more information about the data. I believe that's because of technological limitations.

Modeling the repository requires a modeling language suited to representing the repository elements. The standard for schema modeling is the IRDS standard, an ER-based standard that never really caught on. There are de facto repository schema standards based on OO models, such as the ODMG standard and the ESPRIT metamodeling language. There are even file directory standards you can use for schemas. You need to choose the most appropriate schema modeling language for your particular repository technology.

The schema is more passive than many of the system models in this book. Querying the repository accesses the schema to generate the results of the query, using the modeling capabilities as generators for the result types. Certain kinds of tools can use the schema to generate other systems, such as backup versions and baselines.

Schema reusability comes from the effectiveness of the modeling language. Usually, this in turn derives from the tools you use to build the repository. Some tools are better than others at representing structural information. Relational databases are quite good at simple structure. OO databases are better at complex structures. You should use whatever modeling tools are most appropriate for your repository.

It's interesting to compare project repository schemas with other schemas. Most project management systems have little in the way of schemas, and that interferes with the ability of the tool to retrieve information. The latest generation of project management tools has begun to access relational databases, usually through ODBC or some other high-level interface. This lets them store and retrieve data in relational format. However, most do not take advantage of even basic schema facilities in the relational databases. Most do not allow extension of their schemas. Many don't even store the data automatically in the relational database; they convert it to the database on demand from their internal file structures. The file structures themselves have no schema. This limits their use by both the system and any other tools you might want to apply to them.

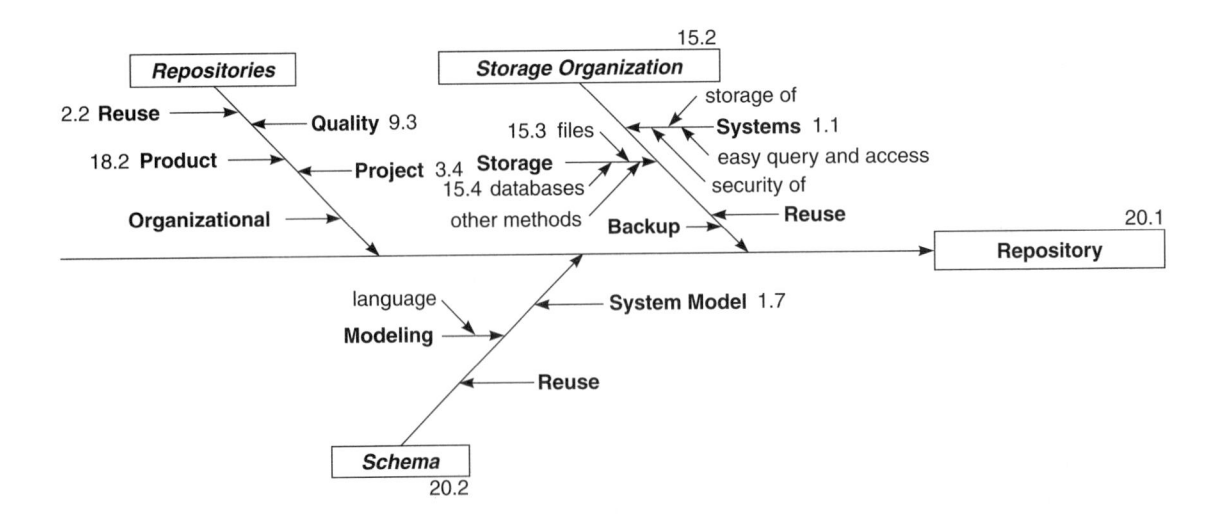

Most of the OO projects I've worked on have had only limited repository facilities and no schemas. I worked with a repository scheme on one project that stored the functional specification as a series of data elements in a file-managed database. The schema was the record description for each record, which you could retrieve on demand to structure a result. This ability was accessible only through the client/server front end that the company marketed, not through any API. The schema worked invisibly through tool system functions to do its basic job, but it provided no great leap in effectiveness for the project. On other projects, most of the systems I worked with were files stored on file servers and accessible only if you knew where to look. Usually there was no schema and no search ability other than the operating system tools for file and text searching. You might regard the directory services features of the network operating system as the schema in this case, as it enabled the basic file-searching tools, but that's it.

Questions to Think About

1. Are there any other logical repositories that you might distinguish in addition to the list presented here?

2. List some systems that repositories do not store. Explain, for each one, why no repository stores it.

3. If you have a paper or online index to document files, is that a schema? Why or why not?

4. Many tool integration environments such as HP Softbench, Atherton Backplane, CORBA, and OLE/COM depend on schemas to operate. How do the schemas vary for the tool systems you have used? Why are there no standards for these (a rhetorical question, really)?

CHAPTER

21 *Development Tool*

The Development Tool

The *development tool* is a hardware or software tool that supports a development task. The development environment contains these tools. Often, applying the tools in your development tasks produces other systems such as drawings or development documents. Acquiring the development tools is a major part of the set of acquisition processes of the project.

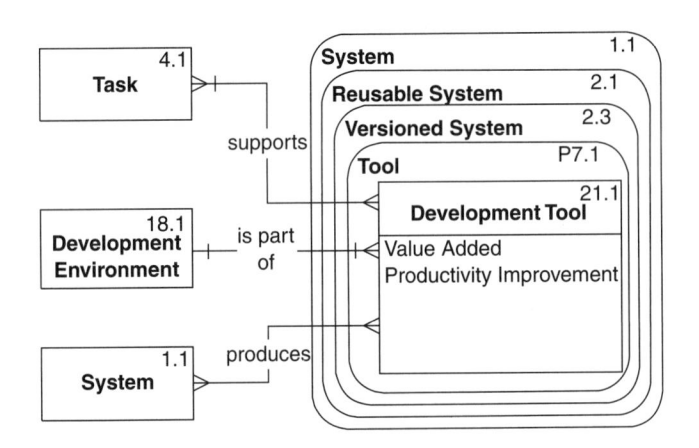

Vision: People getting work done on development tasks
Mission: To provide leverage to effort in achieving development processes

The Development Tool

Objective 21.1: To add value to a task in a development process

Approach 21.1: Acquire, share, and maintain the tool as in Approach P7.1. Focus on the contribution to earning function point value, rejecting the use of tools that do not add substantial value to the deliverable system.

Metric 21.1: Value Added: the amount of value in function points that you generate from tasks using the tool that you could not have generated without the tool

Target 21.1: A value within control limits on an x-R control chart of similar development tools from your organization or industry; the value should reflect a positive internal rate of return on investment as well

Objective 21.2: To improve productivity in executing a development process

Approach 21.2: Proceed as in Approach 21.1, except for focusing on productivity instead of value.

Metric 21.2: Productivity Improvement: the ratio of mean productivity (effort-hours per function point) while using the tool to productivity while not using the tool on similar tasks

Target 21.2: A value within control limits on a p control chart of similar tools from your organization or industry; the value should be materially greater than 1

Development tools include many different kinds of hardware and software:
- Workstations
- File servers
- Network servers and communications equipment
- Compilers
- Linkers
- Debuggers
- Editors
- Profilers
- Video games
- Squirt guns
- Espresso machines
- Online service accounts (to get stock quotes!)

"Quality Tools" section, Chapter 9, p. 163

Whatever it takes to get the software done is a development tool. The following sections look at some of the kinds of tools that are most important for OO software projects.

■ *Note:* There are signs that vendors are beginning to wake up to the possibility of development tools other than design and coding (and testing) tools. Requisite, Inc., is marketing the Requisite product, which it calls "groupware for requirements management." Quality Systems and Software announced a product called DOORS (Dynamic Object-Oriented Requirements System), which provides both requirements management and tracing. I haven't used these products, but the direction is right. Now if they'd just provide the House of Quality....

Design Tools

A design process is one that specifies the structure of your solution to the problem of delivering a software object that satisfies its requirements. High-level design creates system and high-level cluster architectures, while low-level design creates cluster and class architectures and details. There are several kinds of tools that help with OO design.

First, *drawing tools* draw pictures. Pictures are often the best way to present OO designs, which focus on cluster structure and the relationships between classes, clusters, and objects. Most OO methods focus on specific notations for their design concepts. You can use simple drawing tools, such as the one that drew the pictures for this book; or you can use expensive and complex CASE tools with drawing components. Often the complexity of the CASE tool makes drawing easy, since the tool understands much more about the syntax and semantics of OO design. It helps you to do what you need to do.

Second, *reverse engineering tools* help you move older designs or undocumented designs into drawings and extended CASE design systems. A reverse engineering tool reads source code, or even object code, and produces design diagrams and the repository data dictionaries that go with them. Using a reverse engineering tool, you can transform an uncertified system produced by another task into a certified, documented, highly reusable system. You can also produce documentation in your standard OO design method notation for systems developed using other notations or paradigms.

Third, *CASE tools* provide a comprehensive environment for design. They include both drawing tools and reverse engineering tools along with many other tools that support the design process. These added tools include repositories, consistency checkers, design simulators that animate your design, and code generators that produce a first cut at the code that implements your design. A sophisticated CASE tool can let you design your system, implement it, and then later change it and reverse-engineer the changes back into designs.

Design tools have a specific set of risks [Schottland]. These risks are not so much to the tool itself as a system but to the systems to which you apply the tools. The Silver Bullet is a primary risk for design tools: promising the sky and delivering air. The youth of OO tools and the tendency for OO tool vendors to exaggerate their abilities can lead to attempts to apply tools in inappropriate ways. A tool's gotta know its limitations. There is also a risk of not balancing tools and people properly. People can do a lot, but not with inadequate tools. Similarly, tools can be very effective in increasing productivity, but only if people learn how to use them effectively and you have people capable of using them productively. Also, you must make sure that people accept the tools. A common failing of the tool acquisition process for CASE tools, for example, is to buy tools that the manager but no one else in the shop likes. This will result in shelfware, not a design tool. ("Shelfware" is a subclass of tool with no vision, mission, or objectives other than to hold up a wall in an earthquake. If you're lucky.)

"OO Development Risks" section, Chapter 12, p. 210

Coding Tools

OO technology began with coding, the process of implementing an OO design. As the advantages of OO coding became clear, the techniques worked their way back through design methods into analysis methods. There are many tools that support OO coding. Most design methods insist that you can implement your design in any OO language that supports the true features of OO design. That works up to the point where the definition of that set of "true" features corresponds to the set of "true" features in the OO programming language. If this mapping is not one-to-one, you have to invent clever coding techniques that mimic the feature, such as multitasking or varieties of messaging.

Configuration Management System (25.3)

Compilers, Linkers, and Coding Environments

A *compiler* is a language translator that takes your programming language source code and transforms it into machine language instructions on the source operating system and hardware. An *interpreter* is a similar translator that, instead of producing machine code, interprets the source or an intermediate version of it at runtime. The *linker* resolves external addresses and produces executable code from object code. *Dynamic linking* resolves these references at runtime. There are as many variations on these tools as there are products.

Some products look much like their non-OO forebears, such as C++. A design goal of C++, as exemplified by its name, was to be compatible with C [Ellis; Stroustrup]. The early C++ compilers were translators that converted C++ statements into C, and then called a standard C compiler on the C code.

Other products took a different tack. Smalltalk and Java, for example, run on top of a *virtual machine*. This is a software cluster that provides the functions the language needs to do its work. Smalltalk and Java objects access the operating system only through this cluster. To move a system to a different operating system requires only a different virtual machine cluster [Goldberg 1983].

The compiler or interpreter for an OO language hardly ever stands alone. It usually comes as part of a *coding environment.* This is a complex of tools that provides editors, compilers, interpreters, browsers, static analyzers, debuggers, source control, and many other minor coding tools. These tools help you to organize your OO coding. Examples include Visual C++ by Microsoft, the ObjectCenter C++ environment by Centerline Software, VisualWorks for C++ and Smalltalk from ParcPlace-Digitalk, and HP Softbench [Garg].

Reusable Systems

Reuse Repository (2.2)

Of equal status to the coding environment is the set of reusable systems you have available. The reuse repository contains these systems. There are several specific structures of interest to OO programmers.

First, the *framework* is a cluster that provides major functionality, such as the features in a graphical user interface or a set of important data structures. Many OO environments come with frameworks built in. Smalltalk, for example, is more framework than language. The Smalltalk programming language is very simple. Almost anything of interest requires the use of classes from the Smalltalk framework. Learning Smalltalk is mostly learning the framework, not the language [Goldberg 1983]. Visual C++ comes with the Microsoft Foundation Components (MFC) framework. It doesn't by any means require that you use this framework. The coding environment gives you all kinds of tools for doing so, such as Application and Class Wizards that generate most of the code for the use of the framework. Often, frameworks provide an OO wrapper around a technology that is not object-oriented, such as the MFC framework for Object Linking and Embedding OLE, a C functional technology, or the JDBC framework for accessing relational databases from Java. You will often have to choose between frameworks at the same time that you choose between programming languages, as they are usually quite closely integrated. Whether the framework is more important than the language depends on your application.

Second, the *API* is a cluster that gives you an interface to specific technology. One way to look at a framework, for example, is as a collection of APIs that apply to a broad domain. Often, an API is a class or a cluster of classes, such as the OLE framework of MFC. Other APIs provide an interface to a particular tool, such as the ORACLE or SYBASE interface for database managers or the CORBA dynamic invocation interface [OMG 1996].

Third, the *database manager* is a cluster that gives you a persistent object manager. There are an enormous variety of relational, OO, and hybrid databases available, each with its own particular slant on persistence. Relational databases provide

APIs and some OO tools. OO databases integrate with OO languages to remove the impedance mismatch between the OO language and the database API by merging them. Hybrid databases give you the ability to store complex objects while using relational access methods such as SQL [Cattell].

Fourth, the *object request broker* is a cluster that gives you the ability to distribute objects across a network. There are two competing standards for this software cluster, the OMG's Common Object Request Broker Architecture (CORBA) and Microsoft's Component Object Model (COM). I prefer the CORBA architecture [OMG 1996], but both have their adherents, advantages, and disadvantages. There are many implementations of the CORBA, but only one of COM (Microsoft's). Which tool you choose depends on your target operating environment and architectural preferences.

Browsers, Inspectors, and Debuggers

Because of the focus of OO coding on relationships between objects, you need a browser. A *browser* is a tool that shows you the relationships between classes and other systems. The browser lets you navigate from system to system to see objects at the other end of the relationships. You can use the browser to investigate inheritance and containment relationships. Navigating through the inheritance hierarchy lets you determine what code you can reuse through inheritance. Navigating through the containment hierarchy lets you understand how the class or cluster uses its contained systems and what the overall architecture of the system looks like. Browser and inspector technologies are moving forward based on research in how programmers work [Goldberg, pp. 367–368].

An *inspector* is a tool that lets you inspect an object at runtime. In many ways, it is a special kind of *debugger,* a tool that lets you navigate through the runtime system as it operates. Inspectors typically operate outside the operation of the system, while debuggers let you inspect the objects, trace through their operation, and change them as you go. Some kind of debugger is essential for the OO coder, as it is often very difficult to determine what is really going on in a system comprising many small interacting objects. On the other hand, most coders would benefit from a short course in logical debugging, the art and science of developing and proving hypotheses about coding problems. These techniques can be more useful than debuggers at uncovering and solving problems [Myers], and are just as applicable to OO programming as to any other kind.

Prototyping Tools

An intermediate level of OO coding tool is the *prototyping tool,* which lets you rapidly generate your OO system using reusable systems. This prototype may not do everything you want, but it gives you an idea what the system will do. Often, your prototyping tools are your coding tools: the line is not very clear in OO coding. As your reuse repository grows, you will find it easier and easier to prototype using reusable systems. There are prototyping tools, however, that work outside your environment to provide rapid prototyping, usually for prototyping the high-level interfaces and functions. Many of these tools work as client/server development environments, giving you access to databases and graphical user interfaces without diving into lower-level coding at all. Others mix high- and low-level coding to produce clusters and systems that work as both prototypes and deliverable systems.

Profiling and Analysis Tools

Profilers are tools that let you analyze the performance of your system. Code profilers, for example, insert meters in your compiled or interpreted source code. These generate statistics about the amount of system resources you use (CPU time, elapsed time, disk I/Os, and so on). Most database managers have profilers that let you examine SQL statements, system resource usage, and other database-specific performance factors. There are many sophisticated network analyzers, both hardware and software, that let you figure out where problems exist in your network. As CORBA and other distributed object tools become more important, these profilers will provide useful information about their performance on the network.

Documentation Tools

Documentation tools help you to document your code. Most OO languages have comments built in that allow code to be self-documenting. Most OO development processes have standards for these comments, as well as for other coding practices. Most developers comment their code at just the right balance of loquacity and laconism. Of course, each developer disagrees with every other developer on where this balance rests! Generally, an OO developer should build a code system that explains itself to the degree needed for someone else to reuse that code system. One aspect of a code inspection or review should certify that the code system has this level of documentation.

Coding Standard (32.3)
Technical Review (41.4)

Groupware Tools

Groupware tools help coders to work as teams. This is too new an area for many tools to have emerged that are specifically helpful to OO programmers. However, the nature of OO development should help these tools emerge naturally as solutions to team coding problems. The coding and integration of parallel clusters, for example, requires communication and configuration management tools that permit parallel work on shared systems. For example, if one cluster needs to modify another cluster, the coder can check out the other cluster through the configuration management tool built into the development environment. Other teams needing to modify that cluster must then coordinate with the coder that checked out the cluster. As technology in this area develops, you will see tools that aid in this communication process emerge. In particular, since most current configuration managers manage files, not clusters, there is a real opportunity for tool vendors to provide better solutions for OO team coding problems. For example, you should be able to check out a single method from a class for changes. Right now, you would usually have to check out the entire file, which might contain all kinds of methods, global variables, and who knows what else.

A special class of groupware tools includes the various implements that let an OO development team interact on a personal level, such as pagers, beer parties, squirt guns, and other implements of (self-) destruction. I'll leave it to you to determine whether your team benefits or not from these tools.

I worked at a small Silicon Valley start-up populated mostly by very recent Stanford graduates. There were two teams: the young turks and the old turks. The young turks socialized around roller-blading through the halls, Bruce Willis movies, and gym workouts; the old turks socialized around war stories about previous employers. Amazingly, this worked, though with some tension. I read a letter in *Computerworld* about one shop with a development executive who was run down by a developer's bicycle coming around a corner in a hallway. Such activities didn't last, if the story was in fact not apocryphal. Most developers have more sense. I think.

Design Patterns

Design patterns are an interesting innovation that the OO software design community is just beginning to use. Although not strictly OO, design patterns adapt well to the culture of the OO community with their emphasis on reuse and structure. Most design patterns assume an OO design paradigm. A *design pattern* is a tool that you apply to address a recurring design problem. The pattern describes the design problem and the solution using a design language independent of any programming language. The pattern also describes the context of the solution: where and when to apply it, roles and collaborations, what happens when you apply the solution, and the distribution of responsibilities. It provides examples and design and coding tips to guide your low-level design and coding of the solution [Gamma].

Vision: Productive architects reusing well-thought-out designs

Mission: To represent design solutions in a highly reusable, productive format

---

Objective 21.3: To represent design solutions to recurring design problems

---

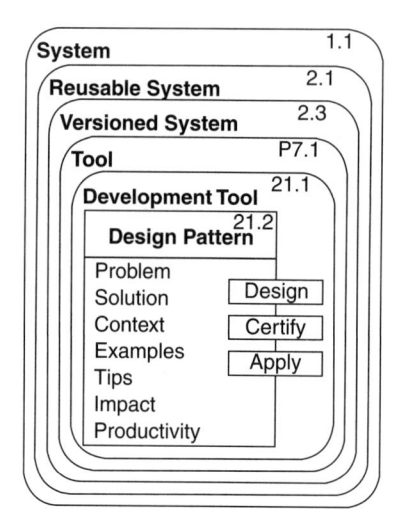

```
                    System              1.1
                  Reusable System        2.1
                 Versioned System         2.3
                Tool                      P7.1
                 Development Tool         21.1
                             21.2
                    Design Pattern
                    Problem
                    Solution      Design
                    Context       Certify
                    Examples      Apply
                    Tips
                    Impact
                    Productivity
```

Approach 21.3: Start with published design patterns [Gamma] and expand the collection in your reuse repository. Focus on design problems that recur often in your development processes. Certify the patterns through technical reviews and apply them in design processes.

Metric 21.3: Impact: an ordinal measure that evaluates how often the design problem the pattern addresses recurs; values High, Medium, Low

Target 21.3: High to Medium High depending on the stage of development of your reuse repository and its collections of patterns

---

Objective 21.4: To provide highly reusable design solutions

Approach 21.4: Develop your design patterns using careful OO design techniques for generalizing the pattern as much as possible. Focus the technical review and certification process on generalization to optimize reuse potential.

Metric 21.4: Reuse potential (see Metric 2.1)

Target 21.4: A reuse potential within control limits on an x-R control chart of similar design patterns for your organization and industry

---

Objective 21.5: To provide productive design patterns

Approach 21.5: Include examples and tips in your design patterns to guide specific implementations. Orient these examples toward the design and coding tools in your development environment. Provide framework or cluster implementations of the patterns in your reuse repository along with the patterns. Parameterize and optimize these implementations to make them as flexible and as high performance as possible to encourage black box reuse of the pattern and its implementation.

Metric 21.5: Productivity on design tasks

Target 21.5: A productivity value within control limits on an x-R control chart of productivity, keeping the productivity at a high level given productivity benchmarks

---

While design patterns are by design independent of any programming language, their approach often assumes a design paradigm, such as OO design or functional design. These assumptions limit the application of the design pattern to certain languages, a fact that the design pattern should note. Most design pattern work assumes an OO design paradigm at this time.

Design patterns can accompany specific reusable systems that implement them. This both documents the solution and provides guidance about when to apply the solution.

Reusable System (2.1)

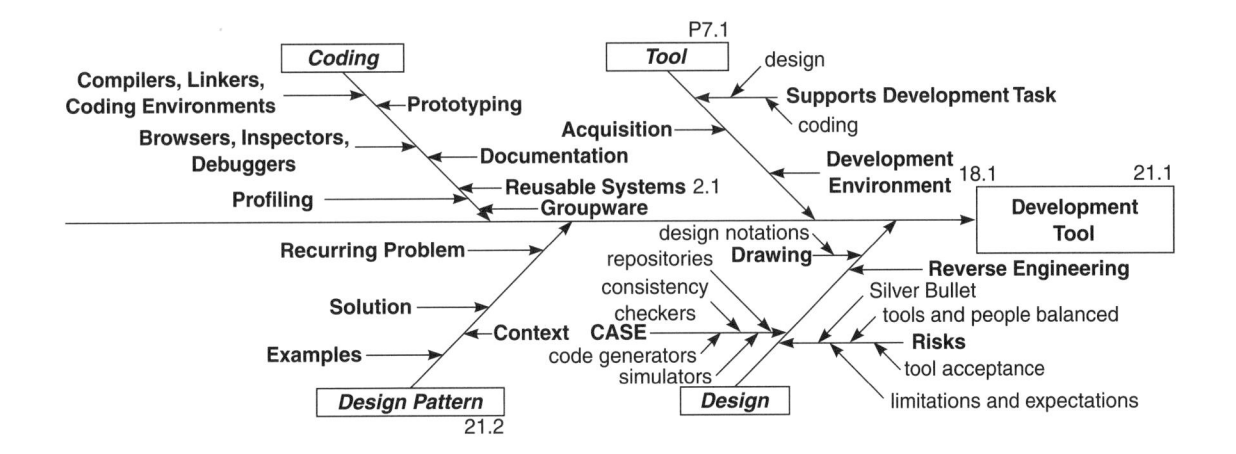

Readings

[Cattell]   R. G. Cattell. *Object Data Management: Object-Oriented and Extended Relational Database Systems.* Reading, MA: Addison-Wesley, 1991.

While this book is an excellent introduction to OO databases and extended relational databases, don't believe everything you read in it. OO database managers vary a great deal in quality and their ability to deliver on their performance claims in specific applications. Make sure the shoe fits before you wear it. *Caveat emptor.*

[Gamma]	E. Gamma, R. Helm, R. Johnson, and J. Vlissides. *Design Patterns: Elements of Object-Oriented Software Architecture.* Reading, MA: Addison-Wesley, 1995.

This is the seminal work on design patterns. It identifies several basic OO design patterns and gives you a design framework in which to develop additional ones.

[Goldberg 1983]	Adele Goldberg and D. Robson. *Smalltalk-80: The Language and Its Implementation.* Reading, MA: Addison-Wesley, 1983.

This is the book that introduced Smalltalk-80 to the programming public. It has some very interesting discussions of the issues with implementing tools for "personal" programming and OO programming.

[Goldberg]	Adele Goldberg and Kenneth S. Rubin. *Succeeding with Objects: Decision Frameworks for Project Management.* Reading, MA: Addison-Wesley, 1995.

This book, among its many other useful features, has an excellent discussion of tools and tool acquisition.

[Johnson]	Ralph Johnson. Documenting frameworks using patterns. *ACM SIGPLAN Notices* 27:10 (October 1992): 63–76.

This is a fascinating paper on one application of design patterns, the documentation and certification of framework software.

[Khoshafian]	Setrag Khoshafian and Marek Buckiewicz. *Introduction to Groupware, Workflow, and Workgroup Computing.* New York: Wiley, 1995.

This book is all about groupware and work-flow tools and environments. It has excellent descriptions of specific tools and methods for applying them.

[Lewis]	Ted Lewis. *Deploying Distributed Business Software.* New York: SIGS Books, 1996.

This is a book about client/server and distributed object development, but it contains good summary descriptions of the various tools you can use in OO development, and especially distributed object development. It also has good sections on groupware and process modeling tools.

[OMG 1996]	Jon Siegel, editor. *CORBA Fundamentals and Programming.* New York: Wiley, 1996.

This is the best book available on CORBA development. It has three chapters that describe specific tools that implement CORBA in various ways. This is the most comprehensive and clearly written book on using and understanding CORBA technology.

[Schottland]	Greg Schottland. Choosing and using design tools. *Object Magazine* (November 1996): 61–63.

This is a well-done column on design tools for OO systems. Not only does it cover the varieties of design tools, but it discusses the issues in tool acquisition and the risks you face in using design tools.

Questions to Think About

1. When would you choose to use a simple drawing tool instead of a complicated CASE tool, and vice versa? Can you design OO software effectively without true CASE tools?

2. Could you develop software without the basic software tools? How does tool sophistication impact software development? Do you need to use sophisticated tools to scale up your efforts to larger OO systems? (Hint: This is a trick question—think about the principles of OO design.)

3. Think about development tools you have used in the past that wound up as shelfware. Why did they go on the shelf? What could you have done differently to prevent their becoming shelfware?

4. When would you build development tools instead of buying them?

5. Why do you think design patterns have emerged in addition to frameworks and other reusable components? Do you think that one or the other approach to solving problems is preferable? Why?

6. How do you think a general simulation tool might help a project manager? (Hint: Simulation tools are best for problems with nonlinear solutions.)

CHAPTER

22 *Information System and Modeling Tool*

This chapter presents several essential project management tools. You use information systems, including project and product management systems, to create and manage project systems. System modeling tools let you build reusable system models, such as process models.

The Information System

The *information system* is a tool that creates and manages information that people use to complete their tasks. The information system stores data in one or more repositories and works as a system of tools interacting to create and manage information.

Vision: People using information to get their jobs done in a project

Mission: To create and manage information that people need to get their jobs done productively

Objective 22.1: To create and manage reusable information that people need

Approach 22.1: Identify systems that you need to create that supply information for a project task. Acquire, share, and maintain an information system that creates the required information. Use the system to obtain information, to assist in decision making, to certify reusability, and to support organizational needs.

Metric 22.1.1: Information Failure: a count of the number of incidents in which a person could not get information needed to do a project job using this tool, including lack of timely information

The Information System 361

Target 22.1.1: A count within the control limits of a p control chart of counts; the value should be low relative to an industry benchmark of information failure

Metric 22.1.2: Necessity: an ordinal, subjective measure of the need for the information that the system creates and manages; values High, Medium, Low

Target 22.1.2: High to Medium, balanced against the cost to the project or organization

Objective 22.2: To increase productivity of information used in project tasks

Approach 22.2: Acquire tools based on projected information productivity. Market the tool and train people to use it effectively. Identify and communicate to potential users the situations that would benefit substantially from using the tool. Improve the tool and its use with improvement plans that take the results of prior use into account as feedback.

Metric 22.2: Information productivity: the ratio of effort spent using the tool relative to total task effort for tasks that use the tool

Target 22.2: A value within control limits on a pn control chart for tasks using the tool

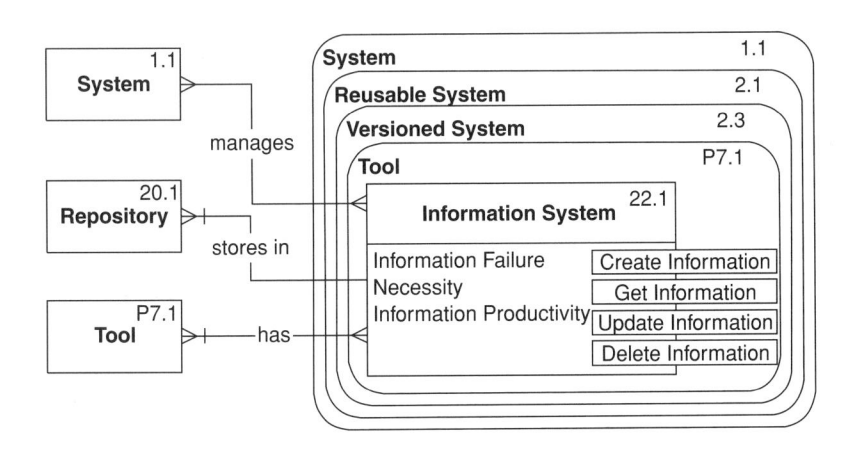

There are many kinds of information system that relate to project management in one way or another [Kerzner, pp. 72–74]:

- Management information systems
- Operating information systems
- Decision support systems
- Financial information systems

- Marketing information systems
- Inventory control systems
- Resource information systems

The organizational environment contains these tools. This chapter goes into detail on two classes of information system, the project management system and the product management system. Related subclasses of this abstract class appear in chapters dealing with their management process (change management and cost management).

Change Management System (24.4)

Cost Management System (38.2)

Information comes in many forms. Much of the information of interest to OO software projects comes from systems that contain the information. The information system accesses those systems in their repositories or on the fly. It transforms the information into the form that the user needs. It lets users create and manage the information as a computer interface to many of the project systems.

■ *Note:* **Information systems existed long before computers. Modern project management, however, has transformed most paper- and people-based systems into computer-based systems. This kind of system is what the computer does best, yielding the most productivity.**

Information systems are systems of tools. Some are monolithic, being one big tool; others are collections of loosely coupled tools distributed over wide-area networks. You should structure information systems to conform to their operational objectives and improve their structure continuously, pushing them ever higher in their contribution to the project.

There are general management support information systems. The best known of these at the time of writing is ManagePro from Avantos Performance Systems. This product not only provides a great interface and standard tracking tools, it gives you advice at every step of the way and lets you customize the tool to your needs. Rumors say that Microsoft will be releasing a new product in 1997 called Team Manager 97. It is supposed to integrate with Microsoft Office 97 and do much of what Exchange and Schedule do besides the kinds of things ManagePro does [Angus].

For all their technological expertise, software development shops seem to have difficulty using information management systems. I worked in one company that tried two different calendar management packages. Both were full-featured groupware systems that let us plan meetings and interact. Both failed miserably, with use falling to zero within months of installation. No one knew how to use these systems to improve productivity, so everyone felt they were a waste of time. This was only partly due to the limitations of the products; it also had to do with the managers not being trained in the tool and the developers not being permitted to have the tool (only managers).

Another company went a little too far in the other direction. Every manager had their own project management software, and maintained their own schedule completely separately. The project manager (me) had yet another separate system. I tried to integrate the schedules at a high level, but the lack of cross-updating in a central repository made it very difficult to keep track of things. Fortunately, this was a functional organization; as project manager, I didn't need to do anything but exhort the managers to meet their schedules.

Dare I mention bug tracking? Every company I've worked in has had a bug-tracking system. Every one has been built, not bought. Every one has been terrible. These systems seem to have the mission of focusing the ire of developers on QA and customer support, or vice versa. The running refrains of "not a bug" or "can't reproduce it" or "user error" get old after a while. I wish I could say that the OO ones were better, but they weren't. One system in particular was incredibly bad, with intolerable performance using a flat-file database over a wide-area network and many kludgy restrictions on data entry and access. Both development and MIS took responsibility for developing a new version; both failed due to lack of management support and consequent low prioritization. The lack of effective bug-tracking tools had a major impact on managers' and developers' productivity. The lack of management support had a major impact on developer, QA, and customer support morale.

The Project Management System

The *project management system* is an information system that creates and manages project-related information. Project management systems are responsible for creating and managing many of the systems in the first few parts of this book: projects, plans, schedules, risk, and even software development.

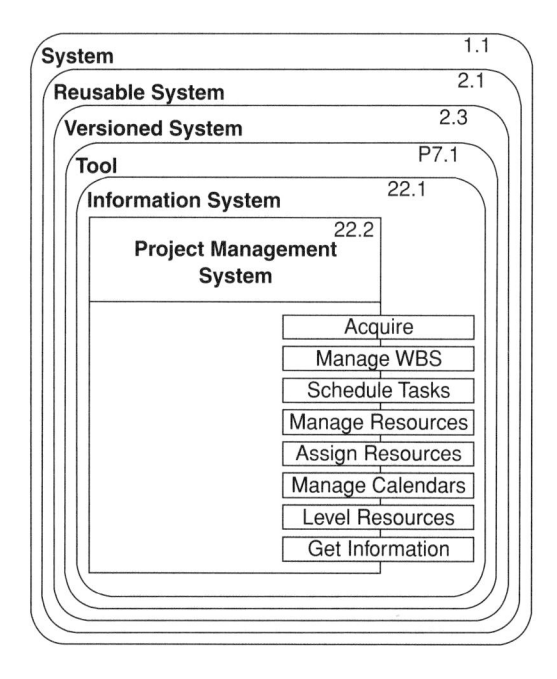

Vision: People using project information to get their jobs done in a project

Mission: To create and manage information about the project and its environment that people need to get their jobs done productively

---

Objective 22.3: To create and manage reusable project information that people need; see Approach 22.1 and Metric 22.1

Objective 22.4: To increase productivity of project information used in project tasks; see Approach 22.2 and Metric 22.2

Project management systems integrate several different tools and systems, usually in one integrated system:

- Projects (3.1), including multiple projects at once
- Time charts (10.2) with their durations (11.2)
- Dependency charts (10.3) with their dependencies (11.3)
- Work Breakdown Structures (8.2) with their tasks (4.1)
- Schedules (10.1) with their schedule tasks (11.1) and milestones (4.12)
- Work calendars (19.1) and their time intervals (19.2) and shifts (19.5)
- Resources (34.1) with their assignments (35.1)

Every project management system has a different way of creating and managing these systems, though most do it in one way or another. Table 22-1 lists the major project management systems I've seen in different software shops.

Acquiring project management systems is much like acquiring any information system. One difference comes from the system complexity. You will invariably need to make features trade-offs between different project management systems and your requirements. One system will fit your requirements except for one important feature; another will have that feature but will have a reputation for crashing Windows, for example.

You should involve anyone in the organization who will use the tools in making the decision. Particularly with groupware tools such as timesheets or progress reports, you need to get consensus on the value of the tool. Look for tools that foster trust rather than structure the environment rigidly. (One project manager, for example, refused to use any tool that told him "Please wait…" instead of what it was really doing.) You must also ensure that the tool will support your process models in action. Use the tool in a pilot project if you can as part of your project improvement plan.

Pilot Improvement Plan (1.5)

If you can, build your project management system out of several different tools integrated loosely or within some kind of tool integration environment. This

Table 22-1 The Major Off-the-Shelf Project Management Systems

Vendor	Product	Comments
ABT Corp.	Project Workbench	One of the only project management systems specializing in software projects, though without special OO features
Apple Computer (Claris)	MacProject	An increasingly out-of-date but easy-to-use product for the Macintosh
Computer Associates	CA-SuperProject	An old standard for DOS updated for Windows
Digital Tools	Autoplan	One of the only tools in the UNIX market; no one seems to know why there are so few UNIX project management systems
Microsoft	Microsoft Project	A new standard; the market leader by far for both Windows and Macintosh systems, even with significant limitations
Primavera Systems	Primavera Project Planner (P3)	A high-end system but worth it
Scitor Corp.	Project Scheduler 7	The best graphical user interface I've seen in a Windows project management system
Time Line Solutions	Time Line for Windows	A full-featured product but quirky

approach is much more likely to yield the best from each vendor rather than your having to make unwelcome trade-offs.

Get senior management support for your tool. Make sure your project sponsor and other important internal stakeholders accept the need for the constraints the tool puts on them and on other resources. Otherwise, instant shelfware.

Here are the top ten reasons project management systems are underused [Thamhain]:

1. People don't know how to use the tools.
2. People get anxious over the misuse of information and methods.
3. Too much work, time, or paper.
4. Tools sap drive and problem-solving initiative.
5. The tool doesn't support current business processes.
6. The control aspects threaten people's freedom, autonomy, or rewards.
7. Some people hate the tool for whatever reason.
8. You bought the tool instead of having it built in-house.
9. Some people think the tool or method is worthless.
10. The tool cost too much.

Multiple Projects

About 1990, the project management system vendors discovered that most of their customers wanted to manage multiple projects at once. The first attempt at doing this in a PC package that I know of was SuperProject in about 1985. Its name shows its solution: integrate projects as tasks, with tasks potentially being super- or subprojects. It confused the issue, however, with resources and files and other system issues, making the solution less than workable. As time went on, systems dealt with the issue of multiple projects in several different ways.

Why is multiple-project planning so difficult? Here are some issues [Levine]:

- Project priorities versus one another
- Dependencies between tasks in different projects
- Resources that projects share
- Calendars that projects share
- Leveling resources across projects
- Reporting across projects, and particularly aggregating cost or schedule data across multiple projects
- Tracking progress across projects (multiple-project timesheets)
- Security and access control (multiple-project managers having access only to their projects, and so on)

To this point, there are two basic ways of satisfying these requirements: subprojects and groups. The subproject approach establishes a master project and several subprojects, while the group approach groups projects together for some particular purpose, such as resource sharing, leveling, or reporting. Each project management system has a different way of doing all this, with each having various quirks and foibles deriving from its unique design. Some designs let you take both approaches.

I believe that you need to look at multiple projects in a more flexible way. The structure of the Project system class has the project inheriting from the complex task. Thus the project is a kind of task, which is a kind of versioned system, which is a kind of reusable system, which is a kind of system. This structure lets you treat any project as a complex task within another project. It also lets you embed project structures in your process models. Most of the issues in the above list have to do with the relationships between other systems and the project and the perspective from which you're looking at the project.

In an OO system, encapsulation takes care of most of this. When you level the resources of a project, those resources include any shared with other projects.

Project (3.1)

If those projects are complex tasks within the current project, the tasks within that project get leveled. Otherwise, they remain static, and you level around them.

Future project management systems are going to have to separate their implementations from their system model. Instead of looking at each project as a file, the project management system should see everything it needs to see when it needs to see it. Instead of loading one project into memory at a time and operating only on it, the systems must work on both in-memory data and persistent data. Working from a system model instead of from the software design or implementation makes many of these issues irrelevant.

I've worked in several environments where management dealt with multiple projects. Virtually everyone ignored most of the issues because they weren't interested in measuring things across projects, only in milestones and interproject dependencies. This allows functional managers to manage their own projects separately, coordinating dependencies in an ad hoc way.

For example, one OO project had one project for each deliverable subsystem (GUI, repository, object model). The three managers coordinated their efforts in weekly meetings on a verbal basis. We did not use the project management system's ability to link tasks across projects because it was too difficult to keep updated and had deleterious effects on our own duration management. That is, the software wouldn't let us manage our projects if we linked them. We struggled along, partially succeeding in avoiding conflicts.

Another OO project divided up projects along functional lines. This was a strong functional organization. QA had a project, Docs had a project, and the three development groups each had a project. As project manager, I had a project as well. We could not link these for several reasons. First, we were all using different software. One manager used an Excel spreadsheet. Another two used Microsoft Project on the Macintosh. A third used Scitor's Project Scheduler on Windows. Of course, we could not link these different tools. But even if we had all been using the same tool, each manager had a completely different process structure and WBS, and the dependencies were not clearly defined. One group had milestones that mattered to them, but not to QA or Docs. Docs had milestones that derived completely from QA milestones that drifted with the sands of the project. We tended to focus on delivery dates rather than on intermediate milestones in that company.

My conclusion is that effective multiple-project management depends on three key elements:

- The management culture has to support *real* project management, not just pay lip service to it.
- The project management systems must be able to *interact*.
- The ability to integrate *process* into project management systems is essential.

WBS, Schedules, and Charts

Virtually all major project management systems integrate a work breakdown structure (WBS) with the ability to represent project schedules in various forms. The dominant metaphor, which started with Time Line when it was a DOS product, is to integrate the WBS with the schedule in the form of the Gantt chart. The advantage of doing this is to see the hierarchy of tasks and the time chart relating to them in the same graphic. These systems usually show dependencies in the Gantt chart as well.

This approach has a couple of major disadvantages, however. The first one is that you cannot manipulate the schedule tasks outside the WBS. For example, say you have the defect tracking system WBS from Chapter 8. You have a major heading for each deliverable, followed by headings for processes, then headings for processes within those, then headings for groups of tasks, then tasks, and so on. If you wanted to sort these by start date, good luck. The project management software won't sort just the simple tasks (those with actual work). The software sorts in the headers as well. Usually, these are tasks with start dates too, but the dates reflect the group of tasks indented below the heading. Also, the display typically can't make the headings vanish or allow the indented tasks to move outside the heading group. When you display the schedule as a PERT chart, this leads to silly displays and layouts that try to show the hierarchy as well as the schedule tasks. This just makes the job harder.

Work Breakdown Structure (8.2)

A second major flaw in this approach is the mixing of accounting with scheduling issues. All these systems combine accounting information with schedule information. The WBS then serves as the "chart of accounts." This leads to the headings being "summary tasks," tasks with cost values that aggregate, or "roll up," values from the tasks contained within them. This leads to all kinds of nonsense with displays, decisions about when to roll up, and many other things that should not be an issue at all with a WBS and schedule.

I eagerly await an OO project management system that properly separates the information and encapsulates it. This would allow me to display the information I want to see, when I want to see it. Right now, I don't know of any tools that let me do this reliably. Of the packages in Table 22-1, only Scitor's product comes close, but not close enough. I am almost to the point where I will abandon the WBS aspect and just put schedule tasks into the project management system.

Resources, Assignments, Calendars, and Leveling

Many parts of this book refer you to resources and resource assignments. I believe managing resource assignments is critical in OO projects for two reasons. First, assigning the right resources to critical tasks is a primary risk management method for OO projects. Second, constraining schedules by resource assignment rather than by duration estimate is much more likely to result in a tight, well-planned, well-controlled project given the iteration and incrementalism of OO projects.

Given that, it can be quite difficult to use project management systems to create and manage the resource subsystem. Every package has resources, assignments, and calendars, but they all do things differently. It is primarily in resource leveling that the software gives you problems. The main reason for this is the sets of assumptions that different packages make to decide how to handle a resource assignment conflict (delay or split the task, and so on). One common assumption, for example, is that two resources working on the same task work simultaneously rather than independently. That means you can't resolve a resource conflict for one resource without involving the other resource (unnecessarily).

A secondary reason for the difficulties in resource management lies in the way project management systems manage calendars and shifts. All of these systems have much the same limitations. They have simplified time management by using very simple, single-level shifts and some kind of exception mechanism for overriding the shift. Time Line lets you associate calendars with projects and resources and has a slightly more interesting shift structure. Project Scheduler lets you, in addition, assign them to tasks. Primavera doesn't have resource calendars but does have task calendars and the ability to specify global and recurring holidays. You pays your money and takes your choice.

- *Note:* One criticism I have of all these systems is their total lack of support for time zones. You'd think in this enlightened age of internationalization that serious vendors would understand that projects happen over several time zones. You're out of luck as I was managing a project sited in California and the U.K.

Claris MacProject has an excellent feature that lets you decide how to resolve resource conflicts while leveling. As it levels, when it reaches a conflict, it prompts you to choose between several alternatives. You can also use priorities and default choices to speed things up. This almost but not quite outweighs the lack of a WBS feature in the product.

Time Line for Windows has a very sophisticated system for resolving resource conflicts. This system does an excellent job of resource leveling.

Project Scheduler lets you resolve resource conflicts in several different ways. This is probably the most flexible of the systems. It provides a resource assignment spreadsheet that lets you assign time on a minute-by-minute basis if you want to. It has a leveling tool button that finds the next resource conflict in the schedule and highlights it for you. It also has automatic leveling that is much like every other product.

- *Note:* One tip for using resource leveling. If you level, you destroy any special delays you put into the schedule. For projects that you are going to level, use the task-scheduling features to fix tasks you do not want leveled. Some systems (Project Scheduler is one) can turn off leveling for specific tasks.

Repository Management

Although there have been some client/server project management systems around for many years (PS/2, for example, which works with ORACLE), most project management systems are client applications using flat files to manage their repositories. This lack of storage sophistication has inhibited these systems in many ways. Most do versioning, for example, by copying the file; you thus must version a project, not anything within it. Also, this is the feature that has caused most of the problems with multiple-project management.

The real problems here are with multiuser access, however. Databases and repositories have transaction management, concurrency and integrity management, rollback and roll-forward recovery, object versioning, and real security. The project management systems have real problems with these things. Most rely on network operating system file managers for what little repository management they offer, though some are more sophisticated (Time Line with its built-in database support, for example).

Several systems have added support for the ODBC client/server interface middleware. This is an API that allows the system to communicate with multiple relational database products. For the most part, this works by downloading the project data into the database on demand. Some systems (Time Line, Project Scheduler 7) work with the database rather than with files. These systems show a somewhat greater sophistication in the features relating to the repository and the data structures within it, but the true advantages of client/server are still remote (that's a joke, son).

I am anxiously awaiting a client/server project management system that takes advantage of distributed object and Web browser technology to offer truly repository-based tools. These tools will allow us to integrate several tools into custom project management systems rather than being constrained by the vision of a single vendor. Multiple operating platforms, too. Nirvana!

Reporting

There are two ways to get information from a project management system. The first is to use the user interface of the tool itself to display charts, forms, and spreadsheets with the project information. The second is to generate a printed or online report with the information.

One benefit of the ODBC interfaces the last section mentioned is the ability to use standard report writers to generate reports. This ability depends on the downloaded data being sufficient to allow the reports you want. Some systems such as Microsoft Project do not download all the data, which can be annoying.

Many project management systems build in a report writer. In some cases, they integrate third-party tools (Time Line has Crystal Reports, for example). In other cases, they have their own tools (Microsoft, Scitor, Primavera, ABT, and so on, all do). I haven't seen any project management system that overwhelms me with its reporting capabilities, though most do a fair job.

There are several problems that crop up in different systems. Some systems have problems with the hierarchical WBS interfering with the report structure that you'd like to see. This is strongly related to the problems I discussed above. Other systems, such as Project Scheduler 6 (I haven't seen 7 yet) have problems with customizing built-in reports. For example, you can't save a particular configuration as a custom Gantt report, only the current settings.

I was working with a team of developers on multiple projects. I wanted Project Scheduler 6 to print a weekly report detailing, for each developer, a list of in-progress tasks for each project on which they were working ordered by start date. It proved almost impossible to get everything I wanted due to the interference of the WBS hierarchy with sorting. Also, you had to sort the data outside the report, which meant resorting it when you had finished with the report. The first release of the product was unusable because sorting the data slowed the report writer close to a complete stop. That was fixed in an update. These kinds of problems are ubiquitous in the report subsystems of all tools.

Some new technologies are starting to appear that should make reporting easier. Project Scheduler 7 advertises a Report Wizard for setting up custom reports. Microsoft Project should be getting this soon. Third-party report writers such as Crystal Reports are also making great strides in usability.

The Product Management System

The *product management system* is an information system belonging to the organizational environment. It contains systems and tools for managing the deliverable objects as products: product tracking and versioning, the customer database, failure tracking, and customer call tracking.

Vision: People using product information to get their jobs done in a project

Mission: To create and manage information about the deliverables that people need to get their jobs done productively

---

Objective 22.5:   To create and manage reusable information about deliverables that people need; see 22.1 for approaches and metrics

---

Objective 22.6:   To increase productivity of information about deliverables; see 22.2 for approach and metric

---

Figure

(Diagram: nested systems — System 1.1 / Reusable System 2.1 / Versioned System 2.3 / Tool P7.1 / Information System 22.1 containing Product Management System 22.3 with components: Track Product, Version Product, Track Customers, Track Failures, Track Requests, Get Information. Product Repository 18.2 "manages" it. Organizational Environment 33.1 "is part of". Organizational Repository 33.3 "manages".)

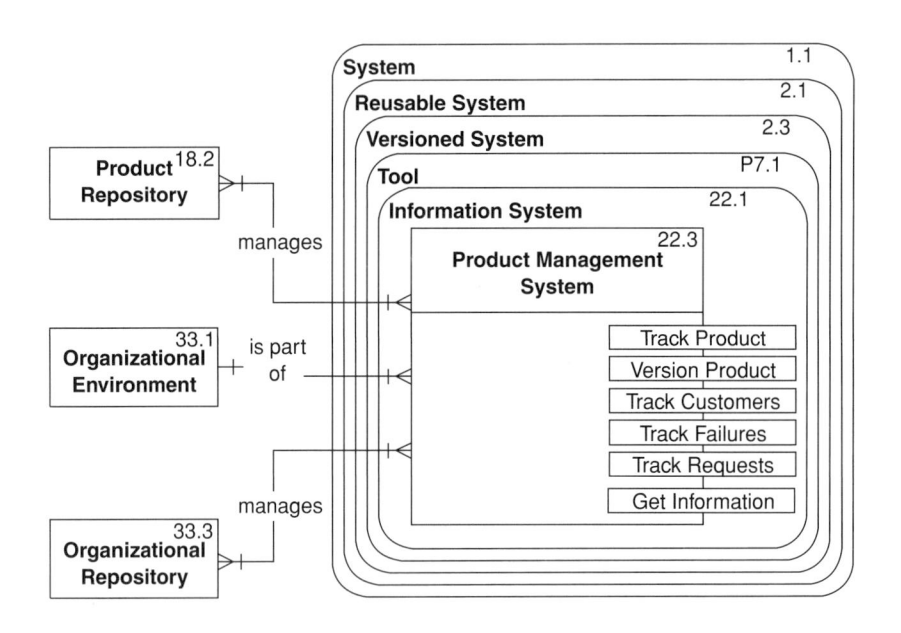

Product information systems are outside the scope of any one project, but most projects need the information they deliver. Also, these information systems are part of the overall system of tools an organization uses for communication outside the project, including team communications, reviews, briefings, negotiations, and other external relationships.

Product tracking and versioning requires more than just a configuration management system; it's really a kind of operating information system. A *product* is a collection of deliverables, often delivered by more than one project. The organization identifies it as a product through its marketing product plans. Product systems reside in the product repository, and product information resides either in the product or organizational repository, or both. Projects use the product information system in three ways. First, other information systems link to the product information in the product or organizational repository. Second, project resources sometimes need information about products to do their work on projects. Third, you may want to reuse parts of the product in a new project. For example, you may want to look at the current version of a product to develop requirements for the next version, and then take some of the parts of the product from the product repository.

Similarly, tracking customers is vital to any organization. You can use the customer system to develop stakeholder expectations by surveys or focus groups. You can link to customer information to release maintenance information to the people who need to know about it. You can analyze customer information to decide things like platform availability and porting strategies for your projects. You can choose beta release prospects and track the results of customer beta testing.

Failure and customer call tracking are customer support applications that automate the support process. As an information system, these applications can contribute directly to your ability to meet stakeholder expectations. Customer calls and failure reports are a primary source of both information about how your products fail and enhancement requests.

- *Note:* You should separate the concept of product *failure* from the concept of a *fault* [Weinberg 1992, pp.186–197]. A failure is a single occurrence of a problem (a "departure from requirements"), either to a customer or to someone internal to your organization. A fault is a defect in a product, such as a design or code flaw. Faults cause failures. By distinguishing failures from faults, you can better prioritize your fixes to faults. Some faults may never cause a failure, even though their potential is catastrophic, due to lack of use or other structural factors. Other faults, supposedly minor, may cause hundreds or thousands of failures because of their prominent location in the system. Distinguishing faults from failures lets you see how many times your product fails. By clearly identifying faults, you can use this information as input to your system improvement plans without any confusion as to occurrence or failure priorities. This also lets you identify problem areas that lead to failures not caused by faults. It lets you remove the thousands of enhancement requests from your fault system as well.

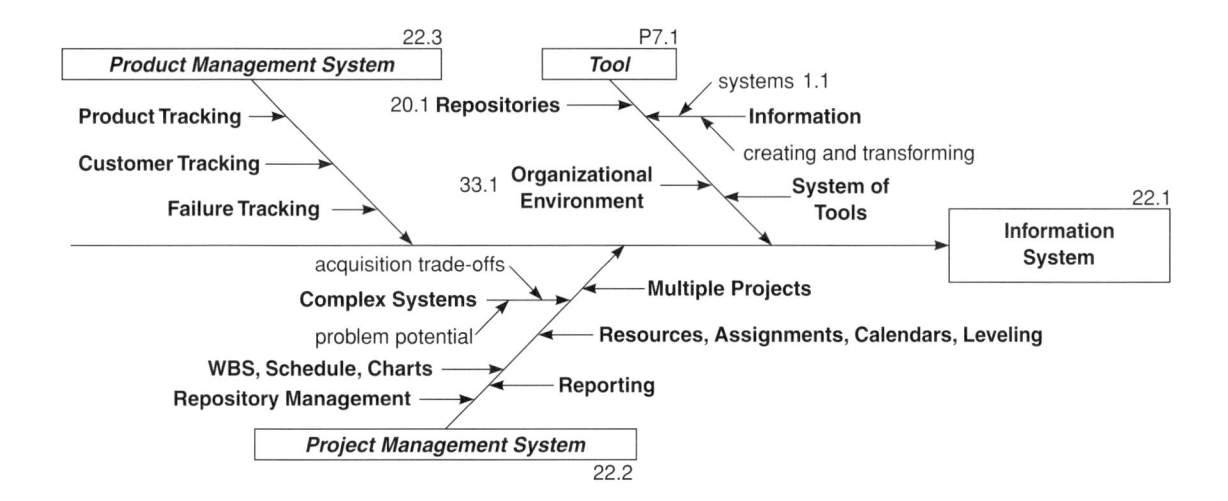

System Modeling Tool

Projects comprise systems. Many of the tasks of project management, as well as development, involve modeling those systems. The *system modeling tool* is a tool that lets you model systems in one way or another.

Vision: Project managers and system designers getting their jobs done

Mission: To provide leverage to effort in achieving system modeling tasks

Objective 22.7: To add value to a system modeling task

Approach 22.7: Acquire the tool using an evaluative procurement process that estimates the value that the tool will add to your work. Train people to use the tool. Work the use of the tool into policies and plans. Improve the impact of the tool on value through improvement plans. Maintain the tool and dispose of it when it no longer can add value to your work.

Metric 22.7: Value Added: the amount of value you generate from tasks using the tool that you could not have generated without the tool

Target 22.7: A value within control limits on an x-R control chart of similar tools from your organization or industry; the value should reflect a positive internal rate of return on investment as well

---

Objective 22.8: To improve productivity in achieving a system modeling task

Approach 22.8: Proceed as in Approach 22.7, except for focusing on productivity instead of value.

Metric 22.8: Productivity Improvement: the ratio of mean productivity (effort-hours per unit of value produced) while using the tool to productivity while not using the tool on similar system modeling tasks

Target 22.8: A value within control limits on a p control chart of similar tools from your organization or industry; the value should be materially greater than 1

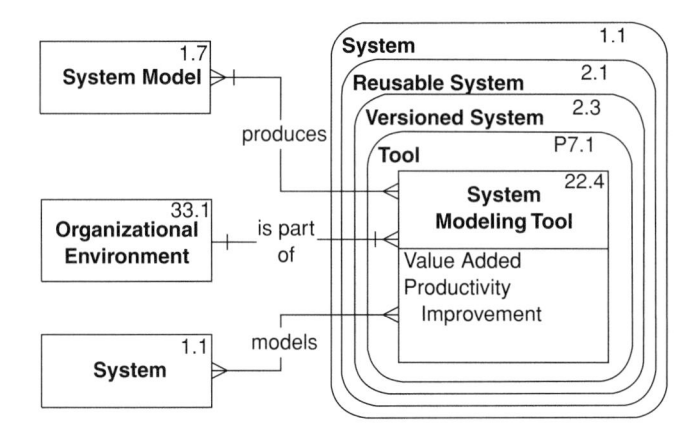

The broadest *system modeling* tools let you model any system. You can use design tools for this purpose. These tools model the systems as though you were going to build them in software. This book is an example. You can also use mathematical or system simulation tools such as GPSS or Dynamo (a language for systems dynamics models [Abdel-Hamid]). You can even use spreadsheet modeling.

There are many *process modeling* tools on the market, as the popularity of business process reengineering (BPR) waxes. Process modeling lets you model your work flows, development processes, and other elements of your business processes. You can model them as flowcharts or other process-centered notations [Garg; Khoshafian; Lewis]. You can often achieve this with CASE tools, since software also uses process modeling in analysis and design tools.

Certain project management systems have begun to integrate process modeling tools into their systems:

- Abt Technology's Methods Architect, which lets you create and maintain a development process model
- LBMS, Inc.'s Process Engineer, with Process Library, Process Manager, Project Manager, and Activity Manager modules to integrate process and project management [Heichler]
- Scitor Corporation (makers of Project Scheduler) and their Process Charter product, which is a process modeling and optimization tool linked with their project management system
- Time Line Solutions' Guide Maker and Guide Line, which let you script the creation of a project

Planning tools let you model plans through spreadsheets, graphics, work breakdown structures, schedules, action lists, checklists, and many other devices. Many planning tools come packaged as project management or decision support tools, which this book terms project information management systems. Other tools stand alone, such as risk analysis tools or calendar systems.

Project Management System (22.2)

Documentation templates help you model documents. This increases productivity through reducing the amount of work you must do to create them. Standard *word processing* or *document publishing tools* let you create and reuse document templates and styles.

Document Template (6.3)

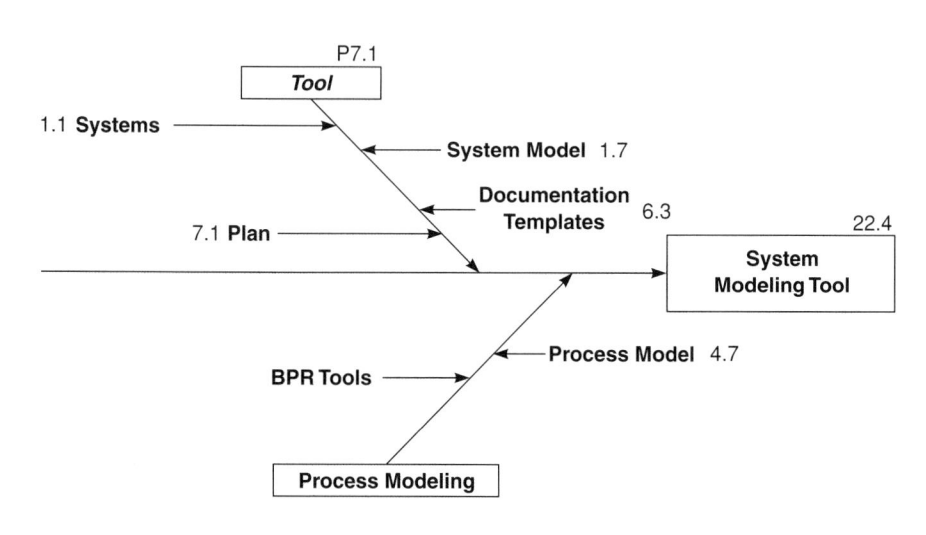

Readings

[Abdel-Hamid] Tarek Abdel-Hamid and Stuart E. Madnick. *Software Project Dynamics: An Integrated Approach.* Englewood Cliffs, NJ: Prentice Hall, 1991.

This book shows the application of Systems Dynamics, a well-known system modeling tool, to software development projects. It shows you what you can do with such tools, moving far beyond simple modeling into nonlinear systems modeling that more accurately represents project systems. While you can disagree with some of the models, the application of the tool is very suggestive.

[Feierstein] Max Feierstein and Jeannette Cabanis. The software selection project: tips from a pro. *PM Network* 10:9 (September 1996): 28–35.

This article has some excellent advice for the selection of project management systems.

[Garg] Pankaj K. Garg and Mehdi Jazayeri. *Process-Centered Software Engineering Environments.* Los Alamitos, CA: IEEE Computer Society Press, 1996.

This collection of readings from conferences on process-centered software engineering, while on the academic side, describes the current research going on in the area of process modeling. It has several interesting articles, including an excellent one on the Hewlett-Packard Softbench tool integration environment. The book does have a slight HP bias with respect to tools.

[PMI 1996b] Project Management Institute. 1996 project management software survey. *PM Network* 10:9 (September 1996): 29–42.

This is the annual project management software survey issue of *PM Network*. The survey contains responses from all the major and many of the minor project management system vendors. Anyone interested in project management should get a copy to keep abreast of what's available. While the features surveyed are basic, it provides an excellent screen for your first-pass selection process. *PM Network* also has a monthly software column that is worth following.

[Thamhain] Hans J. Thamhain. Best practices for controlling technology-based projects. *Project Management Journal* 27:4 (December 1996): 37–47.

This is an excellent article on the tools and methods available for technology project management. In particular, there are excellent sections on why tools fail and what you can do to help your people successfully use project management tools.

Questions to Think About

1. Who maintains your information systems? Is there an IS department or function of some kind in your organization? What are the key elements of the trade-off between acquiring and maintaining these tools yourself and letting IS people do it?

2. Would you rather have a simple project management system that lets you do basic tracking or a complex one that gives you many different features to help plan and manage projects? How would you go about acquiring and sharing each type of tool differently?

3. How important to you is the ability for a project management system to manage multiple projects? How satisfied are you in this regard with the capabilities of your current project management system?

4. Would you benefit from a project management system that had much more extensive resource management features such as organization charting, skills management, and extensive resource availability and cost modeling?

5. Do you distinguish failures from faults in your product management system? If not, what are the consequences?

6. List five different system modeling tools you use. (Hint: Look at the different subclasses of the System Model class.) If you can't, why not? Do you avoid system modeling, or do you just not use tools to do it?

PART EIGHT

Change

Never let the future disturb you. You will meet it, if you have to, with the same weapons of reason which today arm you against the present.

Marcus Aurelius, *Meditations,* 7:8

The weapons of reason for a project are, as always, systems: the change management systems that plan for and manage change. This part discusses change management in general and configuration management in particular. The change management plan lets you plan the processes you need to incorporate changes into your systems. The configuration management plan, a subclass of change management plan, is specific to software: it lets you control changes to software baselines and helps you to configure software releases.

The change management process and its accompanying process model are the major feedback mechanisms in your project. This set of processes, which you set in motion through change requests and baselines in the change management system, let you incorporate changes due to both internal and external forces. The change report lets you track what changes.

The configuration management process and its model are specific to software baselines. The configuration management system provides a rich set of tools, including source control and build tools, that help you to control change and manage baselines. The build report lets you track the results of product baseline builds.

The baseline is the key to all this management. A *baseline* is a particular set of versions of systems that satisfy a set of exit criteria. Document baselines are collections of documents, such as requirements or design documents. Cluster baselines configure clusters, generally before they become part of a product baseline. The latter is a baseline of a software system, capable of delivering value to stakeholders. You use baselines in many different ways to stabilize the systems in your project.

There are several different kinds of product baseline. The prototype baseline is a working system that is not yet ready to deliver to customers. Alpha, field, and beta baselines are prototypes for system and acceptance testing. After such testing, you get a production baseline, the actual working software product that you deliver to customers.

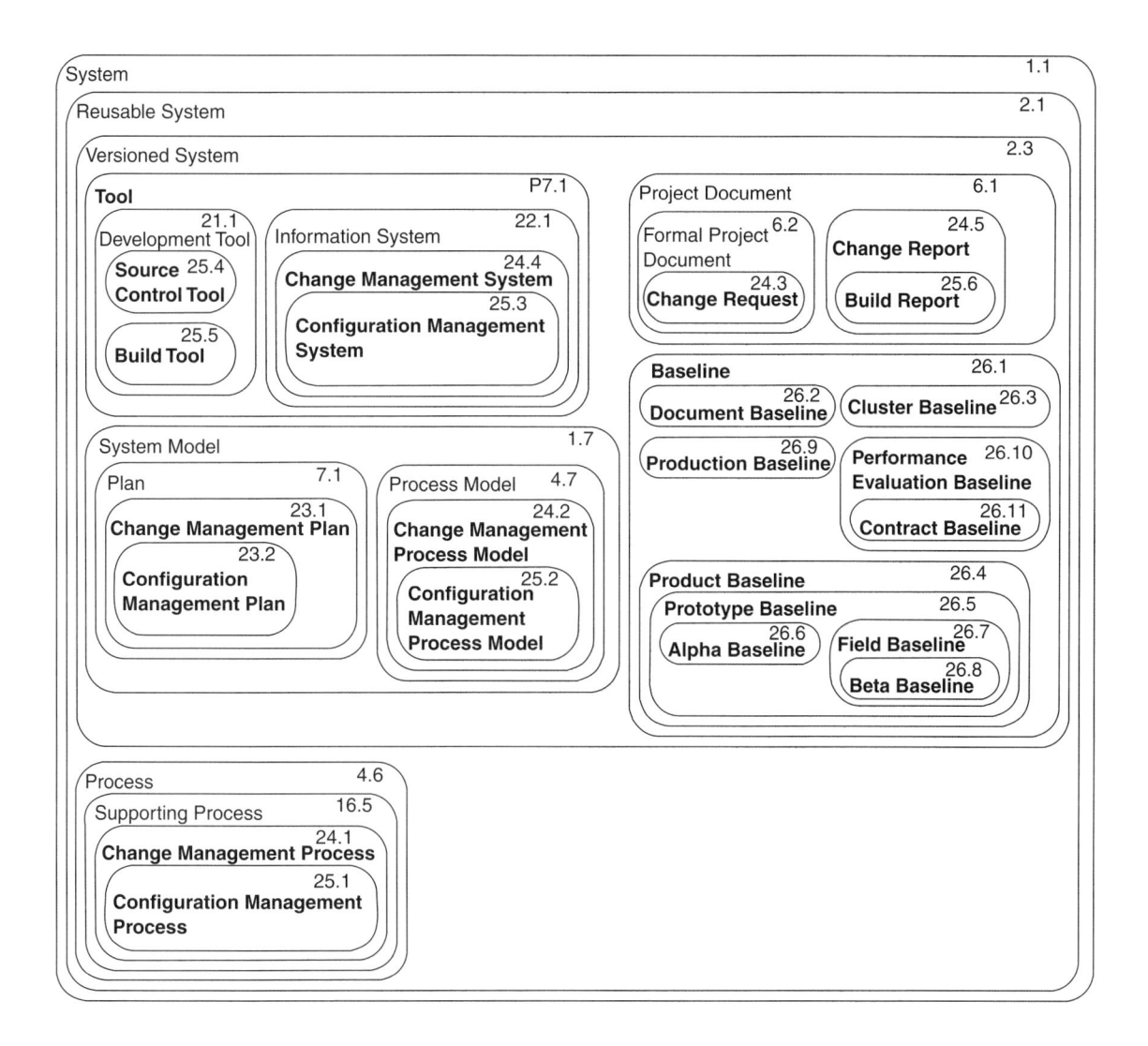

```
┌─System─────────────────────────────────────────────────── 1.1 ─┐
│ ┌─Reusable System───────────────────────────────────── 2.1 ─┐ │
│ │ ┌─Versioned System────────────────────────────── 2.3 ─┐ │ │
│ │ │ ┌─Tool──────────────────────────── P7.1 ┐ ┌─Project Document──────────── 6.1 ┐ │ │ │
│ │ │ │  **Tool**                               │ │  **Project Document**              │ │ │ │
│ │ │ │  21.1                                   │ │  Formal Project  6.2   24.5        │ │ │ │
│ │ │ │  Development Tool    22.1               │ │  Document       Change Report      │ │ │ │
│ │ │ │  ┌──────────┐  Information System       │ │         24.3           25.6        │ │ │ │
│ │ │ │  │ Source 25.4│      24.4               │ │  Change Request   Build Report     │ │ │ │
│ │ │ │  │ Control Tool│ Change Management System│ │                                    │ │ │ │
│ │ │ │  └──────────┘       25.3                │ └────────────────────────────────────┘ │ │ │
│ │ │ │  ┌──────────┐  Configuration Management │ ┌─Baseline─────────────────── 26.1 ┐ │ │ │
│ │ │ │  │ 25.5     │  System                   │ │  **Baseline**   26.2      26.3    │ │ │ │
│ │ │ │  │ Build Tool│                          │ │  Document Baseline  Cluster Baseline│ │ │ │
│ │ │ │  └──────────┘                           │ │         26.9         26.10         │ │ │ │
│ │ │ └─────────────────────────────────────────┘ │  Production Baseline  Performance   │ │ │ │
│ │ │                                              │                       Evaluation Baseline│ │ │
│ │ │                                              │                          26.11      │ │ │ │
│ │ │                                              │                    Contract Baseline│ │ │ │
│ │ │ ┌─System Model────────────────── 1.7 ┐      └─────────────────────────────────────┘ │ │ │
│ │ │ │ Plan            7.1                 │      ┌─Product Baseline─────────── 26.4 ┐ │ │ │
│ │ │ │       23.1    Process Model  4.7    │      │  **Product Baseline**              │ │ │ │
│ │ │ │ Change Management   24.2            │      │  Prototype Baseline  26.5          │ │ │ │
│ │ │ │ Plan            Change Management   │      │        26.6        Field Baseline 26.7│ │ │
│ │ │ │       23.2     Process Model        │      │  Alpha Baseline                    │ │ │ │
│ │ │ │ Configuration       25.2            │      │                      26.8          │ │ │ │
│ │ │ │ Management      Configuration       │      │                   Beta Baseline    │ │ │ │
│ │ │ │ Plan            Management          │      └─────────────────────────────────────┘ │ │ │
│ │ │ │                 Process Model       │                                              │ │ │
│ │ │ └─────────────────────────────────────┘                                              │ │ │
│ │ └───────────────────────────────────────────────────────────────────────────────────┘ │ │
│ │ ┌─Process────────────────────────── 4.6 ┐                                              │ │
│ │ │ Supporting Process        16.5          │                                              │ │
│ │ │               24.1                      │                                              │ │
│ │ │ **Change Management Process**           │                                              │ │
│ │ │               25.1                      │                                              │ │
│ │ │ **Configuration Management**            │                                              │ │
│ │ │ **Process**                             │                                              │ │
│ │ └─────────────────────────────────────────┘                                              │ │
│ └───────────────────────────────────────────────────────────────────────────────────────┘ │
└───────────────────────────────────────────────────────────────────────────────────────────┘
```

Finally, the performance evaluation baseline is one you take to enable measurement of project progress, such as schedule or budget baselines. The special case of the contract baseline lets you evaluate a contractor's progress in his or her contribution to the project, making the baseline a part of the legalities of the contract.

The combination of baselines and change management lets you incorporate feedback and change into your project in a stable, forward-looking way. Using change management, your project stays on track for delivery of value to stakeholders.

- *Note:* The illustration of the class hierarchy contains all the classes this part defines. Other parts of the book define and discuss classes not in boldface.

CHAPTER

23 *Change Management Plan*

The Change Management Plan

The *change management plan* is a plan that describes how a change management process handles changes to a system. It documents the process model and the policies that apply to controlling changes. It generates the change management process from its model to specify any tasks, dependencies, and milestones relating to changes. These tasks can include process changes, document changes, schedule changes, and changes to software and test objects. The plan also specifies the baselines for process milestones in your schedule.

Vision: A change management process brought to a successful conclusion, achieving its mission by controlling change to project systems

Mission: To bring the change management process model for a system to bear on successfully achieving the system mission

Objective 23.1: To translate a change management process model into a set of tasks that control change through a change management process

Approach 23.1: Generate a plan from the change management process model, laying out the tasks, milestones, and dependencies of the process in the required amount of detail. Specify any baselines for the process milestones in the project schedule. Proceed with Approach 7.1 as for any plan.

Metric 23.1: See Metric 7.1

The Change Management Plan 381

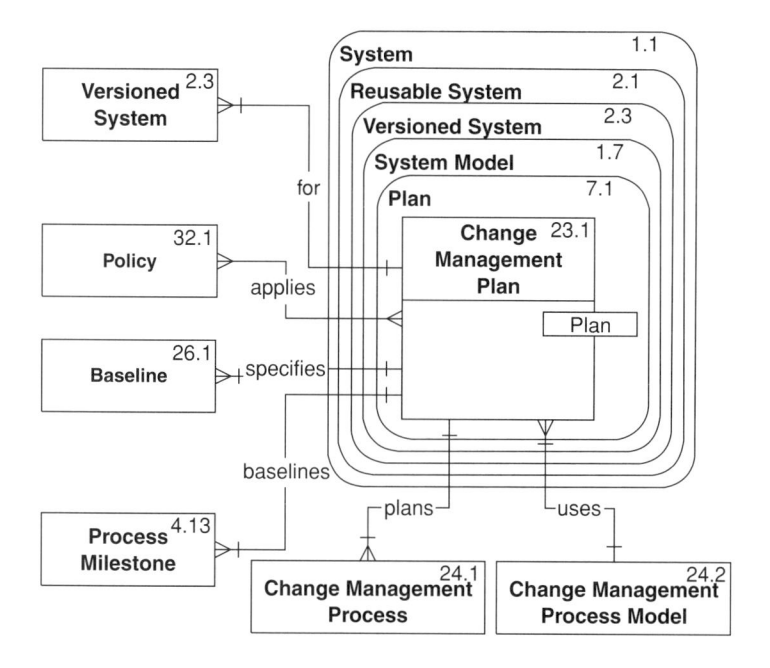

Change management policies address the following issues:

- The version and baseline *identification* schemes

■ *Note:* The version number should be as simple as possible. Avoid overloading this identifier with attributes of the system. This practice, while it may help you to understand the context of a system from its identifier, leads to much complexity in change and repository management. A simple, numeric scheme of increasing integers is really the best approach for both version and baseline identification.

- *Concurrency:* how to control concurrent updating of objects by multiple resources; a check-in/check-out protocol, for example
- Where and when, and with what approvals, to *baseline* the systems in the appropriate repository, specifying the process milestones that result in baselines of varying sorts, including builds
- Where, when, and how to process *change requests* and the resulting changes
- Where, when, and how to produce *change* or *build reports*
- The record keeping you need to do to build an *audit trail* for versions and baselines

- *Security,* access, and classification of systems for sensitive projects; this includes projects that are sensitive for competitive or political reasons as well as national security issues
- Any special issues for *contract baselines* (baselines that are legally binding parts of a contract with a supplier for your project)
- The *tools,* techniques, and methods to use in change management

As you build the project plan, you create a change management plan for each major versioned system that will experience change over its project life cycle. You choose the baseline to suit the particular kind of system (cluster, software system, document, and so on). If you have different models for change management, you can use the different process models to impose different styles of change management on the system.

Planning means generating the tasks, milestones, and deliverables that implement the change management process where the plan requires it. To do this, you must identify the points in the project where change management applies—which baselines at which milestones have what kind of change control. For each of these points, you install a change management process by generating the process in the WBS and schedule through the change management process model. You then adapt any specific process to its situation by adding or removing tasks, milestones, or dependencies. You then assign the appropriate resources to the schedule tasks and level them.

Change Management Process Model (24.2)

The change management plan must also specify an improvement plan to reduce the number and impact of changes to the system. By using a Pareto chart of the number or impact of changes versus the changing systems, you can identify the systems that change more than any other. Focusing on these systems, you can improve your project or process model's capabilities for dealing with change over time.

A change management plan can accompany the reusable system for which it plans. You can also reuse a basic change management plan up to the point where it becomes specific to the individual system (domain reuse limitations). Depending on your versioning scheme, you may need to distribute your reusable systems with their change management plans. For example, if you have systems in your reuse repository with different versioning or baselining systems, you need to have the change management plan there to describe the policies and techniques that the system uses. You will also need to supply any needed tools for accessing the different versions, since some tools store the versions in different storage formats.

Planning for change is not a critical element in a simple project: you just do it. If, on the other hand, you want to do it better, the plan is the primary mechanism through which you can improve your response to change. Without the plan and its accompanying policies and process models, you don't have a hope of improving. As change becomes rampant in the OO arena, you will find the ability to improve essential to being competitive.

The Configuration Management Plan

A *configuration management plan* (CMP) is a change management plan for clusters and software systems. While a change management plan sets up your project for controlling changes, the CMP also helps you to specify your deliverables. Your product depends on containing the right versions of the right software systems, and your CMP assures that this happens.

Vision: Software systems that have the right components at the right time in the right place

Mission: To assure that the configuration of software in the project deliverables is correct at all times

---

Objective 23.2: To specify the process of configuring the set of systems comprising a cluster or software system

---

Approach 23.2: Generate a plan from the configuration management process model. Specify the configuration management methods and tools to use in software development tasks. Proceed with Approach 23.1 as for any change management plan.

Metric 23.2: See Metric 23.1

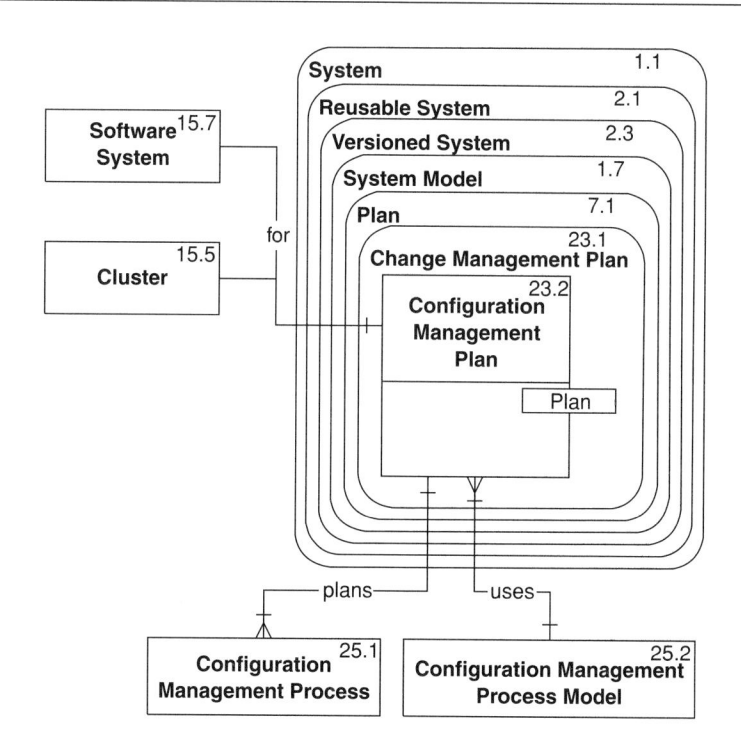

One CMP describes the policies for each software system or cluster. You can have a separate plan for some or all clusters within a system if you choose to have different processes or policies apply to that cluster. You can also reuse the plan for other systems, customizing it as needed. It seldom makes sense to micromanage below the cluster level (classes). It is usually a good idea to stay at the system level in the CMP to keep the complexity at a manageable level, or at least to use one basic set of policies through a reused plan.

There is a specific product baseline for the CMP called a *release*. The CMP identifies the specific releases (alpha, field, beta, production, for example) and their identification scheme. A good choice is a sequential integer scheme. Unless you have strong reasons for additional complexity, a simple name-and-number scheme easily and simply identifies a baseline. The plan also identifies the specific tasks required to produce and deliver the release baseline.

Product Baseline (26.4)

The CMP must take into account the nature of the input baseline. You hardly ever start from scratch in OO projects. If you're not using a reuse repository baseline, you're reusing a previous version of the software system. This baseline may come from a different project or from the reuse repository and hence may have a different configuration management process from that of the current project. The plan must contain policies for updating shared reuse libraries with changes, additions, and fixes.

Baseline (26.1)

The CMP also must contain policies for managing software failures and fault fixes, including approval, verification, and notification policies. Verification is particularly important for fixes, because fixes often generate additional failures due to faults introduced with the fix.

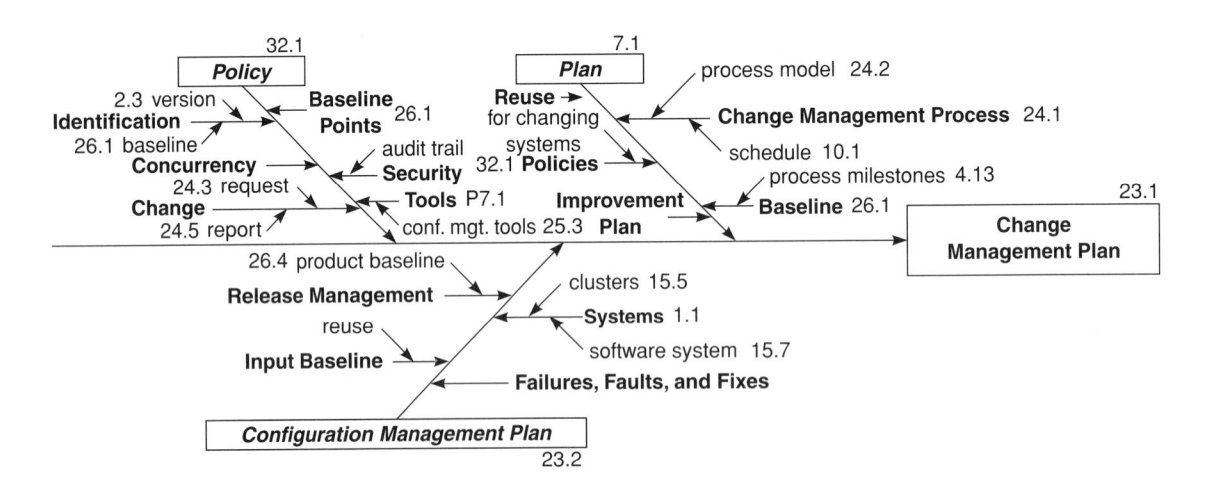

I worked with an excruciatingly bad bug-tracking system on one project that failed to link releases and faults in any useful way. For example, when a developer submitted a fix, he or she would identify the baseline into which the fix was included. But the baseline organization was such that there were multiple paths branched out to several developers. The release, however, assumed that all these merged into a single prototype baseline. Bad assumption, as we gathered about three-quarters of the way through the project when things started breaking. It became almost impossible to figure out which version of which cluster was addressing which fault. The same project had problems with regression testing technology. We had planned to integrate a whizzy new GUI testing tool into our product testing cycle at alpha release. Unfortunately, the vendor failed to supply a version that worked on all the target platforms. As a result, we had to change the plan to accommodate manual testing of the fixes (several hundred of them). The Silver Bullet had missed.

Readings

[Bennatan] E. M. Bennatan. *On Time, Within Budget: Software Project Management Practices and Techniques.* New York: QED Publishing Group, 1992.

This book has a very nice section on the configuration or change management plan (pp. 98–102).

[PMI 1996a] Project Management Institute Standards Committee. *A Guide to the Project Management Body of Knowledge.* Project Management Institute (+1-610-734-3330), 1996.

Although the PMBOK does not define a specific change management plan, it does identify management plans that describe management and the integration of changes into the project (4.3, Overall Change Control, lists the various control tasks, each of which refers to a management plan such as the scope management plan or the cost management plan). Because change is so central to software projects, I have integrated these disparate plans into a single change management plan class. The PMBOK also discusses configuration management briefly (4.3.2.2).

Questions to Think About

1. List five systems outside of the software hierarchy that might benefit from change control. Why do you think most of the literature on change management is based on *software* change management?

2. How do you include change management in your current project plans? How will this change given the recommendations in this chapter?

3. Is it necessary to have a single set of change management policies that applies to all versioned systems? Why or why not?

4. If you reuse a versioned system from the reuse repository and adapt it by changing it, what systems must you modify? (Hint: Your project is not the only place where baselines exist.)

5. How does the release process interact with the change management process in your plans? If you didn't need to manage software releases, how would your change management and CMPs change?

CHAPTER

Change Management 24

The Change Management Process

The *change management process* is a supporting process that coordinates the impact of change for a baselined versioned system. Based on one or more approved change requests, the change management process tasks keep the system on track toward achieving its objectives. It thus serves as the primary route for feedback in the project. The process also uses change reports to keep itself on track, gathering feedback on change status as the process works toward its milestone. The change management system, an information system, automates the change management process.

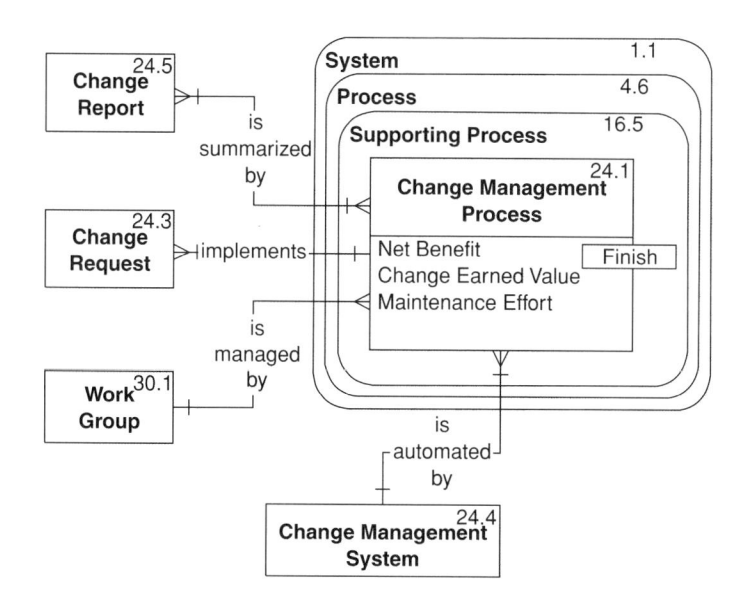

387

Vision: A process that ensures delivery of planned value despite change to a system

Mission: To ensure that the impact of change on a system affects delivery of value in a positive way

Objective 24.1: To determine whether a change is beneficial to the system

Approach 24.1: Convene a change control team for the system to consider change requests. Evaluate the impact of the change on the system and on other systems. Consider the costs and benefits (return on investment or other metrics) to determine whether the change is beneficial to the project. If it is, approve the change; if not, reject the change or defer it to a later time.

Metric 24.1: Net benefit: the benefit from an approved change in value units; this could be the result of a cost-benefit trade-off analysis or of a return-on-investment analysis

Target 24.1: A value within control limits of an x-R control chart for the process

Objective 24.2: To coordinate changes with other systems that must respond to the change, closing the loop with those systems as a transaction

Approach 24.2: Convene a change control team for the system to coordinate change requests. Evaluate these requests for their impact on the different parts of the project system. Plan the appropriate processes and tasks needed to implement the change, integrating the tasks and any milestones or dependencies into the project plan. Add a milestone to the schedule to represent the completion of the change. Monitor the execution of the plan to close the loop on the change. Close the change request when the project reaches the milestone.

Metric 24.2: Change earned value: the earned value from planned changes, where you earn value when you reach the change completion milestone

Target 24.2: An earned value close to planned value within control limits on an x-R control chart of earned-value points

Objective 24.3: To integrate feedback from the environment, and especially the stakeholders, into the system without overloading the system's ability to operate and respond to change

Approach 24.3: Actively gather project data that helps you evaluate the progress of the system, such as progress and problem reports. Include stakeholders in this data gathering through a change request process. Use that information to evaluate

The Change Management Process

the system, and then correct the system's operations based on your evaluation. Integrate corrections with improvement plans where possible to optimize the use of the feedback. In particular, identify high-maintenance systems and improve them using Pareto analysis and control charts.

Metric 24.3: Maintenance effort: the amount of effort you are expending on changing the system that you would otherwise spend on other tasks

Target 24.3: An amount of effort within control limits of an x-R chart of this and similar systems, both from your organization and from other organizations in your industry

---

A special work group or team, the *change control team*, works on the tasks in the change management process. The change control team has the authority to approve or reject change requests. There can be one change control team for a whole project, or you can assign teams as necessary to specific change management processes or groups of such processes. The former approach lets you consolidate change management in a single team, leading to efficiencies and inefficiencies of scale. The team can acquire a global knowledge of the project. It can thus better evaluate costs and benefits and coordination requirements. Change can inundate a single team, however, in a volatile project. For such projects, multiple change control teams can handle the incoming changes, distributing the load. On the other hand, the more teams you have, the more change requires coordination and communication. In either case, the team should represent the major stakeholders interested in the systems under change control.

I worked for a company with an implicit change control process built around bug management. The single change control team was huge, often with 15 or more people in two international locations meeting once a week. Authority resided not in the team but in the quality assurance manager who led the meeting, and even she did not have final authority to approve or reject changes. Everything was negotiable. Because the products the team managed were not well engineered, every week saw dozens, if not hundreds, of additional items, particularly during the release cycle for a product. The combination of a large number of team members and a large number of small change requests led to huge inefficiencies. Twelve people on two continents could sit for two hours without hearing anything that required their input. Most of the changes were not controversial and were either referred to development for minor fixes or deferred, since development had no time for major fixes unless the problem was bad enough.

- *Note:* One suggestion for the situation where you have many changes for one team: have the team deal only with controversial changes, changes that two or more stakeholders disagree over. Team meetings can then deal with these, not with the trivial or automatically acceptable changes, which individual team members can handle.

On a smaller OO project, change management was more informal, with change requests being verbal and the change management system and change control team being the project manager. Because the project was small, one person could keep track of everything going on. It helped that the developers on the project were all experienced and knowledgeable, producing excellent designs and code. Changes generally reflected the occasional fault, stakeholder suggestions, or competitive opportunities.

Change management in a project is the quality pulse of the different project systems. If those systems are out of control, you will find change management out of control or nearly so. If those systems are well understood and in control, change management will be trivial.

- *Note:* There are many more changes in a project than those you have under change management. Because of the iterative and incremental nature of OO projects, change is omnipresent. Everything changes all the time. Not every change needs a change request, review and approval by a change control team, or a change management process. Rolling-wave planning, scheduling, and budgeting, for example, are outside the change management process. If such change results in some kind of material scope change, on the other hand, you should go through a change request and change management process. Rolling change specifies a system in greater detail within normal planning processes. Baseline change creates completely new systems and changes baselines outside of normal processes.

The change management process instigated by a change request, progress report, or problem report results in feedback about the system. This feedback lets you manage the scope and system changes. Evaluating the change request lets you identify the additional systems that the change affects, and the change process then can coordinate the changes to the different systems. This prevents rework. If you don't coordinate changes, a changed system can affect the operation of other, dependent systems, requiring additional, unplanned work.

Coordinated systems can include systems from the statement of work, schedule, budget, quality plan, or risk management plan. You may also have to coordinate changes through contracts with third-party suppliers; this usually involves transmitting the change request to the contractor and tracking it through a contract administration process.

Contract Administration Process (28.1)

A change management process finishes in a milestone indicating successful changes in all the affected systems. A technical review or test suite execution at this milestone lets you close the feedback loop, evaluating the success or failure of the change. Often, this technical review involves a new baseline of the underlying systems and the appropriate review or testing of the baseline at the baseline milestone. A baseline can involve several different changes you make as a group, simplifying the evaluation and feedback of the system. The change management report displays the status of such changes.

A change management process also must handle two exceptional situations: emergencies and unauthorized changes.

An *emergency change* requires immediate action outside the usual policy-driven change management process. You might need an emergency change, for example, if a software failure has shut down a major stakeholder process of some kind. Another example might be a system that is incapable of delivering a product with a critical delivery schedule. A third example might be a sudden change in resource availability due to family emergency, incapacity, or other resource problems. The most important aspect of emergency changes is the review process. When the emergency is over and the dust has settled, a change control team must review the change. If the change requires further work, either to fix additional problems or to coordinate the change with other systems, the team approves a new change management process for the additional work. The team can also back out the change if necessary. To do all this, any change to the system, emergency or not, must result in an audit trail and an ability to reconstruct the initial state of the system (transaction management). Thus, all changes must go through the change management system, regardless of emergency status.

Change Management System (24.4)

- *Note:* If you've set up your configuration of change control teams optimally, the bureaucracy involved in getting a change through should be minimal. Under these circumstances, you should have very few "emergency" changes going through. Emergencies happen, but handling emergencies need not abandon all process if the process is set up right.

An *unauthorized change* results in new systems or baselines without change control team approval. The team must review all such changes, punish the innocent and reward the guilty, and decide whether to roll the changed system back to its original condition. Unfortunately, these changes are the most likely to be done late at night by people who don't use change management systems on principle. Therefore, it is unlikely that the standard transaction management solutions from the change management system will save your bacon. This is yet another reason to back up your baseline systems. The backup can serve as a recovery point for unauthorized changes that circumvented standard change management.

Baseline (26.1)

- *Note:* Backing up a baseline requires a bit more than just standard file backup. You must record the fact that a particular backup contains a particular baseline somewhere to be able to recover the baseline by restoring the appropriate files from the backup storage.

The Change Management Process Model

The *change management process model* represents the structure of the change management process. It contains the set of tasks and work flows that transforms a group of one or more change requests into a new version of the target systems. A set of policies determines how to apply the change management process model to change requests. These policies specify the details of request approval authority and the consequent process generation from the model. All this happens as part of change management planning.

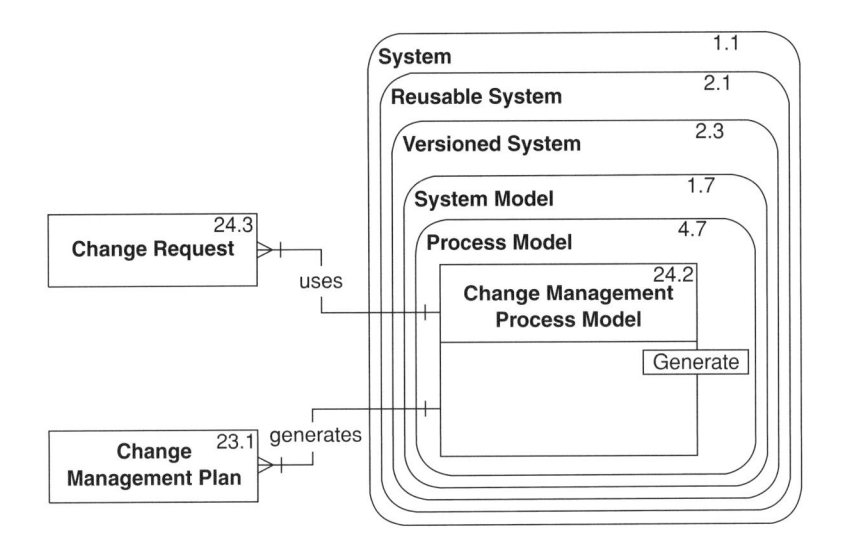

Vision: A valuable, reusable, productive change management process you productively plan from a continuously improving model

Mission: To represent a productive change management process that you want to reuse many times

---

Objective 24.4: To represent the change management process to allow planning with optimal productivity

---

Approach 24.4: Model the standard change management process. Determine what kind of approval is necessary to generating a change process. Identify the specific tasks, work flows for those tasks, and potential risks of failure. Subclass the model for different kinds of versioned systems that you may want to change under change control.

The change management model is abstract. A model for a particular kind of system might specify the exact things you need to do to implement transaction management, such as check-in and check-out procedures, timestamping, or other methods of ensuring recovery and traceability. It can also specify risks usual to the type of change or system involved, such as schedule risk or tool risk. The model must specify the exit criteria for the baseline resulting in the change process milestone, such as a completed regression test for the cluster or a review of scope changes.

Configuration Management Process Model (25.2)

The Change Request

The *change request* is a formal project document that contains a request to change one or more versioned systems in a baseline. The change request is an input into the planning task of a change management plan. When a change control team approves a change request, the planning process sets up a change management process for the requested changes, and the process implements the change.

Vision: A clearly defined, beneficial change in a project system

Mission: To define a beneficial change in a project system

Objective 24.5: To define a change

Approach 24.5: Create a standard document template for change requests. The format should contain sections to identify the systems in a baseline to change, the proposed changes, the reasons for the changes, supporting systems such as cost and schedule estimates and potential resource assignments, and the standard document information (version, names, dates, and so on). There should be a separate approval for content review. A stakeholder submits a change request to the project manager or other designated resource, who assigns the request to a change control team. That team assigns one or more reviewers for the content review, who then review the document and approve or reject its contents as technically adequate or inadequate.

Metric 24.5: Adequacy: a subjective rating on an ordinal scale, with values Worthless, Needs Work, Good, Excellent

Target 24.5: Good to Excellent

Objective 24.6: To propose a beneficial change

Approach 24.6: The change control team reviews technically adequate change requests for costs and benefits, either as a team or by assigning one or more resources to the task. The cost-benefit analysis becomes part of the document, showing the potential of the change to contribute value to the project. This review must include a review of cost estimates, schedule impact, and any other planning issues. When the review is complete, the team should either approve the request or reject it as impractical or of insufficient value to the project. Optionally, you can defer this decision to a later time.

Metric 24.6: Approval: Accept, Reject, or Defer

Target 24.6: Accept, with the ratio of approved to total requests within control limits on a p control chart of reviewed requests

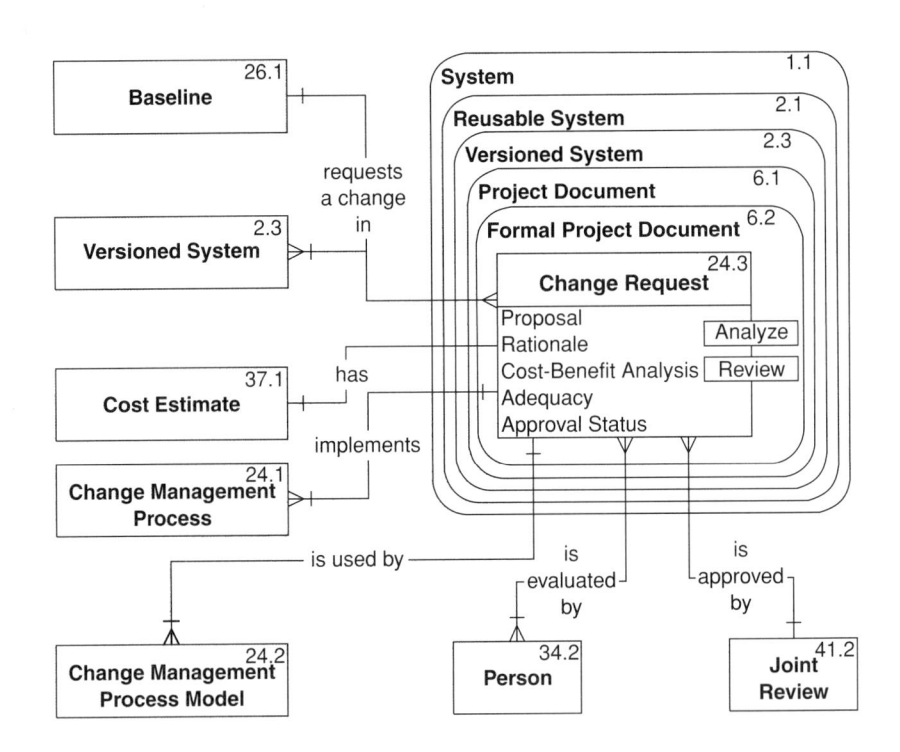

Change requests usually address external requirements such as stakeholder expectations, not internal changes. However, for complex or very large projects, it may make sense to have a change request form for internal changes to designs, codes, or tests as a means of controlling such changes. Also, most change requests are for changes in deliverable systems, not internal systems within the project, but change is change. If you need to control changes to internal systems, put the changes under change control and plan them.

Two specific kinds of requirements-driven or scope change request that apply to software systems are the enhancement request and the fault fix request. Scope changes are changes that affect the statement of work and its work breakdown structure. Other kinds of change request may not relate to requirements or scope at all but to other aspects of the system the request wants to change.

The *enhancement request* identifies one or more failures of the system to address requirements that are not a part of the current project's requirements and proposes a system change to address those requirements. An enhancement request adds value to the system you are delivering.

The *fault fix request* identifies one or more failures of a cluster or software system to function according to requirements, provides a root-cause analysis of the source of the failures, and proposes software changes to address these root causes. A fault fix request fixes a problem in the system you are delivering.

Other kinds of change requests are usually informal, particularly in smaller projects. You can localize such informal change within a project by delegating change authority down to the system. Local managers or teams can then make the change as long as it doesn't affect anyone else. However, in large or complex projects, even changes such as reassigning resources or rescheduling tasks may require formal change requests and approval, depending on the consequences or coordination needs.

The Change Management System

The *change management system* is an information system that manages the information that change management processes require and produce. Where the change management system versions systems under its control, the versions reside in the repository where the system resides. The system stores information it produces in the project repository.

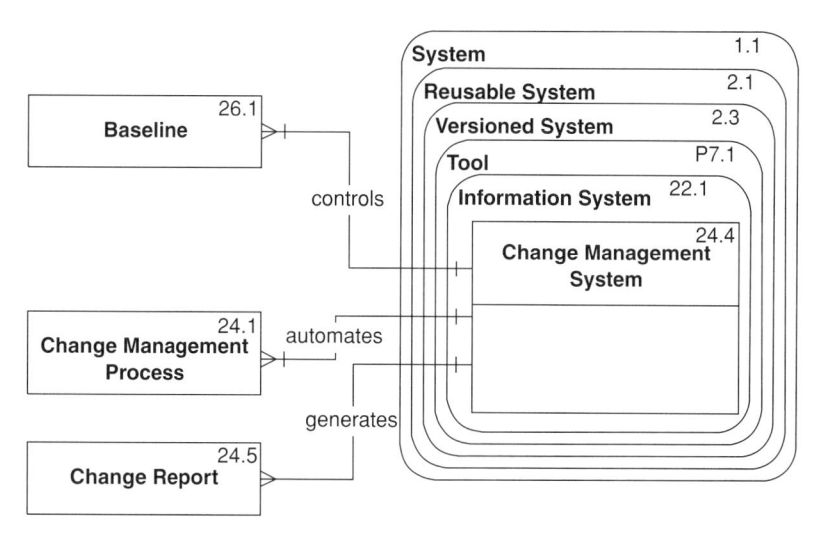

Vision: People using information about change to get their jobs done

Mission: To create and manage information about change that enables people to accommodate change in ways beneficial to the system

Change management systems must support several specific tasks:

- Automation of the change management process, including groupware and work-flow tools that support change requests, reviews, and approvals, including emergency situations
- Transaction management of changes, including checking systems in and out of their repositories and maintenance of version histories capable of restoring the system to a prior state or providing information useful in debugging and resolving problems that arise in changed systems [Evans, p. 38]
- Baselining systems
- Change management process and baseline system audit trail generation that permits auditing of change authorization and tracing of changes to change requests
- System progress reporting, including the status of planned changes to systems

I assume full automation here because this kind of thing is what the computer does best. You can do all this with paper files, but why waste the trees? Even a single PC server with a simple repository database can handle simple change management needs for a small project, and there are many tools you can use to add specific capabilities, such as TP monitors, groupware and work-flow tools [Khoshafian; Lewis], project management tools, and report writers. I have been unable to discover any general change management tools, but there are many tools in the software configuration management arena.

I highly recommend that you have some kind of work-flow software in place that automatically handles the flow of change requests. You should make it as easy as possible for stakeholders to feed information back into the system. Having a work-flow system in place will not only help them to enter information in a timely manner, it will make sure the information gets to the right change control team and that the results have an appropriate impact on the system.

Configuration Management System (25.3)

Information System (22.1)

The Change Report

The *change report* is a project document that describes the status of changes managed by a change control team during a specific period.

The Change Report

Vision: A set of changes contributing value to the project

Mission: To deliver timely feedback to the change control team and other stakeholders on the status of changes to enable the team to manage the changes to completion

Objective 24.7: To report the status of changes during a report period

Approach 24.7: Set the report period, usually a week. For each change under active planning during the report period, report the status of the change and the planning information for the future, if any. Distribute the report to the members of the change control team. The team should review the report, either individually or in a joint review, and should raise any issues suggested by the status feedback and take action on those issues, closing the planning-doing loop.

Metric 24.7: Timeliness: whether the report provides timely feedback that the change control team can use effectively to manage changes to completion; values Timely, Untimely

Target 24.7: Timely

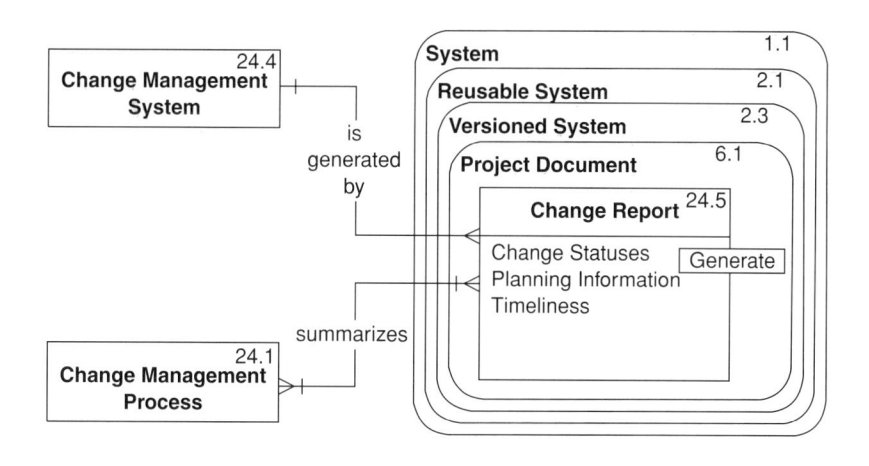

The report should list outstanding change requests and the changes that have occurred during the period. It can also list rejected reports and the reasons for their rejection for the information of all team members or other stakeholders.

- *Note:* This report is a good place to report data useful to improvement plans for change management.

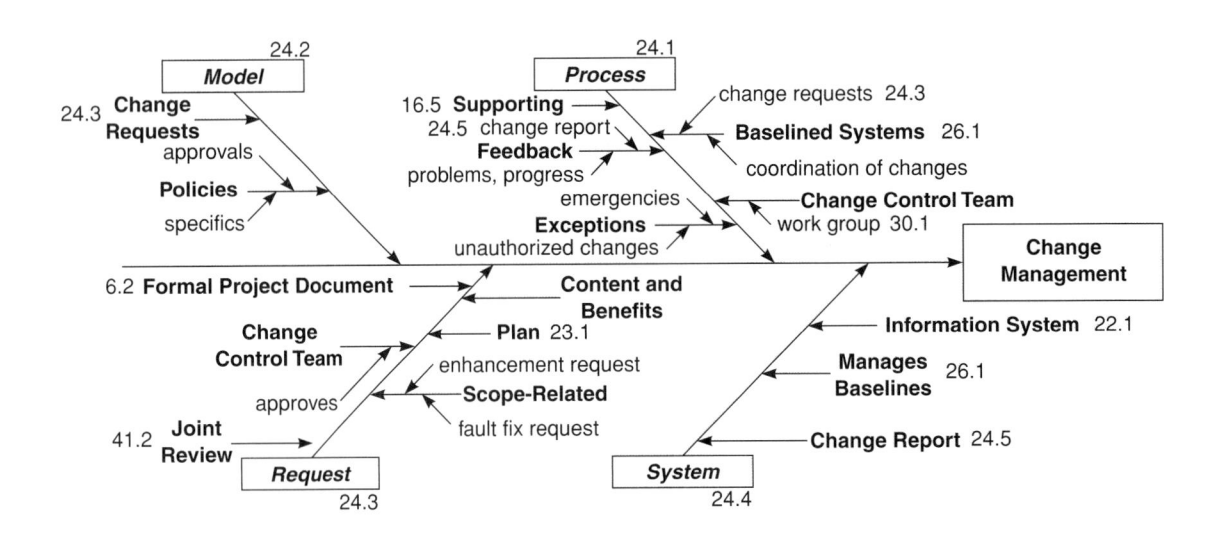

```
                        24.2                          24.1
                       Model                         Process         change requests 24.3
          24.3   Change              16.5 Supporting                  Baselined Systems 26.1
                 Requests            24.5 change report
                   approvals              Feedback                   coordination of changes
                 Policies             problems, progress
                                                       emergencies             Change Control Team
                   specifics                        Exceptions                   work group 30.1
                                                  unauthorized changes                                 Change
                                                                                                       Management
          6.2  Formal Project Document              Content and
                                                     Benefits                   Information System 22.1
                          Change              Plan 23.1
                          Control Team    enhancement request                  Manages     26.1
                                            Scope-Related                      Baselines
                           approves
          41.2  Joint                        fault fix request
                Review                                                        Change Report 24.5
                                 Request                   System
                                  24.3                      24.4
```

Readings

[Evans]   Michael W. Evans, Pamela H. Piazza, and James B. Dolkas. *Principles of Productive Software Management.* New York: Wiley, 1983.

This book is a general textbook on software management. It has an excellent chapter on configuration management (Chapter 3), including good discussions of the purpose behind such management that apply equally to general change management. The discussion of the reasons for using information systems in support of change management is particularly good (pp. 31–38).

[Kehoe]   Raymond Kehoe and Alka Jarvis. *ISO 9000-3: A Tool for Software Product and Process Improvement.* New York: Springer-Verlag, 1996.

Chapter 16 of this book explains the requirements in ISO-9000-3 section 6.2 for document control.

[PMI 1996a]   Project Management Institute Standards Committee. *A Guide to the Project Management Body of Knowledge.* Project Management Institute (+1-610-734-3330), 1996.

The sections of the PMBOK on Overall Change Control (4.3) and Scope Change Control (5.5) are a simple and cogent explanation of how change control and configuration management works in standard project management practice.

Questions to Think About

1. What other mechanisms provide feedback during the project? Why is change management such an important source of feedback?

2. What kinds of specific costs and benefits can you think of for a typical OO project change? Don't limit yourself to software changes.

3. Are there strong benefits to having a single change control team? When do you think this approach would begin to break down?

4. How big an effect do you think unauthorized changes might have on a large project? Why? (Hint: Think about feedback and control and their impact on system value.)

5. Why do you think there are very few general change management tools available?

6. Who should have access to change reports in addition to the change control team?

CHAPTER

25 *Configuration Management*

The Configuration Management Process

The *configuration management (CM) process* is the change management process specific to managing the impact of change on software systems (classes, clusters, and deliverables). The CM process identifies, defines, and baselines software systems. It manages change to and release of such systems. A highly technical process, CM uses sophisticated software tools to manage the ongoing march of change to the software system. The main input into the process is the product baseline for the system; the output is an updated baseline with new versions of some or all software objects and a build report giving the status of all the baselined systems.

Vision: A process that ensures delivery of planned value despite change to a software system or cluster

Mission: To ensure that the impact of change on a software system or cluster affects delivery of value in a positive way

Objective 25.1: To ensure that the software deliverables of the project are complete, consistent, correct, and secure

Approach 25.1: Build a product baseline from the different cluster and software system baselines. Generate and distribute the build report to the appropriate people. Using the various product baselines, test the deliverables with quality assurance validation and verification processes using system test suites. After validating and verifying the system, freeze it and secure it for delivery. Place the source code for the system, including configuration management repository data and tools, in a secure escrow facility or backup location. Create master copies of the deliverables

The Configuration Management Process 401

and deliver them to stakeholders through a production or installation process, which may or may not be a part of your project.

Metric 25.1: Risk of product loss: the risk of losing one or more of the systems of the product baseline, rendering the deliverable valueless

Target 25.1: Very small, within a stated risk tolerance for the product baseline

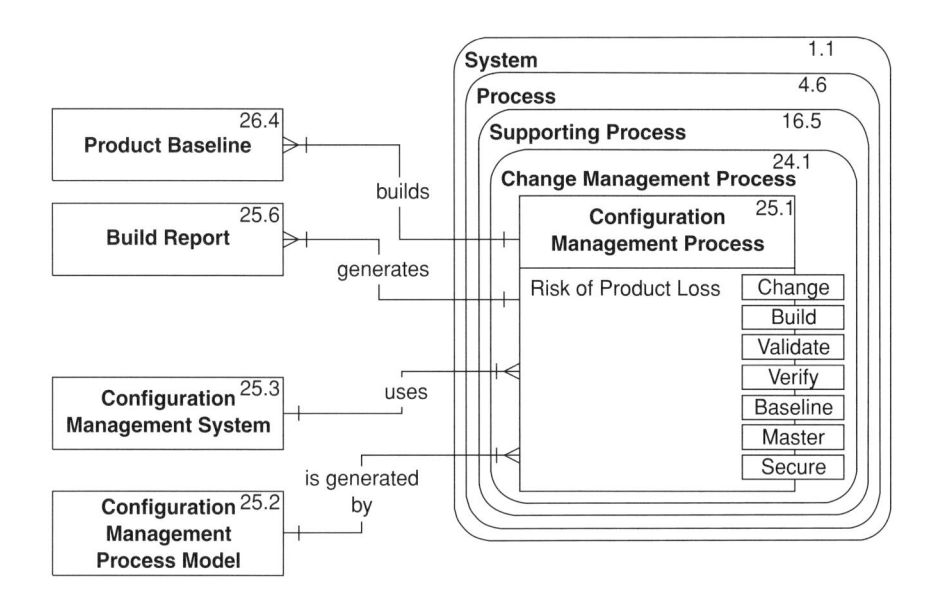

While the change management process aspect of the CM process is the same, the CM process has the additional objective of providing release management for software. *Release management* is the construction of deliverable software systems using product baselines (the system *configuration*). This process is strongly related to change management, as its main contribution is to join together specific versions of clusters and software systems into a product. Once you define a product, you must control change to the product baseline as it goes through system testing, storage, handling, and delivery to stakeholders. The issues are similar to change management but more extreme.

Organization

It is quite possible to separate configuration management from quality assurance, and many companies do just that. Organizationally, configuration management is closer to the developers than to anyone else. Both the practice itself and the tools that implement it are directly of interest to software people. Configuration management is a technically challenging business practice, particularly subject to automation and hence interesting to technical people. It also directly affects the daily work of most developers, being simultaneously the business practice that lets them get their job done by coordinating work among multiple developers and the most bureaucratic of all processes, requiring the most discipline. The love-hate relationship of developers with configuration management, challenge versus discipline, is of long standing. The exact organizational structure for configuration management often depends entirely on chance.

I worked on an OO database management system with an extensive configuration management system built entirely out of UNIX tool scripts. The system not only fully automated the build process, it also automated the porting process that built the system on five target UNIX operating systems. This labor of love by one of the developers on the project ensured that the quality assurance group had no configuration problems to deal with.

On another OO project, I wound up having the program librarian in charge of configuration management reporting to me as manager of the client/server and object model group. Quality assurance didn't want the responsibility, and other development managers had tried and failed to work with the technology and resources involved. The resources migrated into my group because they simultaneously worked on client/server aspects of the system and on these tools.

In a third project, the quality assurance group took partial responsibility for configuration management, taking over the system from the alpha baseline on but ignoring it before that point. The primary development manager took responsibility for version control and baselining the alpha product release. The result of this division was to delay implementation of a real configuration management process. The QA manager and the development manager could not seem to agree on a process model for both version control and release management!

System Loss

A key objective for configuration management is to limit the risk of system loss. Because the product baseline represents the deliverable value of the project, your tolerance for losing this system is close to nil, or at least it should be if the thing has any value. Hard disk crashes, floods, earthquakes—all can result in a catastrophic project failure if you lose your deliverables.

I was working in a high-rise in San Francisco on October 17, 1989. After my muscles unfroze and the building stopped shaking, I looked at my monitor just in time to see an hour of work blip out into blackness as the power died all over the city. The work was on the product baseline for a new OO case tool that represented several person-years of effort and a good part of the future of the company. We lost that hour of change, but we preserved most of the system despite the loss of a rack of backup tapes. It could have been worse.

One of the greatest risks for OO projects is the potential for financial failure. The combination of new technology and lack of experience and training can lead to companies disappearing. This can impact you in two ways. First, if the company that disappears is a supplier for your framework, you are out of luck. Second, if a stakeholder has financial dependencies on your software, and you go away, they may too.

The answer to this problem is escrow storage. When you complete a product baseline, you put it on a portable storage medium (tape or portable disk) and get it to an external facility that stores it and retains the legal right to distribute it to bona fide creditors on demand. The creditor must have a contract provision giving them access to the source code in escrow, and usually a judgment that the provision should be enforced.

Whether your storage is in escrow or is just a secure, off-site storage facility, you must store more than just the product baseline. You must also store the repository and tools you would need to build the system from the source code. In particular, the build tools, the compiler, and the build-related data (make files, project files, configuration management repository data, and so on) and system regression tests should accompany the product baseline into secure storage.

I worked at another company (not an OO project) that had some bad luck, being devoted to providing portfolio management software for savings and loans in 1987, just before the scandal broke. I can't say whether the declining fortunes of savings and loans was at fault, but the cash flow and revenue dried up, throwing us all out of work. The company was bought at bargain-basement prices by its main creditor, a major time-sharing facility. Several of our savings and loan clients had contracts with escrow clauses, which presumably allowed them to continue developing the software after our company disappeared.

The Configuration Management Process Model

Every process needs a process model, and CM is no exception. One difference between the *CM process model* and other process models is the sheer weight of standards and literature that discusses it. Virtually every book on any aspect of software engineering, software project management, or quality assurance for software has a chapter or section on this model.

- *Note:* One consequence of this surfeit of management wisdom is a disconcerting range of differences among standards for the CM process model. They are all quite specific about what CM is and how it does it. Only by stretching your interpretation of various standards and references can you reconcile some of the differences. Here, I don't have the room to present all the models and their differences, so I offer a bare-bones model of CM that should satisfy all standards. However, I suggest that you consult applicable standards carefully when you build your own process model.

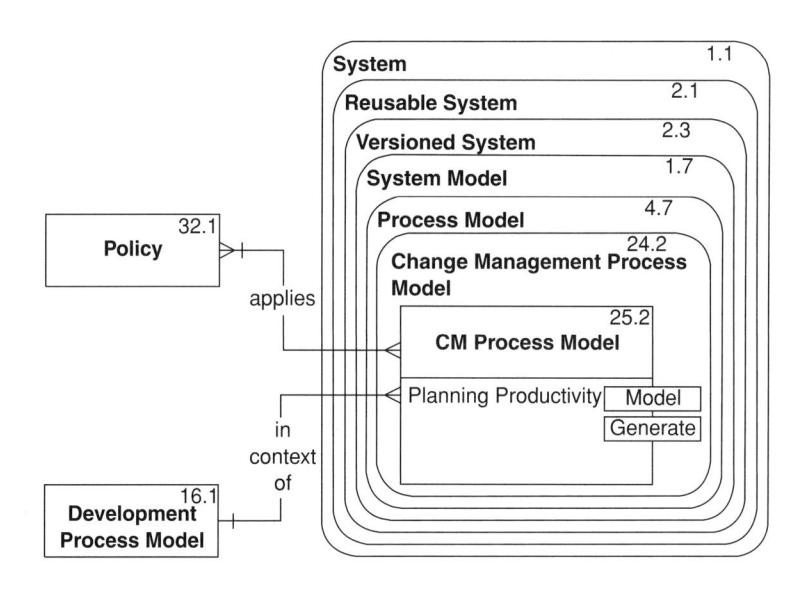

Vision: A valuable, reusable, productive configuration management process you productively plan from a continuously improving model

Mission: To represent a productive configuration management process that you want to reuse many times

---

Objective 25.2: To represent the configuration management process to allow planning with optimal productivity

---

Approach 25.2: Model the standard configuration management process. Specify the approval policies for baseline changes to software. Specify check-in and check-out versioning policies. Specify the change management policies relating to the validation and verification processes. Specify both the ordinary version control tasks and work flow and the release process that kicks in after the first product baseline. Specify the secure storage policies that reduce your risk of baseline loss below tolerance.

Metric 25.2: Planning productivity: effort-hours per change request

Target 25.2: A value within control limits of an x-R control chart of similar change requests

---

There are several standards for the CM model as it relates to change management:
- *ISO-9000-3, Section 6.1:* Configuration Management
- *ISO/IEC-12207, Section 6.2:* Configuration Management Process

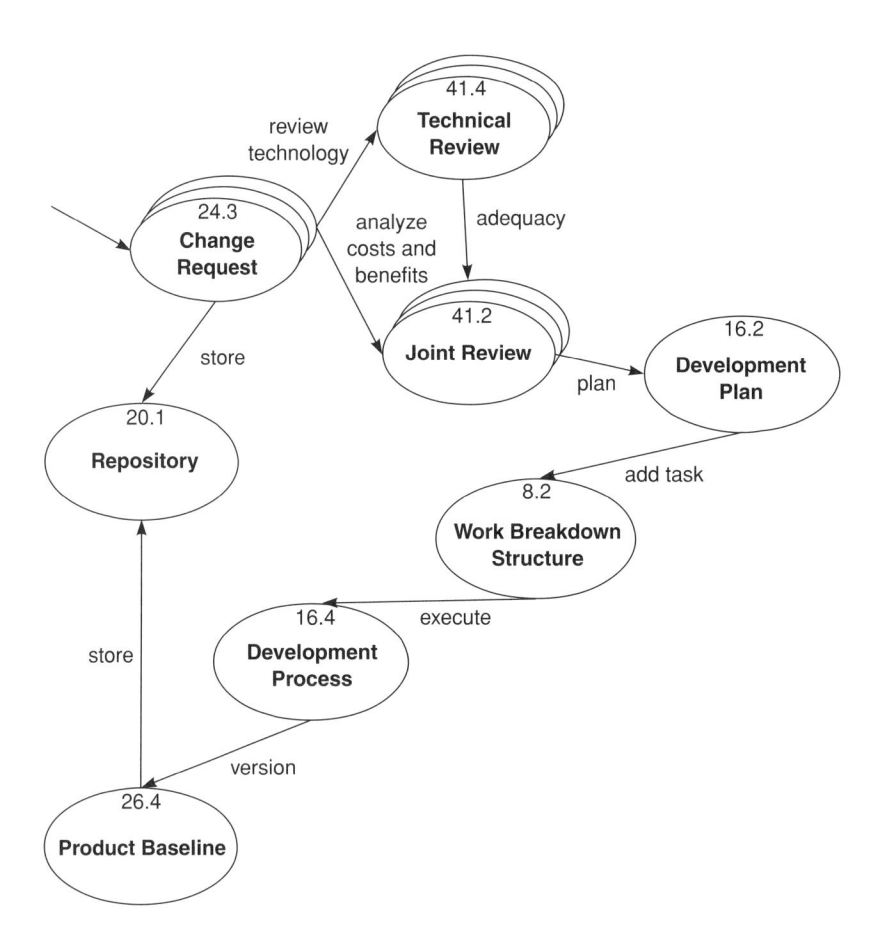

Figure 25-1
The CM change process model

- PMBOK 4.3.2.2: Configuration Management
- IEEE 828: Software Configuration Management

The CM process model is a special case of the change management process model. Figure 25-1 shows an archetypal CM process system model [Bennatan, p. 100; Whitten, p. 269].

The change process starts with a change request, usually either an enhancement request or a fix request. Very rarely, some feedback issue requires software changes to correct a process problem. For example, you might determine that the capabilities of your resources are not up to implementing a particular design, so you propose acquiring a third-party framework instead, halfway through development of the cluster.

Depending on the development process model and on the point of entry into the development process, the nature of authority required to make the change differs. The framework of the CM process model exists within the framework of the development process model. Before a major baseline, developers generally have the authority to change anything and everything about a system, with only technical reviews involved. After a major baseline, such as an alpha product baseline (a "code freeze"), things get more disciplined, with authority residing in a change control team of some kind. Change requests are informal where developers have authority and formal where they do not.

Software change requests, while they include technical material, usually do not have detailed design or code suggestions. Both enhancements and fix requests require a good deal of work to flesh out. That work should be part of the development process after the acceptance of the change request; therefore, you can't have the details in the change request. There should be enough detail for a reviewer to judge the technical adequacy and feasibility of the request, however. It should also have enough detail to generate a cost estimate.

The change request includes the reason for the change, the proposal, and any supporting technical documentation such as requirements or design documents. Before doing anything else, the change control team must evaluate the technical aspects of the proposal. For proposals the size of a cluster, this should be a technical review; for lesser proposals, you assign a resource to evaluate it and report back by a certain time. This report can be a short paragraph or longer, depending on what needs saying. Like any review, however, it should be constructive.

Change Request (24.3)

- *Note:* Often, the technical documentation is a revision of existing documentation. You would usually put the changed elements in the change request and later, as part of the development process that incorporates the change, version the documents with the changes.

After evaluating the technical content, the reviewer(s) may decide to proceed with the proposal. The next stage is to evaluate the costs, benefits, and risks of the proposal to decide whether it adds value to the project. Again, this can be quite sophisticated, involving several people; or it can be a one-paragraph summary. The result should have a recommendation to accept, reject, or rework the proposal. If you rework the proposal, you go through the whole process again. In any case, the team archives the request version in the project repository.

Once the change control board accepts the proposal, they may combine it with other proposals into the development process and risk management plans. These plans then add development and risk control tasks and work flows to the WBS, as in Figure 8-1. The team then coordinates the new work with the project manager to integrate it into the project schedule and assign resources to the tasks. Finally, the project manager executes the development process to incorporate the change.

Work Breakdown Structure (8.2)

- *Note:* The project manager may or may not need to approve the change, depending on your change management and configuration management policies. In a small project, the project manager may be part of the change control team; in a larger project, the project manager may just reserve the right to review team decisions. Your organizational authority structure should reflect your trust and commitment to the processes you've put in place.

Figure 25-2 shows an archetypal release management process model. This system model handles the aspect of configuration management that relates to releasing software deliverables. It interacts with both the development process and the quality assurance process. As the development process winds down toward its major baseline, the configuration process starts up. At the same time, quality assurance goes from a development-centered activity (object and integration testing) to a release-centered activity (system testing, including validation and verification processes as well as capability testing).

The basic systems for release management are the product baselines. How you sequence them and the particular tests and other tasks you use to move them along provides the behavioral structure of the model.

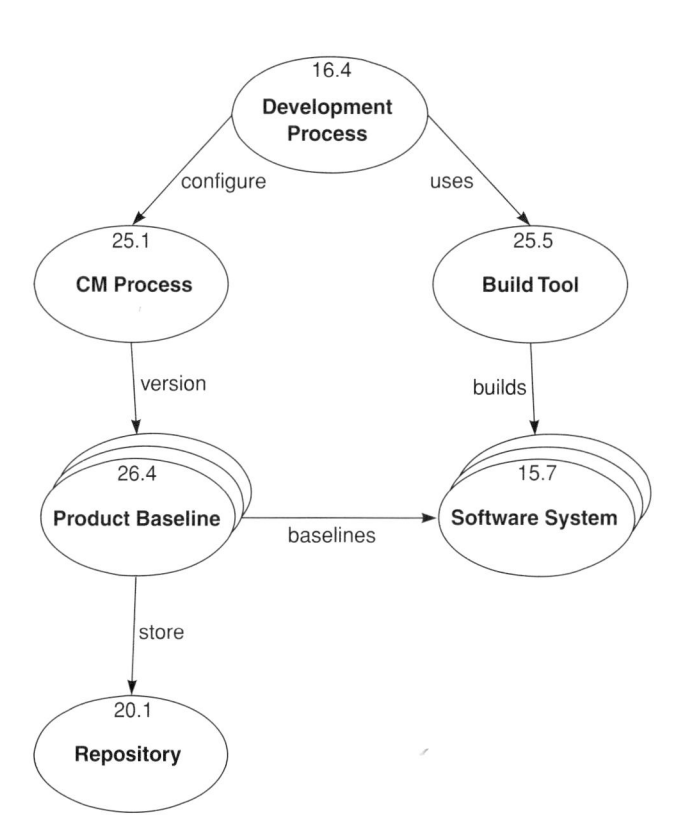

Figure 25-2
The release management process model

The Configuration Management System

The *configuration management system* (CMS) is a change management system that manages all the information about software configurations in your product repository.

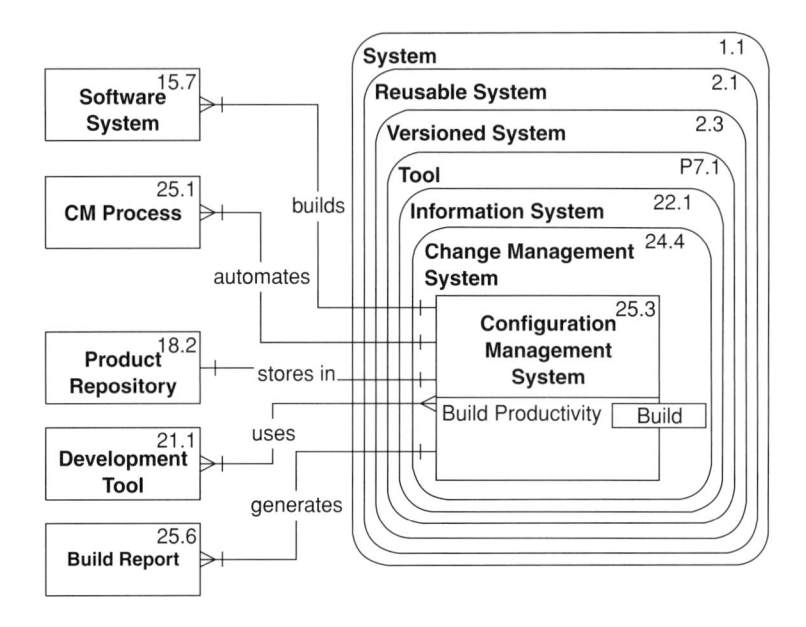

Vision: People using information about the configuration and change of software to get their jobs done

Mission: To create and manage information about the configuration and change of software

---

Objective 25.3: To create and manage information about software configuration (release management)

Approach 25.3: Use the tools in the development environment to specify the configuration of systems for the environment. If you are using a project-oriented development environment, you should incorporate the appropriate systems into your product repository. You should construct a build tool script capable of building your entire system automatically. You should specify the release configuration for product baselines in the product repository. When you build the baseline, generate a build report giving the status of the different components in a deliverable bill of materials. You should use production tools to build a master delivery system (CD-ROM, floppy disks, tape, and so on) and test it. Delivery or installation of this master results in reaching the process milestone for the deliverable.

Metric 25.3: Build productivity: effort-hours per weighted software baseline build, where the weight reflects the size of the system in function points

Target 25.3: A relatively small value reflecting high automation of the task, with the value within control limits on an x-R control chart of software-related baselines

---

Objective 25.4: To create and manage information about software changes (version control)

Approach 25.4: At a point where a cluster begins functioning for the purpose of integration testing, check the software systems into the configuration management system, storing them in the product repository. Use a source control tool to manage checking files in and out of the repository and to synchronize your baseline with the master baseline. Use a build tool to build software after each change to ensure rebuilding all dependent systems. Use difference and merge tools to compare and merge versions of systems as needed.

Metric 25.4: Information failure: see Metric 22.1.1 for the Information System

---

The CMS contains several tools in addition to its repository management features. The source control tool manages the versioning of source code. The build tool manages the building of clusters and systems. The CMS also has built-in reporting for builds that lets you report status on and audit a build.

See the Readings section for suggestions on where to find specifics on the popular configuration management systems available from commercial vendors [Eaton].

If you are using a project-oriented development tool such as MKS Source Integrity, Microsoft's Visual C++, ParcPlace's VisualWorks, IBM's VisualAge, or Object Technology's ENVY/Developer, you should take full advantage of the project-oriented capabilities. In these tools, a "project" is a configuration of software files or systems. You could therefore class at least this aspect of these tools broadly as a configuration management system. Source Integrity has a unique "project sandbox" feature that lets you establish a private configuration automatically as you check files in and out of the master project. You see the master project files until you check out a file, but any changes you make are private until you check the file in. The Intersolv PVCS system supports similar features with less automation.

- *Note:* UNIX, Windows 95, Windows NT, and Macintosh operating systems support *aliases,* files that are references to files in another location. Configuration management systems can use aliases to construct virtual baseline configurations, replacing the references with copies of the files when you check them out. Different systems use this feature in different ways. Also, since this works on the file level, you still have to maintain clusters and higher-level systems manually. This is true in general of configuration management systems: they work with files, not with clusters, which is somewhat limiting for OO systems.

CM systems are as reusable as any information system, with the same characteristics determining reuse potential. Inherent reuse potential depends on the flexibility, robustness, and value of the tools. Domain reuse potential depends on how capable the system is of handling the different kinds of software builds to which you want to apply it. Organizational reuse potential depends on your organizational policies, process models, and discipline.

Since most CM systems have proprietary or special methods for storing information, and there are no standards for such storage, reuse of the information that the CM system manages means reuse of the information system. If for some reason you cannot reuse the CM system, you will almost certainly have to convert the baselines, audit trails, and other information into a different format.

The Source Control Tool

The *source control tool* is a development tool that implements software versioning and release management by controlling the source code associated with classes, clusters, and software systems.

Vision: A continuously improving software development process delivering its software despite concurrent development and changes to source code

Mission: To preserve the state of all versions of a software-related system to permit auditing and recovery of all versions

---

Objective 25.5: To allow concurrent development

Approach 25.5: Use a simple transaction-locking scheme to permit updates of baselined systems. Check systems out when you want to modify them; check them back in when you're finished. If other developers need to make changes while you have a file checked out, coordinate the changes with them and make them in your version. Use the build tool to synchronize your system by incorporating changes made by other developers on a regular basis, preferably daily.

Metric 25.5: Concurrency: the amount of time developers wait for source code locked by other users; this can be fairly difficult to measure if your source control tool does not automatically track such waits; many systems do not

The Configuration Management System

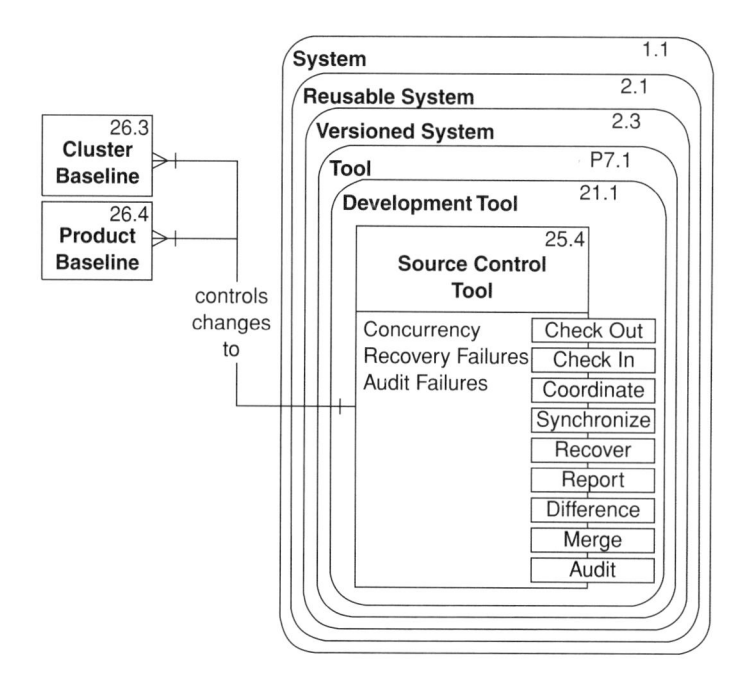

Target 25.5: A low number within limits of an x-R control chart for similar systems

---

Objective 25.6: To allow recovery of prior versions of a software-related system

Approach 25.6: Use the check-in feature of the source control tool to ensure that your changes become a permanent part of the product repository when you end a change transaction. Use the build report or a report writer to find prior versions if you need them, and use the source control tool to retrieve those versions.

Metric 25.6: Recovery failures: the number of times you fail to recover to a given baseline of a software system

Target 25.6: Zero, or a very low number within control limits of a pn control chart

---

Objective 25.7: To permit auditing of changes to a software-related system

Approach 25.7: Use the check-in and check-out facilities of the source control tool to maintain an audit trail, storing timestamps and names of the person modifying the system with each version of the system. By policy, require each change to have an accompanying description, preferably with reference to a change request for baseline changes.

Metric 25.7: Audit failures: the number of versions with missing or inadequate information required by source control policy (timestamp, name, description, change request reference, and so on)

Target 25.7: A low number within control limits of a pn control chart of cluster or software system versions

---

Source code is the original format of a software-related system. This format uses the syntax of the OO programming language. *Object code* is a compiled or partially compiled format that turns the source code into machine instructions or byte codes. *Executable code* is object code with external references linked, either statically or dynamically.

Source control tools let you manage the source code for a system in a master repository. With most source control tools, you can accomplish the following things:

- Check a source file out of the product repository
- Check a source file into the product repository
- Synchronize local files with master files
- Recover a specific version of a file
- Report on the status of a file in the product repository
- See the difference between two versions of a file
- Merge two different versions of a file to produce a new version
- Audit the changes made to a file

■ *Note:* All of these functions work on *files,* not on systems such as clusters. As a consequence, you must interact a bit more with the tool than might otherwise be the case in an OO project.

The UNIX facilities sccs and rcs set the standard for source control tools. The DEC tool CMS (configuration management system) is very popular in the configuration management literature. For PC software, the MKS Source Integrity tool based on rcs, the Intersolv PVCS tool, and Microsoft's SourceSafe are the major tools.

The Build Tool

The *build tool* is a development tool that lets you automate the building of a cluster or software system.

Vision: A fully automated, error-free software build process

Mission: To increase the productivity of building software and the quality of software builds

The Configuration Management System *413*

Objective 25.8: To increase the productivity of building software

Approach 25.8: Use the build tool to automate building.

Metric 25.8: Build productivity: effort-hours spent in building baselines for clusters or software systems

Target 25.8: A value within limits of an x-R control chart of builds

Objective 25.9: To increase the quality of software builds

Approach 25.9: Automate the building process to remove error-prone manual procedures. Ensure that the build tool has all the appropriate dependencies built into it. Ensure that the build tool runs whenever you require a new baseline.

Metric 25.9: Build failures: the number of problems due to oversights or errors in the build process

Target 25.9: Zero

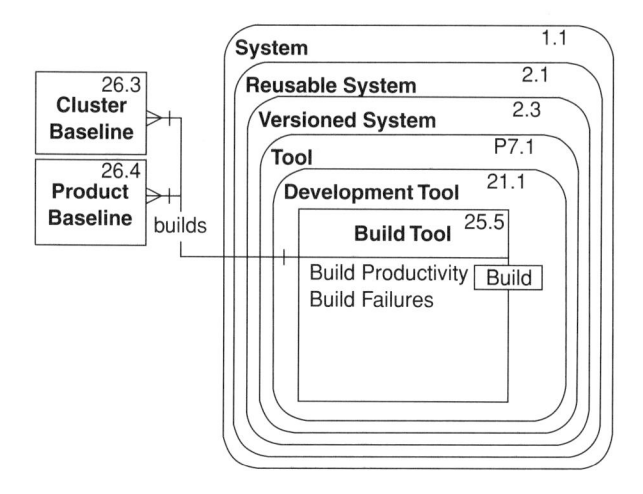

The archetypal build tool, UNIX "make," has been around for many years. Most development environments now include make, but usually with proprietary extensions. Tools such as Visual C++ let you automatically build an entire cluster or software system baseline by clicking on a button in the development environment.

Some programming languages, such as Ada, Smalltalk, and Java, support incremental compilation. This feature lets you compile classes and clusters you change and anything that depends on them without rebuilding the whole system.

Usually, this works with byte-code systems, as these are internal data structures under the control of the compiler.

There is a class of development tools that causes problems for build tools: the precompiler. This is a tool that processes source code to produce more source code. Two examples are the UNIX "yacc" command ("Yet Another Compiler Compiler") and Embedded C [ANSI]. The yacc tool (and its commercial counterparts, such as yacc++ from Compiler Resources and Visual Parse++ from Sandstone Technology) reads a grammar and produces C (or C++) code that implements an LR lexical analyzer and parser for the grammar. The Embedded C precompiler reads source code with embedded SQL statements and translates them to some target API for a database management system.

When you use a precompiler tool, you first precompile your source, and then build the system with the resulting source in your target programming language. The build tools currently on the market generally aren't smart enough to figure out by themselves what needs to be done. With UNIX make, you can add rules for these files that automatically run the precompiler. With PC systems, this can be quite a bit harder, as those systems take full control of the make files and produce them automatically. Until the build tool vendors give you some kind of access to the make file generators in their environments, you may have more manual work to do in building PC systems than you do in UNIX systems.

On an early parser project in an OO system, I developed an extensive set of tools to automate the building of the parser. Because yacc had some limitations with respect to global variables and things that C++ didn't like, I had to use the "sed" editor tool to postprocess the C output of yacc into C++. I packaged all this in a make rule and integrated it into the build system for the overall product, fully automating the build. I would have had much more trouble doing this in Visual C++ and its cousins. On the other hand, I spent most of my time in this project working things out on paper, since the debuggers available for C and C++ could not properly debug the yacc source files because of the code alterations and technological incompatibilities.

The same project used the make facility itself to generate make files ("make-make"). When you added a new software system to the product, you could build the initial make file using make-make with the appropriate set of arguments. This ensured that the resulting make file would have all the appropriate rules and sections needed to build the new software system on various target UNIX operating systems around the network, using the proper libraries and including file directory structure. This approach represents both the best and the worst of the UNIX mentality. It uses standard UNIX commands, not special-purpose programs, to get a surprising amount of work done. On the other hand, the resulting complexity made it nearly impossible to understand either the make-make code or the resulting make files. As long as you were doing things in a standard way, you were all right. When you had special needs (such as the special parsing for OO code above), your productivity suffered.

The Build Report

The *build report* is a change report that describes the structure and status of a particular product baseline release. It lists all the built systems with their identifying version numbers and supplies the status as of the last build, along with the standard change information listing changes for the baseline. There is one build report for each build of the baseline, including unsuccessful and multiple builds.

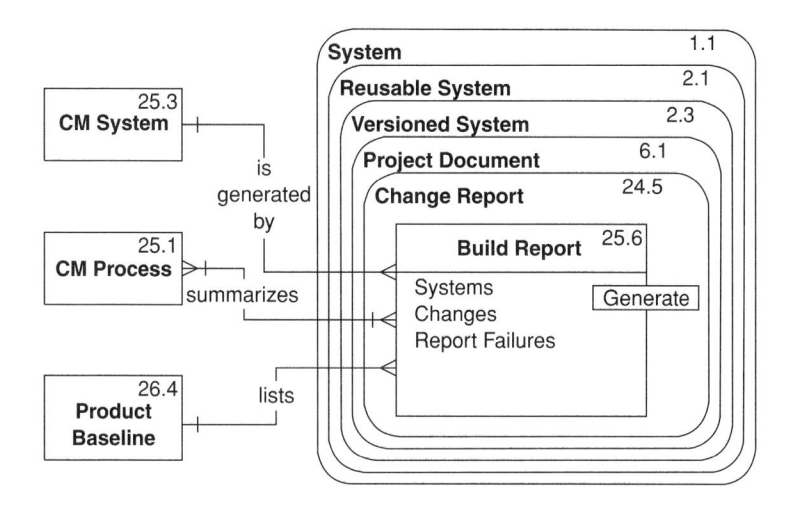

Vision: A group of stakeholders with confidence in the quality of a software system

Mission: To communicate the status of product baseline builds to stakeholders

---

Objective 25.10: To communicate product baseline build status

---

Approach 25.10: Using the information maintained in the product repository by the configuration management system, report on the status of all the components of a baseline build. Communicate the report as the communications management plan requires.

Metric 25.10: Report failures: the number of failures to generate an accurate, useful report

Target 25.10: Zero

The build report communicates the status of a product baseline to anyone that needs to know that status. It also serves as a bill of materials that you can use to communicate a system configuration to anyone who needs to know that information, such as a production facility or development manager. Finally, you can use build reports to form an audit trail for baseline auditing.

Ideally, an OO build report would report on clusters. Current systems now support only file systems, not higher-level objects. As a consequence, you may need query tools to summarize information about particular clusters of files between the system level and the file.

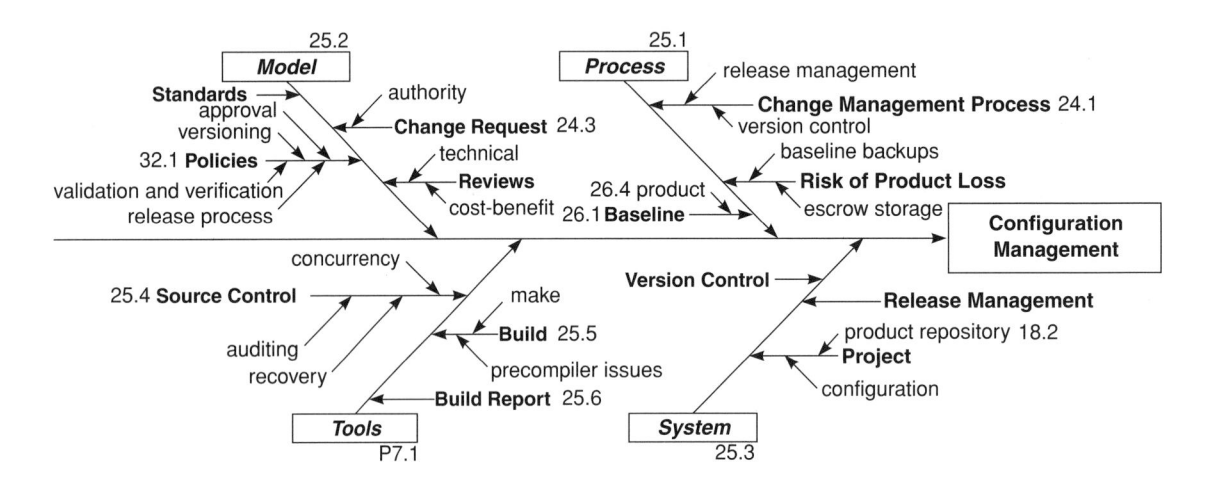

```
                25.2                        25.1
              Model                       Process    release management
       Standards      authority                     Change Management Process 24.1
            approval                                 version control
          versioning  Change Request 24.3           baseline backups
  32.1 Policies       technical                     Risk of Product Loss
                       Reviews       26.4 product   escrow storage
validation and verification cost-benefit 26.1 Baseline                  Configuration
       release process                                                   Management
                        concurrency
                                             Version Control
  25.4 Source Control           make                      Release Management
                                                         product repository 18.2
         auditing          Build 25.5                    Project
         recovery          precompiler issues            configuration
                       Build Report 25.6
                           Tools                    System
                           P7.1                      25.3
```

Readings

Anyone seriously interested in configuration management should read the Usenet news group comp.software.config-mgmt, where many issues of interest are discussed. Consult the FAQs for this group for the basic issues (see [Eaton] below) by searching for "configuration management" on the World Wide Web.

[Babich]   Wayne A. Babich. *Software Configuration Management: Coordination for Team Productivity.* Reading, MA: Addison-Wesley, 1986.

This is a classic reference on software configuration management. Go here to find the gory details on just about anything to do with it.

[Berlack]   H. Ronald Berlack. *Software Configuration Management.* New York: Wiley, 1992.

This is a recent book on software configuration management, updating some of the earlier standard works in the area.

[Bersoff 1980] Edward H. Bersoff, V. D. Henderson, and S. G. Siegel. *Software Configuration Management.* Englewood Cliffs, NJ: Prentice Hall, 1980.

This is another classic reference on software configuration management, although now seriously out of date. It tends to read a bit like a military contractor's reference, but it does define all the basic concepts in a clear manner.

[Bersoff 1991] Edward H. Bersoff and Alan M. Davis. Impacts of life cycle models on software configuration management. *Communications of the ACM* 34:8 (August 1991): 104–117.

This is an excellent article that extends the concepts of the software configuration management discipline into the newer life cycles, including reuse, prototyping, and (weakly) automatic software synthesis.

[Dunn] Robert H. Dunn and Richard S. Ullman. *TQM for Computer Software*. New York: McGraw-Hill, Inc., 1994.

This book has a full chapter on configuration management (Chapter 6). Well written and opinionated, this chapter touches on almost all the issues I raise in this and the following chapter on baselines.

[Eaton] David W. Eaton. *Configuration Management Tools Summary*. Available on Usenet group comp.software.config-mgmt FAQ (Frequently Asked Questions), Part 2, version 3.6. Also available on the World Wide Web through http://www.iac.honeywell.com/Pub/Tech/CM/CMTools.html.

This is a FAQ file available through Usenet or the World Wide Web that gives you all the information you could want about the current raft of configuration management tools. It provides contact information and brief summaries and evaluations for dozens of tools.

[IEEE] The Institute of Electrical and Electronic Engineers. *Software Engineering Standards*. Los Alamitos, CA: IEEE Computer Society Press, 1987.

This book, and its more modern cousins, contains all of the IEEE standards for software engineering. While these standards are interesting, none have been compelling enough to ensure their adoption throughout the software community. They serve mainly as reference models and standards for the definition of the more important terms that software engineering uses. In particular, IEEE-828 is the standard for software configuration management.

[ISO 1995] International Standards Organization. *ISO/IEC 12207, Information Technology—Software Life Cycle Processes*. ISO, 1995.

The section of ISO-12207 on the Configuration Management Process (6.2) defines the basic process for configuration management. This is a particularly clear and complete definition of software configuration management with the exception of a lack of definition of "baseline."

[Kehoe] Raymond Kehoe and Alka Jarvis. *ISO 9000-3: A Tool for Software Product and Process Improvement*. New York: Springer-Verlag, 1996.

Chapter 15 of this book explains the requirements in ISO-9000-3 section 6.1 for configuration management. The standard itself is relatively generic; Kehoe and Jarvis expand the requirements with material similar to that in other books. There is also a separate chapter (23) on the configuration management process that summarizes the issues nicely.

Questions to Think About

1. List some differences between a software change request and other types of change request. What are the implications of these differences for the change management process model versus the CM process model?

2. What are the basic feedback mechanisms in the configuration management process? How does that process serve to integrate feedback into the development and quality processes?

3. Why should you separate technical review from cost-benefit analysis of a change proposal? (Hint: Who serves on the change control team? Who approves change requests?)

4. Some configuration management systems permit "branching," the ability to split a release or version stream into two or more streams, with changes happening in parallel. You can then merge the streams later into a single stream. Is this a good or bad idea? Why?

5. How might you work around the limitations of PC make systems? Can you customize these systems to include special rules for precompilers?

6. List five possible uses for the build report. (Hint: Think about the different people who must deal with a product baseline.)

CHAPTER

Baseline 26

The Baseline

The *baseline* is a versioned system that contains a set of versioned systems. This set of systems satisfies a set of *exit criteria*, standards for reaching a milestone [DeMarco 1982, p. 137]. The change management system creates and manages the baseline. Baselines happen at process milestones, having an intimate relationship with milestone events. They provide the basis for change management after the milestone, letting you control changes to the systems as the project progresses.

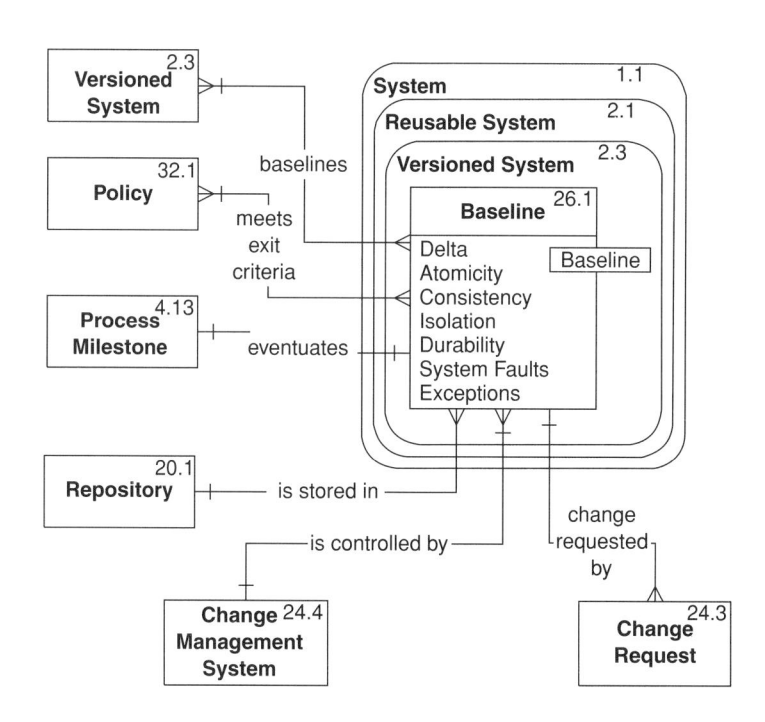

419

Vision: A well-defined set of systems ready for use by future project processes

Mission: To create an explicit set of systems for use as a system by future project processes

---

Objective 26.1: To identify a set of systems explicitly

Approach 26.1: Specify the set of versioned systems by name and version to the change management system, naming the set as a particular version of a named baseline.

Metric 26.1: System faults: number of systems not identified as part of the baseline but later determined to be part of it

Target 26.1: A very low number within control limits of a pn control chart

---

Objective 26.2: To determine the readiness of the system for input to project processes

---

Approach 26.2: Define a set of exit criteria as a standard for the type of baseline or the process milestone.

Metric 26.2: Exceptions to the exit criteria: the count of exceptions allowed for the baseline to exceed the values the criteria specify as required for baselining

Target 26.2: A very low number within control limits of a pn control chart

---

Objective 26.3: To finalize a transaction on the baseline, enabling recovery from later problems

---

Approach 26.3: Store the baseline in the appropriate repository. Ensure through repository or backup technology that you can restore the baseline if required.

Metric 26.3: Durability: the number of attempts at restoring the baseline that fail, indicating how permanent the baseline really is in the repository

Target 26.3: Zero, or a value close to it within control limits on a pn control chart (technology is a random variable at times, even database technology and especially backup technology)

Versioned systems include everything from the project plan itself to the individual systems within the plan. You can baseline milestones, schedule tasks, requirements documents, design components, classes, integration test suites, or system test results, for example. Since a baseline is also a versioned system, you can have baselines of baselines. *Exit criteria* are standards or policies that set targets for risk or other operational objectives of the baseline.

- *Note:* Many discussions in the software configuration management literature focus on software baselines or development document baselines. From the project management perspective, however, software is only a small part of the range of systems that can participate in baselines. Creative subclassing of the baseline class can help you to achieve many operational objectives that depend on change management or the evaluation of change.

Processes drive the creation and versioning of baselines. At a process milestone, the process may request the change management system to create a baseline or to version an existing baseline. The process tells the change system what kind of baseline the milestone requires and what systems to baseline. The milestone event thus results in a baselined set of systems that meet a set of exit criteria.

The creation or versioning of a baseline does several things. The baseline evaluates the exit criteria to determine whether the baseline is valid. If it is, the baseline eventuates the milestone event and uses the change management system to store the valid baseline in the appropriate repository. If the evaluation fails, the baseline informs the process that the milestone has failed and does not create a new baseline or version.

For example, say you can build a software deliverable such as a class hierarchy and its associated test systems and development documents in about four to six weeks of effort. This grouping level provides a clear sequence of product baselines for your work breakdown structure. Each development process for each cluster results in a cluster baseline. The exit criteria for the cluster baseline involve reaching appropriate levels of test model coverage for object and integration test suites. As you iterate on the clusters, each new cluster version results in a new version of its baseline when you finish a development iteration. Some iterations result in unworkable clusters, so the system throws them back to development for rework without versioning the baseline.

As you integrate into higher- and higher-level clusters, you generate new cluster baselines. Eventually, you integrate the system into the software deliverable and generate an alpha baseline, freezing the code. You then do the system test on the baseline, iterating until the software passes the exit criteria for the system test, resulting in a beta baseline. You then go through as many beta tests as you need to, versioning the baseline for each. When the final beta completes successfully, passing its exit criteria, you create a production baseline and ship the product.

Placing a baseline under change control means that you version the baseline when you change anything in it. A process that uses the baseline as input must version the baseline if it changes anything in it. If several processes share elements of the baseline, you must notify all the processes of the changes, especially if they are using copies of the baseline.

Change Managment Process (24.1)

There are three rationales for baselining. The first and most important one is to formalize a collection of systems to place them under change control. The change management process has its own rationale. The second is to ensure that the collection as a system satisfies some exit criteria for a process that produces it. The first objective requires identifying the systems and versions under control; the second requires formal approval or verification through some kind of review or testing. The third is to commit the baselined changes to a repository to provide a base for later recovery if necessary.

■ *Note:* The change management process can be quite loose for some kinds of baselines, such as cluster baselines. Your change management plan should specify the change policies for your different baselines, including the degree of formality.

In many ways, baselining resembles transaction management in database systems. A database transaction is a logical unit of work, a sequence of actions that satisfies the four properties in Table 26-1 [Agrawal; Gray].

The baseline is equivalent to committing a transaction to a database. Baselining supports the ability of multiple people to use and to change the baselined systems. It also supports your ability to later restore the system to a consistent state.

Reusability has a dramatic impact on the baseline, or at least on the structure of baselining through the change management process. To look at most of the literature on baselining, you would think that there is no reuse in software projects. The existence of systems that several other systems reuse distinctly complicates the baselining of those other systems. The reused systems become part of multiple baselines [Bersoff 1991]. Changing the reused system then requires notification of however many systems, projects, and organizations are reusing the software. Change begins to have an exponential impact on reusing systems.

There is one baseline that contains the master version of the reusable system and several other baselines that use it. Those baselines may contain revised versions of the reusable system (*variants*) if the reusing system changes it to tailor it

Table 26-1
ACID Properties of a Baseline Transaction

Property	Definition
Atomicity	All operations become a single unit
Consistency	The state of the system is correct at the end of the transaction
Isolation	The series of actions takes place in the context of a consistent environment
Durability	The resulting systems are permanent, even if the environment has failures

to new requirements or domains or corrects faults. These baselines thus must track not only the link to the original system but a *delta* (set of changes to the original system in the local system). The baselines may use inheritance to adapt the reusable system, resulting in a dependency. When the original system changes, the reusing systems must decide whether to upgrade their versions, to test them with regression suites, or to replace them with new systems. All of these systems and baselines require change management.

The baseline aligns with the architecture of the project systems. Instead of having single baselines for an entire project, you have many baselines for the different collections of systems of interest at different process milestones. The structure of the process models and the systems you build with or reuse in project processes determines the set of baselines.

Baselines are also reusable, versioned systems. Versioning lets you modify a baseline with controlled changes (or uncontrolled ones, for that matter). This usually happens through some kind of incrementalism, the evolution of the collection of systems as you move forward in time. Typically, you make many changes before versioning the baseline.

Reusable systems are part of the baseline for the process that creates them. Certified reusable systems in the reuse repository require change management as does any other system and thus require baselining in that repository. The project thus interacts with reused baselines as well as with internal baselines. The reusability of a baseline depends on the reusability of its components working as a whole. It also depends on the degree to which you must adapt the components as you reuse them.

The Document Baseline

The *document baseline* identifies the components of a project document and puts them under change control. The exit criterion for this baseline is the formal approval of the document as policy dictates, usually with a joint review. When your organization approves the document at the end of the documentation process (or whatever process produces it), the change management system puts the document under change control in the project repository.

Vision: A formal document that serves as the basis for adding value to the project

Mission: To enable any processes that depend on the document through a stable, controlled document

---

Objective 26.4: To formalize a project document

Approach 26.4: Produce the document as part of a project process. Review the document. If the document is acceptable, approve it and baseline its contents, placing them under change control in the project repository. If the document is not acceptable, either reject it or revise it as the review mandates, and then review it again.

Metric 26.4: Changes: number of document changes

Target 26.4: A number within the control limits of a pn control chart of similar documents in your organization and preferably a downward trend indicating improving stability of the documents over time

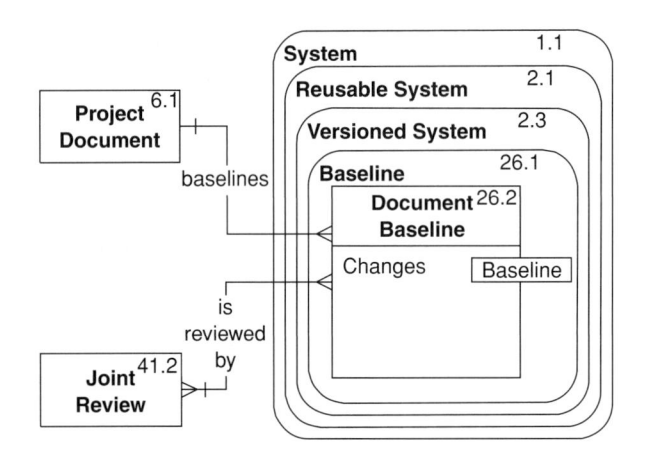

- *Note:* Usually you find only development documents as part of the change-controlled baseline. This more general class lets you decide what documents require change control and which do not. Keep it simple.

The Cluster Baseline

The *cluster baseline* identifies the pieces of a cluster. The milestone occurs when the team developing the cluster finishes a development iteration. Generally, the cluster consists of a set of files that contain class definitions, methods, data objects, and any other software-related systems that the cluster owns. The process milestone is usually an integration milestone with exit criteria comprising object and integration test suite coverage targets.

Vision: A well-defined OO cluster ready for system integration

Mission: To enable iterative development and integration of a cluster

The Cluster Baseline

Objective 26.5: To formalize a cluster into a stable base for iteration and integration

Approach 26.5: After performing the initial development process for a cluster, perform object and integration test suites and review the cluster with a technical review as required by the risk management and quality management plans. Revise the cluster as the review requires, and then use the configuration management system to baseline the cluster, checking in all systems that are a part of it to the product or reuse repository. For iterative development tasks, check out the systems you are changing, and then test and review the changes, revise, and check the systems in, versioning the baseline.

Metric 26.5: Check-in Ratio: the ratio of checked-in systems to total baselined systems

Target 26.5: One; any other value indicates something wrong with either the baseline or the status of the cluster

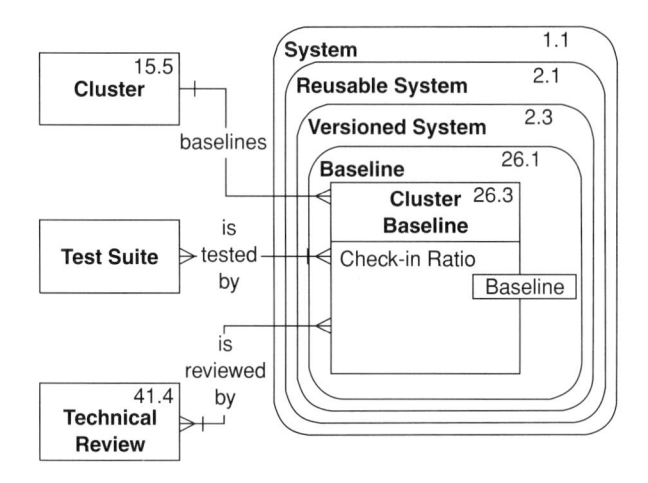

Most cluster baselines do not freeze development. You either iterate on the cluster or integrate the cluster into higher-level clusters. The former results in a version of the cluster baseline. The latter results in a version or creation of the higher-level cluster baseline. Hence, cluster baselines are not under formal change control unless you think they need it. The goal of the baseline is to provide a sound, stable base for iterative development and integration.

The Product Baseline

A product baseline contains one or more viable software systems. This collection functions as a working product delivering stakeholder value. There are several different kinds of product baseline, each with its own exit criteria, mission, and process milestone. Exit criteria for the baseline have some kind of test process and test criteria standards.

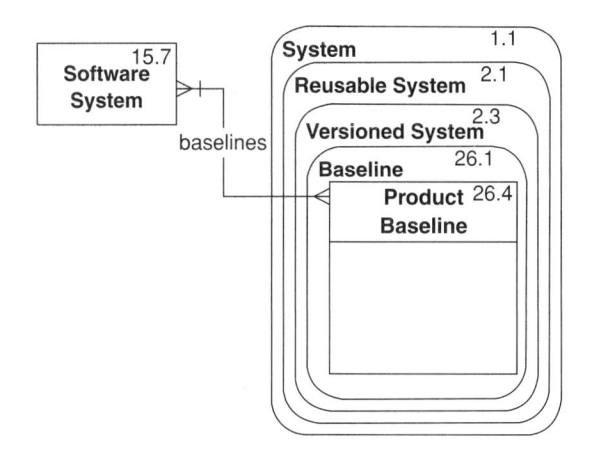

Vision: A working product delivering value to stakeholders

Mission: To provide a stable base for evaluation of a deliverable software system

In OO systems, you see product baselines early in the project. Developers try to bring together reused systems into an early, working whole. This approach provides a productive working environment early on. It also helps to ensure good stakeholder and technical evaluation of the product.

■ *Note:* Most books on software configuration management use the scheme from the U.S. Department of Defense (DOD-STD-2167A). This standardizes one major system baseline, a product baseline, at the end of the development process. The classes of product baseline introduced here reflect my experience in the commercial software industry with its alpha, field, beta, and production releases. Doubtless, other schemes are possible. If yours requires different kinds of product baselines, just subclass.

The Prototype Baseline

The *prototype baseline* is a product baseline that identifies the components of a viable software system that is not yet a production system (a *prototype*). The exit criteria are the test criteria for the cluster (object and integration test suite coverage).

The Product Baseline   427

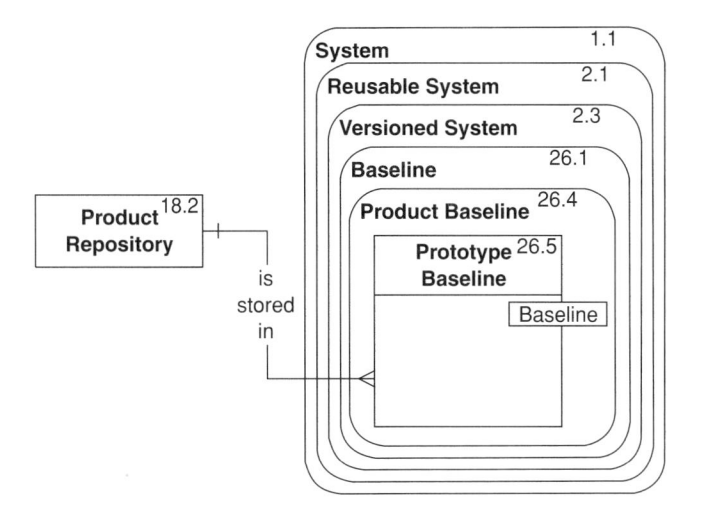

```
                                    System              1.1
                                                   2.1
                                    Reusable System
                                                       2.3
                                      Versioned System
                                        Baseline    26.1
                                                         26.4
    Product    18.2                     Product Baseline
    Repository                             Prototype  26.5
                                           Baseline
                    is                              ┌──────────┐
                    stored                          │ Baseline │
                    in                              └──────────┘
```

Vision: A prototype ready for evolution into a deliverable system

Mission: To enable control of the prototype in evolutionary prototyping

---

Objective 26.6: To formalize the prototype into a stable base for evolution

Approach 26.6: Integrate the various clusters that make up the prototype deliverable. Perform integration test suites and review the system as required by the needs of the prototype. Use the configuration management system to baseline the prototype, storing it in the product repository. This is either an initial baseline (first time) or a version (other times).

Metric 26.6: Reference to the test metric and criteria for the integration test suites

Target 26.6: Targets for the integration test suites

There are two kinds of prototype. The *throwaway* is quick and dirty; the *evolutionary* is quick and clean. Your objective for an evolutionary prototype is to add to it as the project goes on. Also, often you release prototypes to other organizations or to contracting customers for evaluation. These prototypes therefore require change control once you complete the first version. The prototype baseline contains an evolutionary prototype, not a throwaway one.

■ *Note:* Prototypes are reusable within a project. They are not reusable across multiple projects. That means prototypes appear in the product repository but not in the reuse repository. You don't certify the prototype for reuse until you evolve it into a production deliverable.

While evolutionary prototypes require testing, they do not require the level of testing you need for a production system. You must run the integration test for the clusters you integrate into the system. If you have cheap system regression test suites, you can run them to verify the system. You won't find much more testing than that.

Prototype baselines are a critical part of the spiral process. After analyzing risks, you prototype to manage those risks, resulting in a commitment to further development. Baselining the prototype signals a commitment for that project iteration.

> "The Spiral" section, Chapter 16, p. 284

Several OO development projects I worked on had prototypes done through a weekly or nightly build process. Early in one project, the product came together to a point where you could run the graphical user interface and some functionality. This was the first build. From that point on, the developers built the system periodically. Each build had to result in a working prototype, or work stopped until the developers resolved any major problems preventing building or running the system. Usually, this meant everyone in the group having a mass espresso break, because their base for development was no longer functional. On a good day, the release manager was able to restore the previous prototype so that at least some people could get some work done.

One OO project I remember well. We developed a clearly defined iterative process for prototypes. We made various QA and documentation processes dependent on these prototypes, since they were the basis for test planning and preliminary documentation. As the project moved forward, some development managers and developers ignored the prototyping process. They delivered only versions they regarded as final. On looking into this, I realized that each developer was given a deliverable system to do. Instead of delivering prototypes, they delivered complete, frozen code. Also, these systems had architectures that were monolithic and poorly designed from the OO design perspective. The developers had to build these systems as systems rather than as decoupled clusters. The consequence was a series of builds that included the basic system but not the new features of the product. These appeared only at alpha release, far too late to be of any use as pre-alpha prototypes.

- *Note:* You can improve your prototyping ability by improving your OO design ability. If you design well using OO techniques, you can identify the parts of the design that a prototype needs to function as a system. You can then deliver these clusters first, providing the nonessential features as part of the evolution of the prototype. This avoids the all-in-one behavior of the above example.

Reuse, and especially the lack of it, can have a dramatic impact on prototype baselines. In one of my own early OO projects, I was not able to reuse any components for basic data structures such as lists, hash tables, and strings: there weren't any. I wrote all these clusters as templates from scratch. The result was an interminable period during which I tested and debugged these fundamental components using stone knives and bearskins. My manager stopped by every day and politely asked for demos of the new features. The day I finally got all these basic clusters debugged, I was able to add a single cluster that delivered basic functionality, and my manager was ecstatic at seeing something on the screen. He then vanished to tell his fellow executives that we could now demo the great new features of the system!

A third lesson in prototyping: the impact of the deadline. I worked on a RAD project with a client/server tool that promised highly productive prototyping and development. The project was a rush job to deliver an application in time for an annual budgeting process. The impact of this tight deadline was an inability to prototype. The tools had great reuse features, but to use them meant you had to design, think, and implement the system carefully. To avoid having to redo anything, I had to essentially complete the system before doing it. This did result in meeting the deadline, but the postdeadline iterations on the product showed that a prototype or two would have benefited the requirements process. Deadlines and prototypes do not necessarily agree with one another.

The Alpha Baseline

At some point, you turn your evolutionary prototype into a product. The strategy for doing this is to treat the baseline as a system, running system tests. The result is effectively a deliverable prototype: it still has problems, but it is a complete system. The initial baseline for a software deliverable is an *alpha baseline,* a kind of prototype baseline. This baseline usually has exit criteria similar to a cluster baseline but includes a code freeze, putting the baselined systems under rigorous and formal change control, and a system build resulting in a build report.

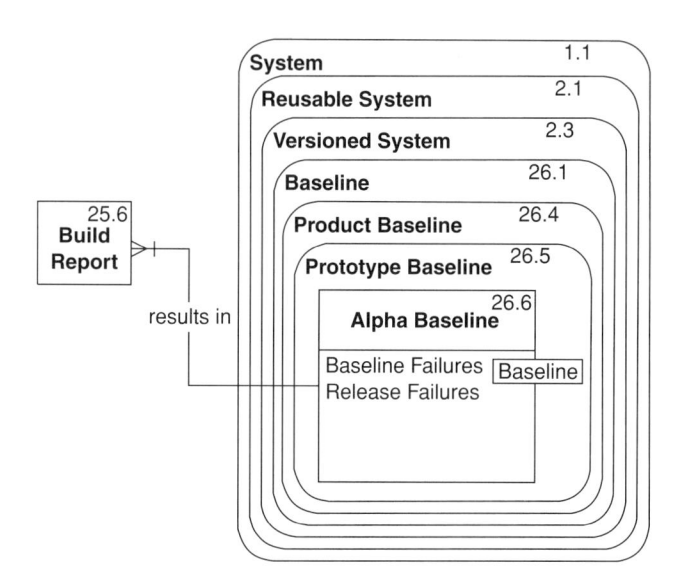

Vision: A prototype evolving into a deliverable system
Mission: To provide a stable base for system testing and release management

Objective 26.7: To provide a stable base for system testing

Approach 26.7: Determine the set of deliverable software systems that are to constitute the product. Ensure that all clusters and other components of these systems are checked into the configuration management system, and then freeze the system. Define the baseline in the configuration management system. Build the working system from the baseline. If the build succeeds, eventualize the alpha milestone; otherwise, revise the baseline components and try again.

Metric 26.7: Baseline failures: a count of test failures during system test caused by a fault that should have been discovered during object or integration testing according to their test criteria

Target 26.7: A count within control limits of a pn control chart for similar baselines

Objective 26.8: To provide a stable base for release management

Approach 26.8: See Approach 26.7. Use the configuration management system to structure the baseline for release, including developing a bill of materials. Identify any missing components that others will supply for future baselines.

Metric 26.8: Release failures: a count of failures after the alpha milestone caused by missing systems (systems whose absence resulted in the failure); excludes unplanned systems whose necessity is discovered during testing or release

Target 26.8: Zero

> ■ *Note:* Some QA departments perform an abbreviated system test as part of the baselining task. This provides a quick check on whether the system is really ready for system testing. The value of this depends largely on the estimated effort for system test.

Once you establish an alpha baseline, you must go through the change management process to make a change to any baselined system. This enables the alpha test process that runs system and regression test suites against the baseline. If you change the baseline, you must run all these tests again, which can be expensive.

You will usually not have many versions of the alpha baseline. The only circumstance where you might is when you retract the system, unfreeze development, and rebaseline the system. This would indicate a major failure in the system testing process of some kind, which you hopefully will avoid through good management earlier in the development process.

In an earlier chapter, I described one alpha baseline scheme promoted by a QA manager that wanted to lock down the system completely at alpha release. The rationale for this severe freeze was twofold. First, QA believed it was essential to test the release as a full deliverable. To do that, they needed all the files present before system test. Second, QA wanted to ensure that developers were not adding or changing anything during the test, which had happened in the past. This had resulted in many delays while QA figured out what was missing from the disk set, what had changed, and so on.

While this process was only slightly inconvenient to the developers, it had a major impact on documentation and other groups. The company was moving to online documentation, for example. This meant that the documentation had to be complete and ready for conversion to online format two weeks before alpha release (the process was complex and error prone). Similarly, the technical services group doing code examples and the marketing group doing tutorial examples and demos for inclusion on the disks had to finish before alpha. This in turn fed back into the development process, as all these external groups competed for developers' time before alpha, getting the help they needed to complete their tasks using not-quite-ready software. This became a major inconvenience to everyone.

Another company had two parallel alpha test schemes. The first was a standard QA-run alpha test. The second was a special variety of alpha feared and loathed by all developers: the presidential test. The project manager would install the new system on the workstation of the president of the company and he would "bang on it for a while." (You could also call this a field test, if your field were wide open with nothing in it.) The resulting problem reports would come back without enough information to identify the problem, much less fix it. After "banging on it" for a while, the president would usually storm into someone's office and berate them for producing garbage that didn't work.

You can guess where we found and fixed the most problems. The company eventually found and fixed its problems, too.

The Field Baseline

The field test process transfers prototype final deliverables to stakeholders in the field for testing under their myriad odd hardware and software configurations. This kind of prototype baseline is the *field baseline*. The stakeholders file failure reports, feeding back the status of the baseline to developers. If field debugging is necessary, developers may change the software in the field, and then bring back changes [Bersoff 1991]. Thus, the field baseline needs formal change control, particularly in situations with parallel testing and fixing. The exit criteria for this baseline is successful completion of alpha system and regression tests signaled by successful test coverage. When you reach the field milestone, the software is ready for field release.

Vision: A deliverable software system free of configuration-related problems

Mission: To provide a stable basis for testing the software under field conditions

Objective 26.9: To provide a stable basis for testing the software under field conditions

Approach 26.9: Complete alpha regression and system test suites according to their test criteria, and then eventualize the field test milestone. Store the baseline in the product repository. Version the baseline for each iteration of field testing.

Metric 26.9: Baseline field failures: a count of the number of failures in the field due to systems missing from the baseline

Target 26.9: Zero

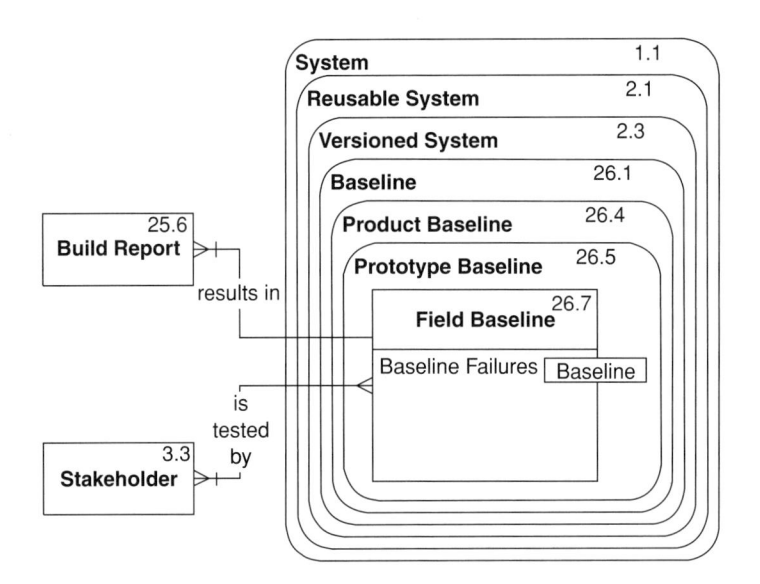

- *Note:* The field baseline is not the beta baseline. See the following section for this special class of field release. Field tests do not necessarily require the kind of monitoring and control that a full beta test requires. An example is Microsoft's style of "beta" test, involving as many as 7,500–15,000 or more beta sites. These field tests are enormously successful at removing configuration faults [Cusumano, pp. 309–313].

While system configuration tests can find many problems, the field is usually much more complex than any company can simulate in system tests. Even a company with as many resources as Microsoft cannot begin to completely test configurations [Cusumano, p. 310]. Giving the software to stakeholders for testing provides a kind of randomized system configuration test.

The baseline itself must have comprehensive change control. Field tests proceed in parallel at many client sites. Since the field baseline is not under version control at the client site, you must coordinate failure reports and fixes through change management. You will need to retest the software after each set of fixes to ensure that it runs correctly. To catch regression faults (unanticipated consequences of fixes), you may need to iterate through the test, sending baseline revisions to all field test sites. Each such release is a version of the field prototype baseline.

- *Note:* You can improve the quality of your field testing through proper random-sample-generation techniques, particularly stratified sampling. This technique lets you randomize within groups of stakeholders selected for their special contribution to the test and weighted accordingly. I'm sure you can identify the cluster of clients who are particularly error prone, for example. Send the prototype to all of this group, and then randomly sample the rest.

Microsoft has pioneered the technique of extensive field testing [Cusumano]. They have combined this with a philosophy of "good enough," releasing software to production when it is good enough to make money. The downside to this approach is the continuing embarrassment of major flaws. Microsoft has just released an upgrade to Windows NT 4.0 as I write that crashes systems and causes more problems than it fixes. While I suppose this is quite in line with my system of following the objectives, I think the approach tends to ignore some major stakeholders: the users of the software. Ultimately, I believe with Boris Beizer that this constitutes *software abuse* [Beizer]. I fervently hope the software industry does not go much further down this path.

The Beta Baseline

The *beta baseline* is a more formal field baseline. The alpha release process applies system test suites in a system testing process. The field release process applies random configuration tests. After each iteration of testing and debugging, you need to evaluate the exit criteria for the beta prototype. A beta test is a kind of field test that has much more developer involvement and control than the usual field test. The exit criteria for the beta prototype usually require a low fault discovery rate.

Vision: A deliverable software system free of configuration-related problems

Mission: To provide a stable basis for testing the software under field conditions

---

Objective 26.10: To provide a stable basis for testing the software under field conditions

---

Approach 26.10: Select a group of stakeholders likely to be able to rigorously test the product. Negotiate a contract with each stakeholder specifying testing responsibilities and remuneration. Assign a resource to manage each test effort as part of the contractual arrangement. Otherwise, proceed as in Approach 26.9.

Metric 26.10: Contract failures: a count of the number of failures to perform according to the beta contract

Target 26.10: A value within control limits on a pn chart of similar baselines

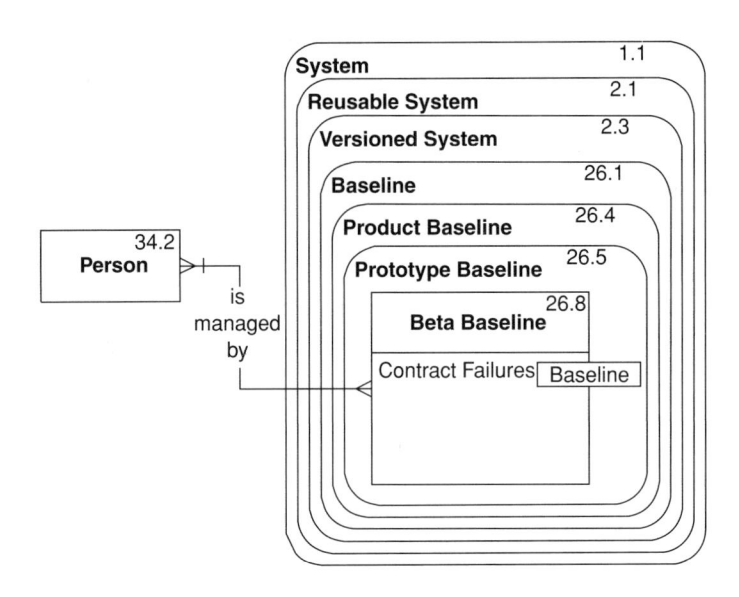

I bet there are companies that do real beta releases; if so, I haven't worked for them. Most companies do limited field testing rather than real beta testing. A beta test means putting a representative in the field capable of debugging and patching the code. Minimally, a technical support representative must track the beta and handle all failure reports, following up with the stakeholder to make sure the test is on schedule.

Ideally, a beta is a *contractual* arrangement, with the stakeholder taking responsibility for acceptance testing for the system and for reporting faults with the system. Some companies have begun to charge for beta test software as part of this contract. Naturally, some companies abuse this by delivering systems that are not viable and then taking no responsibility for supporting them. This is like selling a poke in the eye with a sharp stick and then telling the buyer to pay his or her own doctor bills. Vendors do this for marketing or competitive reasons, often trying to be "first to market." This approach can work for the vendor if the product is a "must-have" system; otherwise, it results in trash can liners.

Beta releases are essentially prerelease versions of the software. As prototypes, they are inherently riskier than production software. Therefore, stakeholders should evaluate the risk carefully before using the software. The most common use for a beta release is to prepare for integration of the upcoming production release.

The Product Baseline

It lets you get a head start on what you need to do to integrate the system into your operations. The second most common use is as a demonstration system for prospective buyers. The third most common use is to test the usability of the system in an extended field usability test.

The nature of the beta test renders it quite unsuitable as a testing strategy. By the time you get to this baseline, you do not want to change the system. Mostly, any changes will be major faults not found earlier or final versions of things such as documentation or examples. You want change control to be very tight on this baseline, with as few versions as possible.

The Production Baseline

The production baseline is a product baseline that completely freezes the system. After beta testing, the software must satisfy the exit criteria for the beta or field test, usually involving the number, discovery rate, and priority of faults in the software. This results in a production baseline. The production baseline becomes the software system you deliver as a product.

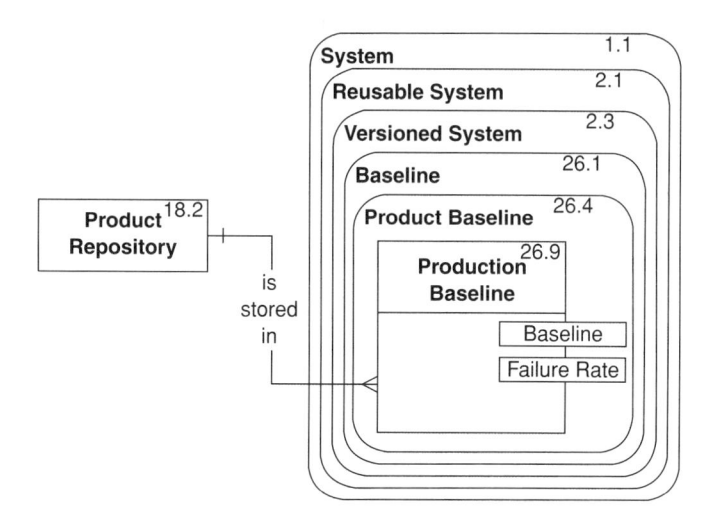

Vision: A software system that delivers value to stakeholders

Mission: To provide a stable definition of the deliverable software product

---

Objective 26.11: To freeze the deliverable software systems for delivery to stakeholders

---

Approach 26.11: Build the production system and store the results in the product repository. Run the system regression test suites on the baseline. On successful completion of the regression test according to its test criteria, eventuate the production milestone.

Metric 26.11: Failure rate: a derived ratio value combining time, number of registered users, number of reported failures in the field, and failure priority to show the weighted rate of failure of the baseline with respect to time and use

Target 26.11: A value within control limits of a pn chart of similar products

---

Metric 26.11 is a major product metric for a software system. The failure rate of the production baseline is the key to your product improvement plans because it directly measures the impact of your product to stakeholders. The production milestone that the baseline eventuates makes strong claims about the reliability of the product. The failure rate provides feedback on those claims.

The production baseline can prove to be the most problematic baseline in this hierarchy. Because of its prominence in the project, virtually every critical path in the project converges on this baseline and its milestone. It must be on the critical path. The result: time pressure, stakeholder pressure, and high risk. The milestone measures the schedule risk; the baseline measures the product risk. Going for the schedule invariably results in lower product quality and a higher risk of product failure in the field.

I worked in one OO project that was an exercise in meeting deadlines. The project sponsor did not prioritize product quality or meeting the stakeholders' expectations other than by delivering a product on time, a business goal. He cut some major features from the product, but coming up on the production milestone, it looked as though the product would not meet the system test criteria. It was just too unstable. We iterated and delivered on schedule, barely, shipping the product to the field only by relaxing the test criteria. The result: several required maintenance releases, some bad press, rather poor revenues, and a hearty handclasp from the project sponsor for meeting our schedule. There were over 3,000 reported faults (not failures, faults) in the product at the end of six months in the field. I shared an office with the maintenance project manager, who favored short haircuts so he couldn't pull his hair out. We learned all the varieties of the human voice saying the word "deferred."

Improvement Plan (1.3)

The Performance Evaluation Baseline

Performance evaluation baselines play an essential role in calculating earned value and other measures of performance such as return on investment. Earned value depends on the estimated value of an object with respect to time, as does return.

The Performance Evaluation Baseline

You will find most systems having to do with time in the project plan, and that is the logical place to look for baselining.

Vision: *A clear picture of the progress of the project according to its plan*

Mission: *To enable evaluation of the performance of the project according to its plan*

Objective 26.12: To enable evaluation of the performance of the project according to its plan

---

Approach 26.12: Store the systems with value and time estimates in the project repository. Maintain these copies as part of the baseline, even when the original objects change as you replan. Use the baseline to calculate the planned and earned value (or other performance measures) of the project at a specific time.

Metric 26.12: Evaluation failures: the count of the number of failures you encounter while trying to evaluate the performance of your project

Target 26.12: A number within control limits of a pn control chart of performance evaluations using similar baselines

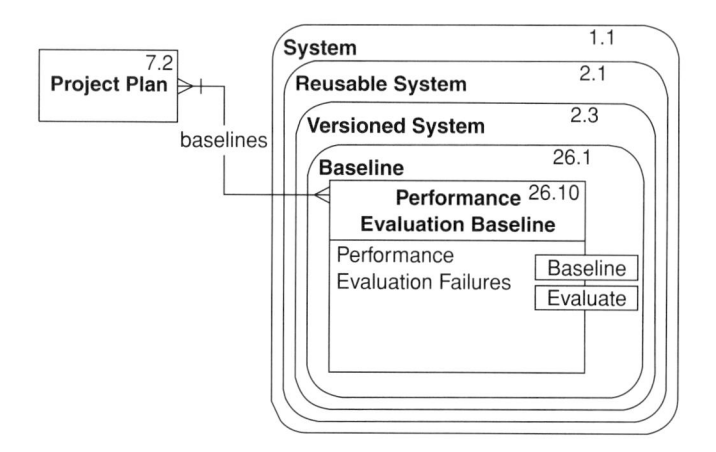

A performance evaluation baseline stores the state of systems containing time and value estimates in the project repository. When it comes time for performance evaluation, you use these time and value estimates to compare to your actual and earned value, usually in the current versions of the systems you baselined.

An OO project, with its heavy reliance on rolling-wave and iterative planning, requires multiple baseline versions. In this situation, your performance measure is relative to the baseline you select as the benchmark for your project. You can, for example, revise your benchmark baseline to be the most recent baseline rather than fixing the baseline at the beginning of the project. Earned value could thus change over the course of the project as the baselined proposed value changed. While this may seem attractive in a really dynamic (that is, horrendously chaotic) environment, it is usually better to benchmark the planned value for the project at the end of the planning stage. If the planned value changes drastically, you should revisit the plan and communicate the changes to the stakeholders in a comprehensive way before changing the benchmark of the project value, since this value relates directly to stakeholder expectations.

■ *Note:* None of the project management systems I've used is particularly good at multiple baselining. Usually, the software supports one or possibly two baselines. When you version the baseline, you must overwrite the previously saved baseline, either in its entirety or task by task. You thus get earned-value calculations but no history or ability to roll back the plan to a previous baseline. I find this limiting because I'd like to use baseline changes in my planning improvement plans. If the project management system doesn't keep them, I can't do that.

Process Milestone (4.13)
System (1.1)
Cost Budget (37.3)

For earned-value calculations, you must baseline the development process milestones in the project plan and the value and summary cost estimates for the systems you deliver at these milestones. At each major process milestone, you then evaluate progress against the benchmark. Calculate the amount of planned value you have earned through process completion and the amount of value you planned to earn by this time or cost expenditure.

For return-on-investment (ROI) calculations, you must baseline either your ROI estimates from your plan, if any, or the elements of the plan you need to calculate estimated ROI (estimated value, cost estimates, investment period, discount rate, estimated cash flows). At each major process milestone, you can calculate the current return on investment updated with actual cash flows and revised cost estimates, and then compare it to the baseline.

Cost Budget (37.3)
Spending Budget (37.4)

For simple schedule or budget performance, you can baseline the schedule tasks, milestones, and cost estimates. You can then calculate the average variance at each process milestone. The variance is the difference between the budgeted time or cost (the baseline) and the actual time or cost at the milestone. You can also compare the actual cost or spending to the cost or spending budget curves. This kind of metric tells you how good your estimates were, but it is not a good metric for project performance; use earned value for that.

The main problem I've experienced with performance baselining comes from a "crashing-wave" style of planning. I've been in several projects, and "managed" a couple, that replaced weekly planning meetings with daily plan-trashing meetings, or nearly so. This usually happens for a very poorly specified project with many missed requirements. It can also happen if your architecture is badly designed and you wind up having to redesign time after time, resulting in massive WBS changes as your project "progresses." Baselines in such projects are meaningless, if not actively detrimental to your sanity. My only recommendation is to get the architecture or expectations under control, and then baseline and evaluate.

This situation can also happen when designers or programmers go completely out of control and start changing everything out from under your plan. You are then, with Alice, just running as fast as you can to stay in the same place. Again, baselines become meaningless.

The worst situation from the performance evaluation perspective is where the autonomy of the individual or team is such as to negate effective planning. That is, you don't have any say in what happens. You turn over the requirements to the developers, and they produce whatever they want to produce. On one OO project I managed with little authority, I even started with the developer's own requirements for the component. With little interaction or status reporting, this developer worked for four months and produced a component that looked completely different from what he had specified. Since he had not updated the specification, the plan, WBS, and schedule baselines were instantaneously rendered useless for evaluation. They were simply not comparable. This situation is like when you wake up in the morning and you can't remember who you are. You have a hard time figuring out what you're doing and how you're doing.

The Contract Baseline

The contract baseline is a kind of performance evaluation baseline that you apply through a contract administration process. This baseline lets you measure the performance of the contractor through earned value at various milestones in the contract administration process.

Vision: A clear picture of the progress of the project according to its contracted baseline

Mission: To enable evaluation of the performance of the contractor according to the contract

---

Objective 26.13: To enable evaluation of the performance of the contractor according to the contract

---

Approach 26.13: Baseline critical process milestones and value and cost estimates for the contract as part of the contract document. Maintain these through a formal change management process. Use the baseline to calculate the planned and earned value (or other performance measures) of the contract at a specific time.

Metric 26.13: Evaluation failures: the count of the number of failures you encounter while trying to evaluate the contractor's performance

Target 26.13: A number within control limits of a pn control chart of performance evaluations using similar baselines

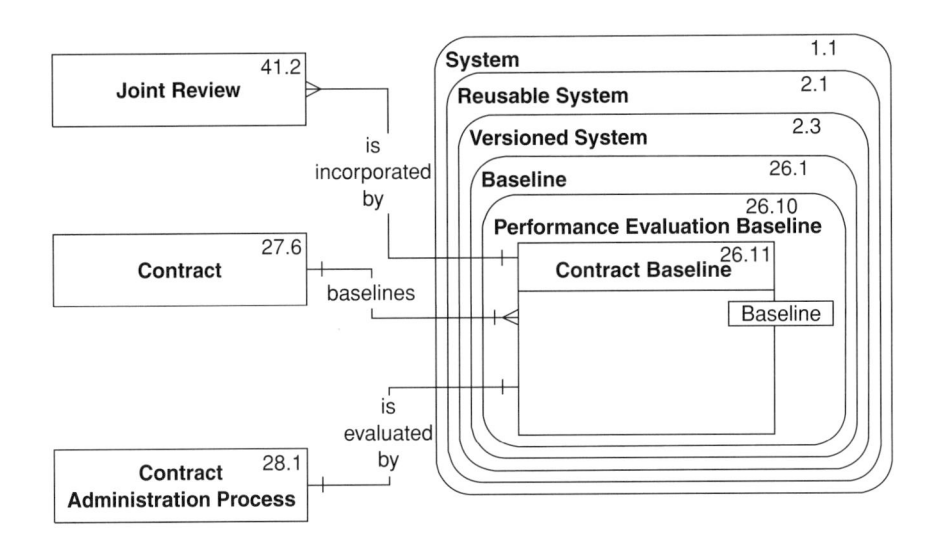

Contract administration involves a great deal of evaluation. As the contract progresses, it is vital that you understand how well the contractor is doing. The contract baseline not only provides this view on the contractor's performance but formalizes it legally into a binding contract. This contract specificity has two major goals. First, it communicates the plan, committing both you and the contractor to deadlines, budgets, and deliverables. Second, it gives you clear and easy-to-enforce legal grounds for contract action in the face of nonperformance.

I've seen many contracts over the 15 years I've been in the software arena. Most have the clarity of a San Francisco summer day (we get a lot of fog here). For some reason, it seems difficult for people to specify in a software contract what they expect. Using a baseline clarifies the performance implications of a contract enormously.

Contract (27.6)
Contract Administration Process (28.1)

You can incorporate the baseline into the contract as part of the contract provisions rather than supplying it on signing. This lets you gather expectations; develop plans, tasks, schedules, and budgets; and write everything up into a project plan. You can then review the plan with the contractor in a joint review, get their acceptance of the terms, and baseline the plan. This contract baseline then becomes part of the contract by reference.

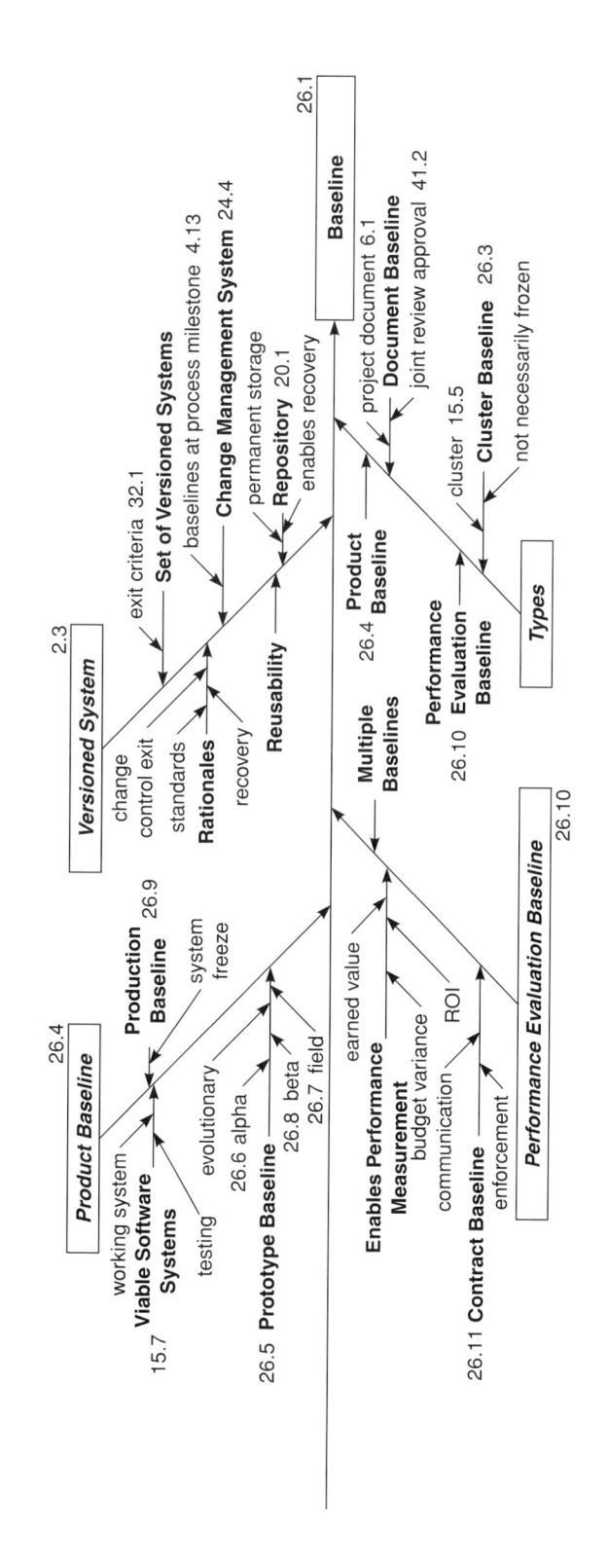

The Contract Baseline

Baseline 26.1

- exit criteria 32.1
- **Set of Versioned Systems**
  - baselines at process milestone 4.13
- **Change Management System** 24.4
  - permanent storage
- **Repository** 20.1
  - enables recovery
- *Versioned System* 2.3
  - change control exit standards
  - **Rationales**
    - recovery
    - Reusability
- *Types*
  - project document 6.1
  - **Document Baseline**
  - joint review approval 41.2
  - cluster 15.5
  - **Cluster Baseline** 26.3
  - not necessarily frozen
- **Product Baseline** 26.4
  - Multiple Baselines
- **Performance Evaluation Baseline** 26.10

Product Baseline 26.4

- **Production Baseline** 26.9
  - system freeze
- 15.7 **Viable Software Systems**
  - working system
  - evolutionary
  - testing
  - 26.6 alpha
  - 26.8 beta
  - 26.7 field
- 26.5 **Prototype Baseline**
- **Enables Performance Measurement**
  - earned value
  - budget variance
  - ROI
  - communication
  - enforcement
- 26.11 **Contract Baseline**

Performance Evaluation Baseline 26.10

Readings

There are very few readings devoted to baselines. Most discussions of baselines mention them in passing while discussing configuration or change management. See the Readings section of the chapter on configuration management for readings that discuss software baselines.

[Bersoff 1991]   Edward H. Bersoff and Alan M. Davis. Impacts of life cycle models on software configuration management. *Communications of the ACM* 34:8 (August 1991): 104–117.

This article describes the impact of reuse, prototyping, and RAD on configuration management. For baselines, there is a particularly good discussion of the sharing issues with reused components and the issues with evolutionary prototyping. There is an excellent model of field-test prototyping and the consequent need for change control on field updates.

[Cusumano]   Michael A. Cusumano and Richard W. Selby. *Microsoft Secrets: How the World's Most Powerful Software Company Creates Technology, Shapes Markets, and Manages People.* The Free Press, 1995.

This book provides an excellent case study of a major commercial software vendor's baselining strategies. In particular, the description of the postdevelopment release process is excellent and eye-opening. Fifteen thousand beta sites!

[PMI 1996a]   Project Management Institute Standards Committee. *A Guide to the Project Management Body of Knowledge.* Project Management Institute (+1-610-734-3330), 1996.

Sections 7.3 and 7.4 discuss cost budgeting and cost control, which involve cost baselines. Section 7.3.3.1 defines a cost baseline as a time-phased budget that measures cost performance on the project. Section 7.4.3.2 discusses budget updates and rebaselining. The approach in the current book calls the time-phased budget a cost budget and discusses it along with the rest of the cost management materials in Part 12. It also takes a very different approach to rebaselining based on the iterative/incremental process architecture of OO projects.

Questions to Think About

1. How do the exit criteria for baselines compare to the exit criteria for process phases in standard development process models?

2. What is the practical difference between creating a baseline and versioning a baseline? (Hint: How do you treat a system and a version of a system differently?)

3. If you change a reusable system in your shared reuse repository, how do you notify everyone who needs to know about the change? (Hint: What kind of record keeping must you do?)

4. What is the practical difference between change management and configuration management? How do you distinguish between systems under change management and systems under configuration management? (Hint: What is the relationship between the change management process and the configuration management process?)

5. Have you ever been a part of a beta test? Field test? Did the test help improve the quality of your software? Why or why not? How many test sites were there, and what was the impact of that number on the success of the test?

6. If you don't evaluate progress on a contract through a baseline, what can you use?

7. How can you develop earned-value measures of a contract amount? What are the prerequisites that need to be in the contract?

PART NINE

Procurement

You pays your money and you takes your choice.

Anonymous

Procurement has often been seen as a cure for insomnia, which is unfortunate as it can be the primary means of ensuring that your OO project makes optimal reuse of available systems. Acquiring systems from outside the project is the essence of reuse, and you need procurement to do it well.

The procurement process and process model organize the whole process of procurement, including the solicitation for proposals through the request for proposal, the assessment of proposals with assessment criteria, and the selection of a seller and signing of a contract to deliver the reusable system. The procurement management plan coordinates this process and the accompanying contract administration process.

This latter process oversees the cooperation between the contracting parties to make sure that the contract results in the expected value to your project. The contract administration process model gives you a reusable process for managing your contracts. The contract administration system is a tool that helps you to manage and store all the information. The contract report helps you to evaluate the progress of the seller in achieving the contract baseline milestones.

```
System                                                    1.1
  Reusable System                                         2.1
    Versioned System                                      2.3
      Tool                        P7.1   Project Document          6.1
        Information System        22.1     Formal Project  6.2   Progress Report  42.1
                                  28.3     Document
          Contract Administration                         27.6                    28.4
          System                             Contract                Contract Report

                                             Request for  27.3      Proposal      27.4
                                             Proposal

      System Model                                                                1.7
        Plan                       7.1   Process Model              4.7
                                  27.7                              28.2   Policy         32.1
          Procurement                      Contract Administration                        27.5
          Management Plan                  Process Model                   Assessment
                                                                    27.2   Criterion
                                             Procurement Process
                                             Model

  Process                                                                         4.6
    Primary Process                                                               16.3
                                  27.1
      Procurement Process

                                  28.1
      Contract Administration Process
```

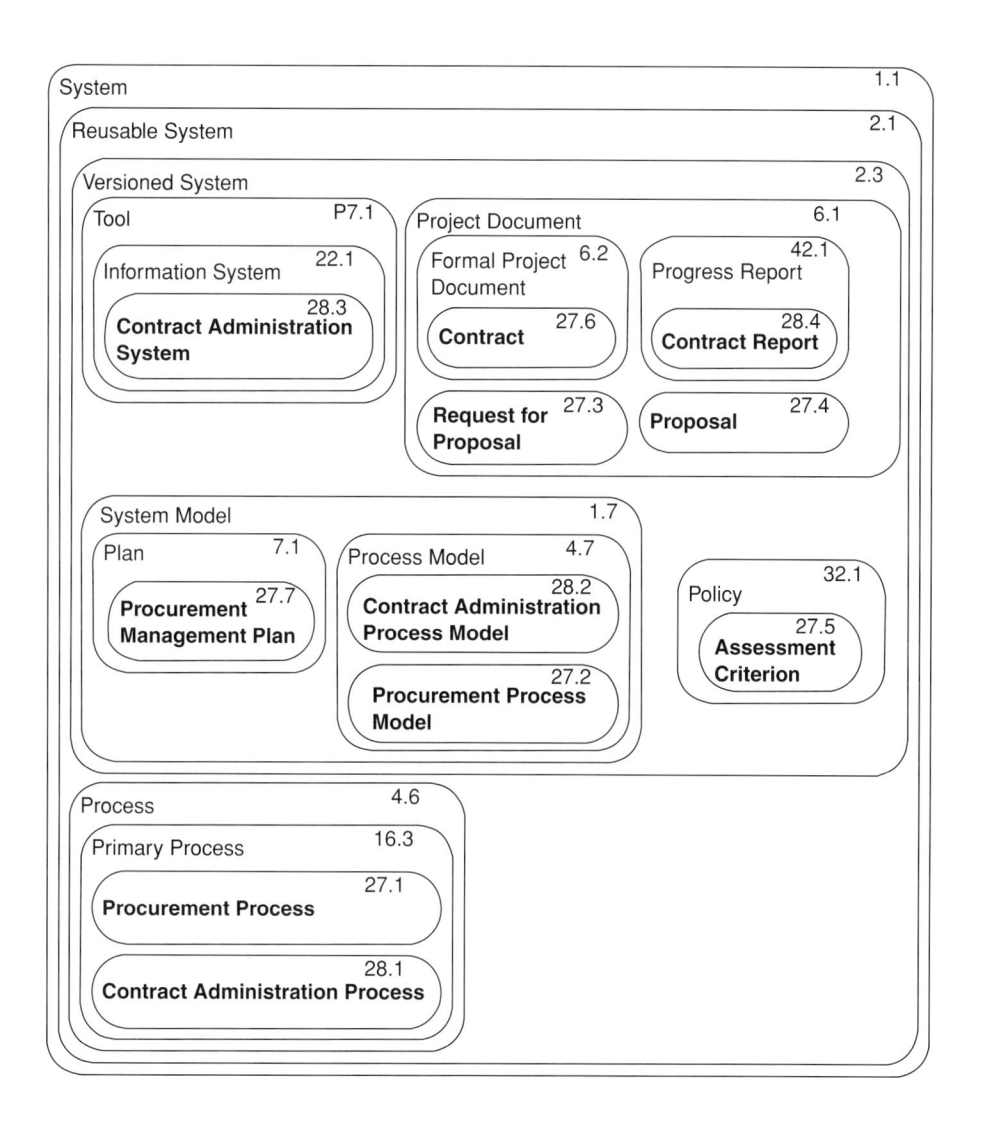

- *Note:* The illustration of the class hierarchy contains all the classes this part defines. Other parts of the book define and discuss classes not in boldface.

CHAPTER

27 Procurement

The Procurement Process

The *procurement process* is the primary process for acquiring products that you reuse in a project. Procurement usually involves contracts and proposals as well as methods for assessing proposals, all specified by policies in the procurement process model. The essence of procurement is reuse. Like any primary process, the objective is to deliver a reusable system. The major difference in the procurement process is that you are *acquiring* reusable systems, either from a reuse repository or from a third-party supplier, instead of building them yourself. Once you put a contract in place, you plan and execute a contract administration process to guide the contract to a successful delivery.

There are many words for the parties in the process. The party that is acquiring the system is the "acquirer," "purchaser," or "buyer." The terms "contractee" (not a word) and "procurer" (a word with a different meaning) aren't used much. The party that is supplying the system can be the "vendor," "supplier," "contractor," or "seller." Which term you use depends entirely on the domain, the nature of the agreement, and the mood of the parties. I will use the terms "seller" and "buyer" here.

Vision: *Reusable systems deployed to best effect in the project*

Mission: *To manage the acquisition of reusable systems for successful reuse in the project*

Objective 27.1: To decide whether to make or buy the reusable system

Approach 27.1: Start with the decision to buy the system instead of making it. Develop a high-level statement of work that defines the system. Evaluate the

The Procurement Process

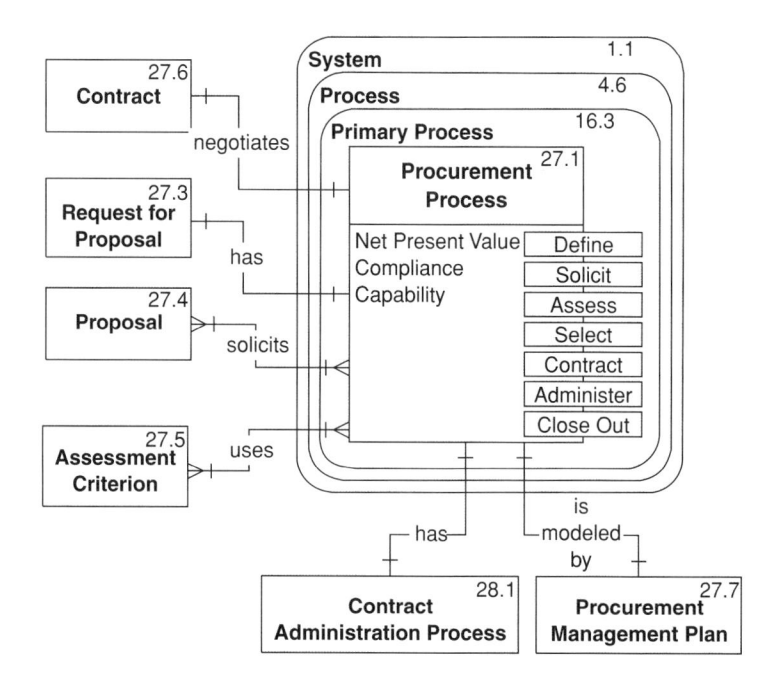

[Diagram: Procurement Process relationships showing System Process → Primary Process → Procurement Process (27.1) with sub-activities Define, Solicit, Assess, Select, Contract, Administer, Close Out; related entities: Contract (27.6), Request for Proposal (27.3), Proposal (27.4), Assessment Criterion (27.5), Contract Administration Process (28.1), Procurement Management Plan (27.7). Attributes: Net Present Value, Compliance, Capability. Relationships: negotiates, has, solicits, uses, has, is modeled by.]

effect of different acquisition methods (off-the-shelf, contract, customization, or enhancement) on the decision. Evaluate as many alternative ways of satisfying the requirements as you can. If necessary, exclude alternatives by a triage method, focusing on those alternatives most likely to provide the highest value. Review the decision process with stakeholders of the system, and in particular with those who will use it, to establish the legitimacy of and support for the decision. Obtain the approvals required for the decision to proceed.

Metric 27.1: Net present value of cash flows

Target 27.1: A positive net present value greater than any feasible alternative

---

Objective 27.2: To improve project productivity through acquisition of externally built systems with high reuse potential for the project

---

Approach 27.2: Create the request for proposal containing the system requirements and business issues. Put the request out to bid, soliciting proposals. Evaluate the reuse potential of each proposal you receive in the context of the requirements (inherent, domain, and organizational reuse issues). Evaluate the certification of the proposal using assessment criteria. Using the proposal compliance metrics, compare the proposals and select one. Contract with the supplier for the reusable system. Put in place a contract administration process to evaluate progress, control change, accept deliverables, and audit the process.

Metric 27.2: Assessment criteria compliance: the degree to which the acquisition process results in reusable systems that comply with the assessment criteria; for numerical criteria, an appropriate aggregate or multiattribute metric; for qualitative criteria, an appropriate subjective, ordinal rating scale such as High, Medium, Low

Target 27.2: A value that suggests a risk within tolerance for the reusable system; that is, the system should comply with the criteria to an extent commensurate with the risk tolerance of the reusing system

---

Objective 27.3: To acquire a needed system with skills, expertise, or resource levels not available within the project organization

---

Approach 27.3: Given the requirements for the system, evaluate your organization to decide whether it has the skills, expertise, and resources to build the system. If not, evaluate an alternative that lets you acquire those skills or resources versus one that acquires the system from an external source. Include in the analysis the benefits of acquiring the skills for future projects, amortizing the cost over those projects.

Metric 27.3: Acquisition capability: a ratio of skills or resources available to those required to build the system

Target 27.3: For a build or enhancement or customization decision, a positive acquisition capability; for an off-the-shelf or contract solution, a negative acquisition capability

---

There are several ways in which you can acquire a reusable system. Table 27-1 lists the different methods and some advantages and disadvantages of each.

- *Note:* If you choose to build the system yourself, you have essentially voted with your feet against reusing available components. As such, you are not procuring, you are developing new systems. Therefore, the procurement process does not deal with the "build" alternative; instead, that is a development process within the project, a different variety of primary process.

Whatever method you use to evaluate your alternatives, you must be careful to understand how you will use the value of the desired system. You can't assume, for example, that the entire value of the system goes to your project. A reusable system is just that: reusable in multiple projects. If the system you are acquiring has high reuse potential, your return-on-investment analysis must allocate both value and cost to multiple projects, not just to your own [PMI 1996a; McTaggart]. That usually increases the value of the system and decreases its cost to your project. A consequence is that the make-or-buy decision usually favors the buy side and procurement over development. Otherwise, reuse wouldn't make much sense. Another consequence is that some systems available through rental, such as computers or other hardware, become targets for purchase instead.

Buying off-the-shelf systems, and especially software systems, requires an extensive evaluation of the product's characteristics. In addition to comparing the functions of the product to your requirements, you must examine several aspects of the package [ISO 1995]. These features of the agreement are part of the certification of the system as a reusable system.

- The product documentation
- Training materials and courses
- Various proprietary rights (copyright, trademarks, trade secrets, patents)
- Licensing terms, especially with respect to multiple use of the system
- Warranty, liability limitations, and consumer protection issues
- Support policies (terms for support, maintenance upgrades, and so on)
- Tax issues

Table 27-1 Acquisition Methods

Method	Description	Analysis
Off-the-Shelf	Commercially available, prepackaged systems or systems from the reuse repository that deliver value immediately on acquisition	Entire cost is in acquisition and training; manageable risk of failure; higher risk of lack of support
Contract	Formal acquisition of system through the work of a third party by contract	Skills and expertise of third party can reduce overall cost and deliver value sooner than the build method; higher risks of acquisition failure, higher maintenance costs depending on support and maintenance contract
Customize	Customization of an off-the-shelf system	More likely to satisfy requirements than off-the-shelf systems; higher training cost, additional cost for customization effort, risk of customization failure, higher maintenance costs
Enhance	Enhance a system already available within the project	Less risk, less cost than other methods; less likely to satisfy requirements, depending on reuse potential of existing system
Combination	Combine any of the other methods to balance risks with rewards	Balanced risks and rewards; higher cost, potentially higher overall risk due to higher complexity of solution

Reusable System (2.1)

Enhancement or customization of an acquired system is a standard way to reuse a system. Although this means you aren't getting the full benefit of reuse and are incurring some maintenance issues, you do benefit to the extent that you aren't building and testing the system from scratch.

I've handled two contracts that involved extensive customization. The first was a client/server interface framework that let you connect your application to various kinds of database managers using a standard language and interface. The seller of this system sold you the source code, and you as buyer needed to customize it to your target file system or DBMS. This permitted early OO systems to integrate database managers into a standard client/server framework. Managing the process turned out to be more difficult than expected, however. The seller had designed the framework as a portable system on the UNIX operating system, and our target platform was Microsoft Windows. The memory management module turned out to have many faults that weren't obvious until you had a 64K memory limit. This easily tripled our work from the original schedule and made the system much less valuable as a reusable system.

The second contract was for the integration of a graphics system into a larger OO client/server interface. Our company contracted for the graphics libraries but needed to customize them to handle various kinds of callbacks and other interactions with the user. Because the user had an extensive programming environment available, they needed deeper access to the underlying graphics libraries than the original company had engineered. This is the kind of situation that you hire really good programmers for; we did, and we successfully integrated the package, though not without various contract-oriented worries. Buying the system instead of developing it ourselves probably generated millions of dollars in extra revenue for our company's products.

The procurement process begins with putting the system out to bid with a request for proposal (RFP). The RFP solicitation contains the initial statement of work and other elements that sellers need to know to be able to bid on the project. Once you select a seller, you must evolve the statement of work as a cooperative effort as part of the contract administration process.

The selection process takes the bids that result from the RFP and uses a decision process to decide among them. You apply your assessment criteria policies to the bids, rating them and balancing pluses and minuses. If you can make the decision objectively using quantitative methods, so much the better; often, you must include some qualitative analysis. You can also often negotiate with different sellers to remove obstacles that prevent the bid from being considered. A big part of the assessment process is your evaluation of the bid against your technical and business requirements. You need to weight these with priority weights to make sure you are not rejecting bids on minor issues that are perfectly satisfactory on the major ones. Again, this selection process is an optimization process. You may need to go through several bidding rounds to finalize your selection for major acquisitions.

Once you select a bid, you then enter the contract negotiation process, and a later section takes that up. Having signed a contract, you start up the contract administration process. When this process completes, with all systems delivered and all invoices paid, you close out the contract, making sure you have a complete audit trail of all the documents and other systems relating to the contract.

The Procurement Process Model

The *procurement process model* contains the process tasks and work flows for the procurement process. Using this model, you generate the procurement management plan that guides the procurement process to a successful conclusion.

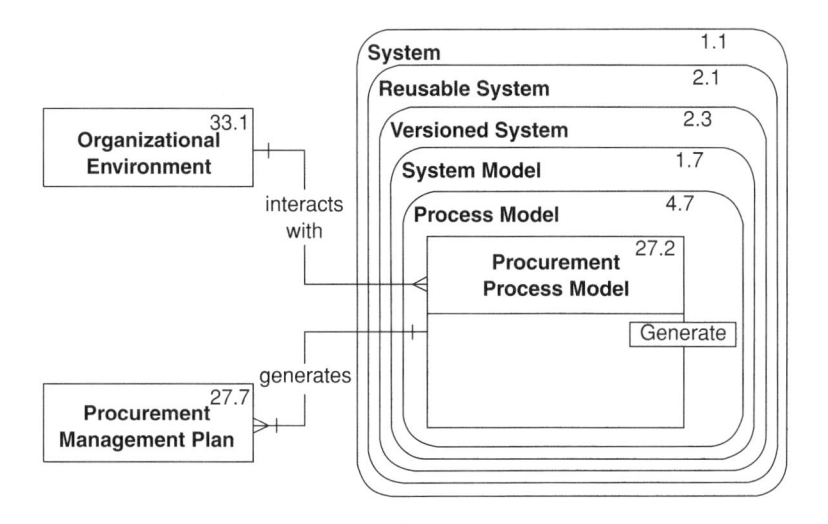

Vision: A valuable, reusable, productive procurement process you productively plan from a continuously improving model

Mission: To represent a productive acquisition process that you want to reuse many times

---

Objective 27.4: To represent the process to allow planning of acquisitions with optimal productivity

---

Approach 27.4: Model the process with the tasks, milestones, and work flows that represent the generic work and structure of the process. Include standard assumptions, contracting policies, organizational responsibilities, communications tasks, and risks. Train anyone who participates in the process in how the process works, and facilitate the use of the process model at the appropriate organizational levels (team, project, functional, and so on). Legitimate the process model in the organization through communication, training, and participative process modeling activities.

The procurement process is usually a central administrative process for a company, and often the financial or operations organization maintains control of this process and its process model. Especially in a functional organization, this means that each project must interact with the organizational environment to obtain reusable systems. A well-supported process model is of great value in making this relationship work.

The same things that make for a well-supported model make for a reusable model. The inherent reuse potential of the model comes from its ability to get the job done productively. If you hate the bureaucracy of your purchasing department, you're probably spending time finding ways not to go through purchasing. This can inspire bizarre behavior, such as buying totally inappropriate off-the-shelf systems or spending large amounts of money on customization of systems that you could contract out with better, and cheaper, results.

Domain reuse depends almost entirely on the quality of the model. If the model adequately represents standard procurement requirements, it should be quite generic and applicable to many different systems. If you include special-purpose tasks and dependencies in this model, you have a model that is less reusable.

Organizational reuse is critical. In most cases, it requires company policy to mandate the use of the procurement model throughout the company. Few operations or purchasing departments understand how to work with technical departments to create spontaneous use of their purchasing models. Unless you are a projectized organization with your own procurement department, count on following the CFO's policies with respect to the procurement model.

The Request for Proposal

The *request for proposal* (RFP) is a project document that solicits proposals, bids, or quotations from prospective contractors.

Vision: A clearly defined and expressed need for reusable systems

Mission: To define a system you need to acquire to a level of detail that makes it possible for third parties to bid on the project

---

Objective 27.5: To specify the technical requirements for the acquired system for bidding

---

The Request for Proposal 453

Approach 27.5: Create a requirements document, a deliverable specification, and a high-level work breakdown structure in a statement of work. Make sure to define clearly any technical systems constraints, such as operating platforms, performance requirements, and so on. Review the statement of work in the usual ways. Approve the statement of work through a joint review with the stakeholders of the system to acquire.

Objective 27.6: To specify the business requirements for the acquired system for bidding

Approach 27.6: Create sections in the RFP that describe the terms and conditions of the contract, subcontracting terms, and instructions for bidders. Review any departures from standard sections from the document template with financial, legal, and project management experts. Specify any restrictions on schedule (milestone requirements) or budget (cost limits). Get approval for the business requirements from a stakeholder with authority to sign the contract.

Metric 27.6: Bidding failures: number of bids that fail to meet business requirements

Target 27.6: A low number within control limits of a pn control chart of RFPs

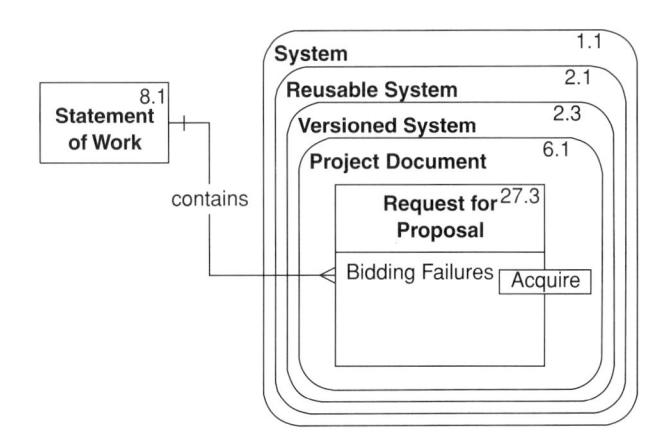

Alternative terms for the RFP are the "invitation for bid," "invitation for quotation," "invitation for negotiation," and "contractor initial response."

The RFP contains the statement of work for the system, which in turn includes a requirements document, a list of deliverable systems, and a high-level WBS. The point of this statement of work is to allow potential sellers to bid, so the level of detail must be enough to permit a seller to estimate the cost and schedule of the system. ISO-9000-3 calls for a "complete and unambiguous" set of requirements. As with any OO system, however, the requirements evolve with the architecture and with the environment. You do need to go deep enough that the bidders can get a good background for understanding what you want. You do not need to develop the final requirements document as part of the RFP.

Contract Administration Process (28.1)

The contract administration process uses this statement of work as the basis for the development process tasks that result in the final statement of work for the contract baseline.

RFPs can be reusable, but only within their limited domains. That is, while you can make inherent and organizational reuse potential high, it is difficult to create an RFP that is not domain specific. The acquisition process for an RFP usually involves looking over old RFPs for similar requirements and terms, providing a better starting place than a straight document template.

- *Note:* The RFP may be on its way out in software contracts. Potential replacements include a simpler requirements-driven survey, a screened shortlist of potential vendors with an abbreviated RFP, a scenario-based approach similar to use cases, and a partnering model [GT Online].

The Proposal

The *proposal* is a project document that contains the response of a contractor to a request for proposal. This may not be *your* project document but someone else's, of course. Also, this document is not a preliminary contract, though it may include one. The form and structure of this document is set by the RFP to which it responds.

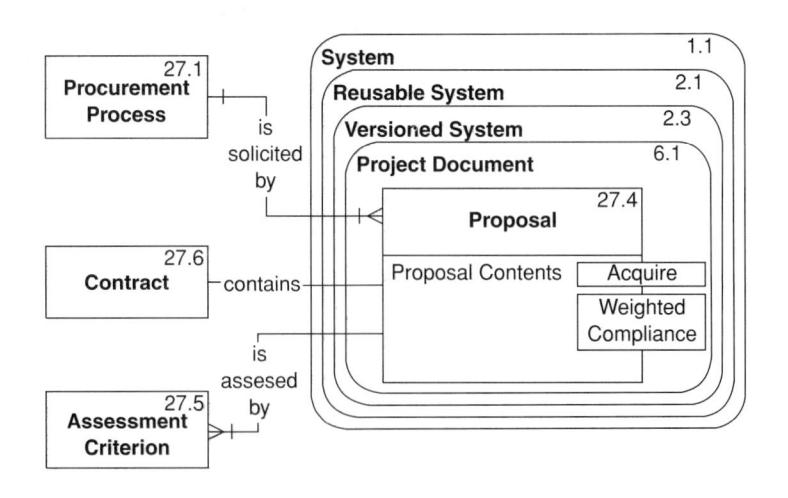

Vision: A clearly defined and expressed proposal to supply a system for reuse in your project

The Proposal

Mission: To present a proposal for the supply of a reusable system

Objective 27.7: To present a proposal for the supply of a reusable system

Approach 27.7: The supplier responds to the RFP with the proposal document by the indicated deadline, if any. You then measure the compliance of the proposal using the requirements and assessment criteria for comparison to other proposals.

Metric 27.7: Weighted proposal compliance: a potentially multiattribute metric that measures how well the proposal complies with requirements and assessment criteria. The weighting scheme weights these components with your priority structure. You must include in the computation some criteria designed to catch lowball bids (see the text for a discussion of this).

Target 27.7: The best compliance relative to all proposals to a specific RFP; possibly, compliance on one or more components better than a certain level indicating the minimal requirement for the criterion

A lowball bid is a proposal that is highly attractive to the buyer and costly to the seller. It represents a seller's attempt to get the work by pretending they can do it for much less than anyone else. Usually, this results in an attempt to create a contract that lets the contractor increase the cost later through change requests or other methods. Sometimes, the contractor will threaten to abandon the contract unless the buyer relents and gives them more money. Obviously, such proposals are totally unethical. Part of the process of evaluating any proposal requires a basic computation of costs, called "should-cost estimates." These estimates give you a ballpark figure you can use to eliminate lowballers. Proposals that come in with negative or minimal profitability for the supplier based on the should-cost estimate are almost certainly an attempt to lowball the bid. Reject these ploys.

In a larger context, you can get proposals that are loss leaders for other business. If the contractor can make a convincing case for this proposal's being a way to attract your business and that later contracts will make up the difference, you might accept the bid. In my experience, however, you should consider most contracts and proposals as separate entities. Things change too fast in this industry to make plans across more than one contract.

A proposal is a reusable system, but only for the bidder, not the buyer. The seller has the copyright on the document. In particular, you cannot reuse the proposal by giving it to another bidder: that's unethical. You can reuse it with the same bidder in a different procurement process, though, if that makes sense. Proposals tend to be very domain specific. As well, parts of the proposal, usually those having to do with cost, expire after some period of time.

The Assessment Criterion

The *assessment criterion* is a policy that contains at least one operational objective and a method for assessing contractor proposals through the metrics of those objectives. Each criterion contributes to one aspect of the overall assessment of the proposal.

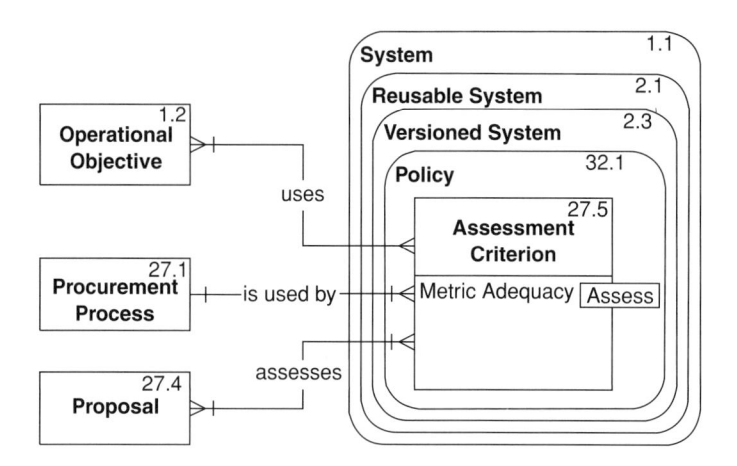

Vision: A clear and decisive assessment of the proposals for an acquisition process

Mission: To evaluate some aspect of a proposal

Objective 27.8: To evaluate some aspect of a proposal

Approach 27.8: Create the policy using metrics development methods suitable for the type of thing you want to measure. State the criterion in a format that an evaluator can easily use to implement the measure. Preferably, supply software for the metric with a storage design and algorithm for computation. Supply one or more examples of application of the criterion to proposals. Certify the criterion for reuse.

Metric 27.8: Metric adequacy: a multiattribute metric that evaluates the ability of the criterion to measure its domain

Target 27.8: An adequacy equal to its potential impact on your decision making

---

The operational objective serves as the basis for the assessment. The goal, approach, metric, and target are all relevant to the assessment. The goal expresses the purpose of the criterion: to assess some specific characteristic of a proposal. The approach explains how the assessment works for this criterion. The metric, applied to the proposal, is the tool you use to measure the criterion to assess it. The target is the operational definition of the criterion: achieving the target means that the proposal passes muster.

Depending on the particular criterion, you can rely on the target to assess the proposal, letting the entire proposal rise or fall on one assessment. Usually, however, you will want to combine several criteria, balancing their measures against each other. Thus the assess task gives you access to the measurement of the individual proposal as well as to the target comparison. So, even though a particular criterion may fail to meet its target, the proposal can still be acceptable if other criteria make up the difference. The procurement process system makes this judgment.

As with any reusable system, if you can create reusable assessment criteria, you'll be more productive in your acquisition processes because you can reuse the criteria in other procurement processes. Inherent reuse depends on the various characteristics of good metrics (Metric 27.8 measures this). Domain reuse depends on the domain generalization you can achieve in the criterion. Organizational reuse depends on the structure and method by which you make your criteria available to other procurement processes, as well as the legitimization of the criterion with other parts of the organization.

"Metric" section, Chapter 1, p. 22

Potential candidates for assessment criteria include any of the following:

- Seller understanding of buyer need
- Cost
- Seller's technical capability
- Seller's management capability
- Seller's financial capability
- Support policy
- Maintenance policy

The Contract

The *contract* is a formal project document that is a mutually binding, legal agreement between two or more parties to limit or compensate risks on both sides. The contract obligates sellers to provide a specified product and buyers to pay for it. Contracts are subject to remedy in the courts or in binding arbitration. Contracts specify the obligations, rights, and risk management methods of the procurement process for the seller and buyer [Fishman; Gordon].

- ■ *Note:* Many OO books, especially ones on design, like to call the relationship between clusters a "contract." That is, when you design an interface, you establish a contract with the users of that interface [Booch 1994; Booch 1996; Goldberg; Meyer; Wirfs-Brock]. This is a nice metaphor in some ways, but you shouldn't take it too literally. Interfaces are not legally binding, and they do not require a contract administration process, nor will they sue you in a court of law if you don't perform. They do require a change management process; in that sense, any baselined system establishes a "contract." Again: real contracts mean law, courts, and major commitments.

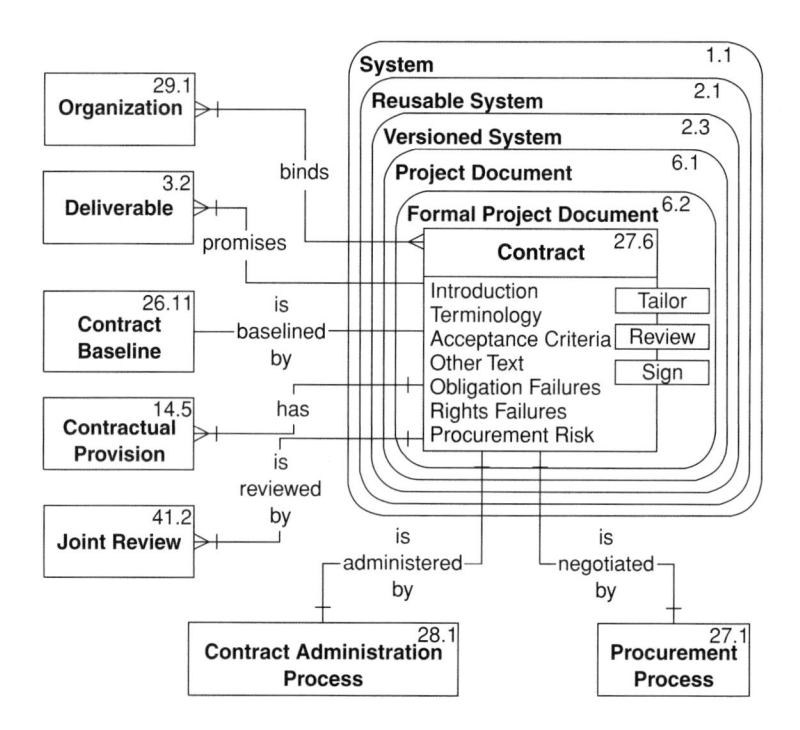

Vision: A win-win procurement process benefiting all the contracting parties

Mission: To clearly and completely express the obligations, rights, and risks incurred by the contracting parties

---

Objective 27.9: To express the obligations of the contracting parties

---

Approach 27.9: Develop contractual provisions that clearly define what the buyer is to pay, what the seller is to supply, and what the timing of those two things is. Make sure you specify the content and format of the deliverables. Add provisions for any special coordination or exchange required between buyer and seller, such as joint reviews, audits, or tools the buyer supplies to the seller. Add provisions that specify limits on subcontracting. Add provisions specifying acceptance criteria for the deliverables and specifying the acceptance process. Add provisions for auditing the seller if required.

Metric 27.9: Obligation failures: the number of problems with obligations that arise during contract administration that the contract does not cover

Target 27.9: A low number within control parameters of a pn control chart of similar contracts

---

Objective 27.10: To express the rights of the contracting parties

---

Approach 27.10: Assess the RFP and proposal for intellectual and other property rights issues. Add contract provisions that state clearly who owns what and what precise rights the parties have with respect to deliverables, tools, and any other system that is part of the procurement process. Be sure to specify the replication rights for software or other reproducible systems.

Metric 27.10: Rights failures: the number of problems with rights that arise during contract administration that the contract does not cover

Target 27.10: A low number within control parameters of a pn control chart of similar contracts

---

Objective 27.11: To express the risks and compensation for those risks to the contracting parties

---

Approach 27.11: Assess the RFP and proposal for risks to property and mission. For each risk above your tolerance, develop a contract provision that manages the risk, either through risk avoidance or risk mitigation.

Metric 27.11: Procurement risk: the risk of the procurement process that the contract controls

Target 27.11: A risk within the risk tolerance of the process

---

Contracts are one of those things that seem to deal with many different things but come down to the issue of risk in the end, much like quality assurance. The essence of a contract is to create a legally binding agreement where one party pays another party compensation for value. This begs the question: why have a contract at all? Because one party risks not getting paid and the other party risks not getting value. The courts are the biggest risk management method around. Unfortunately, they sometimes create as much risk as they manage. The legal process…don't get me started.

Because the contract is fundamentally about risk, the contractual provision is not in this chapter but in the risk management one. Contract provisions manage risks from compensation and value through liability to excessive cost and schedule

Contractual Provision (14.5)

risks. They come down to managing risk either by being very clear about what is expected or by agreeing to rewards and penalties for different situations to create incentives to do the right thing.

Usually, contract provisions that mitigate risk take the form of some kind of compensation. Incentive provisions, for example, compensate the buyer for schedule or cost overruns. Penalty provisions can compensate either party for some undesirable action or inaction by another party.

Contracts require contract administration. A contract that you cannot enforce has two problems. First, any risks you manage through such a contract won't be managed. Second, if the other party can show your lack of intention to enforce the contract, or even a single provision of the contract, you may be at risk later in the courts if you decide to enforce it. Law is a funny thing; until you use it, you never know what it will deliver. Legal enforcement of contracts is both expensive and uncertain. Enforcing the contract as you go is much more likely to be useful in the end.

Table 27-2 lists the various optional cost attributes of the contract. Many of these attributes only appear in government or other very large contracts.

There are as many kinds of contract as there are lawyers to create them, and probably more. From the project perspective, you need to know about the three types in Table 27-3.

For an OO system, the fixed-price alternative is probably the least useful one for both seller and buyer. Because OO systems develop with iterative, incremental methods, a contract that requires complete understanding at the beginning is less likely to result in a good system. Only if you are truly reusing a system does the fixed-price method make sense.

Table 27-2   Contract Cost Attributes [Kerzner, p. 1076]

Attribute	Description
Estimated Cost	The target for the total project budget; this is the value that appears in the contract baseline for final cost
Expected Profit	The target for the seller's profit on the project; this is the value that appears in the contract baseline
Price Ceiling	The maximum amount that the buyer will pay to the seller under the contract
Profit Ceiling and Floor	The maximum and minimum profit for the seller on the project; the profit cannot exceed these values
Maximum and Minimum Fees	The profit ceiling and floor expressed as percentages of the cost, tying the profit to the cost; you can put incentives for lower cost in with a declining percentage scheme
Sharing Responsibility	A division of savings or costs between the buyer and seller; this provides risk management for cost overruns and incentives for cost savings

Table 27-3 Types of Contract [PMI 1996a]

Contract Type	Description	Advantages and Disadvantages
Fixed-Price	The seller fixes the price for its product	Fixes the cost of the system; provides incentive for quick completion; requires complete scope and architecture before setting cost; has a more comprehensive bidding process; incurs higher cost due to contingencies built into estimates; tends to have more change requests
Cost-Reimbursable	The payment to the seller contains reimbursement of documented direct and indirect costs to the seller to produce the required systems	Buyer flexibility; minimization of excessive profit and bidding/negotiation process; no assurance of final cost or incentive to minimize such cost; tendency to allow too much change
Unit-Price	The payment to the seller depends on the number of units of the product or service sold to the buyer	Maximum buyer flexibility and control; some cost advantages; tends to reduce planning to nothing, resulting in higher risk of budget and schedule failure

While the unit-price method can be attractive, it is unusual in the software industry, which normally uses a licensing structure to preserve proprietary rights and limit liabilities. Some pricing structures, particularly for mid-level operating systems such as UNIX or VMS, price on a per-use or per-user basis. For supposedly reusable systems, this pricing structure complicates the return on investment, and it is thus less preferable than a site license or other structure that lets you take full advantage of the reusability of the acquired system. Unit prices work only if you can reuse the resulting system any way you wish; this is unusual in software licenses, though more usual for capital resources.

Unit prices also function well when you are contracting for personal services such as programming: $100 per hour, for example, with the value of the contract depending entirely on how many hours the contractor works. This can be a better deal for the contractor than for the buyer, but it depends. Many software companies can turn an employee into a contractor and save money doing so; this is not ethical, either on the contractor's part or on the part of the company. I worked briefly for one OO company that had very few employees; virtually everyone was a contractor. Most of them were just out of school and getting paid very low wages as a unit price. This allowed the company to hire and fire them with virtually no restrictions, to get the tax advantages of treating the fees as contract expenses instead of as wages subject to employment taxes, and to supply no benefits whatsoever. Another company laid off half of its workforce, then hired many people back as contractors. This is quite common in the software industry; it is also a scandal waiting to happen. (It's also not limited to the software industry, of course.)

Most OO procurements should look mainly at cost-reimbursable structures for systems that require development and fixed-price models for systems that you will reuse without change. Such contracts usually include incentives and penalties to manage the budget and schedule risks.

Because many reusable systems become "products," the sellers sell them at a fixed price or unit price. You buy the framework, reusable components, or OO development tools at the stated or negotiated price and customize them to your needs. Even if you are acquiring components from your organizational reuse library, the chargeback fee is usually a fixed or even unit price based on amortized value. This fixed-price approach works well if you are really interested in reuse and the reusable systems you acquire have high reuse potential in your project. The more you need to customize, the less valuable the fixed-price approach.

- *Note:* This is neither a legal treatise [Gordon] nor a book on the five easy steps to writing your own contract [Fishman]. If you want to know more, get a lawyer, a law degree, or a life, not necessarily in that order!

Almost every contract that gets executed in the world comes from a contract template, usually known as a "form." Standard contracts are a way of life. Part of a company's operations include putting in place standard contracts for the situations it will face. These things are much too complex to recreate from scratch every time you need one. The contract itself is thus usually not reusable, though it has been done; the contract template is highly reusable, typically through adaptation and customization to the specific situation. Writing a good contract form is mostly about using the right language and internal construction (inherent reuse potential), removing any domain-specific language other than that always found when the contract occurs (domain reuse potential), and convincing managers to use the form (organizational reuse potential).

- *Note:* One of the real lessons in life is that *nothing* about a form contract is required. If you approach a procurement process and the other party gives you a draft contract, it's just a piece of paper until you sign it. You can change anything and everything about the contract. Whose language gets used where is a matter for negotiation, and hence it depends on who needs to compromise where to get what he or she wants.

Tailoring the contract is a large part of the procurement process. Whether the contract form comes from the buyer or the seller, both sides must tailor the form to include the obligations, rights, and risks that apply to the specific situation. One of the dangers of using form contracts is that you get complacent about specificity. Don't. Vague, general contract provisions are much less capable of managing the risks they address. Be as specific as possible—but not more so!

It is generally better to construct mechanisms for agreement such as joint reviews with signed approvals than it is to negotiate all agreements in advance and to put them into the actual contract. For example, you could put the requirements for the system into the contract, or you could contract for a process of requirements development ending in a milestone with approval by both parties. This latter course gives both the buyer and seller the flexibility they need to deliver value. A formal change management mechanism is another good candidate for being a contract provision, as are schedules and budgets. You should see the contract as a set of risk management methods or policies that manage risk, not as a detailed road map for the procurement and administration processes. Make sure that the risk management plan for the project includes reference to the risks and risk management methods that the contract provides.

- *Note:* If you discover in the course of integrating the contract into the risk management plan for the project that the contract contributes little to reducing the project risk below its risk tolerance, consider canceling the contract. It probably isn't necessary. You may be able to acquire the system without a contract, or simply not acquire the system at all.

The seller may need something from the buyer to perform the contract, such as tools, initial versions of the software, or interfaces with which the systems will need to work. The contract should specify the terms and conditions, and timing, under which the buyer supplies these systems to the seller. The contract administration process can then manage this through its cooperative efforts to manage the contract.

Acceptance criteria are measurable policies that become part of the contract. When the seller delivers their final product baseline, the buyer applies the criteria to the system to determine whether to accept it and close out the contract [PMI 1996a]. Usually, the acceptance criteria specify the verification and validation tests the system must pass, carefully relating the final system to the requirements. As buyer, you should have an approach for performing the acceptance test, building that into your project schedule through an acceptance process.

All of these jointly agreed-upon elements become a part of the legal contract between the parties, usually by reference in the original contract. The approval process in this case is thus a legal requirement; without approval, the buyer and seller have not agreed to exchange compensation for value. As with any OO baseline or plan, this one will undergo change through rolling-wave planning and incremental-iterative architecture. The difference is that the baseline you are changing has the status of a legal document. That *requires* a change management process that itself has the force of legal agreement behind it. The contractor cannot perform any work that the buyer has not agreed to, either in the original baseline or in an approved change request. Many larger contracts go as far as to include a work-authorization clause in the contract that prevents the seller from starting on approved changes until the buyer's contract administrator authorizes them to do so as part of the contract administration process.

Your contract should contain support and maintenance provisions specific to the situation. Make sure that the support and maintenance covers the time period during which you are likely to reuse the system. Make sure maintenance provides for record keeping and updates when the original system baseline changes, propagating the changes to all the systems that are reusing that system.

Once you tailor the contract, you should review it with various parts of the buyer organization. Get a technical review to make sure the interface and other technical information is correct and feasible. Get a financial review to ensure the adequacy of the financial arrangements and their conformance to the approach of the organization and company to financial management. Get a legal review to make sure the contract language does what it is supposed to do. Get a project management review to ensure that the milestone and budget requirements fit with the project that is going to reuse the contracted system and that the risks and risk management methods align with the risk management plan for the project. Use all of these reviews as a way to communicate the procurement intentions to all parties, providing another feedback mechanism for the project. Finally, get the review and formal approval of the person who will have to sign the contract. This can be a signature on the contract, or if there are further negotiations, a signature on an internal memo approving the negotiating approach.

The Procurement Management Plan

The *procurement management plan* is the plan that you generate from the procurement process model and the contract administration process model. It contains the tasks, schedule tasks, dependencies, risks, and other planning components relevant to your procurement of a reusable system. Its particular job as a plan is to determine what parts of the process model are appropriate for the situation, the type of contract, the organizational and project environments, and the risks the process faces.

Vision: A procurement process that results in successful delivery of a system for reuse within the project

Mission: To bring the procurement process model to bear on obtaining a system for reuse within the project

---

Objective 27.12: To adapt the procurement process model to the situation through applying contingent aspects of the model to the kinds of system and contract involved

---

Approach 27.12: The procurement process selects the type of acquisition method. Planning then determines the structure of work, given this decision. For off-the-shelf systems, determine the purchasing and support-related issues deriving from the licensing or warranty package. For contracted systems, examine the obligations, rights, and risks to determine the most appropriate form of contract and the specific tasks and work flow needed to administer that contract. Use the standard

The Procurement Management Plan

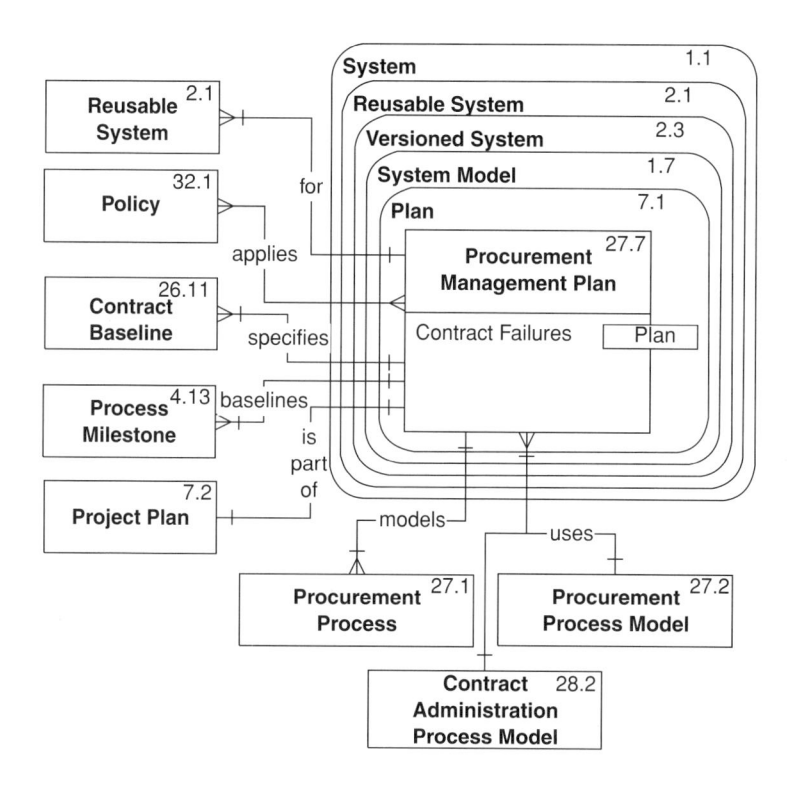

planning techniques to build the WBS, schedule, and budget for the contract administration process.

Metric 27.12: Contract failures: the aggregation of the various types of contract objective failure, summarizing the degree to which the contract failed to align with the obligations, rights, and risks that drove it

Target 27.12: A low number within limits of a pn control chart of similar contracts

---

Objective 27.13: To adapt the procurement process model to the organizational and project environments that will interact with the procurement process

---

Approach 27.13: You must determine the responsibilities of different parts of the organization and incorporate the appropriate tasks and resource assignments into the statement of work and schedule for the project. These responsibilities should become part of the responsibility matrix for the project. You must develop parts of the communication plan for the project relating to communications with contractors, other parts of the organization that must deal with the procurement process, and external entities with an interest. You must also add any tasks to the project for support. This includes your organization supporting the seller and the seller supporting different parts of your organization (training, customer support, or any other such interaction).

Metric 27.13: Change Rate: see Metric 7.2 and apply it to the procurement plan and to the plans it affects (communications, resource, and risk management)

Objective 27.14: To adapt the procurement process model to the risks the procurement process faces, especially the risks involved in changing the requirements or contract obligations

---

Approach 27.14: Identify and quantify the risks that the procurement process faces. Establish a risk management plan for the procurement process, including a change management process for managing changes to requirements, obligations, or responsibilities. Use the standard planning process to incorporate the tasks, schedule tasks, dependencies, and resource assignments from these plans into the WBS and schedule.

Metric 27.14: Risk Rate (see Metric 7.1)

The organizational structure of the project often determines a good deal of the structure of the procurement plan. If you have a separate procurement department, for example, you must carefully determine which responsibilities belong to that team and which belong to other teams. In a large project, the responsibility matrix becomes the focus for such decisions.

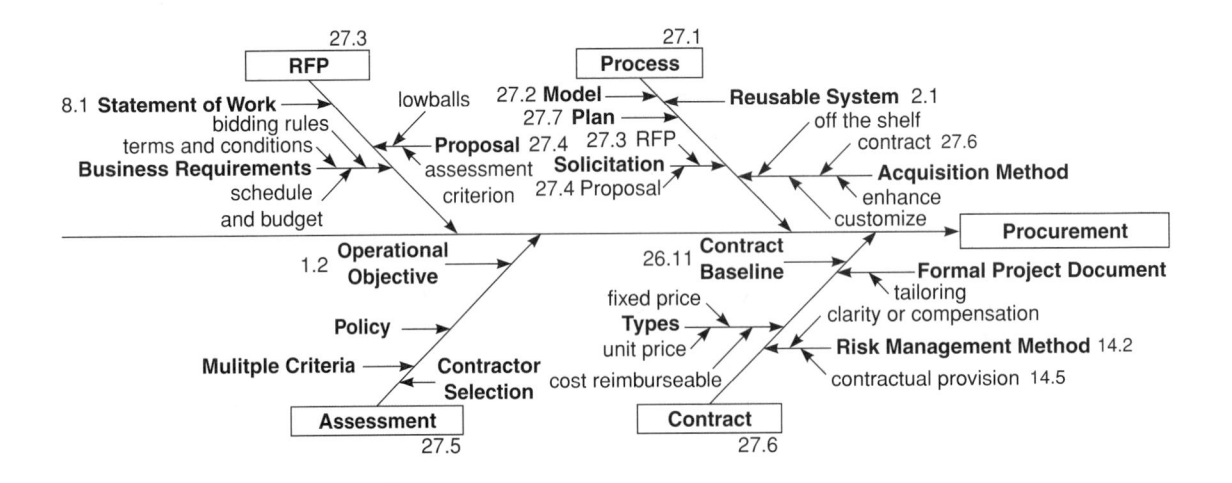

The most important risks associated with procurement are usually either technology limitations or funds limitations. For example, your plan needs to take into account the technological issues with integrating an acquired system into the

larger system. For this reason, the contract usually includes specific reference to both interfaces and technical constraints such as platform requirements. Similarly, if you have a budget for the acquisition, you must assess and plan for risks of exceeding that budget. Where the budget is highly constrained, such as for a government agency with a budget, this becomes a key risk to manage.

Readings

[Bennatan] E. M. Bennatan. *On Time, Within Budget: Software Project Management Practices and Techniques.* New York: QED Publishing Group, 1992.

Bennatan has an excellent chapter on contract software development. This chapter addresses the issues mainly from the point of view of the supplier, and particularly the supplier to government organizations. It has an excellent section on preparation of both RFPs and the proposals that respond to them.

[Fishman] Stephen Fishman. *Software Development: A Legal Guide.* Berkeley, CA: Nolo Press, 1994.

This is a Nolo self-help legal book for software developers. It covers the practical aspects of contracting, mostly from the perspective of the supplier but with comments for the benefit of the buyer. I use this book in most of the contracts I do for my consulting practice.

[Gordon] Mark L. Gordon. *Computer Software Contracting for Development and Distribution.* New York: Wiley, 1986.

This legal treatise is my bible on software contracting. If it isn't in here, it probably isn't legal, so don't do it. The book is full of practical advice as well as the legal theory behind almost every aspect of the software development business.

[ISO 1995] International Standards Organization. *ISO/IEC 12207, Information Technology—Software Life Cycle Processes.* ISO, 1995.

The ISO-12207 standard sections 5.1, Acquisition process, and 5.2, Supply process, are excellent summaries of what happens in a procurement process. The activities that are part of these process descriptions form the basis for the current chapter.

[Kehoe] Raymond Kehoe and Alka Jarvis. *ISO 9000-3: A Tool for Software Product and Process Improvement.* New York: Springer-Verlag, 1996.

This book has a particularly good chapter on acquisition processes and contracts as well as a good chapter on supply. ISO-9000 focuses on acquisition and supply as driving processes for the commercial-quality processes that are its domain.

[Kerzner] Harold Kerzner. *Project Management: A Systems Approach to Planning, Scheduling, and Controlling, Fifth Edition.* New York: Van Nostrand Reinhold, 1994.

Kerzner's Chapter 24 on contracts is definitely oriented toward either construction or government contracting rather than software. The discussion of the process issues is valuable, if a bit difficult to follow at times.

[PMI 1996a]   Project Management Institute Standards Committee. *A Guide to the Project Management Body of Knowledge.* Project Management Institute (+1-610-734-3330), 1996.

The PMBOK addresses an entire chapter to procurement management, Chapter 12. I have taken the categories of contract from this section, as well as some of the logic that extends ISO-12207 to general project management.

[Whitten]   Neal Whitten. *Managing Software Development Projects: Formula for Success, Second Edition.* New York: Wiley, 1995.

Whitten's Chapter 13 on Vendor Relationships has a good overview of the issues in RFPs and contracts, though without much detail.

Questions to Think About

1. Do you think all procurement decisions should be made quantitatively using decision analysis? Why or why not?

2. List five differences between a procurement process that acquires systems from external sources and one that acquires internal systems from different parts of the organization. How do these differences shape the procurement process, and why?

3. Why would it be difficult to include a "complete and unambiguous" set of requirements in the RFP?

4. How should you apply your assessment criteria to a proposal that is the only one in response to your solicitation?

5. How does procurement planning differ from development planning? What are the major risks you undertake through buying a reusable system instead of building it? What major risks do you avoid through this approach?

CHAPTER 28

Contract Administration

The Contract Administration Process

When you decide to acquire a reusable system through a contracting procurement process, you need to establish a *contract administration process* to ensure that the seller meets the contract requirements. The contract administration process is a primary process that includes enabling cooperation between buyer and seller, joint reviews of deliverables, performance evaluation, change management, management of legal requirements, invoicing and payment processing, acceptance and system testing, and auditing.

Vision: A contract that delivers value to the project as planned

Mission: To control the contracted work to ensure delivery of planned value

---

Objective 28.1: To control the contracted work to ensure delivery of planned value

---

Approach 28.1: Determine what kinds of cooperation between seller and buyer are necessary (people, methods, tools, and so on). Integrate communications requirements into the communications plan. Establish the timing, terms, and priorities of cooperative work as a set of contract-specific policies. Schedule and facilitate meetings and joint reviews between seller and buyer people, publishing agendas and minutes. Establish a contract baseline early in the contract administration process. Evaluate the performance of the seller against this baseline on an ongoing basis as contract milestones occur. Establish a change management process for the contract as well as integrating risk management activities into the risk management plan. Authorize work on changes. Check that the seller fulfills all the legal requirements of the contract. Establish an acceptance testing process and conduct it when you receive the appropriate product baseline. As required, schedule and conduct audits of the seller's processes and finances as permitted by contract.

Metric 28.1: Earned value: the amount of planned value actually delivered at a baseline milestone that results in a contract baseline

Target 28.1: An earned value close to planned value within control limits of an x-R control chart of similar contract baselines

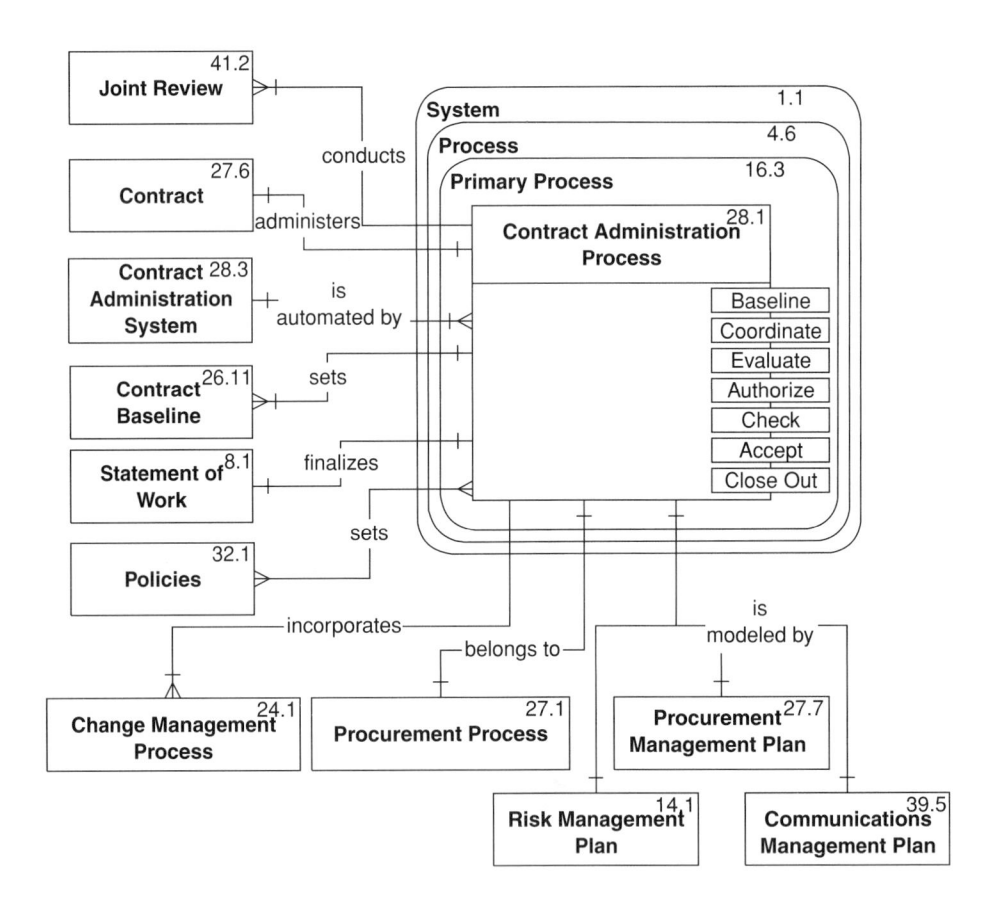

One of the first things you do in contract administration is to facilitate the development of the statement of work. You work together with the seller to refine your expectations as a project stakeholder for this subproject. The seller works out some of the details of their proposed development process by fleshing out the WBS and producing a schedule and budget. The buyer must specify any *interfaces*,

The Contract Administration Process

requirements for elements of the procured system to fit with elements of the larger system, in the requirements document. The buyer should also provide the seller with a dictionary of terms and any other background material that will be of use to the seller's understanding of the project. When both seller and buyer are happy with the statement of work, as approved by a joint review, you baseline it and produce a contract baseline. This baseline usually provides milestones for value and a cost budget against which you can measure performance. It should also provide a comprehensive set of jointly approved acceptance criteria.

Communications planning encompasses a good deal of what you must do to keep the contract moving. If you don't know about it, you can't control it. The communications plan is thus the locus for the feedback activities in the procurement process, with contract administration being the primary mechanism for such feedback. You must integrate your communication needs into the project's communication plan to ensure everything gets communicated.

Communications Management Plan (39.5)

Joint reviews are critical to the contract administration process. Anything that requires approval by both sides should have a joint review. The exception is where the approval does not require any interaction, just a simple exchange of documents or other systems. There will certainly be a joint review to baseline the statement of work, and one for the production baseline the seller is to deliver to the buyer. There will be technical reviews of intermediate baselines that you must initiate and coordinate. You can also have joint reviews for major changes as part of the change management process. It is critical to have agendas and minutes for these reviews. These documents are project documents and part of the contract record.

Meeting (41.1)
Joint Review (41.2)

The contract administrator's daily work centers on coordination and cooperation. There is a section in the ISO-9000-3 standard that defines various characteristics of mutual cooperation:

- Resource assignments for the requirements specification and other joint endeavors
- Methods for agreeing on requirements
- Methods for approving changes to the agreed-upon requirements (a change management process model)
- Efforts to prevent misunderstandings by facilitating communication and transfer of knowledge between the buyer and seller, especially through agendas and minutes of meetings between the parties

The contract administration process sets up a standard change management process for changes to the requirements and to other approved baselines. In particular, if the seller wants to version the contract baseline, they must do so formally using change requests. The buyer must approve such change requests. If the change involves new work, the seller cannot proceed with the work until they receive authorization to do so.

■ *Note:* A change in the contract baseline is a change in the contract. It has legal effect. If your contract calls for completion by a certain date, and you approve another date through a change request, you have just changed your contract completion date. That means if there are any penalties for finishing late, they don't kick in until the changed date.

Contract administration also dots the t's of the contract, checking for the minor legal requirements, milestone dates, and other contract elements. In particular, invoicing and paying invoices according to the contracted terms is critical to keeping the seller happy. The contract management system reports on the status of work at the relevant milestones. The contract administration process incorporates these reports into the ongoing process of performance evaluation of the contract using the contract baseline.

The contract itself represents a major collection of risk management methods. These methods may require more than just the contract. They may require that a contract administrator do something or organize something or communicate something. You need to put any such tasks into the risk management plan along with the contract provisions themselves.

On delivery of the production baseline, contract administration supervises the acceptance test of the product, including joint reviews, testing, and reporting. If the baseline fails the test according to the contract, the contract administration process must work out the sequence of events that follows. Ultimately, should the contract fail, contract administration must bring the issue to the attention of the relevant parts of the organization for further action, including audits. Otherwise, the process notifies the seller of the acceptance of the deliverables, closes out the contract, and archives all the records of the process.

Many contracts in OO projects are simple to administer and do not require extensive cooperation between the parties. Keeping contract administration at an optimal level is difficult even for these contracts, however. I've found that if you don't have a formal process in place, you tend to ignore the contract until something untoward happens. Keeping your contract administration current is a good way to keep the contract on track, no matter how simple it is.

The Contract Administration Process Model

The *contract administration process model* sets the policies for contract administration processes. You may have several contract administration process models in a given project, since there can be several different kinds of contract requiring different management.

Vision: A valuable, reusable, productive contract administration process you productively plan from a continuously improving model

Mission: To represent a productive, comprehensive contract administration process that you will reuse many times

Objective 28.2: To represent the process to ensure comprehensive coverage of all contract-related control issues

Approach 28.2: Develop standard checklists of contract requirements, including deliverable, legal, and business requirements. Develop standard checklists of the different kinds of cooperation required in contracts of different kinds. Refer to change management process models from this process model.

Metric 28.2: Contract administration failures: the number of problems that arise with contract administration due to oversights or missing plan elements

Target 28.2: A low number within control limits of a pn control chart of similar contracts

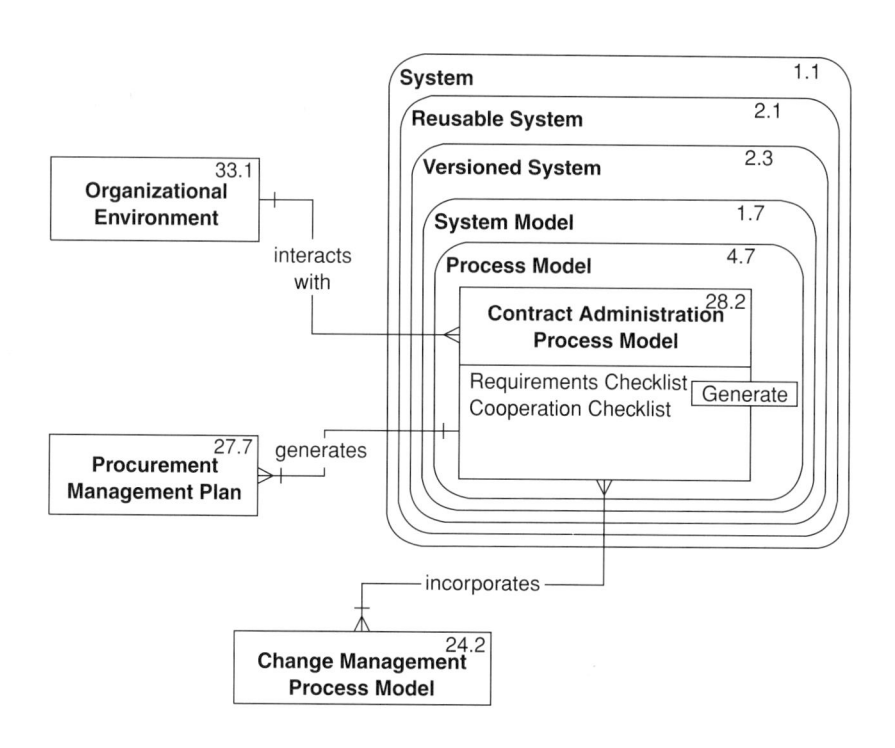

The contract administration process model also specifies a change management process model that the procurement management plan uses to plan the administration process.

The Contract Administration System

The *contract administration system* is an information system that contains contracts and contract-related information, which it stores in the project repository.

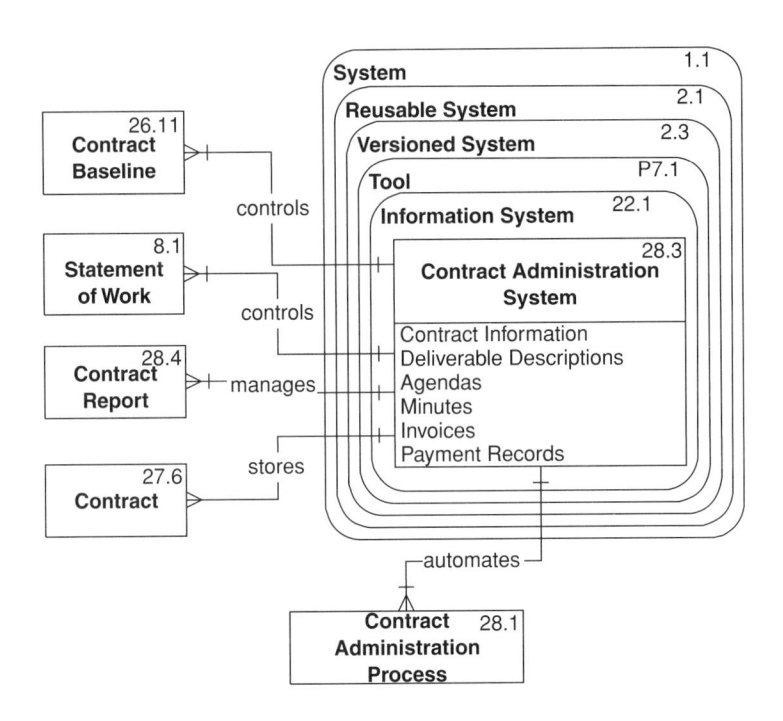

```
System                                                   1.1
  Reusable System                                        2.1
    Versioned System                                     2.3
      Tool                                               P7.1
        Information System                               22.1
          Contract Administration                        28.3
          System
          Contract Information
          Deliverable Descriptions
          Agendas
          Minutes
          Invoices
          Payment Records
```

- 26.11 Contract Baseline — controls
- 8.1 Statement of Work — controls
- 28.4 Contract Report — manages
- 27.6 Contract — stores
- 28.1 Contract Administration Process — automates

Vision: Contract administrators using information to assure contract success

Mission: To create and manage information that contract administrators need to get their jobs done productively

---

Objective 28.3: To create and manage reusable contract-related information that people need

---

Approach 28.3: Store the contract in the project repository with appropriate security and access to those that need to refer to it. Establish a contract baseline for performance evaluation and store that in the project repository as well. Identify additional contract-related information you need to have as part of the contract administration process, such as invoice and payment information. Acquire, share, and maintain an information system that creates the required information. Use the system to obtain information, to assist in contract control, to conduct acceptance testing, and to support cooperative effort.

Metric 28.3.1: Information Failure (see Metric 21.1.1)

Metric 28.3.2: Necessity (see Metric 21.1.2)

The contract management system performs two basic functions: tracking and storage. The tracking features must ensure that the seller and buyer meet all their obligations by the relevant dates. The storage features store the systems that the contract creates:

- Signed contract
- Statement of work approved by buyer and seller
- The contract baseline (in all its versions)
- Any background materials delivered to the seller
- Deliverable item descriptions
- Contract reports
- Change requests for contract or deliverable items
- Agendas and minutes of joint meetings
- Seller invoices
- Buyer payment records

The software for accessing and managing this data consists of the appropriate forms for data entry and update and reports on the status of work results, change requests, and invoices.

The Contract Report

The *contract report* is a progress report from a seller. You should have established a contract baseline early in the contract administration process that represents the plan for the project. The contract reports, which the seller delivers at each contract milestone, must report actual and earned value according to the current contract baseline compared to the planned baseline. It should also contain any change requests from the seller.

Vision: A clear, timely understanding of contract progress against the plan

Mission: To present progress of contracted work against a contract baseline at a contract milestone

---

Objective 28.4: To present progress of contracted work against a contract baseline at a contract milestone

Approach 28.4: When a contract milestone occurs, the seller establishes the appropriate baseline using contracted exit criteria. The seller then gathers the relevant information for performance evaluation as mandated by the contract and delivers it in a report to the contract administrator. The project manager then integrates the earned value from the contract into the earned value computed from other project baselines.

Metric 28.4: Adequacy: an ordinal metric indicating how well the report serves to report progress against the contract baseline: Missing (no report for the milestone), Late (report delivered behind schedule), Inadequate (report has missing elements), Adequate (report is on time and contains all required elements); you can recast this metric as a multiattribute metric in several dimensions, such as time, cost, and earned value

Target 28.4: Adequate

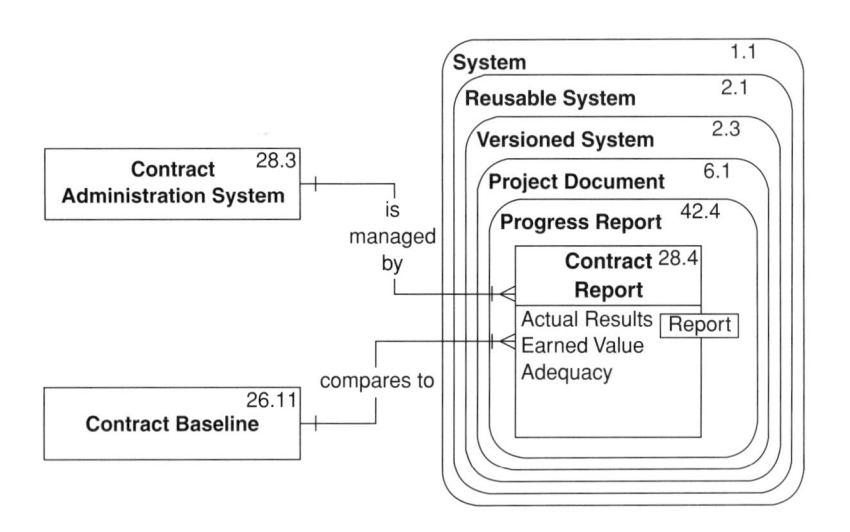

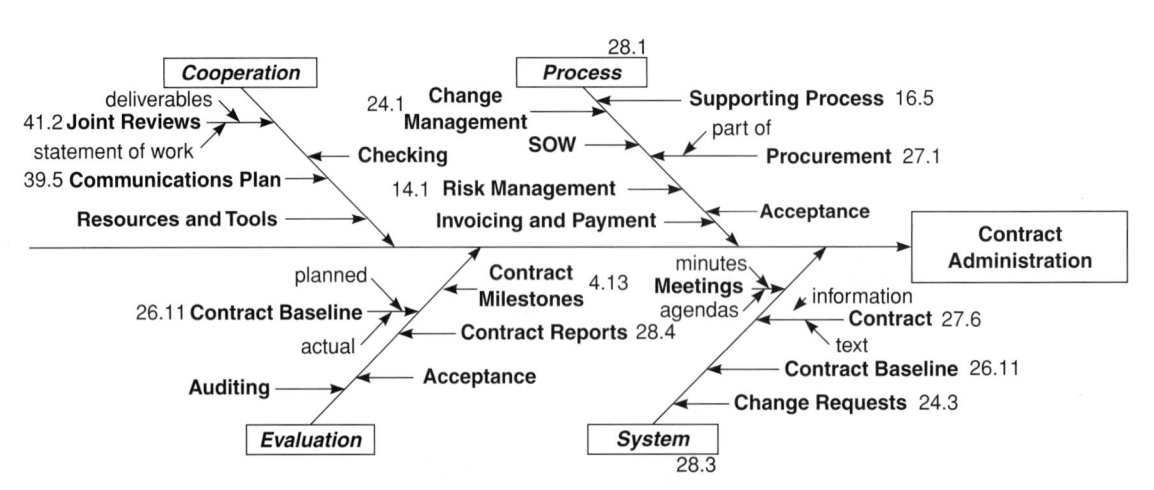

Readings

Most of the literature on software contracting focuses on RFPs, proposals, and contracts and leaves the contract administration to your imagination. It is, however, vital to the success of the contract, and it is a shame that there isn't more written about it.

[PMI 1996a]   Project Management Institute Standards Committee. *A Guide to the Project Management Body of Knowledge.* Project Management Institute (+1-610-734-3330), 1996.

The PMBOK addresses an entire chapter to procurement management, Chapter 12. There are several excellent sections on contract management as part of this process.

[Whitten]   Neal Whitten. *Managing Software Development Projects: Formula for Success, Second Edition.* New York: Wiley, 1995.

Whitten's Chapter 13 on Vendor Relationships discusses the contract administration issues in a highly readable and useful way.

Questions to Think About

1. List several methods you can use to keep contract administration to a minimum. (Hint: Think about OO encapsulation, as well as what you really need to communicate.)

2. When should you consider auditing the seller?

3. Who should actually conduct the acceptance test for the deliverable? What is the practical role of the contract administrator in the acceptance test? What is the seller's role?

4. How would contract administration benefit from a contract management system that included tools for electronic transfer of documents and other information (email, Internet, and so on)?

5. When should the project manager incorporate the earned value for the contract deliverables into the value of the project?

PART TEN

Organization

In a hierarchy, every employee tends to rise to his level of incompetence.

Laurence J. Peter, *The Peter Principle*

The organization is the means by which you can get people to work together in a project. Every project bigger than one person has an organization. With any luck, it will be the right organization. Organizations work through authority and responsibility, commitment and trust. You can organize people according to function in a functional organization, or you can organize them by the structure of the project in a projectized organization. If neither of these works, perhaps the matrix organization will; it's a mixture of the two. In any case, choosing your organization gives you the opportunity to draw it up into an organization chart, which you include with the project plan.

Every organization consists of a set of work groups. Teams are work groups that have a special focus on their mission and on the performance of that mission. You can try to turn a group into a team, but it isn't easy. Part of it depends on the management culture, which is the part of the organizational environment that controls how your organization works. The different cultures organize their processes and work in different ways. Matching the culture to your stakeholders' expectations and risks gives you an optimal chance of completing your mission.

Every organization has policies. Policies constitute the knowledge by which the organization feeds back prior experience into the project. They can also constitute a major roadblock to getting real work done. Design and coding standards are policies that apply specific OO knowledge to your project.

The organizational environment is the external system that contains your organization and its context, including the policies that apply to it, external standards, the market, the political system, and any other outside factor that controls your organization. Each such environment has an organizational repository to store policies, organization charts, and other artifacts of the organization. This environment provides the major source of change for your organization.

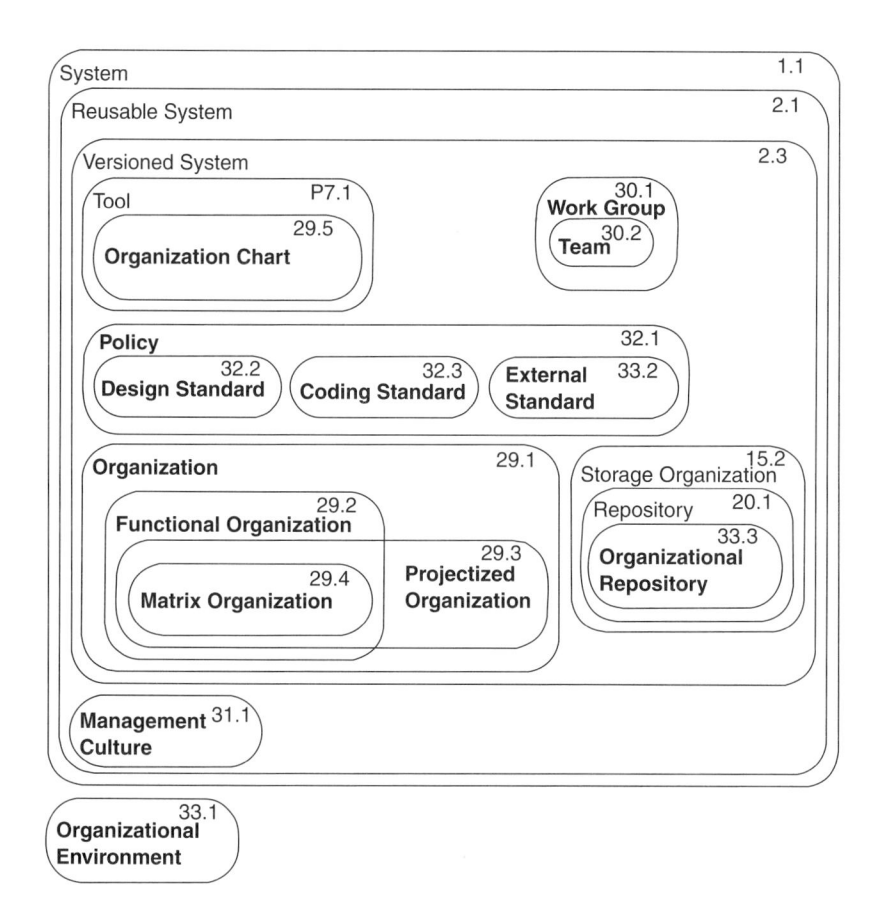

```
┌─────────────────────────────────────────────────────┐
│ System                                          1.1 │
│ ┌─────────────────────────────────────────────────┐ │
│ │ Reusable System                             2.1 │ │
│ │ ┌─────────────────────────────────────────────┐ │ │
│ │ │ Versioned System                        2.3 │ │ │
│ │ │  ┌──────────────────┐    ┌──────────────┐   │ │ │
│ │ │  │ Tool        P7.1 │    │   30.1       │   │ │ │
│ │ │  │          29.5    │    │ Work Group   │   │ │ │
│ │ │  │ Organization     │    │   ┌──30.2─┐  │   │ │ │
│ │ │  │ Chart            │    │   │ Team  │  │   │ │ │
│ │ │  └──────────────────┘    └──────────────┘   │ │ │
│ │ │  ┌────────────────────────────────────────┐ │ │ │
│ │ │  │ Policy                           32.1  │ │ │ │
│ │ │  │   32.2       32.3     External  33.2   │ │ │ │
│ │ │  │ Design     Coding     Standard         │ │ │ │
│ │ │  │ Standard   Standard                    │ │ │ │
│ │ │  └────────────────────────────────────────┘ │ │ │
│ │ │  ┌─────────────────────┐ ┌─────────────────┐│ │ │
│ │ │  │ Organization  29.1  │ │Storage Org 15.2 ││ │ │
│ │ │  │  Functional   29.2  │ │ Repository 20.1 ││ │ │
│ │ │  │  Organization       │ │         33.3    ││ │ │
│ │ │  │              29.3   │ │ Organizational  ││ │ │
│ │ │  │       Projectized   │ │ Repository      ││ │ │
│ │ │  │  29.4 Organization  │ │                 ││ │ │
│ │ │  │  Matrix Org         │ │                 ││ │ │
│ │ │  └─────────────────────┘ └─────────────────┘│ │ │
│ │ └─────────────────────────────────────────────┘ │ │
│ │ ┌─────────────────┐                             │ │
│ │ │ Management 31.1 │                             │ │
│ │ │ Culture         │                             │ │
│ │ └─────────────────┘                             │ │
│ └─────────────────────────────────────────────────┘ │
└─────────────────────────────────────────────────────┘
 ┌──────────────────┐
 │           33.1   │
 │ Organizational   │
 │ Environment      │
 └──────────────────┘
```

- *Note:* The illustration of the class hierarchy contains all the classes this part defines. Other parts of the book define and discuss classes not in boldface.

CHAPTER

29 *Organization*

The Organization

The *organization* is a reusable, structured collection of groups of people that perform work. A good deal of management is organizing people, reversing the natural entropy of a cluster of people. Project management organizes people for the tasks of the project. It also creates policies to standardize operations and to structure communications. The kind of structure you apply depends on the project, the management culture, and the organizational environment. The responsibility matrix ties together the organization and the project by assigning the work in the work breakdown structure (WBS) to groups within the organization.

Vision: A reusable set of work groups productively organized to achieve project objectives

Mission: To organize people into a reusable collection of productive work groups to achieve the project objectives

Objective 29.1: To create a reusable set of work groups

Approach 29.1: Create an organizational structure focused on organizational stability, innovation capability, and value creation. Develop stability through alignment of the organizational structure with the project objectives and the organizational environment. Internally, reduce the turnover rate through reward and recognition of work groups. Develop innovation by creating a culture of innovation through creative optimization of operational objectives. Build on excellence by partnering with groups in the organizational environment to create entirely new things out of reused systems as leaders in your industry. Develop a focus on value creation by measuring value production directly and recognizing the contributions of the work groups to that value creation. Avoid creating organizational systems (work groups or policies) that do not contribute to value creation directly or indirectly. Where the contribution of a system is indirect, be clear on the real contribution, avoiding bureaucratic and wishful thinking. Measure, and measure again.

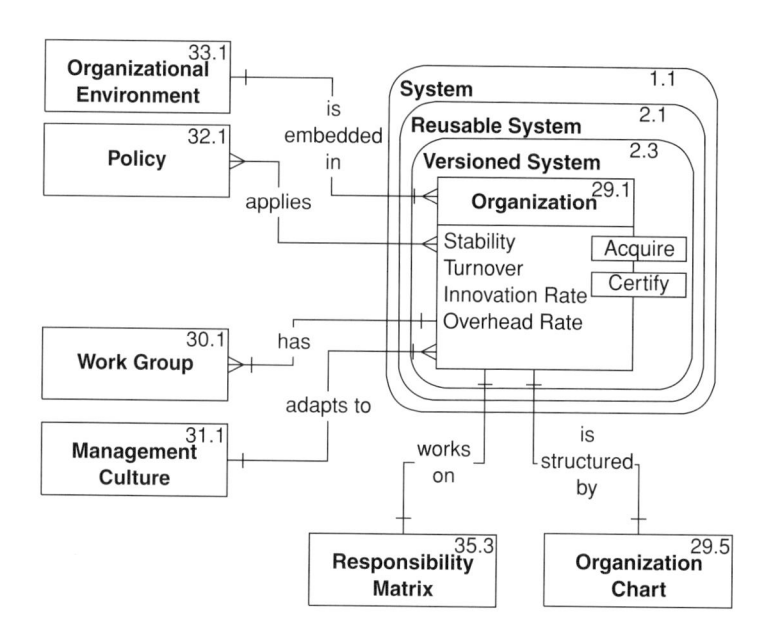

Metric 29.1.1: Stability: the number of material organizational changes (versions) during a quarter (three months) weighted by the number of actual relationships changed in the system in the version

Target 29.1.1: A low number within control parameters of a pn control chart of similar organizations

---

Metric 29.1.2: Turnover: the rate that resources leave the organization per quarter, including voluntary and involuntary exits such as quitting, termination, death or disability, or reassignment

Target 29.1.2: A low number within control limits of an x-R control chart of turnover in similar organizations

---

Metric 29.1.3: Innovation rate: the rate of change of continuous improvement in value creation, which measures the extent to which your improvement plans actually improve your creation of value; you can use the earned value from your progress reports to measure this rate of change by calculating the slope of the curve (the first derivative)

Target 29.1.3: An increasing value within control limits of an x-R control chart of innovation in industry leaders

Metric 29.1.4: Flexibility: an ordinal, subjective measure of the organization's ability to adapt to different situations through structural change

Target 29.1.4: A value within control limits of an x-R control chart of flexibility values

Metric 29.1.5: Overhead rate: the ratio of opportunity cost devoted to organizational systems or relationships that create no value either directly or indirectly during a quarter to total value creation during the quarter; *opportunity cost* is the expected value that the system would have generated had the system been value-producing instead of overhead

Target 29.1.5: A low number within control limits of an x-R control chart of overheads in similar organizations

Objective 29.2: To optimize the work groups' contribution to achieving project objectives

Approach 29.2: Choose an organizational structure that aligns with the project objectives. Organize the work groups into an authority structure with optimal clarity. Create and nurture work groups that productively create value according to the project objectives. Foster communication and other relationships between work groups that help those groups to be more productive and innovative. Ensure that relationships between work groups and the environment focus on either understanding the needs of the environment or reusing systems from the environment.

Metric 29.2.1: Earned contribution margin: the difference between earned value per unit and cost per unit, where the unit is the appropriate measure of system value for systems that the organization produces (function points or sales, for example)

Target 29.2.1: A contribution margin within control limits of an x-R chart of margins for similar organizations

Metric 29.2.2: Clarity: the average of the "fan-in" of the organization's reporting relationships, where "fan-in" means the number of superiors to which an individual resource reports

Target 29.2.2: A number near 1 within control limits of an x-R control chart

Why have an organization at all? Organization is the system's response to people problems. People have differing skills and knowledge. People have different "interpersonal communications" problems (that is, people either yell at each other or don't talk at all most of the time if left to themselves). People have different needs for recognition and structure in their working lives. People have different interests: some are primarily technical, others have an interest in helping people to do things, and still others promote their own interests.

Structuring people into an organization lays the foundation for solving all of these problems and many others related to people. People work best when organized, whether they do it themselves or submit to organization imposed by others. Whether your organization is autocratic, democratic, or any shade of gray in between, you need organization.

The structure of the organization consists of reporting relationships and policies. The reporting relationships constitute the authority structure of the organization. The organization chart expresses these relationships. These charts can be complex, depending on the organizational structure you choose.

The organizational policies set up the constraints on the organization. The company manual provides the part of the organizational environment that imposes external policies on the project organization, but every project has its own set of policies. If you declare a weekly status meeting, that's a communication policy. If you require monthly progress reports from functional managers, that's a progress reporting policy. These policies generally structure the formal communications in the project. You can also set various kinds of targets, such as number of defects or process milestones, as policies.

Authority and Responsibility

An organization is the framework for planning work, allocating people to work, budgeting the costs of work, and explaining and communicating work-related issues. The organization consists of a collection of work groups linked through authority and communication relationships. These so-called "formal" relationships are the structure within which the people form the "informal" relationships between each other, such as trust, commitment, and support.

Work Group (30.1)

Power and legitimacy drive organized activity. Power comes from economic and social position and from knowledge. Legitimacy comes from trust, motivation, and the willingness to delegate and assume responsibility. Power and legitimacy work best when they work together: authority should match responsibility; commitment should equal trust. *Authority* is the power that comes from the position in the organization. The role of the individual in the social organization *legitimizes* the authority of the individual [Hersey, p. 221]. *Responsibility* is the *commitment* that an individual makes to achieve some result. Responsibility comes from the legitimacy of those who hold the responsible person answerable for his or her obligation.

There are two basic kinds of authority in an organization. The lines of authority and responsibility determine the *reporting structure* of the organization, as responsible people report to those who hold them accountable. Accountability thus provides one kind of authority, the authority of a boss and a subordinate. Developers report to managers who report to directors who report to executives. Managers evaluate the performance of their groups. Managers direct the work by telling people what to do. Managers thus take on extra responsibility, that of holding people accountable for their obligations.

A different kind of authority also exists in most software projects: *decision* authority. This is the right to decide whether and how resources should perform some piece of work. Rather than the ability to assign people to work, decision authority is the ability to prevent work from proceeding without a signature or other approval. You must establish the lines of decision authority with policies. An architect, for example, usually must approve a design document as a formal project document by department policy. An executive often must approve a project plan or a functional specification for a project at a major process milestone. These decisions frequently work across the reporting structure. The author of the design document might work for a functional group far from the reporting structure for the architect, and of course the executive lives on a different planet.

Formal Project Document (6.2)

Often, decision authority follows the standard lines of authority in the reporting structure. Most managers can approve their subordinates' purchase or travel requests, for example. As the impact of the decision grows, the high-water mark of approval rises. Large capital purchases, major projects, and other decisions likely to have a strategic impact on the firm get made higher in the reporting structure. Decisions with a large technical impact, such as whether to reuse a framework or how to structure a basic component of a system, require approval high in the hierarchy of the technically competent.

The authority structure of the organization has a clarity determined by the nature of the report graph. A perfectly clear organization is a hierarchical one in which each person reports to exactly one other person, and in which that person makes all decisions. As people begin to refer to more than one person, the clarity diminishes. It can also diminish in the other direction: having people report to no one results in broken authority structures, anarchy.

The meaning of clarity of authority is contextual. A perfectly clear authority structure can be a dictatorship or a democracy depending on the nature of the power and legitimacy involved. Political systems of many different kinds have found, however, that a balanced authority structure is often more acceptable to those governed. It depends entirely on the political culture of the organization and how well your own politics align with it.

A project manager must carefully construct the authority structure to suit the needs of the project and its stakeholders given the organizational environment and the management culture. For example, your organizational environment might require people to bill time to projects. If people work on more than one project, your structure must ensure that you get the full value of each person's work on your project rather than just a bill for services actually rendered to another project. If your management style is highly participative and oriented toward problem solving, you would not want to set up a highly bureaucratic, rigidly hierarchical organization with strong authority and delegated responsibility. If your organization is conservative and risk averse, you should not use an organizational structure that decentralizes authority to such an extent that anyone can take any risk at any time.

The project relates to the organization through the responsibility matrix. This matrix ties the tasks in the WBS to the organizational structure. The clarity of this matrix is a good measure of how well your organizational structure distributes responsibility. If you find it difficult or impossible to develop a responsibility matrix, reorganize your organization—it's not working.

Responsibility Matrix (35.3)

I've wasted quite a bit of time in projects where authority did not match responsibility. I've heard most of the upper-management excuses for this; they're not convincing. They are mostly based on lack of trust and commitment in organizations that have not established the legitimacy of the management. This forces an autocratic pattern of behavior that inevitably draws all the authority out of the project manager, resulting in out-of-control projects. The best projects I've been on have been those that let me do my job as project manager by giving me the authority to do that job. This follows down the line; as project manager, you must delegate the authority to the deliverable teams, going down all the way to the people who get the job done.

Here are two examples of poor authority. I worked on an OO project that used a weak matrix organization. A series of functional managers organized the work but the director of development reserved most authority to himself, delegating some to a chief architect. The functional managers each served as project managers for their piece, and the chief architect and the director exercised all the authority in the project. The result was a classic office politics situation, with the Ins deciding what everyone should do and the Outs not contributing their ideas beyond the boundaries of their coding.

Another OO project used a flat functional structure, with an architect taking on the role of untitled project manager. In conjunction with the VP of development, the architect created a "War Room," posted a schedule, and went back to work as architect. The next six months saw some progress but not much as the tape peeled on the schedule in the War Room. This wasn't abuse of authority as much as absence of authority; there was little project management at all. The functional managers just kept doing stuff in their groups. The consequence was an uncontrolled project that was delivered in very different form six months late. The schedule was still peeling on the wall when I left the firm six months later.

Many of these poor authority situations come about for historical and cultural reasons. The two cases I report above were the result of such factors. In the first case, the company had a very authoritarian culture with little trust in management or by management. In the second case, the company had a laid-back, frat-house atmosphere with a strong culture of independence and antiauthority sentiment. These organizations could not have effective project management without a culture change.

Reusing Organizations

In an environment with multiple projects, not all of them need have the same project organization. Depending on the nature of the project and the way it interacts with the environment, a different project may require a completely different structure. This does run up against an article of faith: that organizations, like most systems, should be reusable.

The reusable system, in this case, is the organization, not the people in the organization in themselves. When you assign a task to the organization, you are reusing the structure of the system. You get versioning reuse as the organization adds, promotes, demotes, and fires people or makes minor changes to reporting relationships. The general reuse potential for the organization system depends on a complex web of factors, including stability, flexibility, innovation, and turnover.

The *stability* of the organization is the degree to which the system relationships remain the same. This partially depends on turnover because some of the relationships are between people and other parts of the organization. Especially in large organizations, however, stability depends as much on higher-level relationships between work groups and policies as it does on people. Another way to put this: organizations have a life of their own. The internal relationships of the organization shift with reorganizations, promotions and demotions, mergers with other organizations, and potentially any number of disruptive changes in the environment. Some companies seem to reorganize every year just to be doing something. This certainly interferes with the reusability of the organizational structure.

The inherent reuse potential of the organization, however, does not depend solely on the absolute rate of change of the organization. Organizations can change without affecting their ability to handle new tasks, after all. The key issue is when the rate of change becomes great enough to absorb a significant amount of managerial resources or to disrupt a significant number of relationships. As the organization itself consumes more resources in a struggle to survive, it loses focus on its work and becomes less effective and productive. Any organization that becomes more focused on its internal relationships is less capable of dealing with the outside world, and hence is going to have problems in delivering value. The degree of stability that you want varies depending on the nature of the environment you face. Too much instability, however, yields nothing—literally.

Balanced against this entropic tendency in the system is the need for *flexibility* and innovation. It is clear that the ultimate survival of an organization depends on its adaptive, evolutionary capabilities: innovation, criticality, and embeddedness

[Moore, pp. 199–207]. The survival crisis comes when the organizational environment enters a mature stage of development. As competition becomes fierce, the system must respond with increasing returns to scale, innovating to stay ahead of the competition. Continuously improving productivity and value production comes mainly from innovation. But while you're innovating and improving, don't forget that the primary purpose for a project is to deliver value. That means criticality: focusing on the critical value that stakeholders want from the project. Make your projects more valuable to stakeholders. Also, embed yourself in your environment. Make deals with stakeholders, especially external ones. Link your project with its environment with intertwining relationships between the people and the products. You can use the synergies of procurement to create relationships with suppliers, leveraging their reusable systems as well. You will note that none of these factors support the stability of the organization.

Measuring *innovation* is tricky. The best measure is Moore's innovation trajectory, a graph relating capital investment to value [Moore, pp. 200–202]. This book transforms that metric into Metric 29.1.3, Innovation. If you measure the rate of change of value creation with respect to time, you see how your organizational system is improving at creating value. This metric is simply the slope of the earned-value curve at each milestone. This is a very general measure that does not take into account the source of the improvement. You can add resources, grow through capital improvements, refine your design and coding practices, radically improve quality assurance, develop new risk management methods, or whatever. If your improvement cycles are weak, your rate of change will reflect only the individual innovations of your people. If your improvement cycles get work groups focused on value, you will see increasing rates of improvement and increasing value over time. If you find yourself at an inflection point where innovation is beginning to decrease, it's time to look at new organizations, new partnerships, or new markets.

Organizational *turnover* is the rate at which people leave the organizational system. The usual metric is exits per year, the number of people who leave the organization in a given year. This includes any exit method, from quitting voluntarily through termination to death or disability. The lower the turnover rate, the more reusable the organization. A low turnover rate means that the institutional memory is strong, that learning curves are more productive, that there are more available skills, and that people need less training [DeMarco 1987]. It means that informal relationships are stronger. It means that improvement plans have more effect due to synergies with previous improvement cycles. You generally get low turnover through the various means you have of making people happy to be in your organization, such as stimulating work, rewards and recognition, training, career advancement, and other techniques for motivating people.

Person (34.2)

The overall impact of organizational structure on the reuse potential of the organization is thus very complex. It depends as much on the environmental challenges you face as on the nature of the organization. To focus on OO software organizations briefly, what do these organizations need? OO software is brand new. OO software organizations are either brand new organizations or organizations that are in motion, moving from some other technology focus to the new OO focus. The business environment in the OO software industry is somewhere between the pioneer and the spreading revolution stage. These two factors combine to require fluid organizations focused on vision and value. The fluidity needs tempering with an ability to scale up to challenges. The most exciting aspect of the OO software organization is its focus on reuse. This focus embeds the organization in a web of reusable systems that permit dramatic innovations in providing value to stakeholders. The ability to recombine systems already created is critical in revolutionary environments, and OO software organizations can only benefit from that.

Certifying an organization for reuse requires evaluating the risk, stating the goals and functions of the system, and describing the responsibility for the system.

Organizational risks come mainly from poor placement in the organizational environment, ineffectual structure, or project policies that get in the way of delivering value [Jones 1991, p. 485]. Jones reports a frequency of 70%, 50%, and 35%, respectively, for these risks in the general software industry. The likelihood of effective reuse is thus relatively low, on average, based on risk.

You describe the goals and functions of the organization with the mission and operational objectives of the system. The organization chart and the job descriptions of the work groups and resources in the organization provide clear descriptions of the authority structure and the responsibilities of each group. These must describe the reality of the organization, not what you hope the responsibility structure will look like.

Work Group (30.1)
Resource (34.1)

■ *Note:* Job descriptions are part of the work group and resource systems.

Responsibility for the organization rests with the organizational environment. To certify responsibility, you must obtain organizational commitments from the executives who control the organization. With the level of change in the software industry and in the OO portion of it in particular, you will find it difficult to get long-term commitments to organizations. Upper-level executives tend to talk about "exit strategies," "incentive options," and "return on investment" rather than about commitment to organizations. Commitment usually goes the other way: executives demand commitment from the organization to deliver software on time and under budget. It is quite enlightening to manage contracts as parts of projects and watch executives deal with legal commitments. Unless they find a way to squirm out of them, contractual commitments constrain executive behavior in ways that organizational commitments do not.

I've worked with several organizations over 10 years in the OO software market. The following paragraphs summarize some of these organizations and how their reuse potential was affected by the different factors I've discussed in the preceding text.

Company A developed CASE tools for OO software development. Its internal development strategy was in transition to OO. We programmed in C, but our internal design was shifting to OO design. The internal structure of the organization was a projectized organization for the most part. Project leaders would work with program managers in marketing to define a product, and then design and build it. The projects were generally six to nine months in duration. When a project finished, the group would turn to another project, but the structure would change. Certain groups were functional in nature (porting groups especially), providing technical resources on demand to other groups. Turnover in these groups was relatively high due to dissatisfaction with a perceived lack of leadership with respect to delivering value to stakeholders. That is, most of the people in the porting groups thought we ought to be doing more with their systems and left because we didn't. As time went on, we reorganized most groups at least once or twice a year to accommodate market changes, changes in people, and project births and deaths. The results of this approach were mixed. Each project got a reasonably focused effort. Reuse was moderate due to the incremental nature of the projects: most transformed an existing system into a new one. Learning was low because of turnover and because of the fluid structure of personal relationships.

Company B was almost entirely focused on a single customer, a large hardware/software company. The product was an OO database management system. The organization reflected the architecture: a UI group, a programming interfaces group, a transaction management group, and so on. The impact of focusing on a single customer was to redirect the efforts of all groups toward a punch list from the customer. This stifled innovation and had a negative effect on the ability of the organization to take on new projects by stabilizing the organization around the punch list. No one could move. Eventually, some did, leaving the company to pursue other interests. The large customer restructured, resulting in almost no revenue for upwards of 20 person-years of effort on the product as the value of the work went down the tubes with the customer.

Company C, a division of a large software company, had a very fluid structure, reorganizing at least four times in two years. The company was focused on a single project and product, a project management system built in C++ with an extensive GUI framework. Turnover was relatively low in the ranks and 100% at the upper levels as the parent company repeatedly wielded the ax. This was an organization where sticking your neck out was not advisable if you liked your head. Internally, the relationships were almost entirely informal. Certain people got their jobs done, others didn't, with or without managers. Middle management played at organization and project management, but real power rested with one or two people who could make anything happen, who kept telling everyone to row harder. The results were clear: the project restructured three times and was a one-year project delivered in four years, long after I'd left the company. The personal and political focus of the organization resulted in a large, useless OO framework that was not portable, causing the cancellation of all but the primary port. The major innovations in the system were mixed in success: a mediocre GUI and client/server implementation, an excellent object model and internal processing system, and totally unportable code. Ultimately, turnover was 100%, the parent company divested the division due to low profitability rates, and everything started from scratch—at least, organizationally.

Organizations That Work

To create an organization with a good chance of reuse, you should follow at least some of the following suggestions.

- Minimize turnover.
- Focus work groups on projects, not functions. I believe the projectized organization is a better way to do this than the functional or matrix ones.
- Focus the organization on stakeholder value, not on technology or personality.
- Emphasize reusable systems, both technological and business, establishing deep, intertwined relationships with your stakeholders and organizational environment. In particular, emphasize the innovative reuse of systems in new, more valuable combinations (it's *open systems, stupid*).
- Eliminate authoritarian political games in favor of commitment and trust between all people and groups.
- Continuously improve everything, including the organization, to increase innovation and value.
- Use growth to add new thinking and technology to the organization, not restructuring and endless looping.

It is not, however, a foregone conclusion that you should emphasize portability in organizations. For example, a completely stable organization with no turnover, no politics, and a total focus on the customer is highly reusable. It is not, however, very adaptable. The stability means that the structure cannot adapt to new conditions in different projects. The general approach of such an organization will not be terribly innovative. You will be able to reuse the organization in any project, but the results may not be as good for the individual project.

For example, the functional organization's major benefit is that it organizes around the process models you have in place to standardize operations. As long as these process models adequately represent the work that needs doing in a project, the organization will succeed. When the project requires something different, the functional organization will not adapt well.

On the other hand, the projectized organization is completely focused on the individual project. This means that reuse potential rides on the domain dimension: how well the organization fits the domain of the new project. While it is less reusable, the projectized organization aligns much better with the needs of the individual project, producing better results.

The matrix organization is a weak combination of both these approaches. If there is a true balance of authority between the project manager and the functional managers in the matrix, then the reuse potential is moderate. You will need to reconfigure the matrix to fit new projects, but you will maintain the organization's stability through the functional organization. Because the authority is diffuse, however, the overhead will probably grow larger than necessary, and you will find it harder to control projects due to the difficulty of integrating feedback into the project.

The Functional Organization

The *functional organization* classically divides responsibility and authority along functional lines rather than project lines. Work groups organize around process models that represent the standard approaches to a given function. The project manager, if there is one, often works as a coordinator or team leader with no authority. Legitimacy rests with the functional manager, who has complete authority. The functional manager deals with all people issues, including career management, compensation, and evaluation. He or she also controls communication.

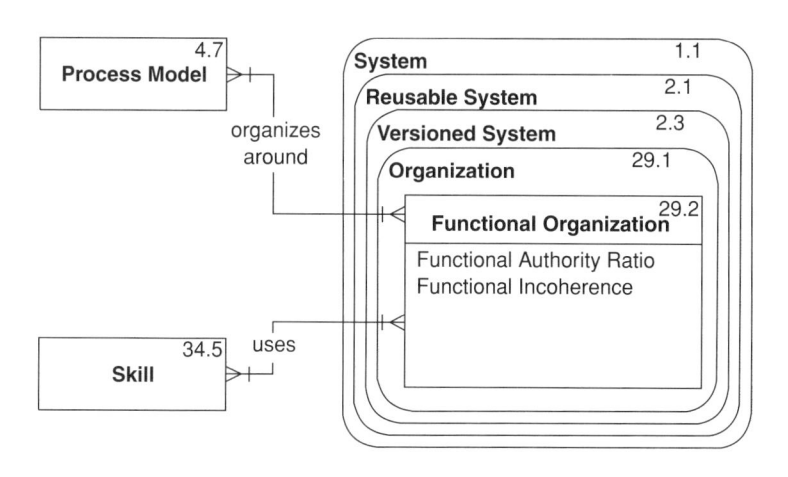

Vision: A clearly organized set of functional teams that perform their functions well in many projects

Mission: To establish clearly delineated authority around functional work, producing teams capable of adding great value to multiple projects

Objective 29.3: To establish clearly delineated authority around functional work areas

Approach 29.3: Organize work teams around process models, such as OO development, C++ or Smalltalk or Eiffel programming, documentation, or quality assurance. Assign a functional manager to each division. Break the departments down into work groups by function and nested process model, establishing managers reporting up the hierarchy as you go. Each work group does the tasks in the WBS from the process for which the group is responsible. Reward and recognize the efforts of each work group based on their demonstrated functional skills and ability to accomplish their process tasks. Structure communication to let each function clearly communicate what it needs to the other functions on which it depends.

Metric 29.3.1: Functional authority ratio: the number of functional reporting relationships over the total number of relationships in the organization

Target 29.3.1: A high value within control parameters of a pn control chart of functional organizations

---

Metric 29.3.2: Functional incoherence: the number of overlaps between work groups in responsibility for process models; a measure of how well the work group organizations reflect the underlying process models, taking into account how well those models in turn represent the work of the project

Target 29.3.2: A low number

The functional organization has two defining characteristics. First, every person in the organization has a single manager with authority over them except for the person at the top of the hierarchy. This provides a major benefit, the clear lines of authority and responsibility. Second, each person works within the boundaries of a single process model. That is, the work groups in the organization reflect the structure of process models that the organization uses. When you use a functional organization in a project, you divide up the work through the process models. A work group performs the tasks you generate from a process model for which they are responsible. The coherence that the process models provide to the organization of the work groups is another major benefit of the functional approach. Figure 29-1 shows a typical organization chart for an OO functional organization.

A functional organization works best when each work group has authority over the process model for which it is responsible. The work group conducts the improvement plans for the process model, keeping the continuous improvement process close to the work. Acquiring the functional model is a two-step process. First, you must determine the set of process models that you will apply in the project. Then, you fit the organization to the set of models, adapting the existing organization to any new or changed process models.

The functional organization has the most reuse potential of any of the three kinds of organization. Because it organizes around process models, it has an internal

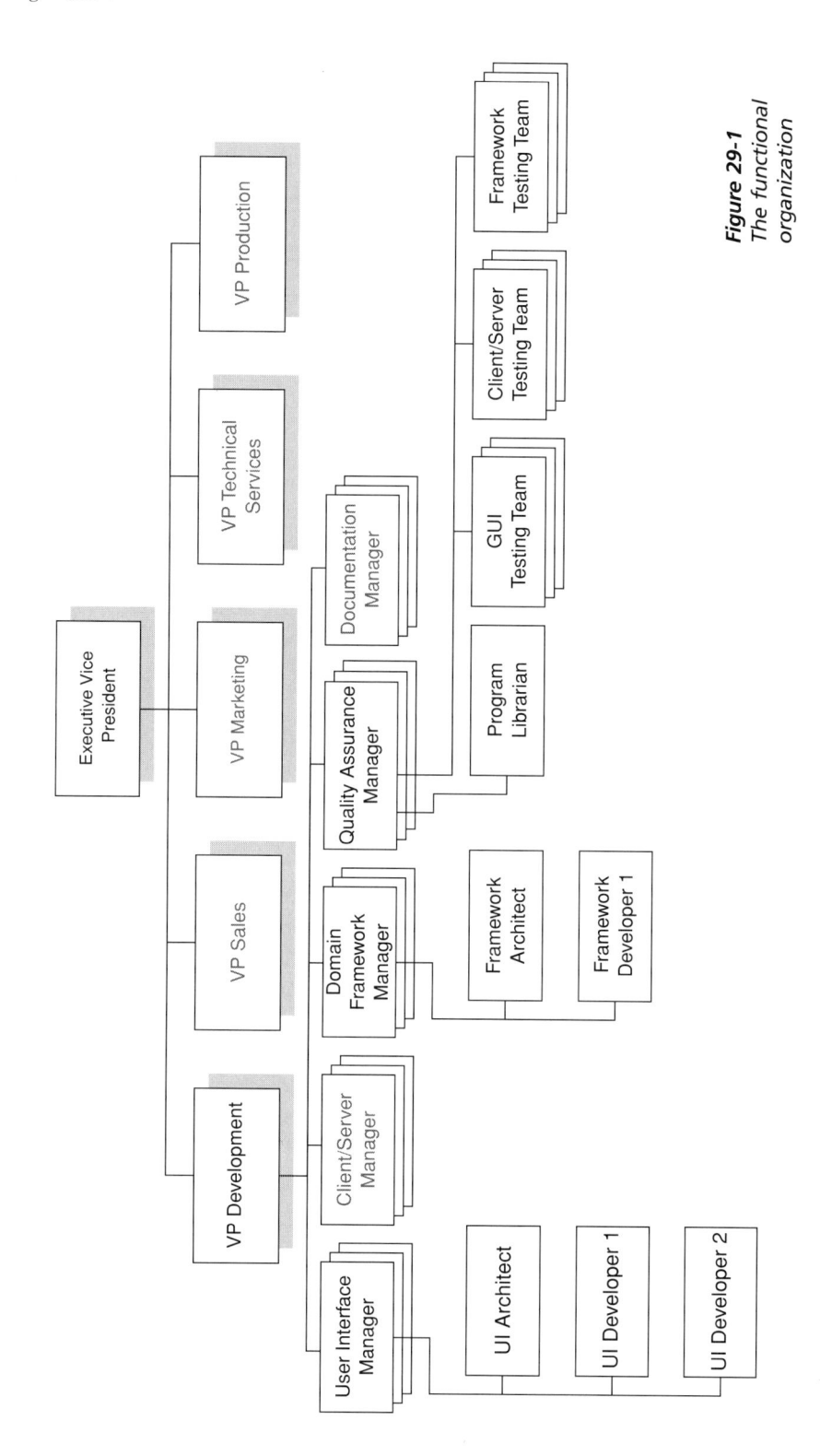

The Functional Organization

Figure 29-1
The functional organization

cohesion that promotes structural stability. As long as the process models accurately represent the work that needs doing, the inherent reuse potential of the functional organization is quite high.

The domain can affect reusability through requiring different sets of skills and different process models, so domain reuse potential comes from the skills coverage of the organization. That is, how many different processes can the organization perform over the universe of possibilities? If your organization has groups for the major kinds of processes you are likely to encounter in your work, then domain reuse potential is high.

Organizational reuse depends on the organizational environment. If your organizational environment emphasizes organizational continuity, you are likely to have high organizational reuse potential for a functional organization. The processes will tend to apply across projects, and you will find support for continuing to use those process models in different projects. For example, such an environment would contain shared repositories and policies that support the functional process models. It would work with organizations to focus on stakeholder needs, leading to process models that take such needs into account. If there is constant turmoil in the environment, or if the environment doesn't invest in the infrastructure needed for continuity, your organizational reuse potential will be low for functional organizations.

When you apply a functional organization to a project, there is usually no project manager at all. Instead, the functional organization just does the project, splitting up the work along functional lines. A manager at some high-to-intermediate level takes responsibility for planning and other project management functions, providing project coordination through management of the functional managers. The different groups are largely independent of one another, and most communication goes through the management chain of command. These projects tend to have quite a few meetings to allow different functional groups to share with each other.

Company C from the above section on "The Organization" had a classic functional structure with some issues. The division of the company had a general manager. He divided the division into marketing, development, sales, support, and quality assurance, each with a director. Each department had internal groups divided up by functional area. Development, for example, had a user interface group, an "engine" group that handled the processing-intensive system programming, and a client/server group that handled database management and object modeling. There was also a single-person system architecture group with no official coding responsibilities.

This was a small organization that worked on one project at a time for the most part. For a six-month period, a different group formed to start up a new project. This group had no internal divisions. When the larger project ran into trouble, and the parent company reorganized the division by firing the general manager and many directors, the new organization merged the two projects and created the functional structure. These functions weren't really organized around process models, but around skills such as UI programming, client/server programming, and algorithm programming. This meant that the groups all shared much the same process but worked on different architectural pieces of the project.

One exception to the clear functional division was quality assurance. While the QA group was separate, certain members of the group worked closely with developers. These QA developers reported to both the QA director and the functional manager, leading to split authority. It did enable the functional groups to integrate high-quality unit and integration testing into the development process. This improved the development work groups' abilities to achieve results, though it led to some curious political battles at the director level.

Another exception was the configuration management function. Historically, the developers had worked out a configuration management process based on a popular PC configuration management tool, PVCS. This tool let you build a repository on a PC network and maintain a local version of the system on your PC with check-in and check-out capabilities. The developer most responsible for the system moved into the client/server group at about the same time as a junior developer moved into the program librarian job full-time. The result was to move the configuration management function into the client/server group. This worked to a certain extent, but the widely differing processes for the two parts of the group were somewhat distracting to me as the group's manager. I worked harder than necessary at doing both jobs.

■ *Note:* Usually, configuration management seems to migrate into the QA group when it achieves full-time status, presumably because the work is much like most QA work and because of the release management component of the work. In the case of Company C, the director of development never considered this because of the political problems he was having with the director of quality assurance. This is a good example of how the organizational environment can foul up the organizational structure.

The biggest issue in this organization, however, was authority. The director of development in particular was strongly authoritarian and unwilling to delegate that authority, though he pretended to do so. The three functional managers were all "provisional," giving the director the ability to demote them without involving human resources. The system architect, who was outside of the formal organizational structure, worked well with the director on a personal level. This led to the architect having more power over the work of the project than the three functional managers. In a way, the architect assumed the role of a project manager in a projectized organization, but informally. He thus had a great deal of authority and little responsibility. The result, as you might predict, was cloudy authority and decision making. No one could finalize a decision until both the director and the architect agreed, but there was no formal process for getting such agreement. As well, there was no formal recognition of the authority issues, so the work groups would make decisions that were later reversed by the architect or director. The level of trust in this organization was not very high, nor was the level of commitment.

The Projectized Organization

The exact opposite of the functional organization, the *projectized organization* centralizes authority in the project manager, with most if not all of the project resources reporting to the project manager. Legitimacy rests with the project manager, who has complete authority. The project manager deals with all people issues, including career management, compensation, and evaluation. The projectized organization's structure reflects the structure of the project: the WBS.

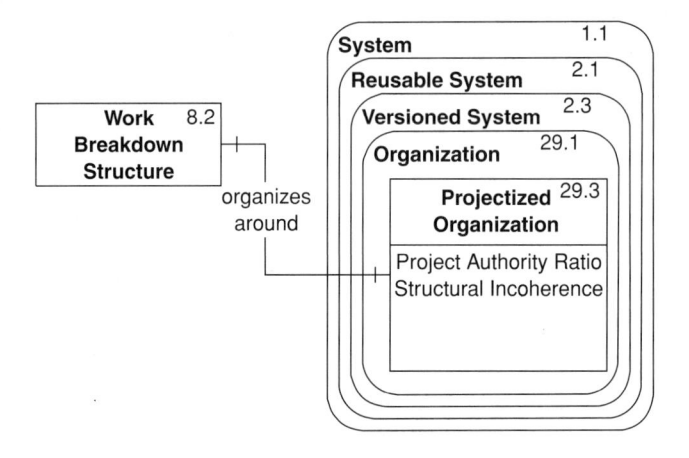

Vision: A clearly organized set of project teams

Mission: To establish clearly delineated authority around project work, producing teams capable of adding great value to a project

---

Objective 29.4: To establish clearly delineated authority around project work

---

Approach 29.4: Organize the work for the project under a single project manager, who has complete authority and responsibility for the project. Divide the work among project resources by organizing them along the lines of the project WBS (deliverable and process). Establish supporting departments or subcontractors that projects share as needed to accommodate needs for less-than-full-time resources or cross-project skills such as knowledge of the corporate reuse repository.

The Projectized Organization

Metric 29.4.1: Project authority ratio: the number of reporting relationships not delegated from the project manager's authority over the total number of relationships in the organization

Target 29.4.1: A high value within control parameters of a pn control chart of functional organizations

---

Metric 29.4.2: Structural incoherence: the number of work groups that overlap WBS subtrees

Target 29.4.2: A low number of overlaps, with the number being within control limits of a pn control chart

---

The most important reason for having a projectized organization is to centralize authority in the person who cares the most about the project: the project manager.

The projectized organization takes its structure from the work breakdown structure (WBS) of the project. The WBS approach that this book takes recommends a WBS with a series of top-level processes corresponding to the processes in the project process model and to the project deliverables. The projectized organization that results from following this structure organizes the work teams either through project processes or as subprojects for each of the deliverables (Figure 29-2) [Bennatan, pp. 62–66]. You assign branches of the WBS tree to these groups, which in turn break them down and assign them to resources.

Work Breakdown Structure (8.2)

This organization is particularly well suited to OO software projects for three reasons. First, the organization adapts to the exact needs of the project, expanding and contracting with the work you plan in the WBS. Instead of forcing squareish functional teams to fit into the round holes of the OO project, you construct the teams you need by hiring resources with the right skills. This allows you to avoid several resource-related risks associated with many OO projects, such as lack of training. Second, the responsibility structure follows the product structure, with each major deliverable and cluster having a single person responsible to the project or group manager for delivery. This makes control easy. Third, the organization can consist of virtual teams producing components. If your company lacks the skills to produce a component, you can solicit proposals from other companies and plug their development efforts into your organization as subprojects. In this way, the benefits of the OO development paradigm become the benefits of the projectized organization as well.

- *Note:* The virtual corporation can make use of the projectized form easily. The project manager belongs to the virtual corporation, with the various organizations reporting to him as the contractual relationships require. While you can organize this as a matrix, with little authority in the project manager, I do not believe this is a good idea; but I have no evidence one way or the other.

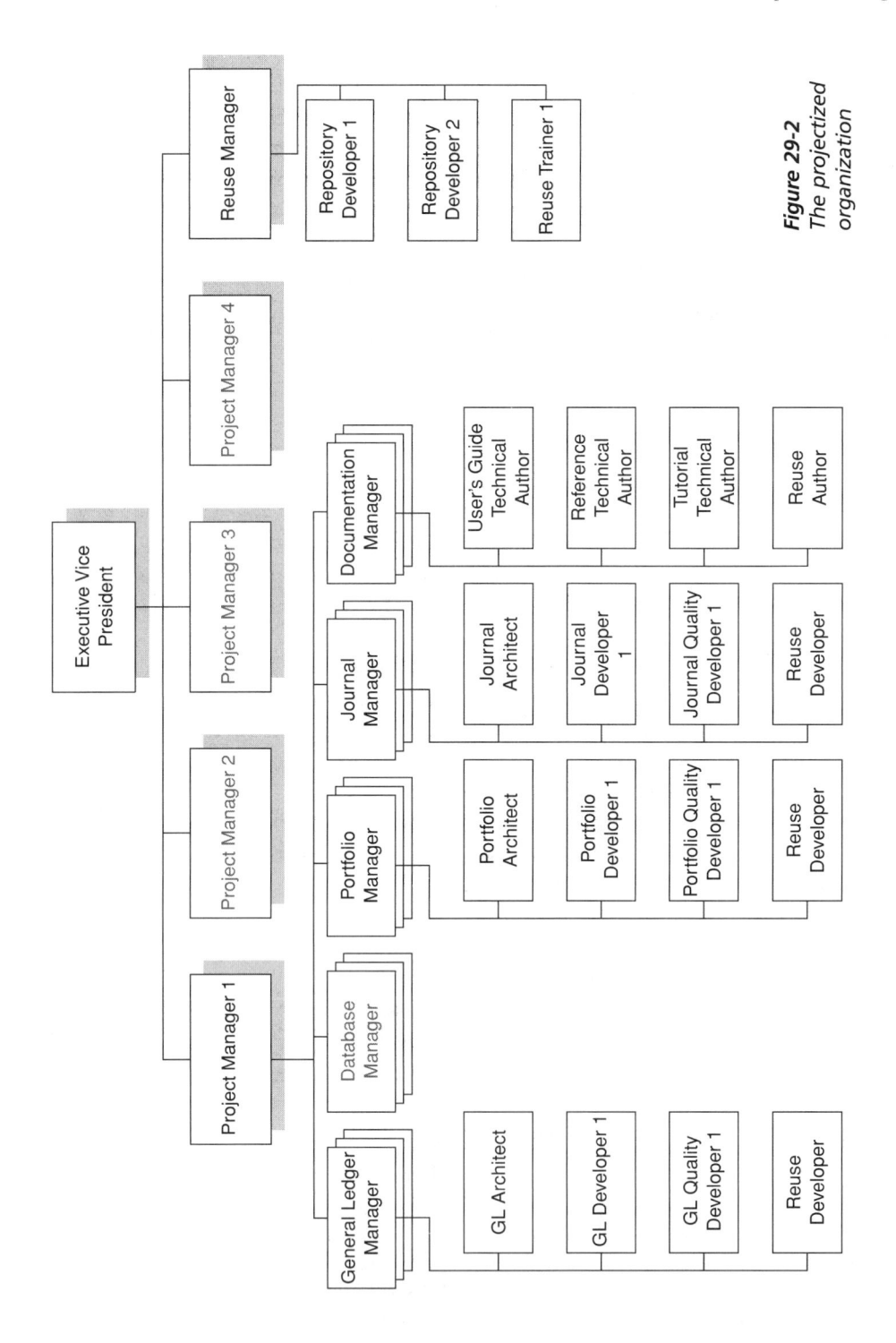

Figure 29-2
The projectized organization

Just as in the functional structure, the authority structure of the projectized organization is clear. Members of work groups report to the group leaders; those leaders report to managers of containing groups responsible for deliverables, who in turn report to the project manager.

You can integrate modern methods of empowerment and work design [Weisbord, Chapter 16] into the projectized organization. Develop the work breakdown structure using participative techniques, getting the available resources involved in developing the project. As your project WBS evolves through your organization's work, the organizational structure evolves with it through the work of the people in the organization. Using these kinds of planning and development techniques is simultaneously the best way to get well-designed software and a well-designed workplace. You can do this with a functional organization too, but the stability expected of such organizations tends to get in your way. In functional organizations, people tend to work with what they have rather than stretching the bounds of the organization.

There are some aspects of work that are best seen as external to the project, such as managing the reusable systems of the company. These support functions go beyond the needs of a single project, optimizing the systems for multiple projects. The functional organization represents these kinds of functions well. Nevertheless, the projectized organization can also take advantage of such a structure by regarding the external group as a contracting organization. The project hires resources from the external group, integrating them into the project work groups that need their skills as subcontractors. In this way, for example, you can hire reuse experts who understand what reusable systems the company possesses and the tools for working with them [Goldberg, p. 256]. These experts can contribute both their knowledge of what exists and their abilities to take new systems and certify them for future reuse in other processes or projects. This matrix-like approach to support functions gives you all the advantages of the projectized organization (authority and responsibility) with all the advantages of the matrix (ongoing knowledge and skills and increasing innovation trajectories for the company as a whole).

A method common among Japanese software companies that market outsourcing services to other companies is to organize several projects under a single project manager [Goldberg, pp. 274–275]. By integrating the different projects into a single project, this approach integrates the reuse function into the project organization as a support department that supplies resources to other parts of the project. This approach will work well for any large company that has several OO projects going on at once.

Reusability takes a much different form in the projectized organization. In the functional organization, reuse depends mainly on stability, similar domains, and organizational legitimacy. Creating a reusable projectized organization lets you relax the assumptions about stability and domain. Instead of relying on the cohesiveness of the functional divisions in your organization, you rely on its ability to adapt to different project requirements. This requires totally different skills than functional ones. It forces people to think about systems and adaptation rather than about functional skills. The best projectized organizations can focus entirely on the project work and organize or reorganize themselves around that work. This makes for fluid internal reporting relationships and communications, so you need to establish the policies and communications methods to accommodate that fluidity. This ensures strong inherent reuse potential.

The best part of such an organization is that it is minimally constrained by domain. The organization can rework itself on the fly to adapt to different domains. It can acquire skills through training or subcontracting and apply those skills exactly where needed without the constraint of a functional organization's separate goals. The flexibility you get from making the organization highly adaptable makes it more reusable across different domains.

To get a projectized organization capable of high reuse potential, you must train the project managers, group managers, and other resources in the skills that will give them the flexibility to adapt to different projects. This means two things. First, you must train most resources in most technical skills, such as analysis, design, programming, and testing. This permits the resources to apply themselves as needed rather than having to reach to a different part of the organization for the expert. Second, you must recruit and train management resources with project management skills. Capers Jones notes that the frequency of project management malpractice in the software industry approaches 15%, with the main causes being lack of criteria for judging performance, lack of project management curricula in schools, poor management recruiting, inadequate on-the-job training, and lack of licensing [Jones 1994, pp. 454–456]. A projectized organization must have both effective technical people and effective management to ensure reusability.

To certify a projectized organization for reuse, you must back up your estimate of the risk of a poor fit with data. Provide data showing how well the project teams did at delivering value. Go one layer down and show how well they did delivering on schedule and on budget as well. Use standardized tests such as the PMI Project Management Professional examination to certify the management team. Develop a document that describes the organization's capabilities and policies. Finally, state the responsibility for the organization's success. How will the organization interact with the organizational environment? How will it maintain itself through the project? What resources does the organization have to back itself up when times get tough? How can the organization guarantee results? With this certification in hand, your projectized organization can make a strong case for reuse on future projects.

The Matrix Organization

The *matrix organization* structure is a mixture of functional and project organization, where the functional managers and the project manager interact to negotiate the work done on the project. The spectrum of matrix organization can vary from a weak to a strong matrix, depending on the degree of authority and legitimacy of the project manager. The exact split of responsibility for people issues depends on the strength of the matrix organization. The functional manager usually gets responsibility for human resource issues and the project manager gets responsibility for work-related issues.

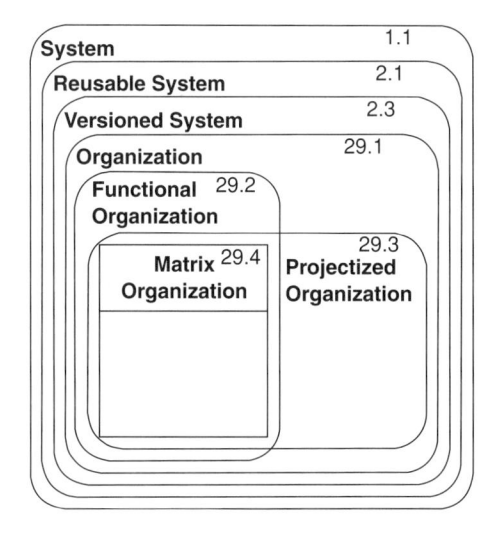

- *Note:* The Matrix Organization class is a rare example of multiple inheritance in this book. The Functional Organization and Projectized Organization classes overlap in the class diagram, showing that the Matrix Organization inherits from both.

Vision: A clearly organized project combining functional teams to address project issues

Mission: To establish clearly delineated responsibility around project work, using functional teams and resources as necessary to create project deliverables

Objective 29.5: To create work groups responsible for specific deliverables

Approach 29.5: Organize resources into a functional structure aligned with process models, as in Approach 29.3. To apply this organization to a project, assign a project manager and project resources to the project tasks in the WBS, with the project manager assuming responsibility for coordinating the resources and tasks. Delegate the project manager enough authority for the tasks and resources to permit effective project management, but keep multiple-project resource planning as the functional managers' authority and responsibility. Train everyone in the skills this kind of structure needs, such as negotiation and teamwork.

Figure 29-3 illustrates the matrix organization, with the project managers managing projects that integrate work groups and resources through a two-dimensional matrix of responsibility.

The matrix organization varies from a *weak matrix*, in which the functional manager has most authority, to a *strong matrix*, in which the project manager has most authority [Kerzner; PMI 1996a]. You can use either the functional authority or project authority metrics to determine the strength of the matrix organization.

In a weak matrix, the project manager is a coordinator or facilitator. In a balanced matrix, the project manager takes on a more active role in planning and controlling, working in tandem with the functional managers. In a strong matrix, the project manager has considerable authority, especially when it comes to project-related decisions and responsibilities, but still leaves some authority to the functional manager for resource allocation and multiple-project planning. In the strong matrix, the functional managers exist primarily to coordinate and supply resources to the project managers.

One way to look at the matrix is to see the project dimension as a profit center and the functional dimension as a cost center. You can add in dimensions for geography, time, and other variables. The more complex the matrix, the less stable it is. This can be an advantage in an unstable environment, but it certainly leads to higher overhead, lower productivity, and increased communications requirements.

The authority structure of the matrix is inherently less clear than that of its parent types. You have two different kinds of manager for each resource, the functional and project manager. In a multiple-project context, you could have resources reporting to several different project managers as well as to a functional manager. You can greatly reduce the potential for conflict by dividing the reporting responsibilities by task. For example, if an OO architect works on three projects and reports to the director of development, the three project managers could have full authority for the schedule and budget issues and the director for the technical issues. Unfortunately, the structure of such issues often precludes such easy division of authority. For example, if two projects have schedule problems, both managers have authority, but the resource has only so much time. This is why most matrix organizations tend toward the weak side, with the single functional manager having the biggest say in what happens. It means less negotiation and stress for the resources as well as faster and clearer decision making.

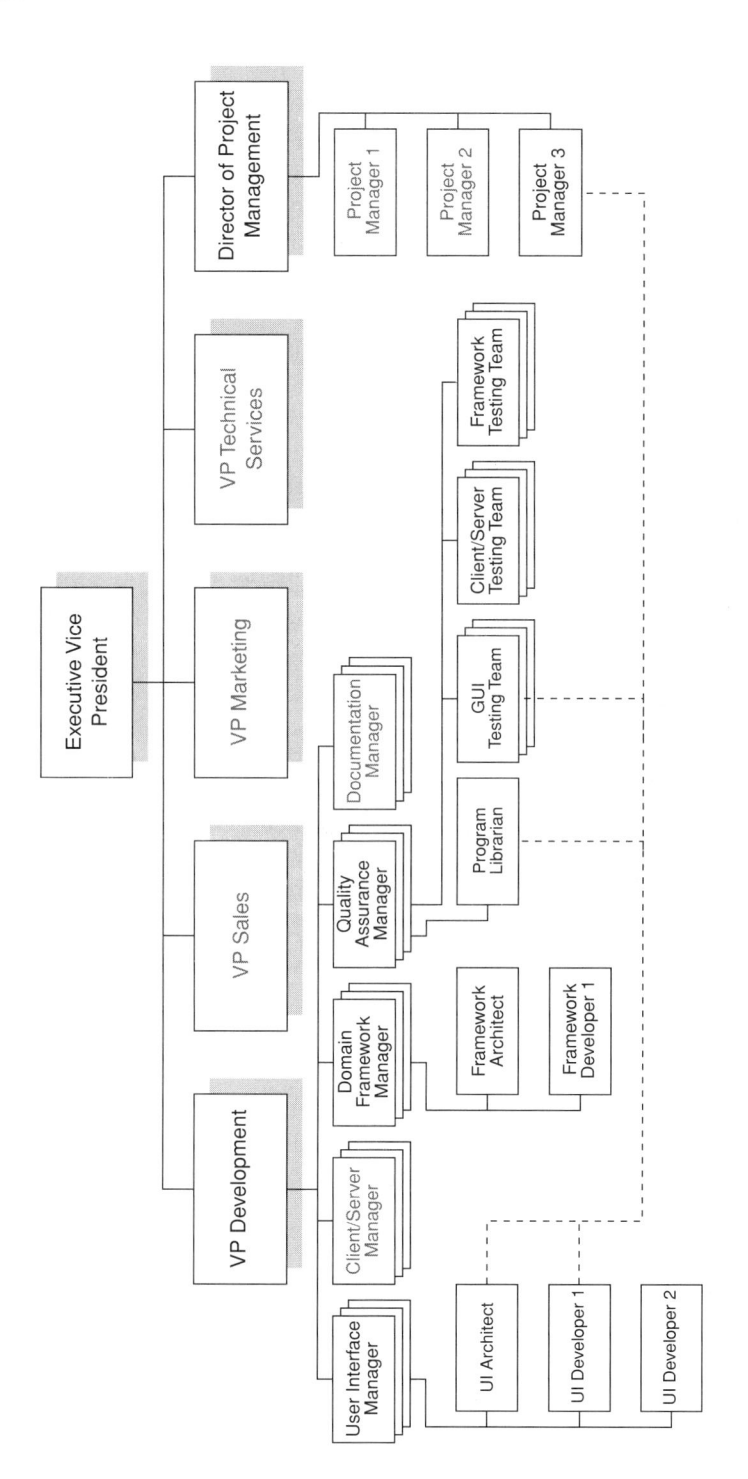

Figure 29-3
The matrix organization

The matrix organization works best for projects with clearly defined tasks and little need for authority, since you organize your matrix around those tasks rather than around the process models or project architecture. This translates to projects with clearly understood requirements, architecture, and legitimacy. Unfortunately, many OO projects aren't like this because of their incremental and iterative nature. Their use of new and unproved architectures and methods can often lead to a lack of legitimacy and support from the functional organizations. In an OO project, you usually wind up with a very weak matrix form that emphasizes the authority of the functional managers. The result is a rather unstable matrix constantly under negotiation as plans change. One characteristic of such projects is the lack of stability in planning.

The primary advantage of the matrix structure is that it combines the reusability of the functional structure with the project focus of the projectized structure. Each person in the organization continues in his or her functional work team through several projects, providing needed stability and reusability. It is easy to share people between projects. Work teams develop strong skills by performing their function on multiple projects.

Another organization I worked with had a weak matrix structure. The functional departments were the usual: core development, client/server development, quality assurance, and documentation. The organization had six or seven projects at a time, which led to having a series of project managers chosen from the set of available scapegoats by the senior manager. Most of these projects were maintenance projects, some were porting projects, and others were projects that moved the product line forward. The project I took charge of was to move the major product of the company into the OO world. It took at least three planning iterations to begin to understand what that meant to the product architecture, which led to much confusion about the work. My role had no authority at all; I was merely a coordinator, combining the development plans and functional specifications of the functional managers into a working whole for which I had responsibility. The priorities of the functional managers dominated the project, as my negotiating position was quite weak. I spent most of my time haranguing the managers to update their plans, report on status, or explain why they delivered something completely different from the specification. All real issues had to go through senior management for resolution. This was not a particularly fun experience for me, which probably explains why I am not in favor of weak matrix management. There may be some project superstars who can make this kind of situation work, but if so, I haven't met any.

I'd like to be able to say the matrix organization inherits the best of both the functional and projectized organization for reuse potential, but it isn't true. Matrix organizations, and especially weak ones, just make the organization less flexible through the lack of authority around the project tasks and the stabilizing effect of the functional groups.

The Organization Chart

An *organization chart* is a tool that describes the project organization. This chart details the authority structure, showing who reports to whom. More sophisticated organization charts may show lines of legitimacy and communication as well as authority, the network of support and trust that underlies the willingness of people to accept responsibility for their work. Teams organized in ways that facilitate legitimacy are more likely to have high motivation and strong ties between the people on the team. The organization chart becomes part of the project plan. Figures 29-1, 29-2, and 29-3 are examples of organization charts. The organizational repository stores the organization chart.

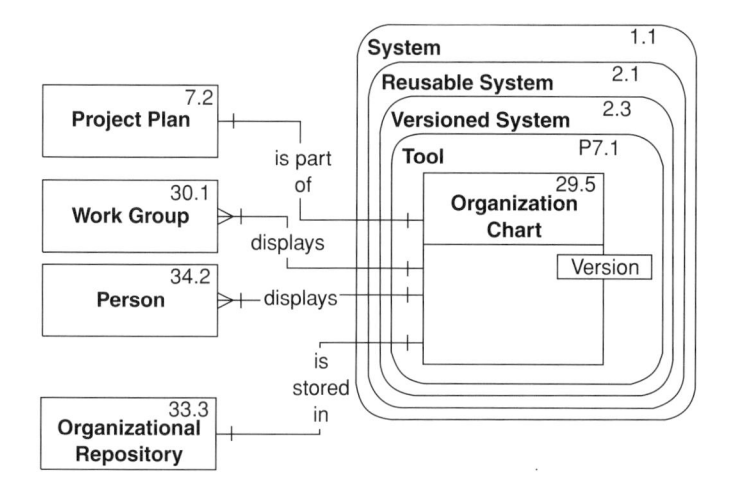

Vision: A clearly defined organizational reporting structure

Mission: To represent the reporting structure of an organization as part of the project plan or organizational environment

Objective 29.6: To represent the reporting structure of an organization as part of the project plan or organizational environment

Approach 29.6: Use a tree-structured graphical modeling tool to represent the nodes and arcs of the organization network graph. Clearly mark the names of the work groups and resources on the chart. Use chart decomposition to represent very large organizations. Maintain the chart as the organization changes to keep the reporting relationships and names up-to-date.

Metric 29.6: Effectiveness: an ordinal, subjective measure of effective communication; users of the chart answer the question, "Please rate the effectiveness of this chart in giving you the reporting structure of the organization." Values: Highly Effective, Moderately Effective, Somewhat Effective, Not Very Effective, Useless

Target 29.6: Highly Effective

I worked in two organizations that deliberately constructed their organization charts with the senior manager at the bottom and the individual resources at the top. The ideology behind this inverted representation is to emphasize the importance of the resources as assets (you know: "People are our greatest asset."). While I admire the thought, neither organization actually valued resources in that way, so the effect reversed the intention.

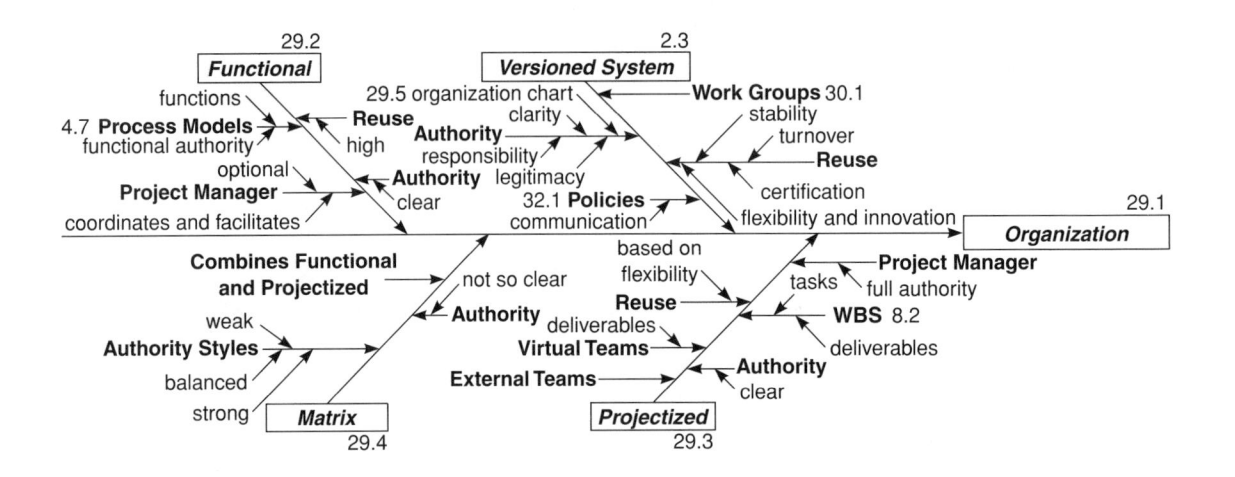

Readings

[Bennatan]   E. M. Bennatan. *On Time, Within Budget: Software Project Management Practices and Techniques.* New York: QED Publishing Group, 1992.

This book contains a nice but short section on organizational structure that describes some variations on the projectized organization. It compares this to the matrix organization and recommends the former to the latter.

[Booch 1996]   Grady Booch. *Object Solutions: Managing the Object-Oriented Project.* Reading, MA: Addison-Wesley, 1996.

Booch recommends the projectized structure for OO projects in a well-written section of his chapter on teams, pp. 200–202. He thinks it vital that the project manager is in charge of the project: "When the pragmatism of a bold project manager finds balance with the intense vision of a hyperproductive architect, the results are magical." He recommends three qualities for such a project manager: being risk averse, being politically sensitive, and being an enlightened dictator.

[Cleland 1983]   David I. Cleland and William R. King. *Systems Analysis and Project Management, Third Edition.* New York: McGraw-Hill, 1983.

This book has an excellent discussion of the organization chart in Chapter 11. It handles both the advantages and limitations of these charts, and then suggests some alternatives. Cleland's Part 4 is also the best advocate for using the matrix organization that I've found, though I remain convinced it is the wrong choice for OO software projects.

[Davis]   Stanley M. Davis and Paul R. Lawrence. Problems of matrix organizations. *Harvard Business Review* (May–June 1978): 131–142.

This article is the classic work on matrix organizational structure. The article focuses on several problems that come from the structure itself, such as anarchy, power struggles, "groupitis," and a tendency to collapse in crunches. The authors suggest preventative measures and treatments for these problems, not altogether convincingly.

[DeMarco 1987]   Tom DeMarco and Timothy Lister. *Peopleware: Productive Projects and Teams.* New York: Dorset House, 1987.

Chapter 16 of this great little book is all about turnover and why it is bad for the organization.

[Goldberg]   Adele Goldberg and Kenneth S. Rubin. *Succeeding with Objects: Decision Frameworks for Project Management.* Reading, MA: Addison-Wesley, 1995.

Goldberg has a comprehensive chapter on the organizational structures for reuse (Chapter 11). The discussion seems to assume a projectized organization making use of reusable software and discusses the need for external reuse organizations in detail. The chapter on team structure (Chapter 12) recommends the alignment of team structure with the partitioning of the problem (p. 280) and has several case studies of specific kinds of teams, such as application teams, framework teams, cross-project teams, and reuse teams. Cross-project teams are very interesting: they act as pollinators, moving from project to project carrying reusable systems, new ideas, and other communications-related systems.

[Kerzner]   Harold Kerzner. *Project Management: A Systems Approach to Planning, Scheduling, and Controlling, Fifth Edition.* New York: Van Nostrand Reinhold, 1994.

Kerzner has an excellent, if verbose, chapter on organizational structures (Chapter 3). He includes some structures I do not, such as the product-oriented structure favored by manufacturing organizations.

[Moore]   James F. Moore. *The Death of Competition: Leadership and Strategy in the Age of Business Ecosystems.* New York: Harper-Business, 1996.

This book on the ecosystem approach to business strategy has excellent case examples that illustrate how organizations can best adapt to different environmental conditions.

[PMI 1996a]   Project Management Institute Standards Committee. *A Guide to the Project Management Body of Knowledge.* Project Management Institute (+1-610-734-3330), 1996.

Section 2.3.3 of the PMBOK summarizes the major organizational approaches nicely from the project management perspective.

Questions to Think About

1. When do you think a major reorganization for a software organization is justified? What kinds of situations might result in such restructuring?

2. How do corporate politics relate to organizational structure? (Hint: Think about power and legitimacy and how they relate to the structure.)

3. Which is more important, making the organization responsive to a project's specific needs or making it as reusable as possible? Why? Are these mutually exclusive choices?

4. Justify the use of a matrix organization over a functional or projectized one. Why do many software projects automatically choose this organization?

5. How would you structure a functional organization for best results in OO projects?

6. Do you think that the organization chart for a project reflects the real authority structure of the project? Why or why not?

CHAPTER 30

Work Group and the Team

The Work Group

The *work group* is a versioned system of resources that is itself a kind of resource. It is part of the larger organization for the project, with the organization chart for that organization describing its authority position. Each work group reports to one or more other work groups and may have any number of work groups reporting to it. The work group takes responsibility and preferably an equal measure of authority for task assignments to members of the group. The work group as a system is therefore responsible for the outputs of the process, and you reward and recognize the group for achieving the outputs. Every group has a policy that describes the work it is supposed to do and the authority it has to do it: a *job description*.

- *Note:* A work group is both a versioned system and a resource. Because resources aren't reusable systems, this represents another of the rare cases of multiple inheritance in the class hierarchy of this book.

Vision: An organized collection of resources effectively and productively delivering value

Mission: To organize groups of resources to bring their skills to bear on project work

---

Objective 30.1: To organize groups of resources

Approach 30.1: Organize the available resources into groups using the appropriate method (functional, projectized, or matrix). Create a job description policy for the group. Determine where there are gaps in the skills required to do the project work, and either subcontract or hire additional resources to expand the work group. If a work group grows beyond a manageable size, divide the group or find a way to manage it using scaleable management techniques if the organizational principle dictates a single group.

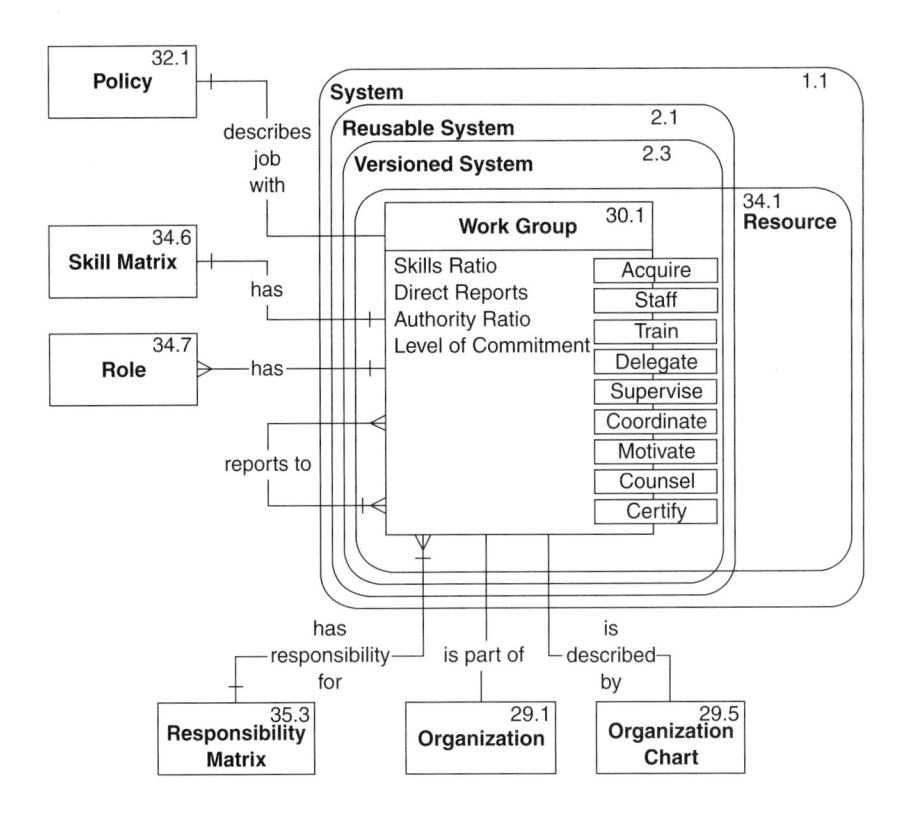

Metric 30.1.1: Skills ratio: the number of skills possessed by group members divided by the number of skills required to do the work the project assigns to the group

Target 30.1.1: One

Metric 30.1.2: Number of direct reports: the number of resources that report directly to the manager of the work group

Target 30.1.2: 7 ± 2, the number of elements a human being can deal with in short-term memory at a single moment

---

Objective 30.2: To create a group that has appropriate authority and responsibility for project work

Approach 30.2: Create a job description for the group that details the responsibilities of the group in the project. If there are elements of this description that you cannot accomplish without reference to your manager, try to get your manager to delegate that authority to you. Delegate authority in this way to resources and groups within your group, aligning authority and responsibility. Give people the tools, and they will finish the job.

Metric 30.2: Authority ratio: the number of responsibilities that the group can accomplish without reference to another group or manager over the total number of responsibilities of the group

Target 30.2: A value close to 1 in functional or projectized organizations, or a suitable value in a matrix organization that makes everybody happy

---

Objective 30.3: To focus the commitment of resources to delivering project work

Approach 30.3: Use situational leadership and other motivational techniques to establish a strong level of commitment to achieving the work of the project. Involve the group members in planning where that makes sense given their capabilities and interests. Direct, coach, train, and integrate the group members as they work on their project tasks. In a word: manage.

Metric 30.3: Level of commitment: the inverse of the average "slack time" of members of the work group, where slack time is the "fraction of project time lost on nonproject activities" [Abdel-Hamid, p. 85, from an article by Boehm], weighted by the ratio of actual hours worked to regular work hours during periods of schedule pressure

Target 30.3: A level of commitment at or around 3.33 (30% slack time and regular working hours) within control parameters of a p control chart for the organization

---

Work groups are the locus for many management tasks and processes because they are the primary units of the organization [Kerzner]. When the organization acquires a work group, the first action after creating a job description and assigning a manager to the group is to staff the group by assigning or hiring resources. The training process applies to the group as well as to the individual and goes on throughout the group's life cycle. The manager delegates responsibilities to the group members and supervises their work on a day-to-day basis. He or she also coordinates their work, prioritizing it and resolving any conflicts that arise. The manager must motivate the group and counsel it when it needs help [Hersey; Weinberg 1994]. The manager and the group must together certify the group for reuse, as the section below on "Reusing Groups" discusses.

"Reusing Groups" section, p. 517

Work Group Structure

The functional organization has work groups that correspond to process models. Each group thus takes responsibility not just for the outputs of tasks but for the entire process. You evaluate the effort of a functional work group at the process milestone. Authority in such a work group covers both the process models and the processes you plan and execute from those models. Part of the group's job description should be to create and maintain the process model through improvement plans. The rest of it is to execute the processes the project plan derives from the process model. The project manager assigns all tasks from the processes to the group, which assigns the tasks to individual members of the group.

The projectized organization has work groups that correspond to tasks in the WBS. Higher-level work groups take responsibility for deliverables; lower-level ones take responsibility for clusters or other deliverable components. In a projectized organization, the project manager delegates the authority over the deliverable to the deliverable groups, who delegate on down the line. The job description of the projectized work group is to produce the required outputs using planned processes and tasks. The project manager assigns the tasks to group members directly.

The matrix organization has work groups taken from functional work groups organized around processes and put into a WBS context by the matrix project manager. The delegation of authority depends on the management style of the matrix, but responsibility and authority are unlikely to match in these work groups. In OO projects I've worked on, the functional managers maintain most authority without delegating it. Usually, the functional manager assigns resources to tasks. If the project manager has an issue with some task, the work group usually refers him or her to the functional manager or managers.

The internal structure of a work group takes the form best suited to the goals and resources of the group. Group structure supports two different aspects of work: delegation and communication.

Responsibility Matrix (35.3)

The group gets responsibility for work through assignment of WBS tasks in the organization's responsibility matrix to the group acting as a resource. The group manager then distributes that work to the group resources through *delegation* of the responsibility and the authority that goes with it to a resource. You thus create a group responsibility matrix that links the group members to specific tasks in the WBS. The structure of the group facilitates this delegation process by setting expectations for the method by which delegation happens.

- *Note:* Delegation assumes a certain amount about the ability and motivation of the resource to whom you're delegating. If the resource is not able to do the work, the task will fail and you will have to take responsibility for that. If the resource is not willing to do the work, the task will fail and you will both have to take responsibility for that. Judging ability and motivation is part of the manager's job [Hersey]. You should choose your group structure, therefore, based on your understanding of the ability and motivation of your group members.

Once work begins, the group members need to communicate within the group to exchange ideas and information. The communication structure of the group has a formal aspect and an informal one. Formal communications happen in team meetings and reviews within the group. Informal communications happen on a personal basis. Either way, the structure of the group again sets the expectations for the methods of communicating within the group.

I have seen four different group structures: democratic, chief programmer, expert, and autocratic.

The democratic group reduces the group manager to a coordinator and administrator. Delegation becomes a matter of group decision making, and the group as a whole assumes responsibility rather than delegating it to an individual [Bennatan, pp. 68–69]. Democratic groups focus on internal communication, sometimes to a fault. The biggest problem with such groups is often the inability to make quick decisions, followed closely by low quality. The structure works best for senior people who understand what they're doing.

The chief programmer group is like a surgical team [Brooks, pp. 32–37]. The manager, or chief programmer, is an extraordinarily talented individual who takes primary responsibility for the work of the group. There should be a second, similar individual with less experience to act as copilot or executive officer. Various other roles (administrator, editor, secretary, program clerk, toolsmith, tester, language lawyer) assist the two primary resources. This group behaves as a complete unit, functionally independent of any other group in the organization. The structure permits the group to achieve a high level of *conceptual integrity* in their work: a unified and integral sense of design and construction of the system deliverables. The chief programmer joins with the other chief programmers to make organization- or project-level decisions with the project manager. This structure reduces the need for internal communication to a minimum, with most actual communication being informal. The structure works best where you have a truly extraordinary individual to act as manager and others available for the other roles.

The expert group is a task force that works on a specific problem that arises during the project [Bennatan, p. 69]. The group usually functions best as a democratic group, but you can vary it as necessary to deal with the issues that arise. Delegation is thus a temporary, need-driven affair, and communication is informal and direct.

The autocratic group is a functional group with a manager qualified mainly by the authority structure to lead the group. This is a typical functional group, with a series of junior-to-middling members and a somewhat more experienced manager coordinating, authorizing, delegating, and directing. You will typically find work groups using this organization during the first stages of team formation. The manager acts as director or coach (teller or seller), bringing the individuals up to a level of ability and willingness to do the job. Delegation serves this team-building process, as the manager directs or coaches the members on work he assigns them.

I've seen all these structures in operation. I've found the chief programmer and democratic teams to be the most effective in OO projects. Because OO projects structure their architecture using a similar kind of conceptual integrity, the chief programmer structure reflects the architecture and is more likely to achieve good results. If your organization has a great depth of experienced and more-than-competent people, the democratic group increases participation. The danger of the democratic group is that with many minds needing consensus, you will compromise the systems and lose conceptual integrity. Democratic groups must carefully control their individualistic impulses and practice egoless decision making.

On a project to develop the first version of an OO database management system, one person took the lead as chief programmer and directed the project. This allowed a small team of developers to complete the project in a year of effort, with excellent results. The organizational structure was flat, with a VP of development (actually more of a marketing position), the core team, and a user interface team. After the release of the first version of the product, the organization grew and hired several relatively inexperienced developers, organizing them into autocratic groups, with members of the former core team taking on management positions. These groups largely failed to achieve results for the next release because of a drastic loss of conceptual integrity. The former chief programmer had become a small cog in the development. Later, he was promoted to being chief architect with no management responsibility, which failed to improve things much.

I've worked in several functional, autocratic teams, sometimes with myself as autocrat, and while these teams achieved results, they were never exceptional. The manager almost always spends far too much time managing. The resources almost always spend far too much time getting experience rather than achieving results. I managed a team developing a client/server engine for a major CASE product that comprised five to six junior developers over a year. I spent most of my time either defining the solutions or acting as program librarian, integrating other people's code, because the developers could not yet take individual responsibility for this. As they gained experience, this situation slowly improved—and they all either became group managers of inexperienced people or left the company!

- ■ *Note:* While I've couched the above discussion in terms of programming teams, the ideas are general. You can apply these structures to any kind of team. I've successfully applied the chief programmer and autocratic group structures to documentation, quality assurance, and marketing groups, for example.

Commitment and Discretionary Effort

Motivation and commitment go hand in hand in most management texts. Motivating people to commit themselves to their work is a big part of a group manager's job. To pin the concept down, though, requires a bit of thought. What exactly is commitment?

The use of slack time and overtime to measure commitment [Abdel-Hamid] will strike many as a poor choice. This measure, originally proposed by Barry Boehm [Boehm 1981b], does have the merit of objectivity. Political science does not offer much in the way of measuring commitment, but other measures might look at subjective support for decisions or other ways of determining the subjective values of the work-group resources. The extra time the resources are willing to spend on the project—*discretionary effort*—is a good approximation for this subjective value. In a work group, as opposed to a team, most resources spend anywhere from 50–70% of their time on project tasks and work regular working hours.

As schedule pressures increase, commitment will increase to some point, and then decline as motivation declines due to overwork or increasing disillusionment with the project or the organization. The logical conclusion is that you should keep commitment up by maintaining a slight-to-moderate schedule pressure using deadlines, setting goals that challenge work groups without exhausting them. You should also provide an escape valve through risk management so that you can keep the schedule pressure at a reasonable level. The best way of doing all this is to involve the group at all stages of planning so that they understand the goal and motivate themselves to achieve it.

There is an extra factor in commitment, though, that this measure does not capture. You usually hear it expressed as working smarter, not harder. That is, commitment implies using your brain in creative work that improves the process. Potentially, then, commitment can actually reduce the amount of work you do. That being said, it doesn't really work that way. As you work smarter, you find time to do the things you couldn't do before, so you work harder, too. The thing about working smarter is that it is so inherently rewarding that it increases your commitment to the work you've improved. You grow into a sense of ownership of the work.

There are organizations that do not value creativity and innovation or working smarter. Generally, I believe those organizations tend to lack real commitment. I worked on an OO project with a group manager who was really into sports metaphors. He believed in the Gipper. He was under the impression that if everyone rowed harder and worked together, they would finish the project ahead of schedule. This was a project that had gone from poor performance to worse performance after three reorganizations. As time went on, this manager began to sense that not everyone on the project was committing themselves the way he wanted. He brought in some commitment consultants to help us work together. We couldn't even commit ourselves to working with the consultants. At the many "come-to-Jesus" meetings that we middle managers had with this guy, he got angrier and angrier at our lack of commitment.

Looking back at this project, I remember the first revelatory burst of light happened in a meeting where I suggested that perhaps doing design reviews would help people understand what was happening. I was savagely attacked, accused of a total lack of commitment, and berated for suggesting such a time-wasting thing. Needless to say, I made no more suggestions, just rowed harder. This sort of thing apparently happened all the time with other group members, too. Eventually, the project emerged, two years late and performing like a slug. The manager was promoted to divisional manager, I still don't know why, and resigned shortly thereafter when the company divested the division to boost profits. Perhaps he just wasn't committed enough.

What lies behind resources' willingness to spend extra time at their project work is treating people like responsible human beings. This is not hard, and involves the following strategies:

- Trust people, and encourage people to trust other people (even senior management). Be deserving of trust by showing respect for people.
- Encourage innovation and creative problem solving.
- Focus on integrating feedback, not microcontrolling people's behavior.
- Help people buy into the vision for the tasks they are to perform.
- Don't ask people to do dumb or purposeless things. At the very least, pay attention to the feedback when people tell you they are doing dumb or purposeless things; don't simply dismiss them as not understanding the big picture. Help them to understand; maybe the big picture is more out-of-focus than you think.
- Make sure everyone understands how they are contributing to the success of the overall project. Give credit where credit is due, especially when you "reuse" ideas or systems from other groups. Make sure that other groups understand how your group contributes, too.
- Reinforce that special feeling people get when they are working wonders.
- Don't ignore the difficult personalities on the team; that just makes them harder for their peers to deal with. Work with them to integrate them, and if that doesn't work, help them to move on to a more satisfying job opportunity.
- Constantly raise your expectations, and don't accept less. If you can't do something, figure out why and improve.
- Don't blame; recover.

In every job I've had, there has always been at least one "difficult" person in each group. Perhaps this is nature's way of distributing stress. In any case, most of the managers in these groups just ignored or, worse, rewarded the person for his or her great contributions. The situation would usually go from barely tolerable to worse until either the person, the manager, or the group became so fed up they quit or engineered the person out of the group.

One person, for example, would dominate design meetings with his brilliant thinking, not permitting anyone else to get a word in edgewise and shouting them down if they did. Another person carefully developed a massive OO data structure, only to be told in a design review that it was much too complex for the task. He went ballistic, stopped talking to everyone, and quit the company shortly thereafter. A third person, much liked by his peers, became convinced the management was out to get him (he was right, actually, but that's another story). He took on a small task on the application framework for our system and spent two months to deliver his revenge: a beautiful, elegant, and very large cluster that handled every possible situation related to the subject. He then resigned and went to another company. A nice guy, just not committed enough, I guess.

This kind of thing tends to happen more often in OO and other advanced technology projects because of the personalities attracted to leading-edge development. Group managers need to learn to handle such people to get their commitment and real work out of them. More importantly, you must ensure that their behavior does not sap the commitment of everyone else in the group. This isn't about bad or good; it's about effectiveness and getting the job done.

Reusing Groups

You don't usually think of it this way, but you are almost always reusing a group. Every time you hire or fire someone or change the structure, you are versioning an existing group. Internal reuse in a project comes from assigning the group or its members to multiple tasks. External reuse means reusing the group in different projects. A work group's potential for reuse depends on the group's capabilities, the domain of the assigned tasks, and the ability of the organization to make use of existing groups.

A group's capability has three aspects: skills, productivity, and commitment. Each resource in the group has a number of skills and a level of proficiency for each. The strength of these skills combined into the group's skill matrix defines the group's capabilities. Strong groups have resources with complementary skills. These groups tend to become *teams*, a special kind of work group. To certify the skills of the group, you develop a skills matrix that shows the proficiencies of the different members of the group for each skill. This matrix tells the acquiring project about the skill level of the group.

Team (30.2)
Skill (34.5)
Skill Matrix (34.6)

As a group improves its productivity, project managers are ever more willing to reuse the group on new tasks. If the group shows a strong commitment to its assignments through working hard to achieve results, again the project manager will reuse the group. Extraordinary commitment leads to the team.

The domain of the assigned tasks must correspond to the domains on which the group is capable of working. Functional groups establish domains through their process models. As they develop and improve their models, their ability to handle a specific domain increases. Projectized groups establish domains on the fly by combining skills to address specific areas of the WBS. A projectized group increases domain capability by increasing the skill set of its resources and their ability to adapt to new situations. A matrix group establishes domains on the fly by using combinations of functional domains available in the functional organization. This may or may not yield a good fit to the domain of the project, which leads to less reuse potential for matrix groups, especially weak ones.

Organizational reuse potential for a group depends on the management culture of the project and its organization. In a small organization, reuse potential is likely to be high for two reasons. First, there aren't that many resources, so every work group stays engaged all the time. Second, communication is much easier, and recognition is wider, so the capabilities and domain understanding of the group is broadly known, making it more likely that you will assign it to further tasks. In larger organizations, however, reuse potential is a function of how well you can advertise the skills and capabilities of your group. Especially in geographically diverse companies, a repository of group job descriptions, work-group Web pages, or other means of getting the message out can increase work-group reuse potential greatly.

Certifying a work group for reuse requires certifying risk, goals and functions, and responsibility.

Work groups provide resources for assignment to tasks. Risks that apply to such work groups include any risk relating to resources, such as lack of training, inability to meet schedules, inability to stick to a budget, and so on. To certify the risk of a group, you collect data on the tasks they deliver and summarize that data with statistics and charts. A group that has successfully completed 95% of its tasks on time and under budget, for example, is certified at the 5% risk level on those factors.

The goals and functions of the group come from its job description. Therefore, the certification of the group contains the job description and any other materials that describe the capabilities and purpose of the group. Listing the skills and biographies of the group members, for example, can be very reassuring and informative to those looking for resources to apply to new projects.

The responsibility for the group comes from two sources. First, every group's level of commitment to its work is its primary demonstration of responsibility. Publishing the level-of-commitment data certifies that responsibility. Second, the manager of the group and the group or groups to which the group reports must take responsibility for the success of the group. Listing this information certifies the group; providing data on historical responsibility of the manager and the next level of management takes this even further.

The Team

A *team* is a work group with a high level of internal legitimacy or commitment. While it takes responsibility, the team focuses more on the strength of its own performance than on accountability. A team's results can often exceed the expectations of the project's stakeholders, while a work group's performance will usually just meet them.

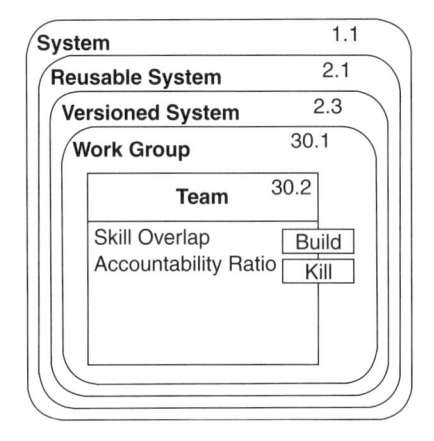

```
System                          1.1
  Reusable System               2.1
    Versioned System            2.3
      Work Group                30.1
        Team                    30.2
        Skill Overlap        Build
        Accountability Ratio Kill
```

Vision: An organization committed to success, delivering great value with great productivity

Mission: To organize resources into a small group of resources with complementary skills committed to a common set of objectives for which they hold themselves mutually accountable

---

Objective 30.4: To organize a group of people with complementary skills

---

Approach 30.4: Identify the group's operational objectives. Staff the group with members that have a mix of skills relevant to the group's operational objectives. Train the team members in needed skills and encourage individual and team skill acquisition. Monitor the skill mix against requirements and feed that information back into the staffing and training processes.

Metric 30.4: Skill overlap: a metric showing the degree of overlap of relevant skills in the group skill matrix

Target 30.4: A low number

Objective 30.5: To organize a small group of people committed to a common set of objectives

---

Approach 30.5: Identify the vision and mission of the team. Staff the group with no more than 20 or 25 members at the maximum. Working with the team members, develop the operational objectives in detail, with approaches, metrics, and targets. Revise the mission and vision as needed, working with the team's stakeholders. Define the group responsibility matrix as a team exercise to distribute the responsibilities of the group to its members so that all members contribute equally to the systems the group produces. Make sure the operational objectives and their metrics effectively measure the progress of the team in fulfilling its responsibilities. Monitor the level of commitment; if it is too low, try reducing the number of team members or redefining the operational objectives for better measurement. Develop the objectives, approaches, and measures continuously throughout the life cycle of the team.

Metric 30.5: Level of commitment (see Metric 30.3)

Objective 30.6: To organize a group of people who hold each other mutually accountable for their common set of objectives

---

Approach 30.6: Accept as much responsibility as possible for work that will involve the joint efforts of the team members. Perform this work in an atmosphere of commitment and trust. Use the operational objective metrics to raise the visibility of team and individual performance. Encourage team members to hold each other accountable. Emphasize the joint work of the team members over individual work, and encourage such work with rewards and recognition of the team as a whole.

Metric 30.6: Accountability ratio: the number of incidents in which team members hold each other accountable for results to the total number of evaluations of results; define accounting relative to the objectives of the group

Target 30.6: A relatively high number close to 1; the number of external evaluations should be relatively small compared to the number of internal evaluations

---

A team is a work group with a high level of internal commitment, both to the project deliverables and to each other. For structural reasons, most teams are resource teams, not higher-level teams of work groups. It's hard to maintain the level of commitment you need in a team across any kind of team boundary, hierarchical or otherwise. It's hard to maintain in a large group of people as well; hence the approach of keeping the team under 25 people, but preferably under 7 or so. Organizationally, you want to have a series of teams working for the organization rather than trying to make the entire organization into a team.

A major task for a team is team building. DeMarco believes you cannot build a team; it just happens while you're holding your breath [DeMarco 1987, pp. 132–133]. I think it is a bit of both; teams generally don't happen behind your back; they happen because you try in a situation where others try as well.

To create an environment conducive to team formation, you need to do the things called for in the team system's operational objectives [Katzenbach]. Identify the mission for the team and staff the team with people having a mix of skills relevant to the mission. Work with those people to establish strong, measurable operational objectives that will achieve the mission. Put systems in place to gather progress data and gather that data, sharing it with the team as often as possible. Work on things for which people can take joint responsibility, and encourage them to take such responsibility [Weisbord, p. 298]. Reward the team, not the individuals. It is important to build in expectations for exceptional performance at every turn, not just promote the team [Katzenbach, p. 13].

There are also things you should not do because they'll kill team formation stone dead [DeMarco 1987, pp. 133–139]:

- Mistrust your team members, managing them as if they were incompetent; a team must have competent people from the beginning
- Impose bureaucratic policies designed to push paper rather than produce systems
- Physically separate the members of the team
- Assign team members to more than one project
- Say that quality doesn't matter, only function or time
- Impose phony deadlines (not challenging ones, just outright phony ones saying "We have to deliver it by this date or we'll be out of business!")
- Break up cliques (that's what a team is!)

Too much supervision is a classic symptom of mistrust, for example. If you find yourself leery of telecommuting or off-site team conferences without you around, you're probably not going to be managing very many real teams.

Two particular things help OO projects: collocation and the war room. On the technical side, because OO teams focus on cohesive clusters of objects, collocation (locating the members of the team physically together) is important. Their close interaction fosters the cohesion that the cluster needs. If you can, having all the teams on a project in a single location is a good idea as well.

On the project side, it is vital to raise the management issues in a direct, clearly communicated way. Because OO projects rely on interfacing and integration of component clusters, you need to have the different teams communicating well. Put in place a war room, such as a room, bulletin board, or even an internal Web site, fully devoted to the team's project. This gives the team both an internal and an external project focus.

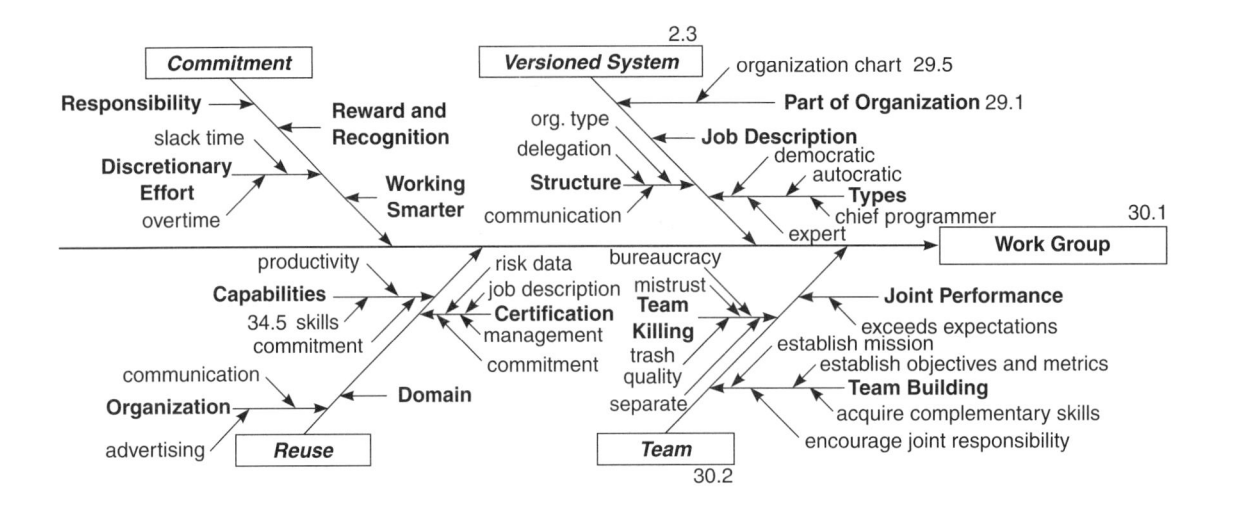

```
                                    2.3
         Commitment         Versioned System    organization chart 29.5
Responsibility                                    Part of Organization 29.1
                     Reward and    org. type
       slack time    Recognition   delegation    Job Description
Discretionary                                              democratic
    Effort                Working   Structure              autocratic
       overtime           Smarter  communication           Types
                                                           chief programmer         30.1
                                                    expert                   Work Group
                  productivity    risk data   bureaucracy
               Capabilities      job description  mistrust    Joint Performance
            34.5 skills         Certification   Team              exceeds expectations
                commitment        management   Killing          establish mission
      communication                commitment   trash          establish objectives and metrics
        Organization                           quality         Team Building
                          Domain              separate         acquire complementary skills
            advertising   Reuse                Team           encourage joint responsibility
                                               30.2
```

Readings

[Bennatan]   E. M. Bennatan. *On Time, Within Budget: Software Project Management Practices and Techniques.* New York: QED Publishing Group, 1992.

Section 5.2 of this book has a good discussion of team structure, from which much of the corresponding section above derives.

[Brooks]   Frederick P. Brooks, Jr. *The Mythical Man-Month: Essays on Software Engineering. Anniversary Edition.* Reading, MA: Addison-Wesley, 1995.

This classic book popularized the concepts of conceptual integrity and the chief programmer team. It remains the best description of these ideas. The appendix on propositions claims that the ideas have survived the test of time since 1975.

[Cleland 1996]   David I. Cleland. *Strategic Management of Teams.* New York: Wiley, 1996.

This is the most current book on the subject of "cross-functional teams," teams with players from different functional areas. It deals with the organizational implications of such teams, discusses team reengineering and benchmarking, and gives many case studies of effective and ineffective teams. While the book is rich in content, its lack of organization and verbosity make it less useful for practical, everyday project management.

Readings

[Darnall]   Russell W. Darnall. Tapping into discretionary effort. *PMNetwork* (August 1994): 54–56.

This short article, taken from the author's book *Achieving TQM on Projects*, is a fictional essay on a group that evaluates its ability to give beyond the call of duty. It summarizes the issues that swirl around motivation, discretionary effort, and commitment very well.

[Dyer]   William G. Dyer. *Team Building: Issues and Alternatives, Second Edition*. Reading, MA: Addison-Wesley, 1987.

This is the classic book on team building. It suffers a bit from an over-academic approach and passive mode language, but the history and concepts in this small book are invaluable aids in conducting or evaluating a team-building exercise. No ropes or rivers to be found.

[Hersey]   Paul Hersey and Kenneth H. Blanchard. *Management of Organizational Behavior: Using Human Resources, Sixth Edition*. Englewood Cliffs, NJ: Prentice Hall, 1993.

This is a leading textbook on organizational behavior. Aside from the One-Minute Management material that Blanchard pushes and you can ignore, this is the best hands-on book on everyday team management I've seen. I've used the situational leadership techniques in several different work groups to excellent effect. I've found it even more effective if you teach the material to the whole team so they know what's going on. The book also has excellent summaries of its competition. Chapter 14 on Group Dynamics shows how to apply situational leadership to team building.

[Katzenbach]   Jon R. Katzenbach and Douglas K. Smith. *The Wisdom of Teams: Creating the High-Performance Organization*. Cambridge, MA: Harvard Business School Press, 1993.

This book is the best book on the team that I've read. It is completely down-to-earth and based on many interviews with successful and unsuccessful teams. If you want to understand what being on a team really means, read the book, and then try some of the methods they suggest to create a team out of a work group. Chapter 3 defines the concept and discusses the various operational objectives in detail.

[Kerzner]   Harold Kerzner. *Project Management: A Systems Approach to Planning, Scheduling, and Controlling, Fifth Edition*. New York: Van Nostrand Reinhold, 1994.

Kerzner's Chapter 5 deals with "Management Functions," the different aspects of team and people management: planning, organizing, directing, controlling, and staffing. It also lumps in communications and other aspects of running the organization. While the discussion of authority and power is confused and contradictory, the material here is instructive in its breadth and is worth reading for the exposure to different views in the field.

[Moody]   Fred Moody. *I Sing the Body Electronic: A Year with Microsoft on the Multimedia Frontier*. New York: Viking, 1995.

This is the best observational study of a software work group (*not* team) that I've read. The work was not an OO project, but the ones I've participated in have similar characteristics to this CD-ROM project. The insight this book gives you into Microsoft's project management style is a nice counterpoint to other books about Microsoft [Cusumano] that focus more on what they *say* they do.

[Weinberg 1994] Gerald M. Weinberg. *Quality Software Management, Volume 3: Congruent Action.* New York: Dorset House, 1994.

Any book by Gerry Weinberg is likely to tell you something about people, groups, and teams and how to manage them effectively. This book is the one that should be on your bookshelf if you are a software manager. It is about transforming your behavior and your team's behavior into congruent action: action that fits the situation, matching thought to behavior. You will find it difficult to navigate your organization into more effective cultural patterns if you do not understand congruent action.

[Weisbord] Marvin R. Weisbord. *Productive Workplaces: Organizing and Managing for Dignity, Meaning, and Community.* San Francisco: Jossey-Bass, 1987.

This book gives you a context for empowering your organization and teams. It provides a thorough introduction to the different schools of management, with fascinating historical insights into why those schools did what they did. It then shows how to build effective, empowered teams that build on the knowledge of the team members to structure work effectively and productively. I took the name of this book from Weisbord. Chapter 15 is an excellent discussion of team building and the factors that contribute to building effective teams.

Questions to Think About

1. List the qualities and skills a chief programmer should have for an OO project. Is it feasible to structure your entire organization as a series of chief programmer teams for OO projects? Why or why not?

2. How might you measure commitment in the absence of schedule pressure?

3. Is the fact that everyone is working 12 hours a day sufficient to demonstrate commitment?

4. Do you think it is better to get rid of (fire, reassign) or to try to help difficult people who disrupt a group? Who should do the helping? the firing?

5. If you were shopping for a group to use on a new project, what would you like to see to help you decide to use a group?

6. It is usually obvious what groups you should use for a project. Why?

7. What kind of organization is more likely to have teams working for it: functional, matrix, or projectized? (Hint: Think about the team focus on objectives.)

CHAPTER 31

Management Culture

The *management culture* is a reusable system that is part of the organizational environment. This system of attitudes, values, beliefs, and norms controls how your organization perceives and structures its behavior, and especially its processes. The system operates through organizational control of system models such as process models and plans. The management culture, along with the rest of the environment, is independent of any particular project.

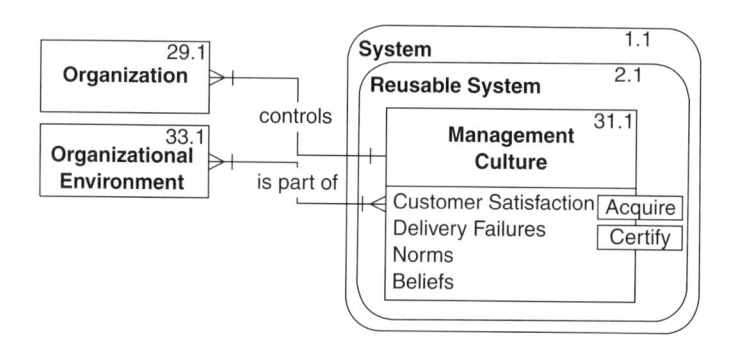

```
                    ┌──────────────────────────────────┐
  ┌──────────┐ 29.1 │ System                      1.1  │
  │Organization│───┤ ┌──────────────────────────────┐ │
  └──────────┘    │ │ Reusable System         2.1  │ │
         controls │ │ ┌──────────────────────┐     │ │
  ┌──────────┐ 33.1│ │ │ Management      31.1 │    │ │
  │Organizational│─┤ │ │   Culture            │    │ │
  │ Environment │ │ │ ├──────────────────────┤    │ │
  └──────────┘ is part of│ Customer Satisfaction │Acquire│
                  │ │ │ Delivery Failures     │Certify│
                  │ │ │ Norms                 │    │ │
                  │ │ │ Beliefs               │    │ │
                  │ │ └──────────────────────┘    │ │
                  │ └──────────────────────────────┘ │
                  └──────────────────────────────────┘
```

Vision: An organization working consistently to deliver value to project stakeholders

Mission: To provide consistency to the delivery of value to project stakeholders

Objective 31.1: To satisfy stakeholder expectations consistently

525

Approach 31.1: Identify your stakeholders. Understand the set of expectations of your stakeholders. Adopt processes and patterns of behavior through system models that align with these expectations.

Metric 31.1: Customer satisfaction: a multidimensional metric that measures how well your stakeholders think you're doing at satisfying their needs

Target 31.1: A relatively high set of values within control limits of x-R control charts of the projects your organization undertakes; note that the control-chart value is not an average, but a measure of consistency

---

Objective 31.2: To produce deliverable software systems consistently

---

Approach 31.2: Identify the risks you face in delivering software systems using your organization. Quantify the risks and evaluate them with respect to tolerances. Identify risk management methods for unacceptable risks. Adopt processes and patterns of behavior through system models that align with these risk management methods.

Metric 31.2: Delivery failures: the number of incidents of a project's failing to deliver a software system as planned; "as planned" means within schedule and budget constraints as well as with the planned functionality that satisfies stakeholder expectations

Target 31.2: A low number within control limits of a pn control chart of the projects your organization undertakes; again, this measures consistency, not average delivery

---

The management culture sets the organizational norms that enable consistent work. Any culture can do this as long as the expectations and risks of the work align with the cultural norms. Once your work diverges from those norms, however, you can run into problems with consistency that can endanger your project and your organization.

- *Note:* The whole approach in this book recommends a certain cultural approach. The twin assumptions of measurement and feedback alone have a huge impact on the management culture. While you are reading the next section, think about the implications of the current approach and its application to your situation. You may discover that you can adopt a culture that doesn't need the methods from this book. This will be true mostly for very small projects and projects that do not take much advantage of the features of OO technology.

There are two ways to acquire a management culture. When you acquire an organization, the culture just comes along for the ride: you reuse the existing culture. Alternatively, you can decide that you need a new culture, and you can change it. The section below on "Successful Pattern Matching" gives you some ideas about when and how to change.

"Successful Pattern Matching" section, p. 532

Certifying a management culture means quantifying risks, specifying the culture and its purpose, and showing the responsibility for the culture.

By measuring customer satisfaction and delivery failures, you provide data that you can use to evaluate the risks of using the culture. Given this data, you can decide whether you need a culture change to continue doing the same thing.

By making the norms and beliefs of the culture explicit through a value statement or a similar document, you can communicate the goals and functions of the culture to potential reusers. The organizational mission and vision are part of this, too, as they generally should reflect the culture that carries out the mission. Given this information, you can decide whether you need a culture change to adapt to potential changes such as increased stakeholder expectations or higher risks.

Culture is usually an implicit part of the working environment. Taking responsibility for a management culture is a first step in making the culture explicit. Usually, upper management takes this responsibility, though the organization as a whole can do so. For example, one approach to quality is summed up by the slogan, "Quality is everyone's job." That implies that the management culture of quality is the responsibility of everyone in the organization. In any case, stating this responsibility through a value statement is a key element of your reuse certification for the management system.

One OO company I worked for had a great CEO and founder who wanted the company to reflect his strong set of values. In my job interview with the CEO, he got out the value statement he had put together for the company to answer one of my questions, and then told me about his commitment to the values. Over the two years I was with the company, I had no reason to doubt that commitment. The values emphasized ethics and humanistic beliefs about the way the company related to the people that worked for it. That places it squarely in the Variable culture, which focuses more on the software developer than on management. There was no mention of feedback, being proactive, or continuous improvement. The company reflected this culture; when it confronted a serious crisis in its ability to adapt to growth, it was unable to respond. The board fired the CEO in a "palace coup," and the company downsized.

The Cultural Patterns

Gerald Weinberg's empirical work on software development organizations lets him categorize organizations into six cultural patterns for management (Table 31-1).

- *Note:* This analysis of culture is similar to the Software Engineering Institute's capability maturity model (CMM) [Humphrey]. While that model imposes the value judgment of "maturity" and scales the cultures, this one does not.

Table 31-1 Software Organizational Cultural Patterns [Weinberg 1992, pp. 23–30]

Pattern	Process	Typical Question/Statement
Oblivious	No faint hint of concept of process	"What software development?"
Variable	No process, superprogrammers	"Just do it."
Routine	Process, but magical, not rational; problems lead to panic and abandoning of process	"Just do it again." "We're behind! *Do* something!"
Steering	Results-driven process	"How are we doing?"
Anticipating	Experience-driven process	"What happened when we did this last time?"
Congruent	Congruent process, where everyone improves everything all the time	"How can we do better?"

"The Capability Maturity Model" section, Preface, p. xx

It also does not impose simplistic and methodologically suspect measures on the culture, which the CMM does. It is a better model for OO project management because the concepts better fit the kinds of tasks such management faces.

The Oblivious Culture

The Oblivious culture probably develops more programs than any other. It is the culture of the "power user," the person who writes macros, scripts, and other small programs to get the primary work done. Spreadsheets, Visual Basic, and UNIX shell scripts are examples of Oblivious work.

Oblivious developers have no notion that they are developing software. They are simply doing their work better by using computers. They don't have any process other than their own self-discipline, and they don't need one. They don't do projects, and they don't use project management. When they have a quality problem and need a deeper solution, they look outside this culture for off-the-shelf or custom solutions from others. Customer satisfaction usually isn't a problem, and projects are as successful as they want to make them—nobody cares but them.

The Variable Culture

The Variable culture is the culture of the superheroic programmer. Managers exist, Dilbert-like, only to throw monkey wrenches into perfectly good programs. Chief programmer work groups often use this culture in smaller projects, and the "skunk works" almost always uses it. These organizations do not usually have a formal process of any kind. They just put groups together into a project and go. The key element is the superstar who can get the job done.

One OO project I worked on was the productization of a prototype that the company founder, a superstar for 10 years, had put together to get into OO technology. He had learned C++ and Smalltalk on his own and applied his own version of OO concepts to the product. The company situation had evolved into a series of maintenance projects that sucked away most of the programming resources from new products, with the result that the superhero coded most of the new system's production code. The fears of the managers were that the project would fail due to poor quality. In fact, the superhero's code, while pasta-like, was relatively defect free compared to code done by others working on the project. It turned out that the functional managers had not paid any attention to the other developers and their process because they were focused on other projects. The biggest problem with this product was the lack of features that would make it competitive. The superhero was interested only in the core technology, which was less than half of what the customers expected from the software system, and nobody else was paying attention.

A *failed* superhero can lead to problems in a Variable culture. A medium-sized OO system I worked on had the bad luck to have a person on the project who thought he was a superhero but was not. For various cultural reasons, management let this clay-footed individual design large parts of the system and implement it. The superhero's coding was less than heroic, and his design wasn't much better. The process came close to a hacking model, the preferred style of the superhero. This led to all kinds of organizational and quality problems that seriously impacted the company's ability to deliver marketable products.

The Routine Culture

The Routine culture is the one many larger organizations find themselves in these days. Routine cultures emphasize the manager over the developer, leading to the supermanager, or management shaman. The shaman, who communicates with the software gods, gives the organization the knowledge he receives from them in the form of procedures. Managers and developers follow the procedures, not because they understand their purpose, but because of belief in their magical powers. This usually goes along with management-by-objectives appraisals and other mystical talismans for success.

The Routine culture's procedures generally work up to the point where something goes wrong. When panic ensues, both the shaman and his followers lose faith in the magic and start doing anything at all that might help. Because Variable shamans think in linear ways rather than thinking about systems and feedback, they often do precisely the wrong thing. When the project dies, and the innocent have been punished through blaming or layoffs, the managers reestablish the procedures and life goes on. This is the culture that led to Brooks's law about adding engineers to a late project making it later. It's also known as the "Silver Bullet" culture, because we all know that silver bullets have certain magical powers....

I've worked in many Routine cultures. The hardest ones to take are the ones where the manager becomes a superhero, valiantly whipping the troops on to greater feats of valor. One OO project I worked on had both a superhero project manager and a superhero chief architect, a kind of shamanistic team. They encouraged each other's interference in the developers' work and made sure that all the lower-level managers followed the procedures they put in place, however worthless. My favorite two procedures were the Wall Chart and the Death Shift.

The Wall Chart started one day when the supermanager sent all the lower-level managers an email message. We were to print out our project plans as huge plotter prints and post them prominently in a hallway. The purpose of this was to inspire everyone to make the schedule (or as the manager put it, "get commitment"). After some investigation, I discovered that the plotter was maintained by a very busy QA developer who used it for testing and kept it disconnected most of the time. He almost knew how to load paper, but not quite. It took about seven or eight person-hours of managerial effort to get three plots up on the wall. The effect on commitment was nil, as far as I could tell. As these plans were almost immediately made out-of-date, I assumed that we would need to put up new ones, but no one ever asked. The Wall Chart had become another failed commitment talisman.

The Death Shift was a few weeks later when the project had slipped beyond even the shamans' abilities to cover up (especially given the Wall Chart). At the aptly called "come-to-Jesus" meeting of the whole organization, the supermanager decreed that we were now working 50-hour weeks and that if we didn't deliver on schedule, it would be 60. The shamans made sure everyone worked weekends and evenings. The result: the project got even later. After a while, no one paid any attention to the Death Shift, and life went on. The process of this project wasn't a process so much as a lifestyle: it went on for years without delivering a system.

Another OO project I worked on followed a kind of waterfall model with formal signatures on things like the requirements document. The shaman in this case had the insight that having everyone sign the document from himself down to the administrative assistants would gain the full commitment of everyone to the project. One developer was so bold as to object to signing, since he didn't believe the product would be marketable due to missing features. They found the bones bleaching out in the desert (just kidding). The project was later canceled by upper management, showing *real* commitment.

One characteristic of a Variable culture pretending to be Routine is a process that no one follows or that is not possible to follow. OO projects often take this approach. The management decrees a waterfall model and then ignores it, not even bothering with the mandated reviews and signatures. The developers do what is necessary to produce a system, and they deliver. The management then says the process is working well, and applies it to the next project.

The Steering Culture

There is one glaring omission in Oblivious, Variable, and Routine cultures: feedback. There are no mechanisms for controlling the project through feedback. The Oblivious culture doesn't even know it's doing a project, much less anything about the results of the project. The Variable culture pays no attention to anything other than the work at hand. The Routine culture knows that if it properly performs its rituals, it will succeed regardless of the real world.

The Steering culture opens a window to its system environment to integrate some feedback into project control. Steering managers strive to understand the purpose of what they do. Having understood the purpose, they can then gather data about what happens and make changes. This basic capability transforms the organization's capabilities by enabling it to adapt to higher expectations and/or risks.

Steering managers seem more competent and are usually more experienced than Routine or Variable managers [Weinberg 1992, p. 29]. Steering organizations use process models and tools to their advantage rather than shelving them. They can adapt these models and tools to new situations by examining the results of their work based on these models and tools. While they are moderately good at adapting to change and solving problems, they aren't very good at being proactive or preventative. The simple feedback techniques they use aren't sophisticated or stable enough to allow prediction.

I have never worked in a Steering culture, though I have friends that have. These cultures exist in larger organizations that have made a real commitment to excellence in some way, usually as a result of an initiative by a very experienced senior manager. Sometimes, the organizations establish this kind of culture bottom up, but this is difficult given that managers by definition drive the culture. The best way to establish this culture is through top-down support and commitment. I have seen one problem with some of the people from these cultures being a little too cocky about their success. They do tend to have a problem with hubris, the ancient Greek sin of pride that inevitably leads to disaster. I've seen the disasters happen when these experienced people go to a Variable or Routine culture and expect things to work the same way. They invariably cause major problems because no one understands or sympathizes with their attitudes and expectations for rational action. This has become something of a problem in OO software as some of the leading companies in the area downsize, releasing many of their software people into the small-company market.

The Anticipating and Congruent Cultures

I'll be honest: there aren't very many Anticipating or Congruent organizations around. Software is still too much of a craft to support processes or tools that can give you the stability you need, and OO software is much worse in this respect.

The Anticipating culture focuses not on reacting to feedback but on creating an organization and environment that anticipate problems and changes. It is a proactive culture that does things that prevent problems rather than cause them. This results in a much more stable environment with few crises. There are all kinds of things that can get you to this point. Probably the most important elements of the Anticipating culture focus on requirements and design. Tools like Quality Function Deployment, stakeholder expectation validation studies, and OO design methods become much more important. These organizations are much more capable of integrating in reusable systems in all parts of the project. Reuse of systems is a major way of avoiding problems. Anticipating cultures tend to be much more efficient and productive at delivering value, and they are much better at dealing with project risks by anticipating and managing those risks.

- *Note:* This book is aimed at creating an Anticipating culture, because I believe this culture is best suited to most OO development by medium- to large-sized organizations. Because of the central focus of OO development on reuse, and because of the iterative and incremental process on which OO development depends to avoid rework, the Anticipating culture is the best choice.

The Congruent culture doesn't just anticipate problems, it improves itself. This is the system that almost achieves *consciousness,* the ability for the organization as a system to *intentionally* act to improve itself and its position in the environment based on an *awareness* of that environment through feedback. This culture institutionalizes continuous improvement at all levels of the organization and project systems.

The Congruent culture's obsession with aligning best practices and reuse with all environmental systems creates a social system that it can easily transfer from project to project. It's kind of like a black hole, with the gravity distortion so powerful that it simply sucks everything in. Success breeds success.

Successful Pattern Matching

Each of the six cultures is appropriate for a given stakeholder profile and a given risk of product failure. If the expectations are low and the project is simple, you can get away with being oblivious to project management. If expectations are many and high and the technology is bleeding edge or the project is very large, you should have a process-oriented culture in the last three categories to ensure

Successful Pattern Matching

success. To a certain extent, the higher risks of OO projects would suggest movement to the Steering or Anticipating culture. Greater risk and expectations might lead to the Congruent culture for a large organization.

You can tell whether you can reuse your culture by measuring Metrics 31.1 and 31.2, customer satisfaction and delivery failures. If either measure varies substantially over different projects, you've got a culture problem that you need to address, and your reuse potential is low. Figure 31-1 shows a possible cultural frontier diagram that illustrates the trade-offs [Weinberg 1992, pp. 40–41]. This diagram is very similar to the strategic position diagrams relating price differentiation versus economic cost that companies use to position their products in a competitive marketplace [McTaggart, p. 117].

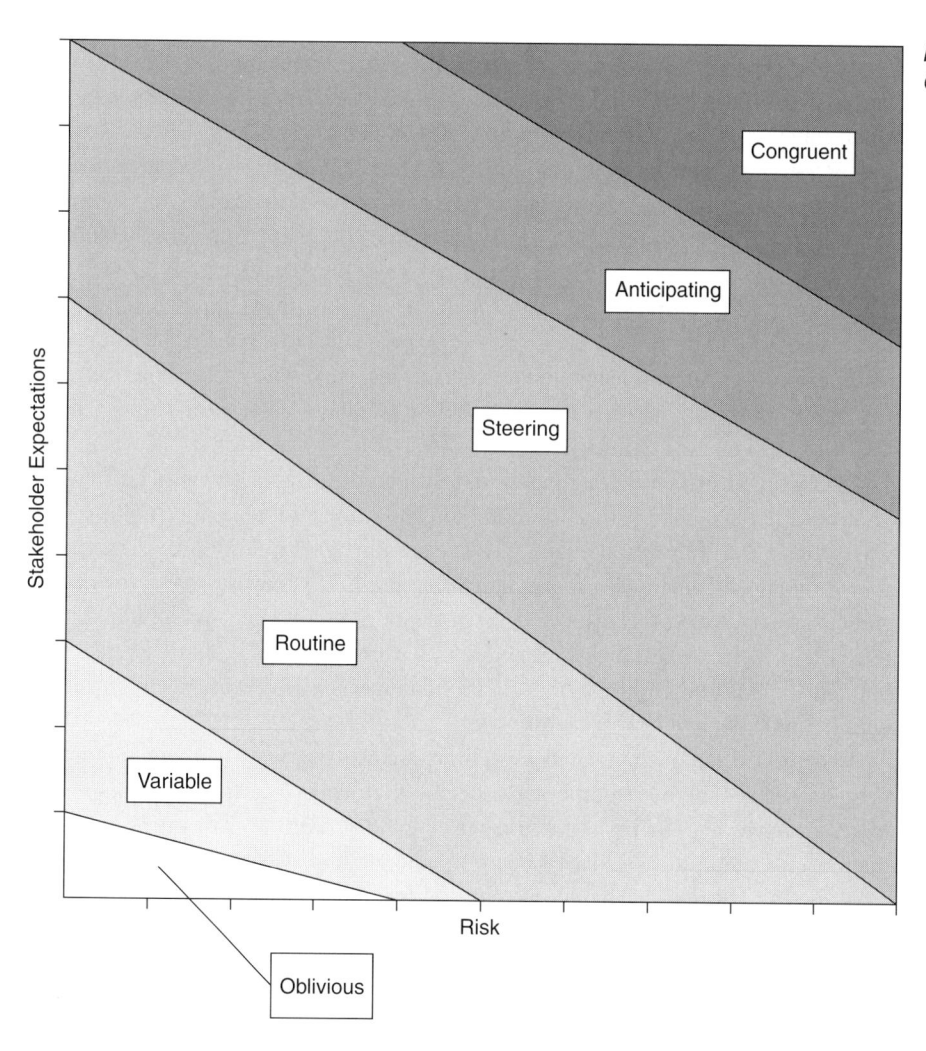

Figure 31-1
Cultural frontiers

- *Note:* To use this diagram seriously, you would need to benchmark your industry or organizational environment through some kind of extensive cultural investigation of risk and expectation, so this is purely illustrative.

It is *vital* to realize that if both measures do not vary substantially and are at reasonable levels, you *do not have a problem*. You should continue using your current culture, whatever it is, because it works for you. Don't fix what isn't broken. One thing: if you're not measuring either of these variables, you don't *know* whether you have a problem. That's worth a little change right there, at least to the extent of a customer survey and a little historical research into past projects.

Making decisions based on past performance is not entirely reliable, however, in an environment where things change radically every day. Yes, you need to measure customer satisfaction. Project success in the past indicates likely future success. But if a giant steps into your market, or your customer base changes radically, or technology makes a leap forward, or your company merges with another, the past is no longer all that matters. Your culture must change to keep up with the change in your environment. Again, your reuse potential is low.

One such change is the coming of OO technology. If your organization has not done OO development, you almost certainly will need to change your culture to adapt to reuse and iteration. If it has done OO development, but not very successfully, then again you will need to change. If your organization is small and your projects not very complex, you can probably get away with using some of the cultures without feedback. However, once your projects start experiencing increasing technical complexity and customer expectations, you will need to manage risk through reuse and other measures that rely on feedback. That means a Steering or, better, an Anticipating culture is the best choice.

Once you estimate your position, you need to evaluate whether to change your culture or to change the situation. You can, for example, reduce risk in many ways other than by cultural changes. For example, you could reduce the expectations of your customers to a more reasonable level. This could drive away higher-end customers, but you could better serve the ones that remain. You could manage technology risks by reuse or other methods, though you may find it difficult in Variable or Routine cultures. You could subcontract risky work to organizations with better skills and less risk. And so on.

If you decide to change cultures, there are as many ways as there are ideas in people's heads. There are some very specific methods you can use with software patterns, however. The basic method for changing a culture is to introduce information into the culture that will break up the vicious cycles of denial [Weinberg 1992, p. 43]. Ultimately, changing a culture depends on establishing trust in those that need to change.

First, you can establish a separate culture within your organizational environment. This culture, suitably rewarded and distinguished, can act as a seed for cultural change in the rest of the organization. This works only if your projects succeed and the rest of the organization recognizes that. That means two things: first, the rest of the organization must agree that you succeeded by their definitions of success, and second, you must communicate your success.

Second, you can engineer changes in the organizational environment by slowly moving that environment to the new culture in an evolutionary way. Pilot projects, small steps forward, sending people off-site for training, and other socialization methods are useful for evolution.

Third, you can radically reengineer the culture through business process reengineering or another revolutionary method. This means calling in consultant facilitators, setting up reengineering projects, working hard to empower the people in the organization, and figuring out how best to organize the new culture. The popular press is full of stories about the failure of reengineering, but it succeeds often enough to represent a viable alternative.

One VP of software development I worked for believed that his organization could move only a bit at a time because of its highly conservative culture and lack of trust in management. He knew that the organization needed to move in the direction of new markets and new technology. The executive staff of the company had decided to reorient the marketing efforts of the company to a new market. New technologies were rapidly emerging in the marketplace that would render our current products useless in a very short time frame.

His solution was two-pronged. The revolutionary part involved consultants, a new development process, and a total focus on schedule. The rationale was that the developers could focus if you told them to deliver on schedule without fail. The process would allow them to see the schedule milestones in a consistent way. The single focus would allow them to change without the distraction of worrying about quality or functionality. The evolutionary part of the plan was to add balls to the juggling act. The company had a single product on two operating platforms. The chief executive put in place a policy to support product versions for 18 months after delivery, resulting in huge maintenance loads. The VP added to this three new operating platforms and a whole new product line with two separate products. The goal (I assume, though I was never told explicitly) was to increase the technical challenge by drastically increasing the risk of failure. This would force the developers to find ways to improve their development practices through adaptation to the higher risks. Combining the emphasis on schedule, the new process, and the radical increase in technical complexity would evolve the culture to a sophisticated, much more capable organization.

In the end, this effort failed. The culture proved too strong. The failure to establish trust and to work in the open with the organization to improve its culture doomed the changes from the start. The organization did deliver software on time, but the quality was terrible and the functionality suffered drastically. The executive committee canceled the new ports and the new product line and retrenched to improve product quality. They had no capability to expand their market to respond to change, however, and the company's revenues suffered correspondingly. And so it goes.

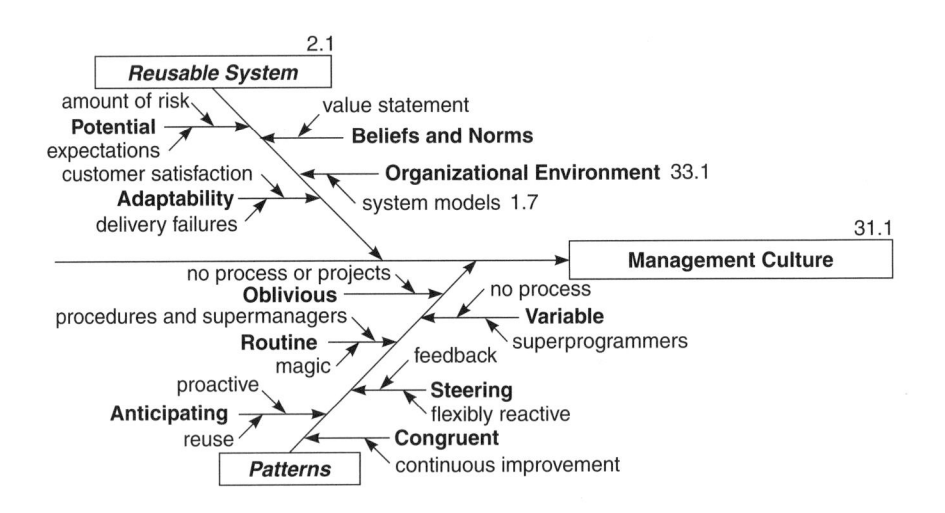

```
                    2.1
              ┌──────────────────┐
              │ Reusable System  │
              └──────────────────┘
    amount of risk ╲    ╱ value statement
       Potential ──→   ←── Beliefs and Norms
     expectations
    customer satisfaction ╲   ←── Organizational Environment 33.1
       Adaptability ──→
     delivery failures ╱   ╲ system models 1.7
                                                              31.1
    ─────────────────────────────────────────────────┌──────────────────────┐
                                                     │ Management Culture   │
              no process or projects ╲               └──────────────────────┘
                  Oblivious ──────        ╱ no process
         procedures and supermanagers ╲  ←── Variable
                   Routine ──→         ╲ superprogrammers
                    magic ╱    feedback
         proactive ╲              ←── Steering
                   Anticipating ──→    flexibly reactive
                 reuse ╱      ←── Congruent
                          ┌──────────┐  continuous improvement
                          │ Patterns │
                          └──────────┘
```

Readings

[Humphrey]   Watts S. Humphrey. *Managing the Software Process.* Reading, MA: Addison-Wesley, 1989.

Humphrey's book contains the capability maturity model version of these cultures, which he bases loosely on Philip Crosby's quality management work. The major differences are the notion of maturity that imposes a value judgment on the cultures, and that you can numerically assess your position on a scale of maturity. I believe you must decide which culture you need to adopt to get the results you want rather than just keeping up with the Joneses.

[Weinberg 1992] Gerald M. Weinberg. *Quality Software Management: Volume 1, Systems Thinking.* New York: Dorset House, 1992.

This book is the inspiration for this chapter. It contains most of the material about the five major management cultures, which Weinberg developed from Philip Crosby's initial categories. Weinberg places these cultures in the context of development system management, rather than project management. The book goes into detail on the various problems that apply pressure to your projects and how to go about changing your culture to get a better handle on these problems.

Questions to Think About

1. List some possible mechanisms by which the management culture controls the organization. What are the implications of each for OO development processes?

2. Why is the *consistency* of work the mission of the culture? What role does consistency play in running an organization?

3. List some values that you might put in a values statement that certifies the culture of an organization.

4. Do you recognize your management culture in the six patterns here? Is it a mix?

5. Think about how each pattern would deal with reusing systems. Can you explain much of the current inability to reuse effectively using the cultural affinity for reuse?

6. Have you ever experienced a culture change? How was the change brought about? Was the result beneficial or not? Was the experience painful or not?

CHAPTER

32   *Policy*

The Policy

A *policy* is a versioned system describing some course of action. A policy suggests or mandates this course of action, influencing and determining decisions and actions that managers and work groups in a project make. The policy is *formal*, encapsulated as a speech act in a legally or procedurally binding document and approved by an authority, and then stored in an appropriate repository.

- *Note: Informal policies,* such as a custom or tradition, are part of the organizational culture or environment. This chapter discusses the formal policies; the chapter on "Management Culture" deals with some aspects of informal policies.

Management Culture (31.1)

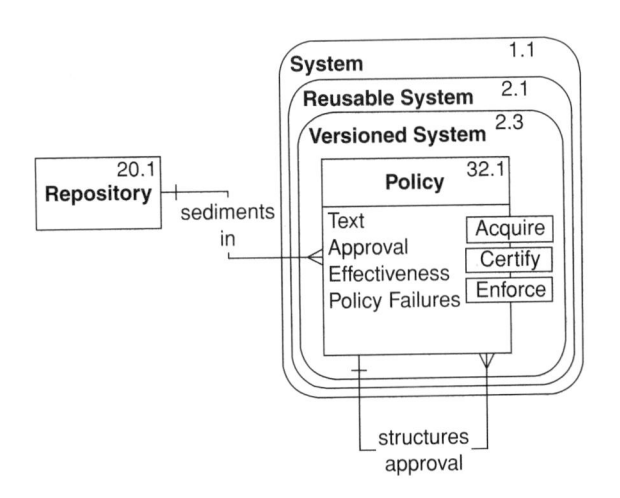

538

Vision: An effective, authoritative body of knowledge about project action guiding and standardizing the way work gets done in projects

Mission: To sediment an item of knowledge required to guide or standardize project action effectively for reuse

---

Objective 32.1: To represent knowledge that guides or standardizes action effectively

---

Approach 32.1: Determine the full scope and content of a guideline or standard for action. Decide whether this policy can effectively guide future action. Decide whether the action should be a guideline or a standard. Create the policy text and gain approval for the policy according to the appropriate organizational decision policy. Communicate the policy and train people in its application. Enforce standards.

Metric 32.1: Effectiveness: the percentage of policy applications that succeed in causing the action to occur, with the intended results corresponding to the mission of the policy

Target 32.1: A number near 100% within control limits of a p control chart of policy applications in an organization

---

Objective 32.2: To sediment an item of knowledge for later retrieval

---

Approach 32.2: Store the approved policy in the appropriate repository. Use the repository searching mechanism to look for applicable policies when you are planning actions in a particular domain of project action or when you are training people in policies that apply to their work. Apply standards and use guidelines as you think appropriate.

Metric 32.2: Policy failures: the number of times you failed to apply a required policy or to find a guideline that might have helped in determining a course of action

Target 32.2: A low number within control limits of a pn control chart of such failures in your organization

---

A *standard* is a policy that the project team *must* observe; a *guideline* is a policy that the project team *should* observe but *need not follow in all cases* [Plum, p. 11]. You must carefully phrase each standard and guideline and give it a distinct, identifying name. You use this name in reviews and automated testing to enforce the standards and guidelines or to identify exceptions to the formal standards approved by an authority.

You acquire policies either by reusing ones already in your repository or by creating new ones. You should create policies only if they contribute to project productivity or to the value that stakeholders receive. Too many policies leads to clutter, making it difficult to identify the important policies you need to use. Too many standards, in particular, can result in bureaucracy—meaningless paper pushing replacing real work. Create a standard only when there is a compelling reason to remove someone's ability to make decisions on their own. Create a guideline only when it really contributes to helping someone do something.

Reusing policies depends on their inherent, domain, and organizational reuse potentials. The inherent potential of a policy depends on people's ability to understand the policy, its practicality in application, and its cohesion of purpose. People are likely to reuse a succinct, well-thought-out policy that really helps them take action. They are also likely to reuse a policy when they understand its mission through a well-written set of operational objectives. The domain reuse potential of a policy comes from the generality of the policy. If a policy applies to a very specific domain, people will use it only in that domain. If it is general and practical to apply in many different situations, people will reuse it a lot. Organizationally, the legitimacy and authority of the policy determines its reuse. A policy that makes sense and that you have communicated well is likely to have the trust of the organization. Conversely, it will distrust policies that cause organizational friction, or senseless ones, or ones that you have hidden well or that you do not support or enforce. If your organization is authoritative about enforcing policies, you will reuse them. If no one in authority pays attention, no one will apply a standard.

I have seen many policies die of neglect. A major OO project spent hundreds of work-hours evolving a development process model that required several different approvals at different points and had many different cross-links to foster communication. Senior management enforced only a few of these policies. Guess which ones were effective and which were not.

You must also have some kind of exception mechanism that lets an authority make an exception to a standard at their discretion. You may exclude from this certain standards, such as those involving human rights or other externally imposed standards. Having an exception mechanism increases the reusability of the policy because it increases its legitimacy. If people think a policy is absolute, they will resent it; it's human nature.

Certifying a policy consists mainly of getting the policy approved. Some policies, such as coding standards, require a review process. Others require only the signature of an authority in the organizational structure. For a standard, approval implies that the approver has considered all the goals, risks, and responsibilities for the policy and has decided that the organization should apply the policy uniformly. The effectiveness of standards depends entirely on the legitimacy of the policy in the organization. For a guideline, approval implies an assertion by an authority that the recommendations of the policy are good, and that people in the organization should take them into account when taking action. It is important in all policies to clearly identify the actions involved and the how-what-when-why-where context in which the actions apply. This lets people understand precisely when the policy applies and what it entails.

Joint Review (41.2)
Organization (29.1)

Table 32-1 shows some of the different kinds of policies you will find in any OO software project, most of which this book mentions in the context of the system affected by the policy.

Some policies I've seen in OO projects have some rather comedic effects. A director believed, for example, that his organization needed to pay more attention to the customers. He put several policies in place that would force people in the organization to meet customers. For example, he started holding focus groups at which managers and developers would present new features to customers and get

Table 32-1 Software Development Project Policies

Policy Type	Description	Classes
Standardization	A policy that requires you to use some system, such as reusable software, process models, tools, external standards, or financial rules	1.4, 2.1, 4.7, 5.2, 9.1, 16.2, 23.1, 24.2, 25.4, 35.2, 27.2, 28.2, 29.1, 30.1, 32.2, 32.3, 33.3, 34.1, 36.1, 41.1
Certification	A policy that specifies what needs to happen to certify something	2.1
Rights	Policies that enforce various kinds of legal or other rights, such as confidentiality, intellectual property, or accessibility	6.3
Security	A policy that protects the system from intentional harm, such as off-site storage policies or wearing badges	25.2
Decision Authority	A policy that specifies who has the right to make a specific decision or approve a specific system	6.2, 29.1
Content	A policy that specifies the nature of the content of a system, such as a document or a change control record	6.1, 25.4
Criteria	A policy that specifies a particular target that the system must reach, such as baseline exit criteria, test criteria, or assessment criteria	9.1, 26.1, 27.5
Time	Policies about the use of time, such as working calendars, shifts, the working hours for a resource, and timesheets	19.1, 34.1, 42.1
Change	Policies that organize and manage the change process and change requests	23.1, 24.2, 24.3, 25.2
Personnel	Policies that apply to people's behavior and rights in the workplace, such as discrimination, harassment, and telecommuting policies	34.1, 35.2

feedback. He had his administrative assistant schedule every person in the development organization, from tech writers to the program librarian, to have lunch with customers on-site for product training. Most of these sessions were remarkable only in the paucity of anything useful that emerged.

Almost invariably, when someone would bring up a criticism of some intended action based on a customer's comment or feedback, this director would respond, "Who said that? Well, they're not the *real* customers, the ones we want to be selling to. Let's focus on them, not our current customers." I never was able to get a list of these intended customers, but it was clear that they loved what the director thought they should have, or would if they ever bought our product. The end result of this was the universal despising of all customer meetings and many earnest pleas to get out of lunches and so on. This kind of policy is symptomatic of the shamanistic approach of the Variable culture.

The Design Standard

The *design standard* standardizes technical requirements that apply to architectural and low-level design with the mission of encouraging the conceptual integrity of the design [Booch 1994; Brooks]. These policies establish known techniques for achieving good OO designs, such as abstraction, encapsulation, and simplicity.

- *Note:* There is *much* controversy surrounding the measurement of design "goodness" with cohesion, coupling, and complexity measures. Anyone putting policies in place that contribute to good design must be familiar with the issues, or you are just doing magic [Champeaux; Fenton; Henderson-Sellers 1996].

Vision: A design process able to apply insights from previous projects and original thought to improve the architecture and low-level design of a cluster or software system

Mission: To sediment knowledge about design of a software system to encourage the conceptual integrity of the design

---

Objective 32.3: To encourage reliable design through coherent, layered abstraction

---

Approach 32.3: Determine a particular practice, method, design tool, or other design-related action that contributes to abstraction. Examine the goals, risks, and responsibilities of the action to determine whether it would have high reuse potential. Determine whether the application of the action should apply in all systems. If so, create a standard. If not, create a guideline.

The Design Standard

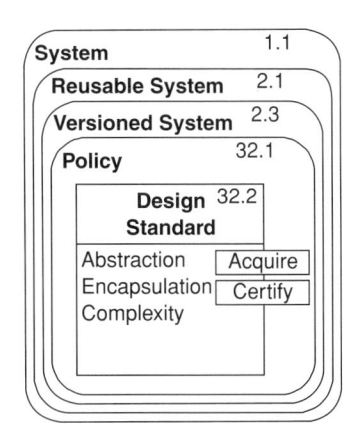

```
System                    1.1
  Reusable System       2.1
    Versioned System    2.3
      Policy            32.1
        Design          32.2
        Standard
        Abstraction    ┌─Acquire─┐
        Encapsulation  └─Certify─┘
        Complexity
```

Metric 32.3: Abstraction: a measure of the degree of abstraction of the systems to which the policy applies; you can approximate this through a cohesion ratio, the number of clusters having abstract data cohesion over the total number of clusters, where "abstract data cohesion" is a metric of the degree to which a cluster represents some kind of abstract data type [Champeaux, pp. 121–122; Fenton, pp. 312–313; Henderson-Sellers 1996, p. 119] (note that this metric is difficult to apply and subjective)

Target 32.3: A number within control limits of a p control chart of similar systems to which the standards apply

---

Objective 32.4: To ensure a clear separation of interface and implementation (encapsulation)

Approach 32.4: Proceed as in Approach 32.3, but analyze the contribution to encapsulation.

Metric 32.4: Encapsulation: a measure of the degree of encapsulation of the systems to which the policy applies; you can approximate this with coupling measures, and as there are several different kinds of OO coupling, this is a metric with multiple parts (class, interaction, and inheritance cohesion each having several specific measures) [Fenton, pp. 309–310; Henderson-Sellers 1996, pp. 110–119]

Target 32.4: Numbers within control limits of the control charts appropriate for their scale

---

Objective 32.5: To encourage simplicity in design

Approach 32.5: Proceed as in Approach 32.3, but analyze the contribution to complexity.

Metric 32.5: Complexity: a measure of the procedural complexity of the systems to which the policy applies; you can approximate this with multiple measures of class and cluster size, properties, inheritance, and other features of OO design [Henderson-Sellers 1996, pp. 120–150]

Target 32.5: Numbers within control limits of the control charts appropriate for their scale

---

Common design policies specify any of the following items:

- The method to use for class, object, interface, and database design
- The CASE tools to use to represent the design
- Patterns, frameworks, and other reusable designs to consider using
- Types of design techniques or patterns to avoid
- Design metrics and targets (cohesion, coupling, and so on)

The most common design standard I've seen in OO projects is the policy that outlaws multiple inheritance. Many projects have found that multiple inheritance leads to clusters that are hard to understand, slow-performing, and difficult to modify [Porter, Tip 229]. It also can lead to significant ambiguities or complexities depending on the language in which you intend to implement it. For example, multiple inheritance in C++ usually leads to virtual base classes, a particularly difficult feature to use effectively. Multiple inheritance usually increases the cohesion of the system, however. Authorities that put more emphasis on strong cohesion tend to allow multiple inheritance or even advocate it for that reason [Meyer].

You do not usually find extensive design *standards* in OO projects other than, perhaps, a mandated GUI or transaction processing framework of some kind. OO design proceeds best when the architects work with open minds. Limiting architects through standardization is usually counterproductive. What you're saying is that they do not have enough design sense to design a rain shelter to keep from getting wet. These kinds of policies are precisely the sort that organizations do not legitimize and hence do not reuse.

Here is one set of design guidelines [Henderson-Sellers 1996, p. 110]:

- A class interface should have only methods, not data attributes or other language features.
- Do not expose the implementation of the class in any way.
- Create an operator in the public class interface only if users of the interface can use it.
- Create only operators that access or modify some class data.
- Minimize the dependencies of a class on other classes.

- Pass all information to another class explicitly.
- Each subclass should make available the entire public interface of its superclass as a subset of its public interface.
- Each inheritance tree should begin with an abstract parent superclass that models the base concept.
- Reusable clusters should maximize their use of inheritance in modeling the problem domain.
- Limit the number of methods that must understand the data representation of the class.

This is reasonably typical of the kinds of guidelines I have seen. In my humble opinion, some of them are wrong. For example, C++ permits you to export exceptions and enumerated types through the public class interface. The first item in the above list would prohibit this, or at least indicate that you shouldn't do it. Why? The item about accessing class data seems all right until you realize that it precludes creating calculation methods relating to the abstract data type that happen not to use data that persists beyond the operation. What about methods that query data from the database rather than class data? Having an abstract superclass in *every* case makes little sense to me. Maximizing inheritance to get reuse is counterproductive as well as meaningless. And what does it mean to "limit" the number of methods that must understand data representations? What *are* data representations?

Perhaps it is best to fall back on measurement for these kinds of standards. If you can formulate a valid metric for the concept, and this is hard for most design concepts, then you can develop a policy that specifies a target for the metric. If not, you have no business developing *standards* for the concept, and your *guidelines* should express a certain humility. You should certainly ensure that designers who are to use the guidelines fully understand them and are willing to use them. Technical reviews of standards and guidelines help with this.

The Coding Standard

The *coding standard* standardizes technical requirements for coding.

Vision: A reliable coding process able to apply insights from previous projects and original thought to improve the implementation of a cluster design and the maintenance and portability of the resulting software

Mission: To sediment knowledge about coding issues to improve quality, maintainability, and portability

---

Objective 32.6: To improve quality of the code in the sense of reducing the generic risk of failure of the code to deliver its value

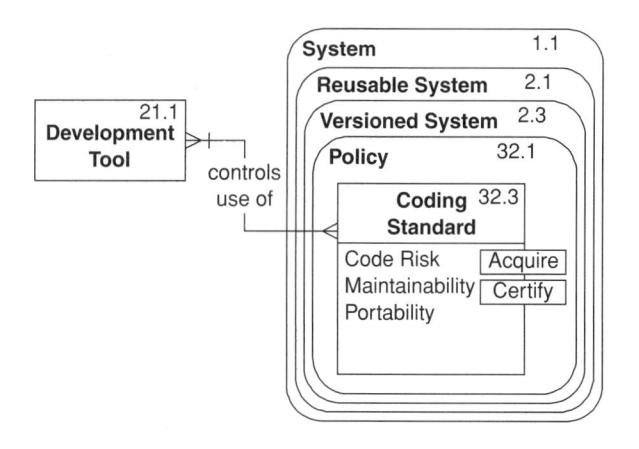

[Diagram: System 1.1 containing Reusable System 2.1, Versioned System 2.3, Policy 32.1, with Coding Standard 32.3 (Code Risk, Maintainability, Portability; operations Acquire, Certify). Development Tool 21.1 "controls use of" the Coding Standard.]

Approach 32.6: Determine a particular practice, method, design tool, or other coding-related action that contributes to lowering the generic risk of failure of coding. Examine the goals, risks, and responsibilities of the action to determine whether it would have high reuse potential. Also determine whether the contribution to risk management is worth the cost of applying the policy. Determine whether the application of the action should apply in all systems regardless of actual risk. If so, create a standard. If not, create a guideline.

Metric 32.6: Code risk: the generic risk that applies to coding

Target 32.6: A value close to the generic risk tolerance for software clusters in your project

---

Objective 32.7: To improve maintainability of the code

Approach 32.7: Proceed as in Approach 32.6, but look at actions that contribute to maintainability.

Metric 32.7: Median effort to repair: the median number of effort-hours it takes to implement a change to restore the code to working order [Fenton, p. 355]

Target 32.7: A number within control parameters of a pn control chart of similar software clusters

---

Objective 32.8: To improve portability of the code

Approach 32.8: Proceed as in Approach 32.6, but look at actions that contribute to portability.

Metric 32.8: Portability: a metric that measures your capability to move the code from one target operating environment to another; one suggestion is:

$$1 - (ET/ER)$$

where *ET* is the effort to port the system and *ER* is the effort needed to create the first system [Fenton, p. 344]

Target 32.8: A value within control parameters of an x-R control chart of similar systems

---

Common coding policies specify any of the following items:

- The coding and configuration management tools to use
- The language-related constructs to use and to avoid
- The restrictions on constructs to ensure portability
- Guidelines for reusing code from other projects
- Standards for code documentation and testing to ensure reusability
- Code metrics and targets (complexity, size, reuse, and so on)

Particularly important standards for coding processes are the coding and configuration management tools to use. You need to standardize on particular compilers, interpreters, frameworks, source control tools, and build tools. Otherwise, cooperative work becomes impossible. These coding standards are essential for any software project.

The OO language and programming tools you use invariably have interesting, dark corners where dragons be. Here are some random examples of coding standards from a published book on C++ coding standards [Plum]:

- *Guideline 1.12:* Declare member functions as `const` to declare that the function does not modify its object.
- *Guideline 2.02:* Justify overloading operators carefully. Preserve the intuitive properties of the operator. Do not implement assignment if it makes no sense. Implement binary operators with both member functions and friend functions so that the operation works in both directions. Implement assignment first, and then implement other operators using that operator rather than duplicating assignment code.
- *Guideline 5.01:* Write all variable names in lowercase using no more than 31 characters. Use initially capped names for your class names, such as MyClass. Explicitly declare all variables. Do not use leading underscores.

There are many programming tips and hints for OO languages that can make your life easier [Porter]. Incorporating major ones as guidelines can help you communicate your tips to others in your organization. One example: C++ explicitly lets you delete null pointers. It is very common for C programmers to spend inordinate amounts of code testing whether pointers are null before deleting them. Finding a small thing like this that influences readability and performance in so much code is a major win and deserves to be a guideline in your coding standards document.

I have two major complaints about coding standards that I've seen. First, if you really intend to have standards, you should enforce them automatically. Before even testing a piece of code, you should run it through a tool such as CodeCheck from Abraxas Software. This software applies a rules file that reports on any standards violations. Before you test or review your code, you should have a clean report on standards. My complaint: nobody does this.

Second, most standards efforts I've seen have invariably standardized everything that the author thought might cause a problem. This inevitably results in onerous coding standards that nobody wants to read, much less follow. In other words, it leads to a lack of legitimacy.

I was at one company that did at least five or six different projects over two years. Early in this period, the VP suggested one of the managers develop some coding standards. He did; the result was total scorn from the functional development managers. Result: no standards for two years. Nobody else would risk social ostracism. Finally, a new VP came in who insisted that the development managers have coding standards, so the main functional manager developed a minimal set and enforced them through reviews (still no CodeCheck, though).

Another company took the approach that an expert knows best. The chief architect developed the 40-page coding standards document and insisted on it being followed. This would have been reasonable except that this guy had some fairly odd ideas about C++, such as prohibiting operator overloading and the use of the "friend" feature. There is always a case to be made for such things; but instead of making a case, he imposed a point of view through his authority. This resulted in a total lack of legitimacy for the standards. Fortunately, this organization did not have code reviews and it did not run CodeCheck, so we'll never know what the compliance rate for this standard was. I can say with assurance that the quality of the resulting code did not benefit as a result of these standards.

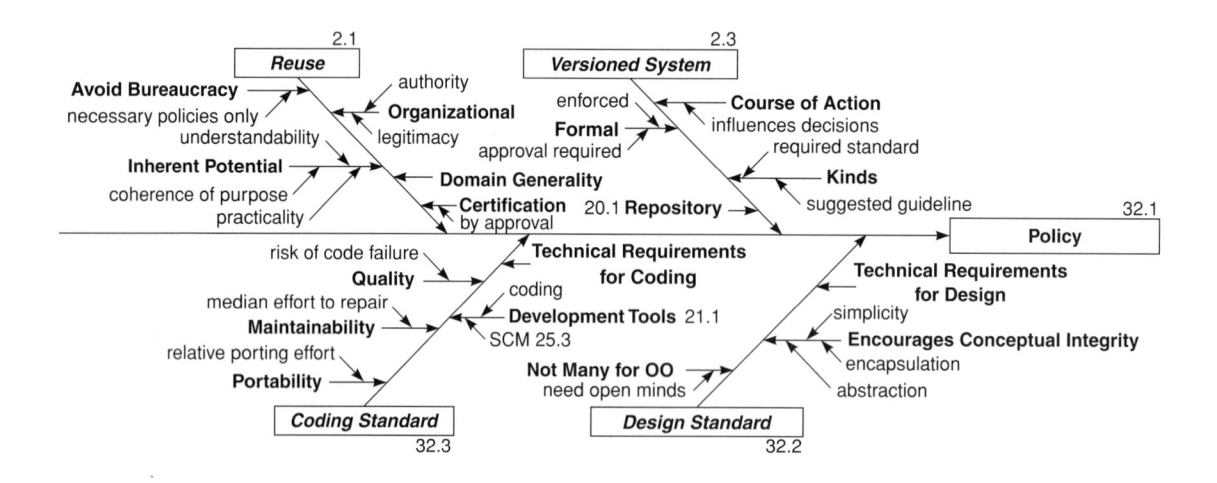

Readings

[Plum]   Thomas Plum and Dan Saks. *C++ Programming Guidelines*. Plum Hall, 1991.

This is a good, if verbose, set of coding and design standards and guidelines that covers most of the interesting issues in C++.

[Porter]   Anthony Porter. *The Best C/C++ Tips Ever.* Berkeley, CA: Osborne McGraw-Hill, 1993.

This is an excellent compendium of issues you have to deal with in C and C++ coding. While the organization is difficult to navigate, using the index usually gets you at or near the right place. The coding examples are worth the price of the book.

Questions to Think About

1. List several ways that you might present policies to people who need to know about them. (Hint: The company manual is not the only mechanism for communicating policies.)

2. Where would you put the various kinds of policy from Table 32-1?

3. How can you determine whether a policy is having its desired effect? (Hint: Measuring the thing it applies to is part of the answer but not the whole answer.)

4. List some possible OO design standards (*required* actions). Can you reliably predict what effect requiring these actions will have on your designs? Does the effect justify the effort to comply with the standard? How did you make that judgment?

5. Are there language- or tool-independent coding standards? If so, what is the relative proportion of such standards to the total number of standards? Why?

6. Can you use the number of standards you need for a language as an index variable to the effectiveness of the development environment? List some positive and negative factors in this application of the metric.

CHAPTER

33 *Organizational Environment*

The Organizational Environment

The *organizational environment* is a system that provides the context for the project and the organization. It contains the organizational repository with the various policies and other elements to which resources refer during their work. It contains the management culture that affects the organization and process structure for the projects. It also contains the external standards and the economic and political factors with which the organization must align itself to do its work.

- *Note:* While the organizational environment is a system, it is not necessarily a strictly purposive one. Also, it is out of the control of the project manager and even of the project organization. Thus, the organizational environment is an independent class in the project management system framework. It has no operational objectives or mission.

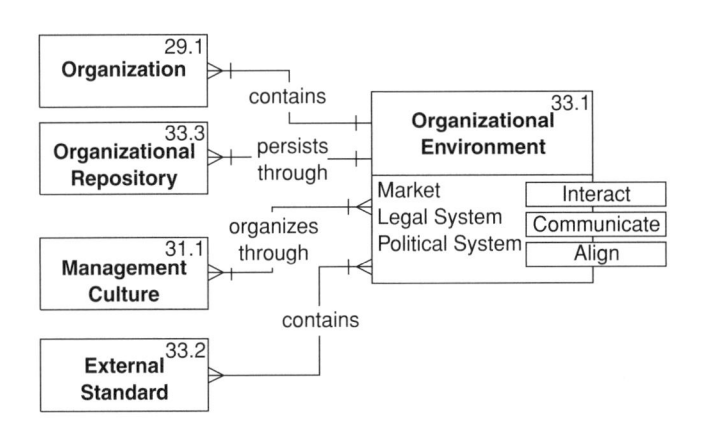

The Market

The economic system in which the organization produces its products, the *market*, has a major influence on the workings of the project system. Deciding to use OO technology is often, for example, a response to the market rather than a simple technological decision. If your competitors trumpet their object-oriented successes, you can choose to trumpet your own or to decry the faddishness of the herd. Which would you pick?

I started programming seriously in a CASE company dedicated to structured analysis tools. Around 1988, this company decided to adapt their tools to the Ada market, which was just beginning to take off. As I examined the various CASE requirements for Ada, including Booch's early work and Buhr concurrency diagrams, I began to see more work on OO technology. Soon thereafter, it became clear that OO technology was becoming an important factor. This was the era of earnest arguments over the true meaning of "object" and "inheritance." As market pressure grew, not only did the company adopt a strategy of marketing to the new OO marketplace, it began to adopt the OO approach in its internal architectures in response to customer opinion.

To better focus the project and the organization on the market, you can use tools such as the competitive position graph that compares competitive position to market economics for system products [McTaggart]. Understanding the strategic implications of your projects also requires a thorough understanding of both your position in your market and the general ecology of the marketplace [Moore].

Most OO software projects happen either in new or rapidly expanding markets. The technology is new, and there are relatively few people around capable of using it. That makes it self-limiting in the short term as a strategic market tool. On the other hand, the rapidity of growth in the OO world, demonstrated both by its press and the impressive market size numbers, point clearly to OO technology having a major impact in markets through the year 2000.

This market impact of OO technology implies that companies using the technology must focus on value creation and the innovation it depends on. You fail if you don't supply value to the customer. Your strategy thus becomes to convince the customer that the OO technology you use is delivering tremendous value they can get nowhere else. As you expand into the market, your strategic approach should establish a critical mass that ensures your survival in the market. Encouraging diversity through varied OO approaches and open systems, building systems through a compelling vision of value, and expanding the market through joint initiatives with other organizations all promote your survival in this stage. The dynamics of these strategic market stages reward the kind of iterative and incremental development strategies that OO development requires. These dynamics also reward the innovative building of new systems out of building blocks supplied by others in the market through reuse. The synergy of working with Microsoft, Sun, Oracle, and other major players in the OO world provides the protection you need to proceed with this bleeding-edge technology to dominate your part of the market.

The market provides many of the reusable products and services that your project reuses. Vendor-supplied tools, subcontractors, and service suppliers are all part of the market environment in which your organization gets its work done. Because reuse is such an important part of the OO approach, your procurement management process is key to your use of OO technology.

Procurement Process (27.1)

In the broader environment, you also need to take international issues into account. If your project team is in different countries, you need to worry about all kinds of things:

- Time zones
- Language differences
- Holidays
- Travel and face-to-face meetings
- Tele- and videoconferencing
- Political and cultural differences

I worked in a company that conducted its OO technology projects using several organizations distributed between the U.S. and Europe. Everyone spoke English, though we had to have French and German speakers to deal with distributors in those countries. The time zone problem was a major influence on our organization, determining the time of meetings (7 a.m.) and their technology (teleconferencing). We went through hell trying to find decent speakerphones. We interviewed a videoconferencing company, which tried to sell us a satellite. Our travel budget was tremendous as managers flew back and forth, harvesting frequent-flier miles. Was all this worth it? Not in the marketplace. We were just spending time and money that would have been better spent in paying a few more developers to get out a more complete product.

The Political System and the Law

The political system imposes its own quirky and convoluted logic on OO software projects through a combination of laws, regulations, and contracts.

Criminal and civil law burdens the organizational environment with a complex web of laws and regulations that the organization must follow or suffer legal penalties. The working world wraps itself in a tremendous array of legal restrictions on what you can do, when, and to whom. Any organization ignores the legal environment in which it operates at its peril. There may be specific laws that affect OO technology; if so, I haven't seen them, but I'm not a lawyer. Individual contracts may impose OO tools on the organization. For example, you may find requirements to use tools conforming to a particular external OO standard such as CORBA or ODMG, or to use specific coding, CASE, or configuration management tools for compatibility reasons.

Government contracting is a legal and economic specialty all its own. I have never worked on a real government contract, though I've spoken and worked with many who have. The bureaucracy and lack of control seem in most contracts to result in less value for the customer—the taxpayer—than might be the case in a purely private arrangement. This area of software development is not yet using OO technology extensively, though that may change as it becomes part of the stable set of tools for general software development.

The quasi-OO technology in Ada provides an interesting example of the impact of government contracting. The Department of Defense adopted Ada as a military standard with the intention of requiring software contractors to use it in all contracts. As any good bureaucracy would, it layered this policy with an exceptions mechanism that permitted contractors to justify using other languages. While Ada is in use in many government contracts, many do not use it, having successfully applied for an exception.

The wider arena of politics, including foreign policy, legislative politics, and even local politics, can have a distinct effect on your OO projects. A project supplying reusable components to a government contractor, for example, may suffer early death when the contractor runs afoul of a minor foreign policy switch [Baker]. A project working for a local government to extend an OO system they wrote in-house may have problems due to funding cuts to the agency or instability in the agency management.

One article on politics and projects suggested the following lessons [Baker, p. 20]:

- Projects based on political initiatives are highly subject to the whims of the political system.

- You need to communicate the value of your project to all stakeholders, and especially to those holding the purse strings and to those who don't support the project.

- The senior management of a company must support the project, especially if the senior management is a political rather than a business position.

- Structuring the project in pieces that can get support from different sources is a good way of maintaining support despite political problems. OO technology should be able to help here.

- The more widespread and compelling the value that the project delivers, the more likely it is to have the support of the political system.

The External Standard

An *external standard* is a policy that the organization adopts as an internal policy. Unlike an internal standard, law, or regulation, an external standard is not mandatory [PMI 1996, p. 24]. Contracts may impose them, but usually it is to your benefit to impose them on yourself through internal standards. The internal policy may mandate compliance with the external standard, or it may construe it as a guideline.

Vision: A project that conforms to relevant external standards to broaden reuse across projects

Mission: To standardize some aspect of technology to permit multiple projects to reuse project deliverables

---

Objective 33.1: To standardize technology for reuse and open sharing of products

---

Approach 33.1: Adopt a standard for a technology such as a programming language, application programming interface, or other software system through either a consensus or a market-driven, de facto recognition of the standard. Communicate the standard to those likely to benefit from compliance. Work with stakeholders of projects to get them to integrate the standards compliance into their expectations for the projects.

Metric 33.1: Conformance: the degree to which a system conforms to the applicable standards; usually this is a metric that the standard itself defines, an ordinal metric that qualifies conformance to a subset of the standard

Target 33.1: A value at a suitable level to establish the legitimacy and credibility of the standard in the marketplace

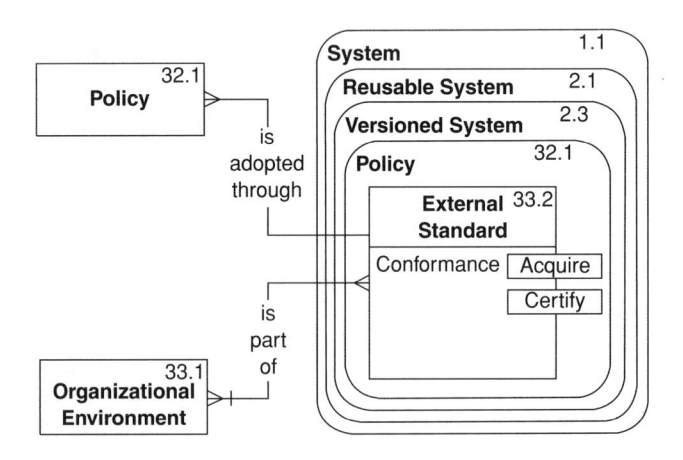

There are several standards relevant to OO projects. There are general standards that apply to all software development:

- *DOD-STD-2167A*, Military Standard, Defense System Software Development
- *ISO/IEC 12207*, Information Technology—Software Life Cycle Processes
- *ISO 9000-3*, Quality Management and Quality Assurance Standards—Guideline for the Application of ISO 9001 to the Development, Supply, and Maintenance of Software

There are standards that you will probably have to deal with, even though they do not contain any reference to OO technology:

- *ANSI X3.135-1992*, American National Standard for Information Systems—Database Language—SQL

There are specific OO technology standards that you must take into account when you undertake an OO project:

- *ISO/IEC 14882*, Information Technology—Programming Language—C++
- *CORBA*, The Common Object Request Broker Architecture and Specification; Revision 2.0
- *ODMG-93*, The Object Database Standard, ODMG-93 v 1.2

You can see regulations, marketing orders, and other contractual agreements as external standards, though at times they may have the force of law. You also have de facto standards that emerge through market forces, such as Windows, C++, and CORBA.

The Organizational Repository

The *organizational repository* stores all the systems that support the organization and its goals as part of the organizational environment. It stores policies, including policies that refer to external standards. Project resources must be able to access all policies and documents to which policies refer. The organizational repository ensures their availability. Often, this repository takes the form of a company library or at the least a company policy manual.

Vision: A set of secure, well-ordered organizational systems that any reuser can easily find

Mission: To enable the secure storage and easy retrieval of organizational systems in an environment

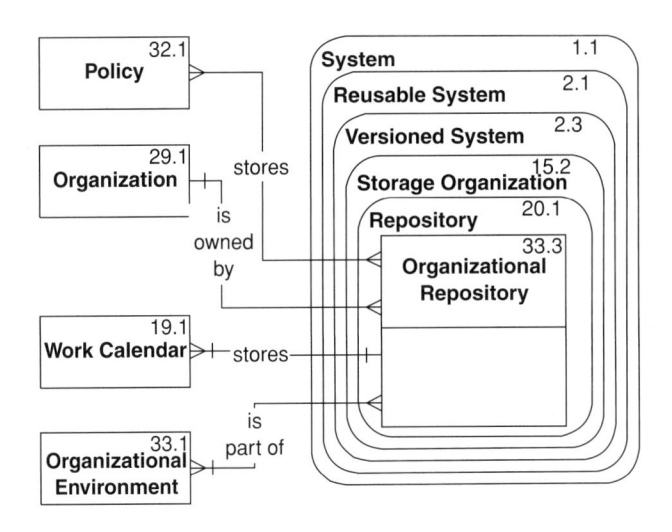

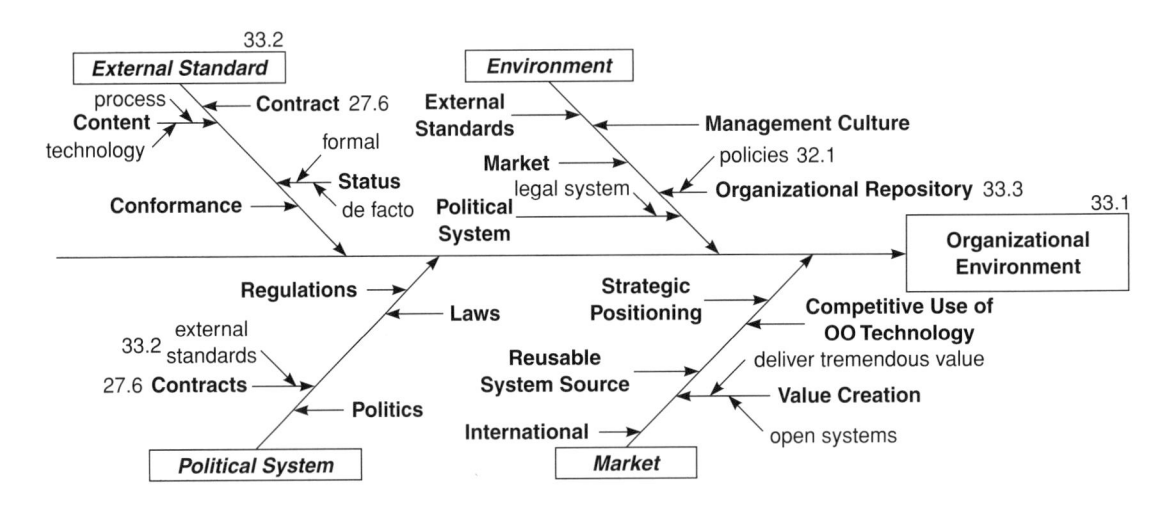

The organizational repository also contains the various work calendars for the organization's resources. These calendars specify things like company holidays, work shifts, and floating holiday and personal-time-off (PTO) policies.

Readings

[Baker] Bud Baker and Raj Menon. Politics and project performance: The fourth dimension of project management. *PM Network* (November 1995): 16–21.

While it has little to do with OO technology, this well-written article zeros in on the true impact of national and international politics on large projects.

[Cattell 1993]   R. G. Cattell, T. Atwood, J. Duhl, G. Ferran, M. Loomis, and D. Wade. *The Object Database Standard: ODMG-93 v 1.2.* San Francisco: Morgan Kaufmann, 1993.

This is the standard for the emerging OODBMS market. If you are going to use an OODBMS, you should look for compliance with this standard, and especially with the query language portion of it.

[ISO 1991]   International Standards Organization. *ISO 9000-3, Guideline for Application of ISO 9001 to the Development, Supply, and Maintenance of Software.* ISO, 1991.

This adjunct standard to ISO-9000 gives you guidelines for applying ISO-9001 to software suppliers. This is the major quality standard that applies to software development. There is no separate standard for OO software.

[ISO 1995]   International Standards Organization. *ISO/IEC 12207, Information Technology—Software Life Cycle Processes.* ISO, 1995.

This standard provides a standard language and framework for software development processes. You will find contracts increasingly specifying compliance with this standard instead of prior IEEE standards.

[ISO 1996]   International Standards Organization. *ISO/IEC 14882, Information Technology—Programming Languages, Their Environments and System Software Interfaces—Programming Language C++.* ISO/IEC Secretariat, December 1996. Available through Global Engineering Documents, 800-854-7179.

This is the only standard for OO programming languages available at the current time, and it's still a draft due for final approval in late 1997. Nevertheless, most tools now conform to this standard, and you should have a copy in your organization if you are coding in C++.

[Kerzner]   Harold Kerzner. *Project Management: A Systems Approach to Planning, Scheduling, and Controlling, Fifth Edition.* New York: Van Nostrand Reinhold, 1994.

Kerzner discusses international project management in Chapter 19, all too briefly, by reproducing a couple of excellent papers by other people. Most of it applies to the cultural issues of dealing with vastly different business practices, personal beliefs, and communication styles.

[McTaggart]   James M. McTaggart, Peter W. Kontes, and Michael C. Mankins. *The Value Imperative: Managing for Superior Shareholder Returns.* New York: Free Press, 1994.

This book on competitive strategy focuses on value for shareholders and how to structure the business to maximize that value through competitive positioning. Many of the lessons apply to projects as well as to businesses.

[Moore]　　　　James F. Moore. *The Death of Competition: Leadership and Strategy in the Age of Business Ecosystems.* New York: Harper-Business, 1996.

This book, a recent bestseller, is part of the new movement toward applying ecology and systems thinking to competitive strategy. Seeing the market as an ecosystem provides unique insights into both external and internal organization of the firm and project.

[OMG 1995]　　Object Management Group. *The Common Object Request Broker Architecture and Specification; Revision 2.0.* Framingham, MA: Object Management Group, July 1995.

This book is the current standard for CORBA. Anyone using CORBA should have this in addition to the after-market books based on it [OMG 1996].

[US DOD]　　　United States Department of Defense. *DOD-STD-2167A, Military Standard, Defense System Software Development.* Washington, DC: U.S. Government Printing Office, 1988.

This standard is the central software development standard for government contracting. Many books hold it up as an example of the bureaucratic nightmare, but 2167A is actually quite flexible and adaptable. It does not assume a waterfall model and allows for explicit exceptions and tailoring to the specific contractor and project. It does get carried away with acronyms, though.

Questions to Think About

1. Is the market for OO technology demand driven or technology driven? That is, do you think the market is demanding OO products, or are companies using OO technology to produce products that the market wants regardless of the specific technology?

2. What economic factors might influence your selection of a vendor to supply OO components? What mechanisms would these factors use to exert this influence?

3. Can you list any legal issues that might apply specifically to an OO software project?

4. How would you phrase a contract provision that required the use of a specific OO technology or external standard?

5. What would be the impact on an OO project of requiring you to conform to the ISO-12205 process standard? What about to the Capability Maturity Model?

6. List five different formats for an organizational repository. Which would you prefer to use?

PART ELEVEN

Resources

You need men, and I have all the men. What am I bid?

John L. Lewis, union organizer, to management at the bargaining table

"Men," of course, was a euphemism for the more politically correct "resource." But the fact remains: your project needs them, by whatever name. A resource can be a work group, a person, or a material resource. A material resource can be a contractor. Resources contribute cost to the project through assignments to tasks in the work breakdown structure.

Every person has a set of skills that enable him or her to do the job. Each work group has a skill matrix that shows how the skills of the resources that play a role in the group combine into the skills of the group as a whole. People acquire skills through training courses.

The staffing plan is the part of the project plan in which you plan for acquiring resources your project needs. Starting with the organization chart, you iteratively build a responsibility matrix that shows the responsibilities of resources for tasks. As you assign the tasks, you estimate the effort for each assignment, which in turn leads to additional staffing plans.

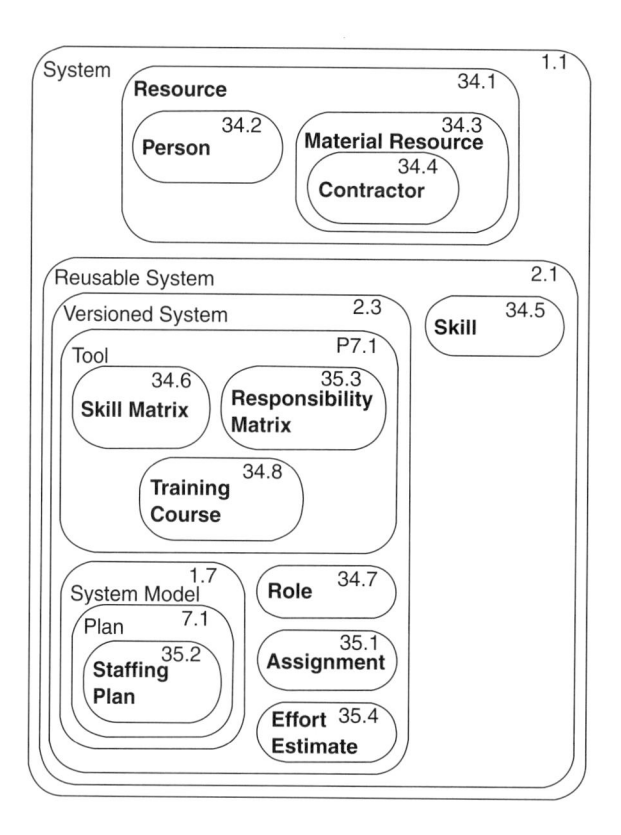

- *Note:* The illustration of the class hierarchy contains all the classes this part defines. Other parts of the book define and discuss classes not in boldface.

CHAPTER

34 Resource

The Resource

A *resource* is a person or thing that contributes cost to a project through assignment to one or more tasks. Resources contribute to multiple projects, each of which is responsible for some portion of the resource cost. Each resource has some number of task assignments, each of which contributes a portion of the resource cost. A work calendar schedules the work time of one or more resources. Every resource should have at least a minimal contingency plan that identifies alternatives to the resource in case of disaster.

Vision: A project that delivers value through the effective, controlled use of people or things

Mission: To apply people and things effectively to the work of the project while controlling costs to an appropriate level

Objective 34.1: To apply people and things effectively to the work of the project while controlling costs to an appropriate level

Approach 34.1: Assign the resource to project tasks that require them as part of the project planning process. Track the cost of the resource for each project.

Metric 34.1.1: Effectiveness: the ratio of task assignments completed successfully to total task assignments

Target 34.1.1: A relatively high value within control limits of a p control chart for the type of resource

The Resource 563

Metric 34.1.2: Total cost: the sum of the cost contributed to all the projects on which the resource works

Target 34.1.2: A total cost within control limits of an x-R control chart for the type of resource

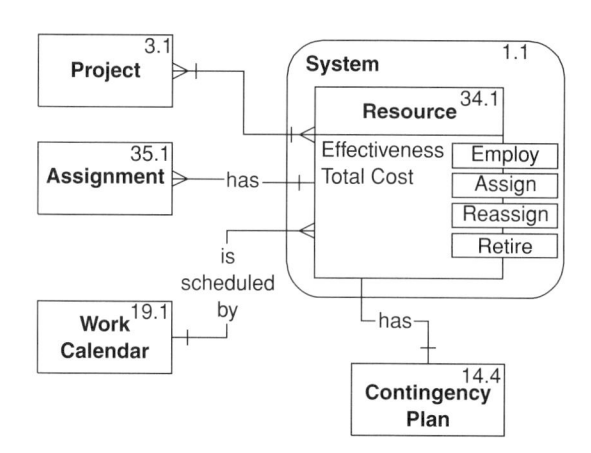

```
        3.1                              1.1
      Project ▷┤      System
                │              34.1
                │      Resource
       35.1     │    Effectiveness ┌─Employ─┐
    Assignment ▷─has─┤ Total Cost  ├─Assign─┤
                │                  ├Reassign┤
                │                  └─Retire─┘
               is
            scheduled
       Work 19.1  by    └─has─┐
      Calendar                 │
                             14.4
                          Contingency
                             Plan
```

The behavior of the resource as a generic kind of system sets up a life cycle for the object. It starts life through being employed in the organization, in the broadest sense of the word. You then assign it to tasks and remove it from tasks. When you have no more use for the resource, you retire it from the organization.

There are three kinds of resource: the person, the material resource, and the work group. The work group is a resource that is also a versioned system, while you do not version or reuse the person or material resource. You can assign and remove tasks from any of these kinds of resource, with differing effects depending on the type of resource. Assigning a task to a person delegates responsibility for working on the task to that person. Assigning to a material resource transfers control over the resource to the person responsible for the task. Assigning to a work group delegates the assignment authority for the work to the group, which then assigns the work to a person within the group.

Work Group (30.1)

The contingency plan is a risk management method that lets you identify what you will do if a risk event happens. In the context of a resource, the risk event is the sudden unavailability of the resource. Booch and Coplien call this the "Truck Number" when applied to a work group: how many catastrophic events it would take to wipe out the team [Booch 1996, p. 197]. If a person gets hit by a truck, or a computer finds its way to Libya by way of your back door, what are you going to do about it? As with any risk, the nature of risk management depends entirely on the risk tolerance. If your tolerance for catastrophe to a particular resource is high, you may not even need a contingency plan.

Person

The *person* ("*labor resource*" to the linguistically challenged) is a resource that contributes labor costs in currency units per work-hour. The person's current *cost rate* is the cost per effort-hour (or other work time unit) at a particular time. As this rate can vary over time, the resource has a *cost profile*. Each person has a work calendar that controls the work time available from that resource, and each person thus has an *availability profile* that varies over time. Finally, each person has a set of skills that can be used in his or her work. Each person plays a set of roles in and contributes to the skills matrix of the work group.

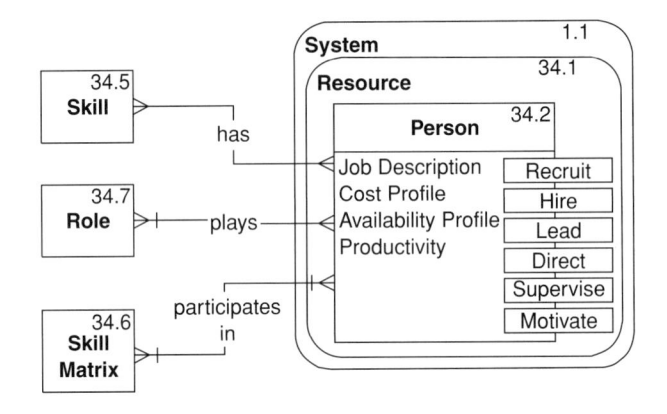

Vision: A project that delivers value through the productive, controlled use of skilled people

Mission: To apply a person's skills productively to the work of the project

Objective 34.2: To apply a person's skills productively to the work of the project

Approach 34.2: Recruit and hire a person according to the staffing plan for the project. Orient the person to the project. Ensure the person's success through leadership, direction, and control of the person's work for the project. When the person's work for the project is complete, retire the person from the project.

Metric 34.2: Productivity: earned value per effort-hour

Target 34.2: A value within control limits of an x-R control chart of people with similar skills

From the project perspective, a *person* is the work time and skills the person makes available to the project. People are many other things as well, but the rest is part of the organizational and personal environment, not part of the project system.

People are not well insulated from their environment, however. A great deal of effective technical and project leadership has to do with recognizing the human elements of work as well as the technical ones. Project managers, or any other kind of manager, doom their projects to failure if they do not take into account the fact that they are managing *people*, not software.

> ■ *Note:* Project management software takes this attitude with a vengeance. I found it difficult at first to understand how resource modeling worked in project management systems until I realized that these systems treat people as pools of skills, not as individuals. I suppose this comes from the origins of this software in the construction industry. In any case, these systems let you specify the number of units of a resource to deploy in an assignment. I believe there should be a fundamental distinction between units and people. I also believe, especially for OO software projects, that people are not interchangeable units. The assignment classes permit you to assign tasks to work groups as well as to people. If you need to represent a pool of people, create a work group out of those people and assign the task to the group. The group itself, however, should be responsible for assigning the work to individuals in the group.

Assignment (35.1)

A *profile* is a list of values and time intervals, one value per interval. This ordered list thus describes the change in a variable over time, such as the change in cost rate or availability. You display the profile as a histogram (Figure 10-1) or line graph. A person has two profiles of interest to a project: the availability profile and the cost profile.

Project Schedule (10.1)

The *availability profile* shows the series of time intervals that describe the amount of work time a person has available. Project management systems let you control this down to the minute through work calendars and other ways of telling the system when the person is available for work.

Work Calendar (19.1)

The *cost profile* shows the series of time intervals that describe the amount of money you pay to a resource for a work unit, usually an hour. Given the weak relationship between yearly salary and work-hours in the software industry, it's not surprising that few software projects actually use cost profiles or, indeed, cost accounting features of project management systems. For example, take the $70,000 salary of an OODBMS developer. To earn this $70,000 in a year, the developer will work how many hours? Answer: as many as his boss wants him to, subject to the laws of physics. This situation is not amenable to costing through cost profiles. Amazingly enough, human resource departments can calculate to the penny how much the company owes you when you get laid off. Usually, you get paid through a pay period, the period that the company agrees to pay for as a matter of custom.

In reality, this is all a matter of convenience for the company; there are very few rules and regulations about pay structure outside of government bureaucracies. At any rate, the pay period thus becomes the unit for the cost profile for a person working on a project. Since this number is usually in parts of months for salaried employees, it usually runs into the problems with month-year intervals versus daytime intervals.

Time Interval (19.2)

■ *Note:* Working as an independent contractor clarifies your mind wonderfully on these subjects, much like diving into a mountain river from a hot spring. "Pay periods" become negotiable through a combination of contract and cajolery. It's fun, though, watching your bank account drain. I think this issue arises because of the difference between *billable* work, work billed to clients as part of contracted work, and *salaried* work, work paid on a pay-period basis regardless of the amount of time actually worked. Projects are traditionally billable work, but that is less true in the software industry.

Recruiting and Hiring OO People

As part of your project planning, you develop a staffing plan that identifies the roles you need to fill on the project. These roles in turn combine into *job descriptions* that your organization works with to fill up its work groups. *Recruiting* is the task of attracting a person who matches this job description. *Hiring* is the task of working with the organization to make a job offer and to help the person make the transition into the organization. *Developing* is the task of training, coaching, counseling, and planning the career of the person.

Staffing Plan (35.2)

The specifics of these tasks are beyond the scope of this book [Licker]. Because the OO software field is new, and because it is growing rapidly, staffing is the focus of some fairly large risks to your projects. It is difficult to find good people who map nicely to your job descriptions. You may find someone who has been coding in C++ for five years but who has no design experience. You may find a great database programmer with no understanding of the object model. You may inherit a work group totally inexperienced in OO methods. You will find it well-nigh impossible to hire a technically informed writer capable of understanding OO concepts. I know; I tried.

Risk (12.1)

Recruiting OO people happens mainly through search firms. While you can find good OO people in other ways, most of them get their jobs through recruiters or through newspaper ads. I worked in one firm that had a policy of not using recruiters. The CEO was a penny-pincher who believed that one good reference from somebody already working at his company was far better than paying a recruiter. Unfortunately, since he had very few good OO people working for him, he didn't get very many good referrals. He got lucky a couple of times, but for the most part the people working in this company had no OO experience. It showed.

Interviewing the person lets you evaluate his or her skills and knowledge, ability to learn, and personality. Which of these is more important depends on the job and the organization. OO projects, though, do need a certain level of facility with the technology. I usually focus more on ability to learn when I'm filling middle-to-lower team slots, and on experience when I'm filling management and leadership positions. Have your team of experts interview the person. Audition people where that's appropriate. If you need an expert in C++ or Smalltalk, have applicants write a small program to show you their skills. If you're hiring a writer, ask the person to make a badly written example into a good one.

This can be overdone. One OO project I worked on had a guy who loved to ask people trick C++ questions based on his own coding experience. If they couldn't answer the question, they were relegated to the trash heap. This has several problems. First, you need to be sure that your approach to solving problems is the right one. On its face, that's an indicator of someone not well suited to either OO development or leadership, but rather to Greek tragedy. Second, C++ in particular is a language that has many hidden crevices and lost cities. Failure to discover one such city is merely indicative of not having explored that area, not of an inability to explore. Third, asking a prospective designer or a writer to solve C++ problems is not likely to be taken well. One person interviewed using this technique was a system designer whose résumé included a major management tool development project. After this interview, the prospect flatly refused to consider further interviews with our organization because of its unprofessionalism.

Hiring OO people is more difficult than you might imagine. First, when you've found someone you want to hire, you need to be sure to make a good first offer. Things happen very quickly when someone good is on the OO job market. These people are worth a premium and generally know it. Work with them. Second, once you get a signed offer letter and tell the new engineer there's no need to dress up anymore, you need to then bring him or her up to speed. That involves all the usual organizational stuff, patriotic lectures and orientations and so on. For OO projects, it may involve a bit more. If you have moved along the path this book suggests toward being an organization that reuses many systems, you have to orient the new hire toward the systems you intend to reuse. It is critical that the new hire learn early on that he or she is expected to reuse systems; otherwise, much time will be wasted reinventing the wheel until he or she finally get with the program.

My favorite example of this is my son's day care center. Most centers take kids when they are out of diapers, for obvious reasons. For working couples with a sudden opportunity brought on by a nanny with a broken foot, this causes problems. This day care center said, no problem. "We just show them what to do, let nature take its course, and they get with the program real quick." He did. A market opportunity. It may not be OO, but you get the picture.

Leading, Directing, and Controlling OO People

The phrase "herd of cats" has come up more than once in my researches into project management. I believe this way of looking at projects does a serious disservice to the profession.

First, jocularity aside, people aren't cats. If your people behave like cats, you have a zoo, not a professional software development organization. If you want to treat people like cats, buy one and give your employees a break.

Second, the whole metaphor suggests that projects are inherently out of control. That is probably true for many organizations that try to exceed the limitations of their management culture. Trying to build a large, complex system with a Variable or Routine management culture is an example. That's not a project management problem, it's a strategic problem for your organization.

Third, congruent management is a complex collection of abilities, techniques, and knowledge that you can apply to the different situations that arise from development work [Weinberg 1994]. Herding cats is, if anything, far too simplistic compared to serious software development management.

What's different about leading, directing, and controlling OO people?

Weinberg defines *leadership* as the process of creating an environment that empowers people [Weinberg 1986]. Hersey and Blanchard, reviewing other writers' definitions, summarize leadership as the process of guiding work toward achieving goals in a given situation [Hersey]. Both of these definitions contribute pieces of the puzzle from very different perspectives. Right now, we're discussing the impact of leading on the individual person. What you do as a leader depends on the situation: who the person is, what the person knows, what the person can do, how willing the person is to do it, and what the task is. Whatever you do, it is some kind of feedback.

There are several issues that constantly arise in OO projects that require leadership.

First, because OO is relatively new, many architects, designers, and coders do not have extensive experience in OO design and implementation. As a result, they tend to do too much—too much design, too much coding. They also tend to do too little testing and definitely do too little reviewing. To lead people, you need to set and communicate the mission and objectives of their work, then create a situation that will empower them to succeed, and then show them that they are succeeding through feedback. In the context of OO software development, that means directing and coaching people, being a hands-on leader who understands what people need to do and what they have actually done. The first thing you need to do, therefore, is to provide expert guidance, either from your own extensive experience with OO technology or by hiring someone with that kind of experience as a team leader or consulting mentor.

I have two examples, one good and one bad. In a project to develop an OO database management system, I worked with several brilliant individuals who also happened to be deeply experienced, both in OO technology and in programming and design. These people needed guidance in a couple of areas, however, because the things they were assigned were brand new and had never been done before. Our manager led us to people and other resources that guided our development to a successful conclusion.

On the other hand, I worked in a project where the main goal was to get out a next-generation commercial project management system based on an innovative OO design. The manager did not understand OO technology or client/server technology, both critical to the project. He had never written a program. He had no clue about motivating programmers. His approach to leadership was to set a goal—in our case, a date—and then browbeat people into meeting that goal.

When people hit technical problems, instead of helping to solve them, he would denigrate the abilities of those doing the work. If the problem persisted despite this assistance, he would criticize the programmers for disloyalty and lack of commitment to the project and to him personally. After a while, this became a self-fulfilling action; we all detested him and hated the project.

Second, getting people to focus on reuse is a leadership issue. In the early stages, just tell people to reuse systems and make it stick. That works if you have systems to reuse but not if you don't. It makes a lot of sense to try to acquire components from outside your project even if it makes marginal sense to build it yourself, because this establishes the pattern of behavior you want to see. You're leading by example. As your reuse repository offers more choices, you need to coach and encourage people to think about reusing those systems. On the other side, you need to direct and coach people in producing systems with high reuse potential. Make sure you have an adequate reuse repository technology, and make sure you have the resources attached to it to make reuse possible and likely. Get rid of any policies (design standards, for example) that get in the way of either reusing software or of producing high-reuse-potential software. Create an environment that empowers reuse, set objectives that encourage reuse, and guide people in ways that motivate them to reuse.

Reusable System (2.1)

Third, remove roadblocks that keep OO technology from succeeding. You face risks such as the Silver Bullet syndrome or the corporate politics risks associated with people thinking too highly or too little of OO technology. Leadership in an OO project must confront these risks actively, managing them to remove the risk from the project environment. If a tool is inadequate, replace it. If there isn't enough money or people to do a job properly, get more money, abandon the job, or find a cheaper, innovative way to solve the problem working with the people involved. OO projects require innovative problem solving by leaders and followers.

Risk (12.1)

Fourth, directing and controlling technical people effectively requires that you understand and use system feedback. Motivating people depends on feedback, as the following section on "Motivating and Retaining OO People" discusses. The best way to keep a project in control is to lead the people in the organization to success by the continuous integration of feedback about their actions [Weinberg 1994].

Motivating and Retaining OO People

The main reason I don't think people are cats is that you can't motivate a cat. You can motivate a dog, you can motivate a rhinoceros, but motivating a cat is a waste of time. If you think motivating people is a waste of time, you shouldn't be a project manager.

The biggest single factor in motivating people in OO projects is the work itself. OO work is inherently interesting and motivating; it's one of the main reasons for its success as a technology. There is status, recognition, and money involved. Just being able to say "I'm an experienced OO developer" is a major motivator. Working on OO projects that really create value for stakeholders gives people a reason to own their work. Keeping a sense of humor and fun in the work is important. Working with the latest tools both enhances people's careers and gives them a chance to expand their skills and knowledge. Working with people at the cutting edge of technology does the same. The more of this you can do, the more motivated your people will become.

I have a company motivation metric that I call the Pig metric. This comes out of early (and non-OO) experiences in some major and minor software companies. The Pig metric measures the number of derogatory references that people inside a company make to their products in personal interactions. One big software company was having growing pains as its reach began to exceed its grasp. The employees of this company, beleaguered by massive numbers of defects, customer complaints, and a "don't tell me" attitude from developers, began to refer to the flagship product as "The Pig." You could tell how people were doing by listening to their often hysterically funny war stories about The Pig. Motivation was not high. Fortunately for this company, all the employees outside the rather cliquish development group left the company, and over the next three or four years, the company outgrew its pain and became tremendously successful. You don't hear a lot of pig remarks there anymore. When I consult with a company, I listen carefully to how they express their regard for their product; if they use words like "pig," I zero in on improving the work itself.

The next biggest factor in motivating people in OO projects is to give them feedback about their work. Recognizing people's good work is critical to motivating them to do more of it. You can do as little as a one-minute-manager back pat or as much as a trip to Hawaii for top performers, but don't just ignore people. Give them feedback. Appraisals are a good way to do this, too, but not in the management-by-objective style of an annual review. You should structure appraisals by the things you want to appraise—process milestones. When programmers reach a major milestone in their work, go over it with them and tell them what you think. Measure and analyze the data with the people involved. Often, appraisal in OO projects works better as a team or group effort, as the group, not the individual, has responsibility for the milestone. Do recognize the individual's role in contributing to the group's success, however.

An OO software company I worked for did reasonably standard management-by-objective performance appraisals on a yearly basis. In doing the set for my group, which had adopted a total quality approach to its activities, I got back several objective proposals that looked aggressive, to put it mildly. One in particular struck me as unusual: this person proposed to complete as many as 12 major projects during the next quarter involving everything from delivering new software tools to finishing a master's degree and getting certified as a tool guru. On my rather restrained response asking him about this, the person replied, "I like to set myself stretch goals." We whittled the list down to five items. At the end of the quarter, he had not completed any of these items, even the ones directly affected by his project work. As we compared notes, I realized that this person had never received feedback from a manager before! He had assumed that these goals were simply communications from him to me telling me what he would like to be doing with his time, not obligations requiring my help and authority to accomplish. My feedback was very direct from that point on, and his performance improved remarkably.

Removing roadblocks is also a big factor in motivation. Most developers feel strongly that management should get out of the way and let them do their jobs. Turn this around; get out of their way, but show them that you are getting everything else out of their way as well. Get them good, highly reusable software systems. Get them good tools. Staff projects adequately. Consult them on cost estimates, and then do what they suggest. Above all, do not put more roadblocks in their way. That's the surest way to sap people's motivation.

Material Resource

A *material resource* is a nonhuman resource belonging to or leased by the organization that contributes fixed or variable costs in units determined by their character. You acquire a physical resource through a procurement process, and then bring it online to employ it in the project. When you no longer have a need for the material resource, you can recycle the remaining units to other projects.

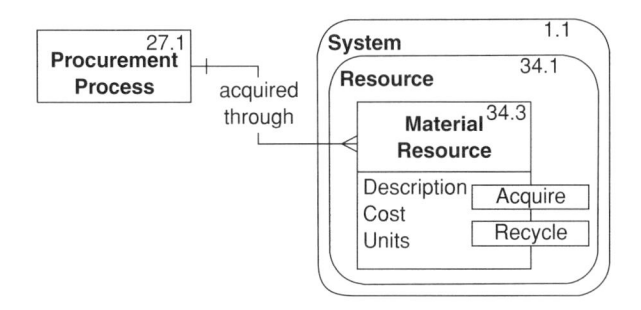

Vision: *A project that delivers value through the effective, controlled use of material resources*

Mission: *To apply materials effectively to the work of the project*

Objective 34.3: To apply a thing to the work of the project

Approach 34.3: As part of procurement planning, list the materials required as part of the statement of work's work breakdown structure. Develop a bill of materials and a procurement plan for acquiring the materials at the proper times. Divide the procurements into appropriate procurement processes to control costs (buying in bulk, for example). Acquire the materials and employ them in the project. Assign the materials to tasks that will benefit from them, removing them if not needed. If the project does not consume the materials, retire the material resource when it is no longer useful.

Material resources can be fixed or variable costs, with the contractor being a special third case of fixed cost.

- *Note:* The principles of managerial accounting are quite clear on fixed and variable costs. Project management software is not. Not one of the packages I have used in 15 years of project management uses the management accounting definitions of fixed and variable cost. I explain in the following paragraphs how the project management systems' use of the terms differs from the standard usage. Accountants beware!

A *fixed cost* is a material resource that contributes its value to the project regardless of the size of the deliverable systems you produce in the project. Virtually all material resources in software projects are fixed costs. Some variations on the fixed cost include a cost that occurs at a single point, a cost that varies with the number of units you use, and a cost that varies with the amount of time you use the resource. Examples: licensing a reusable software system for a fixed price, buying computers, and renting computers, respectively.

A *variable cost* is a resource that contributes its cost with the number of units of value you produce. The most common variable cost in an OO software project is the royalty, a cost you pay when you reuse software in your deliverables by license. Royalties are either a percentage of the price of the product or a fixed amount per unit of the product sold.

My first experience with royalties was with Adobe Acrobat. When Adobe first released Acrobat 1.0, they did it through a distributor, R. R. Donnelly & Sons. To include the Acrobat Reader in your product, you licensed the Reader disk from Donnelly and agreed to pay them $2 per unit you shipped. This lasted about six months before Adobe realized they had shot themselves in the foot and started distributing Adobe Acrobat Reader 2.0 free of charge over the Internet. In the meantime, my accounting department went crazy trying to track the royalties, and I had to supply the license agreement four separate times to different parts of the finance organization. Fortunately, most reuse situations are fixed cost in nature.

An accountant would class people as variable costs, but project management separates them out for special care and feeding. Every project management system has a different characterization of costs. Time Line, for example, talks about fixed, unit, and variable costs, corresponding to the three types of fixed cost above. Scitor's Project Scheduler 6 uses the labor and materials categories, and then adds a catchall "other" category. Primavera Project Planner does not classify the resources but lets you control their behavior through alternative attribute settings such as cost per unit and budgeted amount. Primavera at least gives the accountants a sop through the cost accounting codes it lets you define for the resources. All the other systems rely on WBS codes or similar generic codes for accounting, often permitting accounting only through the built-in work breakdown structure. None of these project management systems are particularly good at cost accounting, though in my opinion Primavera gets closer to it than the others.

Work Breakdown Structure (8.2)

The Contractor

A *contractor* is a material resource that contributes its cost under the control of a contract and a contract administration process. A contractor can be a person working at a desk in your office or a huge corporation halfway around the world. The contractor has a completely different set of behaviors from the other people and things that serve as resources to your organization. The nature of the cost structure depends on the contract, and the nature of the management activities varies with the contractor.

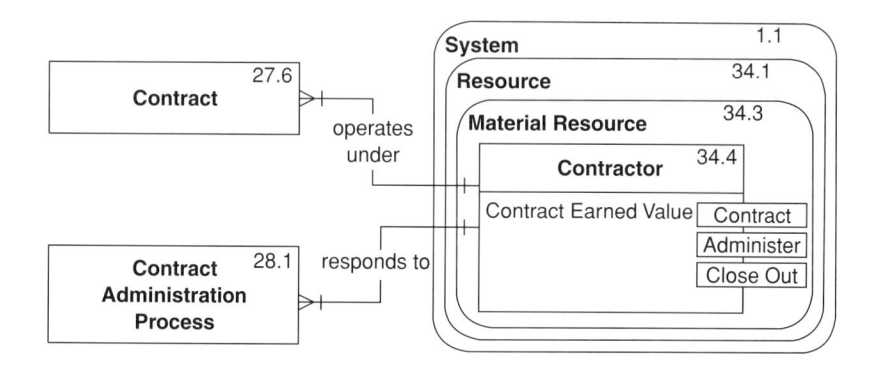

Vision: A project that delivers value through the effective, controlled use of contracted resources

Mission: To contract effectively for part of the work of the project

---

Objective 34.4: To contract effectively for part of the work of the project

Approach 34.4: If you determine to acquire a system through a contract, put a procurement process and a contract administration process in place for the contract. Assign the appropriate tasks to the contractor as part of the contract, listing the tasks in the statement of work for the contract. Treat the contract deliverables as fixed costs, just as though you had bought them off the shelf.

Metric 34.4: Contract Earned Value (see Metric 28.1)

You can manage contractors like people (that is, like employees), but it's generally not a good idea. Even in the case of a single person contracting directly with you, you should use a contract administration process, not an employee development process. The contract contains the entire relationship between you and the contractor, and letting it get beyond that can be ineffective and time wasting. For example, you train your employees in tools and methods they need to do their work. Contractors are responsible for providing such training themselves. If they want you to train them, or you need to train them, that should be part of the contract. Contractors working at your site should participate in whatever social activities you may have, but as guests, not as coworkers. You certainly should not let a contractor work at your site unsupervised, after-hours without some kind of security measures in place. Contractors don't get promoted, and they don't need reward and recognition as team members, just as contractors.

- *Note:* A special case is the contractor you hire to manage a group. This can work, but it implies a matrix organization and the consequent problems with authority and responsibility. I believe you should hire contractors to facilitate but not manage groups. I worked in one organization where the chief architect and project manager was a contract employee. He had one staff member reporting to him. Had he been a better communicator, he might have gotten away with this, but he wasn't. He ran into major conflicts with the functional managers on the project. His project plan was a work of fiction, and no one else in the organization would sign off on it. His staff member alienated the other employees with iconoclastic attitudes and strange working hours; he seemed totally unconnected to the rest of the organization. This company was trying to save money by hiring contractors instead of employees, and nobody was fooled.

A key to managing the resource, as opposed to the contract, is to understand precisely who, what, why, when, and where the contractor connects with your project. It's best if a single person has responsibility for the administration process. Match the person's skills to the job. Assign someone who understands contracts and contract administration, but who also understands the work to be done, the role the contractor performs in the project, and what the results should look like.

This may sound obvious, but the most important thing about managing contractors is to pay them when they expect to be paid. I can't tell you how little motivation you have as a contractor when you are thinking about calling accounts payable rather than how to extend the cWhatever class with the right features. It never ceases to amaze me, as a contractor, when my client gets an invoice and ignores it. Also, trust the contractor until they demonstrate that you cannot trust them. Don't treat the contract relationship as an adversarial one; it's not. Mutual respect is the key to effective contractor resources.

You also have to know when to pull the plug. I worked with a quality assurance department that was responsible for the system test of an OO system built by a third-party contractor to serve as an Internet-accessible interface for their product. From the specification, we built a use-case model of the system we expected to receive. When we got the first release, it was a disaster. In four weeks of system testing, we uncovered 500 faults in the code. After extensive deliberation and negotiation, the company decided to terminate the contract and start over with another contractor. This was a Routine organization, so I am not sanguine that the next time through will prove much better. They'll find the bugs, at least, but they won't learn how to create a better contractual relationship.

The Skill

The *skill* is a reusable, practical ability or facility. Skills are abstractions independent of the people that have them, so more than one person can have a skill. Every skill has a name, a description, and a *body of knowledge,* a relationship to the organizational environment including books, consulting practices, and other repositories of knowledge about the skill. Some but not all skills have training courses that train people to raise their proficiency and competence in that skill. Roles are sets of skills that work groups use. People acquire skills to permit their performing these roles in their work groups.

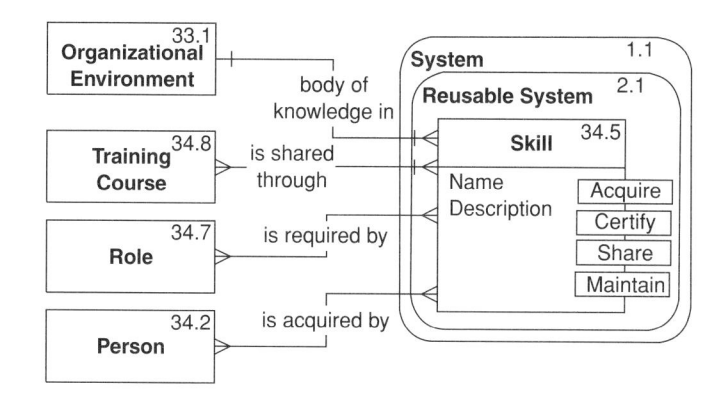

Vision: A set of people capable of productively delivering value to project stakeholders

Mission: To represent knowledge about a practical ability that contributes value to your project

Objective 34.5: To represent knowledge about a practical ability

Approach 34.5: Research the skill using corporate and public libraries, the Web, and other information-gathering tools. Create a repository of skill knowledge in your organizational environment. Include training and consulting options, creating them if they do not exist in the marketplace.

Metric 34.5: Extent: the size of the knowledge base measured in topics; a topic is typically a single section in a document representing an atomic unit of knowledge about the skill

Target 34.5: A value within control limits of an x-R control chart of similar knowledge bases

Objective 34.6: To represent a valuable skill

Approach 34.6: Stay abreast of the technical news and knowledge in your area through magazines, newspapers, technical and professional books, Web sites, and any other knowledge-sharing tool you can find. When two or more sources mention a skill as valuable, investigate it in detail to determine whether your project and organization can benefit from acquiring a knowledge base about the skill. Gather data on pay premiums from market analysis by recruiters and career-oriented newsmagazines and Web sites.

Metric 34.6: Pay Premiums: how much additional money a resource possessing this skill at a proficient level earns. If negative, this means how much money the resource would lose if they did not have this skill.

Target 34.6: A value within control limits of an x-R control chart of similar skills

OO Project Skills

Not all skills are technological; otherwise, this book would not exist. Project management skills are not equally distributed among people on a project. Similarly, every project manager needs general management skills as well as project management skills:

- Leading (direction, alignment, motivation)
- Communicating
- Negotiating (scope, change, contracts, assignments, resources)

- Problem Solving (problem definition, decision making)
- Influencing the Organization

For OO projects, the project manager must have basic skills in OO analysis and design to lead, communicate, and solve problems. If you don't have basic OO technical skills, you will not have any influence over the technical parts of your organization. The OO project manager also needs training and experience in the newer software development processes such as the spiral, fountain, and recursive-parallel models. It's also not a bad idea to have at least a minimal proficiency in OO quality assurance, which serves as a set of primary risk management methods for OO risks.

General technical skills for OO projects include OO methods for analysis and design, general programming language knowledge and specific knowledge about emerging language standards, knowledge of design patterns, knowledge of OO review and testing methods, and an ability to communicate effectively in an OO world.

Specific technical skills might include the following items:

- Relational and hybrid OO-relational database technology
- OO database technology
- OO CASE technology
- Client/server technology [Lewis]
- Graphical User Interface technology
- Work-flow and groupware technology [Khoshafian]
- CORBA (Common Object Request Broker Architecture) [OMG 1996] and technologies such as OpenDoc or IIOP that are CORBA-based
- Internet and networking technology (Web, Java, and so on)

■ *Note:* I debated whether to include ActiveX in this list, but came down on the negative side. ActiveX is, in my opinion, not solely an OO technology. It has some OO features, but non-OO systems can make use of them just as easily. It does, however, compete with technologies such as OpenDoc and other CORBA-based technologies.

A key set of skills relates to the specific software systems that the project produces. As people work on these systems, they acquire a facility with the concepts, structure, and logic of the software itself. This knowledge often determines precisely who is most qualified to work on a task relating to the system. Sometimes this facility with the input software can easily outweigh greater skills in design or coding, particularly so if the scheduling of the task is critical.

In every company I've worked at, development managers have made every effort to keep people working on software systems they have learned. You touch it, you own it. The logic for this seems to be that the knowledge about the specific system is so important to being able to work on that system that virtually no other skill matters. I've seen two problems arise from this approach. First, while you get good complementary skills in your organization this way, you don't get shared skills. Everyone develops expertise in their part of the system, and there it stays. No one else learns it, and when something happens to a critical resource, you need to crash-train somebody. I've seen major delays in delivery when somebody quits or changes jobs and no one else understands that person's code. Second, other skills matter. If you assign somebody with no design skills to a major upgrade of a cluster just because the person worked on the cluster before, you get bad design.

Along the same lines, facility with reusable software from the reuse repository is a highly valuable skill. The people who understand the GUI framework can write their own paychecks. The people who understand the chart of accounts really do write their own paychecks. The people who understand the network and hardware tools are gods that you must propitiate, sacrificing the occasional file in rituals designed to keep them in humor.

Tool knowledge is always valuable. The lack of OO language standards and the vitality of the emerging technology mean that skills in specific tools are very important. Would you rather hire somebody who knows C++ or somebody who knows Visual C++ with MFC? At least if you're developing with the tools, you want a tool expert, not a generalist. Even better, you want someone who has worked with a range of tools and is therefore more versatile. Also, if you are customizing the tools extensively or building tools to work with other tools, you need someone with a high proficiency in the tools.

A particular subset of tool skills supports the roles of project librarian and reuse librarian. The repository and change management tools these roles use are critical to reuse and release management. Maintaining the reuse repository and the product repository requires a thorough knowledge of the repository tools as well as of the systems you maintain in the repositories.

Many vendors are now maintaining extensive knowledge bases and training courses about their tools. Microsoft, for example, distributes their knowledge base both online through their Web site and through the Microsoft Developer Network (MSDN) CD-ROM. If you use Visual C++, Visual J++, or ActiveX, for example, getting MSDN is a way to reuse Microsoft's knowledge about these products.

Skill Processes

Building your organizational skill set requires some analysis of your intended work. As you create your statement of work, you should think about what skills the work requires. Your reuse repository should have a set of predefined skills from which you can choose. If the skill you need is there, you reuse it; otherwise, you must create a new skill. This means giving the skill a name, describing its properties, and relating it to a body of knowledge in the organizational environment.

The inherent reuse potential for a skill depends on the quality of the description and the body of knowledge. If you develop the skill well, others should immediately see its value to their projects and should reuse that skill. If the skill has little or no knowledge base, people won't reuse it because there is no way to acquire it, or because no one else thinks the skill is worth anything.

The domain reuse potential for a skill depends on the specialization that the skill represents. Training in C++ is a very general skill. Training in Visual C++ is more specific. Training in the Microsoft Foundation Class (MFC) library is more specific still. Training in using the ActiveX interfaces with MFC is highly specialized.

The organizational reuse potential for a skill depends on a combination of your repository technology and your organizational culture. If you have a corporate library with good indexing and check-out controls, and if you're connected to the Usenet and World Wide Web, and if you provide a budget for newspapers, magazines, and books for your people, they are much more likely to reuse the skills that these facilities hold. If your organization is insular and doesn't value skill acquisition and training, you will find it difficult to get people to reuse skills. Also, if your organization is crisis managed, no one will have the time, energy, or inclination to add skills to their repertoires.

There are two classes of risk of interest in certifying a skill. First, you should evaluate the skill for its risks in application and training. Are there physical risks—safety issues—associated with training in the skill? How well do the training courses handle these risks? Is a technical skill likely to become quickly outdated? Are there standards for the skill, and does the organization follow these standards? Second, you should evaluate the negative risks: what will happen if the organization does not acquire this skill. For example, take the use of a particular design method. You should evaluate the risk to the reusing project of failing to acquire the skill. Will the project risk technical failure if it does not gain proficiency in the method?

The skill description and knowledge base constitute the certification for the goals and functions of the skill. They answer questions about what the skill offers. Training courses and consulting available on the skill must have certifications of quality or professional certifications.

Certification of the skill also requires that some part of the organization take responsibility for sharing and maintaining the skill. If there are internal courses or consulting for the skill, the certification identifies the work groups that are responsible for this. If the skill requires refresher courses or similar maintenance, who is responsible for making sure people maintain their skills? If a person requires certification in the skill, such as the Project Management Professional certificate or a vendor certification, who is responsible for doing these certifications?

Sharing the skill is critical to its reuse in your system. For OO projects, sharing knowledge about the use of frameworks, programming languages, and other technical skills is essential. Acquiring skills in OO analysis and design through training and mentoring processes helps to spread stronger OO abilities through your organization.

Maintaining the skill requires a constant attention to the knowledge base. You should monitor technical publications to add to the knowledge base for each skill. It is critical to keep the knowledge base current. Just as important is to keep the set of people who have the skill current. You should maintain lists of these people and notify them when the repository gets new information about the skill.

The Skills Matrix

A *skills matrix* is a tool that describes the relationship between a set of skills and the people in a work group or team to certify its ability to do the work assigned to it. The rows are the people in the group, and the columns are the skills that come from the roles in the group, as Figure 34-1 illustrates. The individual cell values are a proficiency rating that describe the level of the skill for the person.

Vision: A reusable work group with the skills it needs to get its job done

Mission: To certify the skills of a work group for reuse

Objective 34.7: To certify the skills of a work group for reuse

Approach 34.7: Construct a matrix for the work group, with the people who belong to the group as rows and the skills that comprise the roles of the group as columns. Combine the same skill from multiple roles into a single column. For each skill, count the number of people who have the skill at the minimum required proficiency level and put the number at the bottom of the column.

Figure 34-1
Skills matrix for OO client/server group

	OODBMS	SQL	Object Modeling	OLE/ActiveX	CORBA	Managing
John	Expert	Functional				
Stewart				Basic		
Adam			Functional			
Mary	Basic	Basic	Functional	Conceptual	Basic	Expert
Meera		Expert				
Reinhard	Basic			Expert		
Alfonso			Functional		Expert	
Pei-Wei	Expert	Basic				Basic
Count	2	2	3	1	1	1

The Skills Matrix 581

Metric 34.7.1: Proficiency: an ordinal metric rating the degree to which the person has acquired the skill; values None, Conceptual, Basic, Functional, Expert, and Guru

Target 34.7.1: A proficiency in each skill at or above the minimum level the roles require

---

Metric 34.7.2: Density: the number of cells in the matrix that have a proficiency of Basic or above over the total number of cells

Target 34.7.2: A density within control limits of a pn control chart of similar matrices

---

Metric 34.7.3: Dispersion: the median number of people who have each skill at the required proficiency

Target 34.7.3: A value between 1 and 2, inclusive, that indicates that the skills are reasonably evenly distributed over the people in the group, allowing for contingency backup skills

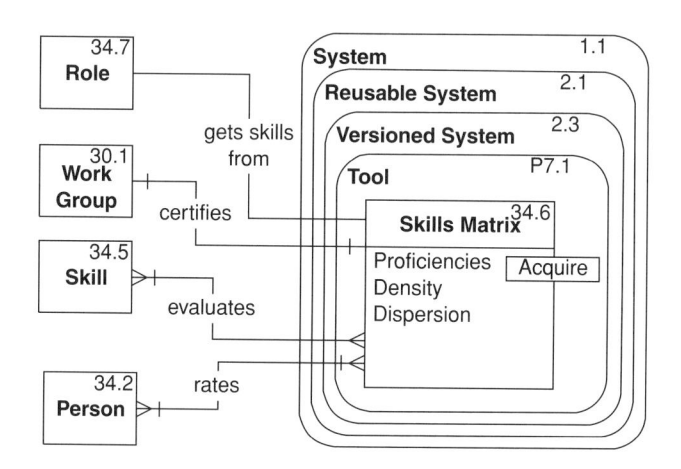

The skills matrix gives you a clear idea of the capabilities of the people in a work group. It also provides a place to keep the proficiencies of the people. You construct the matrix by gathering the skills from the various roles in your work group, and then mapping them to the people in the group by entering their proficiencies.

You use the skills matrix to certify the capabilities of the work group. The proficiencies show how well the people in the group measure up to the skills required to do the work of the group. The density and dispersion metrics give you a way to evaluate the overall nature of the group. The density metric shows you how many

Team (30.2)

people have how many skills at greater than a Basic level. The dispersion metric helps you to evaluate how well the group represents a complementary mix of skills among the people in the group, one of the characteristics of the group that can lead to forming a team from the group.

The Role

A *role* is a relationship between a set of skills, a set of people, and a set of work groups. When you create a work group, you define its structure with a set of roles. When you hire a person, you define his or her job description as a set of roles in a work group. The same skill may be a part of several roles. Roles are thus a central piece of the organizational puzzle. Using roles, you can quickly identify people and work groups capable of doing a piece of work.

Vision: A set of people playing an effective role in the project through their work groups

Mission: To collect a set of skills into a position in a work group that a single individual can fulfill

Objective 34.8: To collect a set of skills and determine the required proficiency levels

Approach 34.8: Analyze the set of tasks you want to be able to accomplish using the work group's people. List the skills you will need to accomplish these tasks. Arrange the skills in clusters that represent coherent combinations. Name each cluster as a role and write the job description for the role, summarizing the skills and listing the proficiency levels required.

Metric 34.8: Cohesion: a subjective, ordinal metric evaluating how well the role makes sense as a cohesive set of skills; values High, Medium, Low

Target 34.8: High

Objective 34.9: To form a position that a single person can fulfill

Approach 34.9: Create the roles for the work group as in Approach 34.9. After forming the role and evaluating the required proficiencies, determine whether a single person could be expected to possess these skills. If not, break the role into separate roles more likely to match candidates for hiring.

Metric 34.9: Hiring risk: the risk that you will not be able to hire anyone to fulfill the role

Target 34.9: A risk that does not cause the role risk to exceed its risk tolerance

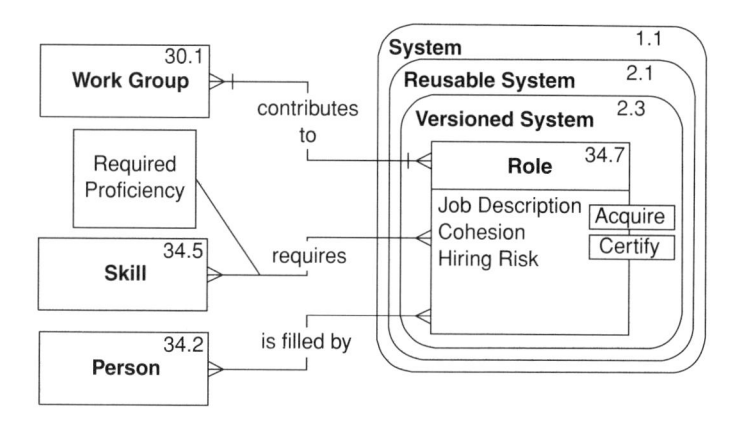

Roles are relationships between people and work groups. They have an additional function in providing a way to describe a mix of skills that makes sense for a single person to perform. Describing work groups in terms of roles lets you abstract the nature of the group from the people who actually comprise it. It also lets you build a set of job descriptions that you can use to hire people into the group. These job descriptions should generally "make sense" in the same way that a class or cluster makes sense. The skills should form a meaningful, cohesive role that is not beyond the capabilities of your potential candidates for the role.

In practical terms, the role also lets the group manager quickly understand how to delegate responsibility within the group. When a work assignment comes to the group, the manager can quickly match the work with the set of skills found in various roles and can assign individual tasks to those roles. Part of this capability requires the role to specify a required proficiency level on each skill. People who take on the role must have a proficiency in the skill at or above that level or must get training to raise their skill level to meet the requirement.

More than one person in a group can perform a role, and a single person can perform more than one role. A person's job description describes all the roles they perform in the group. If there are several people that can perform a role, you can assign a task appropriate for that role to any of them, and each can act as a backup for the others in the group.

The potential set of roles is as large as the potential skills you need in your project. Here are some that come to mind [Booch 1996; Goldberg]:

- Project manager
- Product manager
- Planner
- Internal consultant
- Facilitator
- Administrator

- Chief architect
- Architect
- Analyst
- Group manager
- Technical leader
- Prototyper
- Coder
- Reuse expert
- Technology domain expert (GUI, client/server, CORBA, C++, and so on)
- Application domain expert (banking, programming, medical, and so on)
- Algorithm guru (the one who's always fooling around on the whiteboard)
- Tester
- Design reviewer
- Code reviewer
- Process developer
- Technical support representative
- System administrator

Thomsett identifies two cross-group roles he calls the linking pin and the object consultancy [Thomsett, pp. 143–144]. The *linking pin* is a role that spans two or more work groups to provide a direct communication link between the two groups. You can use the linking pin role to cross-fertilize groups in your project or to coordinate groups in different projects working on similar things. You can also use the linking pin to transfer knowledge from one group to another, such as knowledge about reusable systems. The *object consultancy* is a kind of linking pin that specifically links domain or technology groups outside of the project to groups in the project. For example, if you have a centralized reuse group that maintains the reuse repository, it can provide reuse consultants to project work groups on demand [Goldberg]. If you have a central data modeling organization that maintains your enterprise object model, you can distribute knowledge and integration skills by training consultants in this group and farming them out to the project work groups.

The Training Course

The *training course* is a tool that people use to acquire one or more skills. The course teaches the skills to train one or more people in your organization. Each training session results in a grade for the person taking the training, whatever the grading scheme might be. You acquire training courses through a procurement process if you do not build it yourself.

The Training Course

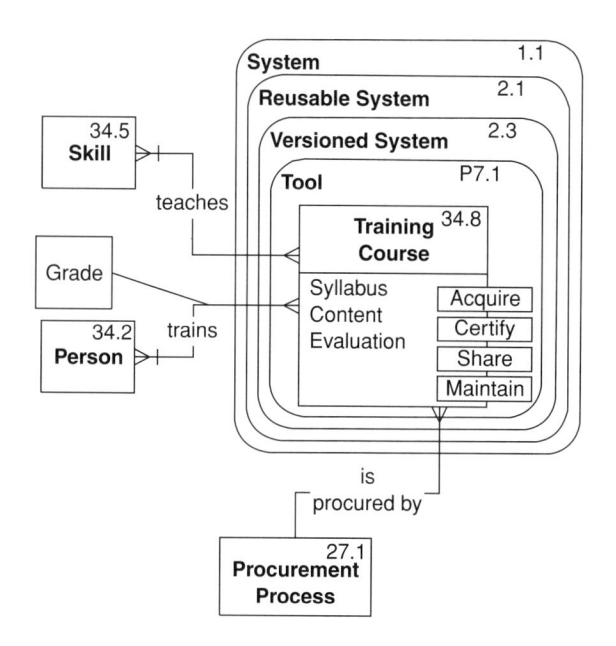

Vision: An organization with the skills it needs to do its job
Mission: To provide an effective means for people to acquire skills

---

Objective 34.10: To provide an effective means for people to acquire skills

---

Approach 34.10: Acquire a training course by either developing one in-house or contracting with an outside vendor to provide the training. Ensure that the outside course content matches the skills you want your people to acquire through the RFP procurement process. Evaluate the course every time a person in your organization takes it to ensure that it continues to contribute to acquiring the skills you need.

Metric 34.10: Evaluation: a metric with multiple components evaluating different aspects of the course, such as content, assignments, appropriate level, instructor's competence, and so on

Target 34.10: An evaluation within control limits on the appropriate control charts for similar courses

---

A critical risk in OO software projects is that you will have inadequate skills for the job. Mostly this is due to lack of either experience, training, or standards. Only time will help experience or standardization, but you can do something about the training.

Acquiring a training course takes one of two routes. You should always look into the available training offerings in the marketplace before developing your own courses to teach skills to your people. Your RFP should describe the skills you want your people to learn and the degree of proficiency in each that you expect the course to reach. Your standard procurement process should then evaluate the resulting bids for acceptability and cost effectiveness. If none of the outside offerings provide what you need at a reasonable price, you then must consider developing your own training course for the skill. You can schedule people for courses either at your site or at the site of the training company or institution.

■ *Note:* I've found that SIGS Publications' *Object Magazine* is a good source of potential training courses, especially in their bimonthly Object Marketplace pullout section and their special annual OO training section. Also check out the directory of object technology on their Web site at http://www.sigs.com/omo. The *Journal of Object-Oriented Programming* is similarly useful.

Training courses come in various formats:

- Lectures
- Seminars
- Boot camps (full-immersion, interactive experiences) [Booch 1996, p. 217]
- Conference tutorial sessions
- Laboratory courses (particularly suitable for tools and programming)
- Video courses (also very suitable for tools)
- Computer-based training (CBT, also very suitable for tools; also includes both written and interactive tutorials available with most tools)
- Paper-based books, periodicals, and tutorials

You need to decide what kind of training course would be the most effective in terms of both cost and content delivery. For anything that requires computer interaction, lab and CBT courses are better. The problem with these courses is that often they do not deliver the degree of proficiency you need. Lecture courses deliver the proficiency but don't give you the practice.

■ *Note:* If you select a lecture course, ensure that it has homework exercises and projects. Stress to people taking the course that they will learn more if they do the exercises. Give them specific time at work to do this, putting your money where your mouth is.

You should set proper expectations for proficiency acquisition. Goldberg and Rubin report that achieving functional or expert proficiency in most OO-related subjects takes 6 to 12 months of work [Goldberg, pp. 406–408]. You should not expect this level of proficiency from taking a single course but from an extended exposure to both course material and work that uses it.

■ *Note:* A common failing in many software companies is to train their people and then to ignore the training by assigning them to tasks that don't use the training. This rapidly obsolesces the training, rendering it worthless.

There are many potential subjects for OO projects:
- OO concepts
- OO analysis and modeling
- OO design, focusing on designing reusable systems
- Framework design
- Development environment tool training, including programming language training
- Project management training with a focus on OO software processes
- Framework and object model reuse
- OO database management systems
- Measuring OO software project processes and artifacts

Certifying a course requires an analysis of the risk that it will fail to deliver the course content in an effective manner. Evaluations help here, of both the course and the instructor. If you sign up for a course without such certification, consider risk management methods such as supplementary materials on the subject, previewing the course, or a money-back guarantee of satisfaction. Make sure that you have a full description, or syllabus, of the course, and that the syllabus clearly describes the course content, its teaching goals, and the level of proficiency you are expected to achieve through the course. Finally, make sure you understand who is responsible for maintaining the course quality and currency. It's never a bad idea to insist on a money-back guarantee of satisfaction for outside courses.

Sharing the course is the process of using it to train people. The first thing you have to do is make sure that everyone in your organization is aware of the certified courses available and what skills they teach. If you have a repository of reusable skills, people can look up skills they want to learn. Through the repository, they can then access the list of courses that teach those skills. You should provide a mechanism in your repository of signing up for courses and recording the results. That is, when a person takes a course, the course instructor should report back to the project the grade for the person (a simple pass/fail is sufficient).

■ *Note:* It is vital that taking a training course be a fully integrated project task. That is, you *must* pay people to take a course designed to improve their skills. This requirement does not include courses that people take for educational or career development purposes, only courses that teach skills your project is going to use. If you don't pay people, you are sending the message that the training is worthless, or, worse, that the skills are worthless.

Maintaining the course requires a constant evaluation and evolution of the course materials. Anyone who takes the course should complete an evaluation and store it in the repository as part of the course certification. You should periodically inspect these to ensure that the courses remain current and certifiable. If the courses are in-house, you should ensure that someone has the responsibility to maintain the course materials to keep them current.

The best courses I've taken are the one- or two-day seminars on specific subjects. DeMarco and Lister's course on Peopleware [DeMarco 1987] and controlling software projects stands out in my memory as one such seminar. The impact of a great teacher and focused material can be dramatic.

The worst courses I've taken have been lecture courses taught by academics. For some reason, university professors hardly ever learn basic teaching skills. To make extra money on the side, many teach university extension or public courses in their subject area. These courses are nearly always terrible, in my experience. I've actually taught classes like this myself. While a lecture can be effective, it is not the best way to present anything but theory and concepts. Successful ones make it through their level of interaction and their assignments. For example, most classes in project management now resemble lab courses more than lecture courses by redoing their lecture formats to include extensive group exercises in class. This gets people involved instead of just having them listen to a talking head.

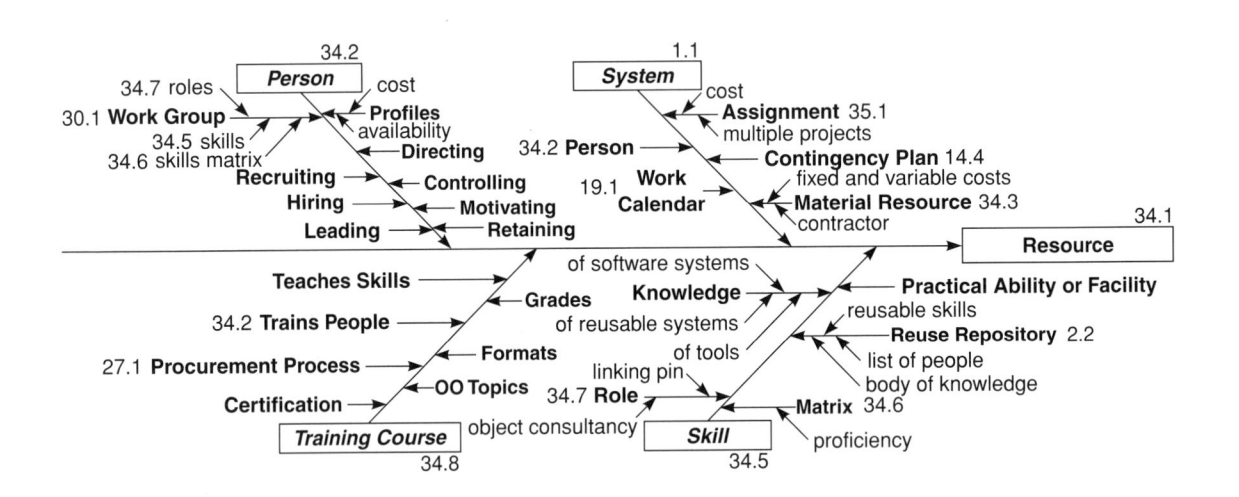

Readings

[Booch 1996]   Grady Booch. *Object Solutions: Managing the Object-Oriented Project.* Reading, MA: Addison-Wesley, 1996.

Booch has an excellent chapter on people and teams. Along with Goldberg, this book identifies the skills and roles most appropriate for OO projects. He puts a bit too much faith in the role of the architect for my taste; I prefer the vision of the system to come from the stakeholders, not the architect. But then, I like to live in my house, not stand outside looking at it in awe of its beauty.

[Goldberg]   Adele Goldberg and Kenneth S. Rubin. *Succeeding with Objects: Decision Frameworks for Project Management.* Reading, MA: Addison-Wesley, 1995.

Goldberg and Rubin have two chapters on training, one a general analysis of the issues and the other a framework for setting up a training program. They clearly identify the specific OO training you should have available to your staff. The book also has an extensive section on roles in teams, although I'm not convinced by the specifics. They define "role" as a set of activities that a person performs rather than as a set of skills, and it gets a bit confusing as you proceed through their examples.

[Kerzner]   Harold Kerzner. *Project Management: A Systems Approach to Planning, Scheduling, and Controlling, Fifth Edition.* New York: Van Nostrand Reinhold, 1994.

Section 4.3 of Kerzner has a nice analysis of the skills a project manager needs: team-building, leadership, conflict resolution, technical, planning, organization, entrepreneurial, administrative, management, and resource allocation skills. Whew. And here I was thinking all I needed to know was MS Project!

[Licker]   Paul S. Licker. *The Art of Managing Software Development People.* New York: Wiley, 1985.

Licker's is the best book on the techniques of management. It provides a comprehensive, well-written overview of the different things you are expected to do as a programmer manager. I usually refer to this book when I want a concise summary of all the things I should be looking at doing (controlling, directing, counseling, and so on). Licker's section on motivation is one of the best I've read.

[Metzger]   Philip W. Metzger. *Managing Programming People: A Personal View.* Englewood Cliffs, NJ: Prentice Hall, 1987.

This is one of my favorite software development management books. While it contributes very little from the OO perspective, Metzger's suggestions for managing are so well phrased and contain so much common sense that I won't hesitate to recommend the book. The illustrations from Daumier are probably worth the price of the book.

[Page-Jones]   Meilir Page-Jones. *Practical Project Management: Restoring Quality to DP Projects and Systems.* New York: Dorset House, 1985.

Page-Jones's book is wonderfully written and full of good, general advice for software projects. In particular, his Section III, entitled "People: A DP Department's Greatest Resource," is one of my greatest resources in helping me to manage people well. His section on failure and firing people is invaluable.

[Weinberg 1992] Gerald M. Weinberg. *Quality Software Management: Volume 1, Systems Thinking.* New York: Dorset House, 1992.

[Weinberg 1993] Gerald M. Weinberg. *Quality Software Management: Volume 2, First-Order Measurement.* New York: Dorset House, 1993.

[Weinberg 1994] Gerald M. Weinberg. *Quality Software Management: Volume 3, Congruent Action.* New York: Dorset House, 1994.

These books provide real insight into both the social and psychological aspects of congruent managing, taking action to move the project toward its mission and vision based on feedback from the situation. Volume 1 is all about how to get feedback going, while Volume 3 is about how to generate the appropriate actions: how to be an effective manager. Volume 2 connects the two with a theory of observation and integration of feedback through measurement. Anyone serious about managing people in software organizations should have this set of books.

Questions to Think About

1. Why are resources defined as contributing cost rather than value to the project?
2. List some alternatives to using recruiters for hiring OO people.
3. Do you think the pay premiums for the different kinds of skills in the marketplace reflect the actual hiring needs of companies doing OO projects? Why or why not?
4. List some roadblocks you've experienced in OO projects. What could your manager have done to remove those roadblocks? If this wasn't done, why not? Are there circumstances in which it is better to have a roadblock than the alternative?
5. What skills do you think an application domain expert should have? (Hint: Knowledge is not enough.)
6. Would you prefer to go outside your organization for training or use video or computer-based training? Why?
7. List some criteria that you might use to evaluate internal and external courses.

CHAPTER

Resource Assignment 35

The Assignment

The relationship between a resource and a task is an *assignment*. The assignment is a versioned system. Assignments to work groups appear in the organization's responsibility matrix and in the staffing plan for the project. Every assignment has a cost estimate that forecasts how much cost the resource will contribute to the task.

Assignments to work groups or people have effort estimates that forecast how much effort each resource will spend on the task. If there is an effort estimate, the cost estimate is the result of multiplying the effort by the cost profile of the resource based on the current schedule baseline; otherwise, it is the cost of the resource multiplied by the units or just the fixed cost of the resource.

Vision: Work distributed through the organization optimizing the effort and cost of the project

Mission: To enable the cost-effective delivery of a task's products

Objective 35.1: To enable delivery of task products

Approach 35.1: Relate the task to the resources that task requires to deliver its products, planning through the staffing plan and mapping the skills required for the task to the resource skills. Estimate the cost and effort the assignment will require. Adjust the availability of the resource in the resource work calendar as you allocate the resource to tasks.

Metric 35.1: Success: an ordinal, subjective measure of how successful the assignment was; the evaluation should be by whoever has responsibility for the task; values Unsuccessful, Barely Successful, Moderately Successful, Highly Successful, and Beyond Expectations

Target 35.1: Moderately Successful; you can use control charts of similar assignments, or assignments to the specific resource, to evaluate the stability of the assignment process

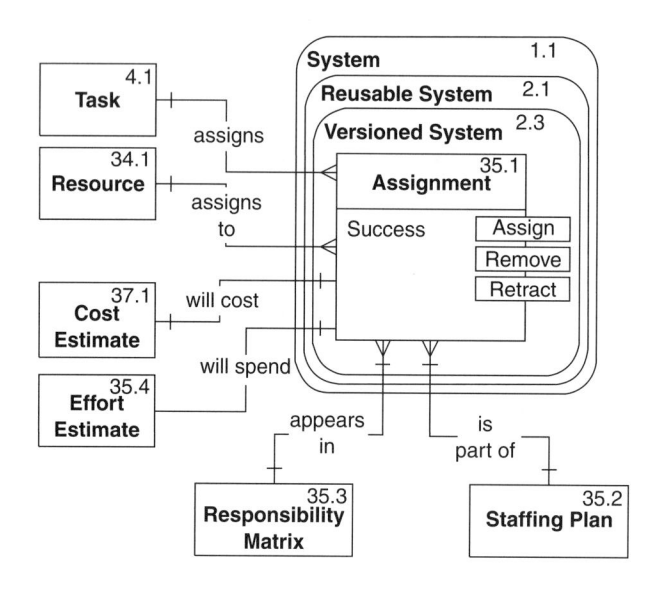

There are many different kinds of assignment, and the classification scheme you use depends on your specific resource management needs.

■ *Note:* Every project management system has a completely different scheme for categorizing assignments, and the schemes appear to be largely incompatible. Most of these schemes represent different approaches to ordering schedule tasks using resource-driven scheduling or resource leveling.

One variation on the assignment is to assign work to roles instead of to resources. That is, when a work group distributes work in the group, the manager allocates the work on a role basis, and whatever person fills the role takes responsibility for the work. This is slightly more ambiguous than assigning to people, because a person can take multiple roles in a project and because multiple people can fill a role in a group. If you are using assignments to control work by people, you should assign work to people; if you are concerned only about responsibility, you can use role assignments.

You must specify whether people need to work on the task simultaneously or can work separately at different times. This can dramatically affect the scheduling of the task, particularly if the people work in different time zones. I managed a team with members in both the U.K. and California, with multiple team members assigned to the same task. For example, freezing a cluster would be done on both sides of the Atlantic simultaneously, requiring work by two team members. I discovered a major flaw in my project management system, Scitor's Project Scheduler 6, when I tried to schedule people for these tasks. The software assumed that if you assign two people to the same task, they both must work at the same time. Because the work calendars overlapped by only an hour, given the time difference, the resource-leveling feature delayed the task three years into the future before I stopped it. Even basic time zone support would make this easier, but the tools I've used haven't had even this.

More common resource constraints on assignments include interdependencies between resources, conflicts between assignments for a resource, mutual exclusion (rare), issues with skills and substitution of other resources, and resource availability. In particular, if your assignments are contingent work-flow assignments with retraction, your resource contingency plans should ensure the availability of resources with appropriate skills to complete the task if the assigned resource cannot.

Work-Flow Model (5.1)

The metric for success of the assignment (Metric 35.1) has nothing to do with the success of the task. From the manager's perspective, you cannot evaluate the success of the people assigned to a task by the success of the task as a whole. The failure of a resource to do its job is only one possible reason for the failure of a task. You could have assigned a person to the task with the wrong skills or proficiency. You could have failed to assign enough resources to the task. The task could have been impossible for technical reasons. In sum, evaluate the assignment on its own merits, not on the ultimate delivery. Assignments enable delivery, not guarantee it.

I worked on a complex OO system that used an extensive and very buggy framework. One assignment was to implement the dialogs for opening and closing the database for the application, replacing the standard File Open and File Close dialogs. As time dragged on, I kept crashing the system over and over every time I tried to display my simple Open Database dialog. I worked with the framework expert over a two-week period to resolve the problem, to no avail. I did figure out the source of the problem, however. The framework interacted with the windowing system at a very low level. It apparently inserted itself in the standard system dialogs for File Open in such a way that you could not replace that particular dialog.

Now, up to this point, this was a technical problem. The effort estimate on this assignment was about two days, and it took three weeks to get to the point of determining that we would not be able to do what the functional specification called for. The director of development and the chief architect of the system decided that despite our demonstrating that the framework was at fault, the failure of the task was a result of my team's lack of loyalty to them, personally. Their view seemed to be that failure was always the result of bad work and evil political intentions, not hard problems. On reflection, I think this mirrored the cultural attitude of the larger company, which I did not understand at the time. The effect of blaming was to reduce our motivation to do other tasks and to reduce our trust in management.

Given the effort estimate, you calculate the cost estimate using the cost profile for the resource. If this is not a person but a material resource, you estimate the cost directly from the number of units you forecast having to use or from the fixed cost of the resource, whichever applies.

The Staffing Plan

The *staffing plan* is a plan that describes how and when you will bring people and work groups into the project organization, how you intend to assign the high-level tasks of the project to work groups, and how you will reassign those people and groups as the project no longer needs them. The staffing plan is a component of the project plan and a result of a standard staffing process model.

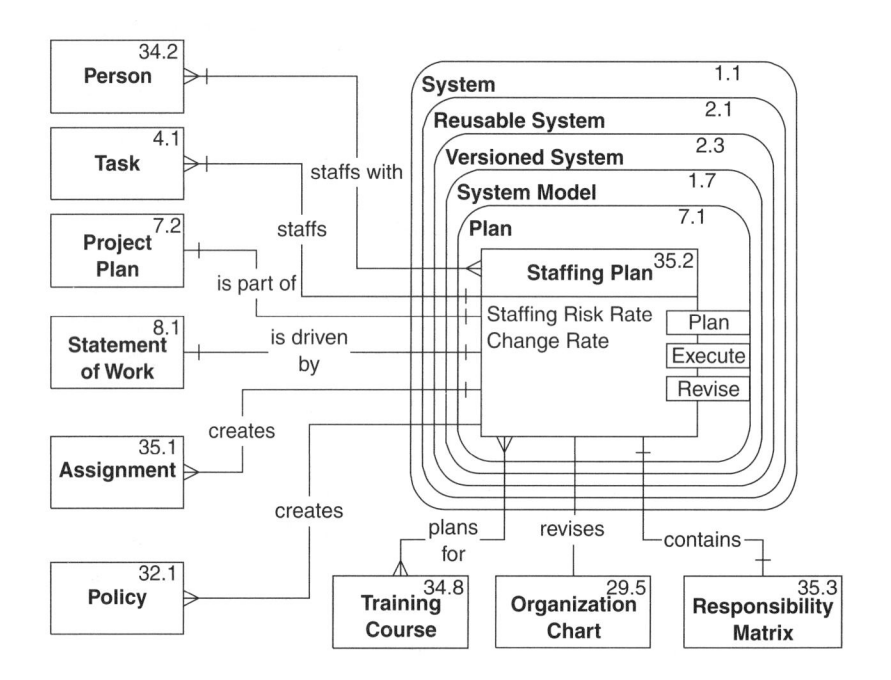

Vision: A staffing process brought to a successful conclusion, providing you with the resources you need to complete the project

Mission: To bring the staffing process model for a project to bear on acquiring the resources you need to successfully achieve the project mission

---

Objective 35.2: To translate a staffing process model into a set of tasks that is likely to provide you with the resources you need for the project

---

Approach 35.2: Set the risk tolerance of the staffing process. Generate a plan from the staffing process model, managing and validating its risks. The resulting plan should include a detailed list of resources you require based on the statement of work, a set of tasks that acquire the resources, a set of high-level assignments of the work breakdown structure to work groups, any needed organizational

The Staffing Plan 595

policies, a detailed training plan, and a clear disposition of resources no longer required. You should produce or version the project organization chart as an output of the planning process. You also must produce the project responsibility matrix. Execute the staffing plan and collect feedback to improve it.

Metric 35.2: Staffing Risk Rate: rate of change of staffing process risk relative to planning effort

Target 35.2: A rate of change that brings the process risk below the risk tolerance of the process in a reasonable time with a reasonable amount of effort

---

Objective 35.3: To provide a mechanism for accommodating staffing changes as the project progresses

---

Approach 35.3: As you execute the project and the staffing plan, collect feedback. As the project changes to require a different set of resources, version the plan, include the new tasks in the work breakdown structure, and execute the plan.

Metric 35.3: Change Rate: see Metric 7.2

The staffing plan deals with assignments to specific resources in the aggregate. It helps to make resource allocation efficient and to improve morale through reducing uncertainty about employment. You should include plans for assigning people to the project on a *contingency* basis as you develop those needs through the risk management plan. You should also include a section on resource development, and especially a training plan that makes reference to the training courses in your reuse repository.

In small-to-medium-sized projects, your staffing plan should show the allocation of resources to roles within work groups based on the required skills for the roles and the skills of the resources. It is during this process that you can make the best use of the reusable skills in your reuse repository. You should also build the resource work calendars and their availability profiles as you complete the resource assignment process. Finally, you should complete a responsibility matrix for the project that shows the high-level assignment of responsibility for WBS tasks to work groups.   **Skill (34.5)**

For larger projects, you cannot plan in this level of detail at the project level. The staffing plan for the large project focuses on the aggregate number of effort-hours that pieces of the project will take and the aggregate resource needs over time, usually specified with a histogram [PMI 1996a, p. 97]. Your responsibility matrix should contain at least the high-level assignments of responsibility to work groups. You should then delegate the specifics of work-group organization and planning to the middle- and low-level managers in charge of the groups. You must coordinate the results of all this delegated planning to ensure that the project plan as a whole reflects the plans of the groups.

You must generate the staffing plan in an iterative process as you complete the other parts of the project plan. These other parts add tasks to the work breakdown structure, which in turn drives the staffing plan as you estimate resource requirements for the tasks. You may have to revise the structure of your organization as your resource load grows, both to reduce the size of work groups to manageable proportions and to accommodate changes in the structure of the work. This will be especially true if you have a projectized organization driven by the architecture of the system you are producing. As this architecture changes, your resource needs and organizational structure will change.

The staffing plan will usually begin with the current organization unless you are building one from scratch, never a good idea if you can avoid it. Depending on your organizational structure, you may have to reorganize an existing organization extensively. In any case, the staffing plan versions the organization chart and the different work groups that you are reusing.

You can reuse a staffing plan in two different circumstances. First, if your project is a maintenance or minor product version project, the chances are good that your current organization and staffing plan will do the job. Second, if your organization has a series of projects that are pretty much the same, as in a software factory, MIS shop, or consulting organization, you may be able to reuse your staffing plan as the projects all look pretty much the same. Otherwise, the most reuse you'll be able to get for the staffing plan is the versioning you do as your resource requirements grow and shrink.

The Responsibility Matrix

A *responsibility matrix* is a two-dimensional chart tool that shows the responsibility relationships between resources in the organization chart and tasks in the WBS. The responsibility matrix, which is part of the staffing plan, shows which resource is directly responsible for which task. Usually this translates into showing some or all of the assignments in the project.

Vision: Resources working on the project with commitment to clear lines of responsibility and authority

Mission: To show which resources take what responsibility for project work

Objective 35.4: To show which resources take responsibility for project work

Approach 35.4: Create a matrix with tasks in the work breakdown structure as rows and work groups and/or people from the organization chart in the project as columns. Show the assignment of the task to a resource by marking the corresponding cell.

The Responsibility Matrix

Metric 35.4: Completeness: the ratio of filled-in cells to the total number of work assignments in the project; you can normalize the total assignment number by the granularity of your matrix (see text)

Target 35.4: One

Objective 35.5: To show what responsibility resources take for project work

---

Approach 35.5: Create the matrix as in Approach 35.5. Create a nominal metric that describes the types of responsibility in your project. For each assignment cell in the matrix, assign one or more codes using this metric to show the type of responsibility.

Metric 35.5: Responsibility failures: the number of problems that arise from a missing responsibility in the responsibility matrix

Target 35.5: A low number within control limits of a pn control chart of failures

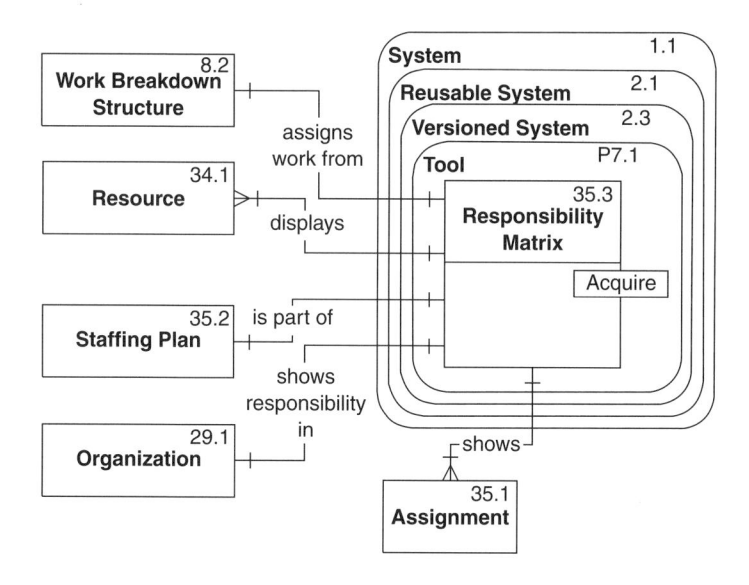

While you can get a grasp of the basic authority and responsibility structures in an organization by looking at the organization chart, that format does not relate responsibility to the actual project work. Especially with a matrix organization, the lines of responsibility may be much more complex than the organization structure suggests. The responsibility matrix can contribute greatly to your understanding of the spectrum of responsibility in the project [Cleland 1983, pp. 303–305]. If you develop this matrix with the work groups that appear in it as part of the planning process, you can increase both the commitment of those groups to the work and the amount of communication about responsibility for work.

■ *Note:* The simpler and more direct your responsibility structure, the better, in my opinion. One of the reasons I recommend the projectized organization for OO development projects is the clarity it brings to the responsibility matrix.

The granularity of the matrix depends entirely on how you intend to use it. You might have a small-to-medium-sized project. You might have a matrix organization with very complex relationships between the functional groups and the project work. Given either of these scenarios, you may want to list all the people participating in the project along the top of the matrix and all the simple tasks in the WBS along the side. If you have a large project, this matrix would be impossible to use to any effect because it would have too many cells for you to easily trace relationships. You may only be interested in the broad distribution of responsibility to work groups. In these scenarios, you can get away with work-group resources along the top and the major complex tasks (design deliverable, test deliverable, and so on) along the side.

■ *Note:* A matrix halfway between these alternatives might show the work groups and the roles within the work groups instead of the individual people. You would use this style if you assign work to roles instead of to people.

Figure 35-1 shows an example of a responsibility matrix for the WBS example in Chapter 8. In this instance, there are three kinds of responsibility. The triangle symbol stands for approval authority: the resource must approve the results of the task at the process milestone. The circle stands for delivery responsibility: the

Figure 35-1
High-level responsibility matrix for DTS project

Legend
△ Approval
○ Delivery
◇ Support

	Project Office	Product Manager	DTS Group	Person Group	Product Group	Problem Group	Tools Group	Docs Group
DTS-1 Analyze Feasibility	○	△						
DTS-2 Plan	○	△						
DTS-3 Develop DTS.EXE	△		○	◇	◇	◇	◇	
DTS-4 Develop PERSON.DLL	△			○			◇	
DTS-5 Develop PRODUCT.DLL	△				○		◇	
DTS-6 Develop PROBLEM.DLL	△			◇	◇	○	◇	
DTS-7 Develop DTSTOOLS.DLL	△						○	
DTS-8 Create User's Guide	△	△	◇	◇	◇	◇	◇	○

resource must deliver the results of the task at the process milestone. The diamond stands for support responsibility: the resource must be prepared to help in delivering. This diagram thus shows how each of the major work groups in the project relates to the tasks. The project office determines project feasibility and plans the project, with the approval of the product manager. The product manager has no delivery responsibilities in the project. The main development tasks (DTS-3 through DTS-8) are the delivery responsibility of a group devoted to that subsystem (a projectized organization). The supporting responsibilities show how the different groups help each other to integrate the system. For example, since all the other subsystems depend on the tools subsystem, the tools group must help all the other groups on all the development tasks. Similarly, since the user's guide is about the whole system, all the development groups must be prepared to help the writers with the guide.

"The Work Breakdown Structure" section, Chapter 8, p. 144

The responsibility matrix gets its reuse potential from the reuse potential of its parts, the work breakdown structure and the set of resources. If you can reuse both of those, you should be able to reuse the responsibility matrix for them. If not, not. In either case, you should certify the responsibility matrix as part of the certification of the staffing plan.

The Effort Estimate

An *effort estimate* is a versioned, quantitative statement of the labor effort that a particular assignment requires. This is a versioned object to enable you to baseline effort estimates and to change and track them as you learn more about the actual resource needs of the task.

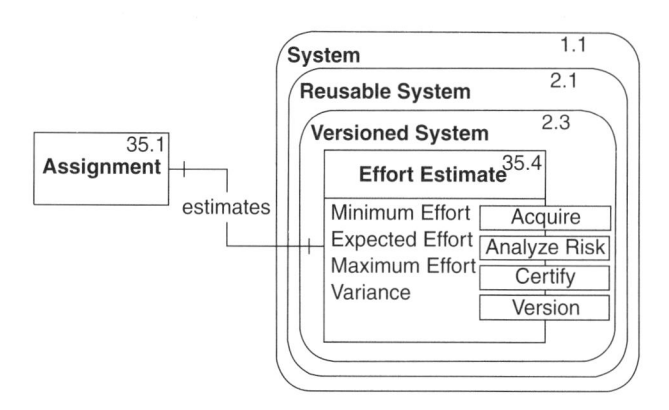

Vision: A project delivered on time and under budget

Mission: To estimate the amount of effort required to complete a work assignment by a single resource

> **Objective 35.6:** To estimate the amount of effort required to complete a work assignment by a single resource
>
> **Approach 35.6:** Ask the resource for the minimum, expected, and maximum number of work-hours they expect the assignment to take. Validate the estimate and adjust it using risk management methods. Track the assignment and record the actual number of work-hours it takes.
>
> **Metric 35.6:** Variance: the expected estimated work-hours minus the actual work-hours at the completion of the assignment
>
> **Target 35.6:** A small variance within control limits of an x-R control chart

The assignment effort estimate is a *bottom-up* effort estimate [Boehm 1981, pp. 338–341]. A *top-down* effort estimate is the estimate you attach to a deliverable system, usually based on its size and various cost-driver factors [Boehm 1981; DeMarco 1982; Fenton; Jones 1991]. As Henderson-Sellers notes, the parametric models that you use to estimate effort and cost at the deliverable level are not very good at this time [Henderson-Sellers 1996, p. 48]. They do not explain very much variance, and they depend on factors that vary widely in different organizations and projects. In particular, none of these models has yet to take the special requirements of OO projects into account. You can use tools such as COCOMO, SPQR, SLIM, and CHECKPOINT to develop cost and effort estimates, but your best use for them in OO projects is as a WAG (wild-ass guess) benchmark to which to compare your bottom-up estimates. If the benchmark differs greatly from your project estimates, you need to reexamine your assumptions.

For example, on one OO project, I used the basic COCOMO model [Boehm 1981] configured for my type of organization to estimate the scope of an OO project. The bottom-up estimates from the developers summed to about one work-year of effort. The COCOMO model, based on an estimate of lines of C++ code, came in at about three work-years of effort for an organization of our size. I went back and realized the developers had not included the testing time for the classes in their estimates, easily doubling their estimates to 2.5 work-years. Testing was not a top priority in this organization, but COCOMO assumes the full validation and verification testing of a defense project in the basic model.

The biggest problem with top-down estimates is their lack of information. By their very nature, they cannot take into account factors such as productivity of individual resources, technical difficulty, and other issues relating to the specifics of each assignment. The best you can hope for is that a combination of the law of large numbers and dumb luck (excuse me, probability theory) will somehow wipe out the variance. This may work for diversifying stock portfolios [Bernstein], but it certainly doesn't work for software estimation [Boehm 1981].

You generally do a bottom-up estimate by getting the assigned resources to give you an estimate. It's a good idea to get the minimum and maximum estimate as well as the expected value. For example, if you ask a developer for an estimate for a coding task, the developer should tell you how many work-hours he or she expects it to take, but also the least and most work-hours it could take. This lets you do some risk analysis and management on the assignment if necessary. Getting some kind of consensus estimate from several sources can yield better end results, but can take quite a bit more work.

There are two common problems with this approach [DeMarco 1982, pp. 33–34]. First, people aren't dumb, right? If you ask someone to estimate how long it will take to do something, he or she will pad the estimates so as not to work hard. If you're working in this kind of culture, estimating isn't going to help, so I wouldn't bother doing it. Just tell people how long it will take to do the task; you'll do just as well in the end. You won't get the work done any faster, but you'll have the satisfaction of knowing that you saved your people from having to make bad estimates. If you work in a Steering culture or one where people take responsibility for their work, they will do their best to estimate correctly, and they will improve their estimates with improvement plans over time.

Second, whatever people estimate, the resulting sum will be too much for the stakeholders, and especially for the project sponsor. The market being what it is, "earlier is better than later," as one not-too-successful CEO put it. In other words, upper management or your boss will insist that the estimates are too high and that they need the project done long before the estimates suggest it will be done. Tom DeMarco has a good line of jokes about this situation. Ultimately, you pays your money and you takes your choice. The right thing to do is to find ways to eliminate work or risk to accelerate the end date of the project. The wrong thing to do is to just reduce the effort estimates. I've seen that done many times, and reality always wins.

The best way to improve estimates in your organization is to do some statistical modeling [Boehm 1921]. After reviewing the literature on estimation and its mathematics, use nonlinear regression and other statistical modeling methods using a statistical package such as SAS or SPSS to develop models that your people can use to estimate their assignments. If your models have no real ability to explain the variance in the estimates, you should immediately undertake an improvement plan to improve estimation, as your estimating is definitely not under statistical control. You should look at both data collection issues and the root causes of bad estimates to determine a new approach, as both contribute heavily to bad estimation.

- *Note:* Effort estimation is not cost estimation. Cost estimates usually apply at the project or subsystem level, not at the assignment level. As the section above on assignments discusses, you get detailed cost estimates for an assignment by multiplying the effort estimates by the cost profiles of the resources given the schedule for the task. Cost estimates for the project generally come from statistical models you apply at the project level given various cost drivers, as bottom-up cost estimating can yield results with entirely too much variance. Cost Estimate (37.1)

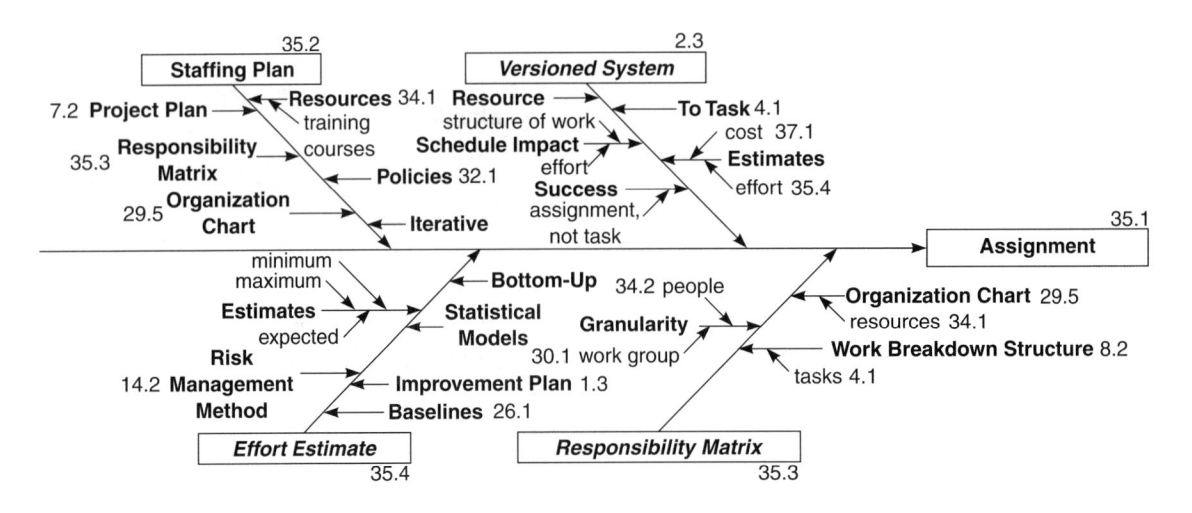

```
                    35.2                    2.3
            ┌─────────────┐         ┌─────────────────┐
            │Staffing Plan│         │Versioned System │
            └─────────────┘         └─────────────────┘
                  ↘ Resources 34.1   Resource      ↙
  7.2 Project Plan →  training       structure of work  → To Task 4.1
                       courses       Schedule Impact ↘     cost 37.1
      Responsibility ↙               effort              ← Estimates
  35.3  Matrix       ← Policies 32.1 Success ↗             effort 35.4
      Organization                   assignment,                                    35.1
  29.5  Chart        ← Iterative     not task                              ┌────────────┐
  ─────────────────────────────────────────────────────────────────────────→│ Assignment │
                 minimum                                                    └────────────┘
                 maximum ↘    ← Bottom-Up  34.2 people
              Estimates →      Statistical     Granularity ↙  ← Organization Chart 29.5
                 expected ↗    Models                            resources 34.1
        Risk                            30.1 work group ↗      ← Work Breakdown Structure 8.2
  14.2 Management          ← Improvement Plan 1.3              tasks 4.1
        Method             ← Baselines 26.1
            ┌────────────────┐             ┌──────────────────────┐
            │Effort Estimate │             │Responsibility Matrix │
            └────────────────┘             └──────────────────────┘
                    35.4                             35.3
```

Readings

Unfortunately, there are very few detailed readings on the material in this chapter. More attention to resource assignments in the project management literature might help project managers get a better understanding of how assignments contribute to the success of their projects.

[Albrecht]   Allan J. Albrecht and John E. Gaffney, Jr. Software function, source lines of code, and development effort prediction: a software science validation. In [Reifer, pp. 218–227]. Originally published in *IEEE Transactions on Software Engineering* SE-9:6 (November 1983): 639–648.

This seminal article does some real statistics on function points, lines of code, and effort estimates. The correlations between function points and effort estimates come in at about 94%. The formula for estimating work-hours from function points is Work-Hours = 54 × Function Points – 13,390. Note that this applies to the software system as a whole, since function points only apply at that level.

[Badiru]   Adedeji B. Badiru. Activity-resource assignments using critical resource diagramming. *Project Management Journal* 24:3 (September 1993): 15–21.

This article presents an interesting, innovative way to look at resources and resource assignments using tools similar to critical path analysis and Gantt charting.

[Boehm 1981]   Barry W. Boehm. *Software Engineering Economics.* Englewood Cliffs, NJ: Prentice Hall, 1981.

Boehm has a very good chapter on alternative models of estimation that includes material on bottom-up estimating (Chapter 22). In general, Boehm gives you a clear idea of what you can do in estimation with reasonably sophisticated statistical tools such as nonlinear regression.

[Champeaux]　　Dennis de Champeaux. *Object-Oriented Development Processes and Metrics.* Englewood Cliffs, NJ: Prentice Hall, 1997 (published in 1996).

Champeaux introduces some interesting algorithms for estimating effort for the various stages of development in an OO project. His methods use artifacts from previous stages and some guesses about constants and multipliers to give you formulas for estimation. The methods do make some assumptions about the specific artifacts you generate and hence about your OO methods, and there is no indication of any empirical validation of the metrics.

[Cleland 1983]　　David I. Cleland and William R. King. *Systems Analysis and Project Management, Third Edition.* New York: McGraw-Hill, 1983.

This standard project management text provides an excellent section in Chapter 11 on responsibility matrices under the name "linear responsibility matrix."

[PMI 1996a]　　Project Management Institute Standards Committee. *A Guide to the Project Management Body of Knowledge.* Project Management Institute (+1-610-734-3330), 1996.

Section 7.1 of the PMBOK is on resource planning. Section 9.1 describes the organizational planning that results in the staffing plan, while Section 9.2 describes the staff acquisition process.

Questions to Think About

1. Why do many project managers drive schedules by the duration of the tasks instead of by the effort that the assignment of resources spends?

2. Examine your preferred project management system's assignment capabilities. How much of what is attached to the assignment is really a characteristic of the resource?

3. Say you were confronted with a project that had several tasks that no one in your organization had the skills to do. List some options for dealing with this situation in the staffing plan.

4. If you developed a very large responsibility matrix, what kinds of tools would allow you to manage and use it most effectively? (Hint: Word processor tables don't make it.)

5. Have you ever experienced a padded effort estimate from a resource? If so, why did the person pad it?

6. How might you use a statistical package to produce better estimates?

PART TWELVE

Cost

> Before we give you billions more, we want to know what you've done with the trillion you've got.
>
> Les Aspin, future defense secretary, in a letter to Caspar W. Weinberger, incumbent

The first thing to do when you begin to manage costs is to establish a chart of accounts. This system provides you with the structure you need to track costs effectively.

Given the chart of accounts, your next move is to establish a budget. Using the staffing plan and your projected need for material resources, you construct cost estimates with a cost estimation tool and build a cost budget. You then analyze how you intend to actually spend the money in your cost budget as cash over time to get the spending budget. Both of these budgets are your cost baselines for the project.

Having established a budget baseline, you build a cost management plan from your cost management process model. This lets you put tasks into the work breakdown structure for managing costs as your project proceeds. Your cost management system gives you the information you need to implement that plan, primarily reporting the earned-cost statistics and the estimated cost to complete the project.

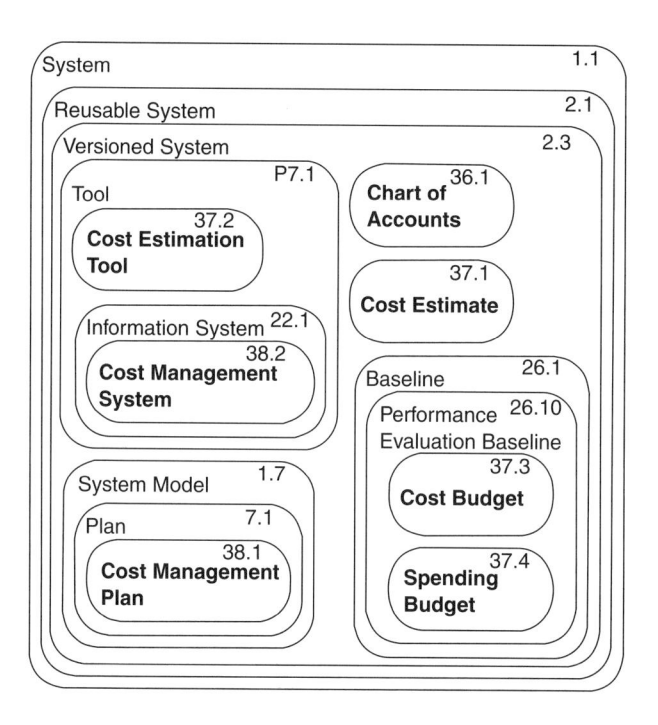

```
┌─ System ──────────────────────────── 1.1 ─┐
│ ┌─ Reusable System ─────────────── 2.1 ─┐ │
│ │ ┌─ Versioned System ─────────── 2.3 ─┐ │ │
│ │ │                         P7.1       │ │ │
│ │ │ ┌─ Tool ──────────┐  ┌─ 36.1 ───┐ │ │ │
│ │ │ │          37.2   │  │ Chart of │ │ │ │
│ │ │ │ Cost Estimation │  │ Accounts │ │ │ │
│ │ │ │ Tool            │  └──────────┘ │ │ │
│ │ │ └─────────────────┘               │ │ │
│ │ │                       ┌─ 37.1 ──┐ │ │ │
│ │ │ ┌─ Information System 22.1      │ │ │ │
│ │ │ │              38.2 │ │ Cost Estimate │ │
│ │ │ │ Cost Management   │ └─────────┘ │ │ │
│ │ │ │ System            │ ┌─ Baseline ── 26.1 ─┐ │
│ │ │ └───────────────────┘ │ Performance 26.10 │ │ │
│ │ │                       │ Evaluation Baseline│ │ │
│ │ │ ┌─ System Model  1.7 ┐│ ┌─ 37.3 ──────┐  │ │ │
│ │ │ │ ┌─ Plan ─── 7.1 ──┐││ │ Cost Budget │  │ │ │
│ │ │ │ │         38.1    │││ └─────────────┘  │ │ │
│ │ │ │ │ Cost Management │││ ┌─ 37.4 ──┐       │ │ │
│ │ │ │ │ Plan            │││ │ Spending│       │ │ │
│ │ │ │ └─────────────────┘││ │ Budget  │       │ │ │
│ │ │ └────────────────────┘│ └─────────┘       │ │ │
│ │ │                       └───────────────────┘ │ │
│ │ └────────────────────────────────────────────┘ │
│ └────────────────────────────────────────────────┘
└────────────────────────────────────────────────────┘
```

■ *Note:* The illustration of the class hierarchy contains all the classes this part defines. Other parts of the book define and discuss classes not in boldface.

605

CHAPTER

36 *The Chart of Accounts*

The *chart of accounts* for a project shows the accounting units from your general ledger to which you will allocate cost estimates and actual costs. You use these accounts by relating them to the tasks in the WBS, packaging the costs of those tasks into account transactions to the general ledger at the appropriate intervals.

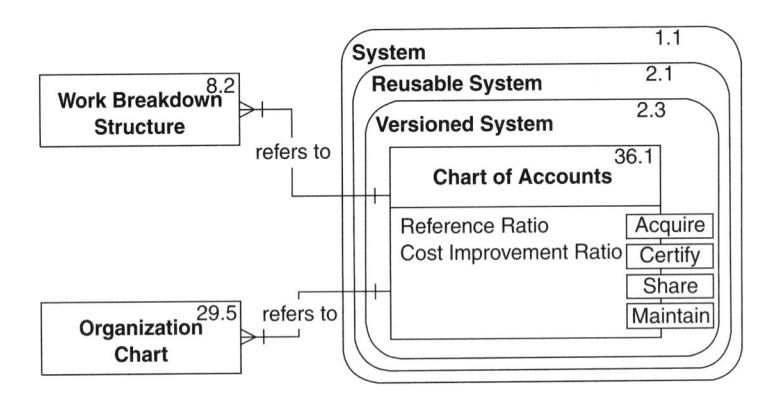

Vision: A project with clearly defined cost accounting

Mission: To provide information to an organization about the cost of its projects

---

Objective 36.1: To provide information to an organization about the cost of its projects to enable cost control or improvement efforts or to obtain reimbursement for costs

---

Approach 36.1: Establish a standard chart of accounts using generally accepted management accounting principles. Base each account on a need for control, improvement, or billing in your organization. That is, each account in the chart of accounts should exist only if it contributes to the mission of the chart of accounts. Bill the contracting organization for costs you accumulate in billable accounts.

Metric 36.1.1: Reference ratio: number of accounts referred to over the total number of accounts in the chart of accounts, where reference is for the purpose of control, improvement, or billing

Target 36.1.1: A relatively high number within control limits of a p control chart of projects using similar charts of accounts

---

Metric 36.1.2: Cost improvement ratio: the amount of money you've saved in the current project by tracking cost accounts

Target 36.1.2: A number sufficiently large to get a project manager a bonus or other reward

---

The major cost management system in the project management world today is the Cost/Schedule Control System Criteria (C/SCSC) system [Fleming]. The system does not propose a specific chart of accounts, but it does make very clear the relationship between the project and the chart of accounts.

Unfortunately, this relationship is perhaps too tight for OO software projects. Much of the project management literature assumes that the relationship between the work breakdown structure and the chart of accounts is one-to-one. This is definitely not true for the kind of work breakdown structure that this book proposes. Here's an example from the Department of Defense C/SCSC Implementation Guide, as quoted by Moder [Moder, p. 141]:

> The lowest level at which functional responsibility for individual WBS elements exists, actual costs are accumulated and performance measurement is conducted, is referred to as the cost account level. While it is usually located immediately above the work package level, cost accounts may be located at higher levels when in consonance with the contractor's method of management.

Now, while all this may have been true for the kind of hardware and construction projects that led to C/SCSC, this relationship is much too constraining for the OO software project. Because of the relationship between architecture and WBS structure, the OO software project uses WBS codes that reflect the structure of work, not the structure of cost. OO projects generally focus on managing work, not managing cost. Therefore, the chart of accounts, the purpose of which is to provide a framework for cost management, is orthogonal to the work breakdown structure.

Responsibility Matrix (35.3)

What C/SCSC tries to do is to equate the responsibility matrix with a "cost account matrix" that shows how individual WBS items accumulate cost to functional departments [Fleming, p. 57]. OO project management should keep these concepts separate, mapping cost and responsibility separately.

Another approach to the chart of accounts is the cost center approach [Kerzner]. Using the organization chart, you establish a hierarchical chart of accounts that establishes an account for each work group in the organization. For example, the engineering division might have the code 2000; structural engineering, 2600; mechanical engineering, 2620; and plastics engineering, 2621 [Kerzner, p. 808]. When you complete your assignments to the simple tasks of the project work breakdown structure, you have a series of cost accounts based on the work groups of the assignments. For example, if the client/server group and the GUI group both work on a work package, there are two cost accounts for work on the package. This lets you roll up the costs through the organizational structure.

The process goes a step further in budgeting. Each assignment budgets a certain cost, and then baselines the assignment. If you need more effort or materials for the work package, you must go through a change request [Kerzner].

The cost center approach is best applied to functional or matrix organizations that support the kind of organizational structure likely to benefit from this style of cost accounting. A projectized project might just as well use the WBS codes directly for this kind of accounting, as the structure should reflect the WBS. Again, while it is perfectly systematic, this approach probably is much more complex than the reasons behind cost accounting would suggest. Again, it is better to keep cost and responsibility separate through a mapping of WBS to cost account.

The result, for cost management, is the need to map the WBS codes to the chart of accounts. When you complete a task, you look up the account or accounts to which you must bill the cost. The more complex this relationship, the more difficult it is to manage cost, so keep it simple. The simplest format is to simply associate an account with each simple task in the WBS. When you finish a task, you accrue the money to the indicated cost account. If you need a more complex relationship, you need to establish a separate cost account matrix that maps assignments to cost accounts, perhaps even showing percentage accrual for each assignment to more than one account. This would be useful only for projects that involved highly bureaucratic billing structures and extensive government auditing.

I've worked on about 15 or 20 software development projects in small-to-medium-sized software companies during my career. Not one of them had any structure for billing work to accounts. The most complex cost accounting had one purpose: to accumulate software development expense as an asset. This is an accounting trick that software companies use to inflate their balance sheet by accumulating cost as assets that ought to be expensed. Not one company cared anything about the costs associated with their software projects, only the general operating budget of the development organization as a whole. You may draw your own conclusions from this. I will say that any reference to "cost estimation" in such an organization is at best misleading.

- *Note:* Only when working for myself have I tracked costs and billed to the contracting organization. In particular, government work involves such billings and requires this kind of accounting in great detail for large projects. To improve your success in such projects, you need to increase the size of the project to the point where the mind boggles, such as the IRS tax tracking systems or the FAA flight control software. You should then be able to avoid cost tracking to any significant degree, to the mutual benefit of your company and the contracting agency, if not necessarily the taxpayer—or the passenger. (A joke.)

What kind of accounts might be helpful in controlling costs? The first and foremost are those that you can use to track earned cost/value. All the project management systems I've used that support C/SCSC or earned value associate these values with the tasks of the project. A more sophisticated approach would collect cost data to look at earned cost for accounts that mean something to your cost containment or improvement efforts. If your work breakdown structure accurately reflects all of your concerns about the way to control costs, then accumulating costs along these lines is adequate; otherwise, you lose information.

"The Project Deliverables and System Earned Value" section, Chapter 3, p. 67

Second, you must collect costs for accounts specified by the Cost Accounting Standards Board, at least if you're dealing with the federal government. You can get reimbursement only for costs you can document according to these standards.

Third, you should collect costs that are necessary to cost-benefit analyses. If you have real data on what it cost the last time, you can much more accurately estimate the costs in your cost-benefit analysis for the next time around. If you don't have costs on the appropriate level, you can only estimate them, which is never as accurate as real history.

Fourth, most costs in software projects are labor costs. Most labor costs in turn depend on productivity. Productivity depends on reuse. Therefore, if you really want to save costs, you should study your cost patterns to discover places that cost a lot but don't reuse software. You should then find ways to improve that situation. This analysis suggests that your cost accounts should divide up along lines that relate to system reuse. Where you suspect you could find a category of reusable systems, establish a hierarchy of accounts.

For example, you might suspect that your object model is the source of a good deal of wasted cost through lack of reuse and rework. As each project proceeds, you notice that the WBS has many more tasks for object modeling and client/server development for object persistence than any other part of the project. By establishing an object model account, you can track the actual costs put into object modeling versus other work on the project. As you introduce reusable application clusters and an OODBMS, you track the resulting costs and see that they are much less than the previous architecture produced. You can then prove to the project sponsor that your innovations are seriously benefiting the organization.

Fifth, and finally, you might consider tracking the costs of the systems approach. That is, track the costs of your improvement plans, process modeling, and other aspects of the overhead of running a project based on the ideas in this book. If you're spending more on improving than producing, ease up.

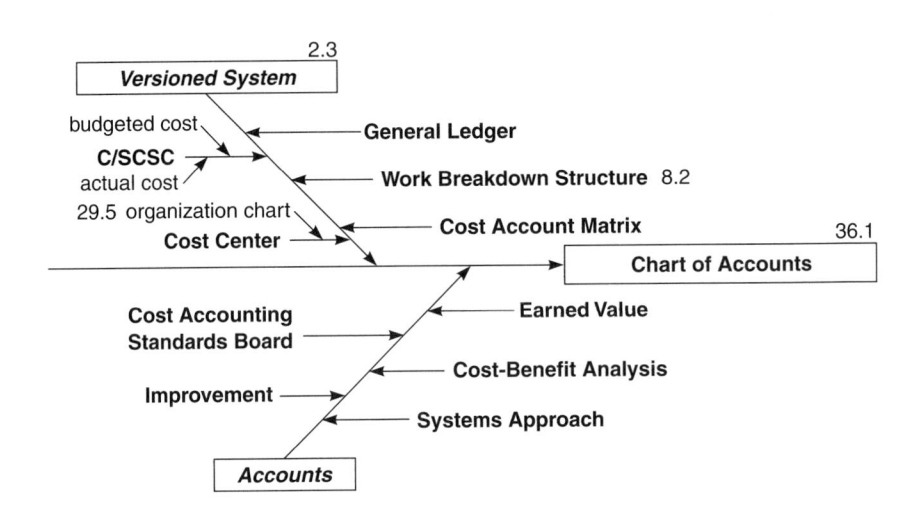

Readings

For constructing a chart of accounts, consult any beginning or intermediate textbook in the field of management accounting.

[Fleming] Quentin W. Fleming. *Put Earned Value (C/SCSC) into Your Management Control System.* Newport Beach, CA: Humphreys and Associates (+1-714-955-2981), 1983.

This book on C/SCSC and earned value has some excellent material on the C/SCSC vision of cost accounts.

[Kerzner] Harold Kerzner. *Project Management: A Systems Approach to Planning, Scheduling, and Controlling, Fifth Edition.* New York: Van Nostrand Reinhold, 1994.

Section 15.3 of Kerzner, entitled "Cost Account Codes," has a complete description of the cost center approach to the chart of accounts, with several graphics and an extended example.

[Moder]	Joseph J. Moder, Cecil R. Phillips, and Edward W. Davis. *Project Management with CPM, PERT, and Precedence Diagramming, Third Edition.* New York: Van Nostrand Reinhold, 1983.

Moder's Chapter 5, on "Project Cost Control," discusses cost control and accounting in the C/SCSC and PERT frameworks and shows how network graphing and project management systems can use these cost accounting frameworks to control costs.

Questions to Think About

1. Why do you think that C/SCSC based the chart of accounts on the WBS?

2. Look at your operations or finance organization's companywide chart of accounts. What percentage of these accounts apply to the kinds of projects that you do? Why do you think that ratio is what it is? (Hint: If your company doesn't have a chart of accounts, bail out NOW.)

3. Why don't software organizations tend to accumulate costs in accounts in a chart of accounts?

4. Have you ever heard of the Cost Accounting Standards Board? If not, why not?

5. Do you think the allocation of costs to accounts is arbitrary? How would you make cost accounting less arbitrary and more purposeful?

CHAPTER

37 The Budget

The Cost Estimate

A *cost estimate* is a versioned, quantitative statement of the resource costs for a task or assignment to allocate to accounts in the chart of accounts. Cost estimates serve as the main input into the cost budget for the project. They also serve as inputs to the contracting process to give both the buyer and seller a starting point for negotiation of the contract price. You can use a cost estimation tool to produce the estimates, which becomes part of the certification of the system for reuse in later projects.

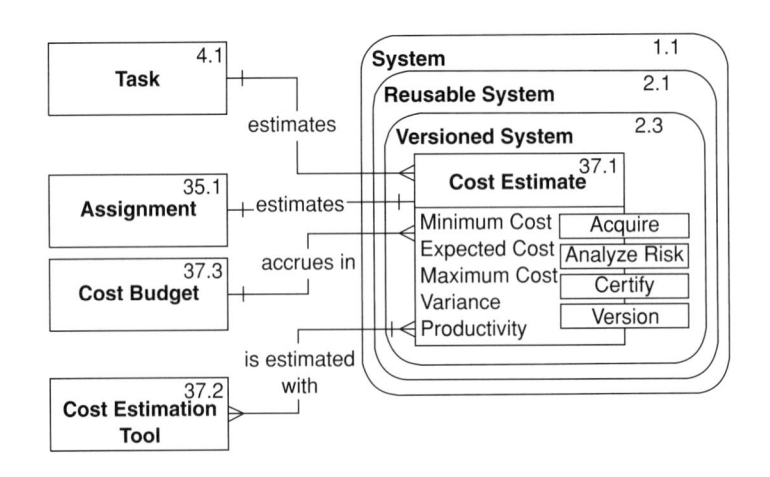

Vision: *A project delivered on time and under budget*

Mission: *To estimate the amount of cost required to complete a work assignment or task*

The Cost Estimate

Objective 37.1: To estimate the amount of cost required to complete a work assignment or task

Approach 37.1: Ask the resources responsible for the assignment or task for the minimum, expected, and maximum cost they expect the assignment or task to take. Validate the estimate and adjust it using risk management methods. Use the cost estimate in budgeting or contracting. Track the assignment and record the actual cost it takes.

Metric 37.1: Variance: the expected estimated cost minus the actual cost at the completion of the assignment

Target 37.1: A small variance within control limits of an x-R control chart

Table 37-1 summarizes the different kinds of cost estimation methods.

The aggregation level of the cost estimate varies with your cost estimation needs [Kerzner]. You can build a cost model for each simple task in the WBS, for example, based on the resource requirements for that task, including the effort estimates. You can estimate costs at a system level based on historical costs associated with estimates of system size (in function points, for example). Cost estimates are usually in a standard currency unit, but you can also use different models of currency conversion, conversion rates over time, and discount rates to model the costs more accurately.

Table 37-1 Cost Estimation Methods [Boehm, Chapter 22]

Method	Description
Algorithmic Model	Functions relating the cost estimate to a number of cost driver variables such as size, organization experience, and so on
Expert Judgment	Consultation with experts on cost estimation, including software cost estimation systems
Analogy	Using data from previous projects to cost similar new projects
Parkinsonian	Estimate the time and the available resources, and then multiply to get the cost
Price to Win	Estimate the price that will win a bidding process, and then set cost to some level under that price, or even at or over if you have a way to recoup the loss over time
Top Down	Have the project manager or an estimating team estimate the project cost as a whole, and then divide it up into pieces according to the WBS
Bottom Up	Have the people responsible for WBS tasks estimate the task or assignment cost and roll up the estimates to the top level, taking into account costs that occur at higher levels such as integration or project management

At the project level, your cost estimate presents your stakeholders with a major piece of the decision they must make. There are two basic risks for cost estimates: underestimating the costs of the project, and overestimating them. Underestimating costs can damage your credibility, waste resources, and cause you to deliver less value than you promised to some stakeholders (those worried about costs). Overestimates might cause premature cancellation or reduction in the scope of the project. When you estimate costs, especially at the project level, you should include quantification of the risk through the minimum and maximum credible values, so stakeholders can properly evaluate the estimate.

- *Note:* One survey showed that two-thirds of major software projects underestimate their costs [Lederer]. This has produced a cultural response in which inaccurate estimate has become acceptable, a "way of life." This is an unfortunate state of affairs, and it is probably worse for OO projects, given the lack of effective cost estimation models for OO projects.

Estimating cost is complex. Cost is relative to the cost profile of the resource and the burden profile (overhead) of the organization. That means your cost depends on your schedule task as well as on your task. If the cost profile for a resource changes during the project, the cost estimate changes if the schedule task includes the change in time intervals. For example, if you assign a rented test machine to a system test, and you then schedule the system test for a certain time interval, and the rental company increases their rates at some point during that interval, your cost estimate must increase. Similarly, if a person gets a raise, or a contractor renegotiates their rates, you need to take that into account. Cost estimates therefore are forecasts as well as estimates. Kerzner believes that projects that last longer than a year cannot expect to estimate costs with any great accuracy for this reason [Kerzner, p. 726].

- *Note:* If you are dealing with international teams, this can get even worse due to currency changes. If one person gets paid in yen and another in lira, the total cost in dollars varies with the exchange rates. No project management system deals with exchange rates in an adequate way at this time, as far as I am aware.

This is one major reason that cost estimation by algorithm requires extensive customization for your organization and project. You cannot use standard industry data because costs and productivity vary so much, both within the industry and across national boundaries. For example, the cost of a project in Silicon Valley may differ greatly from the cost of the same project done in Provo, Utah. It may differ even more from the cost in Bangalore, India. Compensation may vary by as much as an order of magnitude, and burden rate up to 300% [Kerzner].

Also, the higher up you go in the work breakdown structure, the less accurate your estimates will be. Kerzner estimates that "definitive" estimates at the bottom of the WBS vary from –5% to 10%, that process estimates (estimates for an entire deliverable system, or for the major development processes that produce such a system) vary from –10% to 25%, and that project-level estimates vary from –25% to 75% [Kerzner, p. 722]. Your variance targets and risk management must take this accuracy into account. You should not, for example, hold your project cost estimate to a target variance of 5% each way, at least not using standard estimation techniques.

- *Note:* Many software projects are not particularly concerned with cost estimates, only with effort estimates. This can be because the market values time more than money, or because stakeholders see software projects as a kind of overhead rather than as direct costs. In any case, if your stakeholders are not concerned with holding your project to some budget, you should focus your cost estimation at the project level using algorithmic methods, which are the most cost effective, but perhaps least accurate, way to estimate at that level.

If you are serious about cost estimation, either because you use costs as the basis for contract pricing or because your stakeholders have serious concerns about cost, you should use a combination of algorithmic and bottom-up techniques, as in effort estimation. For algorithmic models, use function points and activity-based cost estimation [Jones 1996] modified by simple quantity and risk relationships [Sigurdsen 1996a and b] to develop high-level estimates. For bottom-up models, have the people responsible for the tasks do the estimating, as they are much closer to the costs than anyone else. Use historical data as a benchmark where you can, and apply risk management techniques such as reserves and change management to control the risk to the estimate. Monitor costs closely at the task level, holding people accountable for their estimates [Lederer].

For OO projects, you should use the same baseline techniques in your cost planning that you do in scheduling: the rolling-wave method. As your WBS expands with your greater understanding of what is needed, your cost estimation baselines should expand along with your effort and duration baselines.

The reuse potential of a cost estimate depends on several factors. First, you are much more likely to be able to reuse algorithmic estimates through parameterization of the cost drivers. As you collect more data in your reuse repository, your statistical models will improve in accuracy. Bottom-up estimates depend too much on individual expertise and knowledge to let you easily reuse them. Second, the quality of the data on which you base the estimate is critical to the reusability of the estimate. If your data is spotty or has major flaws, the estimate will reflect those flaws. Third, cost estimates rely on the similarity of the domain to a high degree. If you use an MIS project's estimates to estimate a real-time, embedded system software project, you are unlikely to be successful. Fourth, if your organization's costs (labor and overhead) are too variable to predict over the lifetime of your project, previous cost estimates aren't going to help.

Certifying the reuse potential of a cost estimate reflects these issues. You must specify the methods by which you estimated the cost. If you used a particular cost estimation tool, you must store that information with the estimate, and preferably the tool as well for reproducibility. You must document any assumptions. You must specify the critical facts about the project that created the estimate so that reusers can determine how well the new project fits those facts. You should identify the minimum and maximum credible values to enable reusers to estimate the risk of reusing the estimate. You must provide a guarantee of audited results showing the variance of the estimate from the actual costs. You should provide a clear way to maintain the estimate in the reuse repository.

The Cost Estimation Tool

The *cost estimation tool* lets you estimate the cost of the software system based on economic models of software development, historical data, and data for the current project.

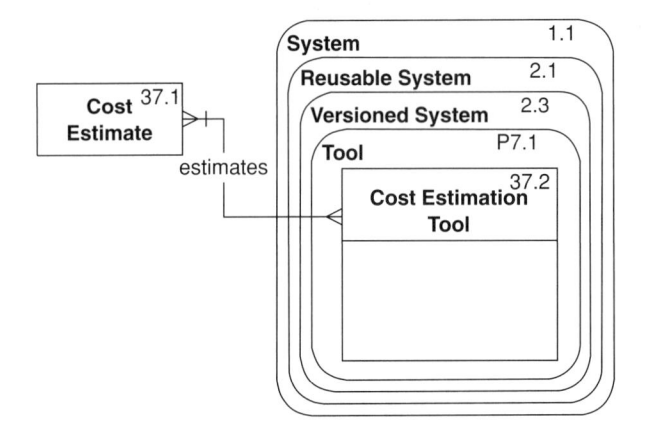

Vision: A project with a systematic and accurate budget

Mission: To help in estimating costs for a project

Objective 37.2: To help in estimating costs for a project

Approach 37.2: Collect historical data about costs in a reuse repository. Use that data with the estimation tool to produce cost estimates for your current project. Baseline the cost estimates at key process milestones. Store the cost estimates with information about the tools that you used to produce them.

Metric 37.2: Estimation productivity: the amount of effort in work-hours that you put into producing each cost estimate for which you use the tool (see the Cost Estimate class)

Target 37.2: A low number within control limits of an x-R control chart of similar effort estimates

---

The Cost Budget

The cost estimation tool assists in developing the cost estimates for the project budget. It can also assist in determining the scheduling of schedule tasks and resource assignments.

There are no tools that I have seen that explicitly deal with OO projects. You may be able to use standard cost estimation tools such as ESTIMACS, SPQR, or CHECKPOINT for these projects [Jones 1994]. To do so, you should examine the assumptions the tool makes and adjust the parameters accordingly. As you use the tool and build your database, these tools should reflect the structure of your OO data to some extent.

The Cost Budget

The *cost budget* is a two-dimensional performance evaluation baseline of time and cost. The cost budget baseline starts with the project start date and ends with the project finish date. The cost is the sum of a baseline of cost estimates given the time scheduling of the tasks. The cost budget thus shows the estimated cost accrued through use of resources during the project. You use this estimate as the basis for earned value (in cost terms, not value) or for the allocation of earned value to the individual tasks, should you wish to do that.

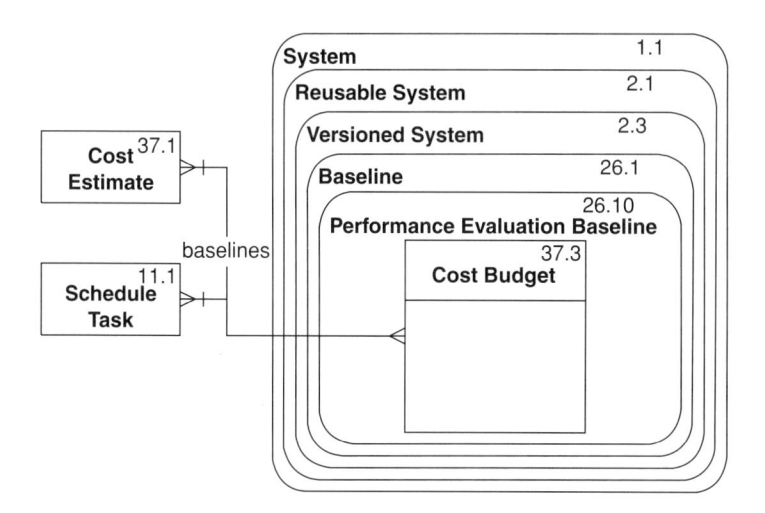

Vision: A clear picture of the progress of the project according to its budget

Mission: To enable evaluation of the cost performance of the project according to its budget

---

Objective 37.3: To enable evaluation of the cost performance of the project according to its budget

---

Approach 37.3: Store the cost estimates in the project repository together with the schedule tasks to which the estimates apply. Maintain these copies as part of the baseline, even when the original estimates change as you replan. Use this cost baseline to calculate the planned and earned cost of the project at a specific time. See Approach 26.13 for metric and target.

To develop the cost budget, you first need to estimate the cost of all the tasks to some level of the work breakdown structure. This means you have estimates for *all* the costs in the project to a certain level of detail. Once you have these estimates, you need to distribute them to schedule tasks to fill out the second dimension of the cost budget: time. As you schedule a task, you accumulate the cost in the time interval that represents the duration of the task. Figure 37.1 illustrates the cost budget baseline, showing the other relationships you use in computing earned cost.

Figure 37-1
The cost budget baseline graph

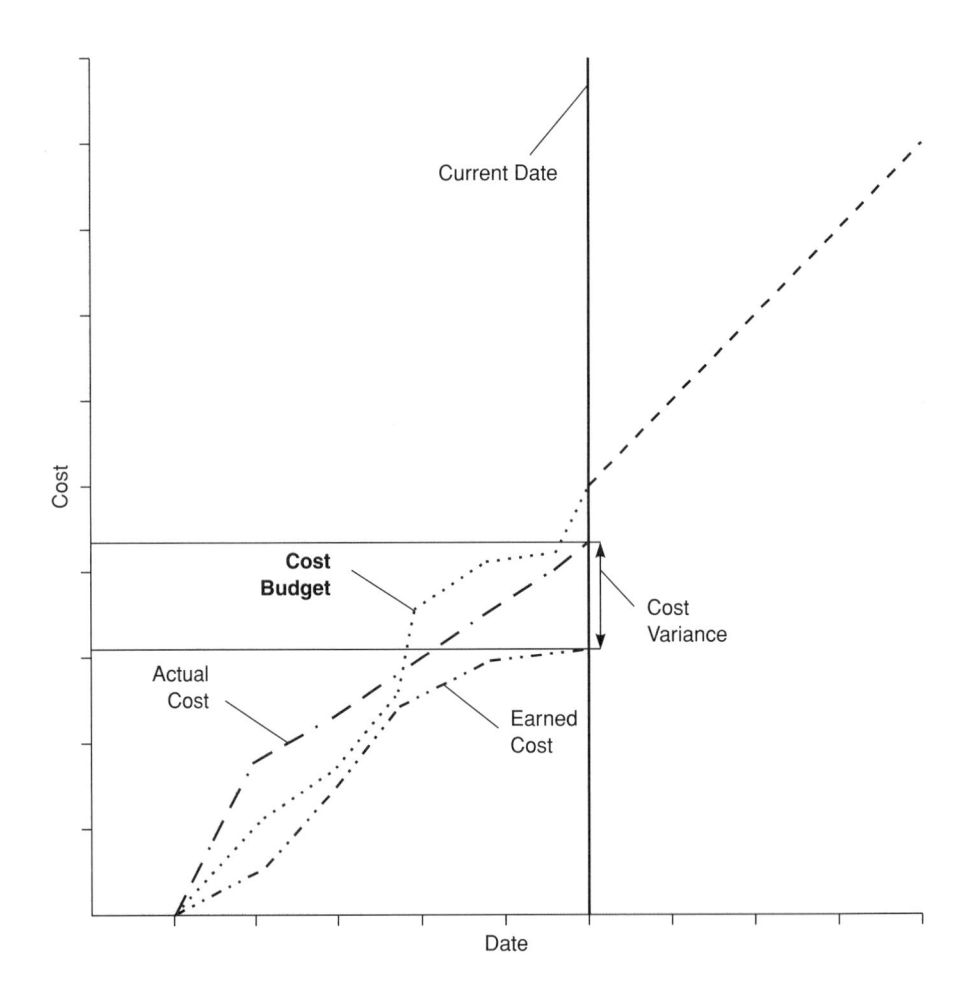

Generally, cost budgets are not very reusable other than as versioned systems. When you rebaseline the budget along with the schedule, you establish an updated version. The only real requirement for this is making sure you have a complete set of cost estimates and schedule tasks to which to allocate them.

The Spending Budget

The *spending budget* is a cost budget that reflects anticipated payments rather than estimated costs. That is, the spending budget tells you when you will *spend* the actual money, not when you expect the project to use the resulting resources. The cost budget thus shows expected resource use costs, while the spending budget shows expected cash flow (Figure 37-2).

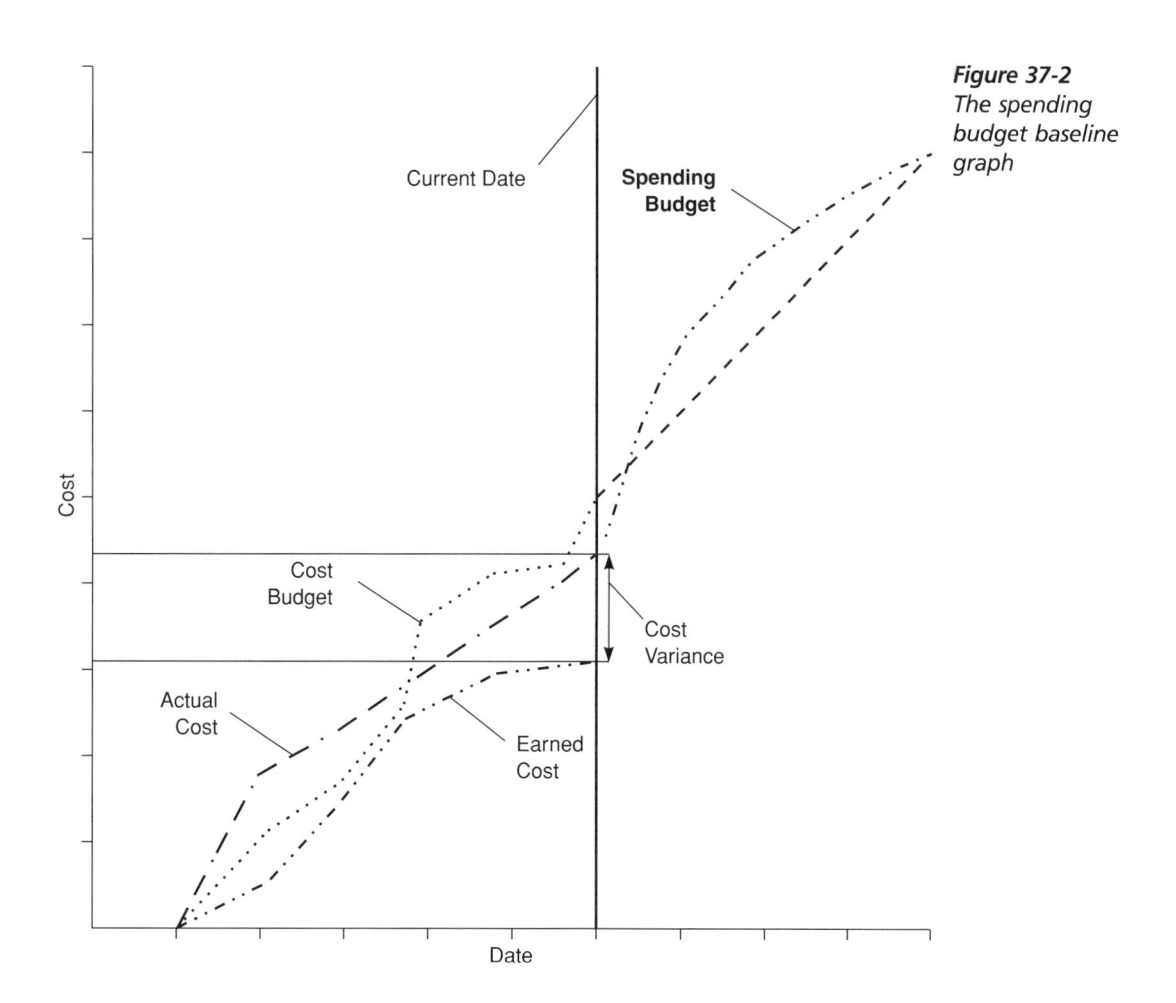

Figure 37-2
The spending budget baseline graph

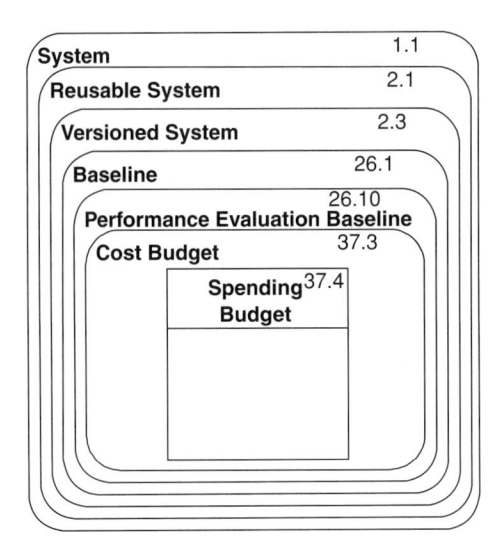

```
┌─────────────────────────────────┐
│ System                     1.1  │
│ ┌─────────────────────────────┐ │
│ │ Reusable System       2.1   │ │
│ │ ┌─────────────────────────┐ │ │
│ │ │ Versioned System   2.3  │ │ │
│ │ │ ┌─────────────────────┐ │ │ │
│ │ │ │ Baseline      26.1  │ │ │ │
│ │ │ │ ┌─────────────────┐ │ │ │ │
│ │ │ │ │         26.10   │ │ │ │ │
│ │ │ │ │ Performance Eval│ │ │ │ │
│ │ │ │ │ Baseline        │ │ │ │ │
│ │ │ │ │ Cost Budget 37.3│ │ │ │ │
│ │ │ │ │   Spending 37.4 │ │ │ │ │
│ │ │ │ │   Budget        │ │ │ │ │
```

Vision: A clear picture of the progress of the project cash flow according to its budget

Mission: To enable evaluation of the cash-flow performance of the project according to its budget

---

Objective 37.4: To enable evaluation of the cash-flow performance of the project according to its budget

---

Approach 37.4: Build a cost budget as in Approach 37.3. Instead of allocating the costs equally distributed over the schedule task duration, allocate them according to when you intend to spend the cash. Again, see Approach 26.13 for metric and target.

You can get a spending budget in two ways. You can allocate the cost estimates in finer detail than in the cost budget by specifying exactly when you intend to spend the money. Alternatively, you can estimate the spending budget directly by aggregating the spending into its natural units. For example, you generally pay salaried and hourly employees in bimonthly pay periods; you pay leases and rents monthly; and you have scheduled payments for loan principal and interest payments. You can show these cash flows directly, accumulating them into the spending budget.

Readings   *621*

■ *Note:* If you take the second approach, you should cross-check the two budgets to ensure that you have accounted for all the cost estimates in the spending budget. Generally, if you look at the final value at the end date of the project, the two should match if you have done everything right.

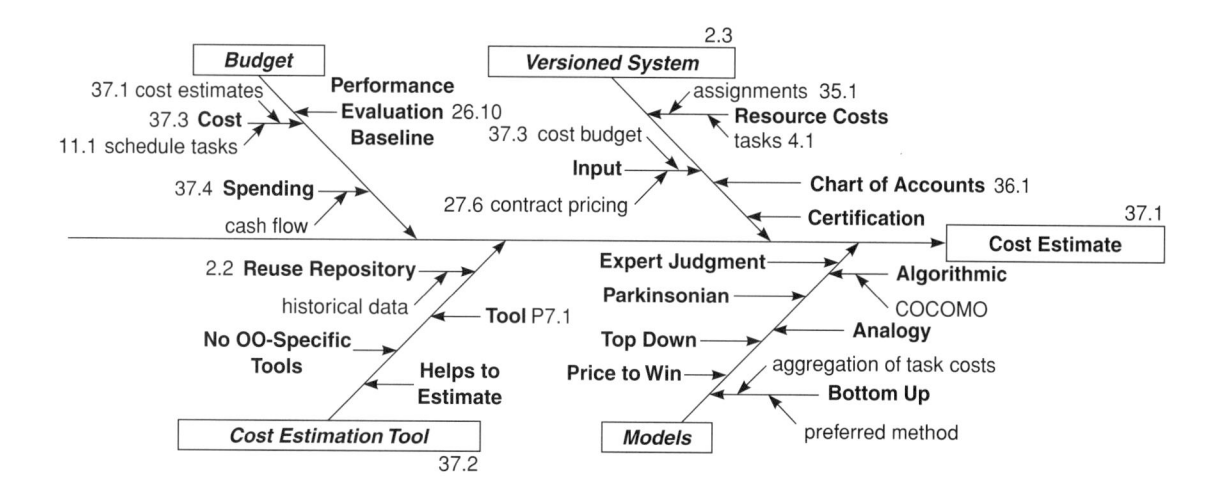

```
                                    2.3
         Budget              Versioned System
   37.1 cost estimates   Performance    assignments 35.1
      37.3 Cost       — Evaluation 26.10  — Resource Costs
   11.1 schedule tasks   Baseline   37.3 cost budget   tasks 4.1
                                      Input
        37.4 Spending                            — Chart of Accounts 36.1
          cash flow    27.6 contract pricing     — Certification              37.1
                                                                         Cost Estimate
     2.2 Reuse Repository       Expert Judgment — Algorithmic
           historical data      Parkinsonian      COCOMO
       No OO-Specific    Tool P7.1  Top Down     — Analogy
            Tools       Helps to   Price to Win   aggregation of task costs
                        Estimate                  — Bottom Up
       Cost Estimation Tool      Models       preferred method
              37.2
```

Readings

[Bennatan]   E. M. Bennatan. *On Time, Within Budget: Software Project Management Practices and Techniques.* New York: QED Publishing Group, 1992.

Bennatan's Chapter 10 gives an excellent overview of the cost estimation process. He discusses in particular the issues surrounding reuse—both software reuse and estimate reuse.

[Boehm 1981]   Barry W. Boehm. *Software Engineering Economics.* Englewood Cliffs, NJ: Prentice Hall, 1981.

Boehm is the fundamental work on constructive cost estimation, the technique of using cost drivers and statistical modeling to develop cost estimation models. Unfortunately, most of his empirical work uses lines of code estimating, which renders his numbers unreliable in the extreme for OO cost estimation. The estimation techniques can be valuable if you do your own studies using better data.

[Fleming]   Quentin W. Fleming. *Put Earned Value (C/SCSC) into Your Management Control System.* Newport Beach, CA: Humphreys and Associates (+1-714-955-2981), 1983.

This book has a detailed Chapter 10 on baselines, with a complete analysis of the process of setting cost budgets for very large projects. It notes the importance of the baseline budget for the whole process of cost control through C/SCSC and earned cost.

[Jones 1994] Capers Jones. *Assessment and Control of Software Risks.* New York: Yourdon Press, 1994.

Jones details several risks involving poor cost estimating and has the best section on estimating tools and techniques I've seen. None of it applies specifically to OO projects, however.

[Jones 1996] Capers Jones. Activity-based software costing. *Computer* 29:5 (May 1996): 103–104.

This short column describes a bottom-up approach to estimating based on function point productivity numbers for different software processes such as requirements analysis and detailed design. He gives a table with empirical data for these processes. Again, these data do not reflect OO projects, so take them with several grains of salt. Also, he uses a fixed productivity number, and productivity may vary with project size.

[Kerzner] Harold Kerzner. *Project Management: A Systems Approach to Planning, Scheduling, and Controlling, Fifth Edition.* New York: Van Nostrand Reinhold, 1994.

Kerzner's Chapter 14 goes into pricing and estimating costs in detail. Much of this material is more appropriate for construction and defense projects than for OO software projects, which are harder to estimate accurately. Kerzner's Section 14.16 on estimating high-risk projects seems very applicable.

[Lederer] Albert L. Lederer and Jayesh Prasad. Nine management guidelines for better cost estimating. *Communications of the ACM* 35:2 (February 1992): 51–59.

This excellent survey report presents its conclusions as management guidelines for conducting cost estimation. While the data is interesting, the survey methodology leaves something to be desired, and some of the conclusions need more context than the article presents. In particular, it seems to assume that estimation techniques are independent of management culture; for example, delaying estimates because the surveyed cultures emphasize single-point estimates rather than rolling-wave estimation.

[Sigurdson 1996a] Arild Sigurdsen. Principle errors in capital cost estimating work, part 1: Appreciate the relevance of quantity-dependent estimating norms. *Project Management Journal* 27:3 (September 1996): 27–34.

[Sigurdson 1996b] Arild Sigurdsen. Principle errors in capital cost estimating work, part 2: Appreciate the relevance of the objective cost risk analysis method. *Project Management Journal* 27:3 (September 1996): 27–34.

These two articles give you some ideas about how to apply statistical modeling techniques to cost estimation in novel ways. They also make clear that you should challenge some widely held assumptions about productivity and risk in cost estimating. I suspect the productivity curve for software projects will show a very different relationship with project size than his oil pipeline example. Instead of exponential increase in productivity, I would expect exponential decline in productivity. Achieving major software reuse might change this relationship drastically, however.

Questions to Think About

1. What level of cost estimate do you think is most appropriate for the kind of projects you do? Why?

2. Why do you think most OO software projects don't focus on costs as much as schedules?

3. Tom DeMarco has pointed out [DeMarco 1982] that the construction industry has estimating books with detailed cost estimate benchmarks for standard tasks and materials. Why do you think no such books exist for the software industry? How about for the OO software industry in particular?

4. Why do estimation tools lag so far behind development tools for OO software?

5. How sensitive do you think your cost and spending budgets are to your schedule? What will happen to your cost and spending baselines if your schedule changes radically?

6. Why should I think that there is likely to be an exponential decline in productivity as the project size increases, the reverse of construction projects? What kind of learning curve does this imply?

CHAPTER 38

Cost Management

The Cost Management Plan

The *cost management plan* is the section of the project plan that describes how you will manage the cost control process. It specifies the cost management information system that tracks and manages costs. It specifies how you will adjust the budget based on your earned-value and cost variance figures. It incorporates the risk management methods for cost risks into the risk management plan, especially any reserves available for mitigation of risk.

Vision: A project brought to a successful conclusion, achieving its mission by delivering its products under budget

Mission: To ensure that you deliver the results of the project at a desirable cost

Objective 38.1: To ensure that the project budgets a desirable cost budget

Approach 38.1: Estimate the cost of the project using a bottom-up costing approach from an appropriate level of the work breakdown structure. Analyze the risks for the estimates. Aggregate the estimated cost and prepare a cost-benefit analysis that establishes a cost target for the project. If the cost target is above the cost estimate, negotiate at the appropriate levels for reductions in cost. If the resulting cost estimate version is still above the target, recommend cancellation of the project; otherwise, baseline the cost and spending budgets from the estimates. Reanalyze the risks, and integrate risk management methods into the WBS through the risk management plan, such as management reserves in the budget. Execute the cost management plan.

The Cost Management Plan

[Diagram showing relationships between Cost Management System (38.2), Cost Budget (37.3), Project Plan (7.2), Risk Management Method (14.2), and nested systems: System (1.1), Reusable System (2.1), Versioned System (2.3), System Model (1.7), Plan (7.1), containing Cost Management Plan (38.1) with Cost-Benefit Analysis, Cost-Benefit Ratio, Cost Variance Ratio, and activities: Plan, Identify Risks, Quantify Risks, Execute. Relationships: "specifies", "tracks", "is part of", "proposes".]

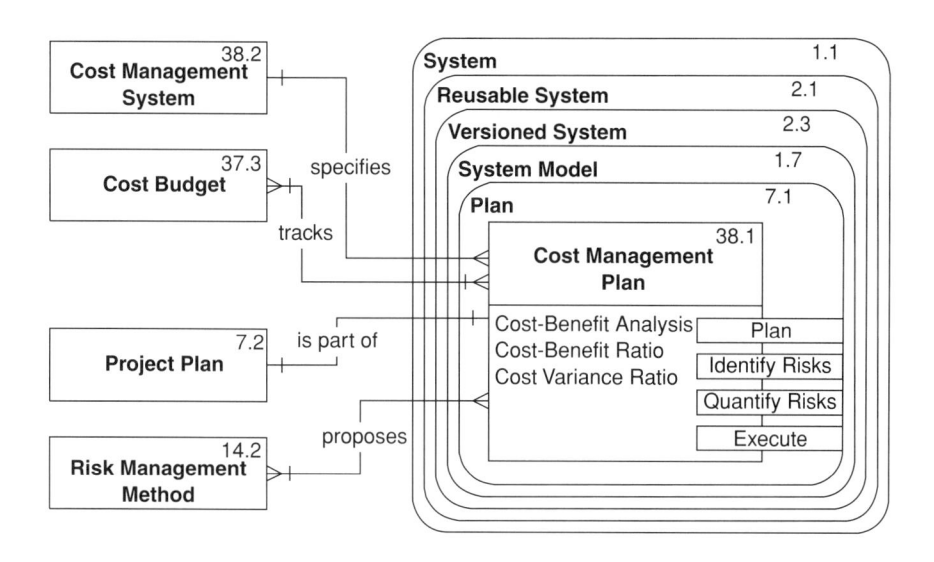

Metric 38.1: Cost-benefit ratio: the ratio of the budgeted cost of the project to the estimated value of the project at the project finish milestone

Target 38.1: A number materially less than 1, corresponding to a return on investment acceptable to the project stakeholders

---

Objective 38.2: To ensure that the project delivers its value under the budgeted cost

---

Approach 38.2: Use the bottom-up approach (38.1) to obtain commitment to the cost estimates at the level of the work breakdown structure most responsible for generating the cost, usually the work package level. Have those responsible for the work packages develop the cost estimates, and then roll the estimates up through the WBS, accumulating the costs. During the revision process, again obtain revised cost estimates from the responsible people, again to obtain commitment. Do not, under any circumstances, impose a cost estimate on a responsible resource over their objections; sell, don't tell. Track costs at the level of the cost estimates, and calculate variances from the estimates at the earliest possible time. If it appears that the cost of a task will materially exceed its estimate, implement any contingency plans you have in place, such as allocating some of the management reserve, or brainstorm new plans. If the actual cost for the project materially exceeds the cost budget at a major milestone, reevaluate the cost budget baseline and its risks to establish a new baseline or, possibly, cancel the project if the resulting cost budget or risks are unacceptable to stakeholders.

Metric 38.2.1: Cost variance ratio: at a milestone, the earned cost (budgeted cost of work performed) minus the actual cost of the work, divided by the earned cost to show the variance as a ratio to the earned cost

Target 38.2.1: A ratio value greater than or equal to zero within control limits of a p control chart for the project's various milestones; a negative value means costs are overrunning the budget, while a positive value means you are under budget; the control limits should tighten for the later milestones in the project, indicating convergence on the budget

---

Metric 38.2.2: Estimate at completion: at a milestone, the total cost from this point on of finishing the project, which is the amount you've already spent plus the amount of the cost budget that applies to work yet to be done:

(Actual Cost / Earned Cost) × Budgeted Cost at Completion

Target 38.2.2: A number that is still acceptable to the stakeholders when compared to the value of the system at the estimated delivery time; the number should vary between control limits of an x-R control chart of milestone estimates during your project

---

"The Project Deliverables and System Earned Value" section, Chapter 3, p. 67

The cost management planning process establishes the cost and spending budgets and the system for tracking progress against those budgets. The C/SCSC earned-value statistics are the key statistics you use to evaluate your cost spending position at a milestone. In particular, if the cost variance ratio is beyond standard control limits, your project is out of control with reference to its budget.

Reporting the earned-cost statistics is the primary task of the cost management system. These numbers have two parts: the earned-cost and cost variance numbers, and the estimate to completion. In Figure 38-1, the cost variance at the milestone is the difference between earned value and planned value. This number tells you how far behind plan you are.

The *estimate at completion* is the cost you will spend to finish the project. This is not the amount you originally budgeted but the actual amount plus the budgeted amount for the work yet to be done. This feedback lets you understand quickly at a milestone what you need to do to control costs in the project. If your estimate at completion exceeds your budget plus any reserves your stakeholders have approved, you need to replan the project to reduce costs. Usually, this means tossing some functionality or improving productivity through crashing or a similar act of desperation. The trick here is to get these numbers early in the project rather than letting the variance creep up on you. Dealing with problems early saves you management time later.

■ *Note:* The simple calculation in Metric 38.2.2 is enough to give you a clue as to how much your project is going to cost at its finish date, but don't take this number too seriously. The formula assumes that the original budget was

The Cost Management Plan

more or less correct and that the cost variance will continue to grow in a linear fashion. Unfortunately, in feedback systems, most things like this are nonlinear. In very large projects, in particular, growth in variance can be exponential. Another approach to estimate at completion is replanning through a thorough review of the remaining work using causal and trend analysis of the cost variance issues your project has experienced to reevaluate the risks. This is quite a lot more work, so you should only do it if the numbers justify it. Also, you should use experienced people to do these analyses, as the major risk here is getting it wrong.

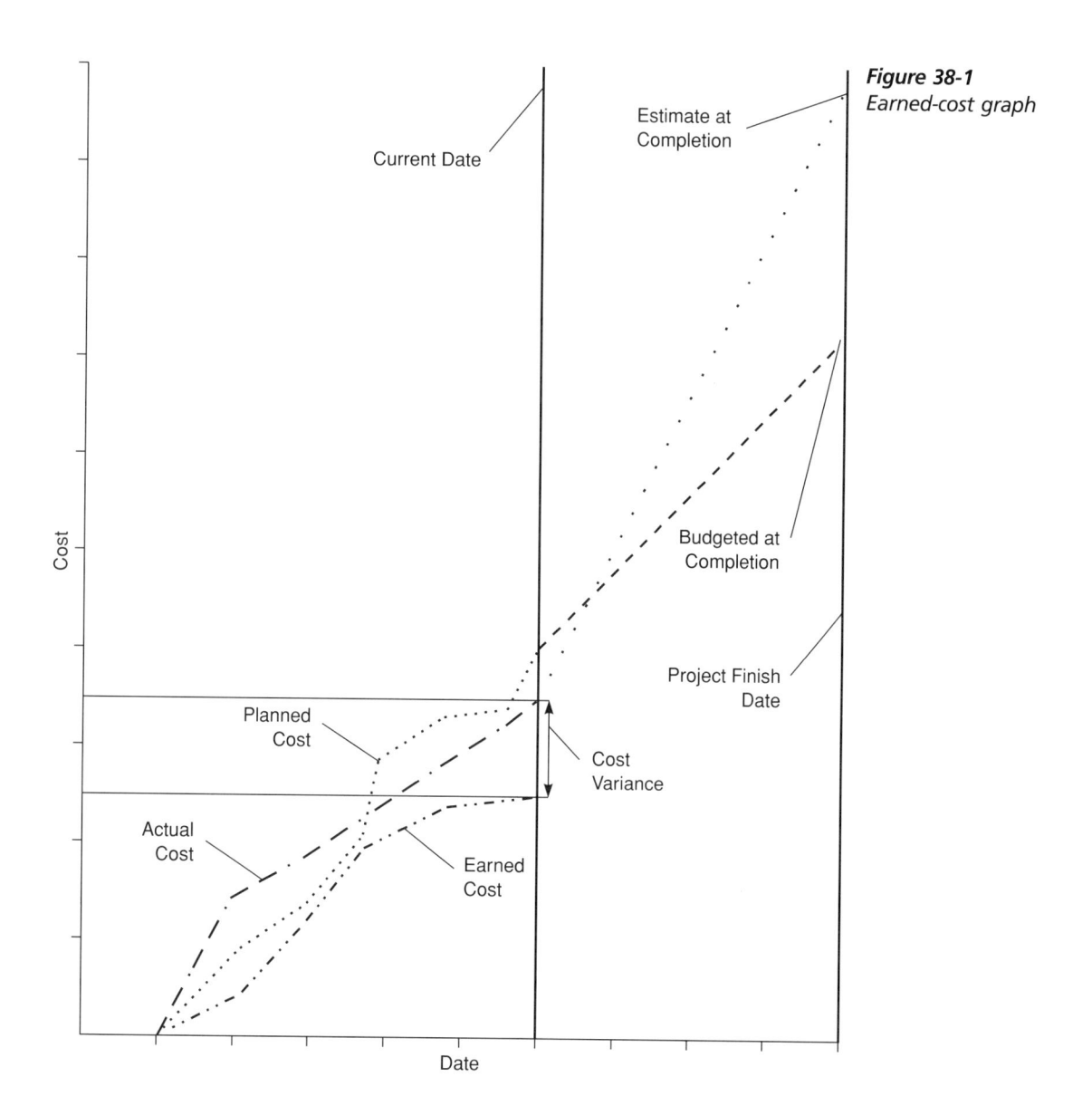

Figure 38-1
Earned-cost graph

The Cost Management System

The *cost management system* is a management information system that contains cost-related information, which it stores in the project repository. The cost management plan specifies the management system. It manages the progress reports that track the costs of the project as well as the cost and spending budget baselines for the project.

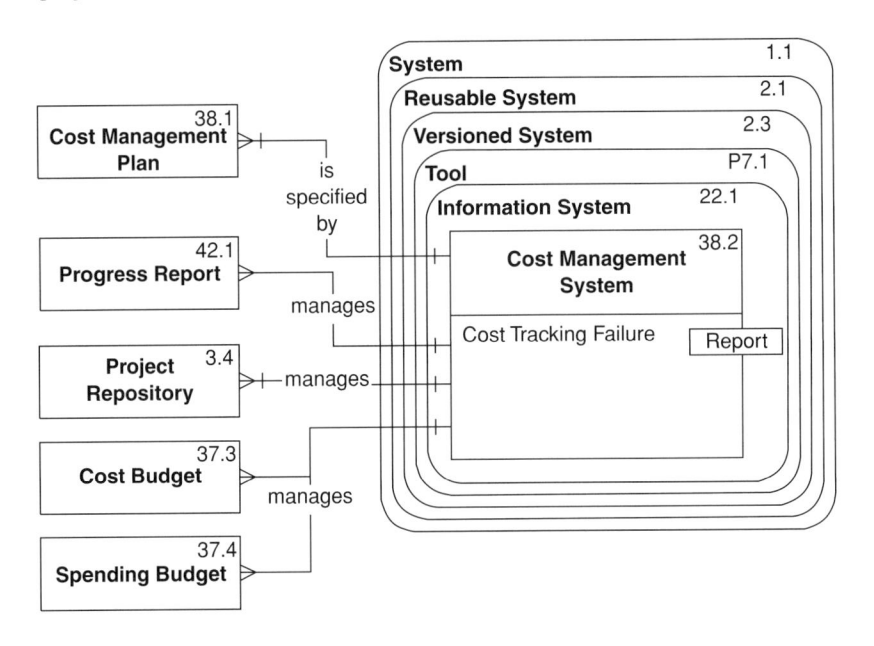

Vision: People using information about costs to keep the project under budget

Mission: To create and manage information that people need to control costs

---

Objective 38.3: To create and manage information that people need to control costs

---

Approach 38.3: Create and store the project cost and spending budgets in the project repository. Create and store progress reports that contain cost information. Generate reports on earned cost and cost variance at designated milestones.

Metric 38.3: Cost Tracking Failures: a count of the number of incidents in which the system fails to accurately measure spent cost for the project at a milestone

Target 38.3: A count within the control limits of a p control chart of counts

Every project management system I've used contains the elements of a cost management system, though not all claim to have fully implemented the full government C/SCSC program. You can generally have one or two cost budgets, track actual costs, and calculate earned cost and estimate at completion using project management software.

Project Management System (22.2)

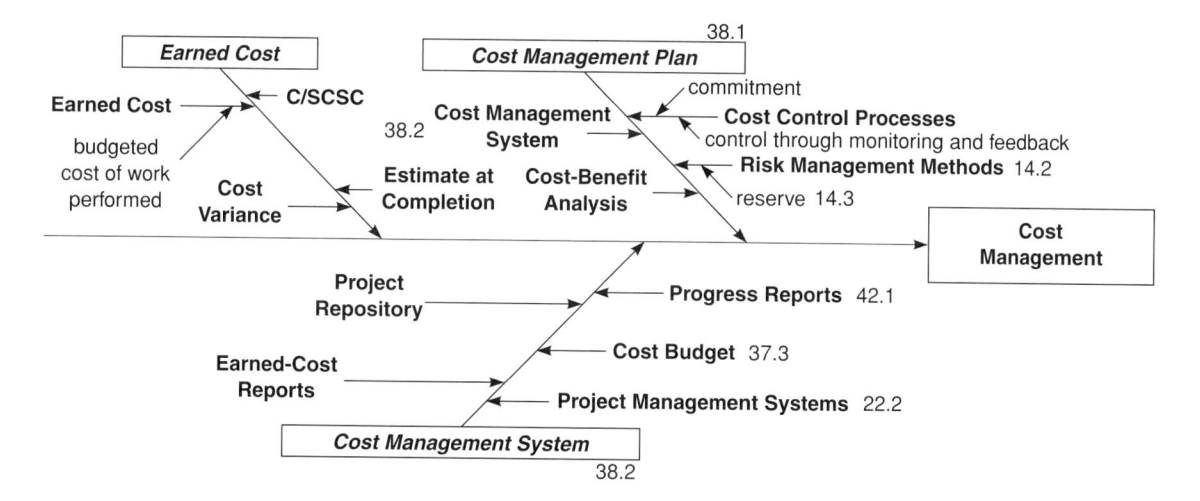

[Fishbone diagram showing Cost Management with branches: Earned Cost, C/SCSC, Cost Management Plan 38.1, Cost Management System 38.2, Cost Control Processes (commitment, control through monitoring and feedback), Risk Management Methods 14.2 (reserve 14.3), Earned Cost (budgeted cost of work performed), Cost Variance, Estimate at Completion, Cost-Benefit Analysis, Project Repository, Progress Reports 42.1, Earned-Cost Reports, Cost Budget 37.3, Project Management Systems 22.2, Cost Management System 38.2]

Readings

[Fleming]   Quentin W. Fleming. *Put Earned Value (C/SCSC) into Your Management Control System.* Humphreys and Associates (+1-714-955-2981), 1983.

This book or any of Fleming's other books on C/SCSC and earned value provide good insights into the cost management process, which is what C/SCSC (the cost/schedule control system criteria) are all about.

[Kerzner]   Harold Kerzner. *Project Management: A Systems Approach to Planning, Scheduling, and Controlling, Fifth Edition.* New York: Van Nostrand Reinhold, 1994.

Kerzner's Chapter 15, "Cost Control," examines budgeting and cost control in great detail, focusing for the most part on earned-value concepts. This explanation of earned value is a good, succinct, and well-written introduction to the formulas and logic of earned value.

[Moder]   Joseph J. Moder, Cecil R. Phillips, and Edward W. Davis. *Project Management with CPM, PERT, and Precedence Diagramming, Third Edition.* New York: Van Nostrand Reinhold, 1983.

Moder's Chapter 5 gives a detailed look at the history and mathematics of cost control in project management as it relates to project networking schemes such as CPM and PERT. The history in particular is a fascinating look into C/SCSC and why project management systems provide the tools they do.

Questions to Think About

1. Most of the software projects I've worked on ignore cost management entirely. When might this approach make sense?

2. Under what circumstances would you cancel a project for reasons of cost?

3. What do you think are the major risks that lead to cost-related problems on a project? (Hint: Where does most of the cost in a software project come from?)

4. What is the relationship between schedule and cost in the earned-value approach to measuring project progress?

5. Why do you think basic project management software tends to ignore cost and cost management?

PART THIRTEEN

Communication

What we got here is a failure to communicate.

The Warden, *Cool Hand Luke*

Communication is one of those things that exists primarily as a reminder that everyone is fallible. When your project is communicating effectively, you operate in blissful knowledge; when communications fail, you operate, if at all, in woeful ignorance. This part gives you an overview of the different kinds of communications that are essential to an OO project and some ideas about communications planning that may make it harder to fail. Otherwise, you risk winding up where Luke did, in a place you don't want to be.

Every communication in a project happens through a communication process, a kind of supporting process in the ISO/IEC-12207 scheme. You plan some, but not all of these. An informal communication process just happens; you don't plan it. You do, however, encourage it to happen, as informal processes probably communicate more information than formal ones. Personal interactions are the most common form of informal communication. You plan formal communications and assign responsibility for the tasks to make it happen. Formal communications plans come from communication process models in the standard process-model/plan/process linkage.

A meeting is the most common kind of formal communication. Getting meetings right is not hard, but you need to know what you're doing, and Chapter 41 tells you. Meetings communicate two ways, with imparting information and getting feedback of equal importance. The joint review is a meeting that gets consensus from several points of view, and management, technical, and improvement reviews are all joint reviews. A communication meeting focuses on imparting information rather than on getting feedback.

The progress report summarizes the data-gathering timesheet to provide status information on contracts, projects, releases, and builds.

```
System                                                        1.1
 ┌ Reusable System                                             2.1
 │ ┌ Versioned System                                          2.3
 │ │ ┌ Process                           4.6   ┌ System Model                    1.7
 │ │ │ ┌ Supporting Process            16.5   │ ┌ Plan               7.1   ┌ Process Model   4.7
 │ │ │ │ ┌ Communication Process      39.1   │ │   39.5              │ │        39.4
 │ │ │ │ │         39.2                      │ │ Communications      │ │ Communication
 │ │ │ │ │ Informal Communication Process    │ │ Management Plan    │ │ Process Model
 │ │ │ │ │   40.1                            │ │
 │ │ │ │ │ Personal Interaction              │ │ ┌ Project Document  6.1
 │ │ │ │ │                                   │ │ │ Progress    42.1
 │ │ │ │ ┌ Formal Communication Process 39.3 │ │ │ Report                 ┌ Storage Organization 15.2
 │ │ │ │ │ ┌ Meeting                   41.1  │ │ │                        │ ┌ Repository      20.1
 │ │ │ │ │ │ Joint Review              41.2  │ │ │ Timesheet   42.2       │ │ Online     43.2
 │ │ │ │ │ │   41.3    Technical  41.4       │ │ │                        │ │ Repository
 │ │ │ │ │ │ Management Review                │ │ ┌ Tool              P7.1
 │ │ │ │ │ │     41.5                         │ │ │     43.1
 │ │ │ │ │ │ Improvement                      │ │ │ Communication
 │ │ │ │ │ │ Review                           │ │ │ Tool
 │ │ │ │ │   41.6
 │ │ │ │ │ Communication
 │ │ │ │ │ Meeting
```

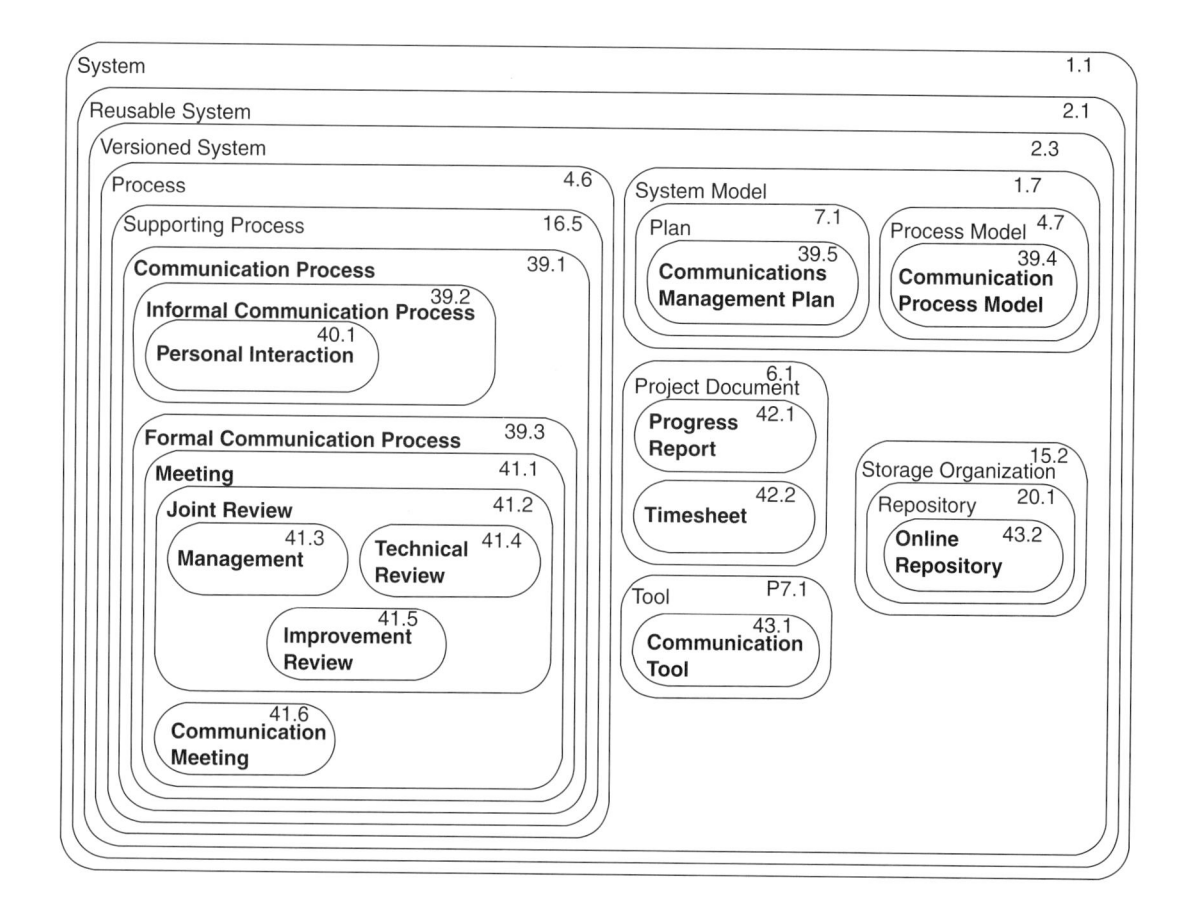

The communication tool enables the communication process. In particular, it enables you to use online repositories of information in creative ways to control your projects.

- *Note:* The illustration of the class hierarchy contains all the classes this part defines. Other parts of the book define and discuss classes not in boldface.

CHAPTER 39

Communication Process

The Communication Process

The *communication process* is a supporting process that enables people, roles, work group, stakeholders, or the environment to communicate with each other. The communication process is the mechanism by which most feedback in the process happens. The project uses many instances of the communication process in the format that best suits the content it wants to communicate: personal interactions, meetings, or progress reports. The communication process uses communication tools. The communications management plan generates the communication process for the project, initiating and managing the flow of information in the project to ensure its successful delivery.

Vision: A process that ensures delivery of planned value through effective communication

Mission: To ensure that project information flows effectively to ensure planned delivery of value

---

Objective 39.1: To ensure the effectiveness of feedback within the project and its direct environment

---

Approach 39.1: Construct the communication tasks appropriate to the particular method of communication. Initiate the communication at the required time. Ensure that the content of the communication is clear and purposeful. Ensure that the intended target of the communication has successfully received the communication.

Metric 39.1.1: Noise: the ratio of useless communication to total communication in the process, where communication is some measure of information content, such as the infon (a measure of semantic information-relating objects) [Devlin]

Target 39.1.1: A value within control limits of a p control chart for the process

---

Metric 39.1.2: Receipt: a binary metric indicating whether the intended target has received the communication, determined either through the communication mechanism (a "return receipt," for example) or through surveying the intended audience

Target 39.1.2: A value within control limits of an x-R control chart for the process

---

Objective 39.2: To facilitate feedback that contributes to planned delivery of value

Approach 39.2: Evaluate the mission and proposed content of the specific communication for its contribution to the value of the project as feedback. Communicate only those things that people need to know to deliver value. Keep it simple.

Metric 39.2: Relevance: an ordinal, subjective metric of the relevance of the communication to the mission of the project; values Irrelevant, Slightly Relevant, Relevant, Very Relevant, Highly Relevant

Target 39.2: Relevant or better

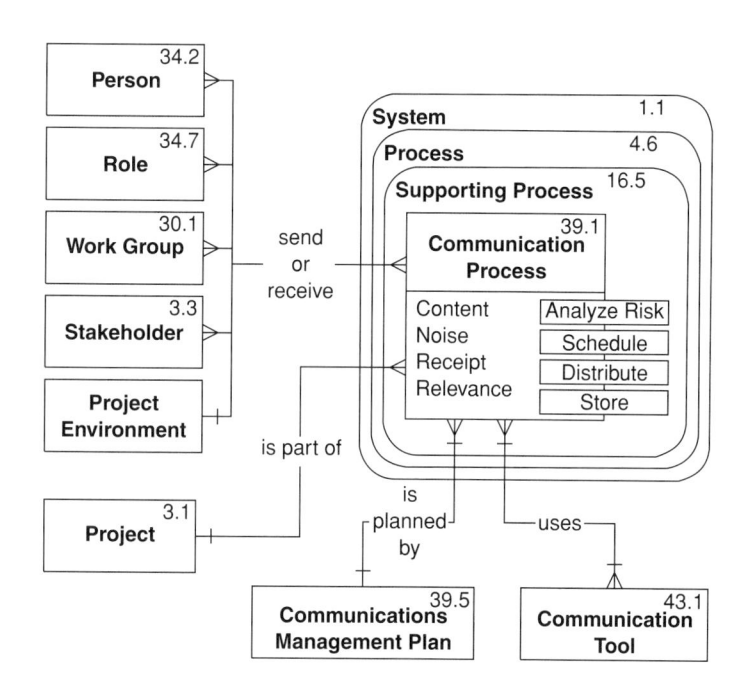

The communication process is a very abstract concept that becomes real only when you adopt a particular form and mechanism. Certain aspects of communication are shared between all the different purposes and media, such as risk, scheduling, distribution, and technology.

The relationship of communication to risk is twofold. First, communication is a mechanism for various risk management methods. To reduce or mitigate risk, you communicate. Second, communication itself is at risk from various kinds of events.

The primary risk management effect of communication is to introduce feedback into the project. Getting information from the environment, the stakeholders, your people, or your processes is the primary way to understand what is going on, both in the environment and in your project. You can then control the project based on that information. Without communication, you cannot control your project.

It is therefore enlightening to read articles and books about communication that never once mention feedback as a purpose of communication [Juliano; Kerzner]. Purposes such as promotion, public relations, increasing awareness, motivation, and training all get heavy play, but not feedback. All of these are interesting reasons to communicate, but they all lead to the main reason: to get feedback from those to whom you are communicating.

The risk of the communications process itself is that it will fail to communicate effectively. The fundamental risk is content ambiguity: the range of different interpretations that the communication targets can give to the communication. Too much ambiguity and you risk not informing; too little, and you risk offending. Aside from ambiguity, the biggest problem with communication is noise, the barriers that interfere with the receiving of information. Physical noise is the result of some problem with the medium of communication: you literally cannot make yourself heard. With technological advances, this is becoming less and less of a problem. Still, telephone lines do fall, networks do get overloaded, and mail does get lost. Other kinds of noise introduce softer issues: the ambiguity of perceptions by different individuals, the personalities that tend to see things that aren't there and not to see things that are, and the emotions in all of us that prevent us from rationally evaluating a communication.

One risk that can lead to communications failure is remote communications failure. When the target of the communication is at a remote site, with no possibility of face-to-face contact, there is often an increase in perception problems that you must overcome. Videoconferencing can help this to a certain extent, but it's still too expensive in its large-group incarnations.

All of these risks have solutions that fill many books, both theoretical and self-help. Learning to communicate effectively is a combination of learning to use all those buttons on your phone as well as to write and speak to the purpose. Those who can communicate are more effective in project jobs than those who cannot.

Scheduling communications happens in two ways. First, when your risk analysis determines that you must communicate a set of facts at some point in the project, you must put tasks into the WBS to accomplish the communication process. You associate these tasks with the relevant schedule tasks through the communications management plan. Second, certain communications are repetitive according to some requirement, such as weekly status meetings. All the project management software I've used supports such repetitive tasks, enabling you to schedule a repeating meeting as a task in your project through your communications management plan. Groupware scheduling software such as Now's Up-to-Date lets you schedule these meetings in a handy, interactive format on your network.

Schedule Task (11.1)

Distributing the communication uses the communication tools to move the information content from the source to the destination. You do, however, have to specify the distribution structure. You must specify to whom the information is to go by setting up mailing lists, distribution lists, or other such mechanisms. All email systems, for example, have the ability to send mail to a previously specified list of addresses. The communication process takes advantage of this kind of technology to distribute the information automatically where possible. The distribution process within the communication process must take place within the context of the organization chart and the access needs of the organization. That is, when you communicate, you must communicate with those who are authorized to receive your communications and respond. If your organization is a heavily authoritarian one with strong lines of command, you may need to reflect those lines in your distribution structure. As well, if the information content in your communication is sensitive or confidential, you must ensure that only those who are authorized to access the information may do so.

The technology underpinnings of all this behavior are becoming second nature to everyone in the software world. The key technology for the communication process is the enabling technology that transfers the information. The next most important technology is the repository technology that lets you save and access the communication on demand. Certain kinds of technology, and especially online browsing repositories, combine these technologies into a single medium.

The Informal Communication Process

An *informal communication process* transmits information that is not necessarily critical to the success of your project. This kind of communication provides a way for people to communicate with very low overhead, leading to increased synergy between the different systems in the project.

Vision: A process that aids delivery of planned value through increased communication

Mission: To help establish synergy between project systems through increased communication

Objective 39.3: To help establish synergy between project systems through increased communication

Approach 39.3: Encourage personal interaction and other forms of informal communication that do not distract people from their work. Organize the environment to facilitate such communication.

Metric 39.3: Information synergy: the degree to which systems are working together better because of informal communications, measured as a subjective ordinal metric; values None, Some, A Great Deal, Very High

Target 39.3: A Great Deal or Very High, depending on the needs of the project for synergy

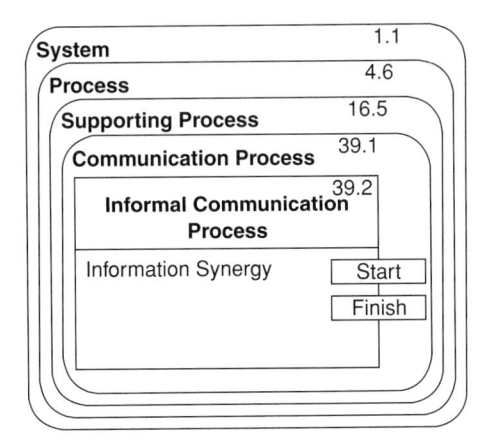

```
System                                    1.1
  Process                                 4.6
    Supporting Process                   16.5
      Communication Process              39.1
                                         39.2
        Informal Communication
                Process
        Information Synergy     [ Start  ]
                                [ Finish ]
```

Synergy is when the component systems of a system work together to achieve effects that the systems working alone could not achieve. Organizational systems achieve synergy through communication as well as the more direct physical interactions in their work. To get *high* synergy in a project, you have to have a culture that lets people interact in both formal and informal ways. The informal communication process is the second half of this culture.

The essence of the informal communication process is to just do it. You need to judge when to start and when to stop; the specific format of the process determines part of this, and the situation determines the rest.

The Formal Communication Process

A *formal communication process* transmits information critical to the success of your project. Because of the importance of the information, you need to plan these communications carefully, which in turn requires a communication process model. Every formal communication process requires a signature from one or more responsible people; every one results in one or more project documents that you store in the project repository.

Vision: A process that ensures delivery of planned value through critical communications

Mission: To ensure that critical project information flows effectively to ensure planned delivery of value

---

Objective 39.4: To ensure the effectiveness of critical feedback within the project and its direct environment

---

Approach 39.4: Identify communications that are critical to the success of the project through risk analysis. Plan the communication tasks using the communication process model. Identify the work group or person who should take responsibility for the communication, assign the process to them, and add it to the project responsibility matrix. Proceed as in Approach 39.1, but when initiating the communication, ensure that the required signatures appear. Use the metrics and targets from Objective 39.1 to measure the success of the communications.

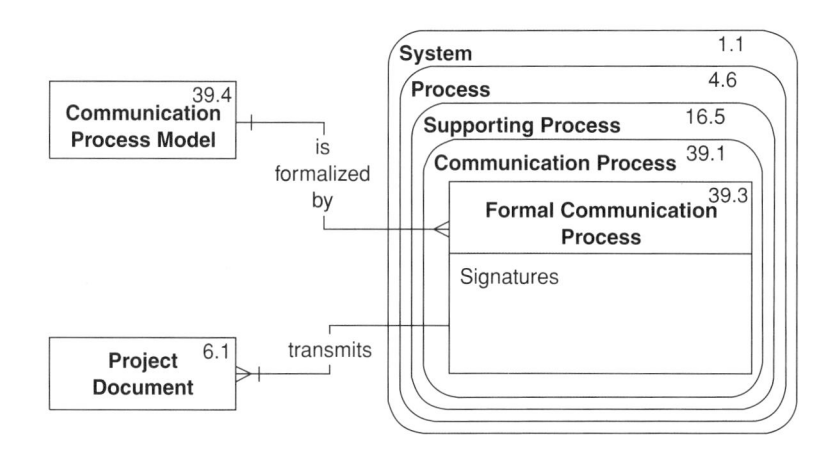

The Communication Process Model

The *communication process model* represents the structure of a formal communication process. It contains the set of tasks and work flows that accomplishes the transfer of a flow of information. A set of policies determines how to apply the communication process model to situations common to projects. Your communication planning uses these policies to set up the formal communications processes that represent the vital information flows in your project. The communication process model interacts with the organizational environment to control distribution and access to the information you intend to communicate.

Vision: A valuable, reusable, productive formal communication process you productively plan from a continuously improving model

Mission: To represent a productive formal communication process that you want to reuse many times

---

Objective 39.5: To represent a productive formal communication process that you want to reuse many times

---

Approach 39.5: Model the standard formal communication process. Determine who is responsible for the communication and who needs to sign it. Identify the specific tasks, work flows for those tasks, and potential risks of failure.

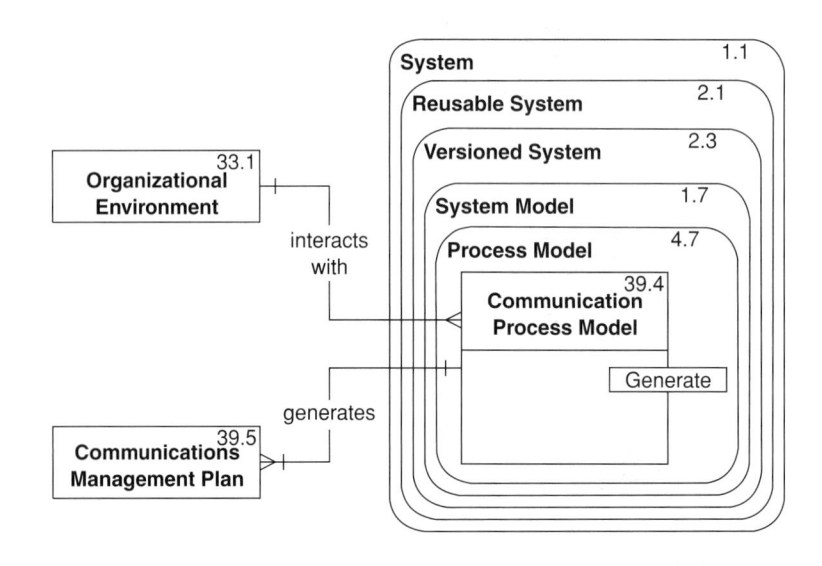

The Communications Management Plan

The *communications management plan* specifies formal project communications and assigns responsibility and timing to them. The plan adds the appropriate formal communication processes (meetings, progress reports, personal interactions) to the work breakdown structure and schedule. Those tasks must specify the different information-containing systems that are the inputs and outputs of the communication processes, such as documents, charts, and schedules. The plan specifies the source and destination of all information as sets of people or roles.

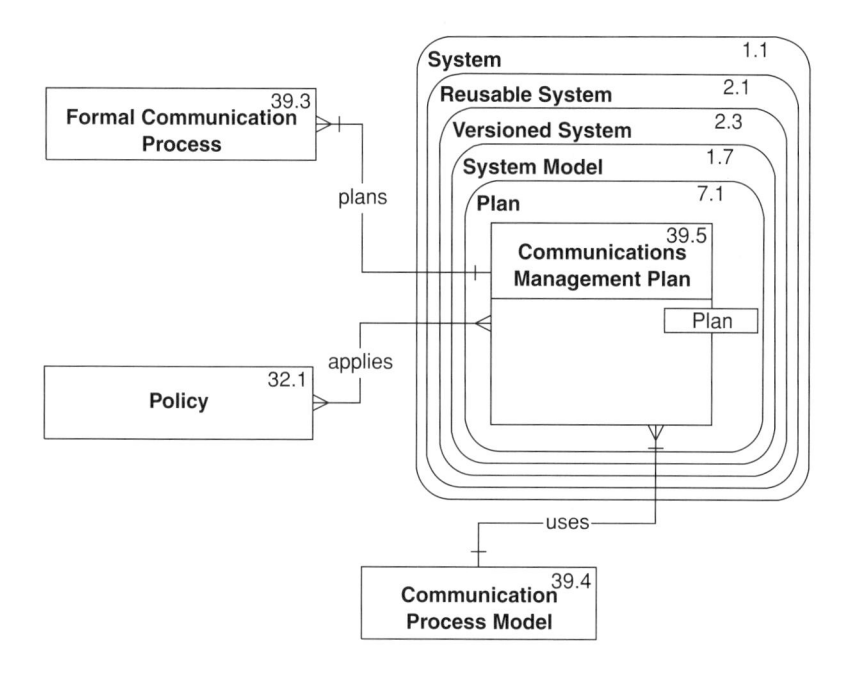

Vision: A communication process brought to a successful conclusion, achieving its mission by moving information to its intended destination

Mission: To bring the communication process model to bear on successfully achieving the mission of the project

---

Objective 39.6: To translate a communication process model into a set of tasks that control the flow of information through a communication process

---

Approach 39.6: Generate a plan from the communication process model, laying out the tasks, milestones, and dependencies of the process in the required amount of detail. Specify any baselines for the process milestones in the project schedule. Proceed with Approach 7.1 as for any plan, using its metric and target.

Responsibility Matrix (35.3)

Your communication plan needs to specify the scheduling and distribution structure of the formal communication processes you want to undertake. You can use a separate communication matrix similar to a responsibility matrix, or you can integrate the communication tasks into the responsibility matrix directly.

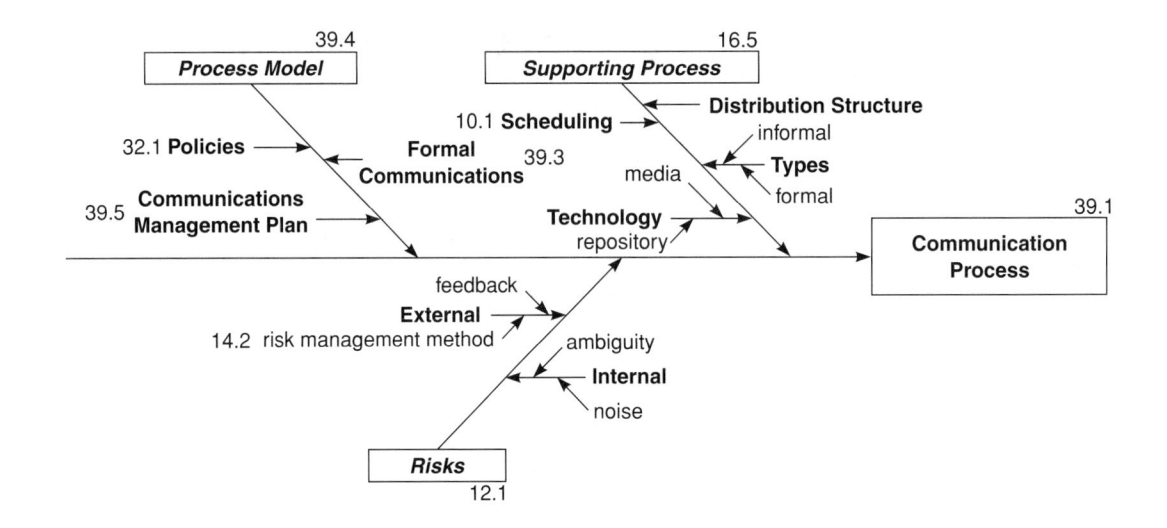

Readings

[Devlin]   Keith Devlin. *Logic and Information*. New York: Cambridge University Press, 1991.

This book is only for those interested in the serious mathematical modeling of information flow. It takes a valuable and unique approach to a subject weighted down with generations of philosophy and computer science, making clear what is information and what is not.

[Juliano]   William J. Juliano. External communication as an integral part of project planning. *PM Network* (February 1995): 18–21.

This short article describes a method of communication planning developed at US West. It proposes a matrix for planning when and how to conduct communication processes based on the kind of communication and the kind of target. While the actual breakdown does not appear to be particularly helpful in planning, the discussion is very illuminating about the issues. In particular, it completely omits the primary purpose of communication: feedback.

[Kerzner]	Harold Kerzner. *Project Management: A Systems Approach to Planning, Scheduling, and Controlling, Fifth Edition.* New York: Van Nostrand Reinhold, 1994.

Kerzner has several sections in his Chapter 5 on communications (5.13–5.16). It serves as a kind of laundry list of potential communications problems and pitfalls and some solutions to them.

[PMI 1996a]	Project Management Institute Standards Committee. *A Guide to the Project Management Body of Knowledge.* Project Management Institute (+1-610-734-3330), 1996.

Chapter 10 of the PMBOK is all about communications management. Sections 10.1 on "Communications Planning" and 10.2 on "Information Distribution" cover the material in this chapter.

Questions to Think About

1. Come up with a scheme for measuring the information content of a communication process. Is this easy or hard? What is "information," and why is it so hard to measure?

2. List five risk management methods that use a communications process. Why is risk management heavily dependent on communication?

3. If the destination for a communication is a role, what problems could affect the communication?

4. Do you think that planning informal communications is useful? Why?

5. Should a communication process model specify the media and format of a communication for every formal communication in the project? What would the impact of such detail be on the reusability of the process model?

CHAPTER

40 The Personal Interaction

The *personal interaction* is the main type of informal communication in a project. The personal interaction connects two or more people in a discussion using some communication tool. It is a key part of the informal communication process in a project. The communications management plan should include a section on encouraging personal interactions.

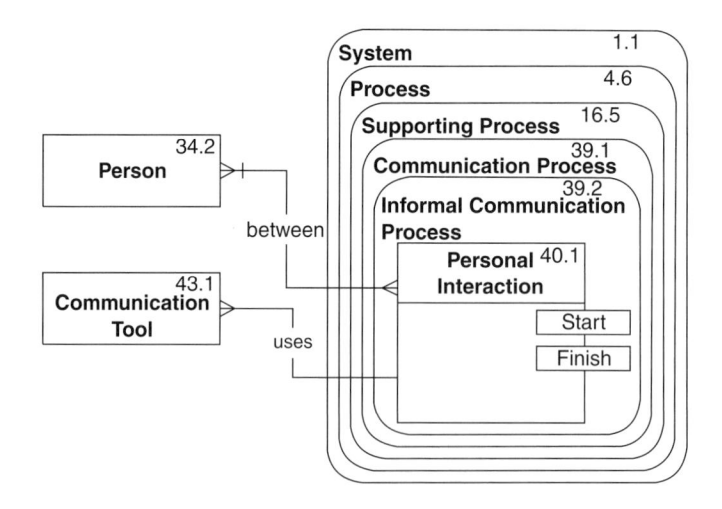

Vision: People interacting with one another to get their jobs done

Mission: To impart information or opinions directly with minimal overhead

Objective 40.1: To impart information or opinions directly with minimal overhead

The Personal Interaction 645

Approach 40.1: Start the interaction at an appropriate time and place using a tool such as the phone, an online browser or chat tool, or just plain talking. Using the appropriate language and references, convey the information you need to communicate to the other people in the interaction. Listen actively to their response to your communication, verifying that they have understood what you communicated. Integrate their response into your work. I don't recommend measuring this process; it's one of those things that is subject to the principle that measurement and motion are mutually exclusive.

Personal interactions seem to bring out the best and the worst in people. The most valuable communications in a project are usually that conversation in the hallway or a phone call to someone. But everything in your life that you would wish unsaid was probably said in a personal interaction. The immediacy and informality are everything.

One of my best learning experiences was an informal debugging session with a master developer. We were working on a UNIX prototype, and there was a problem with the interactions between one part of the system and another. As I worked with my cohort to try to find the problem, we talked about virtually every aspect of the system, while he calmly showed me how to debug a program effectively. I probably should have paid him for the experience.

In another job, I participated in a group "sensitivity training" session taught by a psychologist. This guy had developed a truly awful theory he called "active listening." To put this in context, what most communications people call "active listening" is the practice of feeding back information to the speaker to validate your understanding of what was said [Weinberg 1994]. What this psychologist was selling was the practice of taking control of the interaction by beating your opponent to death, verbally. An interesting approach. He likened it to aikido, which was bizarre, given the usual translation of that term as "the Art of Peace." Perhaps work would be more peaceful if everyone did everything you wanted. In any case, the end result of this session was two people breaking into tears (men, not women, to break a stereotype) and general disgust with management. This approach seemed to have the objective of establishing a codependency relationship between employees and management.

I've worked on several jobs with a management that wanted to discourage personal interactions of various sorts, but mostly those with external people. Sometimes this was because of confidentiality concerns, but more often managers seemed to feel that it was vital to prevent informal interaction with customers or the sales force to prevent developers from promising things they couldn't deliver. I was never very clear whether this was because of the dreadful impact of having to deliver extra value to customers that wanted it or the dreadful impact of not delivering value to customers that wanted it. Perhaps in the end it was not so much what the customer wanted as the need to control the actions of the developer.

There are much better ways to achieve control. Mostly, control comes from getting commitment to the project and its plan. Secondarily, it comes from giving people enough work to keep them busy. Idle hands do have a Parkinsonian tendency to fill in available time. If developers know what they are supposed to do and have had a voice in setting that up, you shouldn't see too many problems from personal interactions with outside people. Finally, most of these situations occur in organizations that don't value feedback. Since management doesn't really know what developers are doing, and generally don't know what customers think of the product, they have to exercise control in more authoritarian ways. The best way to handle this situation is to get the commitment from your team, and then act as the single voice of your team to external people, getting your team's agreement to that as a political strategy for presenting a uniform front [Weinberg 1994, p. 260].

Team (30.2)

One characteristic of the team, as opposed to the work group, is the increased number of personal interactions the team has internally. To build a team from a work group, one thing you must do is to encourage personal interaction. You should also provide a way for people to get away from personal interaction when they need to work alone, either through telecommuting or sensible office space arrangements [DeMarco 1987].

Another place that personal interaction has a big impact is in reuse. How many times have you been standing around in the lunchroom talking about your problems when somebody suggests taking a look at the WhatsIt class, which might work? This happens all the time. The personal interaction is so important for reuse that some authorities go out of their way to emphasize the similarity between their approaches and the personal interaction, such as the concept of the "virtual hallway" [Goldberg, p. 252]. While it is important to provide reuse repositories, linking pins, and organizational structures to facilitate reuse, don't ignore the personal interaction. If people in your organization talk to each other, they will find new and interesting ways to reuse parts of the system. If people don't talk, they won't know what they're missing, and neither will you.

In some organizations, personal interaction is the only way you ever reuse anything. After a couple of months on the job in an early OO project, I got an email from one of the members of my team that he had sent to all the developers in the small organization. He wanted to know if anyone had a C++ list class that he could reuse rather than having to write a completely new one. No one did, but the thought was there!

Readings

[DeMarco 1987] Tom DeMarco and Timothy Lister. *Peopleware: Productive Projects and Teams.* New York: Dorset House, 1987.
Every thinking human resources manager in a software company should read this book and take a test on it. Part II on "The Office Environment" is a wake-up call for companies that want to have productive, happy people working for them.

[Metzger]   Philip W. Metzger. *Managing Programming People: A Personal View.* Englewood Cliffs, NJ: Prentice Hall, 1987.

This little book is all about personal interactions in the context of programming management. While the stories are a little forced at times, the advice is very practical and to the point.

[Weinberg 1994] Gerald M. Weinberg. *Quality Software Management: Volume 3, Congruent Action.* New York: Dorset House, 1994.

This is the best book on personal interaction I've ever read. It is based on the work of the family therapist Virginia Satir, tempered by Weinberg's long experience with programmer psychology and personal interaction. It is mostly about managerial interaction with their employees, but there is plenty of material that applies generally.

Questions to Think About

1. Think about your most enjoyable work experience. Was it a personal interaction or something you did by yourself? Can you draw any conclusions about the effect of personal interactions on your work?

2. How much of your work depends on personal interactions with other people? Would any of those interactions be more appropriate as formal communications planned by a communications management plan? Why or why not?

3. What kind of informal personal interactions are you likely to have with external people such as stakeholders? Is this kind of interaction valuable or harmful to your work?

4. What kind of work do you do best in personal interactions? What kind do you do best working alone? Is there any overlap possible? How would you reorganize your work area or habits to improve the overall quality of your work?

CHAPTER

41 Meeting

The Meeting

The *meeting* is a formal communication process where two or more people simultaneously participate in a communication-oriented task. The meeting is a same-time group effort [Khoshafian; Lewis], though the people involved may not necessarily be in the same place. The meeting uses communication tools both to help conduct the meeting (presentation tools, overheads, and so on) and to enable the meeting for remote participants (conferencing, videoconferencing, and so on). Meetings have two essential project documents: the agenda and the minutes.

Vision: People working together to create value in a project

Mission: To organize a simultaneous group effort to accomplish a set of specific work-related goals

---

Objective 41.1: To organize a simultaneous group effort

Approach 41.1: Determine who should attend the meeting. Prioritize the attendees into essential and dispensable groups, dispensable people being those who should attend but who don't absolutely have to be there. Using networked scheduling tools or some other method, schedule the meeting by getting consensus from the list of essential people, both on the time for the meeting and on its purpose; accommodate the dispensable people up to the point where you are wasting time that would be better spent on real work (two or three iterations should be enough). Ensure that the meeting room and communication tools are available at the scheduled time.

Metric 41.1.1: Reschedules: the number of times the meeting was rescheduled

The Meeting   *649*

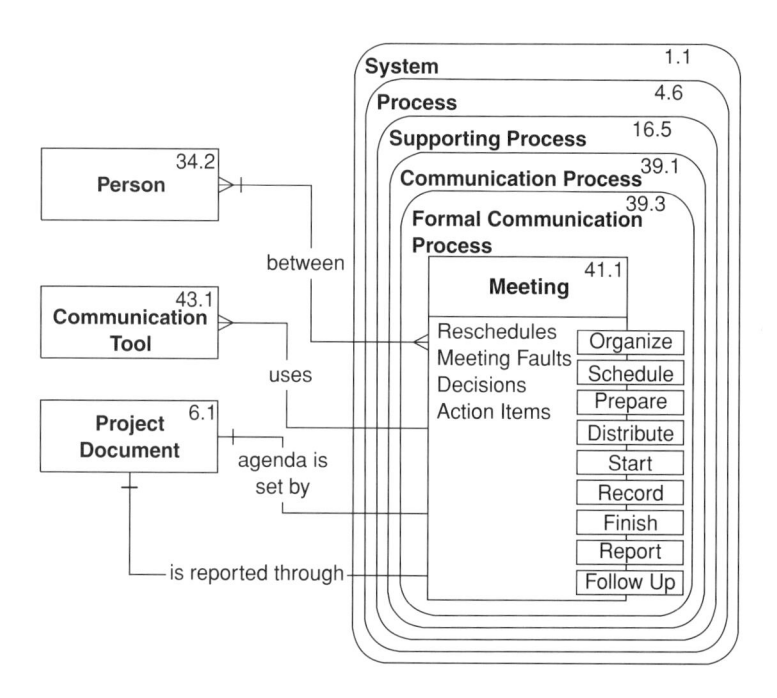

```
                    ┌─System─────────────1.1──┐
                    │ ┌─Process────────4.6──┐ │
                    │ │ ┌Supporting Process 16.5┐
                    │ │ │ ┌Communication Process┐
┌──────34.2─┐       │ │ │ │         39.1    │ │ │
│  Person   │▷──┐   │ │ │ │ ┌Formal Communication 39.3
└───────────┘   │   │ │ │ │ │  Process       │ │ │
                │   │ │ │ │ │ ┌──────41.1───┐│ │ │
           between │ │ │ │ │ │    Meeting   ││ │ │
                │  │ │ │ │ │ ├──────────────┤│ │ │
┌─────43.1──┐   │  │ │ │ │ │ │ Reschedules  ┌─Organize─┐
│Communication│▷┤  │ │ │ │ │ │ Meeting Faults─Schedule─┤
│    Tool    │  │  │ │ │ │ │ │ Decisions    ─Prepare──┤
└────────────┘ uses │ │ │ │ │ Action Items  ─Distribute┤
                │  │ │ │ │ │ │              ─Start────┤
┌─────6.1───┐   │  │ │ │ │ │ │              ─Record───┤
│  Project  │◁──┤  │ │ │ │ │ │              ─Finish───┤
│ Document  │ agenda is        │              ─Report───┤
└───────────┘ set by           │              ─Follow Up┘
      │                        │              └─────────┘
      └─is reported through────┘
```

Target 41.1.1: A low number within control limits of a pn control chart of meetings in your organization

Metric 41.1.2: Meeting Faults: the number of problems that arise with the meeting organization (people not included, room not available, tools not available or not working, and so on)

Target 41.1.2: A low number within control limits of a pn control chart of meetings in your organization

Objective 41.2: To accomplish a set of specific work-related goals

Approach 41.2: Determine the goals of the meeting, and produce an agenda that states the goals. Distribute the agenda before the meeting to the people who will attend and to those interested who cannot attend, including any documents to review. Revise the agenda as required before the meeting, distributing the changes to all who received the original document. Conduct the meeting according to the agenda. Have one meeting participant record the issues raised, decisions reached, and action items assigned during the meeting. That recorder should write up these notes into a minutes document, and then distribute that document to the people who attended the meeting, anyone with an action item assigned to them, and all others with an interest in the issues raised or decisions reached. The project manager should follow up on the action items, integrating them into the statement of work and schedule and tracking them as standard project tasks.

Metric 41.2.1: Off-agenda topics: the number of topics introduced during the meeting that were not on the agenda (not including items brought up under a reasonable agenda heading, even if the discussion was unexpected)

Target 41.2.1: None

Metric 41.2.2: Decisions: the number of decisions made on agenda items

Target 41.2.2: A number greater than zero

Metric 41.2.3: Action Items: the number of action items assigned

Target 41.2.3: A number within control limits of a pn control chart for meetings in your organization

---

Organizing a meeting consists of figuring out who needs to attend and what the agenda will be. The *agenda* is a project document that consists of an itemization of the goals of the meeting, usually stated as meeting topics with a brief description of what the meeting is to consider doing about the topic. These topics should be related, well organized, and reasonably few in number. The agenda states who will attend the meeting and the time and place. As you schedule the meeting, you revise the agenda to reflect changes.

■ *Note:* You do not want to have a meeting unless you must. Meetings are formal occasions that tie up several expensive resources for the duration of the meeting. Consider what you are buying for the money. Also, consider what you could buy for the money if you didn't have the meeting. Robert Lucky once reported a scary number: an organization that had a meeting for every line of code it produced [Lucky]. That is, the number of meetings divided by the number of lines of code was one. While this may be exceptional, it fits with my general experience. Mostly, these meetings do not contribute to any value or productivity and should not happen. You should handle most of these topics as informal personal interactions, not as meetings.

Personal Interaction (40.1)

Scheduling the meeting usually means finding out when everyone can attend. Time management systems such as Now's Up-To-Date can help you with this task by automatically scheduling meetings based on the availability of the participants. In any case, you will usually go back and forth a few times until everyone is happy with the meeting time. You may need to reschedule, but you should keep this to a minimum, as Target 41.1.1 suggests. Too much rescheduling indicates that you don't have the necessary commitment to the meeting goals or that people are too disorganized.

Preparing for the meeting is the process of reserving the meeting room, setting up the conference calls, arranging for the tools, and so on. Once you have finished the agenda, scheduled the meeting, and prepared the room, you should distribute the agenda along with any documents relevant to the meeting to the participants.

You should always start the meeting on time. I think more time is wasted in late starts than any other single aspect of business. If someone isn't there, just start. I wait no more than five or ten minutes for a presenter or some other key person, and then adjourn the meeting and reschedule. Otherwise, you wind up spending a huge amount of money just sitting around. Also, people come and go, causing even more waiting.

Once you've started the meeting, one participant should keep notes, recording any issues raised, decisions made, or action items assigned. These notes become the basis for the *minutes,* a project document that describes what happened at the meeting. If a meeting has no minutes, then nothing happened, and you shouldn't have had the meeting in the first place. When you finish the meeting, make sure the recorder has a list of all the action items by briefly reviewing the list and assigning the items to individuals for further action. The recorder should then write up the minutes and distribute them to the participants and other interested parties, including anyone assigned an action item. The project manager should then follow up on the action items by including them in the project work breakdown structure and tracking them as you would any task.

The Joint Review

A *joint review* is a meeting that involves two or more people with differing views of the object of the meeting. The goal of the joint review is to evaluate task status and task products at a milestone using policies that establish evaluation criteria. At least one participant reviews the work of at least one participant. Certain action items add problem reports to the product management system. If the status and products are acceptable, the review results in the milestone event.

- ■ *Note:* It is vital to understand that the point of a joint review is not to communicate information but to evaluate status and products. You don't review a system to familiarize everyone with it; you review it to judge whether it can achieve its mission.

Vision: Consensual movement toward product delivery

Mission: To produce a consensus on the evaluation of the status and products of a task

---

Objective 41.3: To evaluate the status and products of a task at a milestone

---

Approach 41.3: Identify the task, milestone, and versioned systems that are subject to evaluation and construct the agenda around them. Ensure that the meeting participants understand the evaluation criteria by distributing them with the agenda as well. Schedule the meeting to occur as soon after the task finishes as is practicable. Conduct the meeting, evaluating the status and products of the task using the evaluation criteria. Report the results of the evaluation in the minutes.

Metric 41.3: Evaluation ratio: the ratio of products evaluated to products scheduled for evaluation

Target 41.3: One

Objective 41.4: To produce a consensus on the evaluation in Objective 41.3

Approach 41.4: For each evaluation, vote on the acceptance of the evaluation or note any dissenting views in the minutes. Before finishing the meeting, decide whether to accept the evaluations and products or to reject them. If you reject them, decide whether to allow the task to iterate to produce a reworked deliverable and whether that rework should result in another review. If so, plan the rework and review as action items.

Metric 41.4: Consensus: a Boolean value indicating whether or not the meeting participants concur on the evaluations in Approach 41.3

Target 41.4: True

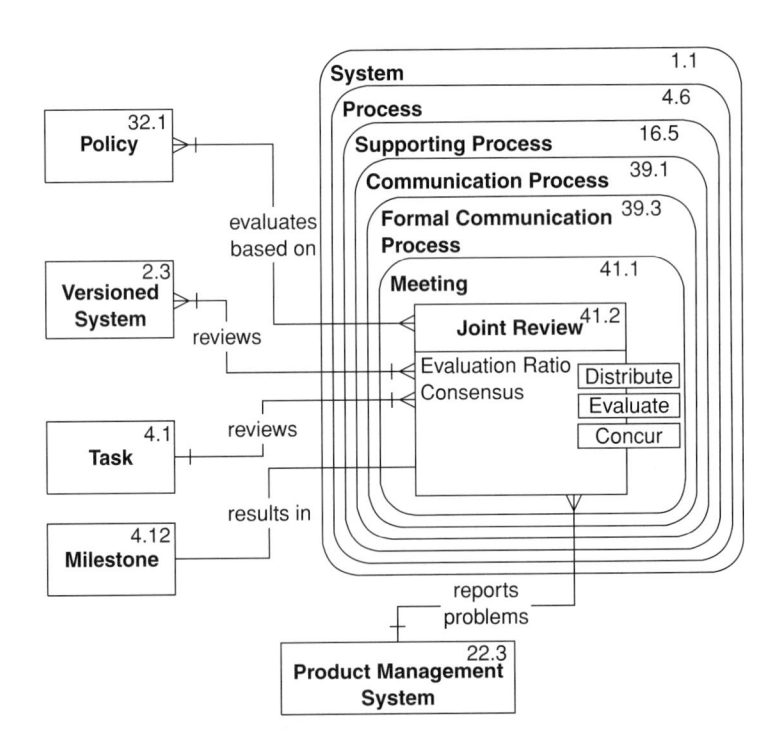

A key decision during a review judges whether the status or product is adequate according to some evaluation criteria. If the outcome is inadequate, the participants must decide whether to permit rework of the product and whether to conduct an additional joint review of the rework results. Both decisions become action items.

- *Note:* The joint review is often seen as a purchaser-supplier review, but this book integrates purely internal reviews into this framework. I can't see any useful distinction between reviews involving external people and reviews with only project people.

The Management Review

A *management review* is a joint review that evaluates project status. The management review thus reviews the project task at a major process milestone.

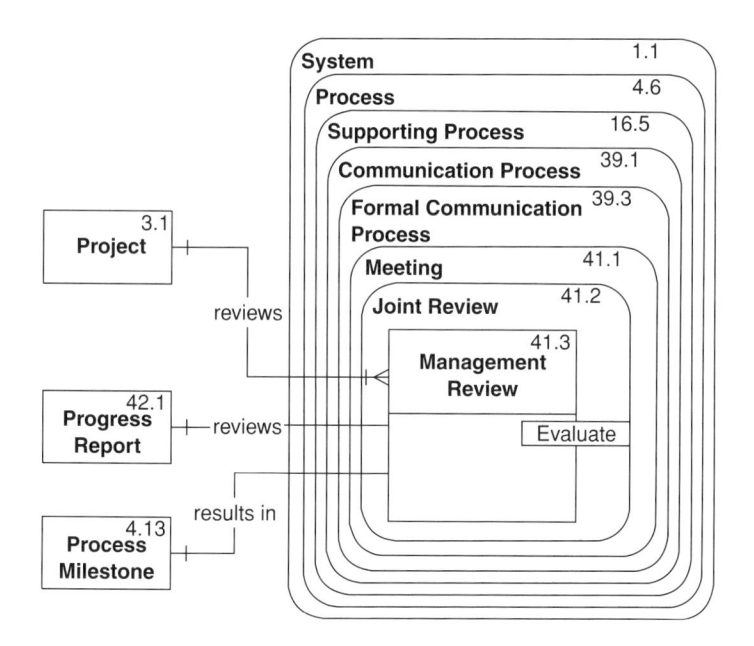

Vision: Consensual movement toward project delivery

Mission: To produce a consensus on the evaluation of the status of the project

A management review evaluates the status of the project in several different ways, depending on the milestone. Typically, the review evaluates how well the project is doing in terms of schedule and budget through earned-value and cost analysis. As well, the management review should evaluate the nature of changes to the statement of work. Finally, the management review should conduct a reevaluation of project risks, with action items relating to additional risk management, should the project be at risk.

The Technical Review

A *technical review* is a joint review that evaluates the products of a development process, usually a software object and/or its documentation.

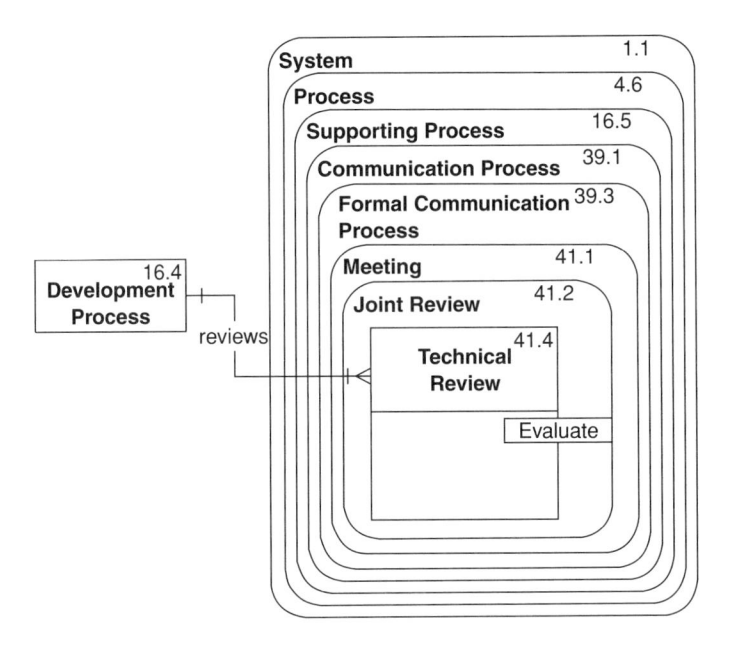

Vision: Consensual movement toward delivery of the products of a development process

Mission: To produce a consensus on the evaluation of the products of a development process

The verification of a product is a quality assurance process that ensures that a product fulfills requirements from a previous task. The purpose of the review is to evaluate the results of the verification process and thereby the products of the development process. ISO/IEC-12207 identifies several different kinds of verification [ISO 1995]:

- Contract verification
- Process verification

- Requirements verification
- Design verification
- Code verification
- Integration verification
- Documentation verification

While each of these kinds of verification differs in content, the criteria for judging them are substantially the same:

- Completeness
- Standards compliance
- Specification compliance
- Changes
- Schedule
- Dependencies met for future tasks
- Process compliance

There are many specific criteria on which to evaluate software and documentation. I prefer to evaluate technical objects using two kinds of criteria. First, I evaluate these objects with criteria that have demonstrated a relationship to either quality or effectiveness of production. Second, I prefer to evaluate objects for standards compliance using objective criteria, and preferably automated, measurable criteria. In code reviews, for example, I prefer to keep to easily standardized criteria that you can check with CodeCheck or a similar static analysis tool.

Policy (32.1)

I have consistently heard, from those who managed me and those who worked for me, that technical reviews are worthless because they don't find problems. Frankly, this is just wrong. Both my own experience and all the scientific research say precisely the opposite. One study reported a range of 50% to 92% of defects detected through inspections [O'Neill]. Another reported 60% defect removal on a consistent basis [Jones 1991, p. 263]. Yet another book reports a ten times reduction in errors reaching each testing stage with a cost reduction of 50 to 80% due to reduced need for testing [Freedman, p. 12].

There are two major issues that lead me to recommend technical reviews over a total reliance on testing. First, the cost of finding defects in software grows dramatically with the progress of the project. A requirements error caught in a requirements review may cost $20 to fix, while the same error caught by an acceptance test after product delivery may cost $1,000 [Boehm 1981, p. 40]. That's a two-order-of-magnitude difference in cost. That doesn't take into account the fact that the error may cascade into many other errors as the project progresses, each one costing you.

The second issue I find compelling is that you can't test software until you have software. And yet many of the task products of a software project, such as requirements and design documents, are the source of many of the major defects in the system. These objects you can only review, not test (at least not yet). Even if you could, the abstraction level of these systems leads me to believe that inspection is a much better way to find problems, because humans are good at the kind of pattern recognition involved in reviews, while computers are not.

I worked with one developer, the founder of the company, who was very good at reading code. We were programming in C, and he could read a function and hand it back to you having identified every single problem relating to pointer dereferences, logic flaws, and oversights. This kind of person is invaluable for quality code.

The problem is, many developers and managers do not get the training in inspection that they need to do adequate reviews. Perhaps that's why many Variable and Routine cultures think reviews are worthless: they are, because the people in those cultures can't do adequate reviews. The problem is, they can't do adequate testing either, so reviews would still be cheaper and more effective than testing.

The Improvement Review

An *improvement review* is a joint review that verifies the effectiveness of a system improvement project. The improvement review requires an approved improvement plan, an ongoing project, and an improvement project progress report that contains data related to the operational objectives of the system being improved. The review presents and evaluates this data and decides on changes to the improvement project.

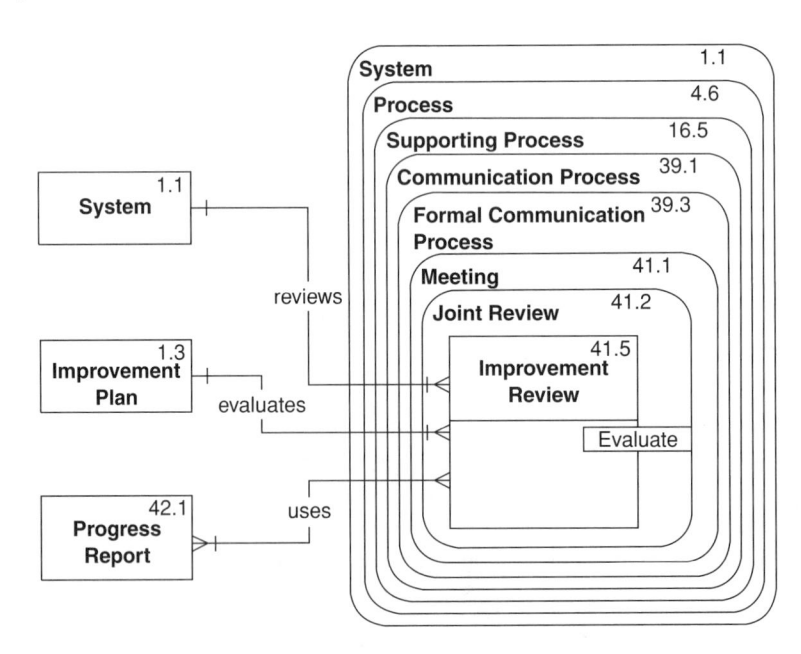

Vision: Consensual movement toward an improved system

Mission: To produce a consensus on the evaluation of the status of an improvement plan

Some candidates for an improvement review include defect prevention, technology adoption, and process improvement projects. The improvement review can also be part of a larger project, where the improvement is a series of tasks within that project.

The Communication Meeting

A *communication meeting* is one in which one or more participants communicate something to one or more participants purely to impart the information. Communication can be two-way, but the emphasis is more on communicating outward and less on feedback.

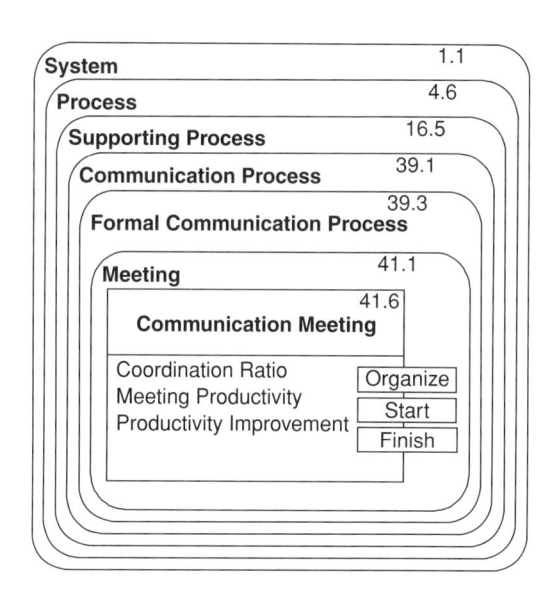

```
System                              1.1
  Process                           4.6
    Supporting Process             16.5
      Communication Process        39.1
        Formal Communication Process  39.3
          Meeting                  41.1
                                   41.6
            Communication Meeting

            Coordination Ratio       [Organize]
            Meeting Productivity     [Start]
            Productivity Improvement [Finish]
```

Vision: People working together to create value in a project

Mission: To impart information to a group of people that will allow them to do their jobs more effectively or productively

Objective 41.5: To increase work effectiveness

Approach 41.5: Put items on the agenda that will align the participants toward some project goal through the coordination of work. Emphasize cooperation and coordination during communication. Be brief and to the point. Through active listening, ensure that the participants have accurately absorbed the content you are trying to communicate. Answer any relevant questions, but keep any discussion focused on the agenda. Create action items for any off-agenda topics that require further discussion.

Metric 41.5: Coordination ratio: the number of agenda topics that contribute to system alignment through coordination of work over the total number of agenda topics

Target 41.5: A number close to 1 within control limits of a p control chart of communication meetings in your organization

---

Objective 41.6: To increase productivity

Approach 41.6: Hold a communication meeting only when you need to communicate information that will improve effectiveness or productivity. Start on time and keep the meeting as short as possible.

Metric 41.6.1: Meeting productivity: agenda topics covered per hour of meeting

Target 41.6.1: A number within control limits of an x-R control chart of communication meetings

---

Metric 41.6.2: Productivity improvement: the degree to which the meeting improves productivity

Target 41.6.2: A reasonable value within control parameters of an x-R control chart of productivity-improving communication meetings

---

Examples of communication meetings include meetings to resolve issues, meetings to help coordinate several people in working on a task, and meetings to gather feedback from team members, stakeholders, or other interested parties.

A *team meeting* is a communication meeting in which a group leader communicates information to his or her group.

- Status of prior action items
- Schedule status
- Changes
- Major issues with group work
- Action items

The team meeting should usually leave room for discussing any team member's issues or concerns, although often these are more appropriate as informal personal interactions. Often the main input to the team meeting is the set of periodic timesheets for the participants.

The *presentation* is a structured communication meeting where the agenda consists of one or more media-assisted expositions on some well-defined subject. You can limit discussion to questions after the exposition or you can be more open. The objective is to communicate a very specific subject to a number of interested people. You will normally use presentation tools such as Microsoft Powerpoint, Lotus Freelance, Corel Presentations, or Harvard Graphics, or simpler tools such as slides, overheads, or flip charts [Rabb].

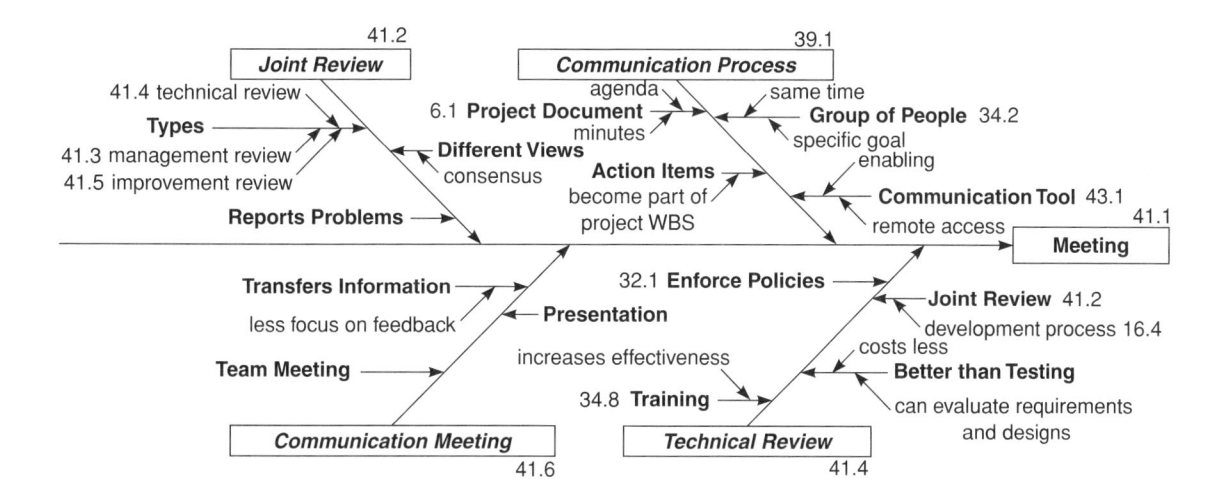

```
                            41.2                    39.1
                       Joint Review          Communication Process
         41.4 technical review                agenda         same time
              Types                  6.1 Project Document        Group of People  34.2
         41.3 management review         Different Views minutes     specific goal
         41.5 improvement review          consensus   Action Items      enabling
                                                    become part of   Communication Tool  43.1
              Reports Problems                       project WBS       remote access     41.1
                                                                                    Meeting

         Transfers Information           32.1 Enforce Policies      Joint Review  41.2
         less focus on feedback              Presentation            development process 16.4
                                                                    costs less
            Team Meeting               increases effectiveness      Better than Testing
                                            34.8 Training           can evaluate requirements
                                                                         and designs
                     Communication Meeting    Technical Review
                            41.6                    41.4
```

Readings

[Freedman]   Daniel P. Freedman and Gerald M. Weinberg. *Handbook of Walkthroughs, Inspections, and Technical Reviews: Evaluating Programs, Projects, and Products, Third Edition.* New York: Dorset House, 1990.

This excellent reference work tells you everything you need to know about technical reviews. It uses a somewhat unwieldy question-and-answer format without achieving the concision of Plato, but it is readable and comprehensive. It contains case studies from different real-world companies to illustrate the processes.

[ISO 1991]   International Standards Organization. *ISO 9000-3, Guideline for Application of ISO 9001 to the Development, Supply, and Maintenance of Software.* ISO, 1991.

Section 4.1.3 of this standard discusses joint reviews in the context of purchaser management (reviews with both a supplier and a purchaser reviewing software).

[ISO 1995]   International Standards Organization. *ISO/IEC 12207, Information Technology—Software Life Cycle Processes.* ISO, 1995.

Section 6.6 of this standard addresses the joint review, including both the management review and the technical review.

[Kehoe]   Raymond Kehoe and Alka Jarvis. *ISO 9000-3: A Tool for Software Product and Process Improvement.* New York: Springer-Verlag, 1996.

Chapter 6 of this book discusses the ISO 9000-3 standard for joint reviews [ISO 1991] in some detail.

[Rabb]   Margaret Y. Rabb. *The Presentation Design Book, Second Edition.* Chapel Hill, NC: Ventana Press, 1993.

This book is invaluable for people who do many presentations. The sections on layout and design are comprehensive, telling you everything you must know to create effective presentations. My only criticism is the lack of material on presentation software, which is becoming ubiquitous in software company presentations these days.

[3M]   The 3M Meeting Management Team. *How to Run Better Business Meetings: A Reference Guide for Managers.* New York: McGraw-Hill, Inc., 1979.

Every manager needs this book. It presents the gamut of knowledge on meetings, with many invaluable details on everything from agendas to meeting leadership to setting up a room for a presentation. This is the best book I've found on the subject.

Questions to Think About

1. List some major differences between the same-place meeting and meetings that don't take place with everyone at the same location. Is there any reason to distinguish the same-time, different-place meeting from the same-time, same-place meeting as a separate class? What would the characteristics of this class be?

2. One technique for generating agendas is to spend the first part of the meeting doing that. Why do you think this chapter doesn't recommend this approach? (Hint: Why does the Distribute task occur before the meeting? What is the relationship between the agenda and the people who attend the meeting?)

3. What are the implications of organizational structure for action items? (Hint: Who takes part in meetings? Who assigns action items?)

4. Can you think of any reason to distinguish joint reviews with external people from reviews within your organization? What would the two classes look like? What would the subclass structure look like?

5. List several possible subclasses of the technical review. What do you use to differentiate between them?

6. Given the operational objectives in the hierarchy of classes terminating in the communication meeting, what is the specific objective of the team meeting? How would you structure the team meeting process given these objectives?

CHAPTER 42

Progress Report

The Progress Report

The *progress report* is a project document that summarizes timesheet information to some required level of detail. The progress report has a double purpose: to communicate the status to stakeholders of the process and to document status for measurement records. For example, you use a progress report for a management review of a process. The underlying goal, as with most communication-related systems, is to enable feedback in the project system. Most progress reports build on previous progress reports to show a trend. The project management system generates the progress report.

Vision: A project making clear progress toward delivering its value

Mission: To summarize the progress of a process toward achieving its mission

---

Objective 42.1: To communicate to stakeholders the progress of a process toward achieving its mission

---

Approach 42.1: Determine the time interval over which you want to report progress. This will usually be the beginning of the process to the as-of date. Gather together the timesheets for the period and any previous progress reports. Add the new information to the previous progress reports in the project management system. Generate the current progress report from the project management system using the current performance evaluation baselines for the process. Add any explanations of significant variances from the plan or interesting trends. Format the report and distribute it to stakeholders through a communication process. If the report is a milestone report, hold a management review to get formal feedback on the process progress.

Metric 42.1: Comprehension: a subjective, ordinal metric describing the understanding of progress shared by the stakeholders, determined by sampling the stakeholders on specific items; values Excellent, Good, Adequate, Poor, Nonexistent

Target 42.1: Good to Excellent

Objective 42.2: To document the progress of a process toward achieving its mission for use in future reports and projects

---

Approach 42.2: Build the report as in Approach 42.1. Store the report in the reuse repository. Measure this objective using Reuse Potential (Metric 2.1).

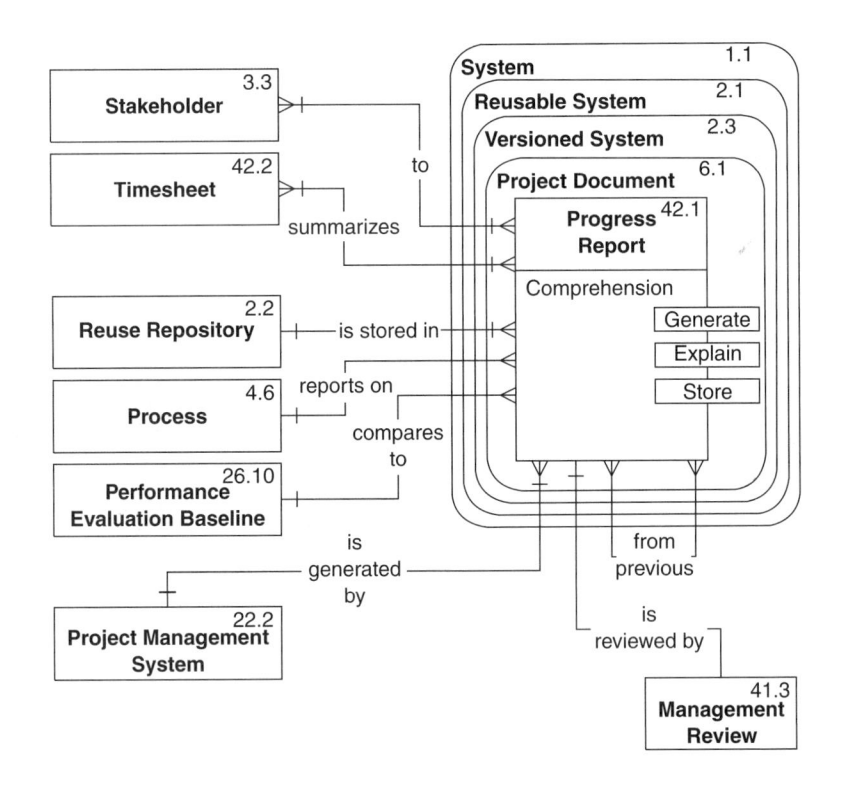

The specifics of the progress summary will vary according to your needs. If you have both a schedule and budget, you will want to have an integrated schedule and cost report that shows both the cost and schedule variances as well as the earned value of the project at a moment. You may want to add a section for causal analysis of the status or performance, especially if there are significant variances from your plan's current baseline. You can use this information to suggest corrective action through the change management process.

"The Project Deliverables and System Earned Value" section, Chapter 3, p. 67

Progress reporting is the key element in controlling the project through the change management process. Progress reporting establishes the status of a project: where the project now stands regarding its schedule and budget. It also establishes the performance of the project through use of earned value and other metrics of project performance. To have effective progress reports, you must have a mechanism for collecting the data to summarize in those reports, such as timesheets. In the context of contracted products, the contractor also supplies progress reports.

Change Management Process (24.1)
Contract Report (28.4)

A *project progress report* summarizes the status of a project, usually including the status and data for metrics on the deliverable objects of the project as well as any milestones or other elements of the project of vital interest to stakeholders. A contract report summarizes the status of a contracted project.

Contract Report (28.4)

Change and build reports are related to progress reports. These reports summarize the changes and bill of materials in system builds.

Change Report (24.5)
Build Report (25.6)

The reuse potential of a progress report depends on its internal characteristics and on your organization's way of reporting progress. Many organizations do not report progress uniformly through earned value or any other measure other than meeting a milestone. This single-minded focus on schedule above all else makes progress reports meaningless after you issue them. Nobody cares about last week's milestone, only about this week's one. The key to reuse potential is thus building a progress reporting system based on a combination of effective baselines and reliable, history-based progress indicators such as earned value and earned cost. Your organization has to both accept and use the report to have any reuse potential.

The certification of a progress report requires some assurance that the numbers are accurate. You must evaluate the risk of bad timesheet data and possibly the risk of tool failure. You can audit timesheets randomly to put a number on the risk of bad data, and you should assess tool reliability through experimentation. The progress report should refer to a comprehensive statement (a policy is good) that describes the report statistics and their interpretation. It should also contain a cogent explanation of the specific report issues, such as unexpected variances in cost, value, or schedule. The responsibility certification should be the signature of the project manager that prepared the report, who must be willing to accept responsibility for any problems with the report in a way consistent with the project manager's code of ethics.

The Timesheet

The *timesheet* is a kind of project document that reports how a person spent effort and money on assignments during the reporting period. The timesheet has a well-defined reporting period and a standard report structure in its document template. A policy determines the reporting period and directs people to submit timesheets at a specific time after the end of each period.

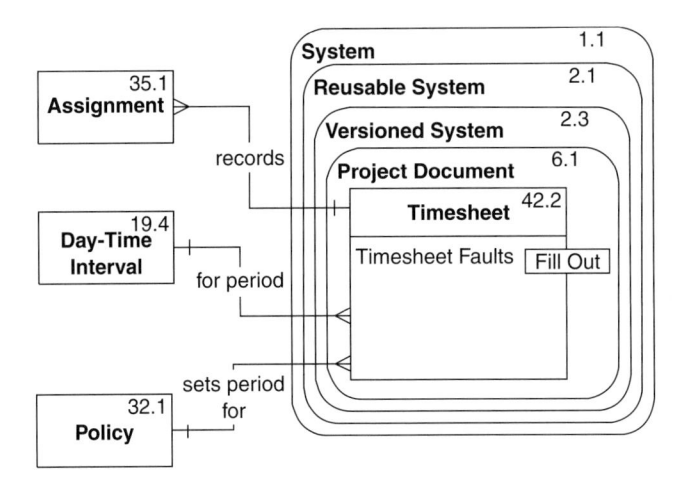

Vision: Clear measures of work done on a project

Mission: To measure the amount of work a person does during a period of time

Objective 42.3: To measure the amount of work a person does during a period of time

Approach 42.3: Create a timesheet from the timesheet document template. Determine the reporting period for the timesheet. For each task you've worked on during the period, note the WBS number, the number of hours you've worked, and any monetary costs for the task. If it's relevant, note the number of overtime hours versus regular shift hours for each task. Specify the currency unit for monetary amounts.

Metric 42.3: Timesheet faults: the number of missing tasks or errors in task numbers or work amounts

Target 42.3: A low number within control limits of a pn control chart of timesheets

This structure may be a document without internal structure, but it can be a series of tables and columns in a relational database or a set of objects. The exact structure depends on your tools and repository schema. There are tools that facilitate submission of timesheets online, such as Time$heet Professional from Timeslips International, or you can use a spreadsheet program.

- *Note:* If your project involves international expenses, you need to make sure that costs are either translated to the appropriate currency or that you note the currency unit on the timesheet.

Timesheets are a widely misunderstood document. Because they resemble punching a time clock, professional workers often feel they are being downgraded to the status of blue-collar workers when management insists on timesheets. I think this comes from two misconceptions. First, management often uses timesheets for purposes that are a mystery to the people who fill them out. Second, management hardly ever insists on accuracy, thus sending the message that the forms are useless bureaucracy. The purpose for timesheets is to gather data on tasks for measurement, nothing else. Accuracy is paramount. You should audit timesheets on a random basis both to make sure people are being accurate and to let people know that the numbers do matter.

I have never seen anyone fired for attendance problems based on their timesheets. For example, I managed a programmer in one OO organization who was very dissatisfied with the company. I noticed within a month that his timesheets were odd; they reported no more than 10 hours a week working on project tasks. I mentioned this to the director of development, who then poured out the sad story of this individual. It turned out that I had been given this problem with no expectation of any resolution, so I was instructed to ignore it. The employee kept filing the accurate timesheets that said he wasn't doing any work, and we dutifully ignored it until he resigned later that year.

One interesting, if irrelevant, use for timesheets is to document costs for a financial accounting practice known as *development expense capitalization*. This creative approach to inflating the company's assets on the balance sheet involves treating project work as a capital expense to be amortized over time rather than appearing on the income statement all at once. As one cogent commentator on the practice [Graham, p. 235] put it, "The magnitude of these items is sometimes proportionate to the ineptitude with which the expenditures were incurred." One company I worked for had accumulated so much capitalized expense it outweighed everything else on the balance sheet, causing them some trouble with security analysts looking at their stock. The company used the timesheet process solely to support this practice. I had to integrate my own timesheet system for gathering project data with their system or risk overburdening my team with useless time reporting.

Timesheets are absolutely vital for measuring effort in a software development organization. Do whatever you have to do to convince your people that the measurement is essential and useful. Show them you value the data by paying attention to it and auditing it. Ignorance, in the case of progress reports, is not bliss.

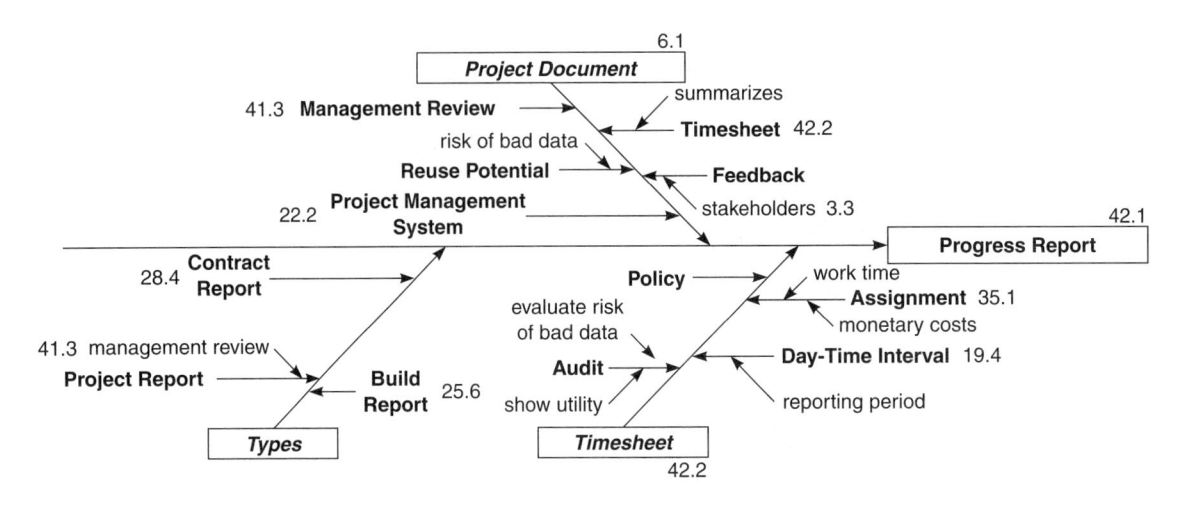

Readings

[Kerzner]　　　Harold Kerzner. *Project Management: A Systems Approach to Planning, Scheduling, and Controlling, Fifth Edition.* New York: Van Nostrand Reinhold, 1994.

Kerzner's Section 15.7 on "Status Reporting" has a good summary of the kind of progress reports stakeholders like to see.

[PMI 1996a]　　Project Management Institute Standards Committee. *A Guide to the Project Management Body of Knowledge.* Project Management Institute (+1-610-734-3330), 1996.

Section 10.3 of the PMBOK is on "Performance Reporting." This section summarizes the issues very succinctly in three pages.

Questions to Think About

1. What criteria would you use to decide whether to include an explanation in a project report about a variance?
2. List some trends in a progress report that might be of interest to management stakeholders.
3. How do changes affect your progress reports? (Hint: What role do baselines play?)
4. How reusable are contract progress reports? What does this depend on?
5. Does your company use timesheets? Compare the techniques your company uses to those suggested here and evaluate them using the class mission.
6. How do the standard expense reports compare to timesheets? What is the purpose of expense reports, and how does their organization reflect that purpose? Do timesheets serve a similar purpose?

CHAPTER

Communication Tool 43

The Communication Tool

The *communication tool* is one you use in a communication process. The communications management plan specifies what kinds of tool to use for particular types of communications in the plan.

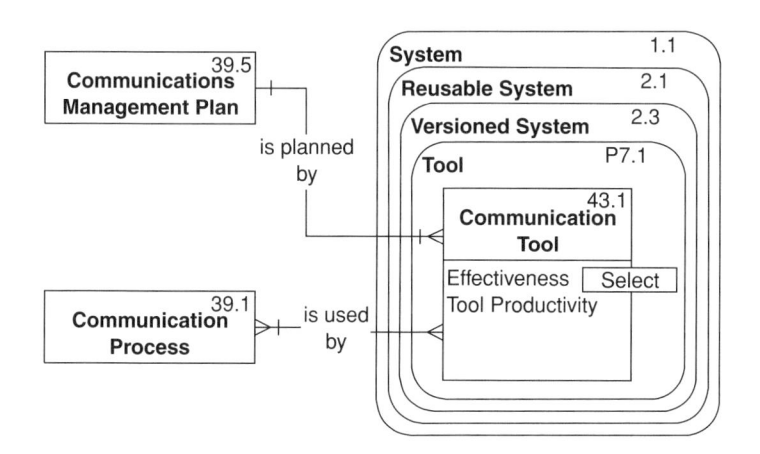

Vision: People communicating without barriers

Mission: To enable effective and productive communication processes

Objective 43.1: To enable effective communication processes

667

Approach 43.1: Match the capabilities of the communication tool to the needs of the communication process. Use the right tool for the job. Use improvement plans to study and improve the effectiveness of the tool in different communication processes.

Metric 43.1: Effectiveness: whether the tool is effective at enabling communication in the communication processes that use it

Target 43.1: Effective

Objective 43.2: To enable productive communication processes

Approach 43.2: Use tools that do not take up work time for setup and use. Use improvement plans to improve the productivity of the tool.

Metric 43.2: Tool productivity: the number of information units per effort-hour of work in setting up or using the communication tool

Target 43.2: A high number within control limits of a pn control chart of communication tools for similar communication processes

---

Certain methods of communication are better for certain types of communication. For example, videoconferencing permits people over a wide area to effectively interact in a review, while mail or even electronic messaging may be much less effective for that purpose. There are many different methods of communication, and several different ways to categorize them. The most obvious is by medium: voice, electronic messaging, online browsers, video, fax, or mail.

Personal Interaction (40.1)

- *Note:* Since it does not represent a technological object, face-to-face communication—personal interaction—does not appear in the following set of tools. It is, nevertheless, the most common method of communicating in projects and appears as a separate class. Perhaps the fact that it does not involve mediating tools explains this success. Not all face-to-face meetings are effective, however.

A *voice* communications tool is one that permits communication by real-time audio conversation between two or more parties at different locations. Voice communications tools include standard, cellular, or satellite telephony equipment. New technologies are becoming available, such as audio conversations conducted through Internet connections. Voice communications are a key component of any communications approach and are usually a standard part of the infrastructure of a business.

Electronic messaging is the ability to send messages in a standard way between computers. The most common use for messaging is electronic mail, which allows written communication between unique mailing addresses. Electronic mail tools often have extended facilities for attaching documents and requesting services. A mail server can respond automatically to well-structured requests sent to it. Mail list servers distribute collections of electronic mail to lists of users. File transfer protocol (FTP) software can initiate transfer of files through messaging. Notification schemes send well-structured messages through networks between computers as notification of events; where the receiving computer recognizes the message, it handles the notification as required.

When using email for communication, pretend you're talking on the phone or face to face. Email can have a tendency to get you in trouble if you don't treat it with respect. Often, people seem to be willing to say things in email that they would not say in person. Also, make sure that the address on the email is the right one before sending it. Sending a very personal note to your entire company happens too often. You can also accidentally send things to the wrong person, having unfortunate consequences. I've seen people send mail to other people criticizing them in very negative terms, when they actually meant to complain to a coworker instead of to the person in question. This can clear the air, but it may do so in ways you don't appreciate. As with any kind of communication, don't assume privacy; make it happen if you need it.

An *online browser* is a software system that enables you to communicate with repositories such as World Wide Web servers of FTP sites using a standard graphical interface. Tools such as Netscape Navigator and Microsoft's Internet Explorer are examples of this exciting new genre of communication tool. Using these tools with an online repository, you can both passively and actively communicate with a worldwide audience.

Online Repository (43.2)

A *video* communications tool permits communication by real-time or recorded video conversation or presentation between two or more parties at different locations. Video recordings can be an effective means of presenting information to many people over a wide area. Videoconferencing can provide communication more effectively than simple audioconferencing, since many cues about information are visual rather than auditory. Video presentations can transmit a presentation simultaneously to many people in real time and can allow feedback through question-and-answer mechanisms.

A *fax* communications tool lets you transmit two-dimensional materials by telephonic means to any number of other people. This is a faster alternative to paper mail. The technology can transmit computer-based images, not just paper.

A *mail* communication tool lets you transmit two-dimensional materials by manual means. This can include government mail services or private package services. The tools that enable mail are usually part of the standard infrastructure of any business.

The reliability of a communication tool is the primary determinant of its reuse potential, followed closely by ease of use. PC fax software, for example, is less reliable than a stand-alone fax and is harder to use to send materials that originate on paper because you need a separate scanner. Using a phone for conferencing is always a challenge. Many phones in offices do not have conferencing capabilities, and the ones that do make it difficult through poor speakers, poor microphones, and difficult-to-use buttons. Transferring a call is nearly always difficult for the technically inadequate software developer (a joke).

Domain reuse for the communication tool is the match between medium and message. Most communication tools have overlaps here, but some are clearly not reusable for certain kinds of communication. You can mail almost anything, but it is very difficult to send pictures over a voice phone line. You can fax pictures, but only if they reproduce well; otherwise, you need to mail them. You can send electronic documents by email, but only if the receiver has the appropriate software for unpacking the document from the mail.

Organizational reuse potential comes from the culture and policy environment of the organization. If you work in a paper culture, you will find it difficult to reuse electronic tools. If you work in a cost-conscious organization, you may find restrictions on the use of phones, faxes, and other expensive communications equipment. Conversely, rich organizations may have their own microwave communications system.

A smallish company I worked for had an international development organization split between the U.S. and Europe. To integrate the organization, we relied on various kinds of communication tools, but the company culture was not up to the task. The phone and electronic systems were the responsibility of the MIS department. For various cultural reasons, MIS could not move very quickly on technology acquisition. We spent a year with an inadequate ISDN network connection that we finally upgraded. More seriously, the MIS organization had real problems maintaining the quirky email system across this link. If you sent a document by email, there was a 50-50 chance of its being received at the other end in a reasonable period of time. At one point things were so bad that my group set up an online repository arrangement into which we would deposit our documents for exchange. We would then copy the documents back and forth on the network. We would notify each other of documents ready for transfer through voice phone calls. This proved to be the only reliable way to get information back and forth for several months until MIS finally addressed the mail system problems.

The Online Repository

An *online repository* is one that you can access through a network or modem connection. There are several types of online repository that serve to communicate information on demand. This can be as simple as a file on a network server or as complex as a bulletin board or Web site. The key point about repositories is that they provide their information on demand rather than notifying you or requiring you to take action. Repositories also serve as warehouses of information, letting you access historical information as well as current information.

Vision: An internetworked set of repositories that actively help people to do their jobs

Mission: To provide an internetworked repository that enables effective communication

---

Objective 43.3: To provide an internetworked repository that enables effective communication

---

Approach 43.3: Set up a repository with associated communication tools that let it operate as a facilitator for communication.

Metric 43.3: Availability: the availability of the online repository as a ratio of time available to the total time in a reference time interval

Target 43.3: A high value within control limits of a p control chart of comparable online repositories

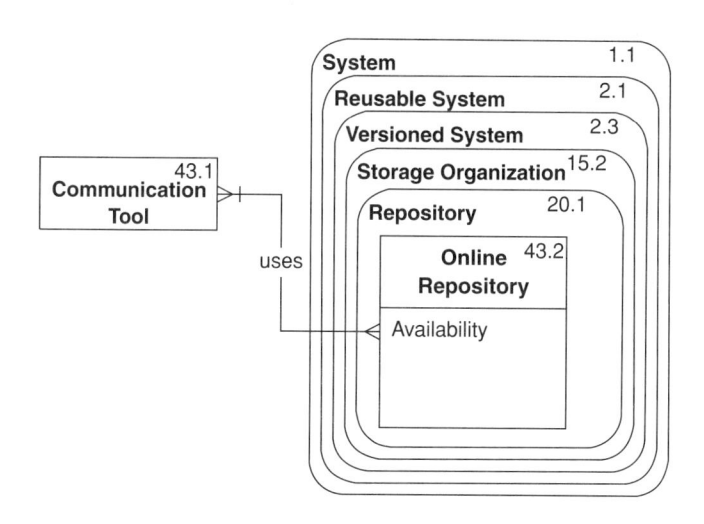

The World Wide Web is a network of linked sites that provide a structured graphical interface for accessing information. A *Web page* is a kind of active, online document that gives you the ability to communicate news and other information very quickly to a wide audience, who see that information when they wish. You can set up Web pages for any purpose at all, with internal and/or external access as you desire. The Web requires Internet access through an Internet Service Provider (ISP), who provides access to the Internet and software tools such as news readers, email systems, and online browsers. Examples: Best, Netcom, and Working Assets Online.

The Usenet *news groups* are repositories of electronic messages that you access in clusters on demand. You can respond in the usual way to the messages, just as though they were electronic mail. You can use the same technology for private news groups on local- or even wide-area networks.

An *online service* is a commercial organization that provides value-added repositories, email, interactive forums, and other online services in addition to Internet access. Examples: America Online, CompuServe, Prodigy, and Knight-Ridder's Dialog.

A *bulletin board* is a server that provides a set of information to you in a relatively unstructured manner. Many companies have bulletin boards that let you access customer support and download documents and software. Most are being replaced with World Wide Web sites on the Internet.

An online *document* is an online file or group of files available for reading through a network. The document can be a standard text file, a file in a special application format (such as a word processor file), or a special online file format with hypertext links (such as Adobe Acrobat).

An online *database* is a slightly more structured version of the online document, with access software available to let you use sophisticated access and display mechanisms to find and look at the information in the database.

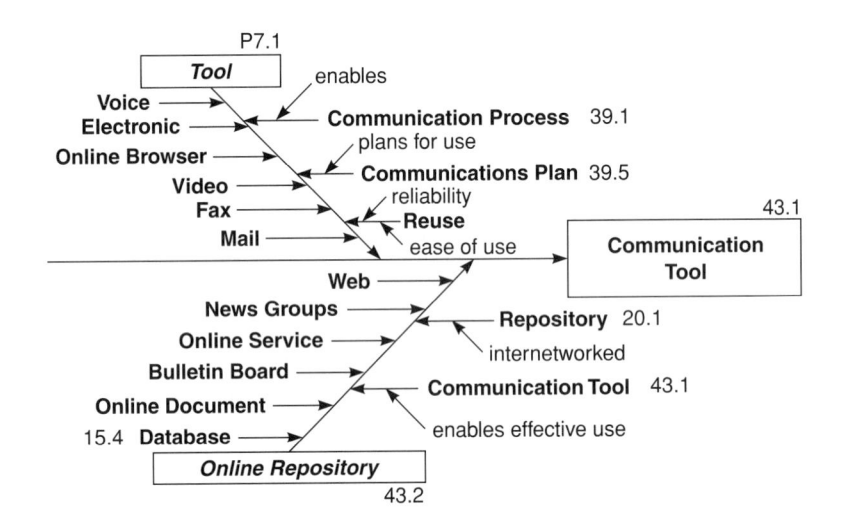

Readings

Consult any of the numerous books on the Internet and World Wide Web for information about those tools, or better yet, get connected!

[Lewis]　　　　Ted Lewis. *Deploying Distributed Business Software.* New York: SIGS Books, 1996.

This great little book summarizes everything you ever wanted to know about client/server and distributed systems, including networking protocols and telephony issues. It's a must-read book for managers barely acquainted with the acronyms ATM, ISDN, OSI, and POTS.

Questions to Think About

1. List several different communications processes you use, and match specific communications tools to them. Why did you choose the tools you did?

2. What kind of communications are private? How can you ensure this?

3. How can you organize communication tools effectively in a projectized organization?

4. Do you think that online documents will totally do away with paper in organizations? Why or why not?

Bibliography

[Abdel-Hamid] Tarek Abdel-Hamid and Stuart E. Madnick. *Software Project Dynamics: An Integrated Approach*. Englewood Cliffs, NJ: Prentice Hall, 1991.

[Agrawal] D. Agrawal and A. El Abbadi. Transaction management in database systems. In *Database Transaction Models for Advanced Applications*, pages 1–31, edited by Ahmed K. Elmagarmid. San Francisco: Morgan Kaufmann, 1992.

[AHD] William Morris, editor. *American Heritage Dictionary*. New York: American Heritage Publishing Co., 1973.

[Albrecht] Allan J. Albrecht and John E. Gaffney, Jr. Software function, source lines of code, and development effort prediction: A software science validation. In [Reifer, pp. 218–227]. Originally published in *IEEE Transactions on Software Engineering* SE-9:6 (November 1983): 639–648.

[Angus] Jeffrey Gordon Angus. Easing group projects: Team Manager can help manage workgroups. *Computerworld* (December 16, 1996): 55–57.

[ANSI] American National Standards Institute, Inc. *American National Standard for Information Systems—Database Language—SQL*. ANSI X3.135-1992. ANSI (+1-212-642-4900), October 16, 1992.

[Arthur] Lowell Jay Arthur. *Improving Software Quality: An Insider's Guide to TQM*. New York: Wiley, 1993.

[Babich] Wayne A. Babich. *Software Configuration Management: Coordination for Team Productivity*. Reading, MA: Addison-Wesley, 1986.

[Badiru] Adedeji B. Badiru. Activity-resource assignments using critical resource diagramming. *Project Management Journal* 24:3 (September 1993): 15–21.

[Baker] Bud Baker and Raj Menon. Politics and project performance: The fourth dimension of project management. *PM Network* (November 1995): 16–21.

[Basili] V. R. Basili and D. Rombach. The TAME project: Towards improvement-oriented software environments. *IEEE Transactions on Software Engineering* 14:6 (1988): 758–773.

[Basili 1996]	Victor R. Basili, Lionel C. Briand, and Walcélio L. Melo. How reuse influences productivity in object-oriented systems. *Communications of the ACM* 39:10 (October 1996): 104–116.
[Beauregard]	Michael R. Beauregard, Raymond J. Mikulak, and Barbara A. Olson. *A Practical Guide to Statistical Quality Improvement: Opening Up the Statistical Toolbox*. New York: Van Nostrand Reinhold, 1992.
[Beizer]	Boris Beizer. *The Frozen Keyboard: Living with Bad Software*. Blue Ridge Summit, PA: TAB Books, 1988.
[Bennatan]	E. M. Bennatan. *On Time, Within Budget: Software Project Management Practices and Techniques*. Woodland Hills, CA: QED Publishing Group, 1992.
[Berard]	Edward V. Berard. *Essays on Object-Oriented Software Engineering, Volume I*. Englewood Cliffs, NJ: Prentice Hall, 1993.
[Berlack]	H. Ronald Berlack. *Software Configuration Management*. New York: Wiley, 1992.
[Bernstein]	Peter L. Bernstein. *Against the Gods: The Remarkable Story of Risk*. New York: Wiley, 1996.
[Bersoff 1980]	Edward H. Bersoff, V. D. Henderson, and S. G. Siegel. *Software Configuration Management*. Englewood Cliffs, NJ: Prentice Hall, 1980.
[Bersoff 1991]	Edward H. Bersoff and Alan M. Davis. Impacts of life cycle models on software configuration management. *Communications of the ACM* 34:8 (August 1991): 104–117.
[Bertalanffy]	Ludwig von Bertalanffy. *General System Theory: Foundations, Development, Applications. Revised Edition*. New York: George Braziller, 1971.
[Biggerstaff]	Ted J. Biggerstaff and Alan J. Perliss. *Software Reusability*. Two volumes. New York: ACM Press, 1989.
[Boehm 1981]	Barry W. Boehm. *Software Engineering Economics*. Englewood Cliffs, NJ: Prentice Hall, 1981.
[Boehm 1981b]	Barry W. Boehm. An experiment in small-scale application software engineering. *IEEE Transactions on Software Engineering* SE-7:5 (September 1981): 482–493.
[Boehm 1988]	Barry W. Boehm. A spiral model of software development and enhancement. *Computer* 21:5 (May 1988): 61–72.
[Booch 1994]	Grady Booch. *Object-Oriented Analysis and Design with Applications, Second Edition*. Redwood City, CA: Benjamin/Cummings, 1994.
[Booch 1996]	Grady Booch. *Object Solutions: Managing the Object-Oriented Project*. Reading, MA: Addison-Wesley, 1996.
[Bossert]	James L. Bossert. *Quality Function Deployment: A Practitioner's Approach*. ASQC Quality Press (Marcel Dekker, Inc., 270 Madison Ave., New York, NY 10016), 1991.
[Bouldin]	B. M. Bouldin. *Agents of Change: Managing the Introduction of Automated Tools*. New York: Yourdon Press, 1989.
[Brooks]	Frederick P. Brooks, Jr. *The Mythical Man-Month: Essays on Software Engineering, Anniversary Edition*. Reading, MA: Addison-Wesley, 1995.
[Carbonell]	Nelson Carbonell. Managing the net risk of your development project. *Object Magazine* 6:12 (February 1997): 58–60.

[Cattell]	R. G. Cattell. *Object Data Management: Object-Oriented and Extended Relational Database Systems*. Reading, MA: Addison-Wesley, 1991.
[Cattell 1993]	R. G. Cattell, T. Atwood, J. Duhl, G. Ferran, M. Loomis, and D. Wade. *The Object Database Standard: ODMG-93 v.1.2*. San Francisco: Morgan Kaufmann, 1993.
[Champeaux]	Dennis de Champeaux. *Object-Oriented Development Processes and Metrics*. Englewood Cliffs, NJ: Prentice Hall, 1997 (published in 1996).
[Charette]	Robert N. Charette. *Software Engineering Risk Analysis and Management*. New York: Intertext Publications, McGraw-Hill, 1989.
[Cleland 1983]	David I. Cleland and William R. King. *Systems Analysis and Project Management, Third Edition*. New York: McGraw-Hill, 1983.
[Cleland 1996]	David I. Cleland. *Strategic Management of Teams*. New York: Wiley, 1996.
[Coombs]	Clyde H. Coombs, Robyn M. Dawes, and Amos Tversky. *Mathematical Psychology: An Elementary Introduction*. Englewood Cliffs, NJ: Prentice Hall, 1970.
[Cox]	Brad Cox. *Object-Oriented Programming: An Evolutionary Approach*. Reading, MA: Addison-Wesley, 1986.
[Cusumano]	Michael A. Cusumano and Richard W. Selby. *Microsoft Secrets: How the World's Most Powerful Software Company Creates Technology, Shapes Markets, and Manages People*. New York: The Free Press, 1995.
[Darnall]	Russell W. Darnall. Tapping into discretionary effort. *PM Network* (August 1994): 55–56.
[Davis]	Stanley M. Davis and Paul R. Lawrence. Problems of matrix organizations. *Harvard Business Review* (May–June 1978): 131–142.
[DeMarco 1982]	Tom DeMarco. *Controlling Software Projects: Management, Measurement, and Estimation*. New York: Yourdon Press, 1982.
[DeMarco 1987]	Tom DeMarco and Timothy Lister. *Peopleware: Productive Projects and Teams*. New York: Dorset House, 1987.
[Deming]	William E. Deming. *Out of the Crisis*. Cambridge, MA: MIT Press, 1986.
[Devlin]	Keith Devlin. *Logic and Information*. New York: Cambridge University Press, 1991.
[Dörner]	Dietrich Dörner. *The Logic of Failure: Why Things Go Wrong and What We Can Do to Make Them Right*. New York: Metropolitan Books, 1996 (originally published in German in 1989).
[Dreger]	J. Brian Dreger. *Function Point Analysis*. Englewood Cliffs, NJ: Prentice Hall, 1989.
[Dunn]	Robert H. Dunn and Richard S. Ullman. *TQM for Computer Software*. New York: McGraw-Hill, Inc., 1994.
[Dyer]	William G. Dyer. *Team Building: Issues and Alternatives, Second Edition*. Reading, MA: Addison-Wesley, 1987.
[Eaton]	David W. Eaton. *Configuration Management Tools Summary*. Available on Usenet group comp.software.config-mgmt FAQ (Frequently Asked Questions), Part 2, version 3.6. Also available on the World Wide Web through http://www.iac.honeywell.com/Pub/Tech/CM/CMTools.html.

[Ellis]	Margaret A. Ellis and Bjarne Stroustrup. *The Annotated C++ Reference Manual*. Reading, MA: Addison-Wesley, 1990.
[Evans]	Michael W. Evans, Pamela H. Piazza, and James B. Dolkas. *Principles of Productive Software Management*. New York: Wiley, 1983.
[Feierstein]	Max Feierstein and Jeannette Cabanis. The software selection project: Tips from a pro. *PM Network* 10:9 (September 1996): 28–35.
[Fenton]	Norman E. Fenton and Shari Lawrence Pfleeger. *Software Metrics: A Rigorous Approach, Second Edition*. Boston: International Thomson, 1997.
[Fishman]	Stephen Fishman. *Software Development: A Legal Guide*. Berkeley, CA: Nolo Press, 1994.
[Fleming]	Quentin W. Fleming. *Put Earned Value (C/SCSC) into Your Management Control System*. Newport Beach, CA: Humphreys and Associates (+1-714-955-2981), 1983.
[Freedman]	Daniel P. Freedman and Gerald M. Weinberg. *Handbook of Walkthroughs, Inspections, and Technical Reviews: Evaluating Programs, Projects, and Products, Third Edition*. New York: Dorset House, 1990.
[Gamma]	E. Gamma, R. Helm, R. Johnson, and J. Vlissides. *Design Patterns: Elements of Object-Oriented Software Architecture*. Reading, MA: Addison-Wesley, 1995.
[Garg]	Pankaj K. Garg and Mehdi Jazayeri. *Process-Centered Software Engineering Environments*. Los Alamitos, CA: IEEE Computer Society Press, 1996.
[Garlan]	David Garlan, Robert Allen, and John Ockerbloom. Architectural mismatch: Why reuse is so hard. *IEEE Software* (November 1995): 17–26.
[Gaudin]	Sharon Gaudin. Microsoft's Java compiler plans unclear. *Computerworld*, December 9, 1996, pages 53 and 58.
[Gause]	Donald C. Gause and Gerald M. Weinberg. *Exploring Requirements: Quality Before Design*. New York: Dorset House, 1989.
[Goldberg 1983]	Adele Goldberg and D. Robson. *Smalltalk-80: The Language and Its Implementation*. Reading, MA: Addison-Wesley, 1983.
[Goldberg]	Adele Goldberg and Kenneth S. Rubin. *Succeeding with Objects: Decision Frameworks for Project Management*. Reading, MA: Addison-Wesley, 1995.
[Gordon]	Mark L. Gordon. *Computer Software Contracting for Development and Distribution*. New York: Wiley, 1986.
[Graham]	Sidney Cottle, Roger F. Murray, Frank E. Block, and Martin L. Leibowitz. *Graham and Dodd's Security Analysis, Fifth Edition*. New York: McGraw-Hill, 1988.
[Gray]	James N. Gray. The transaction concept: Virtues and limitations. *Proceedings of the 7th International Conference on Very Large Data Bases*, pages 144–154. September 1981.
[GT Online]	Grant Thornton. New trends in packaged software selection. *GT Online*, http://www.gt.com/gtonline/homeonl.html, 1996.
[Haag]	Stephen Haag, M. K. Raja, and L. L. Schkade. Quality function deployment usage in software development. *Communications of the ACM* 39:1 (January 1996): 41–49.
[Harel]	David Harel. On visual formalisms. *Communications of the ACM* 31:5 (May 1988): 514–530.

[Hauser]	John R. Hauser and Don Clausing. The house of quality. *Harvard Business Review* 66:3 (May–June 1988): 63–73.
[Hayes]	Frank Hayes. Java makes Microsoft look like IBM. *Computerworld* (December 9, 1996): 58.
[Heichler]	Elizabeth Heichler. LBMS adds workflow, Windows 95 look. *Computerworld* (July 24, 1995): 69.
[Helm]	Leslie Helm. Improbable inspiration: The future of software may lie in the obscure theories of an 18th century cleric named Thomas Bayes. *Los Angeles Times,* October 28, 1996. Available on the World Wide Web at http://hugin.dk/lat-bn.html.
[Henderson-Sellers 1990]	Brian Henderson-Sellers and Julian. M. Edwards. The object-oriented systems life cycle. *Communications of the ACM* 33:9 (September 1990): 142–159.
[Henderson-Sellers 1993]	Brian Henderson-Sellers and Julian. M. Edwards. The fountain model for object-oriented systems development. *Object Magazine* 3:2 (1993): 72–79.
[Henderson-Sellers 1996]	Brian Henderson-Sellers. *Object-Oriented Metrics: Measures of Complexity.* Englewood Cliffs, NJ: Prentice Hall PTR, 1996.
[Hersey]	Paul Hersey and Kenneth H. Blanchard. *Management of Organizational Behavior: Using Human Resources, Sixth Edition.* Englewood Cliffs, NJ: Prentice Hall, 1993.
[Holloway]	Charles A. Holloway. *Decision Making under Uncertainty: Models and Choices.* Englewood Cliffs, NJ: Prentice Hall, 1979.
[Humphrey]	Watts S. Humphrey. *Managing the Software Process.* Reading, MA: Addison-Wesley, 1989.
[IEEE]	The Institute of Electrical and Electronic Engineers. *Software Engineering Standards.* Los Alamitos, CA: IEEE Computer Society Press, 1987.
[IFPUG]	International Function Point Users' Group. *IFPUG Counting Practices Manual, Release 4.0.* IFPUG (Blendonview Office Park, 5008-28 Pine Creek Drive, Westerville, OH 43081-4899, (614-895-7130), January 1994.
[Ishikawa]	Kaoru Ishikawa. *Guide to Quality Control.* Asian Productivity Organization, 1976 (available through UNIPUB, 800-521-8110).
[ISO 1991]	International Standards Organization. *ISO 9000-3, Guideline for Application of ISO 9001 to the Development, Supply, and Maintenance of Software.* ISO, 1991.
[ISO 1995]	International Standards Organization. *ISO/IEC 12207, Information Technology—Software Life Cycle Processes.* ISO, 1995.
[ISO 1996]	International Standards Organization. *ISO/IEC 14882, Information Technology—Programming Languages, Their Environments and System Software Interfaces—Programming Language C++.* ISO/IEC Secretariat, December 1996. Available through Global Engineering Documents, 800-854-7179.
[Jacobson]	Ivar Jacobson, Magnus Christerson, Patrik Jonsson, and Gunnar Overgaard. *Object-Oriented Software Engineering: A Use Case Driven Approach.* Reading, MA: Addison-Wesley, 1992.

[Jézéquel]	Jean-Marc Jézéquel and Bertrand Meyer. Design by contract: The lessons of Ariane. *Computer* 30:1 (January 1997): 129–130.
[Johnson]	Ralph Johnson. Documenting frameworks using patterns. *ACM SIGPLAN Notices* 27:10 (October 1992): 63–76.
[Jones 1991]	Capers Jones. *Applied Software Measurement: Assuring Productivity and Quality.* New York: McGraw-Hill, 1991.
[Jones 1994]	Capers Jones. *Assessment and Control of Software Risks.* New York: Yourdon Press, 1994.
[Jones 1996]	Capers Jones. Activity-based software costing. *Computer* 29:5 (May 1996): 103–104.
[Juliano]	William J. Juliano. External communication as an integral part of project planning. *PM Network* (February 1995): 18–21.
[Karlsson]	Even-André Karlsson, editor. *Software Reuse: A Holistic Approach.* New York: Wiley, 1995.
[Karolak]	Dale Walter Karolak. *Software Engineering Risk Management.* Los Alamitos, CA: IEEE Computer Society Press, 1996.
[Katz]	Barry Katz and Naftali Lerman. Building a three dimensional work breakdown structure. *Data Base* (Summer 1985): 14–17.
[Katzenbach]	Jon R. Katzenbach and Douglas K. Smith. *The Wisdom of Teams: Creating the High-Performance Organization.* Cambridge, MA: Harvard Business School Press, 1993.
[Keeney]	R. L. Keeney and Howard Raiffa. *Decisions with Multiple Objectives: Preferences and Value Tradeoffs.* New York: Wiley, 1976.
[Kehoe]	Raymond Kehoe and Alka Jarvis. *ISO 9000-3: A Tool for Software Product and Process Improvement.* New York: Springer-Verlag, 1996.
[Kerzner]	Harold Kerzner. *Project Management: A Systems Approach to Planning, Scheduling, and Controlling, Fifth Edition.* New York: Van Nostrand Reinhold, 1994.
[Khoshafian]	Setrag Khoshafian and Marek Buckiewicz. *Introduction to Groupware, Workflow, and Workgroup Computing.* New York: Wiley, 1995.
[Lederer]	Albert L. Lederer and Jayesh Prasad. Nine management guidelines for better cost estimating. *Communications of the ACM* 35:2 (February 1992): 51–59.
[Levine]	Harvey A. Levine. The truth about multiproject scheduling: Now it can be told. *PM Network* (January 1993): 22–26.
[Lewis]	Ted Lewis. *Deploying Distributed Business Software.* New York: SIGS Books, 1996.
[Licker]	Paul S. Licker. *The Art of Managing Software Development People.* New York: Wiley, 1985.
[Love]	Tom Love. *Object Lessons: Lessons Learned in Object-Oriented Development Projects.* New York: SIGS Books, 1993.
[Luby]	Robert E. Luby, Douglas Peel, and William Swahl. Component-based work breakdown structure (CBWBS). *Project Management Journal* (December 1995): 38–43.
[Lucky]	Robert W. Lucky. Collaboration. Reflections. *IEEE Spectrum* (November 1992): 15.
[McTaggart]	James M. McTaggart, Peter W. Kontes, and Michael C. Mankins. *The Value Imperative: Managing for Superior Shareholder Returns.* New York: Free Press, 1994.

[Mesarovic]   Mihajlo D. Mesarovic and Yasuhiko Takahara. *Abstract Systems Theory.* Lecture Notes in Control and Information Sciences 116. New York: Springer-Verlag, 1989.

[Metzger]   Philip W. Metzger. *Managing Programming People: A Personal View.* Englewood Cliffs, NJ: Prentice Hall, 1987.

[Meyer]   Bertrand Meyer. *Object-Oriented Software Construction.* Englewood Cliffs, NJ: Prentice Hall, 1988.

[Moder]   Joseph J. Moder, Cecil R. Phillips, and Edward W. Davis. *Project Management with CPM, PERT, and Precedence Diagramming, Third Edition.* New York: Van Nostrand Reinhold, 1983.

[Moody]   Fred Moody. *I Sing the Body Electronic: A Year with Microsoft on the Multimedia Frontier.* New York: Viking, 1995.

[Moore]   James F. Moore. *The Death of Competition: Leadership and Strategy in the Age of Business Ecosystems.* New York: HarperBusiness, 1996.

[Myers]   Glenford J. Myers. *The Art of Software Testing.* New York: Wiley, 1979.

[Narens]   Louis Narens. *Abstract Measurement Theory.* Cambridge, MA: The MIT Press, 1985.

[O'Brien]   James J. O'Brien. *Scheduling Handbook.* New York: McGraw-Hill, 1969.

[OMG 1995]   Object Management Group. *The Common Object Request Broker Architecture and Specification; Revision 2.0.* Object Management Group, July 1995.

[OMG 1996]   Jon Siegel, editor. *CORBA Fundamentals and Programming.* New York: Wiley, 1996.

[O'Neill]   Don O'Neill. Issues in software inspection. Soapbox. *IEEE Software* 14:1 (January–February 1997): 18–19.

[Osgood]   Charles E. Osgood, George J. Suci, and Percy H. Tannenbaum. *The Measurement of Meaning.* Champaign, IL: University of Illinois Press, 1957.

[Ozeki]   Kazuo Ozeki and Tetsuichi Asaka, editors. *Handbook of Quality Tools: The Japanese Approach.* Cambridge, MA: Productivity Press (+1-617-497-5146), 1990.

[Page-Jones]   Meilir Page-Jones. *Practical Project Management: Restoring Quality to DP Projects and Systems.* New York: Dorset House, 1985.

[Phillips]   Lawrence D. Phillips. *Bayesian Statistics for Social Scientists.* New York: Crowell, 1973.

[Plum]   Thomas Plum and Dan Sacks. *C++ Programming Guidelines.* Plum Hall, 1991.

[PMI 1996a]   Project Management Institute Standards Committee. *A Guide to the Project Management Body of Knowledge.* Upper Darby, PA: Project Management Institute (+1-610-734-3330), 1996.

[PMI 1996b]   Project Management Institute. 1996 project management software survey. *PM Network* 10:9 (September 1996): 29–42.

[Porter]   Anthony Porter. *The Best C/C++ Tips Ever.* Berkeley, CA: Osborne McGraw-Hill, 1993.

[Poulin]   Jeffrey S. Poulin. *Measuring Software Reuse: Principles, Practices, and Economic Models.* Reading, MA: Addison-Wesley, 1997.

[Pressman]   Roger S. Pressman. *Making Software Engineering Happen: A Guide for Instituting the Technology.* Englewood Cliffs, NJ: Prentice Hall, 1988.

[Rabb]	Margaret Y. Rabb. *The Presentation Design Book, Second Edition.* Chapel Hill, NC: Ventana Press, 1993.
[Reifer]	Donald J. Reifer. *Software Management, Fourth Edition.* Los Alamitos, CA: IEEE Computer Society Press, 1993.
[Roberts]	Fred S. Roberts. *Measurement Theory with Applications to Decisionmaking, Utility, and the Social Sciences.* Encyclopedia of Mathematics and Its Applications, Volume 7. Reading, MA: Addison-Wesley, 1979.
[Roetzheim]	William H. Roetzheim. *Structured Computer Project Management.* Englewood Cliffs, NJ: Prentice Hall, 1988.
[Rowe]	William D. Rowe. *The Anatomy of Risk.* New York: Wiley, 1977.
[Royce]	Winston W. Royce. Managing the development of large software systems: Concepts and techniques. In *1970 WESCON Technical Papers, Vol. 14.* August 25–28, 1970. Session A, paper A/1. WESCON, 1970.
[Rumbaugh]	James Rumbaugh, Michael Blaha, William Premerlani, Frederick Eddy, and William Lorensen. *Object-Oriented Modeling and Design.* Englewood Cliffs, NJ: Prentice Hall, 1991.
[Scholtes]	Peter R. Scholtes et al. *The Team Handbook: How to Use Teams to Improve Quality.* Joiner Associates (800-669-TEAM, +1-608-238-8134), 1988.
[Schottland]	Greg Schottland. Choosing and using design tools. *Object Magazine* (November 1996): 61–63.
[SEI 1993a]	Mark C. Paulk, Bill Curtis, Mary Beth Chrissis, and Charles V. Weber. *Capability Maturity Model for Software, Version 1.1.* CMU/SEI-93-TR-24. Pittsburgh: Software Engineering Institute, Carnegie Mellon University (http://www.sei.cmu.edu), February 1993.
[SEI 1993b]	Mark C. Paulk, Charles V. Weber, Suzanne M. Garcia, Marybeth Chrissis, and Marilyn Bush. *Key Practices of the Capability Maturity Model, Version 1.1.* CMU/SEI-93-TR-25. Pittsburgh: Software Engineering Institute, Carnegie Mellon University (http://www.sei.cmu.edu), February 1993.
[Siegel]	Shel Siegel with contributions by Robert J. Muller. *Object-Oriented Software Testing: A Hierarchical Approach.* New York: Wiley, 1996.
[Sigurdson 1996a]	Arild Sigurdsen. Principle errors in capital cost estimating work, part 1: Appreciate the relevance of quantity-dependent estimating norms. *Project Management Journal* 27:3 (September 1996): 27–34.
[Sigurdson 1996b]	Arild Sigurdsen. Principle errors in capital cost estimating work, part 2: Appreciate the relevance of the objective cost risk analysis method. *Project Management Journal* 27:3 (September 1996): 27–34.
[Stroustrup]	Bjarne Stroustrup. *The C++ Programming Language.* Reading, MA: Addison-Wesley, 1986.
[Thamhain]	Hans J. Thamhain. Best practices for controlling technology-based projects. *Project Management Journal* 27:4 (December 1996): 37–47.
[Thomsett]	Rob Thomsett. *Third Wave Project Management: A Handbook for Managing the Complex Information Systems for the 1990s.* Englewood Cliffs, NJ: Prentice Hall PTR, 1989.
[3M]	The 3M Meeting Management Team. *How to Run Better Business Meetings: A Reference Guide for Managers.* New York: McGraw-Hill, Inc., 1979.

[Tracz]	Will Tracz. Tutorial: *Software Reuse—Emerging Technology.* Washington, DC: Computer Society Press, 1988.
[US DOD]	United States Department of Defense. *DOD-STD-2167A, Military Standard, Defense System Software Development.* Washington, DC: U.S. Government Printing Office, 1988.
[Wasserman]	Anthony I. Wasserman, Peter A. Pircher, and Robert J. Muller. The object-oriented structured design notation for software design representation. *Computer* 23:3 (March 1990): 50–63.
[Weinberg 1971]	Gerald M. Weinberg. *The Psychology of Computer Programming.* New York: Van Nostrand Reinhold, 1971.
[Weinberg 1975]	Gerald M. Weinberg. *An Introduction to General Systems Thinking.* New York: Wiley, 1975.
[Weinberg 1982]	Gerald M. Weinberg. Overstructured management of software engineering. *Proceedings, 6th International Conference on Software Engineering,* September 13–16, 1982: 2–8.
[Weinberg 1986]	Gerald M. Weinberg. Becoming a Technical Leader: An Organic Problem-Solving Approach. New York: Dorset House, 1986.
[Weinberg 1992]	Gerald M. Weinberg. *Quality Software Management: Volume 1, Systems Thinking.* New York: Dorset House, 1992.
[Weinberg 1993]	Gerald M. Weinberg. *Quality Software Management: Volume 2, First-Order Measurement.* New York: Dorset House, 1993.
[Weinberg 1994]	Gerald M. Weinberg. *Quality Software Management: Volume 3, Congruent Action.* New York: Dorset House, 1994.
[Weisbord]	Marvin R. Weisbord. *Productive Workplaces: Organizing and Managing for Dignity, Meaning, and Community.* San Francisco: Jossey-Bass, 1987.
[Whitten]	Neal Whitten. *Managing Software Development Projects: Formula for Success, Second Edition.* New York: Wiley, 1995.
[Wilson]	David N. Wilson and Mark J. Sifer. Structured planning—project views. In [Reifer], pages 187–193. Originally published in *Software Engineering Journal* 3:4 (July 1988): 134–140.
[Wirfs-Brock]	Rebecca Wirfs-Brock, Brian Wilkerson, and Lauren Wiener. *Designing Object-Oriented Software.* Englewood Cliffs, NJ: Prentice Hall, 1990.
[Zuse]	Horst Zuse. *Software Complexity: Measures and Methods.* Programming Complex Systems: 4. De Gruyter, 1991.

Index

absolute scales, 24
absolute value, improvement vs., 6
abstraction metric, 543
acceptability of document metric, 299
acceptance, 312, 463
accountability ratio, 520
accounting, scheduling mixed with, 368
accuracy and measurement error, 34
acquisition. *See also* procurement
    acquisition capability metric, 448
    defined, 47
    of development environment, 324
    of management cultures, 526–527, 534–536
    planning and, 131–132
    of policies, 540
    procurement process, 276–277
    of project management systems, 364–365
    of reusable systems, 47–48, 448–451
    of reuse repository assets, 55
    of tools, 330, 331
    of training courses, 586
acronyms, 141–142
activity-on-arrow charts, 184, 186
activity-on-node charts, 184–186
actual value, 70, 72
ad hoc work-flow models, 110–112
adequacy metric, 393, 476
administrative work-flow models, 112–113
advancing tasks, 177, 191–192
agenda for meetings, 650
algorithmic model of cost estimation, 613, 614, 615
alignment metric, 293
alpha baselines, 429–431
ambiguity metric, 302, 304

analogy method of cost estimation, 613
analysis tools, 354
ANSI standards. *See* standards
Anticipating management culture, 528, 532
approaches
    defined, 21
    examples, 22
    and goals for metrics, 26
    multiple approaches, 21
    overview, 21–22
approval metric, 394
architectural mismatch, 51, 53
as-of date, 175
assessment criteria compliance, 448
assessment criterion, 456–457
assignments. *See also* resources
    approach, 591
    described, 591
    effort estimate, 599–601
    metric, 591, 593
    mission, 591
    object model, 592
    operational objective, 591
    overview, 10–11, 563, 591–593
    in project management systems, 368–369
    in project schedule, 176, 177
    resource assignment risk, 220–222, 224
    responsibility matrix, 596–599
    risks, 220–222, 224
    to schedule tasks, 192
    staffing plan, 594–596
    summary notation, 602
    target, 592
    vision, 591
atomicity property, 422

attributes
    contract cost attributes, 460
    customer attributes, 306
    defined, 7, 9
    risk attributes, 206–208
audit failures metric, 412
audit process, 157, 279
authority
    authority ratio, 511
    clarity of, 484
    decision authority, 484
    defined, 483
    functional authority ratio, 492
    in functional organizations, 492, 495–496
    in matrix organizations, 502, 504
    policies, 541
    poor authority, 485–486
    project authority ratio, 497
    in projectized organizations, 497, 499
    reporting structure and, 484
    responsibility and, 483–486
    responsibility matrix, 596–599
    structure of, 484–485
    work group structures, 513–514
autocratic work groups, 513–514
availability
    defined, 334, 337
    metric, 671
Average Risk Reduction, 162
avoidance, as risk response, 208–209

backup of repositories, 344
baseline change ratio, 134
baseline failures metric, 430
baseline field failures metric, 432

683

baseline rate of change, 134
baseline value ratio, 145
baselines
   ACID properties of transactions, 422
   alpha baselines, 429–431
   approaches, 420
   beta baselines, 433–435
   for change management plan, 384
   cluster baselines, 424–425
   contract baselines, 439–440
   cost budget baseline graph, 618
   for cost planning, 615
   creating, 421
   defined, 59, 378
   described, 419
   document baselines, 423–424
   field baselines, 431–433
   metrics, 420
   mission, 420
   object model, 419
   operational objectives, 420
   performance evaluation baselines, 436–439
   product baselines, 426–436
   production baselines, 435–436
   project schedule baselining, 180
   prototype baselines, 426–435
   rationales for, 422
   release baselines, 384
   reuse potential, 422–423
   spending budget baseline graph, 619
   summary notation, 441
   targets, 420
   types of, 378–379
   as versioned systems, 420–421
   versioning, 421
   vision, 420
BCWP (Budgeted Cost for Work Performed), 72
BCWS (Budgeted Cost for Work Scheduled), 72
Beizer, Boris, 433
beta baselines, 433–435
beta testing, 434–435
bidding failures metric, 453
black box clusters, 263
Boehm, Barry, 515
bottom-up cost estimates, 613, 615
bottom-up effort estimates, 600–601
branch coverage, 158
Brooks's law diagram, 11–13
browsers, 353
budget. *See also* costs
   Budget Risk, 146
   budgetary reserve, 250
   cost budget, 617–619
   cost estimates, 612–616
   cost estimation tool, 616–617
   performance, 438

   spending budget, 619–621
   undistributed, 250
budget performance, 438
budget risk, 146
budgetary reserve, 250
Budgeted Cost for Work Performed (BCWP), 72
Budgeted Cost for Work Scheduled (BCWS), 72
bug-tracking systems, 363, 384–385
build failures metric, 413
build productivity, 409, 413
build report, 415–416
build tool, 409, 412–414
bulletin boards, electronic, 672
business plan, 66

c control charts, 164
CA-SuperProject, 365, 366
calendar duration, 193, 194
calendars, work. *See* work calendars
capability contribution, 111
capability maturity model (CMM), 527–528
CASE tools
   as design tools, 350
   for document templates, 125
   for process modeling, 375
   for test modeling and scripting, 168
catalog classification scheme, 56
category classification scheme, 56
certainty equivalent, 236–237
certification. *See also* reuse potential
   of cost estimates, 615–616
   of development documents, 301, 314, 317
   of management cultures, 527
   of organizations, 488
   of policies, 540–541
   of projectized organizations, 500
   of reusable systems, 48–50
   of skills, 579
   software development project policies, 541
   of statement of work, 142–143
   system warranties, 49
   of training courses, 587
change control team, 389
change earned value, 388
change management, 387–399
   change management process, 378, 387–391
   change management process model, 391–393
   change report, 396–397
   change requests, 78, 393–395
   overview, 378–379
   resource assignment risks, 222, 224
   summary notation, 398

change management plan
   configuration management plan, 383–385
   described, 130, 380
   improvement plan, 392
   overview, 380–382
   policies, 381–382
   summary notation, 384
change management process, 387–391
   approaches, 388–389
   change control team, 389
   change management system, 78, 395–396
   change report, 396–397
   change requests, 78, 389–390, 393–395
   contract administration process and, 471–472
   described, 378, 387
   emergency changes, 391
   metrics, 388, 389
   milestones, 390
   mission, 388
   object model, 387
   operational objectives, 388
   targets, 388, 389
   unauthorized changes, 391
   vision, 388
change management process model, 391–393, 405–407
change management system
   alpha baselines and, 430
   overview, 395–396
   stakeholders and, 78
change policies, 541
change rate, 129
change report, 396–397
change requests
   approaches, 393–394
   in change management process, 389–390
   in configuration management process model, 406
   described, 393
   enhancement requests, 35
   fault fix requests, 395
   metrics, 393, 394
   mission, 393
   object model, 394
   operational objectives, 393
   overview, 393–395
   stakeholders and, 78
   targets, 393, 394
   vision, 393
changes metric, 424
chart of accounts, 606–611
   approach, 607
   cost center approach, 608
   Cost/Schedule Control System Criteria (C/SCSC) and, 607–608
   described, 606

Index   685

metrics, 607
mission, 606
object model, 606
operational objective, 606
software project costs and, 608–610
summary notation, 610
targets, 607
vision, 606
Check-in Ratio, 425
checksheets, 164
chief programmer work groups, 513, 514
Claris MacProject, 365, 369
clarity metric, 482
class diagrams. *See also* object models
    class hierarchies, 3, 83, 117, 173, 199, 255, 333, 379, 445, 479, 561, 605, 633
    class model notation, 8–9
    for level-of-effort tasks, 89
    with object model notation, 9–10
class model, 7
class model notation, 8–9
classes
    as clusters, 263–264
    defined, 7
    mission, 264
    object model, 263
    root class, 15
    test suite classes, 160–161
    vision, 264
classification schemes, 55–56
closing projects, 67
cluster baselines, 424–425
clusters, 259–264
    approaches, 259, 260
    categories, 262–263
    classes as, 263–264
    cluster analysis vs., 259
    cluster pyramid, 261
    cohesion, 261
    in design document, 315
    hardware processors vs., 259
    metrics, 259, 260
    mission, 259
    object model, 259
    operational objectives, 259, 260
    reusability properties, 262
    software systems vs., 264–265
    targets, 260
    vision, 259
CM process. *See* configuration management process
CMM (capability maturity model), 527–528
CMP. *See* configuration management plan
CMS. *See* configuration management system
code risk, 546
code testing, 158, 166–167
codes, WBS, 149

coding environments, 352
coding guidelines, 547
coding standard, 545–548
coding tools, 351–355
    analysis tools, 354
    browsers, 353
    coding environments, 352
    compilers, 351–352
    debuggers, 353
    documentation tools, 354
    groupware tools, 354–355
    inspectors, 353
    linkers, 351–352
    profilers, 354
    prototyping tools, 353–354
    reusable systems, 352–353
cohesion in clusters, 261
cohesion metric, 259, 582
combining tasks, 177
commitment
    level of commitment metric, 511
    of organization, 123
    in teams, 520–521
    in work groups, 515–517
communication
    communication process, 634–639
    communication process model, 640
    communication tool, 667–670
    communications management plan, 78, 130, 471, 641–642
    during PDCA cycle, 30
    online repository, 670–672
    overview, 632–633
    personal interaction, 644–647
    progress reports, 661–663
    project document and, 122
    time sheets, 663–665
communication meetings, 657–659
communication process, 634–639
    described, 634
    distributing communication, 637
    formal process, 639
    informal process, 637–638
    overview, 634–637
    risks, 636
    scheduling communications, 636–637
    summary notation, 642
communication process model, 640
communication tool
    online repository, 670–671
    overview, 667–670
    summary notation, 672
communications management plan
    in contract administration process, 471
    described, 130
    overview, 641–642
    stakeholders and, 78
comparability of metrics, 25

compatibility
    architectural mismatch, 51, 53
    as cluster reusability property, 262
    of reusable systems, 51, 53
    warranty for reusable systems, 49
compilers, 351–352
completeness metric, 597
complex systems, 15
complex task models, 97
complex tasks, 86–87
complexity, risk and, 218
complexity metric, 544
compliance metric, 113
component risks, 232
comprehension metric, 119, 662
comprehension speed, 269
concurrency metric, 410
configuration management, 400–418
    configuration management process, 378, 400–403
    configuration management process model, 403–408
    configuration management system, 408–416
    in functional organizations, 495
    summary notation, 416
    as supporting process, 279
configuration management plan, 130, 383–385
configuration management process, 400–403
    approach, 400–401
    described, 378, 400
    metric, 401
    mission, 400
    object model, 401
    operational objective, 400
    organization, 401–402
    release management, 401
    system loss risk, 402–403
    target, 401
    vision, 400
configuration management process model, 403–408
    approach, 404
    change process, 405–407
    described, 403
    metric, 404
    mission, 404
    object model, 404
    operational objective, 404
    release process, 407
    standards, 404–405
    target, 404
    vision, 404
configuration management system, 408–416
    approaches, 408–409
    build report, 415–416
    build tool, 409, 412–414

configuration management system
        (*continued*)
    described, 408
    metrics, 409
    mission, 408
    object model, 408
    operational objectives, 408, 409
    project-oriented development tools,
        409–410
    reuse potential, 410
    source control tool, 409, 410–412
    target, 409
    vision, 408
configuration management tools, 409–414
    build tool, 409, 412–414
    development environment and, 324–325
    project-oriented development tools,
        409–410
    source control tool, 409, 410–412
configuration units, 58–59. *See also* versioned systems
conformance metric, 554
Congruent management culture, 528, 532
consensus metric, 652
consistency property, 422
constraints in task model, 95
content metric, 268
content policies, 541
contingency plans, 251, 563
continuous improvement plan, 30, 34–36
contract administration, summary notation,
    476
contract administration failures metric, 473
contract administration process, 440,
    469–472
contract administration process model,
    472–473
contract administration system, 474–475
contract baselines, 439–440
contract failures metric, 434, 465
contract report, 475–476
contractor initial response (request for proposal), 452–454
contractors, 573–575
contracts, 457–464
    acceptance criteria, 463
    approaches, 458, 459
    contractual provisions for risk, 251
    cost attributes, 460
    for customizing acquired systems, 450
    described, 7, 457
    forms (templates), 462
    metrics, 459
    mission, 458
    negotiations, 462–464
    object model, 458
    operational objectives, 458, 459
    in procurement process, 457–464
    in project repository, 79
    risks, 459–460

support and maintenance provisions,
    463–464
targets, 459
types of, 460–462
vision, 458
control
    of personal interactions, 645–646
    as risk attribute, 206
control charts, 163–166
    described, 164
    p control charts, 166, 167
    pn control charts, 165–166
    targets and, 27
    types of, 164
    x-R control charts, 165
controlling people. *See* leadership
coordination, communication and, 30
coordination ratio, 658
cost budget, 617–619
cost estimates, 612–616
    aggregation level, 613
    approach, 613
    complexities, 614–615
    cost budget, 617–619
    cost estimation tool, 616–617
    methods, 613–615
    metric, 613
    mission, 612
    object model, 612
    operational objective, 613
    project level, 613
    reuse potential, 615–616
    spending budget, 619–621
    summary notation, 621
    target, 613
    vision, 612
cost estimation tool, 616–617
cost improvement ratio, 607
cost management, 629
cost management plan, 130, 624–628
cost management system, 628–629
cost performance index (CPI), 282
cost tracking failures metric, 628
cost variance ratio, 626
cost-benefit ratio, 625
cost-reimbursable contracts, 461, 462
Cost/Schedule Control System Criteria
    (C/SCSC), 607–608
costs. *See also* budget
    chart of accounts, 606–611
    contract cost attributes, 460
    contractor payments, 574–575
    cost budget, 617–619
    cost estimates, 612–616
    cost estimation tool, 616–617
    cost management plan, 130, 624–628
    cost management system, 628–629
    cost profile for people, 564, 565
    cost rate for people, 564
    fixed, 337, 572, 573

    for material resources, 571–573
    overview, 604–605
    resource assignment risks, 221, 222
    as risk attribute, 206, 209
    variable, 337, 572–573
    in work calendars, 334
coupling metric, 260
CPI (cost performance index), 282
"creeping requirements," 140
critical path, 184, 190, 213
C/SCSC (Cost/Schedule Control System
    Criteria), 607–608
cultural frontier diagram, 533–534
current date, 175
customer attributes, 306
customer call tracking, 372–373
customer satisfaction metric, 526
customer tracking, 372
customizing acquired systems, 449, 450

databases
    defined, 258
    as design elements, 316
    as functional specification requirement,
        312
    online, 672
day-time intervals, 336–337
debuggers, 353
decision authority, 484, 541
decision theory, 205
delaying tasks, 177, 191
deleting tasks, 177
deliverable systems, 69
deliverables, 67–74
    actual value, 70
    approaches, 68, 69
    earned value, 70, 71
    as emergent properties, 66
    estimated value at completion, 71
    metrics, 68, 69
    mission, 67
    object model, 68
    operational objectives, 68
    planned value, 70
    schedule variance, 71–72
    stakeholder-deliverable matrix, 306–308
    summary notation, 74
    targets, 68, 69
    value variance, 72
    vision, 67
delivery, statement of work and, 141
delivery failures metric, 526
DeMarco, Tom, 601
democratic work groups, 513, 514
density metric, 581
dependencies, 194–196
    approach, 194
    described, 172, 194
    lag time, 194, 196
    lead time, 194

Index 687

metric, 195
mission, 194
object model, 195
operational objective, 194
in project schedule, 174
retraction, 196
target, 195
types of, 195
vision, 194
dependency charts, 183–186
    activity-on-arrow charts, 184, 186
    activity-on-node charts, 184–186
    approach, 184
    critical path, 184, 213
    metric, 184
    mission, 184
    object model, 183
    operational objective, 184
    in project management systems, 368
    in project schedule, 174
    target, 184
    vision, 184
description, as risk attribute, 206
design document, 314–318
    approach, 315
    class and cluster design, 315
    described, 314
    elements, 316–317
    mission, 314
    multiple documents, 316
    object model, 315
    operational objective, 315
    review of, 317
    vision, 314
design guidelines, 544–545
design patterns, 355–357
design standard, 542–545
design tools, 350–351
developing object-oriented software, 273–297
    development process model, 273–279
    fountain process model, 286–288
    genetic process model, 290–295
    hacking process model, 279–281
    recursive-parallel process model, 288–290
    spiral process model, 284–286
    waterfall process model, 281–284
development documents, 298–321
    approaches, 298, 299
    certification, 301, 314, 317
    described, 298
    design document, 314–318
    functional specification, 310–314
    metrics, 299, 300
    mission, 298
    object model, 299
    operational objectives, 298, 299
    overview, 298–301

product documentation vs., 269
product objectives document, 304
requirements document, 77, 140, 301–310
summary notation, 318
targets, 299, 300
vision, 298
development environment, 322–329
    approaches, 322, 323
    configuration management tools for, 324–325
    described, 322
    maintenance, 325
    metrics, 323
    mission, 322
    object model, 323
    operational objectives, 322, 323
    overview, 322–325
    product repository, 325–329
    reuse repository, 53–57
    sharing, 324
    summary notation, 329
    targets, 323
    vision, 322
development expense capitalization, 665
development plan, 130, 274–276
development process, 277–278
    development process model, 273–279
    object model, 277
    summary notation, 295
    tasks, 277–278
development process model, 273–279
    development plan, 274–275
    development process, 277–278
    fountain model, 286–288
    genetic model, 290–295
    hacking model, 279–281
    mission, 274
    object model, 273
    primary process, 276–278
    process policy and the development plan, 275–276
    procurement process, 276–277
    recursive-parallel model, 288–290
    spiral model, 284–286
    supporting process, 278–279
    vision, 274
    waterfall model, 281–284
development task, 94
development tools, 348–355
    approaches, 349
    coding tools, 351–355
    described, 332, 348
    design tools, 350–351
    metrics, 349
    mission, 348
    object model, 348
    operational objectives, 349
    summary notation, 357

targets, 349
types of, 349–350
vision, 348
directing people. *See* leadership
disablement warranty, 49
discretionary effort, 515–517
dispersion metric, 581
distributing communication, 637
document baselines, 423–424
document effectiveness, 269
document publishing tools, 375
document templates, 124–125
documentation. *See also specific documents*
    coding documentation tools, 354
    design document, 314–318
    development documentation vs. product documentation, 269
    development documents, 298–321
    functional specification, 310–314
    online, 672
    product documents, 267–269
    product objectives document, 304
    productivity and, 116
    project document, 79, 118–127
    project process document, 92
    quality evaluation document, 157
    requirements document, 77, 140, 301–310
    in reuse repository, 53
    as supporting process, 279
    templates, 375
domain reusability
    of communications tools, 670
    defined, 46
    functional organizations and, 494
    projectized organizations and, 500
    of work groups, 518
drawing tools, 350
drives, 258
durability metric, 420
durability property, 422
durations, 192–194
    approach, 193
    calendar duration, 193, 194
    defined, 97
    described, 172, 337
    metric, 193
    mission, 192
    object model, 193
    operational objective, 192
    project duration, 193
    relative work duration, 193–194
    risk from poor estimation, 217
    of schedule tasks, 191, 192–194
    simple task model estimates, 97
    target, 193
    vendor duration, 194
    vision, 192

earned contribution margin, 482
earned value
  baselines for calculating, 438
  of deliverables, 70, 71, 72–73
  metric, 470
  schedule variance, 71–72
  value variance, 72
earned-cost statistics, 626, 627
effectiveness
  metric, 181, 184, 345, 506, 539, 562, 668
  as risk attribute, 206, 209
effort estimate, 593, 599–601
electronic messaging, 668–669
email, 668–669
emergency changes, 391
enabled metric, 190
encapsulation metric, 543
enhancement requests, 35
enhancing acquired systems, 449, 450
entity-relationship (ER) notation, 10
environment faults metric, 323
ER (entity-relationship) notation, 10
ergonomics, 312
errors. *See also* failure metrics; fault metrics
  bug-tracking systems, 363, 384–385
  of commission vs. omission, 208
  sources of measurement error, 34
estimate at completion, 626–627
estimated cost, 460
estimated total task productivity, 106
estimated value at completion, 71
estimation productivity, 616
evaluation failures metric, 437
evaluation metric, 585
evaluation ratio, 652
event tree for risk assessment, 232–233
evolutionary prototypes, 427–428
exceptions ratio, 339
exceptions to edit criteria, 420
executable code, 412
executing projects, 67
expectations, 75, 77, 304–306
expected profit, 460
expert judgment cost estimates, 613
expert work groups, 513
extending tasks, 177, 192
extent metric, 576
external standard, 554–555

failure metrics. *See also* fault metrics
  audit failures, 412
  baseline failures, 430
  baseline field failures, 432
  bidding failures, 453
  build failures, 413
  contract administration failures, 473
  contract failures, 434, 465
  cost tracking failures, 628
  delivery failures, 526
  evaluation failures, 437

  failure potential, 292
  failure rate, 436
  information failure, 360
  obligation failures, 459
  policy failures, 539
  recovery failures, 411
  release failures, 430
  report failures, 415
  responsibility failures, 597
  rights failures, 459
failure potential, 292
failure rate, 436
failure tracking, 372–373
fault fix requests, 395
fault metrics. *See also* failure metrics
  environment faults, 323
  meeting faults, 649
  reuse faults, 326, 327
  system faults, 420
  timesheet faults, 664
fax communications tool, 669
feasibility metric, 299
feasibility of projects, 66
feedback
  defined, 28
  directing people and, 569
  feedback effectiveness, 102
  motivation and, 570–571
feedback systems, 15
field baselines, 431–433
field testing, 431, 432–433
  beta testing vs., 434
files, 258
finish date
  Project Finish Date, 174
  of project schedule, 176
  of schedule tasks, 190
fixed costs, 337, 572, 573
fixed-price contracts, 460, 461, 462
flexibility in organizations, 486–487
flexibility metric, 482
float of schedule tasks, 190
flowcharts, 164
formal communication process, 639
formal project document, 122–124
fountain development process model, 286–288
frequency, as risk attribute, 206
fudge factor, reserve vs., 250–251
function points, 265, 266–267
functional authority ratio, 492
functional incoherence, 494
functional organizations, 491–496
  approach, 492
  authority in, 492, 495–496
  configuration management in, 495
  defining characteristics, 492
  described, 491

  metrics, 492
  mission, 491
  object model, 491
  operational objective, 491
  organization chart, 493
  project management in, 494
  quality assurance in, 495
  reuse potential, 490, 492, 494
  targets, 492
  vision, 491
  work groups in, 512
functional specification, 310–314
  approach, 311
  described, 310
  format, 313
  mission, 310
  object model, 311
  operational objective, 310
  reuse of, 314
  review of, 313–314
  system requirements, 312
  vision, 310
functions, 312, 316

Gantt charts, 182–183, 368
generic risks, 207
genetic development process model, 290–295
glass box clusters, 263
glossary of terms, in statement of work, 141–142
goal-question-metric paradigm, 23
goal-seeking systems, 15
goals. *See also* mission; operational objectives
  and approaches for metrics, 26
  of organizations, 488
  overview, 21–22
government regulations, 552–553
graphical user interfaces (GUIs), 168
groupware, 343
groupware tools, 354–355
guidelines. *See also* policies; standards
  coding guidelines, 547
  design guidelines, 544–545
  standards vs., 539
GUIs (graphical user interfaces), 168

hacking development process model, 279–281
high synergy, 638
hiring people, 566, 567
hiring risk, 582
histograms, 164, 178
holidays, 337
House of Quality, 308–310

identified risks, 246
ignoring, as risk response, 209
illustration productivity, 120

Index

illustration size metric, 120
impact metric, 356
improvement, as organizational process, 276
improvement plans, 28–36
   for change management plan, 392
   continuous improvement plan, 30, 34–36
   described, 16, 28
   initial improvement plan, 30, 31–32
   mission, 28
   object model, 29
   overview, 28–31
   PDCA cycle, 30
   pilot improvement plan, 30, 32–34
   process milestone and, 103
   process model and, 92
   single-instance systems, 30–31
   summary notation, 36
   tasks for, 29
   for tools, 331–332
   vision, 28
improvement ratio, 36
improvement reviews, 656–657
incompatibility. *See also* compatibility
   architectural mismatch, 51, 53
   of reusable systems, 51, 53
informal communication process, 637–638
informal policies, 478, 538
information failure metric, 360
information productivity, 361
information synergy metric, 638
information systems
   approaches, 360, 361
   bug-tracking systems, 363
   described, 332, 360
   metrics, 360, 361
   mission, 360
   object model, 361
   operational objectives, 360, 361
   overview, 360–363
   product management systems, 371–373
   project management systems, 363–371
   summary notation, 373
   targets, 361
   types of, 361–362
   vision, 360
infrastructure
   as organizational process, 276
   tools as, 330
infringement warranty, 49
inherent reusability, 46
inheritance, 7, 334
initial improvement plan, 30, 31–32
innovation in organizations, 487
innovation rate, 481
inputs
   in task model, 95
   of tasks, 86
inspectors, coding tools, 353

installation, 312
insurance policy provision for risk, 251–252
interest level weight, 75
interfaces, 312, 316, 470–471
internal consistency metric, 300
international issues, 552
interval scales, 24
interviewing people, 566–567
invitation for bid (request for proposal), 452–454
invitation for negotiation (request for proposal), 452–454
invitation for quotation (request for proposal), 452–454
Ishikawa diagrams, 164
ISO standards. *See* standards
isolation property, 422

joint reviews, 651–657
   approaches, 651–652
   in contract administration process, 471
   described, 651
   improvement reviews, 656–657
   management reviews, 653–654
   metrics, 652
   mission, 651
   object model, 652
   operational objectives, 651, 652
   overview, 77, 651–653
   quality assurance process and, 157
   as supporting process, 279
   targets, 652
   technical reviews, 300–301, 317, 654–656
   vision, 651
Jones, Capers, 206, 212
Journal of Object-Oriented Programming, 586

kaizan, systems and, 14–28
keyword classification scheme, 56

labor resources. *See* people
lag time, 194, 196, 337
lead time, 194, 337
leadership
   defined, 568
   leading people, 567–569
   managing contractors, 574
   reuse and, 569
legal issues. *See also* contracts
   law as organizational environment, 552–553
   standard cautions on document templates, 125
level of commitment metric, 511
level of detail metric, 145
level-of-effort model, 97
level-of-effort tasks, 89
leveling resources, 177–178, 368–369

leverage, communication and, 30
line graphs, 164
linearity and measurement error, 34
linkers, 351–352
linking pin role, 584
lowball bids, 455

MacProject, 365, 369
mail communications tool, 669
maintenance
   in contracts, 463–464
   of development environment, 325
   as functional specification requirement, 312
   of skills, 580
   of training courses, 587
maintenance effort metric, 389
managed risk, 120
management cultures, 525–537
   acquisition, 526–527, 534–536
   Anticipating, 528, 532
   approaches, 526
   blaming and, 593
   certification, 527
   changing, 534–536
   Congruent, 528, 532
   cultural frontier diagram, 533–534
   cultural patterns, 527–532
   described, 525
   metrics, 526
   mission, 525
   object model, 525
   Oblivious, 528
   operational objectives, 525, 526
   overview, 525–527
   reuse potential, 533–534
   Routine, 528, 529–531
   spiral development process model and, 286
   Steering, 528, 531
   successful pattern matching, 532–536
   summary notation, 536
   targets, 526
   Variable, 528–529
   vision, 525
management process effort, 289
management processes, 275–276
management reserve, 250
management reviews, 653–654
management skills, 576–577
market environment, 551–552
material resources
   contractors, 573–575
   overview, 571–573
matrix organizations, 501–504
   approach, 501–502
   authority in, 502, 504
   described, 501
   mission, 501
   object model, 501

matrix organizations *(continued)*
    operational objective, 501
    organization chart, 503
    reuse potential, 491, 504
    strong matrix, 502
    vision, 501
    weak matrix, 502
    work groups in, 512
maximum fees, 460
measurement scales, 22, 23–24
measuring reuse, 43–44
median effort to repair metric, 546
meeting faults metric, 649
meeting productivity metric, 658
meetings, 648–660. *See also* joint reviews
    agenda, 650
    approaches, 648, 649–650
    communication meetings, 657–659
    described, 648
    joint reviews, 77, 157, 279, 471, 651–657
    metrics, 648, 649, 650
    mission, 648
    object model, 649
    operational objectives, 648, 649
    overview, 648–651
    scheduling, 650
    summary notation, 659
    targets, 649, 650
    vision, 648
metamodels (schemas), 344–347
metric adequacy, 456
metrics
    defined, 22
    design issues, 22
    goal-question-metric paradigm, 23
    goals and approaches, 26
    meaningful characteristics of, 25–26
    overview, 22–26
    scales for, 22, 23–24
Microsoft Project, 365, 367
milestone risks, 212–216
    defined, 212
    excessive time to market, 216
    poor estimation, 215–216
    poor project management tools, 215
    poor technical skills, 214
    Silver Bullet Syndrome, 212–214
    stakeholder friction, 214
milestones
    in change management process, 390
    overview, 101–103
    process milestones, 103
    in project schedule, 174
    project schedule constraints, 176
    risks, 212–216
minimum fees, 460
mission
    congruency with, 20
    defined, 15, 19

mission statement, 19
    overview, 19–20
mitigation, as risk response, 208–209
model coverage, 106
modeling
    for plans, 130–131
    for repositories, 345–346
modeling tools, 332
modifying tasks, 177
motivation
    of people, 569–571
    in work groups, 515–517
multiple approaches, 21
multiple inheritance, avoidance of, 7
multiple operational objectives, 20–21
multiple projects, 366–368

name, as risk attribute, 206
necessity metric, 111, 112, 361
negotiating contracts, 462–464
net benefit, 388
news groups, 672
noise metric, 635
nominal scales, 23–24
normalized expectations ratio, 75
notation. *See also* object models; summary
        notation
    class model, 8–9
    object model, 9–11
    summary, 13–14
    system model, 11–13
    for work-flow models, 107
number of direct reports metric, 510
number of problems metric, 193

object code, 412
object consultancy role, 584
Object Magazine, 586
object models
    defined, 7
    notation, 9–11
object systems, 7–8
objective risks, 228–232
objectives. *See* operational objectives
objectivity of metrics, 25
objects, 7, 256–257
obligation failures metric, 459
Oblivious management culture, 528
off-agenda topics metric, 650
off-the-shelf systems, 365, 449
online browsers, 669
online repository, 670–672
online services, 672
open systems, 14–15
operational objectives. *See also* approaches;
        metrics; targets
    approach, 21–22
    changing, 28
    defined, 20

    goal, 21
    metric, 22–26
    multiple objectives, 20–21
    overview, 20–28
    risk assessment, 228–232
    summary notation, 28
    target, 26–28
optimization of project schedule, 177–179
ordinal scales, 23–24
organization charts
    for functional organizations, 493
    for matrix organizations, 503
    overview, 505–506
    for projectized organizations, 498
organizational environment, 550–554
    described, 478, 550
    external standard, 554–555
    market, 551–552
    object model, 550
    organizational repository, 555–556
    political system and law, 552–553
    summary notation, 556
organizational processes, 275–276
organizational repository, 343, 555–556
organizational reusability, 46, 518, 670
organizations, 480–491
    approaches, 480–481, 482
    authority and responsibility, 483–486
    certification, 488
    coding standard, 545–548
    described, 480
    design standard, 542–545
    external standard, 554–555
    flexibility in, 486–487
    functional organizations, 490, 491–496
    goals and functions, 488
    innovation in, 487
    management cultures, 525–537
    matrix organizations, 491, 501–504
    metrics, 481–482
    mission, 480
    need for, 483
    object model, 481
    operational objectives, 480, 492
    organization charts, 493, 498, 503,
        505–506
    organizational environment, 550–554
    organizational repository, 555–556
    overview, 478–479
    policies, 538–542
    projectized organizations, 490–491,
        496–500
    reuse potential, 486–491
    risks, 488
    stability of, 486
    structure of, 483
    summary notation, 506
    targets, 481, 482
    teams, 519–522

Index

turnover, 487
vision, 480
work groups, 509–519
outputs
  in task model, 95
  of tasks, 86
overhead rate, 482
overtime work shift, 337

p control charts, 164, 166, 167
paradigms
  combining system and risk paradigms, 205
  risk paradigm, 204–206
Pareto charts, 164
Parkinsonian cost estimates, 613
paths, 258
pay premiums metric, 576
PDCA cycle, 30
people, 564–571. *See also* skills
  approach, 564
  availability profile, 564, 565
  cost profile, 564, 565
  cost rate, 564
  definition from project perspective, 564
  leading, directing, and controlling, 567–569
  metric, 564
  mission, 564
  motivating, 569–571
  object model, 564
  operational objective, 564
  overview, 564–566
  recruiting and hiring, 566–567
  roles, 582–584
  skills matrix, 580–582
  target, 564
  training course, 584–585
  vision, 564
performance evaluation baselines, 436–439
performance warranty, 49
person. *See* people
personal interactions, 644–647
personnel policies, 541
PERT charts, 183, 368
pie charts, 164
Pig motivation metric, 570
pilot improvement plan, 30, 32–34
planned value
  of deliverables, 70, 72
  schedule variance, 71–72
planning productivity, 404
planning tools, 375
plans, 128–138. *See also specific types of plans*
  acquisition and, 131–132
  approaches, 129
  metrics, 129
  mission, 129

modeling for, 130–131
object model, 128
operational objectives, 129
project plan, 133–137
reuse potential, 132
summary notation, 132
targets, 129
types of, 130
vision, 129
pn control charts, 164, 165–166
policies, 538–542
  acquisition, 540
  approaches, 539
  certification, 540–541
  coding standard, 545–548
  described, 478, 538
  design standard, 542–545
  external standard, 554–555
  informal, 478, 538
  metrics, 539
  mission, 539
  object model, 478, 538
  operational objectives, 539
  reuse potential, 540–541
  software development project policies, 541
  standards vs. guidelines, 539
  summary notation, 548
  targets, 539
  vision, 539
policy failures metric, 539
politics
  as organizational environment, 552–553
  resource assignment risks, 222
portability metric, 546–547
potential for reuse, 44, 46–47
precompilers, 414
preference curves, 236, 237–238
presentations, 659
prevention, as risk attribute, 206
price ceiling, 460
price-to-win cost estimates, 613
primary process, 276–278
Primavera Project Planner (P3), 365
probability, as risk attribute, 206
probability trees
  control decision tree, 234–236
  event tree, 232–233
  for risk assessment, 229–231
problem resolution, as supporting process, 279
process effectiveness, 291
process milestones, 103
process modeling tools, 375
process models
  improvement plan and, 92
  overview, 91–92
  project process models, 92–94

in risk management methods, 249
summary notation, 95
process policy, 275–276
process productivity, 292
Process Representation Accuracy, 96
processes
  described, 90
  overview, 82–83, 90
  planning with, 98–101
  risk from poor definition, 217
  sequence of tasks, 90
  summary notation, 95
  systems approach vs., 4
procurement. *See also* acquisition; contracts; procurement process
  assessment criterion, 456–457
  contract administration process, 469–472
  contract administration process model, 472–473
  contract administration system, 474–475
  contract report, 475–476
  contracts, 457–464
  overview, 444–445
  procurement management plan, 130, 444, 464–467
  procurement process, 143, 276–277, 330, 444, 446–451
  procurement process model, 444, 451–452
  proposal, 454–455
  request for proposal, 452–454
  summary notation, 466
procurement management plan, 130, 444, 464–467
procurement process, 446–451
  acquisition methods, 448–450
  approaches, 446–447, 448
  described, 444, 446
  metrics, 447, 448
  mission, 446
  object model, 447
  operational objectives, 446, 447, 448
  overview, 276–277
  statement of work in, 143
  targets, 447, 448
  for tools, 330
  vision, 446
procurement process model, 444, 451–452
procurement risk, 217, 459
product baselines, 426–436
  described, 426
  mission, 426
  object model, 426
  production baselines, 435–436
  prototype baselines, 426–435
  vision, 426
product documents, 267–269
product management systems, 371–373

product objectives document, 304
product repository, 325–329
   approaches, 326, 327
   described, 325, 343
   internal vs. external, 327–328
   metrics, 326, 327
   mission, 326
   object model, 326
   operational objectives, 326, 327
   physical structure, 328–329
   reuse of, 328
   reuse repository vs., 53
   targets, 326, 327
   vision, 326
product tracking, 372
production baselines, 435–436
productivity metrics, 85, 125, 190, 564
   build productivity, 409, 413
   estimated total task productivity, 106
   estimation productivity, 616
   illustration productivity, 120
   information productivity, 361
   meeting productivity, 658
   planning productivity, 404
   process productivity, 292
   productivity improvement, 331, 349, 374
   project productivity, 323, 335
   text productivity, 120
   tool productivity, 668
proficiency metric, 581
profilers, 354
profiles, 564, 565
profit ceiling and floor, 460
prognosis, as risk attribute, 206, 209
program testing, 158
progress reports
   overview, 661–663
   project progress reports, 663
   summary notation, 666
   time sheets, 663–665
project authority ratio, 497
project deliverables. *See* deliverables
project document, 118–127
   approaches, 119, 120
   described, 118
   document templates, 124–125
   formal project document, 122–124
   formats, 121
   metrics, 119, 120
   mission, 119
   operational objectives, 119
   overview, 118–122
   in project repository, 79
   reusability, 121
   risk management and, 122
   sections of, 120
   summary notation, 126
   targets, 119, 120
   tools for creation, 122, 125

   version number for, 121
   vision, 118
project duration, 193
Project Finish Date, 174
Project Management Body of Knowledge, 130
project management systems, 363–371. *See also* dependency charts; projects; resources; schedules; time charts; work breakdown structures; work calendars
   acquisition, 364, 364–365
   dependency charts, 183–186
   described, 363
   in functional organizations, 494
   mission, 364
   multiple projects, 366–368
   object model, 363
   off-the-shelf systems, 365
   operational objectives, 364
   reasons for underuse, 365
   reporting, 370–371
   repository management, 370
   system modeling tools in, 375
   time charts, 181–183
   tools and systems integrated into, 364
   vision, 364
   work breakdown structures, 144–151
   work calendars, 334–337
project plan, 133–137. *See also specific subsidiary plans*
   approaches, 134, 135
   metrics, 134, 135
   mission, 134
   object model, 133
   operational objectives, 134, 135
   outline with processes, 98–101
   project process model and, 93–94
   project process tasks and, 94
   risk analysis and, 136
   subsidiary plan conflicts, 135–136
   subsidiary plans, 133–134
   summary notation, 136
   system model, 99
   targets, 134, 135
   vision, 134
project process models, 92–95
project productivity, 323, 335
project progress reports, 663
project repository, 53, 78–79, 343
Project Risk Change Rate, 134
project risks, 210–212
   defined, 210
   low stability, 210–211
   poor tools, methods, and tool acquisition, 211–212
project schedule, 174–180
   approaches, 174, 175
   as-of date, 175

   assigning resources, 176, 177
   baselining, 180
   current date, 175
   described, 174
   finish date, 176
   metric, 174
   mission, 174
   object model, 175
   operational objectives, 174, 175
   optimizing, 177–179
   planning, 175–176
   resource leveling, 177–178
   reusability, 179–180
   start date, 176
   target, 174
   vision, 174
Project Scheduler 7, 365, 367, 369
project sponsors, 76–77
project stakeholders. *See* stakeholders
Project Workbench, 365
project-related risks, 200
projectized organizations, 496–500
   approach, 496
   authority in, 497, 499
   certification, 500
   described, 496
   domain and, 500
   metrics, 497
   mission, 496
   object model, 496
   operational objective, 496
   organization chart, 498
   participative techniques in, 499
   reuse potential, 490–491, 499–500
   suitability to software projects, 497
   targets, 497
   vision, 496
   work groups in, 512
projects
   approaches, 64, 65
   business plan, 66
   closing, 67
   complex tasks, 86–87
   deliverables, 66, 67–74
   described, 63
   execution, 67
   feasibility, 66
   initiating, 66
   metrics, 64, 65
   mission, 64
   multiple projects, 366–368
   object model, 64
   operational objectives, 64, 65
   overview, 63–67
   planning, 67
   project repository, 78–79
   risks, 210–216
   stakeholders, 66, 74–78
   summary notation, 67

Index 693

targets, 65
vision, 64
proposals, 454–455
prototype baselines, 426–435
   alpha baselines, 429–431
   approach, 427
   beta baselines, 433–435
   deadline impact, 429
   described, 426
   evolutionary prototypes, 427–428
   field baselines, 431–433
   metric, 427
   mission, 427
   object model, 427
   operational objective, 427
   overview, 426–429
   reuse and, 428–429
   spiral process and, 428
   target, 427
   throwaway prototypes, 427
   vision, 427
prototyping, risk and, 218
prototyping tools, 353–354

QA. *See* quality assurance process
QFD. *See* quality function deployment
   (QFD)
quality approach, 158, 160
quality assurance process, 156–157
   in functional organizations, 495
   as supporting process, 279
quality environment, 162–168
   overview, 162–163
   quality repository, 163
   quality tools, 163–168
quality evaluation document, 157
quality function deployment (QFD),
   306–310
   customer attributes, 306
   House of Quality, 308–310
   stakeholder-deliverable matrix, 306–308
quality management
   quality assurance process model and
      process, 156–157
   quality environment, 162–168
   quality management plan, 130, 154–156
   standards, 156
   summary notation, 168
   test plans, 157–161
quality management plan, 154–156
   described, 130, 154–155
   mission, 155
   object model, 155
   operational objectives, 155
   test plans, 155–156, 157–161
   vision, 155
quality process model, 157
quality repository, 163, 343

quality tools, 163–168
   statistical process control tools, 163–166
   test modeling and scripting tools,
      167–168
   testing frameworks, 166–167

ratio scales, 24
reassignment of work flow, 107
receipt metric, 635
recovery failures metric, 411
recruiting people, 566–567
recursive-parallel development process
   model, 288–290
red flag rate, 245
reference ratio, 607
relationships, 10
relative risk ratio, 244
relative work duration, 193–194
release baselines, 384
release failures metric, 430
release management, 401
release management process model, 407
relevance metric, 635
reliability
   of communication tools, 669–670
   of metrics, 25
repeatability and measurement error, 34
report failures metric, 415
reporting
   build report, 415–416
   change report, 396–397
   contract report, 475–476
   by project management systems,
      370–371
repositories
   approaches, 342
   described, 332, 341
   general class, 341–344
   groupware alternative, 343
   metrics, 342
   mission, 341
   modeling, 345–346
   object model, 341
   online repository, 670–672
   operational objectives, 342
   organizational repository, 343, 555–556
   product repository, 325–329, 343
   project repository, 78–79, 343
   quality repository, 163, 343
   repository management, 370
   reuse potential, 344
   reuse repository, 53–57, 343
   reuse repository vs. product or project
      repository, 53
   risk of data loss, 344
   schemas, 344–347
   storage for, 343
   summary notation, 346
   targets, 342

types of, 343–344
   vision, 341
   World Wide Web as, 343
reproducibility and measurement error, 34
request for proposal, 452–454
   proposals, 454–455
requirements document, 301–310
   approaches, 302, 303
   "creeping requirements," 140
   described, 301
   first version of, 77
   metrics, 302, 303
   mission, 301
   object model, 302
   operational objectives, 301, 302, 303
   quality function deployment (QFD),
      306–310
   stakeholder expectations, 77, 304–306
   in statement of work, 140
   targets, 302, 303
   vision, 301
reschedules metric, 648
reserve, the, 249–251
   budgetary reserve, 250
   defined, 249
   fudge factor vs., 250–251
   management reserve, 250
   schedule reserve, 250
   undistributed budget, 250
resources. *See also* assignments; people;
      skills; work groups
   approach, 562
   availability management, 178–179
   contingency plans, 563
   contractors, 573–575
   described, 562
   effort estimate, 593, 599–601
   leveling, 177–178, 368–369
   material resources, 571–573
   metrics, 562, 563
   mission, 562
   object model, 563
   operational objectives, 562
   overview, 560–563
   people, 564–571
   in project management systems, 368–369
   responsibility matrix, 596–599
   roles, 582–584
   skills, 179, 575–580
   skills matrix, 580–582
   staffing plan, 594–596
   summary notation, 588
   targets, 562, 563
   task model roles, 95
   training course, 584–585
   types of, 563
   vision, 562
responsibility. *See also* authority
   accountability ratio, 520

responsibility *(continued)*
   authority and, 483–486
   defined, 483
   reporting structure and, 484
   responsibility failures metric, 597
   responsibility matrix, 596–599
   in work groups, 512, 513–514, 518–519
results, communication and, 30
retraction of work flow, 107, 196
return-on-investment (ROI), 438
reusable systems, 42–62. *See also* reuse potential
   acquisition, 47–48, 448–451
   approaches, 44, 45
   certification, 48–50
   change management plan with, 382
   as coding tools, 352–353
   deliverables as, 69
   development environment as, 322
   management cultures as, 525
   measuring reuse, 43–44
   metrics, 44–45, 46
   mission, 44
   object model, 45
   operational objectives, 44, 45
   overview, 42–46
   quality planning and, 160
   reusability problems, 50–53
   reuse potential, 44, 46–47
   reuse repository, 50
   sharing, 50
   summary notation, 52
   system reuse certification, 48–50
   targets, 45, 46
   types of reuse, 43
   versioned systems vs., 43
   vision, 44
reuse faults metric, 326, 327
reuse potential
   for assessment criterion, 457
   for baselines, 422–423
   for change management plan, 392
   cluster reusability properties, 262
   for communications tools, 670
   for configuration management systems, 410
   for cost estimates, 615–616
   in development process models, 280, 288
   for document templates, 125
   for documents, 121–122, 124, 301, 314, 317
   as leadership issue, 569
   management cultures and, 533–534
   metric, 44–45
   for organizations, 486–491, 492, 494, 499–500, 504
   overview, 44, 46–47
   personal interactions and, 646
   for plans, 132
   for policies, 540–541
   for procurement process model, 452
   for project schedule, 179–180
   for proposals, 455
   prototype baselines and, 428–429
   for repositories, 328, 344
   for request for proposal, 454
   for responsibility matrix, 599
   for risk management plan, 247
   for shifts, 339
   for skills, 579
   for staffing plan, 596
   for statement of work, 141
   system reuse potential, 293
   for task models, 96
   task risk and, 219–220
   for work groups, 517–519
   for work-flow models, 107–108, 109, 111
reuse repository, 53–57
   acquisition of assets, 55
   approaches, 54
   classification schemes, 55–56
   described, 53, 343
   format of assets, 54
   metrics, 54
   mission, 53
   object model, 53
   operational objectives, 53, 54
   product repository vs., 53
   project repository vs., 53
   search tools, 55–56
   sharing reusable systems and, 50
   summary notation, 57
   targets, 54
   vision, 53
reusers, 77
reusing, defined, 42–43
reverse engineering tools, 350
reviews. *See also* joint reviews; technical reviews
   of design document, 317
   of functional specification, 313–314
   joint reviews, 157, 279, 651–657
   technical reviews, 300–301, 317, 654–656
RFP (request for proposal), 452–454
rights failures metric, 459
rights policies, 541
risk averse preference, 236–237
risk control ratio, 245
risk management, 247–253. *See also* contingency plans
   decision theory in, 205
   risk management methods, 247–252
   risk management plan, 130, 244–247
risk management methods, 247–252
   approaches, 247–248
   contingency plan, 251
   contractual provisions, 251
   described, 247
   insurance policy provision, 251–252
   metrics, 248
   mission, 247
   object model, 248
   operational objectives, 247, 248
   process model, 249
   reserve, the, 249–251
   risk mitigation, 248
   risk reduction, 248
   summary notation, 252
   targets, 248
   vision, 247
   for waterfall development process model, 283
risk management plan, 244–247
   approaches, 244, 245
   described, 130, 244
   metrics, 244, 245
   mission, 244
   object model, 245
   operational objectives, 244, 245
   reuse potential, 247
   revising, 246
   risk quantification, 246
   spiral development process model, 286
   targets, 245
   vision, 244
risk mitigation, 248
risk neutral preference, 236, 238
risk of product loss, 401
risk premium, 237
risk quantification, 226–243
   component risks, 232
   control decision tree, 234–236
   controlling risk, 234–236
   described, 204, 226
   event tree, 232–233
   importance of, 226
   math skills required, 226
   objective risks, 228–232
   probability tree, 229–231
   risk analysis, 227
   in risk management plan, 246
   risk tolerance quantification, 236–242
   summary notation, 236
   types of risk, 227–228
risk rate, 129, 292
risk reduction, 248
risk reduction rate, 292
risk reduction ratio, 248
risk seeking preference, 236
risk tolerance, 238–242
   defined, 16, 17, 238
   equation for, 240
   of project plan, 136
   quantification, 236–242
   of stakeholders, 77–78
   test plans requirements and, 156
risk tolerance quantification, 236–242
   certainty equivalent, 236–237
   equation for risk tolerance, 240

Index 695

preference curves, 236, 237–238
risk acceptance curve, 239
risk premium, 237
risk-adjusted value, 303
risks, 200–225
    from ad hoc work flows, 110
    approaches, 201, 202
    attributes, 206–208
    Average Risk Reduction, 162
    Budget Risk, 146
    code risk, 546
    in communication process, 636
    component risks, 232
    contract administration process and, 472
    contracts and, 459–460
    defined, 18
    described, 200–201
    design tools, 351
    errors of commission vs. omission, 208
    generic, 207
    hiring risk, 582
    identified risks, 246
    managed risk, 120
    metrics, 202, 203, 285
    milestone risk, 212–216
    mission, 201
    object model, 201
    objective risks, 228–232
    OO development risks, 210–224
    operational objectives, 201, 202
    organizational, 488
    overview, 198–203
    paradigm, 204–206
    planning and evaluation of, 131
    political, project sponsor and, 76
    preliminary analysis, 77
    procurement risk, 217, 459
    product loss, 401
    project document and, 122
    project plan and risk analysis, 136
    project risk, 210–212
    Project Risk Change Rate, 134
    project-related risks, 200
    quantification, 204, 226–243
    relative risk ratio, 244
    relative work duration and, 192–193
    repository data loss, 344
    resource assignment risk, 220–222, 224
    as risk attribute, 206
    risk class, 200–209
    risk control, 208–209
    risk control ratio, 245
    risk rate, 129
    risk reduction ratio, 248
    Schedule Risk, 145
    schedule task risk, 216–217
    security risk, 342
    storage risk, 342
    summary notation, 203
    system loss, 402–403
    systems and, 203–206
    targets, 202, 203
    in task models, 95, 96
    task risk, 218–220
    transaction work flows for, 109
    as versioned objects, 203
    vision, 201
    in waterfall development process model, 283
ROI (return-on-investment), 438
roles, 582–584, 592
root causes, as risk attribute, 206, 207
root class, 15
Routine management culture, 528, 529–531

safety, 262, 312
satisfaction metric, 76
scales, 22, 23–24
scatter diagrams, 164
schedule performance index (SPI), 65, 135
schedule reserve, 250
Schedule Risk, 145
schedule task risk, 216–217
schedule tasks, 189–194
    advancing, 191–192
    assigning resources, 192
    delaying, 191
    described, 172, 189
    duration, 191, 192–194
    extending, 192
    finish date, 190
    float, 190
    overview, 189–192
    risks, 216–217
    splitting, 192
    start date, 190
    summary notation, 196
schedule variance, of deliverables, 71–72
schedules. *See also specific types of schedules*
    accounting mixed with, 368
    communication scheduling, 636–637
    dependency charts, 183–186
    described, 172
    for meetings, 650
    overview, 172–173
    performance, 438
    in project management systems, 368
    project schedule, 174–180
    Schedule Risk, 145
    summary notation, 186
    time charts, 181–183
schemas, 344–347
Scitor's Project Scheduler 7, 365, 367, 369
scope of project, 139. *See also* statement of work
security, 312, 541
security risk, 342
sensitivity of metrics, 25
"sensitivity training," 645

sequence of tasks, 90
sharing
    development environment, 324
    responsibility, 460
    reusable systems, 50
    skills, 579
    tools, 331
    training courses, 587
shifts, 332, 338–339
SIGS Publications Web site, 586
Silver Bullet Syndrome, 212–214
simple task models, 97–98
simple tasks
    level-of-effort tasks, 89
    object model, 88
    overview, 86, 87–88
    schedule tasks for, 189–194
    work packages, 88
single-boundary tolerance ranges, 27
single-instance systems, 30–31
single-valued targets, 26
skill overlap metric, 520
skills, 575–580
    approaches, 576
    certification, 579
    described, 575
    maintaining, 580
    management skills, 576–577
    math skills for risk quantification, 226
    metrics, 576
    milestone risks, 214–215
    mission, 576
    object model, 575
    OO project skills, 576–578
    operational objectives, 576
    resource assignment risks, 221
    resources and, 179
    reuse potential, 579
    roles, 582–584
    sharing, 579
    skill processes, 578–580
    targets, 576
    task risks, 219
    technical skills, 577
    training course, 584–585
    vision, 575
skills ratio, 510
software, 256–272. *See also* tools
    bug-tracking systems, 363
    clusters, 259–264
    defined, 254
    developing object-oriented software, 273–297
    objects, 256–257
    overview, 254–255
    product documents, 267–269
    skills, 577–578
    software systems, 264–267
    storage organizations, 257–258
    summary notation, 269

software abuse, 433
software systems, 264–267
　approach, 265
　clusters vs., 264–265
　described, 264–265
　function point counting types, 265, 266
　function point value adjustment factor, 265, 266–267
　metrics, 265
　mission, 265
　object model, 264
　operational objective, 265
　targets, 265
　vision, 265
source code, 412
source control tool, 409, 410–412
special causes of variation, 32–34
special time intervals, 337
spending budget, 619–621
SPI (schedule performance index), 65, 135
spiral development process model, 284–286, 428
splitting tasks, 177, 192
spurious metric, 195
stability
　metric, 481
　of organizations, 486
　as project risk, 210–211
　as source of measurement error, 34
staffing plan, 130, 594–596
staffing risk rate, 595
stakeholder assessment, 140
stakeholder awareness, 202
stakeholder satisfaction, 303
stakeholders, 74–78
　approaches, 75
　effort estimates and, 601
　expectations of, 77, 304–306
　friction as risk, 214
　identifying, 66
　management cultures, matching to, 532–536
　metrics, 75, 76
　mission, 74
　object model, 75
　operational objectives, 74
　project sponsors, 76–77
　requirements document, 77, 140, 301–310
　reusers, 77
　stakeholder complaints, 64
　stakeholder ratio, 64
　stakeholder-deliverable matrix, 306–308
　summary notation, 79
　targets, 75, 76
　types of, 76
　vision, 74
standard work shift, 337
standardization policies, 541

standards. *See also* policies
　coding standard, 545–548
　configuration management process model, 404–405
　design standard, 542–545
　development process tasks, 277–278
　external standard, 554–555
　guidelines vs., 539
　for mutual cooperation, 471
　quality assurance process, 156
　risk and, 204–205, 219
　software development process, 275
　for technical reviews, 654
　time interval data type, 194
start date
　of project schedule, 176
　of schedule tasks, 190
statement of work, 139–153. *See also* requirements document; work breakdown structure
　accepting change and, 140–141
　approaches, 140
　certification, 142–143
　content of, 140–142
　described, 139
　metrics, 140
　mission, 139
　object model, 139
　operational objectives, 140
　in request for proposal, 453–454
　reusability, 141
　roles in project, 43
　summary notation, 151
　targets, 140
　traceability matrix for, 142–143
　versioning, 143
　vision, 139
statistical process control tools, 163–166
Steering management culture, 528, 531
storage
　for contract administration system, 475
　for repositories, 343
　storage organizations, 257–258
storage risk, 342
strategic value ratio, 302
structural incoherence, 497
success metric, 591
summary notation
　development process, 295
　overview, 13–14
SuperProject, 365, 366
support provisions in contracts, 463–464
supporting processes, 278–279
susceptibility, as risk attribute, 206
synergy, 638
system capability index, 35
system faults metric, 420
system improvement plans, 130
system loss, 402–403

system modeling tools, 373–375
　approaches, 374
　documentation templates, 375
　integration in project management systems, 375
　metrics, 374
　mission, 373
　object model, 374
　operational objectives, 373, 374
　planning tools, 375
　process modeling tools, 375
　summary notation, 375
　targets, 374
　vision, 373
system models. *See also* design pattern; document templates; process models; project plan; project process models; task models
　for configuration management process, 405, 407
　most important models, 38
　notation, 11–13
　overview, 36–38
　for project planning, 99
　for work breakdown structures, 100, 148
System Representation Accuracy, 37
system reuse potential, 293
system usability metric, 303
system warranties, 49
systems. *See also* reusable systems; versioned systems
　complex systems, 15
　defined, 14
　feedback or goal-seeking systems, 15
　kaizan and, 14–28
　open systems, 14–15
　processes approach vs., 4
　reusable systems, 42–62
　risk and, 203–206
　as root class, 15
　summary notation, 17

targets
　control charts and, 27
　defined, 26
　goals and, 21
　overview, 26–28
　single-valued, 26
　tolerance range for, 26–27
task models, 95–98
　approach, 95
　classes, 97
　described, 95
　metric, 96
　mission, 95
　object models, 96, 97, 98
　operational objective, 95
　simple task models, 97–98
　summary notation, 98

Index

target, 96
vision, 95
task risk, 218–220
tasks. *See also* assignments; work breakdown structure
    approaches, 85
    in change management systems, 396
    complex tasks, 86–87
    defined, 7, 9, 84
    in development process, 277–278
    for development process models, 285–286
    generation of, 85–86
    level-of-effort tasks, 89
    metrics, 85
    mission, 84
    object model, 85
    operational objectives, 85
    optimizing in project schedule, 177
    overview, 84–89
    project process tasks, 94
    in project schedule, 174
    responsibility matrix, 596–599
    risks, 218–220
    sequence of tasks, 90
    simple tasks, 86, 87–89
    summary notation, 89
    targets, 85
    versioning and reuse of, 86
    vision, 84
    WBS code, 149
    work packages, 88
teams, 519–522. *See also* work groups
    approaches, 519, 520
    building, 521
    commitment in, 520–521
    defined, 478, 519
    destroying, 521
    metrics, 520
    mission, 519
    object model, 519
    operational objectives, 519, 520
    personal interactions in, 646
    targets, 520
    team meetings, 658
    vision, 519
technical reviews. *See also* joint reviews
    described, 654
    of design document, 317
    development documents for, 300–301
    importance of, 655–656
    mission, 654
    object model, 654
    overview, 654–656
    verification types and content, 654–655
    vision, 654
technical skills, 577
templates
    contract forms, 462

document templates, 124–125
    for documentation, 375
test modeling and scripting tools, 167–168
test models, 316
test plans, 157–161
    overview, 157
    quality approach, 158, 160
    quality system objects, 158
    reuse and, 160
    risk tolerance and, 156
    system under test, 155
    test case, 160
    test model, 160
    test script, 160
    test suite, 160–161
test suite classes, 160–161
testability metric, 299
testing frameworks, 166–167
text productivity, 120
text size metric, 120
throwaway prototypes, 427
time charts, 181–183
    approach, 181
    calendar display, 183
    described, 181
    Gantt charts, 182–183
    metric, 181
    mission, 181
    object model, 181
    operational objective, 181
    PERT charts, 183
    in project management systems, 368
    in project schedule, 174
    target, 181
    vision, 181
time intervals, 336–337
    data type, 194
    defined, 336
    mission, 336
    object model, 336
    types of, 336–337
    vision, 336
    in work calendars, 335–336
Time Line for Windows, 365, 368, 369
time policies, 541
time zones, 552, 593
timeliness metric, 397
timesheet faults metric, 664
title warranty, 49
tolerance range, 26–27
tool productivity metric, 668
tools. *See also* repositories; *specific tools and types of tools*
    acquisition, 330, 331
    approaches, 330, 331
    communication tool, 667–670
    configuration management tools, 324–325, 409–414
    cost estimation tool, 616–617

design patterns, 355–357
development tools, 332, 348–355
improvement plan, 331–332
information systems, 332, 360–363
metrics, 330, 331
milestone risks, 215
mission, 330
modeling tools, 332
object model, 331
operational objectives, 330, 331
overview, 330–333
product management systems, 371–373
for project document creation, 122, 125
project management systems, 363–371
project risks, 211–212
quality tools, 163–168
resource assignment risks, 221–222
schemas, 344–347
sharing, 331
shifts, 332, 338–339
skills desirable, 578
system modeling tools, 373–375
targets, 330, 331
task risks, 220
types of, 332
vision, 330
work calendars, 174, 332, 334–337, 340
top-down cost estimates, 613
top-down effort estimates, 600–601
total cost metric, 563
traceability matrix, 142–143
traceability metric, 300
traceability ratio, 140, 265
training
    as organizational process, 276
    "sensitivity training," 645
    training course, 584–585
transaction work-flow models, 108–109
turnover
    metric, 481
    organizational, 487

u control charts, 164
unauthorized changes, 391
understandability property, 262
undistributed budget, 250
unit-price contracts, 461, 462
usability metric, 342
Usenet news groups, 672
user documentation, 312, 316
user interfaces, 312, 316
utility of metrics, 25

validation process, 156–157, 279
validity, 25, 262
value
    absolute value vs. improvement, 6
    actual value, 70
    change earned value, 388

value *(continued)*
  of deliverables, 67, 69–74
  earned value, 70, 71
  estimated value at completion, 71
  goal and, 21
  maximizing vs. optimizing, 5
  overview, 5–7
  planned value, 70
  relativity of, 5
  risk-adjusted value, 303
  schedule variance, 71–72
  value variance, 72
  warranted equity value, 68
value added metric, 330, 349, 374
value performance index (VPI), 65, 135
value ratio, 260
variable costs, 337, 572–573
Variable management culture, 528–529
variance metric, 600, 613
vendor duration, 194
verification process, 156, 279
versioned systems
  approaches, 58
  baselines as, 420–421
  defined, 2
  metrics, 58
  milestones, 101–103
  mission, 57
  object model, 58
  operational objectives, 58
  overview, 57–59
  reusable systems vs., 43
  statement of work, 143
  storage organizations as, 257–258
  summary notation, 59
  targets, 58
  tasks as, 86
  vision, 57
  work breakdown structure as, 146–147
video communications tool, 669
vision
  congruency with, 20
  defined, 15, 18
  overview, 18–19
voice communications tool, 667
VPI (value performance index), 65, 135

warranted equity value, 68
warranties of system reuse certification, 49

waterfall development process model, 281–284
WBS. *See* work breakdown structure
Web, the, as repository, 343, 671
weighted proposal compliance, 455
white box clusters, 263
word processing tools, 375
work breakdown structures, 144–151
  approaches, 144–145
  constructions, 144
  customizing, 100, 148, 150
  generating, 99, 147–148
  importance of, 151
  levels, 149–151
  metrics, 145, 146
  mission, 144
  object model, 146
  operational objectives, 144, 145
  overview, 73
  planning steps, 99–100, 147–148
  in project management systems, 368
  pruning standard tasks from, 151
  in statement of work, 140
  summary notation, 151
  system model, 100, 148
  targets, 145, 146
  as versioned system, 146–147
  vision, 144
  WBS code, 149
work calendars, 334–337
  approach, 335
  availability, 334
  described, 332, 334
  inheritance, 334
  metric, 335
  mission, 334
  object model, 335
  operational objective, 334
  in project schedule, 174
  summary notation, 340
  target, 335
  time intervals, 335–337
  vision, 334
  work time, 334
work groups, 509–519. *See also* teams
  approaches, 509, 510, 511
  commitment, motivation, and discretionary effort, 515–517
  described, 509

  "difficult" people in, 517
  in functional organizations, 512
  in matrix organizations, 512
  metrics, 510, 511
  mission, 509
  object model, 510
  operational objectives, 509, 510, 511
  overview, 509–511
  personal interactions in, 646
  in projectized organizations, 512
  responsibility in, 512, 513–514, 518–519
  reuse potential, 517–519
  roles, 582–584
  skills matrix, 580–582
  structure, 512–514
  summary notation, 522
  targets, 510, 511
  teams, 478, 519–522
  vision, 509
work package model, 97
work packages, 88
work-flow models, 105–114
  ad hoc work-flow models, 110–112
  administrative work-flow models, 112–113
  approaches, 106
  metrics, 106
  mission, 106
  notations, 107
  object model, 105
  operational objectives, 106
  overview, 105–108
  reassignment of the flow, 107
  retraction of the flow, 107
  reuse potential, 107–108
  summary notation, 113
  targets, 106
  transaction work-flow models, 108–109
  vision, 106
World Wide Web, as repository, 343, 671

x control charts, 164
x-R control charts, 164, 165

year-month intervals, 336–337